UNDERSTANDING ORGANIZATIONAL BEHAVIOR

Second Edition

UNDERSTANDING ORGANIZATIONAL BEHAVIOR

Second Edition

Denis D. Umstot

University of Puget Sound

WEST PUBLISHING COMPANY
St. Paul   New York   Los Angeles   San Francisco

Copyeditor: Jeanyne Sletton
Designer: Lois Stanfield

Library of Congress Cataloging-in-Publication Data

Umstot, Denis D.
     Understanding organizational behavior.

     Includes bibliographical references and index.
     1. Organizational behavior. I. Title.
HD58.7.U47   1987   658.3   87–25255
ISBN 0–314–62488–0

To Mary,
my partner in this book and in life

CONTENTS

Preface   xv

PART ONE   WHAT IS ORGANIZATIONAL BEHAVIOR?

1   **Introduction to Organizational Behavior   3**
    Preview Cases: Problems at Chrysler   4
                       Rewards at IBM   4
                       Shock at General Motors   4
                       Shakeup at General Electric   4
                       Apple Computer Loses Its Founder   5
        Perspective: The Best Companies to Work for in America   7
    Managerial Behavior: What Managers Do?   7
    The Nature of Organizational Behavior   9
        Perspective: Learning Processes   13
    Research in Organizational Behavior   14
        Perspective: "On Experimental Design," by Mark Twain   18
    Organizations as Systems   19
    Overview of the Book   24
    Cross-Cultural OB: Exporting Japanese Management to the U.S.A.   25
        Perspective: Two Auto Workers: Toyota versus Ford   27
    Managerial Applications of Organizational Behavior   27
    Cases and Incidents
        Sam Holst, Manager   29
        A Day in the Life of a General Manager   30
    References   32

PART TWO   INDIVIDUAL BEHAVIOR IN ORGANIZATIONS

2   **Understanding Individual Behavior   37**
    Preview Case: Jenni Pike's Crisis   38
    Why Study Individual Behavior?   38
    The Nature of Personality   39
        Perspective: The Two Sides of the Brain   40
        Perspective: Are Organizations and People Incompatible?   46
        Perspective: Individual-Level Barriers to the Advancement of Women
                         in Organizations   47

Personality and Behavior   47
    Perspective: Personal Characteristics of General Managers   50
    Perspective: The Neurotic Organization: A Reflection of the
                    Leader's Personality?   52
Cross-cultural OB: French versus American Characteristics   52
Managerial Applications of Personality Concepts   53
Cases and Incidents
    Barbara Herrick   54
    Analyzing Jenni Pike's Crisis   55
    What Killed Bob Lyons?   56
References   57

3   **An Individual's Perspective: Values and Attitudes   59**
    Preview Case: Jack Blaylock's Lament   60
    Values: The Broad Road Map for Human Behavior   61
        Perspective: Ethical Values: Cheating, Lying, and Bending the
                        Rules   64
        Perspective: What Would Make 11,500 People Quit Their Jobs?   67
    Attitudes and Organizational Behavior   68
        Perspective: Is Job Satisfaction in the United States Changing?   71
        Perspective: The Satisfaction-Performance Controversy   71
    Cross-Cultural OB: Japan as an Example   74
        Perspective: Lifetime Employment in Japan: Myths and
                        Realities   76
    Managerial Applications of Value and Attitude Concepts   76
    Cases and Incidents
        The Graduate's Dilemma   78
        Negotiation Failure in Japan   79
        The Municipal Light Caper   79
    References   80

4   **Perception: What Is Reality?   83**
    Preview Case: The Choice   84
    The Perception Process   85
        Perspective: Getting People's Attention with Symbols and
                        Drama   90
        Perspective: The Self-Fulfilling Prophecy   91
    Problems in Perception   94
        Perspective: Mangerial Myopia: Self-Serving Biases   97
    Impression Management   97
        Perspective: How to Win Friends and Influence People   99
        Perspective: How Top Executives Described Successful Dress   100
    Performance Evaluation and Interviewing   101
    Cross-Cultural OB: Time Perceptions   103
    Managerial Applications of Perception   103
    Cases and Incidents
        The New Supervisor   105
        The Black Managers   106
    References   107

5   **Motivating Work Behavior   109**
    Preview Case: A Tale of Two Cities   110
    An Introduction to Work Motivation   110
    Energizing Behavior   112
        Perspective: When Is Motivating Behavior Impossible?   114
        Perspective: Does a Hierarchy of Needs Really Exist?   115

Directing Behavior   118
Sustaining Behavior With Rewards   123
        Perspective: On the Folly of Rewarding A, While Hoping
                                for B   126
Cross-Cultural OB: Do American Motivation Theories Apply Abroad?   128
Managerial Applications for Motivation Theory   130
Cases and Incidents
        Motivation Overdose: The Workaholics   132
        Rollie on the Assembly Line   132
        Chancellor State University   132
References   134

6   **Motivation Using Behavior Modification and Pay   137**
        Preview Case: Reliance Development Company   138
Motivating with Organizational Behavior Modification   139
        Perspective: Examples of Behavior Modification   141
        Perspective: How the Excellent Companies Use Positive
                                Reinforcement   145
        Perspective: Rules for Using Behavior Modifications in
                                Organizations   151
Motivating With Pay   154
        Perspective: Knowledge-Based Pay   156
Cross-Cultural OB: Three Ways of Dealing with Tardiness   157
Managerial Applications of Behavior Mod and Pay   159
Cases and Incidents
        The Sloppy Secretary   161
        The Ratebusting Saleswoman   161
        Lincoln Electric Company   162
References   163

7   **Job Design and Goal Setting   165**
        Preview Case: The Word Processing Center   166
Job Design   166
        Perspective: Flexitime   172
        Perspective: A Manager's Self-Help Guide to Job Enrichment   174
        Perspective: Looking Back at Topeka   177
Goal Setting   178
Choosing a Motivation Strategy   184
        Perspective: Motivation Techniques: Which Work Best?   185
Cross-Cultural OB: Enriching Jobs at Volvo in Sweden   185
Managerial Applications of Job Design and Goal Setting   187
Cases and Incidents
        Keypunch Operation   189
        The Reluctant Entrepreneurs   190
        Getting Started with Goal Setting   190
References   191

PART THREE   **THE INTERACTION BETWEEN PEOPLE**

8   **Communication: the Link Between Individuals   195**
        Preview Case: The Managerial Treadmill   196
The Communication Process   197
        Perspective: The Grapevine   200
Interpersonal Communication Dynamics   202

Listening Behavior   208
    Perspective: Management by Wandering Around   209
    Perspective: Keys to Effective Informational Listening   213
Nonverbal Communication   213
Cross-Cultural OB: Open Communication in Japanese Owned
        Companies   218
Managerial Applications of Communication Concepts   218
    Perspective: Rules for Communicating in International
                          Business   219
Cases and Incidents
        Lafayette Aerodynamics   221
        What's Happening Here?   222
        Rudolph Carter   222
References   224

9   **Group Dynamics: Individuals Working Together   227**
    Preview Case: The Exit Interview   228
The Nature of Groups   229
    Perspective: Social Networks and the Management of Crisis   235
Group Characteristics   236
    Perspective: "Schmoozing" or "Social Loafing"?   245
Group Development and the Socialization Process   246
Workgroups: Managing Effective Teams   250
    Perspective: Ideal Characteristics of an Effective Work Team   251
Cross-Cultural OB: Socializing New Employees in Japan   253
Management Applications of Group Dynamics   255
Cases and Incidents
        Dennis Calhoun   257
        Acme Wholesale Distributing Company   258
References   260

10   **Conflict, Competition and Cooperation   263**
    Preview Case: Warfare at Advanced Products   264
Understanding Conflict   265
    Perspective: The First-Line Supervisor: Role Conflict in
                          Action   267
Managing Conflict   270
    Perspective: Encouraging Conflict and Confrontation at Intel
                          Corporation   271
    Perspective: How to Be an Effective Third Party   275
Cooperation and Competition   275
    Perspective: Getting to Yes: A Win-Win Negotiation Strategy   279
Cross-Cultural OB: Negotiating Business Deals with the Chinese   280
    Perspective: Constructive Confrontation in Japan   282
Management Applications of Conflict and Cooperation   283
Cases and Incidents
        James Farris   285
        Inflated Performance Appraisals   285
References   286

11   **Management of Stress   289**
    Preview Case: People Uptight!   290
The Nature of Stress   291
    Perspective: Help! My Company Has Just been Taken Over   296
Burnout: A Special Form of Stress   297
Sources of Stress   298
    Perspective: Stress and Women Managers   299

Perspective: Stress and the Air Traffic Controller   301
Managing Stress   302
 Perspective: Shift Work and Stress   303
 Perspective: Participation in Decision Making to Reduce
   Stress   304
Cross-Cultural OB: Executive Stress Goes Global   305
Management Applications of Stress Management   308
Cases and Incidents
 The Finance Professor   310
 Top Executives Thrive On Stress   310
 What killed Bob Lyons?   311
References   311

12 Power and Politics In Organizations   313
 Preview Case: The Powerless Ones   314
Power, Authority and Influence: Getting Things Done   315
Sources of Power   315
 Perspective: Power is Also a Great Motivator   317
Using Power and Influence   319
 Perspective: Power Games in a Large Corporation   321
 Perspective: Nonverbal Signs of Power   324
Political Strategies and Tactics   326
 Perspective: Developing Positive Political Skills   327
 Perspective: Corporate Coup d'Etat   330
The Ethics of Power and Politics   331
Cross-Cultural OB: Power Dynamics in China   333
 Perspective: Power Distance in Various Cultures   334
Managerial Applications of Power and Politics   335
Cases and Incidents
 Research and Development at General Rubber   337
 The Showdown: How Henry Ford Fired Lee Iacocca   337
References   338

13 Problem Solving and Decision Making   341
 Preview Case: Metro Publishing's New Plant   342
The Decision Process: How Decisions Get Made   343
 Perspective: Defining Problems Using the Kepner-Tregoe
   Approach   345
 Perspective: Knee-Deep in Big Muddy: Escalating Commitment to a
   Course of Action   346
 Perspective: Intuitive Decision Making: Using the Right-
   Brain   348
Using Groups for Decision Making   350
 Perspective: Groupthink   351
Participation and Delegation in Decision Making   353
Group Decision-Making Techniques   359
Cross-Cultural OB: Arab Decision Making   365
Managerial Applications of Decision Making   366
Cases and Incidents
 Participation at Moonlight Cosmetics   368
 The Engineering Change   368
 The *Challenger* Launch Decision   369
References   370

14 Leadership   373
 Preview Case: The Second Lieutenant   374
In Search Of Leadership   375

Perspective: Leaders versus Managers: Is there a Difference?   376
Traits and Behaviors of Leaders   377
   Perspective: History of the Assessment Center   379
Social Exchange and Leadership   379
   Perspective: Charismatic Leadership   380
Behavior of Leaders   381
Situational Approaches to Leadership   385
   Perspective: Barriers to Female Leadership   393
Leadership: Summarizing What We Do Know   394
Cross-Cultural OB: How does Leadership Differ?   395
Managerial Applications of Leadership   397
Cases and Incidents
   The Antileadership Vaccine   398
   Bill Kadota's Problem   399
References   403

PART FOUR   THE TOTAL ORGANIZATION

15   Organizational Design and Behavior   409

Preview Case: Synergistic Advertising Systems   410
Purpose, Objectives, and Structure   415
The Organization's Environment   415
Designing the Organizational Structure   419
   Perspective: The Informal Organization   421
   Perspective: Achieve Excellence by Having a Lean Staff   425
   Perspective: Reorganization at General Motors   427
Types of Organizational Structures   430
   Perspective: "Skunkworks"   431
   Perspective: Structures to Encourage Managerial Progression of
                     Women   436
Cross-Cultural OB: Japanese Organizational Structure   437
Managerial Applications Relating to Organizational Design   439
Cases and Incidents
   Advanced Aerospace Research Laboratory   441
   Lee Iacocca Reorganizes Chrysler   441
References   442

16   Organizational Change and Development   445

Preview Case: Great Pacific Shipbuilding   446
The Change Process   447
   Perspective: When a New Manager Takes Charge   450
Unfreezing: Getting Ready for Change   450
   Perspective: Overcoming Resistance to Change: A Classic
                     Experiment   454
Moving: The Change Itself   455
   Perspective: Expectations and Change   457
Refreezing: Making the Change Stick   458
   Perspective: Quality Circles   459
Organization Development   460
   Perspective: The Confrontation Meeting   464
Cross-Cultural OB: Fitting OD to National Culture   465
   Perspective: The Great Soviet Computer Screw-up   466
Managerial Applications of Change and OD   467

Cases and Incidents
 Shift Change   469
 A New Plant Manager   470
References   471

17 Organizational Culture and the Quality of Life   473
 Preview Case: Delta Airlines   474
Organizational Culture   475
 Perspective: The Culture of Excellence   476
Organizational Climate   480
Type Z Organizational Cultures   482
Quality of Work Life   484
 Perspective: Applications of QWL Strategies   486
 Perspective: Considerations for Reinventing the Corporation   489
Organizations of the Future   489
 Perspective: The Contractual Organization: For Fees, Not
   Wages   490
Cross-Cultural OB: The Cultural Relativity of the QWL Concept   490
 Perspective: American Culture: A Shock for Foreign
   Managers   493
Managerial Applications of Organizational Culture and QWL   494
Cases and Incidents
 The Consolidated Life Case: Caught between Corporate
 Cultures   495
References   499

GLOSSARY   503

TOPIC INDEX   517

AUTHOR INDEX   525

PREFACE

For several years after I began teaching organizational behavior my course critiques often included statements like: "The course was really interesting, especially when you consider the *boring* nature of the material." This recurring comment bothered me since I believe organizational behavior is inherently exciting and interesting. When I explored the reasons for such comments, students noted that while I made the lectures interesting, the text was dry, boring, and academic. A review of student ratings of texts seemed to confirm this finding—most texts were rated average at best.

While there seemed to be a number of reasons why students did not like the texts, the main concerns were lack of examples and reading difficulty. It seemed that even though my colleagues and I teach motivation, we were not writing texts to motivate students or positively reinforce the learning experience.

My goal has been to design and to write a book that will involve the reader in the material, hopefully creating interest, challenge, and motivation. The strategy to reach the goal is to relate theory to organizational practice on a continuous basis by providing examples of every concept and theory. In addition, the book is designed to be stimulating and positively reinforcing to read. It not only provides the theory needed to understand human behavior in organizations, but also attempts to provide perspectives that broaden the reader's outlook by exposure to a wide range of ideas, techniques, research, and controversies not always covered in an organizational behavior book.

New Material in the Second Edition

Every chapter has been thoroughly revised and updated to reflect the most current available research, theories, and examples. New or expanded coverage focuses on such topics as self-managing work groups, developing positive political skills, searching for excellence, reward strategies, atttribution theory, and organizational culture. Each chapter contains a section on cross-cultural organizational behavior to emphasize the global nature of the field. Twenty three new perspectives have been added to provide insights into current issues and problems. A managerial applications section at the end of each chapter summarizes what we do know about the topic and provides practical guide-lines for managerial action. While each chapter still contains a number of short cases and incidents, there are ten longer cases for more in-depth analysis. In other words, this edition is a major change from the first edition.

Features

It has been a challenging task to design and write a book that attempts to be interesting and motivating. A number of features have been used to aid in this effort.

Examples   Every theory and concept is illustrated with at least one example. My most challenging task was to integrate an example into almost every paragraph. I found that it was far easier to merely describe a theory than to provide a relevant example of how it applied.

Theoretical Base   Theories and concepts were chosen for their explanatory power, validity, and relevance for practice. A wide variety of theoretical perspectives are used. Systems theory has been used in a number of instances to bring unity to diverse concepts and to show the interrelationship among organizational subsystems.

Research Basis   While this is not what is termed a "research-oriented text," it does have its foundations in state-of-the-art organizational research. Over 1,000 references are cited to provide a strong academic foundation. On the average, approximately one-half of the citations are research studies or reviews. The aim of this text is to inform the reader about what we *do* know about organizational behavior rather than to explain all the doubts and reservations about every theory and research study. This is not to say that research or theoretical criticism has been ruled out—it is still included whenever serious problems arise that need to addressed.

Writing Style   An active, interesting style results in a book that is easy and perhaps fun to read but still rigorous in content. Difficult terms are defined in a clear, straightforward way with examples to help the reader link them to personal experiences and thus be more likely to retain the terms and ideas in long-term memory. A glossary is provided for easy review of definitions.

Perspectives   While the central core of organizational behavior theory is covered in the main text, there are numerous interesting side issues for both theory and practice that cannot be covered in depth or that diverge somewhat from the main theme or thrust of the chapter. Nevertheless, these Perspectives add richness, color, and interest to the study of organizational behavior. Thus, the chapters include a number of Perspectives to perk interest and to generate curiosity. They should be treated as topics that add breadth and diversity and are not necessarily directly linked with the main textual material.

Previews and Opening Cases   Each chapter opens with a set of preview questions or statements to serve as interest-arousers and an outline overview of what is to be covered. In addition, each chapter begins with a case that surfaces issues related to the topics covered in that chapter. Its purpose is to arouse interest and create an organizational example for use in much of the rest of the chapter.

Cross-Cultural Organizational Behavior   An important force in the environment is the international aspect of markets and organizations. Working in this turbulent environment requires that managers understand the similarities and differences in behavior related to culture. Each chapter contains a section that relates cross-cultural topics to the chapter's conceptual material. Examples of some of the cross-cultural topics include: exporting Japanese management to the U.S., the applicability of American motivation theories abroad, power dynamics in China, Arab decision making, and Japanese organizational structure.

Managerial Applications   Since one of the major goals of the book is to help the reader relate theory to practice, I have designed a new section at the end of each chapter that summarizes what we do know about the topic and provides guides for managerial action. I know that these prescriptions may oversimplify the managerial actions needed to resolve many problems. They are, nevertheless, a good starting point for managerial strategy, especially for inexperienced managers.

Current and Authoritative Material   In addition to the essential theoretical foundation, there is a strong emphasis on current topics such as power, politics, stress, organizational culture, change, and cross-cultural topics. In addition, the book reflects the state of the art in research and theory with references being added right up to presstime.

Sexism   I have tried to use examples that display a balanced use of men and women in both traditional and nontraditional roles. In addition, there are a number of Perspectives that specifically address unique problems faced by women in managerial positions.

Cases   In addition to the opening case, each chapter contains at least two short cases that relate to the topic. There are also a number of longer cases that provide opportunities for students to experience more realistically the complexities of organizational behavior.

Acknowledgments

I am very grateful to the many people who have contributed to the development of both the original and the revised editions of the book. In particular, I would like to thank the reviewers who read the entire manuscript and made many valuable comments that resulted in significant improvements in the book:

Hamid Akbari
Northeastern Illinois University
John Anstey
University of Nebraska-Omaha
Thomas Calero
Illinois Institute of Technology
Hugh F.R. Cowley
*Grant MacEwan
  Community College*
John A. Drexler, Jr.
Oregon State University

Cynthia V. Fukami
University of Denver
Fred Heffner
Albright College
Mark A. Mallinger
Pepperdine University
Larry McDaniel
*Alabama Agricultural and
  Mechanical University*
James C. McElroy
Iowa State University

Cynthia Pavett
University of San Diego
Paul Preston
University of Texas-San Antonio
Donald R. Rickert
Saint Louis College of Pharmacy
Bernard Stern
Villanova University
Robert R. Taylor
Memphis State University

Robert J. Vandenberg
Georgia State University
Richard Vorwerk
Governors State University
George C. Witteried
University of Missouri-St. Louis
Paul Wolff
Dundalk Community College
Joseph Wright
Portland Community College

I certainly appreciate the efforts of the staff of West Publishing Company. Editors Dick Fenton and Esther Craig have helped make the planning process for the second edition quite smooth and trouble-free. Esther has been particularly helpful in getting things done when they needed to be with a minimum of hassle. My production editors, Jane Gregg and Cheryl Wilms, have made the complex production process seem almost easy. My copy editor, Jeanyne Sletton, has been very effective in improving the readability, flow, and accuracy of the manuscript.

The University of Puget Sound has also been helpful. John Dickson, Dean of the School of Business and Public Administration, has provided active support, encouragement, and assistance. The administrative assistance provided by Doris Anderson has also been most helpful.

A special thanks goes to Mary Umstot, who read every word of the revised manuscript in all its numerous drafts and galleys. She has been a helpmate, friend, critic, and supporter throughout the development and revision of the book. In addition, she has managed the complex process of obtaining copyright releases.

FEEDBACK IS DESIRED

I would greatly appreciate any suggestions for improving the book or correcting errors. In addition, I would like to find out how well the test bank in the Instructor's Resource Manual works for you. Address corrections or comments to:

Professor Denis Umstot
School of Business and Public Administration
University of Puget Sound
Tacoma, Washington 98416

UNDERSTANDING ORGANIZATIONAL BEHAVIOR

Second Edition

Part One

WHAT IS ORGANIZATIONAL BEHAVIOR?

Chapter One

Introduction to Organizational Behavior

PREVIEW

- What do managers do? How much of their time is spent working with people?
- Which companies are best to work for? Why?
- Is there a best way to manage?
- Which research strategy is better: natural observation, surveys, or experiments?
- How do you suppose Mark Twain used ants to conduct an experiment?
- How was Japanese management used to change an American automotive manufacturing plant?
- Who has the better job; a Japanese or an American worker?

MAJOR TOPICS

Preview Cases: Organizational Behavior in Action

Managerial Behavior: What Managers Do

The Nature of Organizational Behavior

Research in Organizational Behavior

Organizations as Systems

Overview of the Book

Cross-Cultural OB: Exporting Japanese Management to the United States

Managerial Applications of Organizational Behavior

Preview Cases

PROBLEMS AT CHRYSLER

The bad feelings between [Chrysler] and its dealers were astounding. I was amazed and appalled by the way the two sides were talking to each other and by the angry and insulting letters that were being exchanged between the dealers and Chrysler headquarters . . . . Instead of allowing the two sides to harbor grudges and take potshots at each other, we needed to create an environment where somebody from top management could sit down with the dealers and go over all of their complaints and problems, one by one.

And the dealers certainly had plenty to say. They had every right to be angry with management, because they hadn't been treated well at all. For years the company had been shipping them junk and expecting them to sell it. Chrysler's quality had been so poor that dealers got into the habit of expecting to rebuild the cars when they received them. Under those conditions, how could we ask them to be courteous and enthusiastic? How could we ask them to *trust* us?

From *Iacocca: An Autobiography* 1

REWARDS AT IBM

IBM motivates its 405,000 employees by preaching an unwavering religion, rewarding thousands and singling out "the individual," no matter how tiny his contribution. Big units are broken into small departments of a dozen people; one manager for every nine or 10 workers speaks with them constantly . . .

[IBM's marketing representatives, called "reps"] are the main reason for the company's tight hold on the computer market. IBM treats them accordingly, motivating this army of politely aggressive blue suits with tons of cash, intense peer pressure and enough rah-rah rallies to rival a college fraternity . . .

Each January, branches stage glitzy "kickoff" meetings replete with slogans, skits, and mascots. Monthly meetings often close with a dramatic tale about an un-named rep; finally, the person is named and comes forward to accept an award amid crackling applause. "It takes your breath away, it really does," says Diana Ingram, a Chicago rep who has received four awards in less than four years at IBM.

From *The Wall Street Journal* 2

SHOCK FOR GENERAL MOTORS

[While GM has been having difficulty with its modern, newly automated plants—only 70 percent of planned productivity levels have been attained at its Hamtramck (Mich.) plant—it has been shocked by the success of] the Fremont (Calif.) plant that [it] operates as a joint venture with Toyota Motor Corp. Although the New United Motor Manufacturing, Inc. [NUMMI] plant uses out-of-date technology to assemble Chevrolet Novas, its productivity is higher than most of GM's new plants. The key, experts say, is Toyota's management style, which emphasizes thorough training and participative management, lean layers of middle management, and decision-making pushed as close as possible to the assembly line. NUMMI "has shaken GM to the core," says Cole [Director of the University of Michigan's Office for the Study of Automotive Transportation]. "It's making them rethink their whole philosophy about how to be competitive."

From *Business Week* 3

SHAKEUP AT GENERAL ELECTRIC

[In 1981 General Electric's Directors selected a 45–year-old chemical engineer named Jack Welch as its chief executive.] Welch jolted the staid and sprawling conglomerate to life. He chopped 100,000 jobs, a quarter of GE's work force, sank billions into automated factories, and started winnowing the company down to major businesses that dominate their markets, a process that has involved buying or selling over 100 operations . . . .

For the 350,000 people GE employs, Welch has changed what it means to go to work in the morning. He revoked a tacit promise of lifetime employment GE used to make, substituting what he sees as a realistic new deal: "The job of the enterprise is to provide an exciting atmosphere that's open and fair, where people have the resources to go out and win. The job of the people is to take advantage of this playing field and put out 100%." Welch has no

patience with those who pine for the glory years of American business that followed World War II. "The people who get in trouble in our company," he says, "are those who carry around the anchor of the past."

From *Fortune* 4

APPLE COMPUTER LOSES ITS FOUNDER

After months of anger and anguish, Steve Jobs resigns as Apple chairman. He was the brash, brilliant and sometimes bumptious brat of Silicon Valley, a symbol of its high-tech genius and fabulous sudden wealth. Alternately infuriating and inspiring, Steve Jobs co-founded Apple Computer in a California garage nine years ago and helped build it into a billion-dollar business that gave rise to the personal-computer industry. Along the way, Jobs was widely hailed as the prototype of a new American hero—the irreverent and charismatic young entrepreneur.

[On September 17, 1985] an embittered and virtually powerless Jobs resigned as Apple's chairman and from the board of directors, following an anguished break with President John Sculley . . ..

In a characteristically petulant move, the chairman leaked his letter of resignation to the press hours before delivering it to Apple. "The company's recent reorganization," Jobs wrote, "has left me with no work to do and no access even to regular management reports. I am but 30, and want still to contribute and achieve." Apparently intended to arouse sympathy, the tone of the letter and its public release struck some Apple executives as a clear attempt to embarrass them.

From *Time* 5

The organizational situations described relating to Chrysler, IBM, GM, GE, and Apple provide glimpses of the pervasiveness of organizational behavior and its importance for organizational effectiveness. However, most of these cases show what is happening at the highest organizational levels. What kinds of organizational behavior might be found in lower-level management jobs? The following are some illustrative incidents. The last sentence of each incident poses a question. When you finish reading the book, you should be able to answer the questions, and more, based on your knowledge of organizational behavior.

- *Mike Sloan, heavy equipment salesman:* "I'm always looking for a challenge. It seems that I'm not happy unless there are several big deals going at once." Mike is a crackerjack salesman, but would he make a good sales manager?

- *Susan Ling, supervisor:* "It really makes me mad. No matter what I do my people only produce at their own leisurely pace. I know we could easily do one third more work if only my people were motivated. What can I do?"

- *Jake Olsen, foreman* (to another foreman): "I just don't understand these new workers that personnel sent us. They were hired under our program to give disadvantaged workers an opportunity. The problem is that they just can't seem to get to work on time. I've started giving them a day off without pay as punishment, but things have gotten worse instead of better." Is a day off without pay punishment or a reward for these workers?

- *Willard Aimes, management trainee:* "But Mr. Johnson, I thought you said you wanted the reports by the end of the month, not the end of the week. I must have misunderstood." Why do people see the same situation differently?

- *Marsha Wagner, supervisor of the word processing center:* "It's too bad Amanda quit. She was one of the best and fastest typists we've hired in a long time. Why she would put out almost twice as much work as the other typists. But for some reason the others just didn't like her. I think they may have driven her off because she's too good." Do you think Amanda was really that much better or were the other typists "coasting"? Why didn't they like her? How important are group pressures?

- *Sandra Wool, chief of nursing:* "We certainly have a serious problem here between the doctors and nurses. There always seems to be hard feelings between them and I'm afraid the patients suffer. The doctors complain that the nurses won't do what they are told and the nurses say the doctors act like 'little tin gods' and treat the nurses more like janitors than professionals." Is conflict such as this desirable?

- *Tony Ashly, fast-rising executive:* "The way I get things done is through others. One strategy is to do favors for people. That not only makes them friends, but when I need something done I can always cash in a 'chit'." How important are power and politics in organizational life?

- *Chuck Hannick, chief of the plans division:* Hannick was standing at the main entrance to the plans building at 8:00 A.M. just waiting for someone to come in late. Sure enough, several did. He took their names and when he got back to his office he called their bosses and asked for a written explanation about why the people were late. Is this effective leadership behavior?

- *Jack Sloan, chief of manpower* (discussing the results of his reorganization plan with a colleague): "It was a disaster! No sooner had we announced the plan when we had almost a hundred grievances. In addition, several managers said that they opposed the plan and would back the workers. I don't understand . . . the plan was so logical and such an improvement. Why did this rational reorganization plan fail?"

The incidents related above describe a variety of organizational behaviors that are encountered at one time or another by managers. They are only examples of the types of issues we will be addressing in this book. There is great variety in human behavior and this creates complexity, but the same variety also creates interest, stimulation, and challenge.

The nature of this book is threefold: to help you understand the nature of human behavior in organizations, to provide some practical suggestions for improved people management, and to improve organizational performance.

In this introductory chapter, we will find out what managers do, define the field of organizational behavior, describe how research is conducted to support our concepts, and provide an introduction to systems theory as a way of understanding the interrelated nature of organizations. The chapter concludes with an overview of the remainder of the book.

Perspective 1.1

THE BEST COMPANIES TO WORK FOR IN AMERICA[6]

A study of U.S. companies found that some were much better to work for than others. Here are a few examples of the benefits offered by the most desired companies:[7]

- Moog Inc., a small aerospace company in upstate New York, treats its employees to a seven-week paid vacation on their 10th anniversary—on top of their regular three weeks. And the seven-week treat is awarded every five years thereafter—on an employee's 15th, 20th, 25th, 30th, etc. anniversaries.

- These companies have a "no layoff" policy: Delta Airlines, Digital Equipment Corp., Exxon, Hewlett-Packard, IBM, S.C. Johnson, and Proctor and Gamble. They have never—repeat *never*—instituted a general layoff of employees.

- The time clocks at Donnelly Mirrors plant in Holland, Michigan, have been removed—and everyone is on a salaried basis.

- J.C. Penney, Physio-Control, and Quad/Graphics never refer to their people as "employees." At Penney, you're an associate. At Physio-Control, a Redmond, Washington-based Eli Lilly unit that makes medical electronic products, you're a team member. And at Quad/Graphics, a Pewaukee, Wisconsin-based printer, you're a partner.

- Employees at Raychem Corp. receive quarterly bonuses pegged to the company's profitability. The formula is: one-half of the return on sales multiplied by your salary. Assume Raychem netted eight percent on sales in its most recent quarter; your bonus is then four percent; so if you are making $30,000 a year, or $7,500 per quarter, your bonus for the quarter is $300.

There seem to be five common denominators among the 100 best companies to work for, including:

- Making people feel they are part of a team.

- Encouraging open communication.

- Stressing quality, which enables people to feel good about what they are doing.

- Allowing employees to share in the profits, through profit sharing, stock ownership, or both.

- Reducing distinctions in rank, such as eliminating the executive dining room.

The top ten companies, in alphabetical order, were: Bell Labs, Trammell Crow, Delta Airlines, Goldman Sachs, Hallmark Cards, Hewlett-Packard, IBM, Pitney Bowes, Northwestern Mutual Life Insurance, and Time Inc.[8]

MANAGERIAL BEHAVIOR: WHAT MANAGERS DO

There is a lot of variety in what managers do. Some managers have long, high-pressure workdays. Others are able to organize their activities more carefully and hold their workdays to eight or nine hours. For example, a researcher named John Kotter studied a number of general managers in action. Here is how he described two contrasting people:

> Tom Long and Richard Papolis both worked for the same large U.S. corporation [International Computers] and managers at corporate headquarters thought highly of both of them. By most standards, both were performing very well in their jobs and both had very successful careers so far; yet they seemed to operate so differently that some people at corporate [headquarters] (including my contact) wondered how they could both possibly be so effective.
>
> I began to sense these differences even before meeting the two men. When I arrived at Long's office at 8:15 A.M. for our first encounter, scheduled for 8:30, he was

busy with his 7:30 appointment. His secretary gave me coffee and an office to work in until 8:30 sharp. When I arrived at Papolis' office at 8:45 for our 9:00 A.M. first meeting, his secretary gave me coffee and cookies and had me wait in his office; he hadn't arrived yet. At 9:15 he did.

The two men worked in very different environments. Tom's office was modern, tastefully simple, and had clean working surfaces. Richard's office, at least compared to Tom's was chaotic; there were no clean surfaces and the walls were covered with photographs, favorite sayings, and even pictures he had painted.

Tom's day was as well organized as his office. He spent most of his time in scheduled meetings. There was almost always a relatively clear purpose, and Tom was relentless in helping others achieve that purpose. His style had the rhythm and discipline of a first-rate military drill team: one, two, three, four, one, two, three, four.

Richard's day was quite different. He too had scheduled meetings, but they were far fewer in number; he spent much of his time in informal discussions with his subordinates, many of which they (not he) initiated. The pace was sometimes rapid, and sometimes quite relaxed. Voices were sometimes soft and sometimes very loud (Richard would occasionally yell at someone).

The content of their days was also different. Tom was more heavily involved in short-run issues, Richard in middle- and long-run questions. In addition to spending time dealing with subordinates, Tom spent considerable effort on lateral [with colleagues] and upward relations [with bosses], much more than Richard did.

Even the hours they worked varied considerably. Tom worked about sixty-five hours a week, usually starting at 7:00 A.M. and ending at 6:00 P.M. Richard worked about forty hours a week and was proud of it.[9]

Even though these managers behave quite differently, they still have to accomplish a number of common managerial tasks like those illustrated in Table 1.2. To accomplish these tasks they spend most of their time with others. One study found that only 24 percent of a manager's time is spent working alone and that is mostly at home, on airplanes, or while commuting.[10] The remaining three quarters of their time is spent talking, meeting, and listening to others. An obvious conclusion from this data is that the ability to interact and work with people is a crucial managerial skill.

Another result of managerial behavior research, which may surprise you, is that managers at higher organizational levels seldom give orders. They request, cajole, persuade, or intimidate people into doing what they want to have accomplished.[11] A related research effort found that successful managers spend almost half again as much time politicking and socializing as do less successful managers.[12] Thus, an important part of the manager's job involves influencing and leading others.

Managers are inevitably involved in conflict. Two subordinates may disagree over approaches to new product development. Two work groups under the manager's supervision may be at each others' throats because of perceived inequitable treatment. A union shop steward may threaten a grievance relating to a disagreement over work schedules. Successful managers spend proportionately more of their time managing such conflicts.[13] They confront and deal with problems rather than covering them up.

The behaviors we have discussed illustrate only a small portion of all the things managers do. Managers are involved in a wide variety of activities and

Table 1.1

CATEGORIES AND EXAMPLES OF MANAGERIAL BEHAVIORS

Behavioral category	Examples
1. Planning/coordinating	Setting goals Assigning tasks Scheduling
2. Staffing	Interviewing candidates Hiring people
3. Training/development	Coaching subordinates Clarifying roles and duties Orienting new people
4. Decision making/problem solving	Defining and analyzing problems Taking action Developing new products and procedures
5. Processing paper	Reading mail and reports Writing memos and reports
6. Exchanging information	Attending staff meetings Phone calls
7. Monitoring/controlling performance	Inspecting work Walking around—observing Monitoring performance reports
8. Motivating/reinforcing	Giving rewards Providing recognition and feedback
9. Disciplining/punishing	Enforcing rules and policies Formal reprimands "Chewing out" for infractions
10. Interacting with others	Contacting customers and suppliers Community affairs (Rotary Club)
11. Managing conflict	Resolving interpersonal conflicts Improving cooperation and consensus
12. Socializing/politicking	Informal non-work discussions Office humor and jokes Grapevine Playing politics; gamesmanship

SOURCE: Adapted and abridged from Luthans, F., & Lockwood, D.L. (1984). Toward an observational system for measuring leader behavior in natural settings. In J.G. Hunt, D. Hosking, C. Schriesheim, & R. Stewart (Eds.), *Leaders and managers: International perspectives on managerial behavior and leadership.* (p. 122.) New York: Pergamon Press.

topics. At the same time one central theme arises—managers must be able to communicate, motivate, lead, and interact with people. This book is designed to help you improve your knowledge of human behavior in an organizational setting and to improve your people-management skills (*see* Figure 1.1).

THE NATURE OF ORGANIZATIONAL BEHAVIOR

In this section we will define organizational behavior and discuss why it is important for managers. We will then discuss the ways in which organizational behavior can help people manage more effectively.

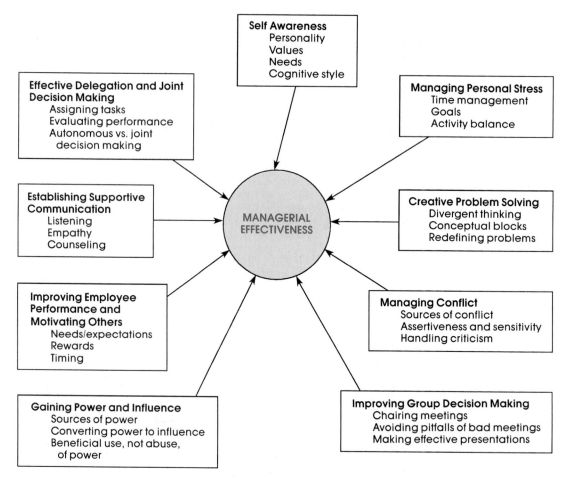

Figure 1.1

SKILLS NEEDED BY EFFECTIVE MANAGERS

SOURCE: Adapted from Cameron, K.S., & Whetten, D.A. (1983). A model for teaching management skills. *EXCHANGE: The Organizational Behavior Teaching Journal, 8,* 22.

What Is Organizational Behavior?

The field of organizational behavior (often called OB or org behavior for short) is a relatively new field that has evolved from the older social sciences of psychology, sociology, social-psychology, anthropology, and political science (*see* Figure 1.2). While the meaning of OB is still evolving, we will define **organizational behavior** as the study of the human aspects of organizations, including individual behavior, group behavior, and their interaction with organizational structure, culture, and processes; with the goal of improving organizational effectiveness.[14]

What Is an Organization?

Several aspects of the definition of OB need clarification. Perhaps the first one is to define an **organization** as a system that coordinates people, jobs, technol-

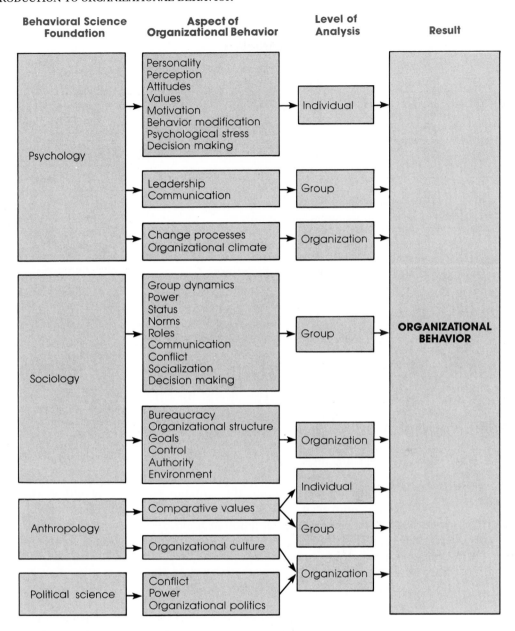

Figure 1.2

THE FIELD OF ORGANIZATIONAL BEHAVIOR

ogy, and management practices to achieve goals. Organizational membership is made up of people, both individuals and groups, whose activities and jobs are structured and coordinated through management. Organizations also use technology—skills, information, techniques—to accomplish their goals and purposes. Finally, organizations work within some identifiable boundary. Examples of elements that fall within the boundary of the organization are payroll and plant facilities. Elements that fall outside the boundary would be suppliers, customers, and the Environmental Protection Agency.

The Contingency Approach

Before reading further you may wish to complete the questionnaire in Table 1.2 to help you understand the contingency approach.

Table 1.2

ORGANIZATIONAL OUTCOME QUESTIONNAIRE

Directions: Answer each question by answering *yes, no,* or *maybe/sometimes:*

	Yes	No	Maybe/ Sometimes
1. Leaders should be equally concerned with their followers and the task.	———	———	———
2. Satisfied workers are more productive.	———	———	———
3. Employees would prefer exciting and challenging jobs.	———	———	———
4. People want to participate in decisions that affect their job.	———	———	———
5. Pay motivates people to work harder.	———	———	———

SOURCE: Adapted from an idea of Pinder, C.C. (1983). Contingency quiz. In D. Hellriegel, J.W. Slocum, Jr., & R.W. Woodman (Eds.), *Organizational behavior,* 3rd edition (p. 19). St. Paul, MN: West.

Much effort in OB is aimed toward understanding and predicting how individuals and groups behave in different circumstances. This often involves more than a simple cause and effect prediction, for different conditions may result in different outcomes. For example, many people may seek more challenging, enriched, responsible jobs, but others may prefer jobs where they feel comfortable and do not have to stretch themselves intellectually. These two groups of people would not respond in the same way to a strategy aimed at enriching their jobs.

This process of determining the situational effects of OB is called the **contingency approach.**[15] Most OB outcomes, such as performance or job satisfaction, depend on the situation at hand. In other words, there is no one best way to motivate, communicate, lead, or design jobs. The best way will depend upon the situation. If you answered *maybe/sometimes* to all the questions in Table 1.2, then you understand that the contingency approach applies to each of them. Later in the book we will discuss what specific contingencies of situations are involved in each of these examples. While there is some controversy surrounding the overuse of the contingency approach, it has served to improve our understanding and prediction of a number of organizational processes.[16]

Organizational Structure, Culture, and Process

People do not exist in isolation in an organization; they interact with the structure, culture, and processes of the organization.

Organizational structure consists of the way tasks are broken down between people, the rules and procedures for accomplishing the task, and the authority and responsibility relationship that exists between people in the organization.[17] Structure continuously interacts with all aspects of organizational behavior; however, it is perhaps most clear in the areas of communication, job

Perspective 1.2

LEARNING PROCESSES

While the entire process of learning is rather complex, there are several concepts that can help improve your learning of organizational behavior or any other subject.[20]

Motivation. You must feel the need to learn. It helps to be interested and motivated. How can the information be useful to you? Examine your reasons for reading this book or taking a course. If you recognize the positive benefits, then you are more likely to learn.

Feedback. You need feedback to correct erroneous perceptions and provide an evaluation of your progress. It is particularly useful if feedback can be given in a nonevaluative manner, such as asking yourself questions about a topic to be sure you understand it or completing the case analysis at the end of the chapter. Exams and tests are also forms of feedback. As distasteful as they may be, they are useful motivators and important sources of feedback.

Practice and repetition. The old saying, "practice makes perfect," has more than a grain of truth in it. Making an outline of the material you want to learn after you have read it helps imprint it on your mind. Frequent reviews are important for they help integrate the concepts and provide additional opportunities to record the information into your long-term memory.

Reinforcement. If you find learning the material is personally rewarding, you will be more likely to retain it. One objective for this book is to try to make the material as interesting and rewarding as possible. Another important source of rewards is the actual chance to put the concepts to work in an organization. Try to use what you learn every chance you can—you will be surprised how much you retain.

design, goal setting, policies and procedures, and reporting relationships (Who is the boss?).

Organizational culture, the topic of Chapter 17, is a broad integrating concept that includes such areas as shared beliefs, philosophies, values, behaviors, and symbols that are characteristic of an organization.[18] Cultures spell out the informal rules that govern how people are supposed to behave. Tandem Computers, one of Silicon Valley's most successful computer companies, was founded on the belief that its greatest resource is people. This culture is widely shared and visible throughout the plant, as evidenced by the slogan, "It takes two to Tandem," the informality (no reserved parking places), and rituals and ceremony, such as the traditional Friday afternoon beer busts.[19]

Organizational processes involve studying how and why activities, results, or states happen—in other words, what steps take place in going from a to b to c.[21] We find examples of processes throughout the book. One process, illustrating the way we learn, is illustrated in Perspective 1.2. Motivation, communication, conflict, and change are other processes we will learn about later in the book.

Organizational Effectiveness

OB is aimed not only at improving your understanding of the way organizations behave, it is also directed toward improving organizational effectiveness. For example, in the opening incidents, a number of problems were raised:

1. How can we select people to get the best fit between the person and the job?

2. How do we motivate employees to perform better?

3. Can problems of stereotyping women and other minorities be overcome? How?

4. What is the most effective way to control or change behavior?

5. How can we get an informal group of employees to accept new members?

6. How may conflict be controlled or reduced?

7. What is the most effective way to supervise?

8. How can we minimize resistance to organizational change?

The answers to these questions and many more are the concern of OB because we want to be able to prescribe better ways to manage organizations. Some of the major organizational effectiveness outcomes that we are concerned with are shown in Table 1.3. We are interested in multiple outcomes rather than each one alone. For example, we may wish to design jobs that simultaneously result in high productivity, high quality, and satisfying jobs.

Now that you have an overview of what OB is all about, we need to look briefly at the sources of our concepts and theories. The next section is concerned with researching OB topics.

RESEARCH IN ORGANIZATIONAL BEHAVIOR

In organizational behavior, we rely upon theories to help us understand and predict behavior. A theory tells us how concepts, variables, or things relate to one another.[22] For example, one relatively simple OB theory says that moderately difficult task goals, if accepted, result in improved performance.[23] This theory says that if we give people difficult goals, they will work hard to reach them, provided they accept the goals in the first place. Such a theory has obvious advantages for managers, if it is true (the theory will be discussed in Chapter 7). It lets us know more about how motivation works, and perhaps more importantly, how to use the theory to change work behavior.

Table 1.3

ORGANIZATIONAL EFFECTIVENESS CRITERIA

Productivity	Output of goods or services per worker.
Quality	Defects per unit produced.
Efficiency	Accomplishing the job with a minimum expenditure of effort and materials.
Job satisfaction	Degree of pleasant or unpleasant feelings toward your job.
Attendance	Number of times and duration of employee absences.
Turnover	Proportion of desirable employees who quit or leave.
Quality of work life	Concern for individual well-being.

The way we test the usefulness and validity of such a theory is through research, the topic of this section. We will cover three basic ways of conducting research: natural observation, survey research, and experimental research. Some understanding of these strategies is needed to evaluate how good the support is for a given concept or theory.

Natural Observation

When a researcher observes and records the natural environment and then analyzes and draws conclusions from these observations, **natural observation, observational research,** or **qualitative research** is being used. Although this strategy is the least rigorous of all research methods, it can address very complex, broad problems and thus becomes quite valuable for looking at the broader aspects of OB. For example, how can we decrease organizational costs and at the same time improve quality of work life for organizational members? Or, how can we change the organization's culture? These questions are too broad to answer with the other research strategies.

One form of natural observation often found in management is comments from successful or knowledgeable insiders, called **authoritative opinions.** For example, Lee Iacocca, Chief Executive Officer for Chrysler Corp., wrote a best-selling book called *Iacocca: An Autobiography,*[24] which gives advice based on his experience as a manager:

> Over the years, I've regularly asked my key people—and I've had them ask *their* key people, and so on down the line—a few basic questions: "What are your objectives over the next ninety days? What are your plans, your priorities, your hopes? And how do you intend to go about achieving them?" [Iacocca calls this goal-setting process the quarterly review system.]
>
> The quarterly review system sounds almost too simple—except that it works. And it works for several reasons. First, it allows a man to be his own boss and set his own goals. Second, it makes him more productive and gets him motivated on his own. Third, it helps new ideas bubble up to the top. The quarterly review forces managers to pause and consider what they've accomplished, what they expect to accomplish next, and how they intend to go about it. I've never found a better way to stimulate fresh approaches to problem solving.[25]

Qualitative research may also be done by academically trained scholars, often with good results.[26] Authoritative opinions, such as those put forth by Peter Drucker, a famous writer on management topics, have been very influential among practitioners and academics alike.[27] The book by Harold Geneen, former Chief Executive Officer of ITT, entitled *Managing,* is also an example of how authoritative opinions can be influential.[28]

Another form of observational research is the **case study,** in which the researcher describes what happened in a particular organization. The best-selling book by Tom Peters and Nancy Austin, *A Passion for Excellence,* is an example of the use of extensive case examples to build theories.[29] Case studies are sometimes written by **participant observers**—academic researchers who join an organization as a member so as to observe in a natural way what is happening in the organization. For example, John Van Maanen actually joined a police force on a full and part-time basis for a number of years. While he observed a range of interesting behaviors, he also noted difficulties in remaining detached and objective and concludes that all such participant-observer research is based on a combination of "passion and judgement"; thus, it is impossible to fully assess its accuracy.[30]

While observational techniques are not as rigorous as other research strategies because they are subject to the biases of the observer, they often provide insights into important issues that would not have been addressed using other research strategies.

Survey Research

Survey research involves the use of questionnaires to gather data about anything that is of concern to the manager or researcher.[31] For example, many organizations regularly measure job satisfaction to find out how well employees like their jobs (*see* Chapter 3 for an example of such a survey). In addition, you might be interested in finding out if employees are experiencing job stress, if they are satisfied with supervisory practices or pay, or if they desire some change in working hours.

Survey responses, which are usually obtained from either a sample or from all employees, may be analyzed in several ways. One way is simply to present percentages for those who respond in a certain way, such as 47 percent favor the new working hour plan. Another common way is to compute the average score for each question, such as a satisfaction level of 7.2 on a scale of 1 to 10. These types of analyses are called **descriptive statistics.**

Another common strategy is to relate one **variable,** or factor that you wish to measure (such as job satisfaction), to another one (such as job performance). This type of analysis is called **correlation.** An important consideration when using correlation is that you can only find out the degree of relationship between two variables; you cannot tell which one is the cause and which one is the effect.[32]

An example of the use of survey research might be using a questionnaire to find out if there is a relationship between job satisfaction and attendance or absenteeism. Our common sense would tell us that people who are satisfied would be more likely to come to work and thus we would predict a moderately strong relationship between these two variables. To accomplish the research, let's assume that the firm has 200 employees and that a sample of fifty was taken. The job satisfaction scores are then calculated and matched with the attendance records of the employees. A correlation coefficient is calculated that will range somewhere between -1.0 and $+1.0$. The closer the correlation to one, either positive or negative, the stronger the relationship. The closer the correlation is to zero, the weaker the relationship.

The plot in Figure 1.3 graphically illustrates the responses of the fifty employees who responded to the survey. The correlation coefficient was calculated with a result of $r = -0.45$, which is a moderately strong relationship between job satisfaction and absenteeism—as job satisfaction goes up, absenteeism goes down. This is the expected relationship and might be an indication that our efforts to improve job satisfaction are linked with the desirable outcome of lower absenteeism. But remember that the correlation relationship does not prove that lower job satisfaction causes absenteeism. Perhaps being

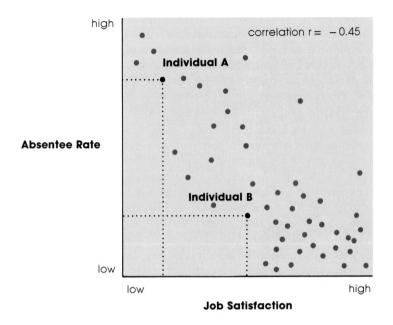

Figure 1.3

RELATIONSHIP BETWEEN JOB SATISFACTION AND ABSENTEEISM

This figure uses hypothetical data. For a research review, see Cotton, J.L., & Tuttle, J.M. (1986). Employee turnover: A meta-analysis and review with implications for research. *Academy of Management Review, 11,* 55–70.

absent makes people like their jobs less rather than the more obvious interpretation. Causation can only be determined through experimental research, the topic of the next section.

In summary, survey research is widely used for organizational purposes as well as for building and testing theory. It is relatively easy to do; and thus costs are low. Problems center around the validity of the survey instruments and problems of determining cause and effect.

Experimental Research

Experimental research is powerful because it allows us to determine cause and effect relationships. In **experiments** the researcher creates a situation, manipulates events, and controls the research environment.[33] There are two basic settings for experiments: field and laboratory. **Field experiments** are conducted in real organizational settings, while **laboratory experiments** are conducted in settings contrived by the researcher. In OB research we see both settings used.

Take a field experiment as an example. Researchers wish to see if enriched jobs result in higher job satisfaction and productivity. The experimental design includes two groups: an experimental group and a control group. Before the jobs of the experimental group are changed so that they are more enriched, productivity and satisfaction are measured for both groups. Then the jobs of the experimental group are redesigned to be more enriched (interesting,

Perspective 1.3

"ON EXPERIMENTAL DESIGN" BY MARK TWAIN[34]

I constructed four miniature houses of worship—a Mohammedan mosque, a Hindu temple, a Jewish synagogue, a Christian cathedral—and placed them in a row. I then marked fifteen ants with red paint and turned them loose. They made several trips to and fro, glancing in at the places of worship, but not entering.

I then turned loose fifteen more painted blue; they acted just as the red ones had done. I now gilded fifteen and turned them loose. No change in the result; the forty-five traveled back and forth in a hurry persistently and continuously visiting each fane, but never entering. This satisfied me that these ants were without religious prejudices—just what I wished; for under no other conditions would my next and greater experiment be valuable. I now placed a small square of white paper within the door of each fane; and upon the mosque paper I put a pinch of putty, upon the temple paper a dab of tar, upon the synagogue paper a trifle of turpentine, and upon the cathedral paper a small cube of sugar.

First I liberated the red ants. They examined and rejected the putty, the tar and the turpentine, and then took to the sugar with zeal and apparent sincere conviction. I next liberated the blue ants, and they did exactly as the red ones had done. The gilded ants followed. The preceding results were precisely repeated. This seemed to prove that ants destitute of religious prejudice will always prefer Christianity to any other creed.

However, to make sure, I removed the ants and put putty in the cathedral and sugar in the mosque. I now liberated the ants in a body, and they rushed tumultuously to the cathedral. I was very much touched and gratified, and went back to the room to write down the event; but when I came back the ants had all apostatized and had gone over to the Mohammedan communion.

I saw that I had been too hasty in my conclusions, and naturally felt rebuked and humbled. With diminished confidence I went on with the test to finish. I placed the sugar first in one house of worship, then in another, till I had tried them all.

With this result: whatever Church I put the sugar in, that was the one the ants straightway joined. This was true beyond a shadow of doubt, that in religious matters the ant is the opposite of man, for man cares for but one thing; to find the only true Church; whereas the ant hunts for the one with the sugar in it.

meaningful, and challenging—*see* Chapter 7). No changes happen to the jobs of the control group. After the changes (called the experimental treatment), the results are measured to see what changes occurred in job satisfaction and productivity. The results illustrated in Figure 1.4 show a significant change in job satisfaction, but no change in productivity.

Experiments offer us precision and control. They are the most rigorous of all research techniques and the only ones from which we can determine cause and effect relationships. However, experiments do not lend themselves to broad-based problems that cannot be manipulated (organizational culture, for example). They may also be so controlled and rigorous that people in organizational settings may react adversely and cause distortions in the results.[35]

Evaluating Research

Critical evaluation of research requires considerable knowledge of research methods and statistics.[36] An important thing for managers to consider is that a

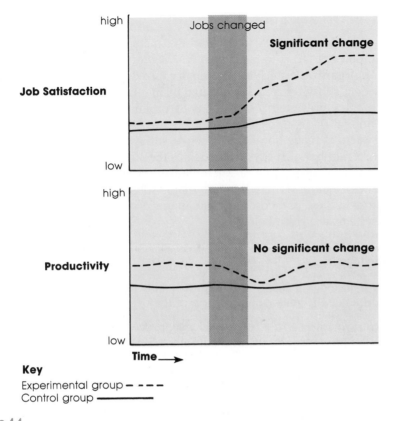

Figure 1.4

**RESULTS OF AN EXPERIMENT TO DETERMINE THE EFFECTS
OF JOB ENRICHMENT ON SATISFACTION AND PRODUCTIVITY**

number of different methods are appropriate for organizational research, but
each has its problems. Observational techniques are good for broad research
issues; survey research offers inexpensive answers to theoretical and practical
questions; and experiments offer rigor and control to determine which factors
are causal. Perhaps the ideal situation is when a number of different research
strategies seem to converge in support of one theory.

ORGANIZATIONS AS SYSTEMS

Even though we tend to separate the topics of organizational behavior into perception, motivation, communication, or group dynamics; in reality, these
topics interrelate and merge together. Every managerial analysis and decision
needs to include a consideration of its impact on other parts of the organization. Managers need to question what will happen to other parts of the
organization's structure, culture, or processes besides the one being changed.
For example, if you are designing a new pay system, it may have an impact on
motivation, organizational goals, leadership behavior, and quality of work life.

What Is an Organizational System?

One way to maintain a total organizational perspective while studying the individual topics of OB is to use a systems view of organizations to tie things together. An **organizational system** is an organized, unitary whole made up of interdependent subsystems and delineated by identifiable boundaries from the environmental suprasystem.[37] Examples of organizational systems might be Rainier National Bank, Apple Computer, Boeing Aircraft, or Shakey's Pizza.

Every system is made up of a number of **subsystems,** just as your body is made up of a number of subsystems, such as the circulatory system or the nervous system. The subsystems of an organization could be divided in many ways. One way separates them into five major subsystems: technical, structural, goals and values, psychosocial, and managerial. Definitions for each of these subsystems are given below: [38]

- *Psychosocial subsystem*—The individual and group behavior of people working together.

- *Goals and values subsystem*—Values, or the broad general beliefs people hold, influence the goals and direction of the organization.

- *Technical subsystem*—The knowledge, processes, techniques, and facilities used to transform inputs into outputs.

- *Structural subsystem*—The structures, procedures, and rules in the organization serve to divide up the tasks and coordinate them. Some examples in this area include time schedules, job descriptions, work rules, communication procedures, and lines of authority.

- *Managerial subsystem*—The central roles of coordinating, planning, controlling, leading, and goal setting are accomplished by managers.

- *Organizational system*—All of the above subsystems compose the organizational system. In other words, an organization is made up of goal-directed people, with values, operating within a structure and technology that allows them to accomplish the organization's purpose.

Figure 1.5 shows that each of the subsystems are interrelated and overlapping and that the managerial subsystem acts as the integrating force.

Environmental Suprasystem

Organizations are also part of a larger **environmental suprasystem** that includes such dimensions as customers, suppliers, competitors, politics, and economic conditions. (These topics are discussed in Chapter 15.) For example an oil company doing business in the turbulent Middle East faces considerably different environmental problems than does a major department store in the United States. However, a Silicon Valley electronics manufacturer may have even greater environmental problems than an oil company because of the extreme amount of international competition in high-technology electronics. Geography is only one factor, among many others, that determines environmental uncertainty and turbulence.

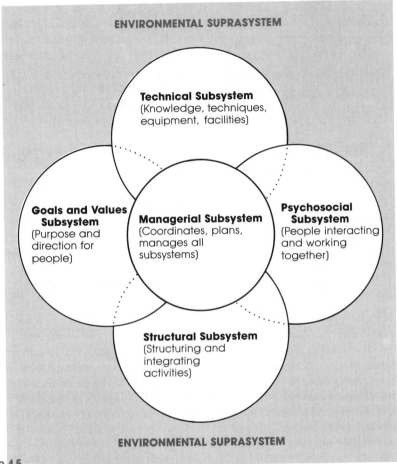

Figure 1.5

ORGANIZATIONS AS SYSTEMS

SOURCE: From Kast, F.E., & Rosenzweig, J.E. (1979). *Organization and Management*, p. 19. Copyright © 1979 by McGraw-Hill, New York. Used with permission.

An Example of the Systems Approach

The Atlas Sign Co. provides an example of how systems concepts apply to organizational behavior. The applicable systems concepts are noted in parentheses. The case concerns the Atlas Sign Co., owned by Jeff Baxter and his brother-in-law, Willie Sanchez, and located in a medium-sized town in northern Florida.

The company was founded in 1951 and had prospered. It specialized in leasing road signs to hotels, restaurants, motels, and other businesses (environmental suprasystem—customers). Businesses that wanted road signs contracted with Atlas on an annual basis to provide the signs (structural subsystem—procedures). Each customer approved a color sketch of the sign and the general geographical location of the sign (technical subsystem—design and placement). By 1958, Atlas had almost sixty employees organized into three divisions: construction, painting, and sales (structural subsystem—division of labor).

The construction division did all the heavy work including digging the holes for the signs, erecting the heavy telephone poles, and building the framing and sign faces (technical subsystem—design and building). The construction crews were generally a pretty tough, hard-drinking lot (psychosocial and values subsystems—macho values). Crews would work hard if they were supervised, but they would take every chance they could to "goof off" and had to be closely supervised by their foremen (psychosocial subsystem—group norms and pressures).

The painters liked to think of themselves as artists and were quite temperamental, so these employees had to be handled with "kid gloves" (psychosocial and managerial subsystems—leadership style and communication).

The salespeople were always trying to beat the company goals (psychosocial and goals and values subsystem—motivation and goal setting). Unlike the construction crews, they required little supervision because their sales dollar values provided a direct measure of their work performance (structural and managerial subsystems—control and motivation).

(For the remainder of this case, you may wish to check your ability to determine which subsystem or suprasystem is involved. Use a separate piece of paper and pre-letter it from a through j. Then following each letter write the system you think applies. More than one system is often involved since they interact. Answers appear at the end of the references at the end of the chapter.)

Until the early 1960s everything went just fine for Atlas. However, a law passed by Congress was to have far-reaching effects on their future (*a*). A new law required all roadsigns to be placed no closer than 600 feet from the highway. This made their standard construction techniques obsolete since much larger signs and lettering would be needed for people to see them from the road (*b*). In addition, it raised the cost per sign astronomically.

At almost the same time another event went almost unnoticed—big chain motels, such as Holiday Inn, were taking over the business once held by big city hotels (*c*). And, to make things even worse, these new chain hotels were using centralized telephone reservation services that made the need for signs somewhat less important than it once had been (*d*). Thus, costs were going up and the number of customers was declining.

About this time Jeff and Willie should have reevaluated their direction to see if there was another product line with more potential, such as neon signs or signs located on the motel's property (*e*). However, they did not notice the changes and continued using the same strategies and techniques they had always used.

As business declined, their first step was to lay off employees. The first ten people were no problem since most of them were transitory. But then they had to lay off one of their long-time employees, Solomon Clark. Solomon had been a bit outspoken and had never gotten along well with his foreman or with the owners (*f*). Solomon protested his layoff by going to the union and filing a grievance (*g*). Although the union had always been pretty weak, the firing gave them a rallying point, and they were able to call a general strike against Atlas (*h*). Since Jeff and Willie were violently anti-union (*i*), they held out for almost ten weeks before they finally gave in to most of the union's demands, including reinstating Solomon Clark (*j*).

Unfortunately, when the strike effects were combined with reduced sales and increasing costs, Atlas Sign went bankrupt within six months—the owners lost everything!

As you can see, there is a great deal of interaction between the subsystems, and it is not always clear which system is the dominant one. In this case the environmental suprasystem was probably crucial. If the owners had paid more attention to what was happening in Congress and in the industry, they might still be in business. The objective of this example is not to make you a systems expert but to alert you to the interactive nature of the material we will be covering in the book.[39]

Table 1.4 shows the topics of the book and the primary organizational subsystems that apply. Keep in mind that there is almost always an interaction between several subsystems.

Table 1.4

ORGANIZATIONAL BEHAVIOR TOPICS RELATED TO SYSTEMS THEORY

Chapter	Subject Matter	Primary Systems Relationships (*See* Legend for key)					
		Psycho-social	Goals and values	Technical	Structural	Mana-gerial	Environ-mental
2	Personality	▦	□			▦	□
3	Values and attitudes	▦	■			▦	▦
4	Perception	■	▦			▦	□
	Impression management	▦	□	□		▦	▦
5	Motivation	■	▦	▦	▦	■	▦
6	Behavior modification	■	□			■	□
	Pay	▦	▦	□		■	□
7	Job design	▦	□	▦	■	■	□
	Goal setting	▦	■	□	■	■	□
8	Communication	■	▦		▦	■	▦
9	Group dynamics	■	▦		□	▦	□
10	Conflict	▦	□		▦	▦	□
	Competition	▦	□		▦	▦	□
11	Stress	■	▦		□	▦	□
12	Power	▦	□		▦	■	▦
	Politics	▦			▦	▦	▦
13	Decision making	▦	▦	▦	▦	■	▦
14	Leadership	▦	▦	□	▦	■	□
15	Organization design	▦	□	▦	■	▦	□
16	Organizational change	▦	▦		■	■	□
	Organization development	▦	▦		□	▦	□
17	Organizational culture	■	▦		▦	■	▦
	Quality of work life	■	▦		□	▦	▦

LEGEND: ■ High Impact ☐ Low impact ▦ Moderate impact   Blank indicates very little impact

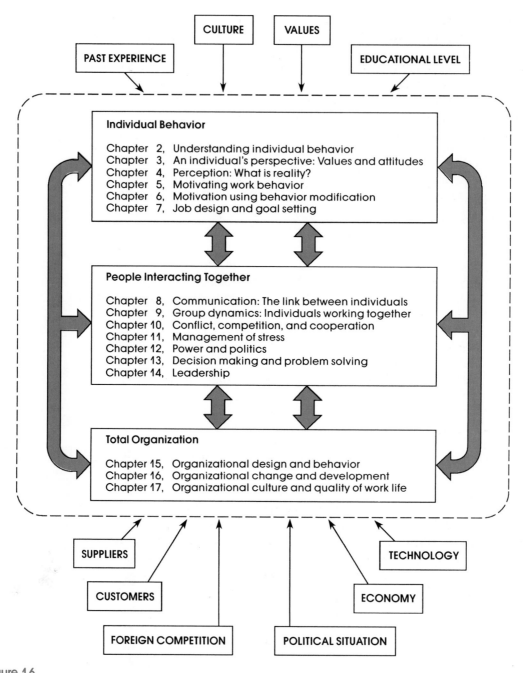

Figure 1.6

OVERVIEW OF ORGANIZATIONAL SYSTEMS

OVERVIEW OF THE BOOK

We will begin our study with the nature of individuals who work in organizations. Personalities, values, attitudes, and perceptions of people influence much organizational behavior, including the important topic of motivation. In the first section of the book, we will cover a number of interesting and applied topics, such as managing one's impression, barriers to advancement of women in organizations, personality characteristics of general managers, and a comparison of Japanese and American values. Figure 1.6 shows how all the topics fit together with each other and the environment.

Our next focus will be how to motivate employees. After learning some theories of motivation we will turn to several ways to apply motivation. The relatively new area of organizational behavior modification will be added to the more traditional strategies of using pay, goals, and job design.

Once we have completed the individually oriented first section of the book, we will examine three important aspects of communication including interpersonal communications, listening behavior, and nonverbal communication. Communication, the link between individuals, will lead us into the next section of the book, which focuses on group behavior.

The study of group dynamics begins the interaction-between-people section. We learn a number of practical concepts for understanding group behavior and find out what it takes to make groups effective. The inevitable conflict that results when people and groups interact will be our next topic. We will learn which resolution techniques to use. One outcome of conflict is often stress, a relatively new topic in OB that concentrates on recognizing and managing the factors that cause stress. Certainly no study of organizations would be complete without the study of power and politics in organizations, a ubiquitous aspect of organizational life.

In the next topic of the section, you will find out how to make more effective decisions. We will cover when to use groups and when to avoid them. We will also cover several useful approaches to decision making. The final chapter in the section deals with leadership. You will find out what makes an effective leader and what leadership strategies seem to work best.

The last section of the book deals more with organization-wide issues. Organizational design discusses the strategies for designing effective organizations. Our attention will then shift to organizational change—we will be concerned with ways to get ready for change and conduct it so it will be effective and lasting. We will also learn about an applied strategy for change called organization development. The final chapter in the book deals with the concept of organizational culture, climate, and quality of work life—critical management issues for the 1980s.

CROSS–CULTURAL OB: EXPORTING JAPANESE MANAGEMENT TO THE UNITED STATES

Cross-cultural organizational behavior topics usually involve cultures of different countries. However, culture can also vary within a country, region, or organization. In this section we will examine how the culture of another country has had an impact on an American business; specifically, we will explain how Japan exported its organizational culture to the United States.

In one of the preview cases, "Shock for GM," we noted that the New United Motor Manufacturing Inc. (NUMMI), run by Toyota Motor Corp., had been successful in turning around an old GM production plant in Fremont, California. In this section we will examine what happened in greater detail.

General Motors closed down its auto-assembly plant in Fremont because of terrible productivity and poor labor relations.[40] The absenteeism rate was 20 percent. There were 5,000 grievances outstanding, an average of one per employee! Wildcat strikes (spur of the moment work stoppages or strikes not related to the union contract) frequently interrupted production. "When GM was here, we hated each other," says Tony De Jesus, president of the new UAW local union at NUMMI . . . "It's true we were partly the blame. There were a lot of drugs and a lot of absenteeism. But we were a reflection of the SOBs we worked for." [41]

Toyota management took over the plant, hired back the UAW employees—including the militant ones—and began construction of the Chevrolet Nova. Two years after startup the plant's 2,500 employees were producing 240,000 cars per year—roughly the same number of cars that it took 5,000 people to produce under GM management. Absenteeism now runs under 2 percent and only two grievances are outstanding.

What caused this turnaround? As our systems perspective would predict, there were a number of factors involved. The Japanese brought in the famed Toyota production system centered around the just-in-time purchasing system, which carefully controls the arrival of subassemblies and parts so that they are received just in time.[42] This cuts down on storage space, ordering costs, and labor costs involved in handling parts several times.

They also used a team approach for designing the jobs of assembly workers. The teams are fully responsible for their jobs. Unlike the GM practice of having industrial engineers determine the best way to do the job, NUMMI employees decide themselves how to set up the job. They come up with better designs than the engineers used to do. For example, in the old GM plant, "the person who installed the windows on the right front doors had to walk from his toolbox to each car three times as it moved along the assembly line. Now, by rearranging the equipment, the worker goes to the car just once and follows along as it passes. The job now requires 11 steps rather than 23." [43] Another advantage of the team approach is that it cuts the number of job classifications so that everyone is qualified in several different tasks. This means that people can readily fill in for one another. Using the team design also increases peer pressure on people to perform—goof-offs are punished by the group.

The culture that permeates the factory is explained by D. William Childs, NUMMI's General Manager of Human Resources: "The Japanese philosophy is to make people an important item, as opposed to the typical U.S. philosophy that workers are just an extension of machines." [44] Employees feel important. They have a voice in what happens and they have responsibility for their jobs. One NUMMI executive says "The difference between now and under GM is like night and day." [45] A union representative says, "We have the same members, the same building, the same technology—just different management and different production systems." [46]

Perspective 1.4

TWO AUTO WORKERS:
TOYOTA vs. FORD[47]

Toyota

Thirty-eight-year old Hisashi Tomiki, a twenty-year employee of Toyota, earns $26,250 per year as a welder and team leader. He gets twenty paid vacation days a year and ten holidays, drives an $8,000 Toyota Cressida and owns a $120,000 tract home. (Toyota loaned him the money for the mortgage). He has never been laid off or worked for another company.

For his first nine years at Toyota he earned little and lived in a small company-owned dorm where no female guests were allowed. After he met and married another Toyota worker, the company found him roomier quarters. He now has three children to support.

While his life sounds relatively good, it is not without problems. Since Toyota does not give sick leave, Tomiki saves half of his vacation for possible illnesses. In addition, he often forgoes his holiday because the company makes him find a workmate to fill in if he takes time off. His workday begins at 8 A.M. and ends officially at 5 P.M., but most of the time he must work another hour of unpaid overtime and he must be in his workstation all ready to go at 8 A.M. Every other week he has to work the swing shift from 9 P.M. until 6 A.M., like it or not, and he doesn't.

Tomiki gets a $3,000 lump-sum bonus twice a year, which he usually saves for a major purchase. He is not resentful that Toyota does not give an even bigger bonus. He figures that the company needs to invest in the future, thus it should not pay workers too much. While he belongs to a union, it is really just part of the company. There have been no strikes at Toyota since the early 1950s when they fired 25 percent of their workforce and broke up the union during an extended strike.

Ford

Michael Dodge has worked for Ford in Ypsilanti, Michigan for sixteen years, but he has been laid off so many times during that period that he has stopped counting. During 1981 and 1982 he only worked six months out of the two-year period. Dodge makes $29,200 per year, owns a $43,200 two-bedroom house, and two cars. He gets three weeks vacation and many company-paid benefits.

While he enjoys his job, Dodge feels like the atmosphere would be better if Ford would treat employees more like family members. He believes that unions and management must cooperate to preserve American automobile industry jobs; however, he thinks the company is too "hardline" in negotiations—more cooperation is needed.

Dodge works the 3 to 11 P.M. shift all the time. He works by himself on the line with no opportunity to interact with others or to work in a team. He is quite concerned about the future. In only four more years he will have made his "twenty" and would then be eligible for a retirement pension if his job were to disappear.

MANAGERIAL APPLICATIONS
OF ORGANIZATIONAL BEHAVIOR

This chapter has provided an overview of the topic of organizational behavior. The cases and incidents provide an inkling of the diversity and richness of the field. Throughout the book this section will provide recommendations for improving your skills and effectiveness as a manager. Here are some insights from the first chapter:

- *Choose a good company to work for.* Your success as a manager will be strongly influenced by your choice of companies. Try to find one that makes you feel part of a team, stresses open communication, and emphasizes quality. Carefully review the organization's culture.

• *Develop your people-management skills.* Since over three quarters of a manager's time is spent working with people, this skill is crucial. To improve your skills, start by learning the concepts presented in each chapter, then try to apply these to your job or situation. The best way to learn skills and to improve your human-resource management abilities is by *doing*, by practice.

• *Recognize that there is rarely "one best way."* Whether you are talking about management styles, job design, motivation, communication, group process, or other behavioral topics, management action is often determined by the situation at hand. Some strategies may be more appropriate than others. Thus you must take a contingency approach.

• *Use theories as your guide for action.* Theories provide the structure and framework for action. Learn them. Use them. Make them a part of your everyday organizational thinking and decision making.

• *Critically evaluate research.* Recognize that different methods of research have differing powers to resolve organizational questions. However, all are useful for providing multimethod evaluation of research questions and theories.

• *Recognize that correlational research does not imply causation.* Only experimental research designs are appropriate for inferring cause and effect; correlations only show relationships.

• *Maintain a systems perspective of organizations.* All organizational systems interact with each other and their environment. Whenever you change one part of the system, expect changes in other parts of the system. Keep the "big picture" in mind.

• *Study culture to improve your effectiveness.* Organizational and national cultures determine how an organization will function and what types of decisions it will make. Careful attention is needed to examine culture because we tend to view the world from our own cultural perspective.

FOR DISCUSSION

1. Using the skills shown in Figure 1.1, evaluate your own skill level on a 1 to 10 scale for each skill.

2. Based upon your organizational experience, think of an example of the contingency approach.

3. Using the learning processes outlined in Perspective 1.2, outline an effective strategy for conducting the organizational behavior class.

4. Is there one factor that is the key to organizational effectiveness? Explain why or why not.

5. How can one evaluate the quality and validity of the natural observation method of research?

6. Explain the meaning of a correlation between job satisfaction and turnover at −0.40.

7. Identify the advantages and disadvantages of each of the three major approaches to research.

8. Pick any organization with which you are familiar and describe it using systems concepts.

9. What cultural differences can you infer from the illustration of Japanese management at NUMMI?

KEY CONCEPTS AND TERMS

organizational behavior	efficiency	correlation
organization	job satisfaction	survey research
contingency approach	attendance	experimental research
organizational culture	turnover	organizational system
organizational structure	quality of work life	psychosocial subsystem
organizational processes	qualitative research	goals and values subsystem
learning processes	authoritative opinions	technical subsystem
organizational effectiveness	participant observer	structural subsystem
productivity	descriptive statistics	managerial subsystem
quality	variable	environmental suprasystem

Cases and Incidents

SAM HOLST, MANAGER

Sam Holst, project manager for the new computer chip at Zoolite Electronics, is upset. Because of a traffic tie-up, he is five minutes late getting to the office. Several of the office employees who see him come in have rather strange looks on their faces. Probably because it was only yesterday that Sam was lecturing them about coming to work on time. Sam thinks to himself that he'll have to set the alarm fifteen minutes earlier.

As he passes his secretary's desk he notices that she is not there yet. Perhaps she too was caught in the traffic. After a few minutes at his desk trying to sort out his day and make his "to do" list, he receives a call from his secretary, Alice. She is in tears. Apparently there have been marital problems at home, and she and her husband are separating. She says she is just too upset to work this week and needs some time off to get herself together. What can Sam say? He knows that the big conference is coming up next week, and he really needs Alice to help him organize it. Sam tells her it is OK to take off, but realizes he's really in trouble.

Sam knows he will have to go to the administrative department to get a replacement for Alice. However, just last week he had a big run-in with Manley, the department head. He'll really have to "eat crow" to get this favor from Manley.

The replacement secretary that Manley sends him is certainly no jewel. She is slow. She has to be told almost everything in great detail to do it right. Oh well, there is all week to get things ready for the conference. But wait, Mr. Robins, the production manager, is on the line and wants Sam to dry-run the presentation for the conference first thing in the morning, so there will be time to change anything that is not just right.

Now Sam has a real problem. He must have his presentation done and charts made by tomorrow morning. He decides that now is the time to call in some chips. George owes him a favor for the bonus Sam swung for him after the electronics module project. Sam calls George, who says, "Sure old buddy, I'll do the charts as a special favor, but I'll have to have them by 2 P.M. today or else they won't be ready for tomorrow morning."

The critical holdup is with Sam's own people—if only they were as motivated as he is. Sam remembers their sullen looks when he came in late this morning. This is a time when he needs an all-out effort from them, but with all the pushing and ranting that he has been doing lately, they probably won't budge without some type of reward. The only trouble is that Sam does not really control pay or anything like that. All he can do is explain the situation to them and hope they will put out for him.

DISCUSSION QUESTIONS

1. What subsystems apply to this case?

2. What research strategy would you use to evaluate the job satisfaction of Sam's work-group?

A DAY IN THE LIFE
OF A GENERAL MANAGER

The GM in this case is Michael Richardson:

7:35 A.M. He arrives at work (he does not have a long commute), unpacks his briefcase, gets some coffee, and begins a "to-do" list for the day.

7:40 Jerry Bradshaw, a subordinate, arrives. Bradshaw's office is right next to Richardson's; he has two sets of duties, one of which is as an assistant to Richardson.

7:45 Bradshaw and Richardson have an informal conversation on a number of topics. Richardson shows Bradshaw some pictures he recently took at his summer home.

8:00 Bradshaw and Richardson talk about a schedule and priorities for the day. In the process, they touch on a dozen different subjects and issues relating to customers, other subordinates, and suppliers.

8:20 Frank Wilson, another subordinate, drops in. He asks a few questions about a personnel problem and then joins in the previous discussion. The discussion is straightforward, rapid, and occasionally is punctuated with humor.

8:30 Fred Holly, Richardson's boss, stops in and joins in the conversation. He also asks about an appointment at 11:00 and brings up a few other topics.

8:40 Richardson leaves to get more coffee. Bradshaw, Holly and Wilson continue their conversation.

8:42 He's back. A subordinate of a subordinate stops in and says hello, the others leave.

8:43 Bradshaw drops off a report, gives Richardson instructions to go with it, and leaves.

8:45 His secretary arrives. They discuss her new apartment and arrangements for a meeting later in the morning.

8:49 He gets a phone call from a subordinate who is returning his call of the day before. They talk primarily about the subject of the report he just received.

8:55 He leaves his office and goes to a regular morning meeting that one of his subordinates runs. There are about thirty people there. Richardson reads during the meeting.

9:09 The meeting is over. Richardson grabs one of the people there and talks to him briefly.

9:15 He walks over to the office of one of his subordinates (corporate counsel). His boss is there, too. They discuss a phone call the lawyer just received. While standing, the three talk about possible responses to a problem. As before, the exchange is quick and occasionally includes some humor.

9:30 Richardson goes back to his office for a meeting with the vice chairman of another firm (a potential customer and supplier). One other person, a liaison with that firm and a subordinate's subordinate, also attends the meeting. The discussion is cordial and covers many topics from their products to foreign relations.

9:50 The visitor leaves. Richardson opens the adjoining door to Bradshaw's office and asks a question.

9:52 His secretary comes in with five items.

9:55 Bradshaw drops in with a question about a customer and then leaves.

9:58 Frank Wilson and one of his people arrive. He gives Richardson a memo and then the three begin to talk about the important legal problem. Wilson does not like a decision that Richardson has tentatively made and is arguing for him to reconsider. The discussion goes back and forth for twenty minutes until they agree on the next action and schedule it for 9:00 tomorrow.

10:35 They leave. Richardson looks over papers on his desk, then picks one up and calls his boss' secretary regarding the minutes of the last board meeting. He asks her to make a few corrections.

10:41 His secretary comes in with a card to sign for a friend who is sick. He writes a note to go with the card.

10:50 He gets a brief phone call, then goes back to the papers on his desk.

11:03   His boss stops in. Before they can start, he gets a brief call. After the call he tells his secretary that someone didn't get a letter he sent and to please send another.

11:05   Holly brings up a couple of issues, and then Bradshaw comes in. The three start talking about Jerry Phillips, who has become a difficult personnel problem. Bradshaw leads, telling the others about what he has done over the last few days regarding this issue. Richardson and Holly ask questions. After a while, Richardson begins to take notes. The exchange, as before, is rapid and straightforward. They try to define the problem and outline alternative next steps. Richardson is not sure what is best so he lets the discussion go on, roaming around and in and out of the topic again and again. Finally, they agree on a next step.

12:00   Richardson orders some lunch for himself and Bradshaw. Bradshaw comes in and generally goes over twelve items. Wilson stops by to say that he had already followed up on their earlier conversation.

12:10   A staff person stops by with some calculations Richardson has requested. He thanks her and has a brief pleasant conversation.

12:20   Lunch arrives. Richardson and Bradshaw go into the conference room to eat. Over lunch they pursue business and nonbusiness subjects; they laugh often at each other's humor. They end the lunch focusing on a major potential customer.

1:15   Back in his office, they continue the discussion of the customer. Bradshaw gets a pad and they discuss a presentation to the customer in detail. Then Bradshaw leaves.

1:40   Working at his desk, Richardson looks over a new marketing brochure.

1:50   Bradshaw comes in again and they go over another dozen details regarding the presentation to the potential customer.

1:55   Jerry Thomas comes in. He is a subordinate of Richardson and has scheduled some key performance appraisals this afternoon in Richardson's office with him present. They briefly talk about how they will handle each.

2:00   Fred Jacobs (a subordinate of Thomas') comes in. Jerry runs the meeting; he goes over Fred's bonus for the year and the reason for it. Then the three of them talk about Fred's role in the upcoming year. They generally agree and Fred leaves.

2:30   John Kimble comes in. The same format is used again. Richardson asks a lot of questions and praises Kimble at times. The meeting ends on a friendly note with general agreement.

3:00   George Houston comes in. The basic format is repeated.

3:30   When George leaves, they talk briefly about how well they had accomplished what they wanted in the meetings. Then they talk briefly about some other of Jerry's subordinates.

3:45   Richardson gets a short phone call. His secretary and Bradshaw come in with a list of brief requests.

3:50   He receives a call from Jerry Phillips. Richardson gets his notes from the 11 to 12 meeting on Phillips. They go back and forth on the phone talking about lost business, unhappy subordinates, who did what to whom, what should be done now. It is a long, circular, and sometimes emotional conversation. Near the end Jerry is agreeing with Richardson and thanking him.

4:55   Bradshaw, Wilson, and Holly all step in. Each is following up on different issues that were discussed earlier in the day. Richardson briefly tells them of his conversation with Phillips. Bradshaw and Holly leave.

5:10   Richardson and Wilson have a light conversation on three or four items.

5:20   Jerry Thomas stops in; he describes a new personnel problem and the three of them discuss it. More and more humor finds its way into the conversation. They agree on an action to take.

5:30   Richardson begins to pack up his brief-
         case. Five people stop by briefly, one or
         two at a time.

5:45 P.M.   He leaves the office.

DISCUSSION QUESTIONS

1. Using Table 1.1 as your guide, what categories of managerial behavior are displayed by Michael Richardson? Which seem most prevalent?

2. Using Figure 1.1 as your guide, what managerial skills are being used by Michael Richardson? Which seem most important?

REFERENCES

1. Iacocca, L. (1984). *Iacocca: An autobiography.* New York: Bantam, p. 172.

2. Kneale, D. (1986, April 7). Working at IBM: Intense loyalty in a rigid culture. *The Wall Street Journal,* p. 21.

3. Mitchell, R. (1986, June 16). Detroit stumbles on its way to the future. *Business Week,* p. 104.

4. Petre, P. (1987, January 5). The man who brought GE to life. *Fortune,* p. 76.

5. Shaken to the very core. (1985, September 30). *Time,* p. 64. For an update on Apple after the departure of Steve Jobs, *see* Apple's comeback. (1987, January 19). *Business Week,* pp. 84–89.

6. Moskowitz, M. (1985). Lessons from the best companies to work for. *California Management Review, 27,* 42–47; Levering, R., Moskowitz, M., & Katz, M. (1984). *The 100 best companies to work for in America.* Reading, MA: Addison-Wesley.

7. Examples quoted from Moskowitz, M. (1985), pp. 42–43.

8. Moskowitz, M. (1985), p. 44. For another approach to determining the best company, see *Fortune*'s annual survey of the most admired companies. In 1987 the list included Merck, Liz Claiborne, Boeing, J.P. Morgan, Rubbermaid, Shell Oil, IBM, Johnson & Johnson, Dow Jones, and Herman Miller. *See* Baig, E.C. (1987, January 19). America's most admired corporations. *Fortune,* 18cf.

9. Kotter, J.P. (1982). *The general managers.* New York: Free Press, pp. 95–96.

10. Kotter, J.P. (1982).

11. Kotter, J.P. (1982).

12. Luthans, F., Rosenkrantz, S.A., & Hennessey, H.W. (1985). What do successful managers really do? An observational study of managerial activities. *Journal of Applied Behavioral Science, 21,* 255–270.

13. Luthans, Rosenkrantz, & Hennessey (1985).

14. For a discussion of definitional issues, see Cummings, L.L. (1978). Toward organizational behavior. *Academy of Management Review, 3,* 90–98.

15. See Cummings, L.L. (1981). Organizational behavior in the 1980s. *Decision Sciences, 12,* 365–377; and Kast, F.E. & Rosenzweig, J.E. (Eds.). (1973). *Contingency views of organization and management.* Palo Alto, CA: SRA.

16. For a critique see Schoonhoven, C.B. (1981). Problems with contingency theory: Testing assumptions hidden in the language of contingency 'theory.' *Administrative Science Quarterly, 26,* 349–377.

17. Payne, R., & Pugh, D.S. (1976). Organizational structure and climate. In M.D. Dunnette (Ed.), *Handbook of industrial and organizational psychology* (p. 1127). Chicago: Rand-McNally.

18. See Pettigew, A.W. (1979). On studying organizational cultures. *Administrative Science Quarterly, 24,* 570–581.

19. Deal, T., & Kennedy, A. (1982). *Corporate cultures.* Reading, MA: Addison-Wesley.

20. Burris, R.W. (1976). Human learning. In Dunnette (pp. 131–146).

21. The classic work in this area is Schein, E.H. (1969). *Process consultation.* Reading, MA: Addison-Wesley. Also, *see* Schein, E.H. (1987). *Process consultation II: Some lessons for managers and consultants.* Reading, MA: Addison-Wesley.

22. Dubin, R. (1976). Theory building in applied areas. In Dunnette (pp. 17–39).

23. Locke, E.A., Shaw, K.N., Saari, L.M., & Latham, G.P. (1981). Goal setting and task performance, 1969–1980. *Psychological Bulletin, 90,* 125–152.

24. Iacocca, L. (1984). *Iacocca: An autobiography.* New York: Bantam Books.

25. Iacocca (1984), p. 47.

26. See Van Maanen, J., Dabbs, J.M., Jr., & Faulkner, R.R. (1982). *Varieties of qualitative research.* Beverly Hills, CA: Sage. Also see the December 1979 issue of *Administrative Science Quarterly,* which is devoted to qualitative research.

27. See Drucker, P.F. (1982). *The changing world of the executive.* New York: Truman Talley/Times Books. And, Drucker, P.F. (1986). *Frontiers of management.* New York: E.P. Dutton.

28. Geneen, H. (1984). *Managing.* New York: Doubleday.

29. Peters, T., & Austin, N. (1985). *A passion for excellence; The leadership difference.* New York: Random House.

30. Van Maanen, J. (1982).

31. See Dunham, R.B., & Smith, F.J. (1979). *Organizational surveys.* Chicago: Scott, Foresman.

32. For a summary of research issues relating to correlation, see Mitchell, T.R. (1985). An evaluation of the validity of correlational research conducted in organizations. *Academy of Management Review, 10,* 192–205.

33. Fromkin, H.L., & Streufert, S. (1976). Laboratory experimentation; and Cook, T.D., & Campbell, D.T. (1976). The design and conduct of quasi-experiments and true experiments in field settings. Both in M.D. Dunnette (Ed.). *Handbook of industrial and organizational psychology.* Chicago: Rand-McNally.

34. Original source unknown. Quoted from Scott, W.E., & Cummings, L.L. (1973). *Readings in organizational behavior and human performance.* Homewood, Il: Irwin, p. 2.

35. Argyris, C. (1968). Some unintended consequences of rigorous research. *Psychological Bulletin, 70,* 185–197.

36. For more information see Stone, E.F. (1978). *Research methods in organizational behavior.* Santa Monica, CA: Goodyear; and Emory, C.W. (1980). *Business research methods.* Homewood, Il: Irwin.

37. See Kast, F.E., & Rosenzweig, J.E. (1985). *Organization and management: A systems and contingency approach,* 4th edition. New York: McGraw-Hill, p. 17.

38. Kast & Rosenzweig (1985).

39. For a more complete description of systems theory, see Kast, F.E., & Rosenzweig, J.E. (1972). General systems theory: Applications for organization and management. *Academy of Management Journal, 15,* 447–465; and Scott, W.R. (1981). *Organizations: Rational, natural and open systems.* Englewood Cliffs, NJ: Prentice-Hall.

40. This section is based on: The difference Japanese management makes. (1986, July 14). *Business Week,* 47–50.

41. The difference Japanese management makes, p. 49.

42. Schonberger, R.J., & Gilbert, J.P. (1983). Just-in-time purchasing: A challenge for U.S. industry. *California Management Review, 26,* 54–68.

43. The difference Japanese management makes, p. 49.

44. The difference Japanese management makes, p. 49.

45. The difference Japanese management makes, p. 49.

46. The difference Japanese management makes, p. 47.

47. Based on: Life on the line: Two auto workers who are worlds apart. (1985, September 30). *Business Week,* 76–78.

Answers to the systems example:
a. Environmental
b. Technical
c. Environment
d. Impact of technology on the environment
e. Goals and values
f. Psychosocial, managerial
g. Structural
h. Structural, goals, and values
i. Goals and values
j. Structural, managerial, and psychosocial

Part Two

INDIVIDUAL BEHAVIOR IN ORGANIZATIONS

Chapter Two

UNDERSTANDING INDIVIDUAL BEHAVIOR

PREVIEW

- How good are you at empathizing? Did you know this skill is vital for managing people?

- Do you seem to turn into a different person when you are hot and irritable? Does your environment affect your personality?

- Which side of your brain is more dominant, the right or the left? Why is the answer important to managers?

- How strong is your self-esteem? A questionnaire will provide a measure of its strength.

- Are there personality barriers that prevent the advancement of many women in organizations?

- What blend of achievement, power, and affiliation motives are related to managerial success?

- Are you an internalizer or an externalizer? Check your self-knowledge by completing a questionnaire.

MAJOR TOPICS

Preview Case: Jenni Pike's Crisis

Why Study Individual Behavior?

The Nature of Personality

Personality and Behavior

Cross-Cultural OB: French vs. American Characteristics

Managerial Applications of Personality Concepts

Preview Case

JENNI PIKE'S CRISIS

Jenni Pike touched her throbbing forehead and thought to herself, "I can't take any more of this, it's driving me crazy. I'll turn in my resignation tomorrow. There has to be a better job than the one here at Interdivisional Enterprises."

Today had been another bad day for Jenni; one of many since she joined the Promotion Department after graduating from a school of business administration.

Jenni's job is to develop promotional ideas for presentation to the senior marketing staff. Although she had always thought of herself as a competent, intelligent person, she was beginning to wonder because only one of her ideas had been approved by the senior staff during the past six months. Since Jenni has always been a high achiever, this lack of success has depressed her. She is beginning to doubt whether she is cut out for a promotion job.

Jenni blames some of her problems on her boss, Fritz Grubb, because he always seems to assign her to difficult products or markets with which she is unfamiliar. For example, her latest product promotion was for electric garage door openers. Jenni knows nothing of garage door openers—she doesn't even have a garage.

And then there is the awful weekly senior staff meeting where Jenni must present her ideas. Most of the senior staff are men and seem to think that women do not really belong in a company specializing in building products. While they do not openly discriminate against her, she feels there is an underlying hostility and distrust for any of her ideas. Thus, she has to work twice as hard to sell something as a male would.

Several times the strain has just been too much. She has become enraged at one of the male staff and told him off. These episodes end in tears and a later counseling session with her supervisor.

"Yes," Jenni thought, "tomorrow I will get even. They won't realize how much I have contributed until I am gone. Revenge is sweet."

How would you like to be in Jenni's position? Most of us would find it pretty uncomfortable. Although there are many complex forces at work in this case, one important theme is the interaction of the job, the social environment, and individual characteristics and traits—personality. The goal of this chapter is to better understand individuals: their self-concepts, their motives, and the roles they play. We will also study how personality affects behavior.

WHY STUDY INDIVIDUAL BEHAVIOR?

There are several reasons for studying the different reactions, responses, and behaviors of people. We need to develop a sense of empathy, and to improve our knowledge of personal problems that may interfere with work performance. We must also select and promote the right people. The study of how individual behavior and attitudes affect organizational theories is referred to as the study of **individual differences.**

To Develop Empathy

Most of us tend to be **egocentric** about what makes people behave the way they do. In other words, we tend to think others have the same feelings, attitudes, motivations, and perspectives that we do. This is seldom true, even between close relatives or spouses. Thus, we are likely to make erroneous judgments and poor decisions because of this faulty way of thinking. **Empathy,** the ability to put yourself in the place of another, is a skill that is quite difficult to develop, but it is very useful for understanding organizational behavior. One of the purposes of this chapter is to help you develop a better sense of empathy.

For Selection and Placement

Since people are different, it follows that some will be more suited for a particular job or company than will others. For example, a person who likes to have everything organized and laid out by the supervisor may be quite unhappy in a job where there is a great deal of discretion and judgment involved. In a typical group of people, we might also find someone who feels frustrated and constrained if too much structure is imposed. Others might be completely indifferent. Managers must consider these differences if they want to be able to pick the right person to hire, promote, or transfer.

To Improve Counseling Effectiveness

One of the tasks of a manager is to counsel and help employees who are experiencing personal difficulties. While the manager is not a psychologist, there are many times when personal problems will interfere with getting the job done. Understanding individuals will help make you more effective at this task.

THE NATURE OF PERSONALITY

In this section we will delve into the nature of personality, including the situational impact on personality. We will discuss the origin of personality, the self-concept, roles, and the social aspects of personality.

What is Personality?

Personality is a stable set of characteristics and tendencies that determine our thoughts, feelings, and actions in combination with the social and biological pressures of the moment.[1] While we all know that people have different characteristics, abilities, and behavior patterns that reflect their personality, when we try to measure these differences we find they are often elusive. Part of the reason is that it is impossible to get "inside someone's head"; to know what thoughts, feelings, and behavioral intentions actually exist. We must depend upon self-reports and inferences based on the behaviors exhibited.

Another aspect of personality emphasizes the similarities among individual behavior rather than the differences. While we are all different in many ways, we also share with others many characteristics, abilities, and behavior patterns. One challenge to managers is to sort through the similarities and differences in the way people respond to organizational changes. For example, if we want to make people's jobs more responsible and interesting, then we must make sure

Perspective 2.1

THE TWO SIDES
OF THE BRAIN[2]

There are differences in many people based upon which hemisphere of the brain is dominant. Unless we have had a stroke, both sides of the brain operate in all of us. We alternate from one side to the other; however most of us favor one side or the other and that influences our personality. People whose left brain dominates are more analytic, systematic, sequential, and verbal. When the right brain dominates, a person will be more intuitive, visual-spatial, sensuous, and holistic. For left-handed people the hemisphere functions are usually reversed.

This theory has several implications for management.[3] People with a strong left-brain orientation may be good for analytical jobs such as planning, engineering, or accounting. On the other hand, top managers need a sense of the overall situation (the "big picture") and good intuition; they should be right-brain people. In addition, it appears that right-brain people are more effective as task force leaders because they pay more attention to making the group work harmoniously and effectively (*see* group maintenance roles in Chapter 9). Another situation where the right brain should be emphasized is in creative activities, such as formulating strategic goals, or developing innovative solutions to problems.

While many people are stronger in either left or right-brain skills, it may be possible to improve a deficiency.[4] We should note that the relationship between brain functions and organizational job assignments is still speculative. Little or no research has been conducted to support these relationships.

---

that the people who must do the jobs have personality traits that fit this design. If many of them do not, our job redesign effort may fail.

The Situation and Personality

The definition of personality also calls attention to the importance of the situation at the moment. People's personalities may show different forms depending on the social or biological pressures that exist. For example, have you noticed how many college students exhibit much different personalities when they are in the presence of their parents than they do in the presence of their peers?

Organizational situations also create pressures on personality. For example, a normally congenial and friendly person may become quite hostile under the right environmental pressures. One incident occurred last August when the air conditioner was broken. Jim, the supervisor of the drafting section, was hot and his clothes were soaked with perspiration. While he was normally quite easy to get along with, that day was different—he was very irritable and uncomfortable. Even the simplest tasks seemed burdensome. Just when Jim was about to go outside and get a breath of fresh air, Duane (one of his subordinates) came in and began asking a lot of questions. As he listened to Duane's numerous questions, Jim became more and more irritated. Finally, he was unable to control his temper any longer. Jim angrily swept some papers off his desk and shouted at Duane in a threatening and hostile manner. Duane beat a hasty retreat wondering what he had done wrong.[5]

While not everyone becomes more aggressive when they are hot and uncomfortable, many people do. Temperature is only one of many environmental and social pressures that may shape personality at any given moment.[6]

How Does Personality Develop?

Two major factors influence personality: heredity and social environment.

Heredity Provides a Starting Point.   Heredity contributes the basic structure for everyone's personality. It determines sex, race, body type, motor skills, and capacity for learning. These characteristics influence our early life experiences and place constraints on our goals and aspirations. For example, a linebacker for the National Football League could not have become what he is without the hereditary potential for a large, muscular body. Likewise, a professional figure skater or ballet dancer must have some genetically acquired athletic coordination to excel. Even though heredity is important for providing the foundation for personality, the most influential inputs probably come from the environment.[7]

Social Environment.   The most powerful determinant of personality is the social environment.[8] As Figure 2.1 indicates, there are a number of social impacts on personality including family, educational experience, and peer interactions. Cultural factors, such as values, language, and religion, also have a strong impact on personality.[9]

How Stable Is Personality?

While personality is relatively stable, we all know of instances where someone has undergone a major change in his or her behavior that reflects apparent

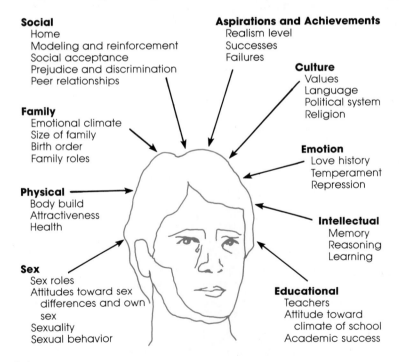

Social
Home
Modeling and reinforcement
Social acceptance
Prejudice and discrimination
Peer relationships

Aspirations and Achievements
Realism level
Successes
Failures

Culture
Values
Language
Political system
Religion

Family
Emotional climate
Size of family
Birth order
Family roles

Emotion
Love history
Temperament
Repression

Physical
Body build
Attractiveness
Health

Intellectual
Memory
Reasoning
Learning

Sex
Sex roles
Attitudes toward sex
  differences and own
  sex
Sexuality
Sexual behavior

Educational
Teachers
Attitude toward
  climate of school
Academic success

Figure 2–1

THE DETERMINANTS OF PERSONALITY

SOURCE: Adapted from the concepts presented in Hurlock, E.B. (1974). *Personality Development.* New York: McGraw-Hill.

changes in personality. The hard-charging, successful Wall Street executive who "retires" at age 40 and becomes a college professor is one example of this type of change. People may go through a developmental process that lasts throughout their lives and includes a number of transitions and stages, as illustrated in Figure 2–2 and described as follows:[10]

• *Early adulthood* (ages 18–30). This stage involves moving from adolescence into the adult world. It includes finding a profession, becoming established, getting married and starting a family. During this period people tend to do a lot of exploring and make choices that will result in long-term life directions. Around age 30 many people go through an anxiety-producing reevaluation of their initial occupational and marital choices. Some people make major changes in direction, while others feel comfortable about their status and settle into a stable period. Preventing undesirable turnover during this stage is a major objective for managers. This is usually done by careful career counseling and open communication.

• *Settling down* (ages 30–40). Once long-term directions are decided upon, stability and control become important. This is also a time when work goals and accomplishments become very important for building a positive self-concept. During this stage it is important for managers to provide sufficient challenge and opportunities for growth and achievement. Another important characteristic of this life stage is that people want to become their own person, which usually involves desires for autonomy and breaking away from old connections. This is a good time for a transfer if the early part of the career has been in one geographic location.

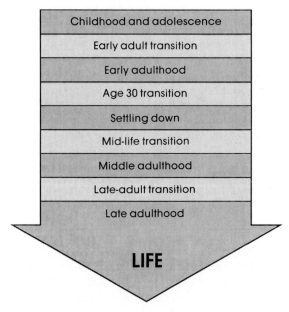

Figure 2–2
LIFE DEVELOPMENT STAGES

SOURCE: Based on Levinson, D.J., et al. (1978). *The Seasons of a Man's Life*. New York: Alfred A. Knopf.

- *Midlife transition* (around age 40). This is often a period of severe re-evaluation and change. A person in this stage might ask: Have I made the right career choice? Have I achieved what I want to achieve? Has my career reached a plateau? Do I want to continue my present life and work situation? The answers to these and other such questions often result in major redirection of life goals.[11]

- *Middle adulthood* (ages 40–60). This is a stage of maturity where life patterns usually become more stable and life goals are more realistic. People in this stage must be managed as mature adults.

Most of us reflect both stability and change over time. Personal aspirations and goals, when combined with situational changes, inevitably result in personal change. However, a number of long-term research projects have shown that people's basic characteristics do not change much. An assertive 19–year–old is highly likely to be an assertive 40–year–old and an assertive 80–year–old.[12]

Self-Concept: The Center of Personality

The self-concept is an extremely important aspect of personality because of its impact on an individual's emotions and behaviors. The **self-concept** is the "totality of the individual's thoughts and actions with reference to himself [or herself] as an object."[13] In other words, the self-concept is the concern we feel for ourselves as an individual. The self is made up of the same types of inputs as personality. It includes your **social identity,** or associations with various groups related to your sex, age, race, social class, and religion. The self also involves certain **dispositions,** or tendencies to react in certain ways based upon attitudes, values, preferences, and personality traits (intelligence, aggressiveness, bravery). In the next chapter we will be discussing how attitudes and values affect behavior.

The self-concept is linked with **self-esteem**—the positive or negative feelings about one's self. The questionnaire in Table 2.1 is a measure of self-esteem that you might wish to complete. People with high self-esteem generally feel good about themselves while people with a weak self-esteem are unsure of themselves and may be easily threatened. People with low self-esteem often choose occupations for which they are not suited because of their fear of failure. In addition, they do not generally perform as well as high-esteem people, and they are less satisfied with their jobs.[14]

In the opening case, Jenni Pike felt a threat to herself after she continually failed to get her ideas approved. She coped with the threat by quitting. While Jenni's problem may have been caused by sexual discrimination, it certainly affected her self-concept. People with low self-esteem need to be handled somewhat differently than people with strong self-esteem. Jenni's supervisor should have paid more attention to building her self-esteem by asking her about her problems and listening carefully. Low self-esteem people may attribute their failures to incompetence when, in fact, external factors beyond their control may have caused the failure.[15] Effective counseling may clarify these types of misperceptions. In addition, people with low self-esteem may need more frequent positive feedback than those who have high self-esteem.

Table 2.1

THE ROSENBERG SELF–ESTEEM SCALE

Directions: For each question circle the answer that best represents your agreement or disagreement with the statement. *SA* means strongly agree, *A* means agree, *D* means disagree, and *SD* means strongly disagree.

1.	On the whole, I am satisfied with myself.	SA	A	D	SD
2.	At times I think I am no good at all.	SA	A	D	SD
3.	I feel that I have a number of good qualities.	SA	A	D	SD
4.	I am able to do things as well as most other people.	SA	A	D	SD
5.	I feel I do not have much to be proud of.	SA	A	D	SD
6.	I certainly feel useless at times.	SA	A	D	SD
7.	I feel that I'm a person of worth, at least on an equal plane with others	SA	A	D	SD
8.	I wish I could have more respect for myself.	SA	A	D	SD
9.	All in all, I am inclined to feel that I am a failure.	SA	A	D	SD
10.	I take a positive attitude toward myself.	SA	A	D	SD

Scoring: If you circled *SA* or *A* for questions 1, 3, 4, 7, or 10, give yourself a 1 for each *SA* or *A* response. If you answered *SD* or *D* for questions 2, 5, 6, 8, or 9, give yourself a 1 for each *SD* or *D* response. Your score will range from 0 to 10. Scores of 6 or below may indicate low self-esteem levels.

SOURCE: From *Conceiving the Self,* by Morris Rosenberg, Copyright © 1979 by Basic Books, Inc. Reprinted by permission of the publisher.

Another incident that illustrates how to deal with weak self esteem is the case of Harvey, a competent computer operator. Through bitter experience, Harvey's boss found out that she had to be very careful about correcting Harvey's behavior. Almost every time he is corrected for even the most minor mistake, he withdraws and pouts for several days. One possible explanation for this behavior is that Harvey has a poor self-concept and low self-esteem. He may be very unsure of himself and quite threatened whenever someone criticizes him. There is no way for us to know the actual causes of Harvey's problem. However, now that Harvey's sensitivity to criticism is known, his boss can be more careful in handling corrections and, perhaps even more importantly, try to reward all desirable and correct work behaviors so that his self-esteem is strengthened. We will discuss strategies for positive reinforcement in Chapter 6.

Sources of self-esteem may differ for men and women. A recent research study found that women's feelings of job satisfaction and self-esteem seemed to decline as the women spent greater amounts of time on the job. For men the opposite was true—the greater the time on the job, the more satisfaction. Perhaps women's self-esteem is influenced more by a variety of on and off-job sources, particularly family responsibilities.[16] Much more research is needed to find out if true differences exist. What do you think?

Protecting the Self Through Defense Mechanisms

People use defense mechanisms to try to reduce their anxiety and frustration when there is some threat to their self-esteem. Defense mechanisms tend to deny reality, distort reality, or push things to the unconscious level. Table 2.2 shows some of the reactions people have when threatened or frustrated.

It is important for managers to realize that obvious behavior does not always reflect the true underlying problem. For example, a person who is angry at the boss may show it by viciously shouting at a coworker. This behavior might be interpreted by the manager as a weakness in getting along with coworkers, while the real problem may lie with the manager. (This is an example of the displacement coping mechanism.) Awareness of the existence of these coping mechanisms will help you more accurately interpret individual behavior.

Table 2.2

PSYCHOLOGICAL SELF DEFENSE: COPING MECHANISMS	
Rationalization	Devising self-satisfying explanations for behavior that would otherwise be unacceptable. An example would be a sales person padding an expense account because "everyone does it."
Displacement	Transferring an emotional feeling for one person or thing to another person or thing. An example would be an angry outburst toward a subordinate as a result of a frustrating meeting with the boss.
Repression	Excluding a feeling, experience, or event from one's consciousness because it is psychologically disturbing. An example is an employee who "forgets" to list a job on her application blank after she was unfairly fired.
Withdrawal or flight	Leaving, either physically or psychologically, whenever a situation becomes threatening or frustrating. Examples would be the sulking salesman who has just lost a big sale or the indignant manager who quits after receiving a "less than perfect" performance appraisal.
Projection	A projection of your own shortcomings to others without admitting that they are true of yourself. An example would be a unsuccessful person who is trying to block the promotion of others in the organization because "they are out to get me."
Negativism	Active or passive resistance or aggression. An example might be the assembly-line employee who is forced to work on Saturday and who sabotages the assembly line to get even.

Adapted and abridged from Costello, T.W., and Zalkind, S.S. (1963). *Psychology in Administration: A Research Orientation.* Englewood Cliffs, NJ: Prentice-Hall, pp. 148–149.

Perspective 2.2

ARE ORGANIZATIONS AND
PEOPLE INCOMPATIBLE?

A number of people think that there may be a basic incongruity between people and organizations. Chris Argyris has argued that organizations have a life of their own that is often diametrically opposed to the needs of their individual employees.[17]

Organizations foster immaturity by designing specialized and fractionalized work, giving orders, evaluating performance, and generally controlling all aspects of the work environment. Organizations often treat people like infants, who begin life by being dependent and submissive, possessing few abilities, and having a short time perspective. Adults, on the other hand, strive toward independence and autonomy, developing their abilities and having a longer time perspective.

Since organizational practices and policies tend to foster dependency and immaturity, the needs of mature individuals are not met. The incongruence between an individual's needs and the formal organization causes individuals to experience frustration, psychological failure, a short time perspective, and conflict. People tend to react to these experiences by leaving the organization (either psychologically or physically), fighting the organization (perhaps by joining a union), or by concentrating their attention on pay, benefits, and time off.

Argyris recommends dealing with the problem by designing organizations to take into account the needs of mature individuals. Jobs should be designed so that people can use their initiative and feel responsibility for work outcomes (job enrichment, the topic of Chapter 7, is one way to do this). In addition, managers should supervise in a mature way so that people feel they are treated as adults rather than children.

Role Playing and Personality

Roles are sets of behaviors that are expected when a person occupies a certain position.[18] We play the role of the student (attentive, hardworking, intellectual), or we may play the role of a union member (ambivalent or hostile toward management, interested in pay and benefits, reluctant to learn new jobs). Some roles are easy to change as we change positions. Other roles, such as those associated with being a man or woman, form a central part of our personalities and are thus more difficult to change (*see* Perspective 2.3).

People Play Different Roles.   People play a number of roles in organizations. They adapt their roles to different organizational situations. For example, a manager will often seem to be level-headed, analytical, good-natured, and people-oriented when dealing with superiors. But to subordinates, that same manager may be a hot-headed, angry, authoritarian. Just like actors, some organizational members are much better than others at role playing. Alert observation of people in different situations and attention to inputs from other sources can provide a more accurate picture of the person.

Roles May Conflict.   Sometimes one role will conflict with another and cause considerable discomfort. For example, a craftsman, such as a finish carpenter, may believe that the proper role to follow is producing top-quality, meticulous work. On the other hand, the supervisor may expect a high quantity of work with only minimal quality standards. Thus the role of the craftsman may conflict with the role of the high producer.

Perspective 2.3

INDIVIDUAL–LEVEL BARRIERS TO THE ADVANCEMENT OF WOMEN IN ORGANIZATIONS

The difficulty of integrating women into organizational leadership positions is a many-faceted problem that involves issues at the societal, institutional, organizational, and individual levels.[19] Several individual-level problems are highlighted in this perspective. Many have to do with roles.

Would you agree that the ideal woman is strong, assertive, powerful, ambitious, and able to produce results? Most people would not. In fact, a woman who displayed those behaviors might be labeled as "pushy."[20] In the United States the ideal woman is generally seen as less aggressive, less independent, less dominant, less active, more emotional and as having great-er difficulty making decisions than the ideal man.[21] When women are viewed in this perspective, it is clear that they may wind up being criticized regardless of their actual performance.[22]

In addition, women are seen by themselves and men as being primarily responsible for the role of caring for children and home and are thus placed at a disadvantage since "their all" cannot be given to their job without sacrificing marriage and children.[23] Women may also prevent their success because they may accept non-line (jobs that are not central to the organization's purpose such as personnel and administration), dead-end, or underpaid jobs.[24]

Another problem is that women and men often avoid close working relationships because they are afraid of implications of sexual intrigue or innuendo.[25] This may mean that women are excluded from informal work groups and may thus be at a disadvantage.

While barriers certainly exist, more and more women are succeeding in managerial positions. There are numerous workshops and books designed to help women overcome the obstacles to success.[26]

Summarizing the Nature of Personality

An individual's personality is made up of all the characteristics and tendencies that make a unique person. In addition, we usually share a number of personality traits in common with others. The situation at the moment may also influence which aspect of our personality surfaces. Our personality, which develops from heredity and social environment, forms during childhood and adolescence and is relatively stable throughout the rest of our life.

A central concept for understanding personality is the self-concept, which reflects our feelings of self-esteem and self-worth. We use defense mechanisms, such as rationalization, displacement, or withdrawal, to cope with threats to our self-esteem. Some people develop a poor self-concept and feel inadequate throughout their lives. This may result in destructive or non-productive behaviors.

Finally, we noted that the roles people play are influenced by their basic personality. Sometimes a role conflict may result that is harmful to the individual or the organization. (This topic is covered in Chapter 10.)

PERSONALITY AND BEHAVIOR

Now we will turn to a review of several personality issues that are useful for understanding organizational behavior. Two major concepts will be covered:

motives and locus of control. In addition, we will summarize what is known about predicting managerial success based on personality characteristics. There are many other interesting and relevant personality issues since the field is rich in theory and research; however, space limits our coverage to those that seem most relevant to organizations.[27]

Motives of Individuals

One way of understanding individual behavior is to look at the motive or need patterns of individuals. A **need** is a tension created by some psychological or physiological deficiency that arouses an individual to try to satisfy that need. The **motive** process is dynamic—"it is an active, goal-directed sequence that begins with arousal and ends with some form of satisfaction."[28] In Chapter 5, we will discuss the relationship between needs and motivation. This chapter concentrates on the personality implications of various motive patterns since some people seem to have particularly strong tendencies toward certain need patterns. Three motive patterns or needs have particular relevance for understanding personality: need of achievement, need for power, and need for affiliation.

Achievement Motive.   David McClelland has spent many years studying people who have high **achievement** needs, whom he calls achievers.[29] Achievers are very concerned with efficiency and getting things done. They take moderate risks and seek feedback on performance. They are concerned with excellence, doing well in competition, creating unique accomplishments, and getting feedback about how well they have done.

> People who are high achievers often gravitate into sales. A sales job provides them with the challenge, moderate risk, and the concrete feedback they need. An interesting problem sometimes results when the high-achieving supersalesperson is promoted to sales manager. The achiever will sometimes become quite unhappy in this supposedly better position, since individual achievement will no longer be possible, and other motives, such as need for power, become more important. The same thing may happen with a top-notch engineer or scientist.

Power Motive.   Higher level managers and leaders need to have a relatively high need for **power,** the desire to influence and control others.[30] Since a large part of a top manager's job concerns influencing, directing, and controlling others, it seems logical that a person with a high need for power would be more comfortable and effective in such a position.

Affiliation Motive.   People with a high need for **affiliation** are particularly concerned with social relationships such as love, friendship, and approval of others. Too much of this motive apparently makes top managers less effective because they lack the courage to make difficult personnel decisions without worrying about being disliked.

Implications of Motive Patterns.   Motive patterns have important implications for personnel selection and placement. When selecting people for sales jobs, high achievement needs are desirable. For higher level management jobs, high power needs combined with a relatively low need for affiliation is a more appropriate combination. We must be aware that different demands and rewards may be associated with supervisory jobs. If these conflict with the motives of the individual, then unhappiness and frustration may result.

Motive Patterns and Long-Term Success in Management

A study of managerial success within American Telephone and Telegraph Co. over a sixteen-year period found that motive patterns were important correlates of managerial success.[31] The study was made of 311 entry-level managers whose careers were followed for sixteen years. At the end of sixteen years, there were 237 managers still remaining in the study. Sixty-one percent of the managers were in nontechnical fields, such as sales, customer service, administration, and personnel. Thirty-nine percent were in technical management fields, such as construction, maintenance, and installation.

The results indicated that nontechnical managers with moderate to high need for power, low need for affiliation, and a high need for self-control were more successful in terms of promotion within the company. At lower management levels, a high need for achievement was also related to success because promotion depends more on individual achievement. However, once the job becomes one of supervising others, achievement is no longer related to success. These patterns did not hold for technical managers. Their success seemed unrelated to motive patterns and more related to their technical competence. For another study on this topic, see Perspective 2.4, Personal Characteristics of General Managers.

Locus of Control

Another aspect of personality that is important to organizations is the locus of control.[32] The discussion of the concepts will be more meaningful to you if you complete the questions in Table 2.3 to determine your personal locus of control level.

Did you score below four points on the Rotter scale? Then you probably feel that you are the master of your own fate; that you can control what you do, where you live, and where you work. You are what Julian Rotter calls an internalizer or someone whose locus of control is internal.[33] If you scored above five points, you may feel that your fate is more a matter of luck or "whatever will be will be." You may feel that circumstances are more in control of your destiny. You may be an externalizer.

Internal and External Locus of Control. When something happens and it is attributed to luck, fate, chance, being under the control of other powerful people, or unpredictable because of the complexity of the situation, then this belief represents an **external locus of control.** If what happens is attributed to a person's own behavior or characteristics, the belief represents an **internal locus of control.**[34]

An example of external locus of control might be Arnie Chang, who just received a lower than expected performance evaluation and reacted like this: "Oh damn! Those fellows up in personnel have done it to me again by changing

Perspective 2.4

PERSONAL CHARACTERISTICS OF GENERAL MANAGERS

John Kotter conducted an in-depth research study of fifteen general managers of U.S. corporations with revenues ranging from around $100 million to $5 billion or more. They included a variety of industries ranging from high technology to banks, retailing, communication, and professional services. He found a number of common personality characteristics summarized below.[35]

Basic Personality

Needs/Motives

- Liked power
- Liked achievement
- Ambitious

Cognitive Orientation

- Above average intelligence (but not brilliant)
- Moderately strong analytically
- Strong intuitively

Temperament

- Emotionally stable and even
- Optimistic

Interpersonal Orientation

- Personable, and good at developing relationships with people
- Unusual set of interests that allowed them to relate easily to a broad set of business specialists

Accumulated Information and Relationships

Information

- Very knowledgeable about their businesses
- Very knowledgeable about their organizations

Relationships

- Had cooperative relationships with a very large number of people in their organizations
- Had cooperative relations with many people in their industry also.

SOURCE: Reprinted with permission of The Free Press, a Division of Macmillan, Inc. from *The General Managers* by John P. Kotter. Copyright © 1982 by The Free Press.

Table 2.3

ROTTER INTERNAL–EXTERNAL CONTROL SCALE (ABRIDGED)

Directions: Circle the response *a* or *b* that best reflects your feelings about the statement.

1. a. Many of the unhappy things in people's lives are partly due to bad luck.
   b. People's misfortunes result from the mistakes they make.

2. a. In the long run people get the respect they deserve in this world.
   b. Unfortunately, an individual's worth often passes unrecognized no matter how hard he tries.

3. a. The idea that teachers are unfair to students is nonsense.
   b. Most students don't realize the extent to which their grades are

   b. Getting a good job depends mainly on being in the right place at the right time.

7. a. When I make plans, I am almost certain that I can make them work.
   b. It is not always wise to plan too far ahead because many things turn out to be a matter of good or bad fortune anyway.

8. a. Who gets to be the boss often depends on who was lucky enough to be in the right place first.

Table 2.3 Continued

b. influenced by accidental happenings.

4. a. No matter how hard you try some people just don't like you.
   b. People who can't get others to like them don't understand how to get along with others.

5. a. I have often found that what is going to happen will happen.
   b. Trusting to fate has never turned out as well for me as making a decision to take a definite course of action.

6. a. Becoming a success is a matter of hard work, luck has little or nothing to do with it.

b. Getting people to do the right thing depends upon ability; luck has little to do with it.

9. a. Many times I feel that I have little influence over the things that happen to me.
   b. It is impossible for me to believe that chance or luck plays an important role in what happens to me.

10. a. What happens to me is my own doing.
    b. Sometimes I feel that I don't have enough control over the direction my life is taking.

Scoring: If you answered *a* to questions 1, 4, 5, 8, or 9, give yourself a 1 for each answer. If you answered *b* to questions 2, 3, 6, 7, or 10, give yourself a 1 for each answer. Now add up the total number of 1s. Your score should range from 0 to 10. A low score indicates a high internal locus of control while a high score indicates a high external locus of control. The average score for college students is about 4.

SOURCE: From J.B. Rotter, 1966, Generalized expectancies for internal versus external control reinforcement, *Psychological Monographs*, Vol. 80 (No. 609). Copyright 1966 by the American Psychological Association. Reprinted/abridged by permission of the author and the publisher.

the form. If we had used the old system, I would have gotten a good rating and been promoted." If, on the other hand, Arnie had reacted from an internal locus of control, he might have responded like this: "I'm disappointed that my performance was not as good as it might have been. I will have to find out what I can do to improve it so I will be promotable."

Using Locus of Control. People with an internal locus of control are especially important in organizational positions that require initiative, innovation, and self-starting behavior, such as managers, researchers, planners, and entrepreneurs. If the task requires complex information analysis and processing, internalizers do the job better.[36] Internalizers are potentially more motivated than externalizers. If you planned to implement a pay system where people are paid "piece-rates" (pay for each unit produced within a given time), then internalizers would be preferable since they believe that the outcomes are under their control.[37] Internalizers would also prefer more freedom from supervision than externalizers, and they would perform better with more personal control over their work environment.

Locus of Control and Business Strategy. A study of thirty-three Canadian firms whose size ranged from sales of less than $2 million to over $1 billion, all located in the Montreal region, found that there was a relationship between the locus of control of top executives and a number of important aspects of corporate strategy.[38] For example, locus of control was negatively correlated with innovation (–.47), risk taking (–.69), and proactiveness (–.82); thus indicating that firms run by internalizers feel more in control of their environments and are more aggressive. Firms run by externalizers, on the other hand, tend to be more risk aversive and fearful of the environment.

Perspective 2.5

THE NEUROTIC ORGANIZATION: A REFLECTION OF THE LEADER'S PERSONALITY[39]

Failing or borderline businesses may be a reflection of the neurotic personalities of their leaders. Organizational culture, strategy, and structure may display the boss' neurotic characteristics. Five **neurotic styles,** or dominant ways of thinking, perceiving, and experiencing, have been identified as linking personality to organizational behavior:

• *Dramatic* This style involves seeking attention and trying to impress people. It may involve excessive displays of emotion and a craving for activity and excitement. Dramatic firms are hyperactive, impulsive, venturesome, and overly uninhibited. Hunches and impressions are the basis for action.

• *Depressive* The depressive style includes feelings of hopelessness, guilt, self-reproach, and inadequacy. Depressive organizations are characterized by inactivity, lack of confidence, passivity, purposelessness, and extreme conservatism. This style results in an overly pessimistic outlook, indecisiveness, and inhibition of action.

• *Paranoid* When a paranoid style governs behavior, suspicion and mistrust inhibit action. A great deal of attention is directed toward intelligence gathering and controls. Information is often withheld because of mistrust and fear that others are out to get us. Paranoid firms have trouble innovating; they tend to be reactive rather than anticipating.

• *Compulsive* This style centers on perfectionism and preoccupation with details. Thoroughness, planning, and conformity to established rules are emphasized. This style inhibits creativity and change; it creates indecisiveness for fear of making a mistake; it fosters overreliance on rules and regulations.

• *Schizoid* The schizoid style describes someone who is withdrawn and who is uninvolved. Reality is not seen as satisfying, so daydreaming and withdrawal become the norm. Emotional isolation is often associated with this style. A schizoid leader leaves a vacuum in leadership that is often filled by political jockeying by subordinates to fill the power void. The organization lacks common direction and is usually divided.

CROSS CULTURAL OB: FRENCH VERSUS AMERICAN CHARACTERISTICS

Since each nation imparts different early life experiences to its young, we should expect personality differences between national cultures. For illustration, the table below summarizes some of the differences between French and American people.[40]

Americans	French
Tend to like people who agree with them.	Tend to be more interested in those who disagree.
Try to impress others because they need to be liked.	Do not feel the need to be liked and are impatient with attempts of those who try to impress.
Assess others by their level of achievement.	Look for the quality of the person and personality.

Americans (Cont.)

Improve self-esteem by acting in accordance with expectations and actions of others; more other oriented.

Social class is very flexible and is less important to self-identity.

Very competitive in sports, business, and education.

Friendly and open.

French (Cont.)

Develop identity and recognition by acting against others; more inner oriented.

Social class and status are important determinants of self-identity.

Not oriented toward competition. May feel threatened by competitive behavior.

Friendly, but cynical.

MANAGERIAL APPLICATIONS OF PERSONALITY CONCEPTS

Now that you have finished the chapter, you should have a better sense of the nature of personality and why people differ. An important point to remember is that while personality is relatively stable, people can change their outward behavior because of the environment—people play different roles in different situations. The self-concept also provides a central concept for understanding why people experience depression and why they behave in ways to protect their self-esteem.

In addition, we have covered a number of characteristics of individuals that might make them more effective managers, such as a moderate to high power motive, a relatively low affiliation motive, and an internal locus of control. These personality concepts provide us with insights into ourselves and others. Here are some specific recommendations for improving your managerial effectiveness:

- *Try to develop empathy.* Put yourself in other people's place. Try to understand their motivations; their personality orientation. This skill will be particularly helpful when counseling employees.

- *Recognize that people go through many different life stages.* The developmental process strongly influences individual behavior. Be aware of its progression in yourself and others.

- *Build self-esteem of your subordinates.* The self-concept is extremely important to our psychological health. People who feel good about themselves will perform better and be more committed to your organization. Give lots of positive feedback to build esteem levels.

- *Identify defense coping mechanisms.* Behavior is not always caused by what it appears to be. Defense mechanisms are ways people cope with threatening situations. Watch for their use as an aid to more accurate interpretation of behavior.

- *Resolve role conflicts when they arise.* Supervisors are frequently the cause of role conflict. When planning or assigning tasks, be aware of this process and try to minimize such conflicts.

- *Recognize the role conflicts faced by women.* Use your knowledge of sex-role conflicts in counseling your female subordinates. If you are a woman, try to work through these conflicts on a conscious level.

- *Consider motive patterns for personnel decisions.* Make sure that a person's motive pattern is consistent with the requirements of the job.

- *Use locus of control in assigning tasks.* Give tasks that require self-starting, innovative behavior to internalizers.

FOR DISCUSSION

1. How stable is a person's personality? Has your personality changed in the past two years? Five years? How?

2. Choose someone you know who is about twenty-five, thirty-five, forty-five, and fifty-five years old and compare their situations with those predicted by the model in Figure 2.2.

3. Describe some situational factors that may influence personality. Do any of these factors affect your personality?

4. What are the implications of the left-brain, right-brain study for organizations?

5. Would a manager use different supervisory strategies for a person with a high self-concept and one with a low self-concept?

6. What does Argyris mean when he says that organizations and people are basically incompatible?

7. How may roles cause problems for managers?

8. McClelland highlights three important motives: achievement, power, and affiliation. Analyze which motives are more important to you. Does this profile fit that of a manager?

9. Why would someone with an external locus of control have a more difficult time being an effective manager?

10. What solutions would you propose for curing each type of neurotic organization?

11. In light of the differences in French culture, what major changes in managerial behavior would be needed?

KEY CONCEPTS AND TERMS

personality	affiliation motive	repression
role	locus of control	withdrawal
motives and needs	self-concept	projection
left-brain, right-brain functions	defense mechanisms	negativism
achievement motive	rationalization	neurotic styles
power motive	displacement	

Cases and Incidents

BARBARA HERRICK

She is thirty; single. Her title is script supervisor/ producer at a large advertising agency; working out of its Los Angeles office. She is also a vice president. Her accounts are primarily in food and cosmetics. "There's a myth: a woman is expected to be a food writer because she is assumed to know those things and a man doesn't. However, some of the best copy

of razors and Volkswagens has been written by women."

She has won several awards and considerable recognition for her commercials. "You have to be absolutely on target, dramatic and fast. You have to be aware of legal restrictions. The FTC gets tougher and tougher. You must understand budgetary matters: will it cost a million or can it be shot in a studio in one day?"

Men in my office doing similar work were being

promoted, given raises and titles. Since I had done the bulk of the work, I made a stand and was promoted too. I needed the title, because clients figured that I'm just a face-man.

A face-man is a person who looks good, speaks well, and presents the work. I look well, I speak well, and I'm pleasant to have around after the business is over with—if they acknowledge me in business. We go to the lounge and have drinks. I can drink with the men but remain a lady. (Laughs.)

That's sort of my tacit business responsibility, although this has never been said to me directly. I know this is why I travel alone for the company a great deal. They don't anticipate any problems with my behavior. I equate it with being the good nigger.

On first meeting, I'm frequently taken for the secretary, you know, traveling with the boss. I'm here to keep somebody happy. Then I'm introduced as the writer. One said to me after the meeting was over and the drinking had started, "When I first saw you, I figured you were a—you know. I never knew you were the person **writing** this all the time." (Laughs.) Is it a married woman working for extra money? Is it a lesbian? Is it some higher-up's mistress?

I'm probably one of the ten highest paid people in the agency. It would cause tremendous hard feelings if, say, I work with a man who's paid less. If a remark is made at a bar—"You make so much money, you could buy and sell me"—I toss it off, right? He's trying to find out. He can't equate me as a rival. They wonder where to put me, they wonder what my salary is.

Buy and sell me—yeah, there are a lot of phrases that show the reversal of roles. What comes to mind is swearing at a meeting. New clients are often very uptight. They feel they can't make any innuendoes that might be suggestive. They don't know how to treat me. They don't know whether to acknowledge me as a woman or as another neuter person who's doing a job for them.

The first time, they don't look at me. At the first three meetings of this one client, if I would ask a direction question, they would answer and look at my boss or another man in the room. Even around the conference table. I don't attempt to be—the glasses, the bun, and totally asexual. That isn't the way I am. It's obvious that I'm a woman and enjoy being a woman. I'm not overly provocative either. It's the thin, good nigger line that I have to toe.

I've developed a sixth sense about this. If a client will say, "Are you married?" I will often say yes, because that's the easiest way to deal with him if he needs that category for me. If it's more acceptable to him to have a young, attractive married woman in a business position comparable to his, terrific. It doesn't bother me. It makes me safer. He'll never be challenged. He can say, "She'd be sensational. I'd love to get her. I could show her what a real man is, but she's married." It's a way out for him.

Or there's the mistress thing: well, she's sleeping with the boss. That's acceptable to them. Or she's a frustrated, compulsive castrator. That's a category. Or lesbian. If I had short hair, wore suits, and talked in a gruff voice, that would be more acceptable than I am. It's when I transcend their labels, they don't quite know what to do. If someone wants a quick label and says, "I'll bet you're a big women's libber, aren't you?" I say, "Yeah, yeah." They have to place me.

DISCUSSION QUESTIONS

1. What types of role conflicts does Barbara face?

2. Does she see a threat to her self-concept? How is she coping?

3. How does locus of control apply here?

ANALYZING JENNI PIKE'S CRISIS

Refer back to the opening case for this chapter and explain how each of the following concepts apply:

1. Which side of the brain was Jenni more likely to favor? Why?

2. What methods was she using to protect her self-esteem?

3. Was Interdivisional Enterprises (Jenni's company) incompatible with her? Why?

4. What roles seem to be important to Jenni?

5. Does she face special problems because she is a woman?

6. Is Jenni an externalizer or an internalizer?

WHAT KILLED BOB LYONS?

Those who knew Bob Lyons thought extremely well of him. He was a highly successful executive who held an important position in a large company. As his superiors saw him, he was aggressive, with a knack for getting things done through other people. He worked hard and set a vigorous pace. He drove himself relentlessly. In less than 10 years with his company, he had moved through several positions of responsibility.

Lyons had always been a good athlete. He was proud of his skill in swimming, hunting, golf, and tennis. In his college days he had lettered in football and baseball. On weekends he preferred to undertake rebuilding and repairing projects around the house or to hunt, interspersing other sports for a change of pace. He was usually engaged, it seemed, in hard physical work.

His life was not all work, however. He was active in his church and in the Boy Scouts. His wife delighted in entertaining and in being with other people, so their social life was a round of many parties and social activities. They shared much of their life with their three children.

Early in the spring of his ninth year with the company, Bob Lyons spoke with the vice president to whom he reported. "Things are a little quiet around here," he said. "Most of the big projects are over. The new building is finished, and we have a lot of things on the ball that four years ago were all fouled up. I don't like this idea of just riding a desk and looking out the window. I like action."

About a month later, Lyons was assigned additional responsibilities. He rushed into them with his usual vigor. Once again he seemed buoyant and cheerful. After six months on the assignment, Lyons had the project rolling smoothly. Again he spoke to his vice president, reporting that he was out of projects. The vice president, pleased with Lyons' performance, told him that he had earned the right to do a little dreaming and planning; and, furthermore, dreaming and planning were a necessary part of the position he now held, toward which he had aspired for so long. Bob Lyons listened as his boss spoke, but it was plain to the vice president that the answer did not satisfy him.

About three months after this meeting, the vice president began to notice that replies to his memos and inquiries were not coming back from Lyons with their usual rapidity. In addition, he noticed that Lyons was beginning to put things off, a most unusual behavior pattern for him. He observed that Lyons became easily angered and disturbed over minor difficulties, which previously had not irritated him at all.

Bob Lyons then became involved in a conflict with two other executives over a policy issue. Such conflicts were not unusual in the organization since, inevitably, there were varying points of view on many issues. The conflict was not personal, but it did require intervention from higher management before a solution could be reached. In the process of resolving the conflict, Lyons' point of view prevailed on some questions but not on others.

A few weeks after this conflict had been resolved, Lyons went to the vice president's office. He wanted to have a long private talk, he said. His first words were, "I'm losing my grip. The old steam is gone. I've had diarrhea for four weeks and several times in the past three weeks I've lost my breakfast. I'm worried and yet I don't know what about. I feel that some people have lost confidence in me."

He talked with his boss for an hour and a half. The vice president recounted his achievements in the company to reassure him. He then asked if Lyons thought he should see a doctor. Lyons agreed that he should and, in the presence of the vice president, called his family doctor for an appointment. By this time the vice president was very much concerned. He called Mrs. Lyons and arranged to meet her for lunch the next day. She reported that, in addition to his other symptoms, her husband had difficulty sleeping. She was relieved that the vice president had called her because she was beginning to become worried and had herself planned to call the vice president. Both were now alarmed. They decided that they should get Lyons into a hospital rather than wait for the doctor's appointment that was still a week off.

The next day Lyons was taken to the hospital. Meanwhile, with Mrs. Lyons' permission, the vice president reported to the family doctor Lyons' recent job behavior and the nature of their conversations. When the vice president had finished, the doctor concluded, "All he needs is a good rest. We don't want to tell him that it may be mental or nervous." The vice president replied that he didn't know what the cause was, but he knew Bob Lyons needed help quickly.

During five days in the hospital, Lyons was subjected to extensive laboratory tests. The vice president visited him daily. He seemed to welcome the rest and the sedation at night. He said he was eating and sleeping much better. He talked about company problems, though he did not speak spontaneously without encouragement. While Lyons was out of the room, another executive who shared his hospital room confided to the vice president that he was worried about Lyons. "He seems to be so morose and depressed that I'm afraid he's losing his mind," the executive said.

By this time the president of the company, who had been kept informed, was also becoming concerned. He had talked to a psychiatrist and planned to talk to Lyons about psychiatric treatment if his doctor did not suggest it. Meanwhile, Lyons was discharged from the hospital as being without physical illness, and his doctor recommended a vacation. Lyons remained at home for several days where he was again visited by the vice president. He and his wife took a trip to visit friends. He was then ready to come back to work, but the president suggested that he take another week off. The presi-

dent also suggested that they visit together when Lyons returned.

A few days later, the president phoned the Lyonses' home. Mrs. Lyons could not find him to answer the telephone. After 15 minutes she still had not found him and called the vice president about her concern. By the time the vice president arrived at the Lyonses' home, the police were already there. Bob Lyons had committed suicide.

DISCUSSION QUESTIONS

1. Were there personality factors that could have accounted for Bob Lyons' death?
2. Could Bob's boss have behaved differently?
3. What coping mechanisms did Bob display?

REFERENCES

1. Maddi, S.R. (1980). *Personality theories: A comparative analysis.* Homewood, Il: Dorsey, p. 10. Also see Gough, H. (1976). Personality and personality assessment. In M.D. Dunnette (Ed.), *Handbook of industrial and organizational psychology.* Chicago: Rand-McNally.

2. Ornstein, R.E. (1972). *The psychology of consciousness.* New York: Viking Press; and Springer, S.P. (1981). *Left brain, right brain.* San Francisco: W.H. Freeman. For an opposing view to the split-brain theory, see Levy, J. (1985, May). Right brain, left brain: Fact and fiction. *Psychology Today,* pp. 38–44.

3. This discussion is based on Mintzberg, H. (1976, July-August). Planning on the left and managing on the right. *Harvard Business Review,* pp. 49–58; and Nugent, P.S. (1981). Management and modes of thought. *Organizational Dynamics,* Spring: 45–59.

4. See Agor, W.H. (1984). *Intuitive management: Integrating left and right brain management skills.* Englewood Cliffs, NJ: Prentice-Hall.

5. Adapted from an incident reported by Baron, R.A. (1977). *Human aggression.* New York: Plenum, p. 125.

6. Terborg, J.R. (1981). Interactional psychology and research on human behavior in organizations. *Academy of Management Review, 6,* 469–576. For detailed discussions of environmental and social

inputs to personality, see Baron (1977), and Maddi (1980).

7. Price, R.A., Vandenberg, S.G., Iyer, H., & Williams, J.S. (1982). Components of variation in normal personality. *Journal of Personality and Social Psychology, 43,* 328–340.

8. Price, et al. (1982).

9. Levine, R.A. (1973). *Culture, behavior, and personality.* Chicago: Adline Publishing.

10. Levinson, D.J., et al. (1978). *The seasons of a man's life.* New York: Alfred A. Knopf.

11. For an article that describes career counseling for such transitions, see Rice, B. (1985, January). Why am I in this job? *Psychology Today,* pp. 54–59.

12. Costa, P.T., Jr., & McCrae, R.R. (1980). Still stable after all these years: Personality as a key to some issues in adulthood and old age. In P.B. Baltes and O.G. Brim, Jr. (Eds.). *Life span development and behavior* (Vol. 3). New York: Academic Press. For a good summary of the research supporting relative stability in personality see Rubin, Z. (1981, May). Does personality really change after 20? *Psychology Today,* pp. 18–27. Additional issues are developed in Peele, S. (1984, December). The question of personality. *Psychology Today,* pp. 54–56.

13. Rosenberg, M. (1979). *Conceiving the self.* New York: Basic Books, p. 9.

14. See Brockner, J., & Guare, J. (1983). Improving the performance of low-esteem individuals: An attributional approach. *Academy of Management Journal, 26,* 642–656.

15. Brockner and Guare (1983), p. 653.

16. Sekaran, U. (1985). Understanding the dynamics of self concept of members in dual career families. *Academy of Management Proceedings '85,* pp. 350–354.

17. Based on Argyris, C. (1957). *Personality and organization.* New York: Harper; and Argyris, C. (1973). Personality and organization theory revisited. *Administrative Science Quarterly, 18,* 141–167. Also see Moore, T. (1987, March 30). Personality tests are back. *Fortune,* 74cf.

18. Graen, G. (1976). Role-making processes within complex organizations. In M.D. Dunnette (Ed.), *Handbook of industrial and organizational psychology* (pp. 1201–1246). Chicago: Rand-McNally.

19. Martin, P.Y., Harrison, D., & Dinnitto, D. (1983). Advancement of women in hierarchical organizations: A multilevel analysis of problems and prospects. *Journal of Applied Behavioral Science, 19,* 19–33.

20. Martin, et al. (1983).

21. Broverman, I., Vogel, S.R., Broverman, D.M., Clarkson, F.E., & Rosenkrantz, P.S. (1972). Sex-role stereotypes: A current appraisal. *Journal of Social Issues, 28,* 59–78; and Aterborg, J.R. (1977). Women in management: A research review. *Journal of Applied Psychology, 62,* 647–664.

22. Martin, et al. (1983).

23. Martin, et al. (1983).

24. Stacey, M., & Price, M. (1981). *Women in Politics and Power.* London: Tavistock; and Martin, et al. (1983).

25. Quinn, R.E. (1977). Coping with cupid: The formation, impact, and management of romantic relationships in organizations. *Administrative Science Quarterly, 22,* 39–45; and Martin, et al. (1983).

26. For example, see Hunsaker, J., & Hunsaker, P. (1986). *Strategies and skills for managerial women.* Cincinnati: South-Western.

27. For a thorough review of personality theories and concepts see Pervin, L.A. (1984). *Personality: Theory and research* (4th ed.). New York: Wiley; and Babladelis, G. (1984). *The study of personality: Issues and resolutions.* New York: Holt, Rinehart and Winston.

28. Bavelas, J.B. (1978). *Personality: Current theory and research.* Monterey, CA: Brooks/Cole, p. 61.

29. McClelland, D.C. (1953). *The achievement motive.* New York: Appleton-Century-Crofts; and McClelland, D.C. (1965). Toward a theory of motive acquisition. *American Psychologist, 20,* 321–333.

30. McClelland, D.C., Atkinson, J.W., Clark, R.A., & Lowell, E.L. (1975). *Power: The inner experience.* New York: Irvington-Halsted-Wiley; and McClelland, D.C., & Burnham, D.H. (1976, March-April). Power is the great motivator. *Harvard Business Review,* pp. 100–110.

31. McClelland, D.C., & Boyatzis, R.E. (1982). Leadership motive pattern and long-term success in management. *Journal of Applied Psychology, 67,* 737–743.

32. Spector, P.E. (1982). Behavior in organizations as a function of employee's locus of control. *Psychological Bulletin, 91,* 482–497; and Phares, E.J. (1976). *Locus of control in personality.* Morristown, NJ: General Learning Press, p. 45.

33. Rotter, J.B. (1966). Generalized expectancies for internal versus external control reinforcement. *Psychological Monographs, 80* (No. 609).

34. Rotter (1966), p. 1.

35. Kotter, J.P. (1982). *The general managers.* New York: The Free Press. For another perspective on personalities of chief executives, see Levinson, H. (1980, Jul.-Aug.). Criteria for choosing chief executives. *Harvard Business Review,* pp. 113–120.

36. Spector (1982).

37. Spector (1982).

38. Miller, D., Kets de Vries, M.F.R., & Toulouse, J. (1982). Top executive locus of control and its relationship to strategy-making, structure, and environment. *Academy of Management Journal, 25,* 237–253.

39. Adapted from Kets de Vries, M.F.R., & Miller, D. (1986). Personality, culture, and organization. *Academy of Management Review, 11,* 266–279; and Kets de Vries, M.F.R., & Miller, D. (1984, October). Unstable at the top. *Psychology Today,* 26cf. Also see Miller, D., & Dröge, C. (1986). Psychological and traditional determinants of structure. *Administrative Science Quarterly, 31,* 539–560.

40. Adapted from Harris, P.R., & Moran, R.T. (1987). *Managing cultural differences,* 2nd edition. Houston: Gulf Publishing, 447–452.

Chapter Three

AN INDIVIDUAL'S PERSPECTIVE: VALUES, ATTITUDES, AND BEHAVIOR

PREVIEW

- How does value programming happen?

- What values are important to you? Fill out the questionnaire and compare your values with others.

- Are you a theory X manager or a theory Y manager? Find out how these values affect organizations.

- Why would 11,500 air traffic controllers quit their jobs over a value issue?

- Is a "happy employee a productive employee"?

- What are some strategies for changing attitudes and behavior?

- Do employees in Japan really have a job for life? Find out more about Japanese management practices.

MAJOR TOPICS

Preview Case: Jack Blaylock's Lament

Values: The Broad Road Map for Human Behavior

Attitudes and Organizational Behavior

Attitudes, Values, and Organizations: Some Conclusions

Cross-Cultural OB: Japan as an Example

Managerial Applications of Value and Attitude Concepts

Preview Case

JACK BLAYLOCK'S LAMENT

"Maybe it's time for me to retire," lamented Jack Blaylock, founder and chief stockholder of the Blaylock Venetian Blind Co. "It seems that everything is going wrong these days. When I first started the business in 1946, after I got out of the Army, it was rough financially, but at least then I didn't have any trouble with my employees.

"Yes, those were simpler times. As long as you took care of people and paid them regularly, they really put out. And, if you wanted to fire someone, you just went ahead and did it. Today things are really different. People don't work as hard as they used to and they get upset when you try to look out for their interests.

"For example, back in the mid-sixties I used to take really good care of all 330–plus employees. I knew them all by name and usually knew their wives and children, too. We used to have regular picnics when everybody would come and have a good time. And if somebody got sick, I would make sure that they were taken care of. Unfortunately, all that changed when the employees voted union in 1975. I was certainly upset that they would do that to me—especially after I had treated them like my

own children. In fact, I got so mad that I fired the ringleaders, but the government folks wouldn't let me do that so I had to take them back.

"Nowadays, people just don't seem to care whether they work or not. In fact, I've heard that some people make more from welfare than they do on the job. Back when I was younger and there was a depression on. You really worried about losing your job because if you did, you would have to go back to the soup lines or sell apples to survive. And on the other hand, the boss was really the boss back then. If you didn't like somebody's work it was easy to give him his 'walking papers.' You can't do that any more. Now if you want to fire someone you have to have a lawyer. There are so many government regulations—grievance procedures, affirmative action—that you just don't boss your own business anymore.

"But worst of all, I just don't understand the younger generation. A few years back when most of the guys wore long hair it really got my hackles up. If I had had my way I would have gotten some barber shears and cut it all off. Unfortunately, I tried to order people to wear short hair, but the union forced a wildcat strike. Seems like you just can't win.

"See why I think it's time to retire? I just don't seem to be able to run my own company any more."

$\mathbf{J}$ack Blaylock is having a difficult time coping with value systems that differ from his. His employees' values often conflict with his and cause him a great deal of frustration and discomfort. Values and attitudes are important determinants of individual behavior. Values about people and work influence behavior in a variety of organizational situations. They are related to supervisory style and reactions of subordinates. They influence how successfully people can respond to changes in organizational conditions. The study of values is also particularly crucial for understanding cross-cultural differences—an increasingly important skill with the growth of international business.

In this chapter we will examine the impact of values and attitudes on organizational behavior and what we might do to resolve value conflicts and to change attitudes.

VALUES: THE BROAD
ROAD MAP FOR HUMAN BEHAVIOR

What Are Values?

A **value** is a broad, general belief about some way of behaving or some end state that is preferable to the individual.[1] Examples of values might be: leading an exciting life, having a comfortably rich existence, being courageous, being honest and ethical, living in a peaceful world, having personal freedom, or being a top-notch business manager. Values guide actions and judgments in many different situations and beyond people's immediate goals to more ultimate end-states of existence.[2]

Values are a form of **belief,** or personal conclusions about what is true or not true or what is beautiful and good about the world.[3] Beliefs are organized within our minds into a more or less organized system that we will refer to as a **value system.** Before proceeding with our discussion of values, you may wish to complete the questionnaire in Table 3.1 so that you can compare your values to those of others.

How Are Values Formed?

Since values are part of personality, they are formed in much the same way. The term **value programming** has been used to describe this formation process.[4] Figure 3.1 shows some of the sources of value programming. With such a wide variety of sources, we might expect that no two people would hold exactly the same values. Yet there probably is a great deal of similarity between the values of people of the same age, ethnic origin, geographic location, or family. One might even be able to generalize certain value orientations to people in certain age groups.[5] For example, those people who grew up during the Great Depression in the 1930s are sometimes obsessed with financial security and staying out of debt. In contrast, many people who grew up in the 1950s are generally less concerned about financial security, believing that installment loans and credit cards are a way of life. Obviously, not all people conform to these overly simplified generalizations; value programming is far more complex than this.

Changes in Values

While the values of most people tend to be relatively stable by the time they reach adulthood, the values of each generation undergo a never-ending change process from one generation to the next. One study of the influence of television on values found that the basic beliefs, attitudes and behaviors of a large number of viewers changed as a result of one thirty-minute television program.[6] Several major value changes that have the potential for wide-ranging impact on organizations are discussed below.

ROKEACH VALUE SURVEY

The following eighteen values are listed in alphabetical order. Your task is to arrange them in order of their importance to *you*, as guiding principles in *your* life. Place a 1 beside the item that is most important, a 2 next to the second most important item, etc., until you have reached number 18.

	A Comfortable Life a prosperous life
	An Exciting Life a stimulating, active life
	A Sense of Accomplishment lasting contribution
	A World at Peace free of war and conflict
	A World of Beauty beauty of nature and the arts
	Equality brotherhood, equal opportunity for all
	Family Security taking care of loved ones
	Freedom independence, free choice
	Happiness contentedness
	Inner Harmony freedom from inner conflict
	Mature Love sexual and spiritual intimacy
	National Security protection from attack
	Pleasure an enjoyable, leisurely life
	Salvation saved, eternal life
	Self-Respect self-esteem
	Social Recognition respect, admiration
	True Friendship close companionship
	Wisdom a mature understanding of life

After you have completed the survey, you may wish to compare your ranking with the average for a number of college students who have taken this survey. You will find these results at the end of the references in the back of this chapter.[7]

SOURCE: Adapted from Rokeach, M., "Beliefs, Attitudes, and Values," San Francisco: Jossey-Bass, 1968 & 1972. By permission of author & publisher. Copyrighted by Milton Rokeach, 1967, 1972. Permission to reproduce granted by publisher, Halgren Tests, 873 Persimmon Ave., Sunnyvale, CA, 94087.

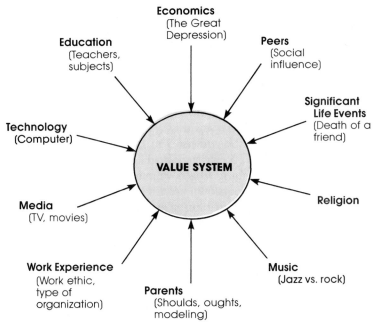

Figure 3.1

SOURCES OF VALUE PROGRAMMING

SOURCE: Adapted from the concepts of Massey, M.E. (1980). *The people puzzle: Understanding yourself and others.* Reston, VA: Reston.

Less Value Placed on Materialism.   Research by Daniel Yankelovich, a psychologist who specializes in conducting polls for government and industry, shows that people are questioning the Western passion for efficiency, cost effectiveness, and control by statistics. People are less interested in success in terms of material possessions, money and status.[8] Instead, they are more interested in self-fulfillment, being creative, spending more time with friends, and enhancing self-understanding.

More Equality for Women in the Workplace.   Yankelovich also found that people are becoming much more liberated in their view toward the division of labor between the sexes. Most respondents felt that the roles and aspirations of men and women need not be radically different.

The Desire for Self-control.   Another change with major implications for organizations is that people are saying they are "entitled" to more "social rights," including a say in decisions that affect their jobs and a job that is pleasurable and satisfying. In other words, they are demanding psychological incentives as well as economic ones.[9]

Coping With Value Changes.   As values change, organizations must develop coping strategies. If people are more interested in job satisfaction, then job enrichment may be needed (*see* Chapter 7). If more leisure time is desired, then more flexible work weeks and longer vacations may be necessary. If employees

Perspective 3.1

ETHICAL VALUES: CHEATING, LYING, AND BENDING THE RULES[10]

A survey of over 24,000 readers of *Psychology Today* (not a random sample) concerning their ethical behavior and values yielded some interesting results. The following shows the proportion of people who admitted doing these behaviors:[12]

• Taken home office supplies or other materials in the past year   68%

• Taken sick days from work although well enough to go in during the last year   47%

• Tried to save money on tax returns by lying or withholding information (in the past five years)   38%

• Made personal long distance calls at work in the past year   37%

• Cheated on an expense account in the past year   28%

Does this mean that a great many people hold the value that dishonesty is O.K.? While there is no direct answer in this research, the responses to a scenario of an everyday ethical problem—driving away after scratching another's car without telling the owner—provide some insight. Forty-four percent of the respondents said they would leave, but 89 percent said it is probably unethical. Matters got even worse if the possibility of getting caught was nil—52 percent would leave.[11] Thus, there seems to be a gap between values and behavior in this case.

A number of companies, including General Dynamics, Chemical Bank, and American Can, now run ethics workshops to alert employees to ethical dilemmas and to clarify values for coping with them.[12]

---

are more concerned with fair treatment, then new procedures may be needed to provide due process.[13] If people are less honest, then strategies are needed to protect the organization from loss.[14]

Before reading the next section you may want to complete the questionnaire in Table 3.2 to identify your values relating to certain work situations. This data will help you relate to the concepts being discussed.

Human Nature and Management: Theory X and Y

One aspect of a person's value system that is particularly important in organizational settings is the nature of a person's values concerning human nature. These values are usually hidden and taken for granted. However, people often access and act according to these values while working in the organization.[15] For example, some people tend to believe that employees are basically competitive, hateful, uncooperative, lazy, and irresponsible while others are more optimistic and believe that employees are industrious, responsible, cooperative, and motivated.[16]

What Is Theory X and Theory Y? Douglas McGregor described two contrasting views of people held by industrial managers as **Theory X:** people are essentially like machines that are set into action by external forces and **Theory Y:** people are an organic system whose behavior is affected not only by external forces but by intrinsic ones.[17] Your scores on the X–Y Questionnaire give a rough indication of your beliefs about the nature of people in work situations. A moderate to high score (five or above) on the Y scale indicates a

Table 3.2

THE X–Y QUESTIONNAIRE

Directions: The following are types of behavior a supervisor (manager, leader) may exhibit toward subordinates. Using the scale below as a guide, mark the number that corresponds to the way you would behave in in the situation described.

1	2	3	4	5
Make a great effort to do this	Tend to do this	Do not know what I would do	Tend to avoid doing this	Make a great effort to avoid this

_____ 1. Closely supervise my employees to make sure they do the job right.
_____ 2. Develop goals for my subordinates and then leave them pretty much alone.
_____ 3. Look for ways to give my subordinates more responsibility.
_____ 4. Use punishment to correct undesirable behavior.
_____ 5. Encourage my subordinates to set their own goals and objectives.
_____ 6. Take over whenever there are indications that the job is slipping.
_____ 7. Allow subordinates to share in making important decisions.
_____ 8. Use rewards as a way to get people to work.
_____ 9. Give my subordinates as much freedom to do the job as possible.
_____ 10. Look for ways to give people more challenging and interesting jobs.

Scoring: If you answered 4 or 5 to questions 1, 4, 6, or 8 give yourself a one for each answer and call it your *Y* subtotal. Then, if you answered 1 or 2 to questions 2, 3, 5, 7, 9, and 10 give yourself a one for each answer and add it to your *Y* subtotal to get your *Y* score. Your *Y* score should total between 0 and 10. Continue scoring below.

Y Score = _____

Now if you answered 1 or 2 to questions 1, 4, 6, or 8 give yourself a one for each answer and call it your *X* subtotal. Then, if you answered 4 or 5 to questions 2, 3, 5, 7, 9, and 10 give yourself a one for each answer and add it to your *X* subtotal to get your *X* score. Your *X* score should also total between 0 and 10.

X Score = _____

Keep your *X* and *Y* scores in mind when reading the section in the text about theory *X* and *Y*.

SOURCE: Adapted from the concepts of Theory X and Theory Y presented in McGregor, D. (1960). *The human side of enterprise.* New York: McGraw-Hill.

tendency toward Theory Y while a moderate to high score on the X scale indicates a tendency toward Theory X. It is possible that you hold both Theory X *and* Theory Y views if you scored about equally on each scale. This indicates that our view of people is made up of many beliefs, some of which may even be contradictory. A more complete description of Theory X and Theory Y is provided in Table 3.3.

Understanding Theory X and Theory Y.   The terms Theory X and Theory Y are widely used in most organizational settings, especially at managerial levels. The two views are not meant to imply that Theory X is tough, demanding management while Theory Y is weak, permissive management. A manager holding Theory Y views may be just as demanding as a Theory X manager, although there will probably be differences in style and methods.

Table 3.3

THEORY X AND THEORY Y VIEWS OF HUMAN NATURE

Theory X: The traditional view of direction and control.

1. The average human being has an inherent dislike of work and will avoid it if he can.
2. Because of this human characteristic of dislike for work, most people must be co-erced, controlled, directed, and threatened with punishment to get them to put forth adequate effort toward the achievement of organizational objectives.
3. The average human being prefers to be directed, wishes to avoid responsibility, has relatively little ambition, and wants security above all.

Theory Y: The integration of individuals and organizational goals.

1. The expenditure of physical and mental effort in work is as natural as play or rest.
2. External control and the threat of punishment are not the only means of bringing about effort toward organizational objectives. Man will exercise self-direction and self-control in the service of objectives to which he is committed.
3. Commitment to objectives is a function of the rewards associated with their achievement.
4. The average human being learns under proper conditions not only to accept but to seek responsibility.
5. The capacity to exercise a high degree of imagination, ingenuity, and creativity in the solution of organizational problems is widely, not narrowly, distributed in the population.
6. Under the conditions of modern industrial life, the intellectual potentialities of the average human being are only partially utilized.

Adapted from D. McGregor, 1960. *The human side of enterprise*, pp. 33–34, 47–48. Copyright © 1960 by McGraw-Hill, New York. Used with permission.

For example, a Theory X manager would employ much tighter supervision and control than would a Theory Y manager. There would be more tendency for the Theory X manager to behave in a distrusting, suspicious manner. Motivation would be through fear, imposed goals, and pay. A Theory Y manager, on the other hand, would be more likely to use participative goal setting and joint planning to give the subordinate direction. The Theory Y manager would trust the subordinate and grant quite a lot of freedom (within the limits of the goals). Motivation would be primarily through opportunities for people to grow, to learn, and to achieve.

How do you suppose employees react to these two contrasting management systems? For an example of how Theory X views caused serious organizational problems, *see* Perspective 3.2.

Resolving Value Conflicts

The conflict between FAA managers and striking controllers described in Perspective 3.2 is certainly an example of a value conflict. When values conflict, serious organizational repercussions can occur. Thus, dealing with value conflict is an important process.

Another example of value conflict is Jack Blaylock's lament, related in the opening case of this chapter. Jack held paternalistic values; he believed that his employees should be treated just like he would treat his own children. But his employees did not seem to respond favorably to this type of treatment. In fact,

Perspective 3.2

WHAT WOULD MAKE 11,500 PEOPLE QUIT THEIR JOBS?[18]

In August 1981, 11,500 air traffic controllers walked off their jobs on an illegal strike against the Federal Aviation Administration (FAA). The strikers, who could only be employed by the FAA, knew that the President was determined to defeat the strike. Even when they were given an opportunity to return to their jobs, they did not. To find out why the controllers behaved in such seemingly irrational behavior, the Secretary of Transportation commissioned a research study.

The results of the study indicated that while there were a number of complex contributing factors, a central cause was the Theory X (autocratic) management style of the FAA. The research showed that the striking controllers were in the lower 6 percent nationally on the Theory X Scale—they were quite Theory Y oriented. In contrast to these mostly younger strikers, the supervisors split into two groups. Forty percent of the supervisors were very low on the X scale, while 50 percent of them were very high. Thus the difference in values between the controllers, who had a Theory Y orientation, and the senior supervisors, with a Theory X orientation, made a clash inevitable.

The study concludes that "organizational conditions and management practices [Theory X]—together with their end products of alienation, dissatisfaction, and stress, not peer pressure—caused 11,500 separate individuals to decide to strike."[19]

we might expect employees of the 1980s to value self-reliance, responsibility, autonomy and self-control. These values are in direct conflict with Jack's. In the confrontation, Jack lost—the employees voted in a union to protect them.

Dealing With Individual-Level Value Conflicts. Since an individual's values are deep-seated and hard to change, the best way of dealing with them is to live and let live. Unless there is some overwhelmingly strong reason for a value confrontation, why not let people have their own values. Even though you may like your own value set, there is no reason to think that only you have the straight line to the truth.

And yet sometimes a value conflict may have an important adverse impact on the organization or upon you as a person or manager. In that case, a confrontation is necessary. When confronting another, one good technique is to confront the other person with solid evidence that the conflict has some tangible effect on yourself or the organization.[20] If the person can see that it does, it is quite possible that he or she will understand your position and modify his or her behavior, if not the basic value itself. If the other person does not see the tangible effect, the conflict will probably continue, or it must be resolved through force.

While force or power may be the only alternative for solving a value conflict, it is a dangerous strategy that may result in alienation and anger. Sometimes the individual and the organization both lose in this confrontation. (*See* Chapter 10 for more information on conflict resolution strategies.)

Dealing With Conflicts Between Groups of People. The controllers' strike described in Perspective 3.2 is an example of a widespread, organizational-value problem. This type of value conflict is especially difficult to resolve. It may take major changes in people, structure, and personnel resources to resolve such systems-wide values problems. Strategies may include problem solving (discussed in Chapters 10 and 13) and organization development (discussed in Chapter 16).

Dealing With Intrapersonal Value Conflicts.   A more difficult type of value conflict may be an **intrapersonal** one (within a single person). For example, many women executives face a conflict between career values and family values, which has resulted in higher career exit rates for women. An excerpt from a recent article, entitled "Why women managers are bailing out," states:

> A career-minded 25–year old dynamo is often more concerned about marriage and a family a few years later. Brooke Banbury-Mashland, a management specialist at Data General Corp., and Daniel Brass, a Penn State professor, studied 94 MBA women whose average age was 30. They found marriage had overtaken career as what women valued most. The authors concluded: "As more of the women married, careers did not increase in importance, but the importance of marriage increased significantly." [21]

Intrapersonal value conflicts are often impossible to resolve without counseling. They are deep-seated and very resistant to change. Sometimes a career-development workshop that focuses on examining values will clarify and resolve these types of conflicts.

The study of values is a key element in the process of understanding individuals. In the next section we will discuss how attitudes emerge from values and how they influence our behavior.

ATTITUDES AND ORGANIZATIONAL BEHAVIOR

Attitudes are a tendency to react in some favorable or unfavorable way toward some person, group, or idea.[22] Attitudes differ from values in that they focus on a specific object, whereas values are very broad, general beliefs about some end state. Often, attitudes are an outgrowth of values. Examples of attitudes might be: typists are boring people, supervisors cannot be trusted, unions are bad, bankers are stuffy people. (For more examples, *see* Table 3.4). Note the attitudes focused on typists, supervisors, unions, and bankers—they are all quite specific when compared to such values as honesty or an exciting life. Both attitudes and values tend to be implicit guides for action in that people often act in accordance with their values and attitudes.

Attitudes involve a preferential response tendency. We tend to feel satisfied or dissatisfied, positive or negative, favorable or unfavorable toward the object of our attitude. Each of the attitude examples in Table 3.4 shows this preferential response tendency: "I really love my job," or "This is a real rip-off." In organizational settings, attitudes tend to be centered around the job, supervisor, pay, benefits, facilities, promotions, coworkers, and other similar dimensions. Obviously, it is important for us, as managers, to find out the nature of people's attitudes and, if needed, attempt to change them to a more positive direction.

Table 3.4

EXAMPLES OF ATTITUDES

Union representative	"You just can't trust management. My job is to push the union position regardless of its merit."
Office employee	"My boss just doesn't care about us. He will walk right past you in the morning without even saying hello. That really turns me off."
Military officer	"One of the best things about the military is that you get to meet so many new and interesting people."
Foreman	"Let's face it. You have to treat these workers like some faceless robots or they will take advantage of you."
Bricklayer	"I really love my job. I can look around town and see hundreds of buildings that were built with my own two hands. I wouldn't trade this job for anything."
Cook	"Hey man, this is a real rip-off. They expect us to do everything around here and then only pay us minimum wages."
Chief executive officer	"You've got to work through people to get the job done. We've got some of the most competent people I know. They can be trusted to do the job right."

Measuring Attitudes

Sometimes we can tell the attitudes or "feel the pulse" of an organization by simply listening and observing. This method may be good for small organizations, but when an organization gets larger there is always the possibility that a vocal minority may be the loudest source of information. Thus, there is a distinct possibility that such a sample may be biased and may not reflect the attitudes of the entire organization. More accurate information can be obtained through systematic use of attitude questionnaires.

Using Questionnaires to Measure Attitudes.   Almost everyone has filled out some type of attitude survey. A pizza house wants to know if you like thick or thin crusts. A stereo designer wants to know if you like a black or gold front for your receiver. Likewise, organizations are interested in a number of issues. Do you like your job? Are you thinking about quitting? Is the pay reasonable? Do you get good food and service from the company cafeteria? Do you respect your boss? Do you like your coworkers? Are promotions fair? Organizations want to know the answers to these questions in order to evaluate the impact of system changes, to pinpoint the need for future changes, to evaluate the status quo over time, or perhaps just because someone simply wants to know. To get a feel for an attitude questionnaire, you may wish to fill out the one provided in Table 3.5.

To do a thorough job of designing a **valid** (Does it measure what it is supposed to measure?) and **reliable** (Does it measure consistently?) questionnaire, you need an expert. However, there are a number of well-validated questionnaires that measure such areas as job satisfaction, pay satisfaction, or attitudes toward supervisors.

Table 3.5

JOB SATISFACTION SCALE

Directions: If you are now working, respond to the questions in relation to the job you are doing. If you are not working, think of some job you have done in the past and respond in relation to that job. Indicate how satisfied you are with each aspect of your job listed below using the scale provided. Write the appropriate number in the space beside each statement.

1	2	3	4	5
Very dissatisfied	A little dissatisfied	Neutral	Somewhat satisfied	Very satisfied

---

_____ 1. The job itself.
_____ 2. The amount of pay and fringe benefits I receive.
_____ 3. The amount of personal growth and development I get in doing my job.
_____ 4. The kinds of things I have to do on this job.
_____ 5. The degree of respect and fair treatment I receive from my boss.
_____ 6. The degree to which I am fairly paid for what I contribute to this organization.
_____ 7. The amount of independent thought and action I can exercise on this job.
_____ 8. The overall quality of supervision I receive in my work.

Scoring: Compute four job satisfaction indices by combining these questions:

a. Add questions 1 and 4 to get
    General Job Satisfaction = _____
b. Add questions 2 and 6 to get
    Satisfaction with pay = _____
c. Add questions 3 and 7 to get
    Satisfaction with growth = _____
d. Add questions 5 and 8 to get
    Satisfaction with supervision = _____

Scores of 7 or above indicate relatively high satisfaction while scores of 5 or below indicate low satisfaction.

SOURCE: Adapted from J.R. Hackman and G.R. Oldham, 1975, Development of the job diagnostic survey, *Journal of Applied Psychology* 60:159–170. Copyright 1975 by the American Psychological Association. Reprinted/adapted by permission of the author and the publisher.

Job Satisfaction

Since job satisfaction is one of the most important and frequently measured work attitudes, we will examine it in more detail. **Job satisfaction** refers to the degree of pleasurable or unpleasurable feelings that one has toward a job or job experiences.[23] People who are satisfied with their jobs will make statements like this about their jobs: "I love it," "It's a great job," or "I wouldn't exchange this job for any other." People who don't like their jobs will say: "I really hate this job," "I would quit right now if I could," or "I never feel good about this lousy job."

A general job satisfaction scale such as the one in Table 3.5 (questions one and four) measures attitudes relating to overall or **global** satisfaction. Managers are also interested in attitudes toward specific facets or aspects of the job, such as satisfaction with supervision, pay, and growth. Questions can be designed to measure these attitudes and more, as illustrated by the remaining questions in Table 3.5.

Perspective 3.3

IS JOB SATISFACTION IN THE UNITED STATES CHANGING?

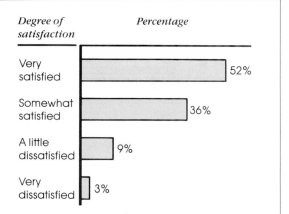

An evaluation of job satisfaction levels of American workers revealed there has been little change for the past twenty years.[24] Overall levels are shown.

While it appears that most people are satisfied, there was less satisfaction for blacks than for whites. There was no difference in satisfaction between men and women. Older and more educated people were both more satisfied. White collar employees were more satisfied than blue collar ones with managers, and professional-technical people tied for the highest levels of satisfaction.

Job Satisfaction and Work Behaviors

The most extensively studied job attitude is job satisfaction. Many researchers have searched for a link between job satisfaction and performance, reasoning that "a happy employee is a productive employee." For many years, no consistent relationship was found between job satisfaction and employment. Recent results are more promising;[25] however, the overall result is far from settled.[26] Perspective 3.4 explains this controversy.

Perspective 3.4

THE SATISFACTION–PERFORMANCE CONTROVERSY

- *Point—Satisfaction Improves Performance.* Many managers feel that a happy worker is a productive worker. Since both high satisfaction and high performance are desirable outcomes, then they ought to go together. One analysis of job satisfaction research found a correlation between job satisfaction and performance of .31 for twenty different organizations involving 3,140 employers.[27] Another review of the research concludes that there is more evidence to support the satisfaction-improves-performance relationship than is often credited.[28]

- *Counterpoint One—Performance Improves Satisfaction.* Another view is that when people perform well and they are properly rewarded, they will be satisfied.[29] One reason for developing this view is that a number of research reviews have found no relationship or a very weak relationship between satisfaction and performance.[30]

- *Counterpoint Two—Both of the above?—or none of the above?* Either approach may be working depending upon the situation.[31] A social exchange process may cause people who are satisfied to reciprocate by rewarding (through high performance) their benefactors. Or, perhaps satisfaction and performance are codetermined by a third variable—rewards, such as pay, recognition, and promotion.[32] Thus, counterpoint two indicates that the reward relationship may be the most crucial one.

Attitudes and Behavior

Do Attitudes Predict Behavior?   Some experts believe attitudes predict behavior while others believe they do not. Since an attitude is a predisposition to
react, doesn't reaction predict behavior? While it usually does, the reaction
could be internal within the person with no visible external behavior. The
situation will also influence whether attitudes result in behavior. For example,
if you live in a small town with high unemployment, you may be much less
likely to quit even when you are quite dissatisfied with your job. Another factor
that complicates behavior prediction is that people hold many attitudes, some
being stronger than others. Thus, it is hard to tell which one or ones are driving
behavior at a given moment.

Job satisfaction seems to be related to performance and to a number of
other important organizational outcomes, such as absenteeism,[33] turnover
(quitting the organization),[34] and the decision to retire.[35] These behaviors are
very important to organizational managers since the costs of absenteeism,
turnover and premature retirement can be high. For example, if 5 percent of
your work force is consistently absent, you may have to hire additional people
to fill their positions, and union contracts and federal laws may require you to
pay the absent employees as well. Turnover is even more costly, especially if the
job requires time to train a person to perform. Training costs and personnel
system overhead costs may make replacing people very expensive.

Research also shows job satisfaction is related to **employee citizenship,**
which entails such behaviors as helping coworkers, accepting orders without
complaint, making constructive statements about the work unit, and
promoting a positive work climate.[36] Such positive work behaviors certainly
make the job of the manager easier and contribute to a more effective
organization.

Job satisfaction may also be related to life satisfaction and physical and
mental health.[37] Thus, job satisfaction is related to many important
organizational behaviors. Improving and maintaining high levels of job
satisfaction is an important objective for managers. Figure 3.2 illustrates many
possible causes and outcomes related to job satisfaction.

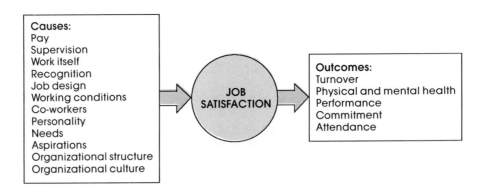

Figure 3.2

CAUSES AND OUTCOMES RELATED TO JOB SATISFACTION

Commitment to the Organization

Another important attitude is **organizational commitment,** a composite of several factors, including belief in the organization's goals and values, willingness to expend extra effort for the organization, and the desire to stay in the organization.[38] Organizational citizenship, discussed earlier, is also closely related to commitment. People who are committed to the organization will be major assets when compared to those who are not. Japanese employees, who will be discussed later in the chapter, certainly show a high degree of organizational commitment. In fact, this is seen as a major competitive advantage for Japanese organizations.[39]

Commitment results from a combination of many factors that are not fully understood.[40] One important factor is feelings of long-term job security. Mergers and staff cutbacks are causing layoffs of white-collar employees who once thought they had a career-long commitment. A cover story in *Business Week* highlighted this problem with the headline: "The end of corporate loyalty?". They reported that 65 percent of salaried employees were less loyal than they had been ten years ago.[41] The article gives an example of a fifty-seven-year-old married man who was nudged into early retirement and said:

> "I was hurt. After 34 years with the company, I was surprised that it came down to an economic relationship between the two of us. I thought I was in a family kind of thing."[42]

What impact would this forced retirement have on 30-year-old employees? Most likely, their commitment would decline; who knows when it could happen to them.

Other factors that may result in higher commitment include opportunities to participate in decisions (*see* Chapter 12), chances to exercise responsibility and autonomy in their jobs (*see* Chapter 7), a decentralized organizational structure (*see* Chapter 14), and a positive organizational culture (*see* Chapter 16).

As you can see in Figure 3.3 there are many positive outcomes associated with organizational commitment. One of the more important ones is job satisfaction.[43] In addition, attendance and turnover are consistently related. Loyalty and job-related effort will also be affected. Clearly, these outcomes are important and effort must be expended to improve and maintain high levels of organizational commitment.

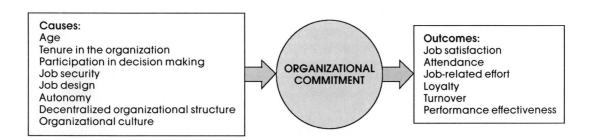

Figure 3.3

CAUSES AND OUTCOMES RELATED TO ORGANIZATIONAL COMMITMENT

Changing Attitudes

Managers are often interested in changing attitudes. A great deal of company effort is frequently put into this task. Unfortunately, not all these efforts are successful. Although attitudes are certainly easier to change than values, they are still relatively hard to influence or change.

A number of attitude-change techniques are available, including group pressures (*see* Chapter 9), behavior modification and reinforcement strategies (*see* Chapter 6), and impression management (*see* Chapter 4).[44] One additional strategy is cognitive dissonance theory, discussed in the following section.

Cognitive Dissonance Theory. Dissonance theory concerns the way people organize their thoughts, beliefs, and attitudes. **Cognitive dissonance** exists when two attitudes, beliefs, values, or behaviors are not consistent with each other.[45] The assumption behind dissonance theory is that people try to keep their thoughts internally consistent with their attitudes, values, and behaviors. If some event is psychologically inconsistent, then the resulting dissonance is usually quite uncomfortable for the individual, and thus every effort will be made to reduce the inconsistency.

Using Dissonance to Change Attitudes. To change attitudes using dissonance theory, one has to create a dissonant situation that will force or encourage the person to resolve the dissonance in some desired direction. In the following example high pay is used to create a favorable attitude toward an otherwise boring job:

Sandra Ming, after trying for a very long time and with considerable effort to get a job at the Blaylock Venetian Blind Company, is finally hired. She then finds that working for the company is not anything like what she expected it to be—the job is quite routine and boring, although the pay is good. After expending the effort to get the job and bragging about it to all her friends, she has to do something to resolve the uncomfortable feeling of dissonance. She could quit, but that would make her even more uncomfortable when she had to explain it to her friends. Sandra could also decide that the job isn't so bad after all—and, since it pays so well, it is now really great.

In this case the dissonance resulted from the conflict between her attitude about the company before she was hired (very favorable) and the reality of the company after she was on board (boring job). She reduced the dissonant element (a routine and boring task) by concentrating on the consonant element (good pay).

CROSS–CULTURAL OB: JAPAN AS AN EXAMPLE

Value differences become even more pronounced between different countries with varied cultural backgrounds. For illustration, we will briefly examine some Japanese values that result in quite different work behaviors—and often superior work performance—from that of American employees. Anthropologists who have compared the two cultures note a number of key differences between Japanese values and American values.[46]

Paternalism

The Japanese people tend to become very closely attached to the people in their work organization. They in effect become members of an organizational family. They form deep attachments to their work organization so that they become part of the organizational household. In addition, there is a normal parent-child relationship between the employer and the employee. The parent is seen as a person with ability, status, and personal attraction who looks after the weaker child. This relationship is seen as quite natural and desirable by both parties.

Out of these paternalistic organizational values grows the **lifetime employment** policy that is common to many, but not all Japanese firms (*see* Perspective 3.5). The feeling often expressed is that the "enterprise is the people" or "this is my company." In fact, the employer and employee are sometimes bound by ties as close and firm as those shared by husband and wife.[47] Paternalism and lifetime employment are two-way ties that meet the needs and values of both the organization and the Japanese people. This results in strong feelings of commitment among Japanese employees.

Jack Blaylock, in our opening case, might have been delighted with these Japanese employees. Unfortunately, his younger American employees did not share the value that organizational paternalism is a desirable end state. In fact, they were concerned with just the opposite—individual freedom and self-control.

Hierarchy

One's position in the hierarchy depends mostly upon seniority; you have to wait your turn. The Japanese world is divided into three basic categories: seniors, juniors, and one's colleagues.[48] It is interesting to note that "colleagues" takes on a somewhat different meaning than in the United States. Colleagues are people who graduated with you and entered business in the same year. Thus, as you can see, the system is very much seniority-oriented.

While everyone takes their "proper station," the roles they play may be quite flexible. For example, in the Japanese decision-making system, most people in the organization, regardless of rank, have an opportunity to put their input into the decision. It would be quite proper for a junior manager, right out of business school, to make an input into a decision that would ultimately go to the chief executive of the company.

Implications for American Managers

We have covered only a few of the many value differences between Japan and the United States. For almost any culture, differences exist that are important management considerations for interacting with that culture. For example, an American multinational corporation must carefully consider cultural values before operating in any foreign environment.[49] In addition, it is becoming more and more common for Japanese and other foreign companies to build subsidiaries in the United States. This means that many Americans may be working for Japanese bosses. Careful study of values will make managers more sensitive to motivation and leadership problems in such organizations.

Perspective 3.5

LIFETIME EMPLOYMENT IN JAPAN: MYTHS AND REALITIES[50]

Many employees in Japanese business and industry have a job guaranteed for life once they are on the payroll. While they are on the job, they have practically complete job security, which is endangered only in the event of a severe economic catastrophe. They are also paid on the basis of seniority, with little variance for the type of job, until management levels are attained after working ten to fifteen years for the same firm. However, there are a number of people who do not enjoy lifetime employment:

• Women are always considered "temporary" rather than "permanent" employees, so they are exempted from the benefits.

• In many "traditional" Japanese businesses, such as workshop industries producing lacquer, pottery, and silk, workers are hired and paid by the hour.

• Even in the "modern" industries there is a slowly shrinking, but substantial (perhaps 20 percent) body of employees, who, by unilateral management decision, are considered "temporary" and remain in that category for many years.

• Most people who have lifetime employment are forced to retire at age fifty-five with a relatively small pension. These people may then become temporary employees or open their own businesses.

Perhaps even more important are the lessons in management that we might learn from the Japanese, for they have developed some extremely effective management strategies.[51] If we are to evaluate critically Japanese techniques for possible application in an American setting, then we need to be able to tell how values relate to management. For example, lifetime employment and paternalistic values allow Japanese managers more freedom to design costly training programs. Japanese firms place very strong emphasis on extensive (often three months long) training programs for new employees. They can afford to do it because they know that their employees will stay with them for a very long time. If we in the United States were to sink as much money into training new employees as the Japanese do, we might find the cost prohibitive because of our higher employee turnover rates.

MANAGERIAL APPLICATIONS OF VALUE AND ATTITUDE CONCEPTS

Values and attitudes are particularly important for understanding individual-level behavior in organizations because they affect the way people behave and the way they perceive the world. In the next chapter, we will examine perception and see how values and attitudes act as filters that determine where we direct our attention. Much later in the book we will focus on how values influence the whole organizational culture (*see* Chapter 17).

An understanding of values and attitudes gives us a framework for understanding how people feel about their jobs, their supervisors, their pay, and many other important organizational variables. If we understand the basic nature of values and attitudes, then we can measure them and possibly change them. This should lead to more precise management strategies and a more effective organization.

Values and attitudes are the glue that holds organizations together. Shared values and attitudes help focus energy on common organizational goals. Here are some guides for management application:

- *Treat your employees as unique individuals.* Since people hold a wide variety of values, managers must treat their employees as separate individuals when designing jobs, constructing pay systems, or appraising performance. The more these systems can be tailored to the individual, the more effective they will be.

- *Keep up with changes in work values.* Managers need to stay attuned to what is happening to values. For example, the increasing importance of self-control means that jobs need to have adequate autonomy and that flexible working hours may be an important strategy (*see* Chapter 8 for details).

- *Managers need to reinforce the importance of high ethical standards.* Manage through example, through education, and by properly rewarding people who display high standards.

- *Use Theory Y values.* Theory X values are becoming increasingly more incompatible with today's work force, as illustrated by the disastrous air traffic controller strike. Theory Y values can be fostered by increasing participation in decision making and giving employees freedom within the constraints of organizational goals and values.

- *Use persuasion to resolve value conflicts.* These types of conflicts are difficult, or even impossible to resolve. If confrontation cannot be avoided, focus on persuasion strategies by trying to convince the employee that the conflicting values have an adverse and tangible effect on the organization. If this does not work, force may be the next resort, but chances of failure are high. Intrapersonal conflicts can sometimes be resolved by having the employee attend a values clarification or career development workshop. Counseling is also an option here.

- *Use attitude surveys to take the organization's pulse.* Attitude surveys are extremely important tools for managers. They allow managers to find out what people think, to evaluate reactions to potential changes, to diagnose problem areas, and to prevent deterioration of important attitudes. All managers should learn how to conduct attitude surveys.

- *Take action to improve and maintain high levels of job satisfaction.* One of the most important goals for a manager is to reach and maintain high levels of job satisfaction in his or her work unit. Job satisfaction is linked with a wide variety of important outcomes, including performance, attendance, turnover, commitment, and even mental and physical health.

- *Seek high levels of organizational commitment.* Your people will be more loyal, supportive of organizational goals and values, and have a willingness to go above and beyond what is normally expected.

- *Use attitude-change strategies when appropriate.* Changing attitudes requires a variety of techniques, including the effective use of communication, rewards, perceptual processes, and group dynamics. One strategy is to use cognitive dissonance to create favorable attitudes by offering something that is the opposite of what is expected.

- *Use those aspects of Japanese management that fit your organization.* While paternalism, as practiced by Japanese organizations, does not seem to fit with American values, organizational loyalty and commitment are important goals for any organization. Thus, some type of mutual, long-term commitment between the manager, the organization, and the employee is desirable.

FOR DISCUSSION

1. How are values related to personality?

2. What is the difference between beliefs, values, and attitudes?

3. Choose some person who is approximately twenty-five years older than you are. Compare similarities and differences in values between yourself and that person.

4. Describe a Theory X and a Theory Y manager. What would be the impact of each of these managers in a research lab? In a prison?

5. Do you think that the Japanese practice of "lifetime employment" is exportable to America? Explain your position.

6. What organizational advantages and disadvantages result from Japanese cultural values?

7. Conduct a mini research study on ten working people to find out how satisfied they are with their jobs. How do your results compare with those in Perspective 3.3? How might you explain the differences?

8. What is the relationship between job satisfaction and performance?

9. Explain the relationship between organizational commitment and job satisfaction. What can be done to change these two attitudes?

10. Use cognitive dissonance to try to change someone's attitude. Did your strategy work? What problems were encountered?

11. What are the benefits and problems associated with lifetime employment?

KEY CONCEPTS AND TERMS

values	Theory Y	value conflicts
attitudes	employee citizenship	paternalism
value programming	cognitive dissonance	hierarchy
job satisfaction	organizational commitment	lifetime employment
Theory X		

Cases and Incidents

THE GRADUATES' DILEMMA

Jammie and Bill have been constant companions over the past six months—they are deeply in love. They met in an organizational behavior class and have hit it off ever since. After their graduation in June, they plan to be married.

But they have encountered one problem. There is a conflict about what positions Jammie and Bill should accept. Jammie's combination of undergraduate chemical engineering and master of business administration has made her particularly attractive to a number of major corporations. The best offer she has received is for an exciting position with a major oil company headquartered in New York City. The pay is quite good, almost $45,000, with a certain raise if she works out.

Bill, on the other hand, has an undergraduate degree in philosophy. In spite of his M.B.A., he still does not have many job offers. In fact, the only decent offer he has received is from a publishing house in St. Paul. The salary will be $16,000. Jammie has also had an offer from a chemical firm in Minneapolis with a starting salary of $28,000.

While she is impressed by both companies, the one in New York is much more exciting.

Bill is afraid that if they go to New York he will have to rely entirely on Jammie. The idea of becoming a "house husband" does not appeal to him.

DISCUSSION QUESTIONS

1. How should Jammie and Bill resolve this dilemma?
2. What value issues are involved?
3. Would it make any difference if Bill were the engineer with the New York job offer?

NEGOTIATION FAILURE IN JAPAN

A large American electronics distributing company had identified a potential market for a new type of test equipment being manufactured in Japan. They anticipated that the product would be very successful. After preliminary contacts with the Japanese manufacturer, they dispatched a team of four managers to Tokyo to negotiate a contract for $8 million worth of test equipment. Even though both sides were interested in a successful conclusion to the negotiation, it failed. Here is a partial summary of what happened:

When the Americans arrived, they immediately opened the conference by suggesting that everyone be called by their first names, a practice common within their firm. In addition, they pressed the person who was the leader of the Japanese negotiation team for immediate decisions on various parts of the contract (Tokyo is a costly city to visit and the American team was anxious to conclude negotiations as fast as possible).

Negotiations dragged on for several weeks with the American team becoming increasingly frustrated because of the delays. Finally, after three weeks, they presented the Japanese team with an ultimatum—either sign a contract or they would find another supplier. The Japanese were offended by this move and elected not to sign the contract even though it would have been quite beneficial to them.

DISCUSSION QUESTIONS

1. What value issues seem to be involved here?
2. How might the American team have reacted so that a more favorable outcome would result?

THE MUNICIPAL LIGHT CAPER

The following article appeared in the *Hamilton Harbinger* newspaper:

NEWMAN SUSPENDS 16 AT MUNICIPAL LIGHT

PRIVATE DETECTIVES TURN UP "ABUSES"

City Light Superintendent Charles Newman disclosed yesterday he has suspended sixteen field employees and reprimanded two for abusing coffee break periods.

Newman said he hired a private detective firm to shadow Municipal Light crews for one week after getting complaints from citizens that some men were taking extended coffee breaks at their Hamilton cafés.

The investigation also turned up possible abuses of coffee break times by "fifteen to eighteen" employees of the Hamilton Engineering Department, according to George Everest, principal assistant city engineer for operations.

However, Everest said he cannot say if there are any actual violations in his department until he has had each reported case checked out. This is being done now.

The three cafés involved, Everest said, are near 2d Avenue and Barstow Street, 7th Avenue N.E. and Interlake Way, and N. 34th Street and Stevens Way N.

Newman said two Municipal Light employees were suspended for ten days without pay, five were suspended for two days and nine for one day. Two others received letters of reprimand.

The superintendent said at least one of the disciplined employees also was disciplined in a similar investigation three years ago for the same thing.

Everest said his department also has to discipline employees from time to time for coffee break time abuses.

The private detective agency placed the three locations under surveillance during the work week of October 30 through November 3 and made its reports according to vehicle license numbers.

The private eyes timed the length of time crews spent in the cafés. Normal time allowed for coffee breaks is fifteen minutes in the forenoon and afternoon, Everest said.

Newman said: "We talked to our people involved and they admitted the abuses. The severity and frequency of the violations varied."

Newman stressed that the infractions involved only a small minority of Municipal Light workers and "I continue to be amazed at the dedication of 99 percent of our employees."

He said those abusing lunch or coffee break periods not only are gypping the city—"they also are cheating on their fellow employees.

"I will not stand for this."

He said most of the violators "had been around for a while." He said that if any "extenuating circumstances" turn up later, the disciplinary actions will be rectified.

"We're not against coffee breaks—just the abuse of them," Newman declared. Although the place has been disguised, this incident really happened.

DISCUSSION QUESTIONS

1. What values do you think the City Light Superintendent holds?

2. How do you think his actions affected the employees?

3. Do you think the attitude of the employees toward management changed?

4. What impact do you think the action will have on performance?

REFERENCES

1. This definition is similar to the one used by Rokeach, M. (1968). *Beliefs, attitudes and values.* San Francisco: Jossey-Bass, p. 124.

2. Rokeach (1968), p. 160.

3. Rokeach (1968), p. 1.

4. Massey, M.E. (1980). *The people puzzle: Understanding yourself and others.* Reston, VA: Reston.

5. Massey (1980).

6. Ball-Rokeach, S.J., Rokeach, M., & Grube, J.W. (1984, November). The great American values test. *Psychology Today*, 34cf.

7. For a more thorough assessment of your personal values, see Simon, S.B., Howe, L.W., & Kirschenbaum, H. (1972). *Values Clarification: a handbook of practical strategies for teachers and students.* New York: Hart.

8. Yankelovich, D. (1981). New rules in American life: Searching for self-fulfillment in a world turned upside down. *Psychology Today*, 15(4), 35cf. Also see Brody, M. (1985, November 11). Meet today's young American worker. *Fortune*.

9. Yankelovich (1981).

10. Based on Hasset, J. (1981). But what would be wrong . . . *Psychology Today*, 15(11), 34cf.

11. From Hasset (1981), p. 41.

12. Otten, A.L. (1986, July 14). Ethics on the job: Companies alert employees to potential dilemmas. *The Wall Street Journal.* Also see What's wrong: Hypocrisy, betrayal and greed unsettle the nation's soul. (1987, May 25). *Time.*

13. See Ewing, D.W. (1982, November-December). Due process: Will business default? *Harvard Business Review*, pp. 114–122.

14. See the summary of a study by Cherrington, D.J., & Cherrington, J.O. (1981). How to keep them honest. *Psychology Today*, 15(11), 50cf.

15. Sullivan, J.J. (1986). Human nature, organizations, and management theory. *Academy of Management Review, 11*, 534–549.

16. Knowles, H.P., & Saxberg, B.O. (1971). *Personality and leadership behavior.* Reading, MA: Addison-Wesley.

17. McGregor, D. (1967). *The professional manager.* New York: McGraw-Hill, pp. 79–80.

18. Bowers, D.B. (1983, Winter). What would make 11,500 people quit their jobs? *Organizational Dynamics*, pp. 5–19.

19. Bowers (1983), p. 17. For an update on the status of the fired controllers, see Lowenstein, R. (1986, August 1). For fired air traffic controllers, life's OK, but not like old times. *Wall Street Journal.*

20. See Gordon, T. (1977). *Leadership effectiveness training, L.E.T.* New York: Wyden.

21. Taylor, A. (1986, August 19). Why women managers are bailing out. *Fortune*, p. 19. Also see Nelson, D.L., & Quick, J.C. (1985). Professional women: Are distress and disease inevitable? *Academy of Management Review, 10*, 206–218.

22. Rokeach (1968) & Bem, D.J. (1982). *Attitudes, beliefs, and human affairs* (2nd ed.). Belmont, CA: Brooks-Cole.

23. Locke, E.A. (1976). The nature and causes of job satisfaction. In M.D. Dunnette (Ed.), *Handbook of industrial and organizational psychology* (p. 1300). Chicago: Rand McNally. Also see Wanous, J.P., & Lawler, E.E., III (1972). Measurement and meaning of job satisfaction. *Journal of Applied Psychology, 56*, 95–105.

24. Weaver, C.N. (1980). Job satisfaction in the United States in the 1970s. *Journal of Applied Psychology, 65*, 364–367. For another view about changes, see Cooper, M.R., Morgan, B.S., Foley, P.M., & Kaplan, L.B. (1979, January-February). Changing employee values: Deepening discontent? *Harvard Business Review*, pp. 117–125.

25. Petty, M.M., McGee, G.W., & Cavender, J.W. (1984). A meta-analysis of the relationship between individual job satisfaction and individual performance. *Academy of Management Review, 9*, 712–721.

26. Locke (1976).

27. Petty, McGee, & Cavender (1984). Also see Herzberg, F., Mausner, B., Peterson, R.O., & Capwell, D.F. (1957). *Job attitudes: A review of research and opinion.* Pittsburgh: Psychological Service of Pittsburgh.

28. Organ, D.W. (1977). A reappraisal and reinterpretation of the satisfaction-causes-performance hypothesis. *Academy of Management Review, 2*, 46–53.

29. Porter, L.W., & Lawler, E.E., III (1968). *Management attitudes and performance.* Homewood, Il: Irwin.

30. Greene, C.N., & Craft, R.E., Jr. (1977), The satisfaction-performance controversy—revisited. In H.K. Downey, D. Hellreigel, & J.W. Slocum (Eds.), *Organizational behavior: A reader* (pp. 187–201). St. Paul, MN: West.

31. Organ (1977).

32. Podsakoff, P.M., & Williams, L.J. (1986). The relationship between job performance and job satisfaction. In E.A. Locke (Ed.), *Generalizing from laboratory to field settings.* Lexington, MA: Lexington Books. Also see Greene and Craft (1977).

33. See Steers, R.M., & Rhodes, S.R. (1978). Major influences on employee attendance: A process model. *Journal of Applied Psychology, 63*, 391–407; and Watson, D.J. (1981). An evaluation of some aspects of the Steers and Rhodes model of employee attendance. *Journal of Applied Psychology, 66*, 385–389.

34. Cotton, J.L., & Tuttle, J.M. (1986). Employee turnover: A meta-analysis and review with implications for research. *Academy of Management Review, 11*, 55–70; and Mobley, W.H. (1982). *Employee turnover: Causes, consequences, and control.* Reading, MA: Addison-Wesley.

35. Schmidt, N., & McCune, J.T. (1981). The relationship between job attitudes and the decision to retire. *Academy of Management Journal, 24*, 795–802.

36. Bateman, T.S., & Organ, D.W. (1983). Job satisfaction and the good soldier: The relationship between affect and employee "citizenship." *Academy of Management Journal, 26*, 587–595.

37. Locke (1976).

38. Morrow, P.C. (1983). Concept redundancy in organizational research: The case of work commitment. *Academy of Management Review, 8*, 486–500; and Reichers, A.E. (1985). A review and reconceptualization of organizational commitment. *Academy of Management Review, 10*, 465–476.

39. Sengoku, T. (1985). *Willing workers: The work ethics in Japan, England, and the United States.* Westport, CN: Quorum Books.

40. See Reichers (1985); Mowday, R.T., Porter, L.W., & Steers, R.M. (1982). *The psychology of commitment, absenteeism, and turnover.* New York: Academic Press; and Steers, R.M. (1977). Antecedents and outcomes of organizational commitment. *Administrative Science Quarterly, 22*, 46–56.

41. The end of corporate loyalty? (1986, August 4). *Business Week.*

42. The end of corporate loyalty (1986), p. 42.

43. Bateman, T.S., & Strasser, S. (1984). A longitudinal analysis of the antecedents of organizational commitment. *Academy of Management Journal, 27*, 95–112.

44. See Zimbardo, P.G., Ebbesen, E.B., & Maslach, C. (1977). *Influencing attitudes and changing behavior* (2nd ed.). Reading, MA: Addison-Wesley. Also see Bem (1982).

45. Festinger, L. (1957). *A theory of cognitive dissonance.* Evanston, Il: Row, Peterson.

46. For an analysis of Japanese culture, see Nakane, C. (1970). *Japanese society.* Berkeley, CA: University of California Press. Also see Thurow, L.C.

(Ed.). (1985). *The Japanese management challenge: Japanese views,* Cambridge, MA: MIT Press.

47. Nakane (1970).

48. Nakane (1970).

49. Harris, P.R., & Moran, R.T. (1987). *Managing cultural differences,* (2nd ed.). Houston: Gulf.

50. There are many good books and articles on Japanese management. I recommend Keys, J.B., & Miller, T.R. (1984). The Japanese management theory jungle. *Academy of Management Review, 9,* 342–353; Hatvany, N., & Pucik, V. (1981, Spring). Japanese management practices and productivity. *Organizational Dynamics,* pp. 5–21; Yang, C.Y. (1984, November-December). Demystifying Japanese management practices. *Harvard Business Review,* pp. 172–182; and Drucker, P.F. (1981, January-February). Behind Japan's success. *Harvard Business Review,* pp. 83–90.

51. See Pascale, R.T., & Athos, A.G. (1981). *The art of Japanese management: Applications for American executives.* New York: Simon and Schuster; and Ouchi, W.G. (1981). *Theory Z: How American business can meet the Japanese challenge.* Reading, MA: Addison-Wesley.

Rokeach Value Survey, Table 3.1: Rankings based on the responses of college students in 1983.

Value	Ranking
Self-respect	1
Family security	2
Happiness	3
True friendship	4
Freedom	5
Wisdom	6
Sense of accomplishment	7
Inner harmony	8
Comfortable life	9
Exciting life	10
Mature love	11
World at peace	12
Salvation	13
Pleasure	14
Social recognition	15
Equality	16
World of beauty	17
National security	18

Chapter Four

PERCEPTION: WHAT IS REALITY?

PREVIEW

- Why is it that two people can observe the same event and see entirely different things?

- Why do we see some things but ignore others—why do we selectively perceive?

- How can stereotypes act as invisible barriers to achieving equal treatment for blacks, Hispanics, women, and other minorities?

- What is a self-fulfilling prophecy and how does it work?

- Why does the halo effect cause so many problems in performance appraisal?

- Does the way you dress really make a difference in how well you succeed in organizations?

MAJOR TOPICS

Preview Case: the Choice

The Perception Process

Problems in Perception

Impression Management

Performance Evaluation and Interviewing

Cross-Cultural OB: Time Perceptions

Managerial Applications of Perception

Preview Case

THE CHOICE

Lacy Vanscott, who has been the Assistant Secretary of Defense for Electronics for six months, felt he was finally getting the hang of the job. Half a year ago, when the Secretary had called him at Xeron Electronics and asked him to take the job, he had been flattered.

Lacy thought to himself: "Who would have believed that the Army Lieutenant of only twelve years ago would now be the Assistant Secretary! Obviously, I made the right decision to get out of the service and get my masters in electrical engineering from M.I.T. And, the fact that the Secretary and I were both undergraduates at Yale didn't hurt either."

Lacy leaned back in his high-backed executive chair, lit up his pipe, and returned to his current major problem—choosing someone to head the Satellite Communications Division, called SCD for short. Ever since last week when John Oshiyama announced he was leaving for Harvard Aerospace Industries, Lacy knew he would have a problem picking John's successor. Each of the three SCD branch chiefs seemed well qualified. Herb Zawalski was a conscientious, low-key individual whom Lacy did not know much about. Dave Sands was a sharp-dressing, alert, high-visibility person who was always "Johnny-on-the-spot." The third possible choice was Wilma Marlow, who seemed quite competent despite the rumor that she is the "token woman" in SCD management. Whom should he choose?

Lacy turned his chair around and gazed out the window at the Potomac River. He was almost distracted by the sailboat gently moving up the river, but he forced himself to concentrate on the selection problem.

"Dave always seems to come to my mind first whenever I think of someone to promote. Why? Dave always looks competent and self-assured. He wears the right clothes—you know, dark grey pinstripes, with vest, dark tie, and wing-tipped shoes. Dave also makes it a point to come around and talk about sailing at the beginning of each week. He is also a Yale graduate, although I can't remember his major. But what about his performance? Well, I don't remember very much good or bad so I have to assume he runs a 'tight ship.' On the other hand, I do remember hearing about some grievances filed by some of his employees—disgruntled troublemakers, no doubt. Overall, its very hard to shake my very favorable impressions of Dave."

Actually, Dave's department is always on the verge of collapse. He is gone much of the time talking sailing with other enthusiasts. When he is there, he is openly ignored because of his lack of technical expertise and his general incompetence as a supervisor. He was a zoology major and seems to have little interest in or talent for electronics. He responds to the slights by blaming all his problems on his incompetent employees. He feels that he is quite competent, but he has been stuck with a bunch of dunderheads. He hopes that he will get the promotion because he can get away from these troublesome employees and, perhaps secretly, he can spend more time concentrating on sailing.

Lacy continued his line of thought, "Now Herb, he's something else. He looks like he buys his suits from the bargain basement and in the summer he even wears an open shirt. He certainly doesn't project an executive image. Also, I don't see Herb as often. He never stops by for a social chat like Dave does. On the other hand, Herb's division is the most complex in SCD and he seems to handle all the problems quite well. He has an engineering degree from one of the far western universities and, I believe, an MBA from one of the local night schools."

In reality, Herb is a very conscientious and competent manager and engineer. His people respect him and will go out of their way to do things for him. Herb is so concerned with getting the job done that he does not find much time for small talk. Neither is he very interested in clothes. He would probably wear the same suit all week if his wife did not remind him to change. Herb perceives Dave as an incompetent supervisor and cannot imagine working for him.

Lacy turned to his last alternative: "What about Wilma? If I don't choose her, will she complain to the equal opportunity people? I'd sure hate to go through one of those messy investigations. And let's face it, Wilma's just too pushy. She would have everybody up in arms within a month. Although I've never heard anything bad about her management, I'm sure she would be very hard on her subordinates. Also, I can't forget that time about two months ago when she called me, in an obviously emotional state, and asked if she might have a couple of days off for personal reasons. I think she might just break down when the pressure gets tough. We need someone who is stable in such an important position."

But in reality Wilma is a quite competent candidate. She is no more pushy than men who have similar positions. Her people respect her and certainly "put out" the work for her. She is also technically competent with a dual major in electrical engineering and management. The only unprogrammed time she has had to be absent in the last three years was when her mother died. She had been quite close to her and had been pretty broken up.

A few days later, Lacy faced the deadline for a decision: "Well, I guess I'm going to have to 'bite the bullet' and make my decision. The way I see it the only real choice is Dave. Herb's appearance and lack of sociability make him unsuitable for a high-level position. Wilma, being a woman, is just too emotional for the position. That pretty much leaves Dave as the only choice."

Within the next three months both Herb and Wilma left the federal government for lucrative jobs in private industry. Dave stayed on until the next big satellite communications program fell flat on its face. When he left he found a good position with an advertising firm on Madison Avenue.

The accuracy and soundness of Lacy's decision to promote Dave depended on the accuracy of his perception of Dave, Herb, and Wilma. Because we have more accurate information about the three candidates, we know that Lacy made a mistake. But as far as Lacy is concerned, he made the best decision possible using information and observations that were quite accurate and real to him. Thus, a very key aspect of perception is that *reality is in the mind of the perceiver.*

In this chapter, we will discuss the perception process, including factors within the person and the object being perceived that cause selective perception. Then we will turn to two major problems that may be associated with perception: stereotyping and the halo effect. We will also discuss ways that people manage others' perception of themselves using impression management. Finally, we will highlight several organizational implications for perception including performance appraisals and interviews.

THE PERCEPTION PROCESS

There are many sorts of stimuli in the environment. The way we make sense of all that data is through the perceptual process. In this section we will discuss the perceptual process in terms of how characteristics of the individual perceiver, the object being perceived, and the situation all interact to result in perception. Since we cannot attend to every possible sensory input, our minds only select or allow certain inputs to predominate at any one time—a process called **selective perception.**

Before proceeding with the discussion of the perceptual process, test your perception by counting the number of *F*'s in the statement below:

Finally, we have an example of finished research that is the result of years of scientific study combined with the experience of a lifetime.

How many *F*'s did you count? Three? Four? Most people who have not done the exercise before find four; however, the correct answer is eight! If you counted less than eight, you were probably selectively perceiving the statement without the four instances where the word *"of"* appears. Most people read right over such words as "of" without even perceiving them.

Perception is the process of filtering, organizing and interpreting information about the environment.[1] The overabundance of information in the environment means that we must filter and interpret it so that it makes sense. Figure 4.1 illustrates this perceptual process. In our opening case, Lacy was perceiving many different types of information about each of his three candidates for promotion. He first filtered the information (we noted that he filtered out some important information too), then he organized and interpreted it in his mind and came to conclusions about each person's suitability for promotion.

The perceptual process is also influenced by a number of factors related to the object or person being perceived, the person doing the perceiving, and the situation where it all takes place. The next part of this section will cover these three major areas: object, person, and situation factors. The final part of this section will examine the way people link events to the environment using what is called an attribution process.

Object Factors That Cause Selective Perception

Why do we notice some objects and entirely miss others? Basically, it all boils down to the "standout effect." For something or someone to be perceived it has to come to our attention. Some of the characteristics of objects or people that tend to subdue or bring things to our attention are covered in the following paragraphs and summarized in Figure 4.2.

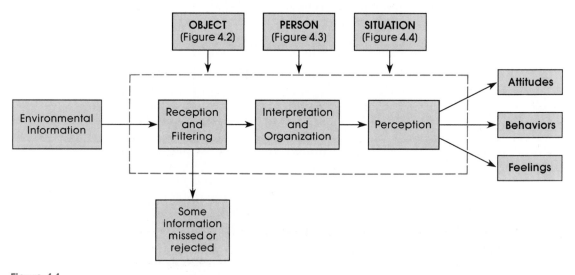

Figure 4.1

THE PERCEPTUAL PROCESS

Object Factors	Organizational Example
Novelty	An executive consistently wears a bow tie.
Contrast	A single female executive applicant among fifteen males for the job.
Size	A large office to create perceptions of power.
Intensity	A textile company sends 200 people to a conference in Italy.
Proximity	An assistant located next to the CEO is perceived to be powerful.

→ **PERCEPTUAL PROCESS** (Figure 4.1)

Figure 4.2

OBJECT FACTORS IN PERCEPTION

Novelty. Something that is different is perceived more easily than something that is familiar. For example, a single problem incident, such as catching an employee smoking pot on the job, might be more easily perceived and remembered than the normal good performance of the employee.

Contrast. This close relative of novelty exists when something or someone stands out against the background. In organizational settings, contrast is sometimes desirable and sometimes not so desirable. Safety signs should be designed with bold, contrasting letters and colors; otherwise, they will just blend with the environment and not be seen. (This may happen anyway because they are too familiar.) Another example of contrast is the Transamerica Building (called the Transamerica Pyramid) in San Francisco, shown in Figure 4.3. Its contrasting pyramidal shape causes it to stand out. Transamerica makes very effective use of this contrast in its advertising.

Size and Intensity. Remember Jeff Baxter, owner of Atlas Sign Company, whom we discussed in Chapter 1? He knew that the bigger the sign and the bigger the lettering, the more likely people were to see it. He also knew that when he used bright, intense colors like red and orange, people were likely to pay more attention. A status-seeking corporate president might ride in a silver Rolls Royce limousine that combines both size and intensity. The size and intensity of architecture is often used to get people's attention.

Proximity. We tend to group people together because of their physical or time proximity. People in a particular department, such as accounting or sales, are seen as relatively similar because of their proximity. Time proximity can also cause perceptual distortion. For example, shortly after a new manager is hired, sales start a downward trend. The new manager could have been the cause, but there are also a number of other explanations, such as a change in market conditions.

Figure 4.3

THE TRANSAMERICA PYRAMID

Photo courtesy of Transamerica Corporation, 600 Montgomery St., San Francisco, CA, 94120.

Person Factors that Cause Selective Perception

We also have perceptual filters that are related to our personality, values, attitudes, needs, and past experiences. These filters change, distort, or block sensory inputs. Figure 4.4 summarizes the person factors that affect perception. Any or all of these factors may be operating at a given time. Person factors also affect how we organize and interpret the signals we receive.

Self Concept. People who have a high self-concept (*see* Chapter 2) and feel good about themselves will tend to see things in a more optimistic and positive light than will someone with a low self-concept.[2] For example, an insecure supervisor is more likely to view capable and ambitious subordinates as a threat.

Values and Attitudes. What would an authoritarian manager with Theory X values (*see* Chapter 3), perceive if he or she happened to find an employee reading a book on communication during the regular workday? Would the employee be perceived to be goofing off on the job and deserving of a reprimand? Or, would the employee be perceived as someone who is trying to improve and thus should be praised? We would predict that the Theory X manager would react in the former way—the positive aspects of the employee's behavior would not be seen. A Theory Y manager, in contrast, would be more likely to perceive the situation positively.

Salience. When you are hungry, you can smell food for a considerable distance—it is relatively important to you and is thus **salient** at that time.

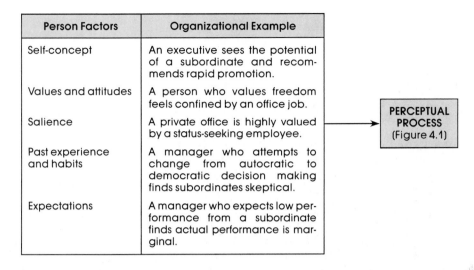

Person Factors	Organizational Example
Self-concept	An executive sees the potential of a subordinate and recommends rapid promotion.
Values and attitudes	A person who values freedom feels confined by an office job.
Salience	A private office is highly valued by a status-seeking employee.
Past experience and habits	A manager who attempts to change from autocratic to democratic decision making finds subordinates skeptical.
Expectations	A manager who expects low performance from a subordinate finds actual performance is marginal.

Figure 4.4

PERSON FACTORS IN PERCEPTION

When you are full, you may not pay any attention to food smells. Thus your needs at the moment have a strong influence on what you perceive. If your needs for esteem and praise are salient, you will be particularly attuned to behavior of your boss that reflects either praise or criticism.

Past Experience and Habits.   Your past experiences and habits will affect your perception. For example, a foreman who constantly rides his workers may reach a point where the workers tune out the foreman's comments entirely. Another case might be an overly conscientious school principal who calls frequent fire drills. The students and teachers may become so accustomed to the drills that when a real fire occurs, they may not respond quickly.

Expectations.   Sometimes we hear only what we expect to hear because of what is called a **preparatory set** or **expectancy.**Our previous experience or a strong desire to see something come true causes us to distort the inputs to fit the pattern we want to occur. An example of how expectations influence behavior is the story of Craig Branson, an up-and-coming young manager with a medium-sized computer firm, who learned about this form of perceptual distortion quite painfully.[3]

Craig had been commuting back and forth on weekends between New York, his home base, and Pittsburgh, a temporary base, with the company picking up his expenses. When he married, he asked his boss if he could bring his wife to Pittsburgh at company expense. His boss said, "Sure, company policy permits you to turn in expenses for you and your new wife up to the average amount you have been spending on hotels, planes, and other reimbursable expenses."

Craig was elated. He figured that when he turned in his expenses for an amount equal to the average of his past total expenses, he would be able to bank most of his salary. All went well for about a month until Craig's boss noticed the same high amount of expenses on the voucher. He called Craig and chewed him out for padding his expense account, saying, "It can't possibly cost

Perspective 4.1

GETTING PEOPLE'S ATTENTION WITH SYMBOLS AND DRAMA

Tom Peters and Nancy Austin, in their book *A Passion for Excellence*, assert that **symbol and drama management** are crucial skills for the manager. Here are some examples they cite:

Corning Glass had focused its energies on decorative glass for most of its history. Now it was faced with a declining market. Arthur Houghton was the newly appointed chief executive officer. He wanted to move Corning toward higher technology. His approach? He went to the warehouse containing some of the most beautiful glass Corning had ever produced (it was lying fallow in inventory). He had a sledgehammer with him. He proceeded to smash several million dollars' worth of glass to smithereens. He

wanted to make it clear that he was up to something new. He did!

When [Renn Zaphiropoulos] assumed a more senior position within the Xerox group [he was determined to get rid of the status-oriented private parking spaces. He located the nearest hardware store and took off with one of his executive assistants in tow]. Upon arriving, he took two crisp twenty-dollar bills out of his wallet, bought two one-gallon cans of black paint and a paint brush. He returned to the office. And then, in front of his office building, the chief executive stripped off his coat, rolled up his sleeves, opened a paint can, and while the cameras rolled (two phone calls had summoned the video people) he began to paint out the labels on the executive parking spots.[4]

These dramatic and symbolic actions got peoples' attention and they remembered them for long periods of time. These two examples illustrate a powerful strategy for overcoming perceptual problems.

you that much to live! I'm bringing you back to the home office until you learn not to fudge on your expense account."

Craig had made a mistake when he perceived the boss' statement as "the average amount of your past expenses," rather than "*up to* the average amount of your past expenses." The boss had expected that during an extended stay the expenses would go down while Craig thought this was an opportunity to make some additional money legally. Craig heard what he wanted to hear because of his set of expectations.

Situation Factors in Selective Perception

While most of the perception process is focused around object and person factors, there are many possibilities for these to interact with the situation at hand. For example, a person giving a business briefing may be perceived quite differently if the briefing is in front of the CEO as compared to the person's immediate boss. We will discuss three major situational factors: selection, similarity, and organization (*see* Figure 4.5).

Selection.   We select objects to pay attention to that we are comfortable with and we filter out those that we are uncomfortable with—a process called **selection.** A good example of this perceptual factor is the parochial viewpoints of functional managers in an organization. Let us assume that four managers have joined in a task force to solve an important organizational problem, such as declining sales of a personal computer. The marketing manager will see the

Perspective 4.2

THE SELF-FULFILLING PROPHECY

One powerful impact of expectations and perception is the **self-fulfilling prophecy** or SFP.[5] A SFP may occur when our expectations about ourselves or others cause us to behave in such a way that our expectation actually comes true. Our initial expectation may be either true or false. There is considerable evidence that this effect does in fact exist.[6]

The SFP process begins when the perceiver forms some type of expectancy about the behavior of himself, herself, or another person. An expectancy is formed based on a limited sample of behaviors such as the ones described in our opening case. Once the expectancy is formed the behavior of the perceiver will be influenced by the expectancies. If a person is expected to perform poorly, the behavior will encourage that poor performance. If the expectations are for superior performance, then the perceiver will encourage this type of behavior.

Nonverbal cues (facial expressions, body posture, tone of voice) are particularly important factors for reinforcing the expectancy and creating SFP.[7] Subconscious signals often are primary factors in the process.

Organizational implications for SFP are great. If a boss has high expectations regarding a person's performance, then the person may actually perform in a superior way. However, SFP inevitably creates contrast effects because only one or a few people are typically singled out for high or low expectations.[8] Thus, the usefulness of SFP for changing employee behavior is limited because "favorites" are often singled out as targets for expectancy effects. In addition, an interviewer who expects a person to perform well because of his or her educational background may be eliciting an SFP that could result in discrimination against those with other educational backgrounds.[9]

problem as lack of enough resources for advertising. The production manager will blame it on too many cuts in her quality-enhancement program. The research and development person will probably say that the design with the most modern advances was not chosen. The human resources person may lay the blame on lack of funds for performance bonuses. Each of these managers filters or selects information that fits within his or her range of comfort and blocks out other possible inputs.

Similarity. We also tend to try to fit the environment into a scheme with which we are familiar. We may group things or people together even if they do not belong together. We may perceive a person much differently if he or she is a union member then we would if he or she were a member of management. Often people are grouped into stereotypes because of ethnic background, color, or sex (stereotypes will be discussed later in the chapter). While grouping sometimes causes problems, it is also a way of remembering and coping with the environment.

Organization. People tend to view things as logical, ordered, consistent systems. When we perceive information we try to fit the information into some existing pattern. This process is called **perceptual organization.** The Atari Corporation introduced the first programmable home video player in 1976, ushering in the sale of video games. Their sales went from $39 million in 1976 to $2.7 billion in 1982. Atari saw the world in terms of an ever-increasing explosion of video games. They ignored signals that personal computers were fast overtak-

Situation Factors	Organizational Example
Selection	At a contract negotiation, labor wants control over job assignments. Management feels this is its prerogative.
Similarity	Blue-collar workers are perceived to be incapable of making their own quality control decisions
Perceptual organization	A manager ignores important information because it does not fit the organizational plan.

PERCEPTUAL
PROCESS
(Figure 4.1)

Figure 4.5

SITUATION FACTORS IN PERCEPTION

ing video games. This data did not fit in their perceptual organization and was thus not fully perceived. Unfortunately, in 1983 Atari lost half a billion dollars and was sold in 1984 just short of bankruptcy—a costly perceptual error for Atari.[10]

Attribution Theory and Perception

Attribution theory can be applied to many aspects of human behavior, including performance appraisal, motivation, and leadership. However, it is fundamentally a perceptual process. **Attributions** involve the way we perceive and interpret the causes of behavior.[11] Attributions apply to three general areas: (1) our perception of what or who caused a specific event, (2) our assessment of responsibility for a specific event or outcome, and (3) our evaluation of the personal qualities of persons involved in the event.[12]

Figure 4.6 illustrates how the attribution process works. The process begins with our perception of behavior, either our own or someone else's. We then evaluate the behavior based upon our perception of three types of information cues: consistency, distinctiveness, and consensus. In work situations, **consistency** refers to the degree to which a person behaves in the same way over time. **Distinctiveness** refers to the degree to which a person behaves in the same way over a variety of other situations or tasks. **Consensus** refers to the way others behave in the same situation—it is the basis for comparison.

For example, when a supervisor evaluates the performance of a subordinate the evaluation is based on a number of interrelated perceptions. If the subordinate is performing poorly and usually does, we have high consistency. However, if the poorly performing subordinate usually performs quite well, then we have low consistency. Similarly, if the poor performance is associated with most tasks done by the employee, then low distinctiveness applies. On the other hand, if the low performance is linked only to a unique or unusual task, high distinctiveness is the correct category. Finally, if all other employees doing similar jobs are also performing poorly, then high consensus is attributed; whereas, if most other employees are performing well, low consensus would be inferred.

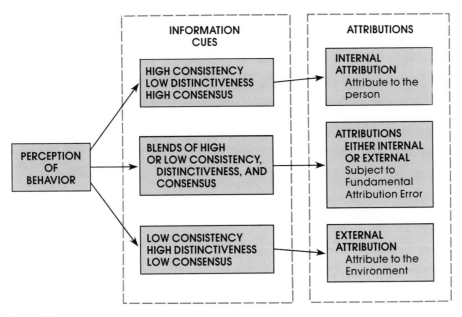

Figure 4.6

ATTRIBUTION THEORY

To illustrate how consistency, distinctiveness, and consensus work together to create attributions, consider the following example:

> Eva, a manager of the actuarial department of a medium-sized insurance company, has observed that the performance of one of her employees, Mike, is only 75 percent of what most employees produce in her department. She reviews her records and confirms that Mike produces at this low level regardless of the number of different job assignments he is given. She decides that Mike's poor performance is attributable to internal reasons, either his lack of motivation or lack of ability. She decides to write an unsatisfactory performance appraisal.

In this case we have a clear example of an employee with high consistency, low distinctiveness, and high consensus. Not surprisingly, the theory predicts that the supervisor will blame the employee for the poor performance. This type of diagnosis of factors within the individual is called an **internal attribution.**

Consider one more example:

> Vernon, manager of an actuarial department in another insurance company, has observed the output of one of his employees, Katie, to be only 75 percent of the performance goal. He notes that the output of his other employees is also below par to about the same extent. Katie's work history reflects generally quite high performance—the problem seems to have originated recently. The current task is quite unusual and is considered to be especially difficult. Vernon decides that something in the environment (such as a new computer model) is causing the poor performance and that it is not Katie's fault.

Here we have an example of low consistency, high consensus, and high distinctiveness. Katie is a poor performer, but her past records are good, she is not alone, and her job is particularly difficult. In this case we would predict that Vernon would attribute her performance problems to environmental reasons. This process is called **external attribution.**

Of course there are many situations that fall between these two extremes. However, regardless of the information cues, there is a tendency toward internal attribution.[13] This problem is sometimes referred to as the **fundamental attribution error.**[14] In addition, much of the information that is used to evaluate consistency, consensus, and distinctiveness is subject to perceptual distortion. Thus, the attribution process is imperfect and is another source of perceptual distortion.

In the next section, we will turn to several major organizational problems that arise from the perception process.

PROBLEMS IN PERCEPTION

In the previous section, we noted a number of places in the perception process where distortion and selectivity can arise. Although perceptual distortion often serves a positive purpose for the individual by simplifying the environment, it may cause problems for the organization. Two of the most important and far-reaching perceptual problems, stereotyping and the halo effect, are discussed in this section.

Stereotyping

A **stereotype** is a generalization about a class or group of people. "Stereotypes are not necessarily incorrect, illogical, or rigid . . . although they may be less verifiable than generalizations about impersonal categories such as dogs or molecules."[15] Stereotypes may also be seen as oversimplified pictures of reality that make it easier for us to interpret and understand our complex world.[16]

When we generalize about women, blacks, old people, hippies, redheads, Germans, or Jews, we are stereotyping. Most people, except the "Archie Bunker-types" (a stereotype itself), seem to have a rather flexible approach to stereotyping. In other words, if they find an exception to their stereotype, they will accept that deviation but continue to hold the general stereotype. For example, if a stereotype is held that women are more likely to be passive and submissive, and then there is an encounter with an active and aggressive woman, she will probably be seen as an unusual exception—the one in a hundred that does not fit the rule. The overall stereotype usually remains unchanged. Thus, stereotypes are particularly difficult to change even in the face of evidence that they are inaccurate.

Problems With Stereotyping.   Remember in the opening incident when Lacy saw Wilma as being too "pushy" and emotional? His stereotypic view of women was probably distorting his perception of Wilma. On the other hand, the stereotype of a well-dressed Yale grad may have worked in Dave's favor to get him the promotion.

Stereotypes often involve hidden prejudice that gets in the way of organizational affirmative action programs. (Affirmative action programs are designed to insure that women and other minorities, who have been discriminated against in the past, have at least an equal opportunity for all hiring, promotion, and pay decisions.) If Wilma had wanted to, she might have filed an affirmative action complaint against Lacy, although this is seldom done at higher managerial levels because even if she won, it would then be difficult if not impossible for her to work effectively with Lacy.

Decisions based on imperfect or even invalid stereotypes often cost organizations more than they realize. The departure of Herb and Wilma from the Department of Electronics proved very costly in terms of lost talent, leadership, and experience. And if Dave is really as incompetent as he seems, then the failure of the satellite communications system might also be attributable, at least in part, to Lacy's error in perception.

Self-fulfilling Stereotypes.   Another rather insidious possibility is that if a manager believes strongly enough in a stereotype, then it may become a self-fulfilling prophecy (*see* Perspective 4.2) for the people involved—they may actually come to behave in the way the stereotype predicts.[17] The **self-fulfilling stereotype** process works in much the same way as the self-fulfilling prophecy—the generalized beliefs and attitudes that form our stereotypes reinforce our own behavior and the behavior of the target of our stereotype so that actual behavioral outcomes are consistent with the stereotype.

One way the self-fulfilling process works is that people tend to notice, observe, and remember the characteristics that fit the stereotype, while ignoring those that do not. Thus, selective perception tends to maintain the stereotype and cause self-fulfilling behavior.[18]

An example of this behavior might be a supervisor who treats black employees as if they were less competent than the whites (because of a racial stereotype or prejudice). This unfavorable stereotype may mean that blacks are unwittingly given less challenging work experiences and thus are not as well rounded as their white peers. Since less is expected of them, they may even perform at a lower level, thus confirming the stereotype.

The Halo Effect

When someone is good in one area and then on the basis of this strength is assumed to be good in all areas, the person is said to wear a halo. The term **halo effect** means that a general impression permeates evaluations in other areas; or that a person is rated the same in many areas because of one overall feature that is perceived to be related to these areas.[19] In practice this means that individual rating categories tend to be distorted because of the halo effect.

Take, for example, the opening case. Dave's sociability may have created a halo effect that resulted in Lacy's decision to promote him. Another form of the halo effect is created when a person who was once rated outstanding continues to be so rated in spite of a decline in performance. (In the section on impression management we will cover some strategies for harnessing this bias to your advantage.)

The halo effect works in reverse, too. If a person is once labeled as a poor performer or troublemaker, it is difficult to overcome that unfavorable image.

Controlling the Halo Effect

In performance appraisal, in promotion decisions, and in selecting new employees, it is important to control the halo effect. There are a number of methods, including specifying performance criteria, increasing rater familiarity with the ratee, using multiple raters, and by training for raters.[20]

Establishing Performance Criteria. One of the best ways to do this is to specify clearly what behaviors and performance criteria an individual must meet. For example, Lacy might have established something like the following criteria for the selection of the satellite division chief:

1. Effectively supervises employees.

2. Maintains costs within budget.

3. Makes accurate decisions.

4. Communicates effectively with Congress.

5. Is technically competent in satellite technology.

6. Is a good team member.

Increasing Rater Familiarity. The more the supervisor knows about the subordinate's behavior, the more accurate the ratings are likely to be. In our opening case, one of the major problems was that Lacy did not know either Herb or Wilma and thus made erroneous ratings of their overall behavior based on a very limited and distorted sample of their performances.

Use Multiple Raters. When possible, using several people who are familiar with a person's performance to rate that performance can reduce the halo effect.[21]

Improve Training for Raters. While the evidence is weak that training can reduce rating distortions, two techniques appear promising.[22] Supervisors can keep diaries that detail the day-to-day performance of subordinates so that a detailed, factual reference is available for rating. Another strategy is to train supervisors to be critical. Most of us would prefer to rate someone leniently to avoid unpleasant confrontations.

Reducing Halo: A Pessimistic Conclusion. In spite of our desire to reduce halo effect, few strategies seem to have much power. Since there are multiple opportunities for perceptual distortion during the rating process, we may continue to expect a fairly high degree of inaccuracy. Prevention of the halo depends on awareness. Managers must ask themselves: "Does this person actually behave the way that I am rating him or her? Have I observed his or her specific behavior for this factor? What is his or her actual performance level?"

Perspective 4.3

MANAGERIAL MYOPIA:
SELF–SERVING BIASES

A perceptual distortion that is related to both stereotyping and the halo effect is the tendency to generalize based on incomplete and biased information. When managers allow this bias to enter their decision processes, they are said to have **managerial myopia,** or a view of the future that is blurred because of their self-serving biases. The result of a research study into the effects of biases on managers' predictions of organizational growth concluded that: "self-serving biases are a wide-ranging phenomenon that can affect managerial decision making through the process of overly optimistic planning."[23]

Interviews were conducted with forty-eight presidents of manufacturing firms to find out how accurately they predicted the firm's future performance relative to competition. Fifty-six percent of the executives predicted they would do better than their actual performance while only 8 percent predicted they would do worse than they actually did—in other words, there was a strong tendency to overpredict performance.

The researchers conclude that managers perceive themselves to be more capable than they really are, and this bias affects their ability to predict organizational performance realistically.

Using another concept from the chapter, the self-fulfilling prophecy, one might ask if it is more desirable for a manager to be optimistic and overconfident or to be accurate and realistic?

IMPRESSION MANAGEMENT

So far we have been discussing problems with perceptual distortion and filtering. Now we will turn to the application of perception techniques to control the image we project of ourselves. **Impression management** is the process of behaving in ways that create and maintain desired perceptions of ourselves.[24] In other words, we try to control the image we project of ourselves.[25] Another way of thinking about this concept is to use the terms self-presentation or self-projection, since impression management has to do with the ways we present ourselves to others. This self-presentation process is an integral part of our self-concept and personality (*see* Chapter 2). Figure 4.7 shows some of the many ways we consciously or unconsciously create impressions.

We can learn a number of practical lessons from the study of impression management.[26] First, people who create a favorable impression may be more successful in gaining entry to the organization via the interview process. They may then obtain promotions by making a good impression on their bosses.[27] Second, effective leaders need to be able to create the proper impression to maintain their influence. A third major consideration is that impressions can be controlled and managed by an individual, thus offering an important way to influence one's success.

All of us have engaged in some type of impression management. For example, have you ever cut your hair or worn a nice suit to get a good job? Favorable and accurate impressions are very important for organizational success. In our opening case, Herb's casual dress was certainly a major reason why he did not get selected for the promotion. Even if you do not want to use im-

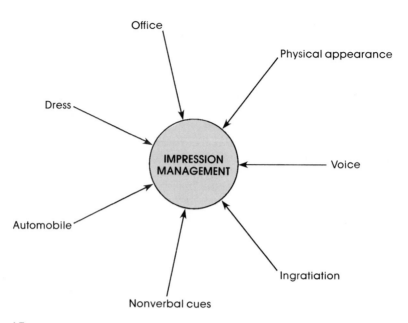

Figure 4.7

IMPRESSION MANAGEMENT

pression management—some people think it's manipulative—you should be aware that others are employing the techniques. Knowledge of impression management might have prevented a mistake like promoting Dave.

In the remainder of this section, we will cover three major aspects of impression management: ingratiation, appearance and dress, and nonverbal impressions.

Ingratiation: Getting People to Like You

The word ingratiation has a somewhat negative connotation even though the techniques are widely used. **Ingratiation** means that an individual is making a conscious effort to increase another person's liking for him or her.[28] If it is done with sincerity and finesse, ingratiation can be very effective for both persons. However, if it is obviously motivated only by the desire for personal gain, such behavior is considered to be manipulation and is detested by most people. Yet the target of the ingratiation may be quite flattered and may respond positively toward the ingratiator, even though aware of the strategy.

There are a number of tactics used to increase liking, most of them verbal.[29] In addition to those listed below, you might refer to some of those listed in Perspective 4.4.

- Use flattery, compliments, and other techniques that enhance the self-image of the other person.

- Conform to the other's opinions, judgments, and behaviors. Remember that we tend to like those who are similar to ourselves.

Perspective 4.4

HOW TO WIN FRIENDS

AND INFLUENCE PEOPLE

Impression management is not new. Over fifty years ago Dale Carnegie published a best-selling book, *How to Win Friends and Influence People*, that contained these six rules: [30]

1. Become genuinely interested in the other person.

2. Smile.
3. Remember that a person's name is to that person the sweetest and most important sound in any language.
4. Be a good listener. Encourage others to talk about themselves.
5. Talk about things that interest the other person.
6. Make the other person feel important—and do it sincerely.

- Present and describe yourself favorably. Present a favorable self-image and acclaim your accomplishments. But beware of too much self-praise; modesty may be more effective strategy.

- Render favors to the other person. Gifts and rewards to others tend to increase their liking for you.

- Apologize for possible offenses. Be the first to give in.

Dress and Impressions

Clothes are one of the most important factors in impressions. Everyday when you arrive at the workplace, your clothes are the first thing others notice. Even in a brief encounter, we normally observe what the other person is wearing, make judgments about that person, and behave in accordance with the judgment.

One important aspect of personal appearance is whether it is appropriate or inappropriate to the situation at hand. Sports clothes in an office may be just as inappropriate as a wool suit on a tennis court. If a person is wearing entirely inappropriate clothes, we may form our strongest impressions based primarily on his or her clothes.

It was interesting to observe the change in President Carter over the first three years of his term. At first, he was very informally dressed, sometimes in open shirts and sweaters. Later, when he felt a need to change his image, he began wearing conservative, dark suits with conservative shirts and ties. He apparently believed that the conservative image made him appear more "presidential."

President Reagan, on the other hand, always seemed to wear clothes that fit the situation. In Washington, he wore finely tailored dark suits, while on his ranch, he dressed in an informal, western style. His appearance always seemed appropriate to make a good impression.

Dress for Success. John Molloy's book, *Dress for Success*, and his syndicated news columns on dress are extremely popular in many organizational circles. An example of the type of advice given by Molloy is as follows. [31]

Perspective 4.5

HOW TOP EXECUTIVES DESCRIBED SUCCESSFUL DRESS

Clothing consultant and syndicated columnist, John T. Molloy, queried 100 top corporate executives in medium to large organizations to determine their attitudes about appropriate dress. The following excerpt from *Dress for Success* shows Molloy's research strategy for this study and his results (be sure to critique his research methods): [32]

> I showed the executives five pictures of men, each of them wearing expensive, well-tailored, but high-fashion clothing. I asked if this was a proper look for the junior business executive. Ninety-two of the men said no, eight said yes.
>
> I showed them five pictures of men neatly dressed in obvious lower-middle-class attire and asked if these men were dressed in proper attire for a young executive. Forty-six said yes, fifty-four said no.
>
> I next showed them five pictures of men dressed in conservative upper-middle-class clothing and asked if they were dressed in proper attire for the young executive. All one hundred said yes.
>
> I asked them whether they thought the men in the upper-middle-class garb would succeed better in corporate life than the men in the lower-middle-class uniform. Eighty-eight said yes, twelve said no.
>
> I asked if they would choose one of the men in the lower-middle-class dress as their assistant. Ninety-two said no, eight said yes.

No question then: The tie is a symbol of respectability and responsibility; it communicates to other people who you are, or reinforces or detracts from their conception of who you should be. While the most appropriate tie, worn correctly, naturally cannot insure your success in business or in life, it certainly can—and should—give the right signals to keep you from being regarded as a no-class boob.

We find more and more people looking like the conservative, successful business executive that he describes. Molloy's emphasis, based on research (*see* Perspective 4.5 for an example of his somewhat unconventional research), is to describe effective dress, not what is good or bad taste in dress. His assumption is that if you are perceived to be powerful, successful, and attractive, then you will enhance your chances of promotion and corporate success. Molloy also published another book entitled, *The Woman's Dress for Success Book,*[33] aimed at aspiring female executives. Other studies, although few in number, tend to confirm Molloy's views on dress and impressions.[34]

Verbal and Nonverbal Impressions

Every time you speak, you are making yet another important impression. Voice quality, pitch, accent, speed, articulation, and content reveal a great deal about you and are important to the impression-forming process. Verbal behavior, while not impossible to change, is much more difficult to change than dress.

Nonverbal impressions are also crucial for controlling impressions.[35] For example, during your initial contact with another person you may go through the ritual handshake. If your handshake is limp, your face is unsmiling, and your eye contact poor, the other person will probably get a very aloof and unfavorable impression of you. In contrast, if you have a firm, warm handshake, with a smile and good eye contact, the other person will probably feel very favorable toward you. We will discuss nonverbal communication more fully in Chapter 8.

Implications of Impression Management

The positive application of the perception process is becoming more important to organizations in a number of ways. Impressions help create halos that may impair or enhance the performance appraisal system. Dress makes a substantial difference in how people are perceived and how people act in response to their perceptions. Impressions are also important when dealing with customers and other contacts outside the organization. Representatives of the organization should make impressions that are appropriate for that organization. Thus, skillful impression management can contribute to organizational effectiveness.

Organizational Impression Management

Much of our discussion of impression management has focused on how individuals manage their impressions through ingratiation, appearance, and nonverbal cues. Another important consideration is that organizations need to be concerned about the impressions they make as well. The way an organization is perceived also depends on the way its employees look and act, and the image it projects based on its name, its facilities, and its advertising. Can you imagine a banker in Boston or Chicago dressing in an open-necked shirt with no coat? And what about a computer salesman in Dayton who is dressed in blue jeans and cowboy boots? While both of these examples are extreme, there are often important decisions to be made about what type of impression the organization wants to project. In addition, corporations are spending millions to spiff up their images through name changes and advertising.[36]

Organizational-level impression management requires careful analysis of the impacts of impressions, and a clear idea of whom the organization is trying to impress.

PERFORMANCE EVALUATION AND INTERVIEWING

Two important processes closely linked with impression management—performance evaluation and interviews—are discussed in the following sections.

Performance Evaluation

Organizations must often rely on subjective performance evaluations because we cannot always measure the objective performance of people. For example, most managers' jobs involve a number of different skills and behaviors (i.e., ability to work with people, problem-solving ability, communication skills) that cannot be measured by direct, objective measures like units produced or items sold. This means that perceptual distortions like stereotyping, the halo effect, the self-fulfilling prophecy, and leniency are inevitable and must be carefully avoided or minimized. In addition, raters typically do not have the opportunity to observe thoroughly all the behaviors that are relevant to job performance.[37]

Democratic Leaders Give More Favorable Ratings.   Another possible problem in performance appraisal is the setting and the leader's style. A laboratory experiment using 678 Temple University students found that leaders who use democratic leadership will use noncontrolling influence tactics, will be more likely to attribute self-motivation to subordinates, and will thus form a more favorable employee evaluation.[38] Autocratic leaders, on the other hand, would use controlling tactics and perceive that employees were not self-directed. Thus, performance was evaluated less favorably. One conclusion to this experiment is that Theory Y values that result in more democratic practices may also result in more favorable performance appraisals because managers attribute self-motivation to their employees.

Reducing Performance Appraisal Errors.   Training people in the types of errors that may occur is the most commonly used method for reducing rating errors. Supervisors are presented with examples of common rating errors, and are then encouraged to avoid them. Once this information has been conveyed, the most effective way to further decrease errors is to conduct practice and feedback sessions so that raters can learn from experience. In a recent literature review, five out of six studies increased rating accuracy using this training method.[39]

We have already discussed several other methods for minimizing errors in performance evaluation, such as establishing clear performance criteria and increasing rater familiarity.[40]

Interviewing

Interviewing is a key method used for selecting new employees, reassigning existing employees, and providing feedback on performance to employees.[41] In addition, many one-on-one communication interactions in organizations might be considered to be interviews. Almost everyone has had or will have some type of interview experience when pursuing a job. Here again, stereotyping and the halo effect are ever present. In addition, there are other problems that are more likely to occur in an interview, such as differences in the frame of reference between the interviewer and interviewee caused by their differing values systems, experiences, and attitudes.[42]

Self-fulfilling Prophecies.   The self-fulfilling prophecy, discussed earlier, can also affect selection interview.[43] Interviews form an evaluation of the interviewee based on pre-interview information, such as application blanks, resumes, and references. If the pre-interview evaluation is favorable, then it is likely that the final evaluation will be favorable. Here is how the process might work:

A recruiter from Loadstar Corp. reviews the records of a prospective recruit, Lori, and evaluates her as quite impressive. During the interview itself the recruiter shows more signs of approval and fewer signs of disapproval. In addition, Lori is told that she is an impressive candidate. As a result, she tends to perform up to these expectations, thus confirming the recruiter's pre-meeting impressions. In addition, the recruiter is more likely to notice and selectively recall information that is consistent with the pre-meeting impression and reject information that is not. Thus, Lori is likely to receive an offer and, because of the positive interview experience, she may be more likely to accept.

Impression Management. The importance of impression management in the interview process cannot be overemphasized. Dress and nonverbal cues are particularly important. Research supports common sense in this area.[44] People who use positive self-descriptions, present an attractive appearance, use enthusiastic nonverbal behaviors, and exhibit some degree of tactical conformity are more likely to receive job offers.

CROSS–CULTURAL OB: TIME PERCEPTIONS

Time is perceived quite differently in other parts of the world. In the United States, time is considered to be linear—it has a past, present, and future. We also measure time quite precisely—every minute, five minutes, fifteen minutes, and so forth. In contrast, much of the Arab world perceives time in three general categories: no time at all, now (which varies considerably in duration), and forever (too long).[45] Arab students in the United States often find the adjustment to Western time difficult and frustrating.

In Latin America and much of South America, time also has a somewhat different meaning. Lack of punctuality is considered to be a badge of success; someone of high status is expected to arrive late.[46] A recent study compared time perceptions between 107 students at California State University at Fresno with those of 91 students at the federal university in Niteroi, Brazil (a medium-sized city across the bay from Rio de Janeiro). Students were asked when they would consider a friend late or early for lunch. Americans said the friend would be late if the time was missed by nineteen minutes. Brazilians gave their friends thirty-three and one half minutes. In terms of earliness, Americans considered twenty-four minutes the absolute earliest, while Brazilians found fifty-four minutes acceptable.[47]

Another study by the same authors compared the pace of life in six countries.[48] They found that the pace of life was fastest in Japan, followed by the United States, England, Italy, Taiwan, and Indonesia. While this study was rather simplistic, it does show indications of very significant differences throughout the world. Any business person who has attempted to negotiate a contract with the Chinese knows that their perception of time and their pace of doing business are much different than ours.[49]

MANAGERIAL APPLICATIONS OF PERCEPTION

The most far-reaching impact of perception in organizations is that it affects the way individuals perceive the workplace and their interaction with their work. Since perceptual reality is in the mind of the perceiver, distortions often occur. Employees may perceive inequities in pay, assignments, promotions, racial or sex treatment, or discipline. In fact, almost all organizational situations offer the potential for perceptual distortion. Here are some ways to improve management of perception:

- *Clear communication helps clarify perceptions.* Managers need to communicate information clearly about organizational processes to prevent misunderstandings. In addition to the usual communication techniques (to be discussed in Chapter 8), participation in decisions aids in clarifying perceptions.

- *Avoid perceptual blocks and sets through awareness.* Awareness of the various aspects of the perceptual process helps us be on guard for possible distortions or selective perception; however, no one can completely eliminate these tendencies.

- *Use dramatic actions to get people's attention.* People will remember dramatized events. Although this strategy is powerful for overcoming perceptual blocks, do not overuse it.

- *Use the self-fulfilling prophecy to improve effectiveness.* Managers can have a strong influence on the performance of their subordinates through the SFP. Try to use it to create positive rather than negative performance expectations.

- *Recognize that everyone has their own parochial views.* People tend to see the world through their own experiences. Be aware that marketers will view things quite differently from production people.

- *Avoid the fundamental attribution error.* Remember that when appraising performance, we tend to attribute poor performance to problems with the individual rather than external causes. Try to balance your analysis of problems to minimize this effect.

- *Take care to recognize and avoid stereotyping.* Treat people based on their qualifications and performance rather than how you expect them to behave because of their sex, race, or other factor. Avoid self-fulfilling stereotypes.

- *Recognize the halo effect.* When evaluating performance, try to avoid perceiving someone as effective or ineffective because of some personal characteristic. However, the halo can add to impression management by creating a favorable first impression.

- *Pay attention to the impressions you create.* Take care to dress appropriately for the situation. Watch your nonverbal behavior, especially hand shakes, eye contact, and smiles. Beware of overuse of ingratiation—it may backfire.

- *Be aware that people perceive time differently.* Personal clocks vary even within a culture. They are radically different between cultures. Try to understand others' time concept to prevent frustration and to improve your empathy.

FOR DISCUSSION

1. Pick an example of some event or circumstance that happened to you lately and resulted in a misperception. What perceptual factors (object, person, situation) seem to best explain why you did not accurately perceive the situation?

2. Describe the factors that cause selective perception.

3. Based on your personal experience, relate an example of the self-fulfilling prophecy. What factors seem to be primarily responsible for it?

4. How can stereotypes affect the success of minorities in organizational situations?

5. Explain the relationship between the halo effect and impression management.

6. What can be done to minimize the impact of stereotypes and the halo effect?

7. What impression do you intend to make when starting a new managerial job or being promoted to a higher position? How will you dress differently? Will your behavior change?

8. How is the concern of perception related to organizational performance and job satisfaction?

9. What is your perception of time? Compare yours with those of your friends. Explain any differences.

KEY CONCEPTS AND TERMS

attribution	self-fulfilling prophecy	perceptual organization
consistency	person factors	proximity
contrast	selective perception	salience
distinctiveness	object factors	selection
perception	stereotyping	self-fulfilling stereotypes
expectations	managerial myopia	similarity
fundamental attribution error	novelty	impression management
halo effect	preparatory set	symbol management
ingratiation		

Cases and Incidents

THE NEW SUPERVISOR

Having just graduated from college a few months earlier, Denise began a career in her field of computer science and business at a medium-sized hospital. Part of her job responsibilities involved supervising three data-entry clerks, two part-time and one full-time. After spending a few weeks introducing herself to the position and environment of the company, Denise realized that her predecessor had been a very flexible supervisor. In fact, she had left the supervisory duties to her own boss, who had spent little or no time worrying about the data-entry clerks.

Since no direct supervision was given, these employees came and went as it was convenient to them. The part-time employees completed their quota of time and more or less kept a regular schedule, which worked out fine. On the other hand, the full-time employee, Julie, tended to abuse this flexibility. While other full time employees in the office started work at 8 A.M., she came to work after she had dropped off her son at school, between 9:15 and 9:45 A.M. Then, when everyone else went home at 4:30, Julie claimed that since she did not take a "formal lunch break," she could leave when they did. Besides causing jealousy among other workers in the company, this practice violated company rules, which state that employees are required to take their alloted breaks, including lunch. Julie was given one half hour unpaid lunch and two fifteen minute paid breaks. She never officially left the office to take a break, but being a smoker, she took many small cigarette breaks throughout her shift. A walk to the cafeteria for a salad "to-go" also was not considered a "lunch break." Thus, Julie received eight hours of pay per day for a seven-hour work day.

To further complicate things, Julie would quite often announce to Denise that she was leaving early to pick up her son since he had only a half day at school. She would *try* to make it back to work later in the afternoon for an hour or so. Or there was the time Julie told Denise, "I'm leaving in one half hour for the rest of the day," at noon. Since no explanation was offered, Denise pried for a reason and was told, "My husband and I had a fight this morning, which is why I was late, and we are going to work it out this afternoon."

If this were not frustrating enough to Denise, she was told by Julie that all the time she missed was made up by the overtime she had saved up. Of course, Denise had no way to track this overtime since Julie kept taking work home on her own and then announcing later that she had worked overtime.

THE BLACK MANAGERS

Bill's division was part of a company newly acquired by a large multinational enterprise located on the West Coast. Hired through a headhunter by the new parent, he was the first black manager in his division. Between the time Bill was appointed and the day he walked into his office, an executive who had opposed Bill's selection had been promoted and as a vice president was two steps above Bill as his boss's boss. Despite Bill's repeated requests, his immediate superior gave him no written objectives. But all of Bill's colleagues told him they liked his direction.

The only indication that race was even noticed was a comment from a sales manager whose performance Bill's division relied on: "I don't normally associate with blacks." Bill learned later that other managers were telling his boss that he was hard to work with and unclear in his plans. His boss did not confront Bill with these criticisms, just hinted at possible problems. Only later did Bill put them together into the indictment they really were.

After six months, out of the blue, he was put on probation. According to Bill's superior, the vice president said he "did not feel Bill could do the job" and suggested to him that Bill accept severance pay and look for other work. Bill decided to stick it out

Denise had been in her position for almost two months and had one more month before a review would establish whether she would become a permanent employee. Her boss was aware of the personnel problems occurring with Julie and was sure to notice how well Denise handled the situation. With office space restrictions, Denise was currently working in the same office as Julie, which emphasized the importance of avoiding any animosity between the two.

DISCUSSION QUESTIONS

1. What factors in the perception process might make Denise and Julie see the situation quite differently?
2. Do you believe that Julie thought she was "slacking off?"
3. Assuming you were in Denise's place, what would you do to change Julie's behavior?
4. What impact would Julie's behavior have on others in the office?

Case written by Dawn Umstot. Used with permission.

for pride's sake; he knew he could do the job. His work and educational records had proven him to be a winner.

During the following six months, his division performed ahead of plan. Bill was getting compliments from customers and colleagues. His boss assured him that he had proved his worth, and the probation would be lifted. It was. A few months later, Bill's boss finally agreed to set written objectives and scheduled a meeting with him. But when Bill walked into his superior's office, he was surprised to see the VP there too. The purpose of the meeting was not to set objectives but to place Bill back on probation, or give him severance pay, because he did not "seem to be the right man." Bill left the company and started his own business.

Bob was an ambitious person who changed employers when passed over for promotion. After a year at his new job, he saw that white managers he thought to be inferior performers were being promoted above him. Actually, many of the company's black managers were becoming vocal about a perceived pattern of favoritism toward white managers, who were faring better on appraisals, assignments, promotions, and pay. So that his superiors would see him in a positive light, Bob didn't associate openly with other black managers—but he privately encouraged their efforts to speak up. They should be the "bad guys" while he played the "good guy" in the hope that at least one black might be the first to crack the color barrier at a high level.

In meetings with black managers, senior executives would say that they recognized that blacks were not moving up fast enough, but it takes time and the blacks should not be too pushy. Bob told the white executives, "I don't see why you're even meeting with those guys. They're a bunch of complainers." Two months later, Bob was the first black to be promoted to the executive level.

DISCUSSION QUESTIONS

1. Why are these black managers perceived less favorably than white managers?

2. Why was Bill told he did not "seem to be the right man?"

3. Are expectations such as the self-fulfilling prophecy or the self-fulfilling stereotype applicable here? Why or why not?

From Jones, E.W. Jr. (1986, May-June). Black managers: The dream deferred. *Harvard Business Review,* pp. 87, 90. Used with permission.

REFERENCES

1. For in-depth coverage of perception, see Levine, M.W., & Shefner, J.M. (1981). *Fundamentals of sensation and perception.* Reading, MA: Addison-Wesley. And Schiff, W. (1980). *Perception: An applied approach.* Boston: Houghton Mifflin.

2. Lewicki, P. (1983). Self-image bias in person perception. *Journal of Personality and Social Psychology, 45,* 384–393.

3. Based on an incident related to Senger, J. (1980). *Individuals, groups, and the organization.* Cambridge, MA: Winthrop.

4. Peters, T., & Austin, N. (1985). *A passion for excellence.* New York: Random House, pp. 274–275.

5. Eden, D. (1984). Self-fulfilling prophecy as a management tool: Harnessing pygmalion. *Academy of Management Review, 9,* 64–73. Merton, R.K. (1948). The self-fulfilling prophecy. *Antioch Review, 8,* 193–210. Darley, J.M., & Fazio, R.H. (1980). Expectancy confirmation processes arising in the social interaction sequence. *American Psychologist, 35,* 867–881.

6. Eden (1984); and Rosenthal, R., & Rubin, D.B. (1978). Interpersonal expectancy effects: The first 345 studies. *Behavioral Brain Science, 1,* 377–386. Also see Jones, R.A. (1977). *Self fulfilling prophecies: Social, psychological, and physiological effects of expectancies.* Hillsdale, NJ: Erlbaum.

7. Schneider, D.J., Hastorf, A.H., & Ellsworth, P.C. (1979). *Person perception,* Reading, MA: Addison-Wesley.

8. Eden (1984), p. 71.

9. Dipboye, R.L. (1982). Self-fulfilling prophecies in the selection-recruitment interview. *Academy of Management Review 7,* 579–586.

10. Sutton, R.L., Eisenhart, K.M., & Jucker, J.V. (1986, Spring). Managing organizational decline: Lessons from Atari. *Organizational Dynamics,* pp. 17–29.

11. Heider, F. (1958). *The Psychology of interpersonal relations.* New York: Wiley.

12. Lord, R.G., & Smith, J.E. (1983). Theoretical, information processing, and situational factors affecting attribution theory models of organizational behavior. *Academy of Management Review, 8,* 50–60.

13. Kelley, H.H., & Michela, J.L. (1980). Attribution theory and research. In M. Rosenzweig and L. Porter (Eds.). *Annual Review of Psychology, 31,* 457–501.

14. Reeder, G.D. (1982). Let's give the fundamental attribution error another chance. *Journal of Personality and Social Psychology, 43,* 341–344.

15. McCauley, C., Stitt, C.L., & Segal, M. (1980). Stereotyping: From prejudice to prediction. *Psychological Bulletin, 7(1),* p. 196.

16. McCauley, et al. (1980).

17. Snyder, M. (1982). Self-fulfilling stereotypes. *Psychology Today 16(7),* 60 cf. Also see Skrypnek, B.J., & Snyder, M. (1982). On the self-perpetuation nature of stereotypes about women and men. *Journal of Experimental Social Psychology 18,* 277–291.

18. Snyder, (1982).

19. Cooper, W.H. (1981). The ubiquitous halo. *Psychological Bulletin 90,* 218–244.

20. Cooper (1981). Also see Landy, F.J., & Farr, J.L. (1980). Performance rating, *Psychological Bulletin 87,* 72–107.

21. Cooper (1981). Also see Holzbach, R.L. (1978). Rater bias in performance ratings: Superior, self, and peer ratings. *Journal of Applied Psychology, 63,* 579–588.

22. Bernardin, H.J., & Buckley, M.R. (1981). Strategies in rater training. *Academy of Management Review, 6,* 205–212.

23. Larwood, L., & Whittaker, W. (1977). Managerial myopia: Self-serving biases in organizational planning. *Journal of Applied Psychology, 62* (2), 198.

24. Schneider, D.J., (1981). Tactical self-presentations: Toward a broader conception. In J.T. Tedechi (Ed.). *Impression management theory and social psychological research.* New York: Academic Press.

25. Schlenker, B.R. (1980). *Impression management.* Monterey, CA: Brooks/Cole.

26. The following section is based on Gardner, W.L., & Martinko, M.J. Impression management in organizations. Unpublished paper, Southern Illinois University at Carbondale.

27. Forsythe, S., Drake, M.F., & Cox, C.E. (1985). Influence of applicant's dress on interviewer's selection decisions. *Journal of Applied Psychology, 70,* 374–378.

28. See Schlenker, *Impression management;* and Jones, E.E. (1964). *Ingratiation: A social-psychological approach.* New York: Appleton-Century-Crofts.

29. Ralston, D.A. (1985). Employee ingratiation: The role of management. *Academy of Management Review, 10,* 477–487; and Jones (1964).

30. Adapted from Carnegie, D. (1936). *How to win friends and influence people.* New York: Simon and Schuster. (This is the earliest of numerous editions.)

31. Molloy, J.T. (1975). *Dress for success.* New York: Warner, p. 77.

32. Molloy, (1975), pp. 35–36.

33. Molloy, J.T. (1978). *The woman's dress for success book.* New York: Warner.

34. See Schlenker, (1980), Chapter 9; and Cash, T.F., & Janda, L.H. (1984, December). The eye of the beholder, *Psychology Today.* And Solomon, M.R. (1986, April). Dress for effect. *Psychology Today,* 20 cf.

35. See Edinger, J.A., & Patterson, M.L. (1983). Nonverbal involvement and social control. *Psychological Bulletin, 93,* 30–56. And Buck, R. (1983). *Nonverbal behavior and the communication of affect.* New York: Guilford Press.

36. See Fisher, A.B. (1986, July 21). Spiffing up the corporate image. *Fortune,* pp. 68–70.

37. Smith, D.E. (1986). Training programs for performance appraisal: A review. *Academy of Management Review, 11,* 22–40.

38. Kipnis, D., Schmidt, S., Price, K., & Stitt, C. (1981). Why do I like thee: Is it your performance or my orders? *Journal of Applied Psychology, 66,* 324–328. Also see Hogan, E.A. (1987). Effects of prior expectations on performance ratings. *Academy of Management Journal, 30,* 354–368.

39. Smith (1986).

40. Landy and Farr (1980).

41. See Cederblom, D. (1982). The performance appraisal interview: A review, implications and suggestions. *Academy of Management Review, 7,* 219–227.

42. Zima, J.P. (1983). *Interviewing: Key to effective management.* Chicago: SRA. Also see Arvey, R.D., & Campion, J.E. (1982). The employment interview: A summary and review of recent research. *Personnel Psychology, 35,* 281–322.

43. Dipboye, R.L. (1982).

44. Gardner and Martinko (1986); and Wortman, C.B., & Linsenmeier, J.A.W. (1977). Interpersonal attraction techniques of ingratiation in organizational settings. In B. Staw & G.R. Salancik (Eds.). *New directions in organizational behavior.* Chicago: St. Clair Press, pp. 133–178.

45. Hall, D.T. (1959). *The Silent Language.* Garden City, NY: Doubleday.

46. Levine, R., with Wolff, E. (1985, March). Social time: The heartbeat of culture. *Psychology Today,* p. 29 cf.

47. Levin with Wolff (1985).

48. Levine with Wolff (1985).

49. See Pye, L.W. (1986, July-August). The China trade: Making the deal. *Harvard Business Review,* p. 74 cf.

Chapter Five

MOTIVATING WORK BEHAVIOR

PREVIEW

- Why is motivation one of the most troublesome problems for managers?

- When is it impossible to motivate work behavior?

- How can the social environment influence motivation?

- What work outcomes do you value? Find out by filling out a questionnaire.

- Which rewards are most powerful: those from sources within the person or those from the environment?

- Why is equity a crucial element of the motivation process?

- Do American theories of motivation work if you are assigned to a job in another country?

MAJOR TOPICS

Preview Case: A Tale of Two Cities

An Introduction to Work Motivation

Energizing Behavior

Directing Behavior

Sustaining Behavior with Rewards

Cross-Cultural OB: Do American Motivation Theories Apply Abroad?

Managerial Applications of Motivation Theory

Preview Case

A TALE OF TWO CITIES

Ferndale Jim Matsumoto, head of the Public Works Department for Ferndale, was upset. He tossed the Refuse Utility Division study on his desk in disgust. The study concluded that yet another refuse collection crew and truck was needed. This was the second new truck and crew this year and funds were tight. Squeezing another $200,000 out of the city council would be very difficult. But if the garbage was not picked up, everyone would get in an uproar. If only he could motivate the crews to make five more stops a day, then no new crew or truck would be needed.

Going from 110 to 115 stops would not seem to make that much difference. Yet the last time he tried to get the crews to increase their production, it resulted in a wildcat strike (a one-day work stop-

page) that almost got him fired. The crews work a forty-hour week and resist overtime, even at double-time rates—they say the work is too tiring to work overtime. Perhaps their current pay of $12.33 per hour is so high that they do not care about money? If only he could find some way to motivate the crews, life would be much simpler and more pleasant.

Martinsville Things were different in Martinsville. Refuse service is contracted to the Quickpik Company headed by Marlo Bennett. Her crews are paid $8 per hour for the first 100 stops and then $.50 per stop for anything over 100. But in contrast to the Ferndale crews, who must be on the job eight hours a day, the Martinsville crews can go home as soon as their stops are completed. It usually takes them about six hours for 200 stops! The Martinsville crews make more money for working less time, and they are highly productive.

Certainly one of the most common managerial problems is how to motivate employees. If you take a poll of workers in almost any organization, most will say they are working at considerably lower than their full potential. On the other hand, the supervisors of these workers may say that they have tried "everything" to get them to be more productive, to use more of their potential.

The key to improving motivation is to obtain greater use of people's capabilities without exploiting them. However, motivating employees is not easy. There are no simple, foolproof methods that can be applied to everyone. What works in Martinsville might not work in Ferndale, depending on the individuals involved and the situation.

Our task in this chapter is to gain an understanding of the basic concepts of motivation. To do that we will use an approach that divides motivation into three general areas: energizing behavior, directing behavior, and sustaining behavior. Then, in the next two chapters we will learn about some techniques that are used to motivate people, such as behavior modification, pay, and job redesign.

AN INTRODUCTION TO WORK MOTIVATION

In this introductory section, we will define motivation and look at some fundamental relationships between motivation and performance.

What Do We Mean by Motivation?

When we speak of motivation, we are interested in *behavior* as opposed to attitudes. What we are interested in is why people work faster or harder, why they come to work on time, why they produce high quality work, or why they decide to join or leave our organization. **Motivation** is the process that causes behavior to be energized, directed, and sustained.[1]

Behavior is normally **energized** or aroused by an unfulfilled need or desire. A desire for money, promotion, time off, social contacts, or job challenge can all affect motivation. Once energized, the behavior must be **directed** in some way by making sure the effort is channeled where it is needed or desired. Finally, the desired behavior is **sustained** through rewards and feedback. We want people to keep on performing over the long run. Figure 5.1 shows a model representing an overview of the motivation process.

Motivation and Job Performance

Have you ever been highly motivated to make an *A* in a course only to wind up with a *B* or *C*? Obviously, performance depends upon more than just motivation—you must have the **capacity** to perform. Capacity to perform means that you must also have the ability, aptitude, skill, training, tools, and technology to be able to perform.

To illustrate how performance depends upon capacity as well as motivation, return to the opening example. A refuse collector for Quickpik Co. has to lift cans weighing over 100 pounds all day long. Not everyone can do it—some people simply lack size and strength. Training is probably less important than ability for refuse collectors because the job is relatively simple and easy to learn. However, tools and technology are crucial. If the collectors were limited to old-fashioned open trucks rather than the modern trucks with hydraulic trash compactors, they would not perform nearly as well. It is doubtful that fifty stops a day could be completed. Thus, one must have the capacity to perform as well as the motivation or inclination.

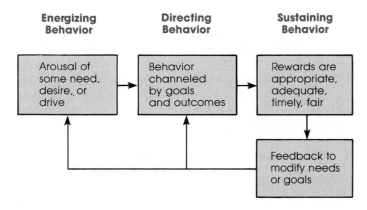

Figure 5.1

MODEL OF THE MOTIVATION PROCESS

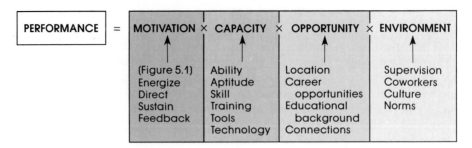

Figure 5.2

GENERAL MODEL OF PERFORMANCE

The **organizational environment** and culture must also support the motivation process. For example, if you worked in an organizational culture where people were lax and uncaring, it is highly unlikely that you would be motivated. In addition, you must also have the **opportunity** to perform. If you are a business-school graduate, but working as a taxi driver, it is unlikely that you will be able to show how much you know. The model in Figure 5.2 illustrates this relationship.

While our emphasis will be directed primarily at motivation, such factors as capacity, organizational environment, and opportunity should always be considered as possible causes of performance problems.

ENERGIZING BEHAVIOR

In this section, we will cover two major approaches to explaining what energizes behavior: needs and social forces.

Needs—An Energizing Force

What Are Needs?   A **need** is tension created by a deficiency that arouses an individual to behave in the direction of accomplishing some goal.[2] Hunger is a basic physiological need for food. If you are hungry, you are motivated to do something that will result in eating—you will drive to the restaurant or you will prepare and cook some food. Once satisfied, hunger is no longer a motivator, or for the moment, a need. The refuse collectors in Ferndale were more motivated by a need for rest after the eight-hour workday than they were by a need for the extra money that overtime work would bring.

Categorizing Needs.   There are a number of different classification schemes that attempt to put needs in categories to simplify understanding. Two approaches that are often used by managers are Maslow's Need Hierarchy Theory and Alderfer's ERG Theory. We will discuss both of these theories later in this section. Both these theories limit the number of needs they consider (five for Maslow; three for Alderfer) and combine a number of needs together. A more

Table 5.1

A PARTIAL LIST OF NEEDS THAT ARE RELEVANT TO ORGANIZATIONS

Need	Description
Achievement	To do one's best; to accomplish something difficult and significant.
Affiliation	The desire for relationships with others; to share and do things with friends; to love; to relate to others on an interpersonal basis.
Autonomy	To seek independence, freedom; to avoid domineering authority; to be unattached; to resist coercion and restriction.
Esteem	Self-respect and respect from others; to have a good reputation; to have prestige and status.
Growth	To develop; to learn; to experience new skills and knowledge; challenge.
Physiological	The basic needs of the body to stay alive: food, water, air, temperature.
Power	To control one's environment; to be dominant; to direct and control others; to supervise others; to be regarded as a leader.
Safety	To seek freedom from the threat or reality of physical or psychological harm; to live in a secure environment.
Self-actualization	The desire for self-fulfillment; to realize one's potential; to become everything that one is capable of becoming; to achieve fulfillment of one's life goals; to realize the potential of one's personality.

SOURCE: The table is based on a variety of sources including Maslow, A.H. (1943). A theory of human motivation. *Psychological Review, 50,* 370–396. Alderfer, C.P. (1972). *Existence, relatedness, and growth.* New York: The Free Press. Senger, J. (1980). *Individuals, groups, and the organization.* Cambridge, MA: Winthrope.

complete, but still partial, list of needs that seem relevant for organizations is presented in Table 5.1.

Maslow's Need Hierarchy Theory

Maslow's Need Hierarchy Theory is probably the best known and most widely used need theory of motivation.[3] Maslow classifies needs into five sets: **physiological, safety, love** (or affiliation), **esteem,** and **self-actualization** (*see* Table 5.1 for definitions). As shown in Figure 5.3, these needs are arranged in a **hierarchy** that begins with basic physiological needs and ends with self-actualization. While the hierarchy is a general guide, it is not rigid. Many people will show patterns that do not precisely follow the hierarchy and some researchers question whether the hierarchy even exists (*see* Perspective 5.2.)

Need Satisfaction.   The strongest need at the moment, say, hunger, will predominate until it is gratified. Then the next need in the hierarchy will take over, since a gratified need is not a motivator. However, just because another

Perspective 5.1

WHEN IS MOTIVATING WORK BEHAVIOR IMPOSSIBLE?

A review of motivation theory and practice concludes that it may not always be possible to motivate behavior, even if we know how. There are circumstances that make it exceptionally difficult for a motivational system to work, including the pay system, the coworkers, the technology, or the union. If a manager has to answer *yes* to the following four questions, then some other form of behavior-change strategy other than motivation may be appropriate: [4]

1. Is the reward system rigid and inflexible? In other words, are people and tasks grouped into such large categories for reward purposes that the rewards are not seen as being related to performance?
2. Is an individual's behavior dependent on the actions of others rather than his or her own behavior?
3. Is there turmoil in the work environment, such as changes in people, jobs, or expected work behaviors?
4. Are social pressures the major determinants of what people are doing on the job?

need in the hierarchy becomes predominant does not mean that the previous ones on the hierarchy have been 100 percent satisfied. A more common case would be for all needs to be partially satisfied. Figure 5.4 illustrates this process.

For example, take Jane Hernandez, a new engineer for Solar Electronics Company, who wants to gain the respect of other engineers and establish a good reputation. Jane's need profile at the moment might be something like this: physiological needs, 90 percent satisfied; safety needs, 80 percent satisfied;

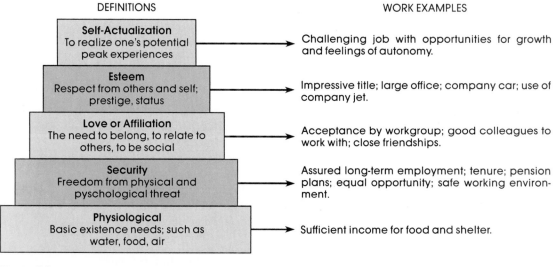

Figure 5.3

MASLOW'S HIERARCHY OF NEEDS

Perspective 5.2

DOES A HIERARCHY OF NEEDS REALLY EXIST?

Little evidence exists to support the notion that Maslow's hierarchy of needs exists. An extensive review of the literature found that a hierarchy tended to exist only between deficiency needs (physiological, safety, and social) and growth needs (esteem and self-actualization).[5] Does this mean the theory is invalid? Possibly. It is certainly not as robust as we might desire. But, there are also some other competing explanations:

1. The theory may not be testable using traditional research methods. For example, Maslow developed his theory based on deduction and clinical insights with a very special group of people—self-actualizers. Thus, it may not be possible to evaluate the theory using research designs that differ greatly from Maslow's design.
2. It is very difficult to develop questionnaires that measure such elusive variables as needs.

From a practical standpoint, his theory is a logically appealing, easy-to-remember framework for understanding human need processes in organizations.[6]

love needs, 70 percent satisfied; esteem needs, 40 percent satisfied; and self-actualization needs, 10 percent satisfied. Thus, esteem needs may be the predominant need or deficiency at the moment for Jane. However, once her esteem needs have been satisfied, she may be more interested in self-actualization—a need that Maslow says can never be completely satisfied.

Alderfer's ERG Theory

The ERG theory collapses Maslow's five levels into three—existence (E), relatedness (R), and growth (G)—hence the ERG theory.[7] Physiological and safety needs are combined into existence, and esteem and self-actualization are

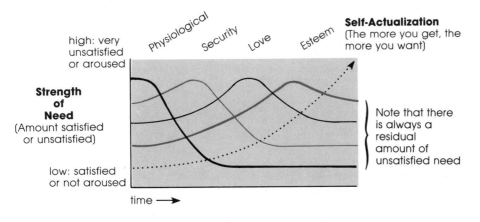

(Hypothetical pattern of need arousal.)

Figure 5.4

MASLOW'S HIERARCHY OF NEEDS SATISFACTION PROCESS

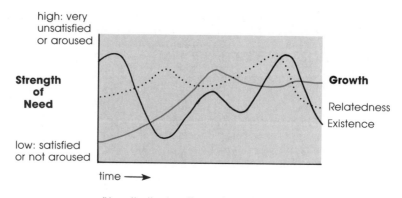

high: very
unsatisfied
or aroused

**Strength
of
Need**

Growth

Relatedness

Existence

low: satisfied
or not aroused

time ⟶

(Hypothetical pattern of need arousal.)

Figure 5.5

THE ERG APPROACH TO THE NEED SATISFACTION PROCESS

combined into growth. Other than the differing categorization system, two main differences exist between Alderfer and Maslow.

Frustration—Regression of Needs.   Maslow says that we progress from one need to another in the hierarchy. While Alderfer agrees with this process, he also says that if we are continually frustrated in our attempts to satisfy a need, then we will give up and redirect our efforts toward some lower need. For example, if an electrician's needs for growth are frustrated, he or she will probably give up and regress to the pursuit of social needs.

Multiple Needs Operate Simultaneously.   ERG theory says that people may experience several needs simultaneously. For example, a person may be hungry and at the same time need love and affection. Figure 5.5 illustrates this process. You might contrast this approach with Maslow's shown in Figure 5.4. Note how peaks occur simultaneously in Alderfer's model.

Applying Need Theory: an Example

Jim Matsumoto, Head of Ferndale's Public Works Department, might rethink his refuse collection motivation problem using Maslow's concepts. His first step might be to talk to the informal leader of the refuse collectors, Mac Gorst (An **informal leader** is someone who is not officially appointed but who nonetheless serves as the leader of the group.) What follows is the way Jim handled the problem.

Jim: "Mac, why don't you want to work overtime to help me resolve our collection problem?"

Mac: "Well, we're really dragging after eight hours of work. All I can do is go home and flake out on the couch. In fact, I don't usually make it through the good TV programs before I fall asleep in my chair. No sir, I've had enough with forty hours! Even though I could use the money, I just can't take anymore." (Sounds like Mac's physiological or existence needs are predominant.)

Jim: "Then what about establishing a goal of say five or ten more pickups a day for each crew—still working forty hours?"

Mac: "Here in private I can tell you that I could do it. But if the other guys were to know I said that they would really be mad. A lot of men feel that if we agree to do more we will be continually asked to up the goals until we are working so hard we are falling out like flies." (Mac is still concerned about physiological needs, but now it sounds like the affiliation or relatedness needs could be threatened. Do we have several needs arising at once as ERG would predict?)

Jim: "Is there some way to get a contest going that might pit crew against crew to determine a winner?"

Mac: "That might be fun, but what would the payoff be for us?" (The idea appeals to Mac's esteem needs, but he has reservations.)

Jim: "Maybe we could develop a goal, say 125 pickups a day, and have each crew try to meet the goal as fast as they could. When the goal is met, they might take off for the rest of the day. Maybe you would have more energy left for the evenings." (Jim is appealing to the esteem [growth] and physiological [existence] needs, and by encouraging team cohesiveness he may be improving satisfaction of affiliation needs.)

Mac: "Yea, that sounds interesting. I'll talk to the rest of the guys and get back to you."

The example makes it sound easier to analyze needs than it really is. Needs are very complex and often difficult to understand. Nevertheless, they do serve as one of the primary ways behavior is energized. In the next section, we will cover another way behavior is energized using social cues.

Social Influences as Energizing Forces

So far we have discussed forces or drives within a person that energize behavior. Another important energizing force that originates in the organizational environment is the social situation. The **social influence** approach suggests that "people are aroused by the presence of others and the knowledge that other people are evaluating them." [8] Social cues, in the form of expectations, are given off by coworkers, supervisors, or subordinates. These cues then become powerful energizing forces for motivating behavior.

The example we just reviewed with Jim and Mac in Ferndale can be extended to illustrate the social influence approach. When Mac expressed concern about how his fellow workers would react to an increase in the performance goal, he was probably responding to social pressure. Mac knows the expectations of the group, and since he is the informal leader, he is under considerable pressure to support the group. If he were to agree unilaterally to an increase in workload, he would probably be ostracized from the group. Thus, Mac is motivated to maintain behavior at the level sanctioned by the group.

Later (Chapters 9, 12, and 14), we will learn much more about such social influence processes as group dynamics, power, and leadership. Now that we have considered some forces that energize behavior, we will turn to the forces that direct behavior.

DIRECTING BEHAVIOR

Why do you choose to behave in one way rather than some other one? Why do you choose to attain one goal while ignoring another? One way of answering these questions is to consider what forces and processes direct or channel behavior. Two theories will help us explain this process: expectancy theory and goal theory.

Expectancy theory is concerned with why we choose certain paths to obtaining an outcome that will result in a satisfied need.[9] The central focus of the theory is on **expectancies,** which are beliefs, based on perception, that a particular behavior will result in an outcome. Expectancies are normally expressed as probabilities (ranging from 0 to 1.0), or chances, (ranging from 0 to 100%) that a certain outcome will be obtained.

Goal theory comes into action after a path has been chosen—goals concentrate energy on the end result that we are trying to obtain.[10] Our discussion will focus first on expectancy theory and then turn to goal theory.

Expectancy Theory: Making Choices

There are three major aspects of expectancy theory: the relationship between effort and performance, the relationship between performance and outcomes, and the valences associated with a given outcome. We will discuss each of these aspects in the following paragraphs.

The Effort-performance Relationship.   Expectancy theory begins with what is called the **effort-performance expectancy;** that is, if you expend the effort, what are the chances that you can perform? This effort-performance expectancy ties in directly with the model discussed earlier of performance as a function of capacity (ability, skill, technology), environment, opportunity, and motivation. If you do not feel you have much chance of performing because of either capacity, opportunity, or environment, then you will be unlikely to expend the effort.

For example, say you are installing a new computer-based information system for your financial analysts to improve their performance. However, two months after installation, you find that very few of the analysts are using the system. When you ask why, you get a variety of answers that boil down to a lack of understanding about how to use the system. Thus, the analysts have not been expending the effort because they perceive that they would not be able to perform the task without considerable frustration and effort. The new system may be quite easy to learn and use, but if the analysts think it is difficult, then they are much less likely to make the effort to try to get the new system to work.

Performance-outcome Expectancies.   The **performance-outcome expectancy** says that if you perform, what are the chances that you will get the outcome you want? In other words, individuals expect outcomes (rewards or punishments) to be associated with behaviors, and they evaluate their chances of obtaining these outcomes before they decide to behave.

For example, assume you are a market researcher in a large wood products firm. If you do an outstanding job on the market research report, will you obtain your desired outcomes; such as praise and promotion (which will satisfy your esteem needs)? Or, do you perceive that no one will care about the report or that you may even get taken to task because management will not like the results (undesirable outcomes)? If praise and promotion are perceived to be more likely, then you will probably direct your energies toward finishing the report. If indifference or punishment seem probable, you may not be motivated to finish the report.

Outcomes can occur at multiple levels. You might consider money to be a first-level outcome because you might use the money to obtain second-level outcomes like a new car or stereo (*see* Figure 5.6 for examples of outcomes that can be satisfied by money). Outcomes are not always associated with money. There are an almost infinite variety of outcomes including such results as praise, group approval, sense of accomplishment, vacation time, and educational opportunities. Eventually outcomes satisfy some need or needs. For example, the outcome money buys a stereo that helps satisfy the needs for growth and relatedness.

Valence of Outcomes. Some outcomes are desirable, like praise and promotion, while others are undesirable, like punishment or being ignored. Thus, each outcome always has a valence associated with it. **Valence** is simply how desirable a given outcome is perceived to be by a certain individual. Outcomes have different valences for different people—not everyone values the same outcomes. The valences are determined by an individual's needs, values, and perceptions.

Valences can be either positive or negative depending upon the desirability or undesirability of the outcome. They also vary in strength since some outcomes are much more important than others. For example, if we used an arbitrary range from $+10$ to -10 to represent the strength of a valence, we could more clearly identify the relative power of the outcomes associated with the market researcher's job referred to earlier. Praise might be very important with a valence of $+7$. Promotion, a crucial outcome for someone with high growth needs, might have a valence of $+9$. Being ignored might have a valence of -3 while being punished might have a -8 valence.

It is now possible to combine all the expectancy theory dimensions into the model illustrated in Figure 5.7.

Using Expectancy Theory

Managers tend to find expectancy theory quite useful for understanding the general nature of the motivation process. In the following paragraphs we will discuss several implications for practice that arise from expectancy theory.[11]

Find Out What Rewards an Employee Values. If you know which outcomes are important to an employee or group of employees and how important each

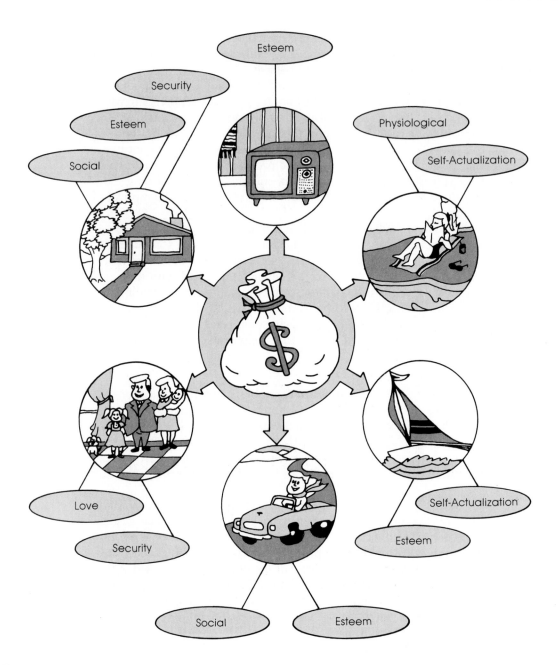

Figure 5.6

ONE OUTCOME, SUCH AS MONEY, CAN FULFILL OTHER OUTCOMES

is in relation to the other (the valences), then you may be able to offer outcomes that will be strong enough to motivate. For example, we saw that we could motivate the Ferndale refuse collectors solely by offering time off. That's handy information. Had we not found this out, we might have been tempted to offer them a plan similar to the one in Martinsville—both time off and more money! So expectancy theory can also teach us to offer only enough to

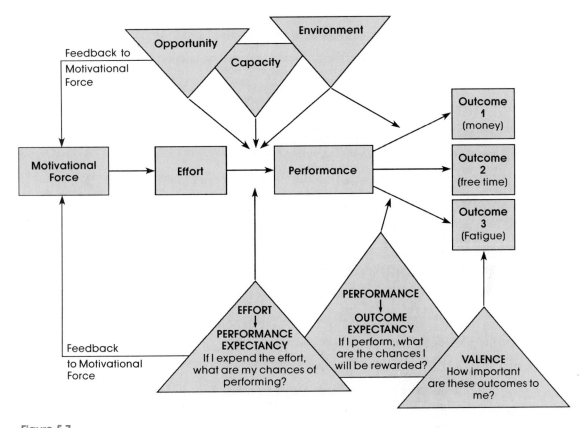

Figure 5.7

MODEL OF THE EXPECTANCY THEORY PROCESS

motivate. Table 5.2 shows how you might find out which rewards are important.

There is another related implication. Often, employees will value different outcomes and have considerably different valences for outcomes. When this happens, we have a serious problem in that what motivates one person may not work for another. In this situation, we must design motivation systems that offer flexibility and choice to the employee—often a difficult task that may involve designing the choice of a number of different rewards for performance.[12]

Link Desired Outcomes to Desired Performance.   If you find that your employees value promotion and yet promotion is based solely on seniority, then you are not effectively using your motivation resources. You need to redesign the promotion system to make sure it is linked to performance. Then, when an employee performs well there will be a high probability of promotion (perception that performance will lead to outcomes) and a much stronger force toward motivation. If employees seek responsibility, growth, and achievement, then some form of job enrichment might be in order. (Chapter 7 contains a detailed description of job enrichment.)

Table 5.2

WHAT WORK OUTCOMES ARE VALUED?

Directions: Rank-order the outcomes you prefer starting with the most preferred outcome as 1 and winding up with the least preferred outcome as 10.

_____	1. Achievement or sense of accomplishment
_____	2. Interpersonal relationships or friendships
_____	3. Job or company status
_____	4. Job security
_____	5. Opportunity for growth
_____	6. Pay or monetary rewards
_____	7. Provision for family
_____	8. Recognition from community and friends
_____	9. Responsibility or control
_____	10. Support for hobbies or avocational activities

To compare your rankings with others, turn to the end of the references in the back of this chapter.

SOURCE: Adapted from Rand, T.M. (1977). Diagnosing the valued reward orientations of employees. *Personnel Journal, 56,* 451 cf.

Use Social Influence.   Group membership and acceptance can be a very potent outcome with a high valence because of the energizing force of social influence. Groups have the power to provide or withhold approval, assistance, friendliness, and inclusion. Thus, if groups can be directed toward organizationally desirable outcomes, they can be an effective motivation strategy.

The example related earlier involving Jim Matsumoto's discussion with Mac Gorst, the informal group leader in Ferndale, involved the use of group forces to improve motivation. If Mac thinks the group will go for an idea, such as the early quitting idea, then he can exert a great deal of influence that may result in the idea being accepted. On the other hand, Mac is not about to bring an idea, such as the one to establish a goal of five or ten more pickups a day, to the group. He might be severely chastised for even considering such an idea. Of course, Mac knows this and will avoid the idea.

Goal Setting

Goal setting is a way of channeling an employee's energy and efforts toward an outcome that is desirable for both the employer and employee. **Goal setting** is the process of developing, negotiating, and formalizing targets that an employee is responsible for accomplishing.[13] An outcome, in expectancy-theory terms, and a goal may be the same. In fact, in many cases a goal is a first-level outcome.

If goals and first-level outcomes are pretty much the same, how do they differ? Goals concentrate effort and direction in a single outcome, while expectancy theory predicts that many diverse outcomes will govern behavior. Hence, goal setting seems as if it would be a cure for our motivation problems. All we have to do is select the outcome, set the goal, and motivated work behavior results. Too bad it is not this simple. There is one big ringer—the goals must be **accepted** for them to motivate.

If Jim Matsumoto simply tells the refuse crews that there is a new production goal of 110 pickups per day, they will probably not accept the goal. They can cope with the nonacceptance in a number of ways. They might just ignore the goal and say, "Sure, boss, we'll try our best," but expend the same amount of effort as previously with no improvement in production. Or they might react by getting angry and calling a wildcat strike, which might result in a public outcry and major problems for Jim. Thus, the key to goal setting is getting goals accepted by those who have to do the work. Goal setting strategies will be discussed more fully in Chapter 7.

Now that we have seen how people channel their energies through the expectancy model and goal setting, we are ready to examine how behavior is maintained.

SUSTAINING BEHAVIOR WITH REWARDS

Equitable and timely rewards are the key to sustaining behavior—people work for the outcomes they value or find rewarding and avoid those outcomes they find punishing. Thus, reward management is a key part of the motivation process. In this section we will discuss sources of rewards and their fairness. In the next chapter we will discuss strategies for administering rewards using reinforcement techniques and pay.

Sources of Rewards

While rewards can come from a number of sources, it is useful to distinguish between those that come from the person or the job itself, called **intrinsic rewards,** and those that come from others such as the boss or coworkers, called **extrinsic rewards.**[14] Intrinsic rewards include such factors as a sense of accomplishment, feelings of creativity, and a positive sense of having performed with excellence. An architect who feels a sense of accomplishment when a building is completed is experiencing an intrinsic reward. These types of rewards are long-lasting and often fulfill a need for esteem, self-actualization, and psychological growth.

Extrinsic rewards are given to you by others. They include such factors as pay, recognition from supervisors or the workgroup, fringe benefits, and promotions. People seem to react differently to self-administered, or intrinsic rewards than they do to other-administered, or extrinsic, rewards.[15] Intrinsic rewards may have longer-lasting effects and be more effective for sustaining motivation than extrinsic rewards.

Another interesting interaction between intrinsic and extrinsic rewards is that extrinsic rewards, such as pay, enhance performance on routine tasks, but may degrade performance on more interesting, challenging, intrinsically-rewarding tasks.[16] This means that if you have an interesting, enriched task, let intrinsic rewards suffice; but if you have a routine task, use extrinsic rewards for better performance.

Herzberg's Motivation-Hygiene Theory

One of the most controversial motivation theories is Herzberg's **Motivation-Hygiene Theory.**[17] The theory states that what motivates people is achievement, recognition for a job well done, the work itself, responsibility, and advancement. In addition to these motivating factors there are a number of factors associated with job dissatisfaction, called the hygiene factors. Examples of hygiene include supervision, salary, company policies, coworkers, and working conditions. These types of items are called hygienes because they are necessary for a good working environment, but they do not motivate. Herzberg's motivators may be roughly equated with intrinsic factors and his hygienes with extrinsic factors.

Herzberg's research technique involved interviews that told participants: "Start with any kind of story you like—either a time when you felt exceptionally good or a time when you felt exceptionally bad about your job." [18] These incidents were classified as factors leading to satisfaction if they related a good story and to dissatisfaction if they related a bad story. By categorizing the content of each story, they were able to put the events into factors, such as achievement or salary. The relative frequency of the factors could then be plotted on a bar chart as shown in Figure 5.8.

Motivators.   Herzberg's theory specifies that we concentrate on the motivators, not the hygienes, if we want people to be motivated. His reasoning is that the **motivators**—achievement, recognition, the work itself, responsibility, and advancement opportunities—are more long-lasting and powerful in their effects. In expectancy theory terms, we might say that the motivators have high valences associated with them. Thus, if we wish to have sustained motivation, the motivator factors are what should be emphasized.

Hygienes.   His research found that **hygienes**—supervision, status, company policies, working conditions, salary, and so forth—do not have an effective, long-term impact on motivation. The following quote from an interview with Herzberg illustrates how he views this part of his theory: [19]

> The hygiene factors are always short term, like the length of time you're not dissatisfied with your salary. It takes about two weeks for the effects of a raise to wear off . . . . The hygiene factors are all subject to the "what have you done for me lately" syndrome. A colonel bucking for general in the Army feels as deprived status-wise as a private bucking for corporal. A colonel is the zero point. If you get a $4,000 increase in salary and the next year they give you a $2,000 increase in salary, psychologically you have taken a $2,000 cut.
>
> By contrast, the motivators are long term and don't go back to zero. I write a book and I achieve some growth. If I don't write another book, I don't get back to where I was before. When I achieve, that achievement never disappears . . . . You see, with the hygiene factors, you've got to have as much as, or more than, you had before to notice any difference, but with the motivators, you do not have to have as much as before to know the difference and feel the growth.

The controversy surrounding Herzberg's theory revolves primarily around methodological issues that show his two independent and separate factors may

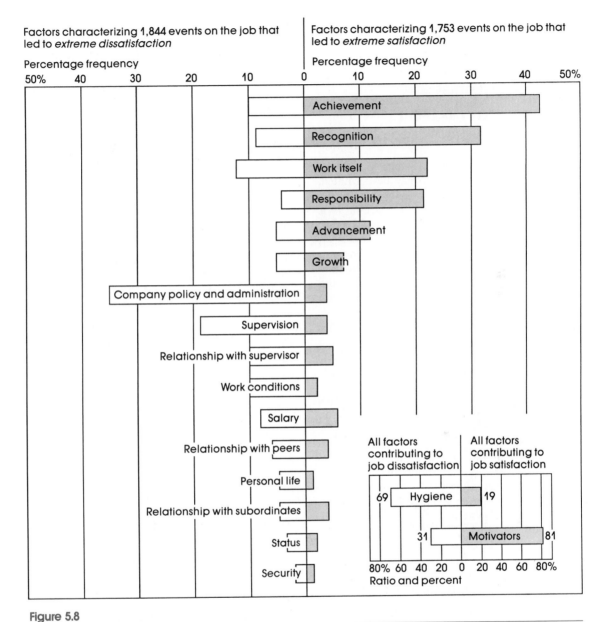

Figure 5.8

MOTIVATION AND HYGIENE FACTORS

SOURCE: Reprinted by permission of the *Harvard Business Review.* An exhibit from "One More Time: How Do You Motivate Employees" by Frederick Herzberg (January/February 1968). Copyright © 1965 by the President and Fellows of Harvard College; all rights reserved.

only exist when the research technique cited above is used. When other methods are used results often fail to confirm the two separate factors.[20] In spite of the problems with the theory, it has been influential in focusing managers' attention on the intrinsic aspects of the job as potential motivators. It has also helped popularize job enrichment, the topic of Chapter 7.[21]

Perspective 5.3

ON THE FOLLY
OF REWARDING A,
WHILE HOPING FOR B

War *as an Example*

If some oversimplification may be permitted, let it be assumed that the primary goal of the organization (Pentagon, Luftwaffe, or whatever) is to win. Let it be assumed further that the primary goal of most individuals on the front lines is to get home alive. Then there appears to be an important conflict in goals—personally rational behavior by those at the bottom will endanger goal attainment by those at the top.

But not necessarily! It depends on how the reward system is set up. The Vietnam war was indeed a study of disobedience and rebellion, with terms such as "fragging" (killing one's own commanding officer) and "search and evade" becoming part of the military vocabulary. The difference in subordinates' acceptance of authority between World War II and Vietnam is reported to be considerable, and veterans of the Second World War often have been quoted as being outraged at the mutinous actions of many American soldiers in Vietnam.

Consider, however, some critical differences in the reward system in use during the two conflicts. What did the GI in World War II want? To go home. And when did he get to go home? When the war was won! If he disobeyed the orders to clean out the trenches and take the hills, the war would not be won and he would not go home. Furthermore, what were his chances of attaining his goal (getting home alive) if he obeyed the orders compared to his chances if he did not? What is being suggested is that the rational soldier in World War II, *whether patriotic or not*, probably found it expedient to obey.

Consider the reward system in use in Vietnam. What did the man at the bottom want? To go home. And when did he get to go home? When his tour of duty was over! This was the case *whether or not* the war was won. Furthermore, concerning the relative chance of getting home alive by obeying orders compared to the chance if they were disobeyed, it is worth noting that a mutineer in Vietnam was far more likely to be assigned rest and rehabilitation (on the assumption that fatigue was the cause) than he was to suffer any negative consequence.

. . . In light of the reward system used in Vietnam, would it not have been personally irrational for some orders to have been obeyed? Was not the military implementing a system which *rewarded* disobedience, while *hoping* that soldiers (despite the reward system) would obey orders?

From S. Kerr, 1975, On the folly of rewarding A, While hoping for B, *Academy of Management Journal 18*:769–71. Copyright © 1975 by Academy of Management, Mississippi State University. Reprinted with permission of author and publisher.

Fairness of Rewards: Equity Theory

Have you ever done a thorough job of preparing for an exam only to have your roommate, who did not study at all, do better than you did? Were you motivated to continue your thorough preparation for that course? Most likely you were not. If people are not rewarded fairly and equitably for the work they do, then they will be extremely dissatisfied with their rewards, and behavior will not be sustained. Whether *equity* exists depends upon the perceived relationship between your inputs and the rewards or outcomes you receive when compared to some other person's inputs and rewards.[22] The equity relationship can be diagrammed as shown below:

$$\frac{\text{Yours}}{\frac{\text{Rewards or Outcomes}}{\text{Inputs}}} = \frac{\text{Comparison Others}}{\frac{\text{Rewards or Outcomes}}{\text{Inputs}}}$$

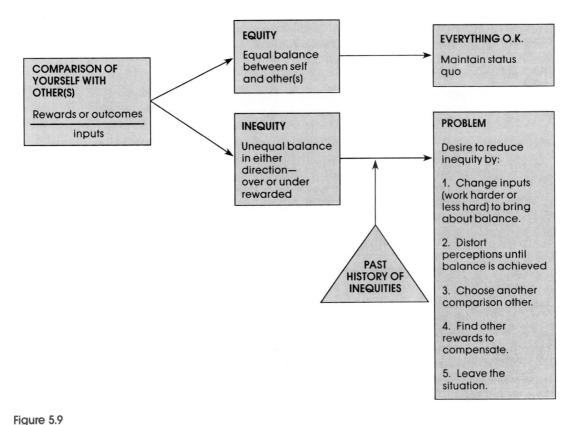

Figure 5.9

THE EQUITY PROCESS

A key element of equity theory is that you are comparing your inputs (education, effort, skill, motivation) and rewards (pay, recognition, achievement, praise) with a "comparison other's" inputs and rewards. A **comparison other** is any person or group of people you perceive you should be compared with.[23] For example, college professors often use other college professors as the comparison others rather than a business executive. We usually choose people who are similar to us as comparison others.

Outcomes of Inequity.   The ideal reward position is perfect equity. Inequity in either direction—over rewards or under rewards—creates discomfort and tension, although the tolerance for over reward is probably higher than under reward. Inequity can be resolved in a number of ways. Inputs can be distorted so that the person perceives his or her inputs are greater or lesser than they really are. Outputs, or performance, may also be increased or decreased to balance the equation.[24] As Figure 5.9 indicates, inequity can also be reduced by distorting perceptions until equity is achieved, choosing another person or group for the comparison other, finding additional rewards to compensate, or leaving the situation.

Past History of Inequity.   Another aspect of equity theory is that past inequities may affect future reactions to inequitable situations.[25] An example might be an employee who was denied a day off when he or she believes that others have been granted this time off in the past. This person may react much more violently than would be expected, not because of the denial but because of a history of inequities that have built up to such a degree that the person explodes. These past inequities might have involved a missed promotion, an unexpectedly low bonus, and lack of praise for doing a good job.

Equity, an Example.   It would seem that $12.33 an hour for the Ferndale refuse collectors would be a more-than-fair wage. And yet, what if the Leesburg refuse collectors, who also work for the city and who also have 110 pickups a day, were receiving $13.50 per hour. Would the Ferndale collectors be dissatisfied? The answer would depend on whether they considered Leesburg collectors to be a comparison other. If Leesburg were Ferndale's sister city just across the river, then it is very likely that inequity would be perceived. On the other hand, if Leesburg were in another state, 100 miles away, then the wage differential would not be a problem.

But what about Ferndale Municipal Hospital's nurses—they make only $8.25 per hour. If they compare themselves with the refuse collectors, they may perceive that they are grossly underpaid. If they compare their pay with Leesburg nurses, who make $8.00 per hour, they may consider themselves fairly paid. It depends on perception and especially who the comparison other is.

CROSS–CULTURAL OB: DO AMERICAN MOTIVATION THEORIES APPLY ABROAD?

For many years the United States has been exporting management education, including motivation theory. Do the theories discussed in this chapter apply universally, or are they a product of our own peculiar culture? Two sides of this debate are described in the following paragraphs.

No, American Theories Do Not Apply Abroad

A prominent Dutch, cross-cultural researcher, Geert Hofstede, has asserted that since American theories are a product of our individualistic, masculine-oriented society, they are not applicable to much of the rest of the world.[26] For example, our emphasis on growth, achievement, and the job itself—as illustrated by Herzberg—are not universally applicable throughout the world. His research concludes that much of the world can be divided into four relatively separate quadrants as illustrated in Figure 5.10. The quadrant where America falls is oriented toward achievement and growth. However, the other three quadrants focus on security or social outcomes, or a combination of the two. This means that the types of outcomes that have high valences for Americans, such as opportunities for promotion and a chance to show what we can do, may not apply in other cultures.

For example, people in Sweden may be much more interested in social outcomes; therefore, an approach to motivation might involve opportunities for people to work together as social units. In Japan, where security predominates, motivation through lifetime employment would seem to apply.

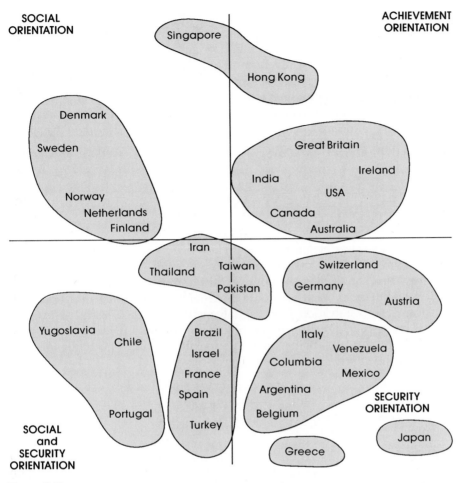

Figure 5.10

MOTIVATION ORIENTATION OF SELECTED COUNTRIES

SOURCE: Adapted from Hofstede, G. (1980). Motivation, leadership, and organization: Do American theories apply abroad? *Organizational Dynamics*, Summer, p. 54.

Yes, American Theories Do Apply Abroad!

Differences in culture are obvious, but much of the motivation theory still applies. For example, Thailand falls in Hofstede's security-social quadrant. However, Thais may be just as achievement-oriented as Americans, *but* achievement may be defined differently. Achievement may mean success which may mean taking care of one's family in Thailand. The boundary between social and achievement may be blurred.[27]

Applying Motivation Theory Abroad: Some Caveats

Certainly there are cultural differences between countries. Lifetime employment works well in collective Japan, but is not popular in individualistic America. But perhaps many of the basic theories may apply. For example, Maslow's hierarchy of needs simply describes the major types of needs that energize behavior. Thus, it may not be surprising that some people in some cultures are more motivated by social needs than they are by achievement needs. The key here is that the basic theory still explains the motivation process. Expectancy theory also seems quite applicable across cultures, although valences, outcomes, and expectancies would certainly be vastly different for an American and a Greek. People everywhere respond to fairness; thus, equity theory would seem to apply. The theory which is perhaps the most culture-bound is Motivation-Hygiene. This theory is entirely based on good and bad incidents happening within the American culture. Caution should be used when using the theory in other cultures.

MANAGERIAL APPLICATIONS FOR MOTIVATION THEORY

The discussion in this chapter makes it clear that there is a great deal of complexity in predicting and managing work motivation. There is no single "master theory" that can explain the entire motivation process. Thus, we must turn to a series of theories, each providing a partial and sometimes overlapping explanation of the motivation process. Categorizing the theories into those that focus on energizing, directing, or sustaining motivation provides a loose overall framework for understanding their interlocking nature. The following hints summarize the implications for managerial action:

- *Motivation must be managed.* Managers need to take an active role in designing and implementing motivation systems and monitor the motivation process on a daily basis. Motivation does not just happen, it is skillfully planned and executed.

- *Find out what needs and outcomes are wanted.* Managers need to be sensitive to the differing needs of their subordinates. Try to find out which outcomes are valued and how important they are. If possible, rewards should be tailored to individual employees. If this is impractical, flexibility should be designed into the system so that employees can choose their own rewards.

- *Clearly link performance and rewards.* Behavior is most strongly energized when people can clearly see that valued outcomes will result if they perform. Systematically rewarding superior performers with promotions, pay, or other valued rewards helps clarify this link. In addition, you get what you reward. Do not expect people to be motivated without rewards or with rewards that are not tied to performance.

- *Improve people's capacity to perform.* Since performance often depends on ability, aptitude, skill, training, tools, and technology, these determiners of performance should be carefully reviewed for adequacy. Training programs, tools, and technology are potentially powerful ways of improving performance with no change in motivation levels.

- *Provide opportunities to perform.* Give people a chance to show what they can do. Use a Theory Y view of people's work motivation as a basis for trust.

- *Develop a positive organizational culture.* People work best in a culture where everyone values achievement and motivation; where leaders exhibit trust and share power. Celebrate and reward outstanding motivation.

- *Use social influence strategies.* Since the need for social approval is important for most employees, situations can be designed where group pressures can be used to motivate employees and provide rewards to keep their behavior sustained. This strategy can only work in a positive organizational culture.

- *Establish goals to direct behavior.* Clear goals serve to direct behavior toward ends the manager wants accomplished. This relatively simple strategy is quite effective for clarifying expectancies and insuring accurate rewards for performance. Involve people in goal setting to help gain goal acceptance.

- *Reward people equitably.* The best motivation system will fail without fair and equitable rewards because people get very uncomfortable or even alienated when rewards are not fair. Be sure people are aware of all the rewards they are getting, such as fringe benefits. Remember that perceived fairness is as important as objective reality.

FOR DISCUSSION

1. Since performance is a function of capacity and motivation, what can you do to select people who have the potential to perform?

2. The text asserts that there are instances when motivating behavior is extremely difficult or impossible. Do you agree? Disagree? Can you think of an instance where motivation was virtually impossible?

3. Which needs (shown in Table 5.1) seem most relevant for energizing your own behavior?

4. Compare and contrast Maslow's hierarchy of needs with Alderfer's ERG theory.

5. Using the method of expectancy theory process shown in Figure 5.7, outline the motivation for directing your behavior to attend college.

6. What are some practical ways that a manager can use expectancy theory.

7. Explain the difference between intrinsic and extrinsic rewards. Which do you prefer? Why?

8. Explain how equity theory works. How is the comparison other determined?

9. Can you think of an example of the folly of rewarding A, while hoping for B?

10. What are the most important elements to consider when managing the motivation process?

11. Based on Figure 5.10 and the text discussion, how would you motivate employees in Mexico?

KEY CONCEPTS AND TERMS

motivation
capacity to perform
expectancy theory
need
Maslow's Hierarchy of Needs Theory
ERG Theory

frustration regression
effort-performance expectancy
performance-outcome expectancy
valence
goal setting
intrinsic rewards

extrinsic rewards
Herzberg's Motivation-Hygiene Theory
motivator factors
hygiene factors
equity theory

Cases and Incidents

MOTIVATION OVERDOSE: THE WORKAHOLICS

A "workaholic" may work a 100–hour week—and love it—according to Marilyn Machlowitz,[28] who has done research on these unusual people. A workaholic may arrive at 6:00 A.M. and leave at 7:00 P.M. with a briefcase full of work to do at home. There is no such thing as the "thank-goodness-it's-Friday" syndrome for the workaholic. On weekends they get anxious to get back to work and may have brought enough work home to tide them over. Vacations are a real drag. Workaholics would just as soon not take one and, if they have to take one for some reason, they may wind up climbing the walls before it is over. Machlowitz found fifteen characteristics that are common to workaholics:

- an ongoing work style
- an ability to work anywhere
- a broad view of what the job requires
- initiative
- a sense of scarcity of time
- the use of lists and time-saving gadgets
- long work days
- little sleep
- quick meals
- an awareness of what their work effort can accomplish
- overlapping of work and leisure
- an inability to enjoy idleness
- a dread of retirement
- a desire to excel
- an intense energy

DISCUSSION QUESTIONS

1. Using the motivation theories discussed in the chapter, determine why a person might work so hard.

2. What outcomes do workaholics seem to value?

3. Should we purposely try to find workaholics for organizational positions?

ROLLIE ON THE ASSEMBLY LINE

A fact of life that Rollie discovered at this stage was that while most assembly-line jobs were hard and demanding, a few were soft touches. Installing windshields was one of the soft ones. Workers doing this, however, were cagey when being watched and indulged in extra, unneeded motions to make their task look tougher. Rollie worked on windshields, but only a few days because Parkland [the foreman] moved him back down the line to one of the difficult jobs—scrabbling and twisting around inside car bodies to insert complicated wiring harness. Later still, Rollie handled a "blind operation"—the toughest kind of all, where bolts had to be inserted out of sight, then tightened, also by feel alone.

That was the day Parkland confided to him, "It isn't a fair system. Guys who work best, who a foreman can rely on, get the stinkingest jobs and a lousy deal. The trouble is, I need somebody on those bolts who I know for sure'll fix'em and not goof off."

DISCUSSION QUESTIONS

1. Why do you think Rollie is motivated to do the tough jobs?

2. What are the rewards or punishments for being a competent, dependable worker?

3. How could the reward system be designed to remedy this problem?

4. What impact would a change in the reward system have on quality control?

From Hailey, A. (1973). *Wheels.* New York: Bantam, pp. 242–243.

CHANCELLOR STATE UNIVERSITY

THE SETTING

Chancellor State University is a large, urban university in the Midwest. Although the University experienced rapid growth in the 1960s and 1970s, overall enrollment had stabilized. The School of Business Administration, however, had continued to grow, drawing students away from programs in the School of Education and the College of Arts and Sciences as well as attracting new students concerned with future vocational opportunities. The faculty and administration of the business school were pleased to see the enrollment growth as it signaled acceptance of their degree programs, but the enrollment expansion also created strong pressure to expand the business faculty.

Under normal circumstances, faculty expansion would simply have meant an active recruitment effort by school administrators. But the situation at Chancellor State was representative of a national phenomenon of enrollment growth in business schools that had resulted in a strong demand for doctorally qualified faculty in the face of a relatively short supply. Thus, faculty recruitment at many business schools had become a priority activity, rather than merely one of the many administrative responsibilities of deans and department heads.

At Chancellor State, Fred Kennedy, Chairman of the Management Department, had been actively seeking new faculty members for his staff, which had the heaviest course load in the school. As is often customary in academia, the faculty in the Department of Management participated in recruitment, spending considerable time meeting with the faculty candidates in an effort to evaluate their candidacy for a faculty position. Faculty members could then make recommendations as to whether or not the prospect should be tendered an offer to join the staff.

THE CONFERENCE

It was late in February, and several prospective faculty members had visited Chancellor State for campus job interviews. Early one Friday morning, Kennedy was in his office reviewing the job files of prospective faculty members. He looked up as he heard the voice of Larry Gordon, an assistant professor of management who was now in his third year at Chancellor State.

"Good morning, Fred," said Larry, as he walked into the Department office. "Do you have a couple minutes? I want to talk with you about something."

Fred gestured to him to come into his office.

"Sure, Larry, what's on your mind?"

After entering Fred's office, Larry closed the door, indicating to Fred that this was not to be just a casual, friendly, conversation.

"Fred," Larry began, "I was wondering what you thought about the prospective faculty member we had in here for an interview last week. I've been talking with a couple other faculty members about him, and they're not really all that impressed. He seems to be OK, I guess, but we may be able to do better. Are we going to make him an offer? If we do, he's sure not worth top dollar in my opinion."

"Well, I've received some of the written evaluations back from the faculty, and they seem to be fairly positive," replied Fred. "They're not as favorable as they could be, but the other faculty seem to think that he would be acceptable and that he could work out pretty well on our staff. His academic credentials are not bad, and he has had some good experience. Given the state of the market for business faculty in his specialty, I expect that we'll extend an offer to him. By the way, I know that he already has a couple of offers in hand from our competition."

Fred could readily see that Larry was not pleased to hear all of this. From their earlier conversations, Fred could anticipate Larry's next comment.

"Yeah, O.K., I can see that we could use him, but what kind of money are we offering in these new positions?" questioned Larry. "I don't mean to pry into somebody else's business, but what sort of salary is the department offering our new faculty?"

Fred winced at this question. He had in the past made no secret about general salary ranges for new faculty members. In fact, this information was generally known throughout the school. But this had become a very sensitive issue in the last few years, given the rapid increases in starting salaries for new business faculty members.

"Well, Larry, I guess you know that we're paying competitively for our new faculty. With our enrollment increase we've got to increase our teaching staff, and to do that we're probably going to have to meet the market," Fred responded.

Larry was obviously not satisfied with this response and was becoming irritated with the conversation. "Fred, I assume that by 'meeting the market' you mean that we're going to offer this guy two to three thousand dollars more than some of us who have been here for several years are now making. This new guy has not yet finished his doctorate, has very little teaching experience, has no publications, and, in my opinion, is not as good as a lot of our current faculty. How much can you justify paying for an unknown quantity? I think it's just unfair to the present faculty to offer him more money than many of us are making. When is somebody going to do something for us? Fred, I'm not unhappy here in this department, but I'm sure going to keep my eyes open for other opportunities. I feel sure that I could move to another school at a higher rank and increase my salary significantly. You may think I'm wrong and maybe I shouldn't feel this way, but this situation is just not fair!"

Fred sighed and tried to calm Larry down. "Larry, I know what you're concerned about, and

I'm certainly sympathetic to the problem. After all, this salary compression issue affects me in the same way it does you. I can assure you that I have reservations about paying the kind of money we are for new faculty in light of our existing faculty salaries, but I don't believe that we can attract the kind of faculty we want by paying less than competitive rates. Although this seems to create some internal inequities, I hope that we'll have sufficient salary increase money to make some adjustments to reduce these discrepancies. Certainly I want to be able to reward and retain our productive people . . ."

Larry, feeling a little embarrassed by his earlier emotional statement, interjected: "I know you've got other problems, Fred, and I didn't mean to lash out at you. I know it's not really your fault, but a lot of the other faculty are talking about this salary issue. It surely doesn't help morale any when a new, inexperienced assistant professor is hired for more than some of the associate professors are making."

"Yes, I'm well aware of this, Larry, and I'm making the Dean aware of it as well. We're certainly going to do what we can to try to resolve this salary compression problem," Fred responded.

As Larry moved toward the door, he continued to make his point: "Well, I hope you can do something soon because it's most inequitable at the present time. People are pretty upset about it, and it's likely to cause the department some turnover problems in the future. No one likes to be treated unfairly. I'll see you later, Fred. I've got to run to class. Maybe we can talk about it again later."

As Larry walked out of his office Fred reflected on their conversation. It reminded him of other discussions he had had previously with several other faculty members. In fact, Larry had hinted at his dissatisfaction before, but had not been so outspoken about it. Yes, the salary compression problem was reaching a crisis. No longer was it a matter of the "new hires" nearing the salaries of some present faculty; it was a matter of their exceeding them. Never in his experience had Fred recalled a labor market for faculty that was this chaotic.

Fred had puzzled over this dilemma before, but he had not been able to come up with a solution for the problem. He wondered if, in fact, there was a solution that would enable him to hire the new personnel he wanted without offending some of the present staff. Maybe it's just one of those "no win" administrative situations, he mused. Perhaps this was something that could be discussed with the other department chairmen and the Dean as some of them had basically the same problem. Maybe then, he would have a better idea of how to deal with the situation. He certainly hoped so!

DISCUSSION QUESTIONS

1. Using your knowledge of motivation theory from Chapter 5, explain what is happening in this case.

2. Based on Figure 5.9, explain how the equity process is operating. What predictions do you have about outcomes?

3. Is the pay strategy functional for the university?

Case prepared by Thomas R. Miller, Professor, Memphis State University. Reprinted by permission.

REFERENCES

1. This definition is based on Steers, R.M., & Porter, L.W. (1983). *Motivation and work behavior* (3rd ed.). New York: McGraw-Hill, p. 3. It is also similar to the one used by Mitchell, T.R. (1982). Motivation: New directions for theory, research, and practice. *Academy of Management Review, 7,* 80–88.

2. See Steers and Porter (1983) for a good overview of need theories.

3. Maslow, A theory of motivation. In Maslow, A.H. (1970). *Motivation and personality* (rev. ed.). New York: Harper and Row.

4. Adapted from Mitchell (1982), p. 86.

5. Wahba, M.A., & Bridwell, L.G. (1976). Maslow reconsidered: A review of the research on the need hierarchy theory. *Organizational Behavior and Human Performance, 15,* 212–240. Salancik, G.R., & Pfeffer, J. (1977). An examination of need-satisfaction models of job attitudes. *Administrative Science Quarterly, 22,* 427–456. Miner, J. (1980). *Theories of organizational behavior.* Hinsdale, II: Dryden. And Rauschenberger, J., Schmitt, N., & Hunter, J.E. (1980). A test of the need hierarchy concept by a Markov model of change in need strength. *Administrative Science Quarterly, 25,* 654–670.

6. Schwartz, H.S. (1983). Maslow and hierarchical enactment of organizational reality. *Human Relations, 36,* 933–956.

7. Alderfer (1972).

8. Mitchell (1982), p. 84. For more complete information on the social influence approach to motivation, see Sussman, M., & Vecchio, R.P. (1982). A social influence interpretation or worker motivation. *Academy of Management Review, 7*, 177–186. And Salancik, G.R., & Pfeffer, J. (1978). A social information processing approach to job attitudes and task design. *Administrative Science Quarterly, 23*, 224–253.

9. Vroom, V.H. (1964). *Work and motivation.* New York: Wiley. For reviews of expectancy theory, see Mitchell, T. (1974). Expectancy models of job satisfaction, occupational preference, and effort: A theoretical, methodological, and empirical appraisal. *Psychological Bulletin, 81*, 1053–1077. And Mitchell, T.R. (1980). Expectancy-value models on organizational psychology. In N. Feather (Ed.), *Expectancy, incentive, and action.* Hillsdale, NJ: Erlbaum and Associates.

10. Locke, E.A. (1980). Toward a theory of task motivation and incentives. *Organizational Behavior and Human Performance, 3*, 157–189. For reviews, see Tubbs, M.E. (1986). Goal setting: A meta analytic examination of the empirical evidence. *Journal of Applied Psychology, 71*, 474–483. And Locke, E.A. (1978). The ubiquity of the technique of goal setting in theories of and approaches to employee motivation. *Academy of Management Review, 3*, 594–601.

11. Some of the ideas in this section were based on those in Nadler, D.A. & Lawler, E.E., III (1983). Motivation: A diagnostic approach. In J.R. Hackman, E.E. Lawler, III, & L.W. Porter (Eds.). *Perspectives on behavior in organizations* 2nd ed. New York: McGraw-Hill.

12. For ways to individualize pay systems, see Lawler, E.E., III (1976). New approaches to pay administration. *Personnel, 53*, 11–23.

13. Umstot, D.D., Bell, C.H. & Mitchell, T.R. (1976). Effects of job enrichment and task goals on satisfaction and productivity: Implications for job design. *Journal of Applied Psychology, 61*, 381.

14. Deci, E.L. (1972). The effects of contingent and noncontingent rewards and controls on intrinsic motivation. *Organizational Behavior and Human Performance, 8*, 217–229.

15. Hamner, W.C. (1979). Motivation theories and work applications. In S. Kerr (Ed.), *Organizational behavior* (pp. 41–58). Columbus, OH: Grid.

16. Daniel, T.L. & Esser, J.K. (1980). Intrinsic motivation as influenced by rewards, task, interest and task structure. *Journal of Applied Psychology, 65*, 566–573.

17. Herzberg, F. (1966). *Work and the nature of man.* Cleveland: World. For a summary of his theory, see Herzberg, F. (1968). One more time: How do you motivate employees? *Harvard Business Review, 46*(1), 53–62.

18. Herzberg, F., Mausner, B., & Snyderman, B.B. (1959). *The motivation to work.* New York: Wiley, p. 35.

19. Quote from: A conversation with Frederick Herzberg. (1979, July). *Management Review,* p. 41.

20. See House, R., & Wigdor, L. (1967). Herzberg's dual-factor theory of job satisfaction and motivation: A review of the empirical evidence and criticism. *Personnel Psychology, 20*, 369–380. And Kerr, S., Harlan, A., & Stogdill, R. (1974). Preference for motivator and hygiene factors in a hypothetical interview situation. *Personnel Psychology, 25*, 109–124.

21. See Herzberg (1968), for details of how Motivation-Hygiene Theory applies to job enrichment. For an update on Herzberg's concepts see (1982) *The managerial choice: to be efficient or to be human.* Salt Lake City: Olympus Pub. Co.

22. Adams, J.S. (1965). Inequity in social exchange. In L. Berkowitz (Ed.). *Advances in experimental social psychology* (Vol. 2). New York: Academic Press. Carrell, M.R., & Dittrich, J.B. (1978). Equity theory: The recent literature, methodological considerations, and new directions. *Academy of Management Review, 3*, 202–212. Mowday, R.T. (1983). Equity theory predictions in organizations. In Steers and Porter (1983), pp. 91–113. Huseman, R.C., Hatfield, J.D., & Miles, E.W. (1987). A new perspective on equity theory: The equity sensitivity construct. *Academy of Management Review, 12*, 222–234.

23. For a discussion of "referent others," see Goodman, P.S. (1974). An examination of referents used in the evaluation of pay. *Organizational Behavior and Human Performance, 12*, 170–195.

24. Mowday (1983). In Steers and Porter.

25. Cosier, R.A., & Dalton, D.R. (1983). Equity theory and time: A reformulation. *Academy of Management Review, 8*, 311–319.

26. Hofstede, G. (1980). Motivation, leadership, and organization: Do American theories apply abroad? *Organizational Dynamics, Summer*, 42–63.

27. See Hunt, J.W. (1981). Applying American behavioral science: Some cross-cultural problems. *Organizational Dynamics, Summer*, 55–62. Hunt does not take the position that American theories are universal, but he does argue that some of Hofstede's (1980) positions are unsound.

28. Machlowitz, M.M. (1980). *Workaholics.* Reading, MA: Addison-Wesley.

Answers to questions posed in Table 5.2:
What Work Outcomes Are Valued?

Outcome	A*	B*	C*
1. Achievement or sense of accomplishment	2	2	2
2. Interpersonal relationships or friendships	9	8	9
3. Job or company status	7	7	8
4. Job security	10	10	4
5. Opportunity for growth	1	1	1
6. Pay or monetary rewards	5	6	6
7. Provision for family	3	5	3
8. Recognition from community and friends	8	9	10
9. Responsibility or control	4	3	7
10. Support for hobbies or avocational activities	6	4	5

*A = Upper management
 B = Middle management
 C = Hourly employees

Chapter Six

MOTIVATION USING BEHAVIOR MODIFICATION AND PAY

PREVIEW

- Can behavior mod, a technique that has proven successful for changing behavior of rats and pigeons, be applied to organizations?

- How do the excellent companies motivate their employees?

- When should punishment be used or avoided?

- Why don't salaries motivate better work performance?

- Why do merit pay and piecework pay systems often pay?

- What is knowledge-based pay?

- Why would a Japanese employee work on a vacation day?

MAJOR TOPICS

Preview Case: Reliance Development Company

Motivating with Organizational Behavior Modification

Motivating with Pay

Cross-Cultural OB: Three Ways of Dealing with Tardiness

Managerial Applications of Behavior Mod and Pay

Preview Case

RELIANCE DEVELOPMENT COMPANY

Reliance Development Co., referred to as RDC by most of its employees, is a young company that was founded after the sky-high interest rates of the early 1980s made many homes unaffordable for the average buyer. RDC capitalized on this market by building large numbers of low-cost, energy-efficient small homes. The homes were attractively designed and reasonably priced and there were plenty of buyers. The company had succeeded beyond the wildest dreams of the four founding partners—it was now a multimillion dollar business with over 400 employees.

The four founders of RDC are meeting this morning to try to solve a problem: The framing costs have been rising and now exceed estimates by 20 percent. (Framing is the basic skeleton of a house, including the studs, floors, and rafters. It is done by a special type of carpenter, called a framer.) Since the company is committed to keeping the costs down, something must be done. The key to their success has been cost consciousness. RDC has been able to build a good quality home for less money than their competitors. If costs are allowed to rise, their competitive edge may be lost.

The directors who are meeting this morning are John Rosenberg, President; Helen Knapp, Vice President for Finance; Roy Steele, Vice President for Production; and Ronda Cole, Vice President for Sales. All are recent graduates of undergraduate or graduate schools of business—they are familiar with motivation theories and concepts.

John: Helen tells me we've exceeded our framing costs by 20 percent on the last block of ten houses. What can we do about it?

Roy: The big problem seems to be quality—that is, too much quality. Several of the new guys we've hired were finish carpenters before. They think that each joint should be perfect; that everything should be perfectly level and square. You know we don't need that level of quality in framing. The house will be just as good, strong, and saleable with a much lower level of quality. I've told them several times to speed it up; to lower their stan-

dards, but to no avail. Worse yet, the old framers seem to have caught the "quality fever." They are also working more slowly and carefully. We can't just fire the lot of them because of the shortage of carpenters. They are hard to find. We will incur some terrific interest expenses if we slip behind schedule because of a shortage of carpenters. Plus, it would throw our other crews out of schedule and delay everything. I'm just not sure what we can do about the problem. Maybe we've just got to live with it and raise our prices.

Ronda: It looks like we have a classic motivation problem here: How do we motivate the crews to work faster with lower quality? Perhaps we could give a bonus for each house that is done on time or early?

Helen: If we pay a bonus, we're still going to be in a cost bind. Somehow we've got to toe the line on costs. And I don't think we can raise our prices. Our competitors are getting pretty close already.

John: Are they being oversupervised? Perhaps their jobs could be changed so they would feel the responsibility for costs?

Roy: Well, they sure don't seem to give a damn about costs. If we could just do something to instill a sense of responsibility for costs; but they can't seem to get this quality thing out of their heads. I believe they probably think of their jobs as already pretty enriched. Maybe that's the reason they're so concerned about quality—they're craftsmen and intend to do a first-class job, whether it's needed or not.

Helen: What about using behavior mod on them? I seem to remember from my org behavior course that if we can develop a schedule or plan for rewards and punishments we can change almost any behavior.

John: Yes, but behavior mod always kind of turned me off. You know, all that manipulation and control stuff. I'm for using a more humanistic motivation technique. What about goal setting? I've heard that it's been successful in a number of industries.

Roy: Isn't goal setting a rather simplistic approach to a complicated problem? I don't think that the framers would go for goals that we imposed on them; and if you ask them to set a goal, they would probably set one even lower so they would have more time to do a real quality job.

Do you have an answer for RDC's behavior problem? If not, perhaps the concepts in this and the next chapter will clarify some issues and help you when you run up against behavioral problems. As you can see from the RDC example, motivation is rather complex with no simple answers. In the next two chapters we will cover four widely used motivation strategies: organizational behavior modification, pay, job design, and goal setting. A basic understanding of these techniques will give you some insight into solving more complex motivation problems, such as the one faced by RDC. The key is to use the practical knowledge presented in this and the next chapter.

MOTIVATING WITH ORGANIZATIONAL BEHAVIOR MODIFICATION

The most basic goal of motivation is changing behavior. While there are many strategies to accomplish this goal, one of the most powerful is **behavior modification** (or behavior mod, as it is often called)—the process of changing behavior by managing the consequences that follow some behavior. While behavior modification has been around for a long time, its use for modifying work behavior is quite recent.[1] Behavior modification applied to organizational situations is often termed **organizational behavior modification** (or "OB mod" for short.)

The key to applying OB mod is to decide which behaviors to target for change, what rewards to use, and how often to give rewards. This section will cover each of these topics along with an evaluation of the pros and cons of using OB mod. The chapter begins with an overview of the behavioral change process.

The Behavior Modification Process

Before we begin with the strategies for changing behaviors, it will be useful to put behavior mod in a conceptual framework. The **S–O–B–C model** is one useful way of looking at the behavior modification process.[2] It recognizes four parts of the process: *S* is, for stimulus; *O*, for the human organism or person; *B*, for behavior; and *C*, for consequences. Figure 6.1 outlines the S–O–B–C process and the next few paragraphs define the terms.

Stimulus.   The *S* in the model stands for stimulus, which includes any environmental cue that plays a role in eliciting behavior. Examples might include

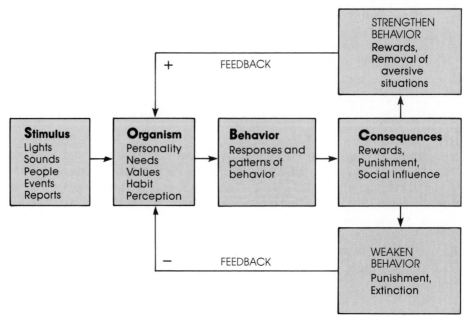

Figure 6.1

THE BEHAVIOR MODIFICATION PROCESS

SOURCE: Adapted from the S–O–B–C model developed by Davis, T.R.V. and Luthans, F. (1980). A social learning approach to organizational behavior. *Academy of Management Review, 5,* 281–290.

noise, a coworker's comment, a machine's actions, or a paycheck received. The stimulus is a cue for behavior, not necessarily the direct cause.

Person or Organism.   The *O* part of the model stands for the person, including motivational patterns, personality, perception processes. Much of what we discussed in the last chapter about motivating behavior with expectancy theory and need theory applies to this part of the model.

Behavior.   The *B* aspect of the model, behavior, includes speech, nonverbal cues, and movements. In organizations, we are particularly interested in work behaviors such as production, arriving for work on time, talking between two employees, not coming to work, or quitting the job.

Consequences.   The *C* part is also environmental since it refers to the consequences that result from behaving, such as praise or reprimands. This is a critical part of the model because behavior is very much a function of the rewards, punishments, or other outcomes that follow a given behavior. Some types of consequences strengthen behavior while others weaken behavior. We will discuss this process more fully later in the chapter.

Contingencies of Reinforcement.   Systematically changing the interrelationships between environmental cues (S), persons (O), task performance or behavior (B), and consequences of reinforcements (C), is often referred to as managing the **contingencies of reinforcement.**[3] If a reward is contingent upon

Perspective 6.1

EXAMPLES OF BEHAVIOR MODIFICATION

While behavior modification has numerous possible organizational applications, examples of the most common uses are presented below:

- *To improve system performance* Emery Air Freight saved an estimated $3 million a year by using a behavior mod strategy that involved carefully measuring performance behaviors, charting these behaviors, and positively rewarding improvements. Behavior mod was used in three main areas: sales and sales training, operations, and containerized shipments. An example of a behavioral change is that on-time deliveries were happening only 30–40 percent of the time before OB mod and 90–95 percent of the time after behavior mod.[4] A research review that examined twenty-six studies to determine the impact on production found that all of the experiments improved production and that the average percentage increase was 64 percent.[5]

- *To improve attendance* When OB mod concepts are used to evaluate attendance behavior, we find that people are often rewarded for not coming to work because of sick pay or recreation programs. A large hardware store used a system where those people who had been at work and on time were eligible to participate in a monthly drawing for a major prize such as a color television. As a result "sick leave payments decreased by 62 percent and absenteeism and tardiness were down by 75 percent."[6] A summary of six research studies found an average decrease in absenteeism of 29 percent with a range from 2 percent to 50 percent.[7]

- *To reduce accidents* A behavior mod incentive program to reduce accidents among bus drivers resulted in a 25 percent decrease when compared to a control group that did not receive the incentives. Incentives (average value $5) included free gasoline and bus passes, plus the personal congratulations of the director of operations.[8]

- *For training* Programmed instruction methods are often based on behavior modification techniques. The trainee proceeds from one question to the next with immediate feedback about how accurate the answers (behaviors) are. This type of training has been used by IBM to train computer programmers, by Maytag to teach electronics skills, and by Zenith to teach sales representatives the features of their television sets.[9]

good performance, then it serves to motivate future performance. If rewards are not contingent upon performance, then they will not motivate behavior. The key parts of this process are knowing what behaviors represent good performance and developing a strategy for rewarding desired behaviors so that they will be strengthened. The first step in this management process is to target behaviors we may wish to change and then develop consequences that either strengthen or weaken the targeted behaviors.

Targeting Behavior for Change

The first step in applying OB mod is to identify the critical performance-related behaviors, called **target behaviors.** These are behaviors chosen by the manager for emphasis or focus. If OB mod were used to solve RDC's problems in the opening example, the first step would be to pinpoint those behaviors management wished to change. Perhaps the behavior might be the number of hours it takes for two framers to complete one house. It is important to concentrate on actual, specific behaviors—something that can be measured, observed, described, and counted.

Another example of targeting is the case of Helen Knapp, Vice President of Finance for RDC, who is having trouble with one of her employees. Here is how Helen describes her troublesome employee, Marline Godell:

"I'm fed up with Marline. She is sullen and hostile. Her constant talking annoys me and others. She has a very poor attitude and often talks back. And, she does poor quality work when and if she works at all."

What are the target behaviors here? It's hard to tell for sure, but the words "sullen," "poor attitude," and "annoys me," are not specific enough to begin targeting. Later, when Helen has learned to be more specific in targeting behavior, she describes Marline's behavior as follows:

"Marline talks almost constantly. In a one-hour period, I observed her to spend forty-eight minutes talking. She constantly frowns, I almost never see her smile. She is absent two or three times per month and late an average of twice a week. Her error rate of 8 percent is much higher than the other clerk's average of 3 percent and the standard of 5 percent."

Now we have some specific behaviors that might be targets for change:

1. talking frequency

2. frowns; doesn't smile

3. absent

4. late

5. error rate

Charting Target Behaviors.   The next step is to measure current behavior precisely. We need to know not only what behaviors to target, but how much and how often the behavior is happening. To accomplish this task systematically, we must measure and chart the frequency of behavior on some time dimension. This means we must **chart** how many hours it takes a carpenter to complete a house; or in the case of Marline's problems, how often she talks, how often she smiles, how many days per month she is absent, how many minutes or times she is late per week, and what percentage error rate she maintains in one month.

Normally, we would not attempt to change a large number of behaviors at one time because it gets too complex. We would target a few critical ones for charting and change. Perhaps, we would start with Marline's low quality or her tendency to come in late. Charting is usually done for a single employee who is the target for change (*see* Figure 6.2 for an example of charting the late behavior of a draftsman.) However, charting can also be done for an entire work unit or organization to measure organizational behavior from an overall perspective (*see* Figure 6.3 for an example).

Charting serves two purposes. First, it provides a way of observing actual behavior to see its scope and dimensions. For example, Helen may perceive that Marline never smiles when in fact Marline often smiles except when Helen is around. Thus, a frequency count might show less of a problem with this behavior than Helen perceived. The second purpose of charting is to provide a **baseline** (a trend over a period of time to serve as the base) for measuring

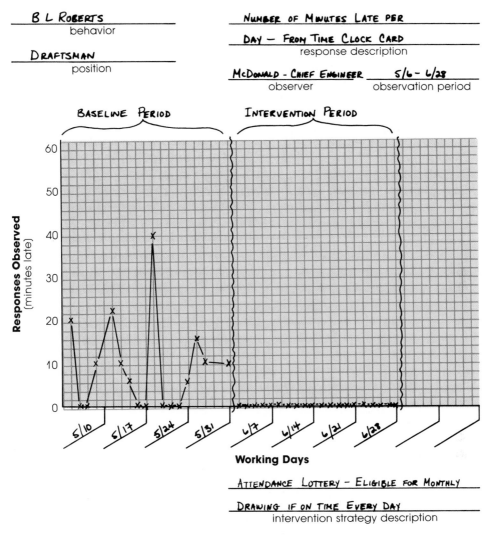

Figure 6.2

**BEHAVIORAL CHART FOR AN
INDIVIDUAL EXPRESSED IN NUMBER OF MINUTES LATE**

SOURCE: From *Organizational Behavior Modification* by Fred Luthans and Robert Kreitner. Copyright © 1975 by Scott, Foresman and Company. Reprinted by permission.

change. The only way we can tell if our change strategy is working is to observe actual changes in behavior over time. Referring to Figure 6.3, note the improvement in the on-time behavior of B.L. Roberts after an attendance lottery was started.

Strategies for Managing Reinforcement

ce we have charted the targeted behavior, we get down to the crux of the problem: developing the contingency relationships between behavior and consequences. The consequences that will increase behavior are positive reinforce-

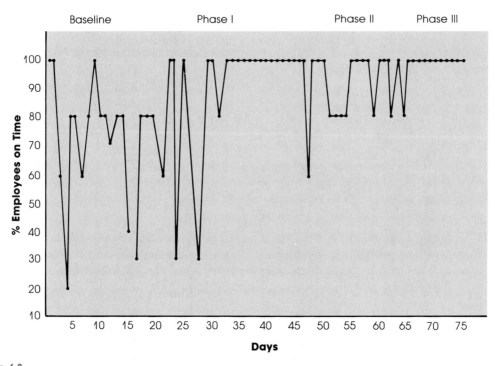

Figure 6.3

BEHAVIORAL CHART FOR AN
ORGANIZATION EXPRESSED IN PERCENTAGE OF EMPLOYEES ON TIME

SOURCE: From L.M. Miller, 1978, *Behavior Management: The New Science of Managing People at Work.*
Copyright © 1978 by John Wiley & Sons, Inc. Reprinted by permission of John Wiley & Sons, Inc.

ment (application of a desirable consequence) or negative reinforcement (removal of an aversive consequence.) The strategies for decreasing behavior are extinction (doing nothing) and punishment (application of an unpleasant, repugnant, or aversive consequence). Each of these consequences is described in the following paragraphs.

Positive Reinforcement.   When a desirable or pleasant outcome occurs after some behavior, the tendency is for us to repeat that behavior in the future. In other words **positive reinforcement** strengthens the response. Examples of positive reinforcement might be praise, doing a job particularly well, money, or simply a smile. It is important to note that all reinforcement strategies are specific to a given individual and situation. For example, RDC's framers would consider the completion of high-quality work as positively reinforcing. Management, on the other hand, might see a high quantity of work to be positively reinforcing. Another example of individual differences might be the refuse collectors in the last chapter who considered time off to be positively reinforcing. Others might find time off to be punishing.

Punishment.   When something bad or undesirable happens to you, the tendency is to avoid the behavior that caused it. **Punishment** is the application of an aversive or unpleasant stimulus that results in a decrease in the behavior.

Perspective 6.2

HOW THE EXCELLENT COMPANIES USE POSITIVE REINFORCEMENT

Peters and Waterman, authors of the best-selling book, *In Search of Excellence,* found that positive reinforcement was a major strategy employed by the excellent companies. Here are some examples they cite:

• Heinz Foods celebrates the "perfect failure." Why would anyone want to celebrate a failure? They say that since "research and development of new products is inherently risky, the only way to succeed at all is through lots of tries, and that a good try that results in some learning is to be celebrated even when it fails. As a by-product they legitimize and even create positive feelings around calling a quick halt to

an obviously failing proposition, rather than letting it drag on with resulting higher cost in funds and eventual demoralization." [10]

• IBM designs its sales quotas so that 70 to 80 percent of the salesforce can meet them and join the "Hundred Percent Club." One of IBM's competitors designs its sales compensation so that only 40 percent of the salesforce could reach their quota. This means that the other 60 percent feel like losers; they feel punished. Tom Peters says: "Label a man a loser and he'll start acting like one." [11]

• Tupperware's sales power is reinforced by Monday night "Rallys." During the Rally everyone marches onto the stage in reverse order of last week's sales—it's termed the "Count Up." All the while their peers are celebrating them by participating in "All Rise." Almost everyone receives some type of reward, pin, or badge if they have performed at all. Because of all the hoopla and applause, the event takes on a positive tone and people work hard to be included. [12]

Examples of punishment are reprimands, assignment to unpleasant duties, frowns, and fines. [13]

While punishment tends to decrease behavior, there are often undesirable side effects. We have all experienced the stomach-churning effects of punishment. It can arouse very strong emotions that can interfere with performance. There is also the possibility that the person who is punished may try to get even through sabotage or a work "slow down." Consequently, most experts recommend avoiding punishment except when there is an immediate need to stop some behavior, such as when safety is involved. [14]

Avoidance.   When people wish to escape or avoid some aversive situation or outcome, their behavior will be strengthened if they avoid the unpleasant situation. **Avoidance** (often called negative reinforcement or escape conditioning) means the removal of an unpleasant stimulus that results in an increase in behavior. This strategy is often confused with punishment, although the two differ rather sharply. Punishment is the application of an aversive stimulus, which later results in a decrease in behavior. Negative reinforcement involves the threat of or actual existence of an aversive stimulus before the behavior occurs. Any action that causes the unpleasant stimulus to be removed provides a sense of relief. Thus, in the future the behavior that resulted in getting rid of the aversive stimulus is more likely to be repeated.

An example of avoidance might be a manager who requires all subordinates to attend an early morning meeting whenever performance of the organization falls below a certain level. Subordinates would then work very hard to avoid the unpleasant early morning meetings and strive for a higher level of performance. The actual requirement of the meeting is punishment; however, the behavioral patterns that result from trying to escape the meetings is an example of avoidance.

Extinction.   When nothing happens, when no reinforcement or punishment follows a behavior, that behavior may decrease and eventually stop—a process called **extinction.** Ignoring someone is a conscious strategy of extinction.

For an example of the extinction strategy, say you have a secretary who just loves to spend the first fifteen or twenty minutes of each morning relating various stories about the previous evening. In the past, you have been politely listening, nodding, and smiling; in other words you have been positively reinforcing the behavior. But you would like to stop the behavior and decide on extinction as your strategy. You ignore all conversation after the first two or three minutes unless it pertains to work. After a few minutes without the reinforcement of your listening and responding, the secretary stops the conversation. Of course, there are limits to extinction because others may continue to reinforce the behavior even though you have stopped.

More examples of the contingencies are presented in Table 6.1.

Table 6.1

EXAMPLES OF TYPES OF CONTINGENCIES

Type of Contingency	Behavior	Managerial Action	Expected Outcome
Positive Reinforcement	Subordinate completes an accurate and thorough report	Praise the employee and make a note on the employee's performance appraisal	Increased performance
Avoidance	Angry verbalization by a valued employee about having to punch a time clock	Allow the employee to keep his or her own time record	More positive verbal support for the company
Punishment	Failure of a subordinate to wear safety glasses required by company regulations	Verbally reprimand and fined	Employee will wear glasses in the future, but may be alienated from manager and company
Extinction	Coworker frequently drops by your desk and interrupts your work	Keep on working with little or no interaction with the interrupting coworker	Decreased interruptions from the coworker

Using Reinforcement Strategies

Sometimes, an even more effective strategy is to use a combination of strategies, like positive reinforcement for desired behaviors and extinction or punishment for undesirable behaviors. The key issue is to decide whether you want to increase or decrease a behavior. Once that decision is made, you must select the appropriate strategy or combination of strategies as illustrated in Figure 6.4 and the specific reward or punishment to accompany the strategy.

For example, take the case of a large chain of department stores that wants to improve responsiveness of their salesforce.[15] To accomplish the objective, they use "mystery shoppers" who are really trained members of the management staff. Let's look at two strategies for dealing with salesforce behavior:

- *A negative approach*—the salesperson is sent a reprimand through channels for "not treating the customer well." As a result the salesperson feels punished and does not specifically know what to do to improve. As a result the person may learn to "avoid customers" rather than "improve treatment of customers."

- *A positive approach* —The mystery shopper tells the customer that he or she has "just acted in the best traditions of the company" in responding to Mrs. Snyder's complaint. This employee is going to feel good and will try to beat the bushes to find more Mrs. Snyders to treat well. In this case the employee learns that praise is associated with successfully dealing with customer problems.

Avoid Negative Strategies. Normally, negative strategies should be avoided because of the possibility of such undesirable side effects as alienation, dissatisfaction, emotional turmoil, conflict, and even sabotage. Threatening punishment to control behavior is almost like using blackmail—avoid it whenever possible because of the problems it causes. However, there are times when be-

CONSEQUENCE

		Reward Something desirable or pleasant	Aversive Stimulus Something unpleasant or undesirable
CONTINGENCY STRATEGY	**Apply**	POSITIVE REINFORCEMENT (behavior increases)	PUNISHMENT (behavior decreases)
	Withhold or Remove	EXTINCTION (behavior decreases)	AVOIDANCE (behavior increases)

Figure 6.4

CONTINGENCY STRATEGIES

SOURCE: Adapted from Luthans, F. (1981). *Organizational behavior* (3rd ed.). New York: McGraw-Hill, p. 251.

havior is so disruptive or dangerous that punishment must be used to achieve a rapid stop to the behavior, but even then it may be a good idea to use a positive reinforcement-punishment combination.

Which Rewards to Use?   There are many rewards to choose from. Table 6.2 provides a list of many common ones. The key is to find the rewards that work, are easy to administer, and are cost effective for the organization. Recognition, praise, and feedback are among the most common rewards. In a behavior modification program at Emery Air Freight (*see* Perspective 6.1), managers were taught to administer 150 kinds of recognition and praise, such as: [16]

- "Keep up the good work, Murray."

- "Great going, Joe."

- "I liked the ingenuity you showed just now getting those crates into that container. You're running pretty consistently at 98 percent of standard. And after watching you, I can understand why."

- "Let me buy you a cup of coffee."

Table 6.2

POSSIBLE ON–THE–JOB REWARDS FOR REINFORCING BEHAVIOR

Negotiables	(exchange for other rewards)
	Money
	Stocks and stock options
	Movie and theater tickets
	Vacation trips
	Time off with pay
	Profit sharing
Job-related	More job responsibility
	More task variety
	More feedback on job performance
	Opportunities to learn and grow
	Make decisions about work schedule and pace
	Recognition for achievements
Social	Pat on the back; compliments on work
	Smile; friendly greetings
	Verbal or nonverbal recognition or praise
	Friendly greetings
	Assignment to a desired work group
Consumables	After work wine and cheese parties
	Coffee break treats
	Dinners for two at company expense
	Beer parties
	Free lunches
Status	Office size
	Company car
	Office furnishings, chairs, desks
Visual and auditory	Office with a window
	Chance to redecorate work environment
	Plants

Schedules of Reinforcement

There are a number of different ways you can schedule the rewards we discussed in the last section. You can reward every desired behavior (called a **continuous** schedule); or you can reward based on a certain number of desirable responses (called a **ratio** schedule); or you can reward after a specified time period, (called an **interval** schedule). Since rewards, such as the ones shown in Table 6.2, are often expensive and difficult to administer, the ratio or interval methods are most commonly used. In the sections below, we will discuss combinations of these schedules with examples of each.

Fixed Interval.   When there is a fixed time period between reinforcements, we have a **fixed interval schedule.** For example, performance appraisals in most organizations are done annually (a fixed interval). With this type of reinforcement, behavior seems to increase as we get closer to the known time of reinforcement. For example, a person may perform rather sluggishly throughout much of the year, but when it gets close to performance appraisal time the person becomes a "ball of fire." A weekly or monthly paycheck is another example of a fixed interval schedule, since the pay comes at the same time period throughout the year. With fixed interval strategies, performance tends to improve just prior to reinforcement and fall off after reinforcement. If reinforcement stops, behavior will decrease rather rapidly.

Variable Interval.   When a reward is given at variable times (variable around some average time), then we have a **variable interval schedule.** An example of a variable interval schedule might be a boss who makes an inspection of work facilities twice a week, but with no specific times for making the inspections. This schedule keeps behavior, such as cleaning work areas, at higher levels because people do not know when they will be inspected (or reinforced)—thus they are always ready.

Fixed Ratio.   In a **fixed-ratio schedule** reinforcement is given after some fixed, or specified, number of responses. For example, fruit pickers on a farm who are paid by the bushel for the fruit they pick are working under a fixed-ratio schedule. In fact, almost all **piece-rate** pay systems (where people are paid for each piece produced) are fixed-ratio schedules. Another example might be a firm that gives an extra day of vacation for each thirty days worked without an absence or tardiness. Fixed-ratio schedules are powerful behavior modifiers, but if the rewards are removed behavior will decline very rapidly.

Variable Ratio.   Under the **variable-ratio schedule** an employee would perform the desired behavior a variable number of times before being reinforced. The reinforcement will vary around some average number of behaviors. For example, an office computer salesperson knows that on the average two sales will be made for every twenty-five calls; however, the salesperson does not know which customers will order. The slot machines in Atlantic City are geared for a variable ratio payoff. Each time you pull the handle there is a chance, say one in ten, that there will be some type of payoff. The payoffs may come after inserting one quarter or 100 quarters. Ratio schedules are the most

Table 6.3

SCHEDULES OF REINFORCEMENT

Schedule of reinforcement	*Nature of reinforcement*	*Effects on behavior when applied*	*Effects on behavior when perceived*	*Example*
Fixed interval	Reward on fixed time basis	Leads to average and irregular performance	Quick extinction of behavior	Weekly paycheck
Fixed ratio	Reward consistently tied to output	Leads quickly to very high and stable performance	Quick extinction of behavior	Piece-rate pay system
Variable interval	Reward given at variable intervals around some average time	Leads to moderately high and stable performance	Slow extinction of behavior	Monthly performance appraisal and reward at random times each month
Variable ratio	Reward given at variable output levels around some average output	Leads to very high performance	Slow extinction of behavior	Sales bonus tied to selling X accounts, but X constantly changes around some mean

SOURCE: From *Introduction to Organizational Behavior* by Richard M. Steers. Copyright © 1981 Scott, Foresman and Company. Reprinted by permission.

powerful sustainers of behavior; it declines very slowly if the reinforcement is removed.[17]

Table 6.3 provides examples of the four schedules of reinforcement.

How Often to Reward?   There is one other important consideration when designing OB mod programs: the frequency of reward. Rewards can be administered **continuously**—every desired behavior can be reinforced—or they can be administered on an **intermittent** or **variable basis.** Normally, a behavioral change strategy will begin by reinforcing every desired response. A secretary may be complimented every time an error-free letter is typed. Then, the rewards are gradually tapered off to a variable-ratio or variable-interval schedule. Instead of praising the secretary for every perfect letter, you begin skipping a time or two until you move to a schedule where you reinforce on the average every three perfect letters, but you do the reinforcement on a random basis. The gradual movement from continuous rewards to a more variable reward pattern is called **shaping.**[18]

Vicarious Reinforcement.   Gambling casino owners are very much aware of the danger of players (particularly inexperienced ones) not being reinforced

Perspective 6.3

RULES FOR USING BEHAVIOR MODIFICATIONS IN ORGANIZATIONS[19]

• *Rule 1: Don't reward all people the same.* Pay people based on their performance rather than rewarding all the people the same. When everyone is paid the same, the behavior of high-performing workers is being extinguished, while low performers are being rewarded.

• *Rule 2: Failure to respond has reinforcing consequences.* Doing nothing shapes behavior, too. Managers need to examine the consequences of doing nothing because it is an extinction strategy.

• *Rule 3: Be sure to tell a person what must be done to get reinforced.* The behaviors that are desired should be clear to the employee. Goals and standards should be specified and the rewards readily apparent.

• *Rule 4: Be sure to tell people what they are doing wrong.* If a manager fails to specify why a person is being punished or why a reward is being withheld, the person may associate the contingency with some past behavior rather than the target behavior.

• *Rule 5: Don't punish in front of others.* Punishing in front of others results in double punishment since the person not only receives the punishment but also must experience a loss of face in front of the group. In addition, the people who witness the punishment may also feel punished vicariously.[20]

• *Rule 6: Make the consequences equal to the behavior.* Be fair; do not over reward or under reward behavior. (See the discussion of equity theory in Chapter 5.)

---

quickly enough. They know that continuous reinforcement is the quickest method of establishing desirable behavior (in this case, putting money into the machine). However, to institute a continuous method at the outset would require either that the machine be rigged (which is against the law) or that they lose money. To approximate as closely as possible a continuous reinforcement schedule, the owners employ a concept known as **vicarious reinforcement,** or reinforcement through another person's experiences. Each machine is wired into a central control. Then, when any machine hits the jackpot, sirens wail, lights flash, and bells ring. This lets everyone else in the casino know that reinforcement is possible—for those who continue to insert money! Vicarious reinforcement can also work in organizational situations, such as a monthly "big winner" in a sales contest.[21]

An Example of OB Mod

Rick Gomez, a production foreman in the Rockard Machinery Manufacturing plant, noted that production for the past month was down.[22] He believed that the problem was centered around workers taking unscheduled breaks. Rick had observed people wandering around and going to the bathroom at times other than during the authorized break (10:00 to 10:15 A.M. or 3:00 to 3:15 P.M.) Thus, the target behavior was taking unauthorized breaks. Rick carefully observed the behavior over the period of a week and noted each instance of an unscheduled break. He found that indeed the workers were taking unauthorized breaks, mostly about 9:00 A.M., 11:00 A.M., 2:00 P.M. and 4:00 P.M.; in other words, in the hour between the schedule breaks. When asked why they were taking an unscheduled break the usual excuse was having to go to the bath-room—"I just couldn't wait."

From a behavior mod standpoint, Rick figured that the workers were being negatively reinforced for their behavior (they were escaping from a dull, boring, hot job) and at the same time they were being positively reinforced for the behavior (they had an extra chance to smoke, to socialize, to rest). Thus, there was a powerful force toward maintaining and strengthening the behavior.

What should Rick do? In most organizations where the managers are not fa-miliar with behavior mod, they would attempt to punish the offenders. This would be difficult because it is hard to prevent people from going to the bathroom if they really have to go, and how do you know if they do or don't? While punishment or the threat of punishment might decrease the undesirable behavior, it might also result in union grievances, production slowdowns, quality problems, or sabotage.

Rick solved the problem by computing the dollar value of the group incen-tive pay that was lost because of unscheduled breaks. He then fed this informa-tion back to the workers while pointing out that staying on the job meant money to them all. In this case, Rick was successful—the workers decided that money was a stronger reward than socializing with friends and withdrawing from the job. However, it is possible that the incentive reward would not be strong enough to offset the other behavior. If this had been the case, Rick would have the difficult problem searching for other reinforcers to resolve his problem.

Summary of Behavior Mod Application Steps

Now that we have covered the major aspects of OB mod, let's summarize how it is applied by referring to Figure 6.5. Behavior is first targeted for change [1] and charted [2] to formulate a baseline for measuring behavioral change. Then, depending upon whether the behavior is desirable or undesirable [3], a change strategy is chosen. For increasing desirable behaviors, we can use either positive reinforcement or avoidance [4]. For eliminating undesirable beha-viors, we use extinction and/or punishment [5]. A schedule of reinforcement (fixed interval, fixed-ratio, variable interval, or variable-ratio) must also be chosen. If the actual behavior we have been charting changes [6], then all we have to do is keep up the same reinforcement contingencies and schedule [7]. But, if the behavior does not change, we must select another contingency of reinforcement, or another schedule of reinforcement or both [8]. The process is continued until the desired behavioral response is obtained.

Is Behavior Modification Ethical?

Do managers have the ethical right to manipulate and control their employees' behavior? This issue is a central focus of Skinner's book, *Beyond Freedom and Dignity*.[23] It has also been a concern of a number of organizational theorists.[24] It can be argued that behavior mod strategies ignore the individuality of peo-ple, restrict freedom of choice, and ignore the fact that people can be motivated by intrinsic rewards.[25] Each of these arguments has some merit, but the

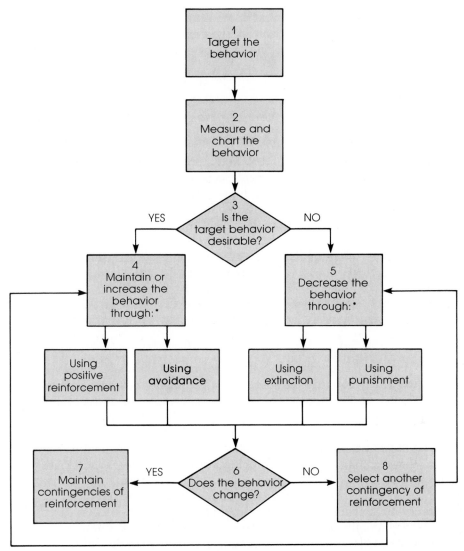

*A schedule of reinforcement (Table 6.3) must also be designed.

Figure 6.5

BEHAVIOR MODIFICATION APPLICATION

position of the critics often misrepresents and distorts the recommendations of behaviorists.[26]

On the positive side the argument runs like this: since a manager's task is to manage the behavior of employees so that they accomplish organization objectives, behavior mod is a natural and inevitable part of the managerial process. Skinner argues that we are constantly affecting others' behavior whether we intend to or not. Every time we smile, frown, criticize, or praise, we are reinforcing or punishing a behavior. We are all conscious or unconscious behavior modifiers. If so, why not recognize and understand what we are doing and make sure we reinforce those behaviors that are desirable?

An important aspect of any management strategy, including OB mod, is to avoid the misuse of behavioral control. In fact, if managers misuse behavior mod, they may find that workers will "no longer allow themselves to be pushed around," [27] but instead insist on fair and equitable treatment.

MOTIVATING WITH PAY

Pay is one of the most widely used, and often misused, rewards applied to motivate work behavior. Pay is simple because it can serve to reinforce so many needs. One person may want money to remodel a house while another may want money to buy a car. Most people find money to be desirable and positively reinforcing. Money can serve to fulfill our basic needs for shelter and food. It can and does serve as a status or esteem-related reward for many people, especially at management levels. But money costs the organization—it directly affects the bottom line. Thus, it may be one of the most costly ways of motivating people unless the increased performance pays for the increased pay.

In this section, we will briefly examine four major pay strategies: wages and salaries, merit pay, piece rates, and commissions.[28]

Wages and Salaries

Hourly, weekly, or monthly pay seldom motivates work behavior except for the decision to join or leave the organization—a very important consideration. The reason salary does not motivate is that wages and salaries are usually not *tied to performance.* For example, a carpenter with RDC receives $10 per hour while an office worker receives $1,800 per month. Each is paid regularly as long as they maintain some minimal level of performance. When there is no monetary incentive to perform, people are likely to perform only at a minimal acceptable level. Of course, people are often motivated by other factors such as the possibility of promotion or recognition; or, in the case of RDC's carpenters, by doing high quality work that resulted in feelings of satisfaction.

For pay to motivate, it must be tied to performance. In the next section, we will look at how merit pay attempts to do this.

Merit Pay and Performance Bonuses

To solve the problems posed by wages and salaries, we try to design **incentive systems**—those that will provide an incentive to perform. The first of three we will discuss is **merit pay,** a system used primarily with white-collar workers, that attempts to link pay with merit or performance. People who have performed the best this year will get, for example, a 20 percent pay raise, while those who are mediocre performers will get no raise. While this scheme sounds easy enough, it does not always work in practice.[29] The central problem is measuring work performance. As we observed in Chapter 4, performance appraisals are often distorted because of perceptual problems, such as stereotyping and halo and are thus imperfectly tied to performance.

There are a number of reasons for poor performance appraisals in addition to perceptual errors. For example, supervisors are sometimes more interested in keeping their employees happy than in improving performance. In addition, pay may not be seen as a reward if the person perceives inequities (see the discussion in Chapter 5 on equity theory). Even a pay raise may seem to be a threat if it is not as much as expected or lower than the raises of others.[30]

But, in spite of these difficulties, merit pay can be properly designed to motivate, and some organizations have been successful with this approach.[31] The key is to use a fair and accurate performance appraisal system, such as management-by-objectives (to be discussed in the next chapter). When merit pay is clearly tied to performance, it does motivate effective work behavior.

Bonuses Tied to Performance.   Senior managers' salaries are usually, but not always tied to organizational performance measured by such factors as return on equity, return on assets, or earnings per share. In 1985, CEO salaries consisted of 50 percent salary, 25 percent annual bonus based on the year's performance, and 25 percent long-term incentive based on a longer period of performance, such as three to five years. For example, the highest paid executive in 1986 was Lee Iacocca, Chairman of Chrysler who received almost $11 million in salary and current year bonuses and $9.6 million in long term compensation.[32]

Bonuses for lower and middle-level managers are not as common since their contributions may not be as directly related to performance as those of their bosses. A survey by Hay Management Consultants found that only 11 percent of the 600 companies queried used pay for performance bonuses at lower levels of the organizations. It is simply more difficult to tie pay to performance for many jobs. In addition, a middle-level manager making $40,000 per year may be afraid to risk 20 or 25 percent of his or her pay in a bonus system.

There have been a number of significant successes in pay-for-performance systems for lower-level salaried and hourly employees using **gainsharing,** an incentive plan that focuses on reducing costs or increasing sales or profits using employee involvement. Employees generate ideas and suggestions for improvements and a financial formula is worked out so that the resultant gains are shared by all employees.[33] Gainsharing has the advantage of getting work force involvement in improving the "bottom line," rather than just top management.[34]

Piece-Rate Pay

When someone is paid for the number of pieces or units that are produced, it is called **piece-rate** pay. In theory, a fixed-ratio reinforcement schedule, such as earning $1 for each toaster produced, should be a powerful motivator. It can be, but seldom is.

The problem with piece rates revolves around *standards*. How much time should one be allowed to produce one toaster? Say the standard says it should take ten minutes for a skilled employee to make a toaster. If the piece-rate is $1 for each toaster completed, then the skilled employee should make about $6 per hour. Ideally, the company would like to see each employee produce more,

Perspective 6.4

KNOWLEDGE–BASED PAY

A new approach to pay that is receiving wide attention is **knowledge-based pay** (KBP).[35] An employee is paid based upon the knowledge and skills possessed. When first starting out, the person receives a flat hourly rate. As more skills are learned, the hourly pay rate is increased. Pay increases are directly contingent upon mastery of a specific skill. KBP is usually combined with a number of other organizational strategies, such as participative management, job enrichment (*see* Chapter 7), or sociotechnical systems (*see* Chapter 15).

Since people are rewarded for increasing their knowledge and skill, these are the primary outcomes of the reinforcement strategy. KBP creates an environment that makes rotating workers from job to job the norm, thus giving managers considerable flexibility. Direct hourly wage costs are higher in KBP plants, but there

are often savings in reduced turnover, lower costs of absences, and increased productivity. Training costs are also higher due to the added effort to teach everyone the entire array of jobs in the plant.[36] We would expect that not everyone would find this method positively reinforcing. If one has high needs for esteem and growth, then KBP will probably be viewed as motivational; if not, then it will be seen as a source of dissatisfaction and punishment.

One American car manufacturer has recently gone to KBP.[37] Workers in their unionized plants are divided into teams that average about twelve people. New employees enter at the standard entry hourly rate. The new worker is then rotated throughout the group's area of responsibility until all the jobs are learned. Once all the jobs for the *entire* group are learned, the person gets a raise. Another pay increase can be obtained by transferring to another group and learning all the skills associated with that group. Results are positive, especially in terms of increased flexibility for managers and for decreased resistance to job changes.

---

say seven to eight an hour. But what if almost everyone produces twelve toasters per hour with what seems to be little effort? And what if the foreman makes only $10 per hour—$2 less than the average employee? Something has to give. What usually happens is that management says, "Whoops, we made a mistake. The rate should be $.50 per toaster, not the overly generous dollar." It is pretty easy to predict what will happen. The employees will be disgruntled, they will feel betrayed and punished, they will cease to respond to piecework as a motivation scheme.

Thus, piece-rate pay schemes may not result in improved performance because workers may perceive that performance will not lead to the desired outcomes in the long run.[38] Even when an individual believes that performance will lead to outcome, group members may exert so much pressure that the individual conforms (more information on these group issues will be covered in Chapter 9).

Commissions

Many sales positions are paid on a **commission** or commission-plus-salary basis. The pay is usually based on a percentage of the value of the total sales made by the individual; for example, 5 percent of every sale made by the car salesperson goes to the individual as pay. Some of the same problems discussed under piecework apply to commission pay schemes. It is possible to find an organization's best sales representative making more than the boss. Thus, informal limits to sales commissions are sometimes established and enforced.

Another problem with commissions is that they foster competition between salespeople, and that can cause friction. For example, in a furniture sales business the salespeople were stealing each others customers, thus causing a great deal of friction and conflict that was alienating customers. In this case there may be a tendency for the short-term goal of commission maximization to overrule the perhaps more important long-term goal of customer satisfaction.

In spite of these problems, commission-pay systems can work quite well, especially when a salesperson works alone. Many sales jobs do not require teamwork, and thus, group pressure to perform is often lower than with piecework. Commissions provide immediate and direct link of pay with performance (behavior and contingency are linked), and they may provide a gauge of achievement for the high-achieving individual who often gravitates to sales.

Conclusions About Using Pay for Motivation

Most wage and salary systems do not motivate behavior because they are based on a fixed interval schedule with little direct ties to work performance. Merit, incentive, and commission pay all seek to rectify this problem by linking pay with performance. Knowledge-based pay links pay with numbers of skills learned and results in increased flexibility for managers. While there are problems with evaluating performance and setting standards that may frustrate our efforts to design these systems, these incentive systems can and often do serve as effective motivators of work behavior. The key is to link pay unambiguously and fairly with the desired work behavior. One effective way to do this is by setting clear goals, the topic covered in the next chapter.

CROSS–CULTURAL OB: THREE WAYS OF DEALING WITH TARDINESS

Tardiness for work is dealt with quite differently in the United States, Great Britain, and Japan.[39] In the United States, late-to-work behavior is usually dealt with by reprimands or by docking the employee's pay. Employees sometimes call in sick rather than get a reprimand for being late.

In Great Britain, a worker who is a few minutes late may take a different approach. For example, one worker was observed to head straight for his work quarters where he enjoyed a cup of tea and smoked his pipe rather than starting to work.

The reason for this behavior is that in Great Britain people are paid by the quarter hour. Thus a person who is two minutes late might as well relax since he or she will not be paid for the next thirteen minutes. In addition, the union structure makes it difficult for management to take more serious action against the late British worker. The reinforcement system is designed, perhaps unintentionally, to foster this behavior.

Table 6.4

REWARD SYSTEMS FOR THE UNITED STATES AND JAPAN

	United States	*Japan*
Relation of salary benefits to individual performance	*High:* Attempts are made to reward outstanding individual performance directly.	*Low:* Individual performance is not formally evaluated for ten years after entering the firm; salary progression is automatic.
Compensation differentials	*Large:* The combinations of salaries, fringes, and "perks" of office sharply differentiate rewards among supervisors at different levels.	*Small:* There are small differences in salary levels, and few "perks" of office.
Salary levels	*Relatively high:* Salaries, compared with those in nonbusiness firms, are high.	*Relatively low:* Fringe benefits are liberal, but salary bases are low.
Degree to which group bonuses and profit sharing are used	*Relatively limited:* Bonuses and profit sharing are a small part of total compensation except for CEOs and division managers.	*Extensive:* Bonuses can be sizeable; they are paid every six months or year.
Criteria for promotion	Criteria are relative performance and minimum educational degree (such as B.S. or M.B.A.).	Criteria are ranks, seniority, education, successful passing of examinations.
Rate of promotion	*Rapid:* Where performance is outstanding, rapid advancement is the rule.	*Slow:* Only time is considered; first review may be after ten years.

SOURCE: Abridged from Melcher, A.J., & Arogyaswamy, B. (1982). Decision and compensation systems in the United States and Japan: Contrasting approaches to management. In *Management by Japanese Systems* edited by Sang M. Lee and Gary Schwendiman. Copyright © 1982 Praeger Publishers. Reprinted and excerpted by permission of Praeger Publishers.

In Japan, tardiness is often handled quite differently. Upon reporting for work the late worker is apt to say, "Make today one of my paid holidays." However, the worker will continue working all day and even work the overtime shift without compensation. (People who are on holiday cannot collect overtime.)

What accounts for these strange behaviors? In the United States a person who calls in sick is often paid for that time off. Compare a day off with the other possibility—a reprimand for lateness. It is no contest which behavior will win.

The Japanese behavior is perhaps most bizarre from a Western point of view, but consider the following factors. Japanese employees take only 40 percent of their paid holidays. Even then, many of these holidays are spent sick in bed. Many Japanese workers feel such a strong obligation to their company and coworkers that they do not want to let them down by taking their vacation, even though they are entitled to it. Since the typical employee has extra vacation days, it is much better to take one when tardy rather than creating a reputation for being a "lazy bum," who is not mentally prepared for work and thus desecrates the workplace. However, by working on a paid holiday, one earns the reputation of an industrious, dedicated worker. Since group acceptance, status, and loyalty are important reinforcers, it is not surprising that this behavior is common.

While this comparison of behaviors across three cultures shows great diversity, people in all three instances were responding to the reinforcers they found to be desirable. In other words, the principles of organizational behavior modification can explain the behaviors in all three instances. Reward systems are often tied to the culture. For example, examine the differences in compensation and promotions between the United States and Japan in Table 6.4.

MANAGERIAL APPLICATIONS OF BEHAVIOR MOD AND PAY

This chapter revolves around people's behaviors in response to various reinforcements. Managers need to be very clear what they are reinforcing when they make a decision regarding rewards or punishments. Since managers are constantly shaping the behavior of their subordinates, it is crucial that they focus attention on the process. The following points summarize some of the major managerial applications of the reward processes discussed in the chapter.

• *Use behavior mod to solve behavioral problems.* Whenever specific behaviors can be identified, they can be targeted for change by the manager. For example, research shows that performance can be improved, attendance enhanced, and accidents reduced.

• *Make your goals clear to your employees.* Be sure people know what they must do to get the reward. Provide feedback to let them know how they are doing.

• *Use positive reinforcement as your primary strategy.* Pay careful attention to reward selection since different people will respond to different types of rewards. Be sure to reward the behavior you want—do not reward people for absences unless you do not want them to come to work.

• *Avoid punishment whenever possible.* Since negative strategies often have undesirable side effects, avoid them whenever you can. If you must punish, do it in private since public punishment results in vicarious punishment for all those present.

• *Remember that failure to respond has consequences.* When a manager does nothing, employees will take it as extinction or even punishment. In either case, behavior is liable to decline when ignored.

• *Carefully manage the timing of rewards.* Generally, immediate rewards are more powerful, although the variable ratio schedule can result in long-term behavior reinforcement. A variety of rewards and reinforcement schedules may be the best approach.

• *Do not expect wages and salaries to motivate.* Since most wage and salary programs are not related to performance, do not expect them to improve work behavior. However, wages do serve to attract and retain people and they are related to feelings of equity or inequity.

• *Whenever possible, tie pay to performance.* Use bonuses, merit pay, piecework, or commissions to improve work performance. However, be aware of the problems associated with these systems. Gainsharing plans may overcome some of the difficulties associated with incentive pay by using group processes and involving the entire work force.

FOR DISCUSSION

1. How does the S–O–B–C process, shown in Figure 6.1, relate to motivation theories discussed in Chapter 5?

2. What managerial problems seem most susceptible to behavior mod strategies? Why?

3. Identify some behavior you wish to change. Precisely target the behavior and actually record the frequency of behavior on a chart. What problems did you encounter?

4. What is the difference between avoidance and punishment?

5. Weigh the pros and cons of all the reinforcement contingency strategies.

6. How does a manager determine which reward is appropriate for changing behavior?

7. How often must behavior be reinforced to maintain or increase it? Which reinforcement schedule is the most long-lasting?

8. Do you believe that behavior mod is ethical? Defend your position.

9. Design a pay system for a fast-food restaurant that would be motivating.

10. When would knowledge-based pay be appropriate? What are the advantages and disadvantages of such pay?

11. Under what circumstances is pay not motivating?

12. How does behavior modification explain the contrasting behaviors associated with lateness in the United States, Great Britain, and Japan?

KEY CONCEPTS AND TERMS

organizational behavior modi-
    fication
S–O–B–C model
contingencies of reinforcement
target behaviors
charting behaviors
positive reinforcement
punishment

avoidance
extinction
vicarious reinforcement
fixed-interval schedules
fixed-ratio schedules
variable-interval schedules
variable-ratio schedules

shaping
incentive systems
merit pay
gainsharing
knowledge-based pay
piece-rate pay
commission pay

Cases and Incidents

THE SLOPPY SECRETARY

Helen Greco has recently been promoted to the position of Senior Analyst for the Research Directorate with a federal space agency. She has a personal secretary, Gladys Moore, who types research reports and correspondence, and does other normal secretarial duties. Gladys is a career civil servant. She has worked for the agency for over ten years. She is personable and performs most of her secretarial duties quite well.

But Gladys has a serious problem with typing accuracy. She types extremely fast—over 100 words per minute—but she makes many errors. She is not good at proofreading so most of the errors go undetected until Helen reviews the report. With two to three errors per page, Helen finds she is quite frustrated trying to find and correct them. Then, upon retyping, she has to carefully read again because new errors crop up. Helen has talked to Gladys and urged her to be more careful, but her performance has not changed. It is almost impossible to fire a career civil servant like Gladys, and a transfer is out of the question.

DISCUSSION QUESTIONS

1. How could behavior modification be used to improve Gladys' error rate?

2. Design a behavior mod program to correct the problem. Specify the steps that would be taken.

THE RATEBUSTING SALESWOMAN

Of the six people in the boy's department of a large department store, one stood out as a ratebuster: Mrs. Brown. She was small physically and very active. She had worked for the store for eight years. The other people in the department were quite cool towards Mrs. Brown since they thought she was a *"saleshog."* In other words, she would do her best to get every sale she could even at the expense of the other clerks.

The pay system was based on an hourly rate plus commission. The amount of commission was based on a quota for the current year based on the past year's performance. Clerks were paid only the hourly rate until the quota had been reached and then they were paid a commission of 5 percent of total sales for every sale they made above the quota. Commissions were paid monthly.

Mrs. Brown's sales were consistently almost twice as much as the other people in the department. Her high sales were attributable to several tactics:

- She learned when special sales were scheduled and called her customers about possible layaways.
- She acted as if she had an exclusive right to any customer that she had ever served before.
- She would skip lunch and breaks so she could be on the lookout for affluent new customers.
- She would lay claim to as many customers as possible. If she was serving one person and a likely customer came through the door, she would lay their merchandise aside and greet the new customer even though other salespersons were not busy.

DISCUSSION QUESTIONS

1. Did this pay system motivate? Why?

2. Is the system appropriate for this type of organization?

3. What dysfunctional consequences from Mrs. Brown's behavior do you predict?

4. Could the system be redesigned to be more effective?

Adapted from an example given by Dalton, M. (1974). The ratebuster: The case of the saleswoman. In P.L. Steward & M.G. Cantor (Eds.). *Varieties of Work Experience: The social control of occupational groups and roles* (pp. 206–214). New York: Schenkman.

LINCOLN ELECTRIC COMPANY

Lincoln Electric Company is the world's largest manufacturer of arc-welding equipment—primarily electric welding machines and electrodes. The company employs approximately 2400 workers in its two main plants near Cleveland. Lincoln is reported to have a 25.4 percent share of the welding equipment market (more than twice that of its nearest competitor), and that figure is expected to remain stable through 1987. It also markets its products through more than seventy company-owned distribution centers in thirty-six states and claims to have one of the largest distribution networks in the country. Lincoln has been so successful that it dictates the price structure of the welding industry.

The company was founded in 1895 by John C. Lincoln. James F. Lincoln, John's younger brother, joined the firm in 1907 and is largely responsible for the company's innovative labor practices and unique culture. He was a firm believer in the principles of hard work and individual initiative. These principles are reflected in the company motto: "The actual is limited; the possible immense." Lincoln also believed that those who work hard and perform well should share in the benefits of their labor. Each employee is expected to be loyal to the firm, and the company is obligated to share the benefits gained from improved sales and productivity. It was long Lincoln's position that the welfare of the firm and its customers is related directly to the welfare of the employees.

In 1914, for example, James Lincoln established a committee of elected employee representatives to advise him on company operations. In 1915 the company gave each employee a paid life insurance policy. An employee's association was established in 1919 to provide health benefits and social activities. A piecework wage system providing paid vacations and cost-of-living adjustments was in place by 1923 and, in 1925, an employee stock purchase plan was initiated. By 1944, Lincoln employees benefited from a number of progressive personnel programs, including a pension plan, a policy of internal promotion, and guaranteed employment. Perhaps the best-known aspect of the "Lincoln System" is the Lincoln bonus plan.

In 1934 the company was faced with reduced sales and increasing demand from employees for more hours of work. In an effort to boost productivity, an annual bonus plan was adopted whereby employees could boost their compensation significantly, depending on their base salary and merit rating and overall company profits. That year the bonus averaged 30 percent of wages and, since then, a bonus has been paid every year, sometimes amounting to 50 percent of wages. In 1981 Lincoln's incentive bonus plan paid an average of $22,008 per employee over and above regular wages and benefits.

The values of hard work, loyalty, security, sharing, and thrift that are at the core of Lincoln's culture survive today. For example, in addition to the advisory committees and compensation and benefit systems already mentioned, the organization emphasizes equality. All employees use the same plant entrance and eat in the same cafeteria. There are no assigned parking spaces and no separate office buildings. The corporate offices have few, if any, status distinctions. Desks and office furnishings are uniform and seem to date from the 1940s. There are few private offices and few of the amenities one would normally expect to find in a corporate headquarters. Not even the president's office is carpeted. A visitor gets the impression that everything is functional and well maintained but that not a penny is spent on unnecessary or frivolous furnishings.

These values are also evident in the manufacturing areas. Employees always seem to be busy and engaged in purposeful activity. There is very little social interaction or wasted time. Plenty of in-process inventory is available at each work station so that employees get the feeling that there is plenty to do. Most workers take no coffee breaks, and little supervision is required.

The corporate culture is also reflected in the structure of Lincoln Electric. Communication channels to management are open, and no doors are closed to workers. Lincoln never has had an organizational chart and encourages people to take problems to whomever they feel is best equipped to help them. Supervisors have wide spans of control because there is little need for routine supervision.

DISCUSSION QUESTIONS

1. What energizes, directs, and sustains behavior at Lincoln Electric?

2. How does the value system relate to motivation?

3. Why has Lincoln Electric been so successful over such an extended period of time?

From Martin, H.J. (1985). Managing specialized corporate cultures. In R.H. Kilmann, M.J. Saxton, R. Serpa, and associates (Eds.). *Gaining control of the corporate culture* (pp. 149–159). San Francisco: Jossey-Bass. Used with permission.

REFERENCES

1. For reviews of the application of behavior mod to organizations, *see* O'Hara, K., Johnson, C.M., & Beehr, T.A. (1985). Organizational behavior management in the private sector: A review of empirical research and recommendations for further investigation. *Academy of Management Review, 10,* 848–864. Hamner, W.C., & Hamner, E.P. (1976). Behavior modification on the bottom line. *Organizational Dynamics, Spring,* 3–21. Babb, H.W., & Kopp, D.G. (1978). Applications of behavior modification in organizations: A review and critique. *Academy of Management Review, 3,* 281–292.

2. Davis, T.R.V., & Luthans, F. (1980). A social learning approach to organizational behavior. *Academy of Management Review, 5,* 281–290.

3. Hamner and Hamner (1976).

4. See At Emery Air Freight: Positive reinforcement boosts performance. (1973). *Organizational Dynamics, 1,* 41–50.

5. Hopkins, B.L., & Sears, J. (1982). Managing behavior for productivity. In W. Fredericksen (Ed.). *Handbook of organizational behavior management.* New York: Wiley-Interscience, pp. 393–425.

6. Babb and Kopp (1978).

7. Kempen, R.W. (1982). Absenteeism and tardiness. In Fredericksen (pp. 365–391).

8. Hayes, R.S., Pine, R.C., and Fitch, H.G. (1982). Reducing accident rates with organizational behavior modification. *Academy of Management Journal, 25,* 407–416. Sulzer-Azaroff, B. (1982), Behavioral approaches to occupational health and safety, in Fredericksen (pp. 505–538).

9. Babb and Kopp (1978), p. 285. Also see Mirman, R. (1982). Performance management in sales organizations. In Fredericksen (pp. 427–475).

10. Peters, T.J., & Waterman, R.H. (1982). *In search of excellence.* New York: Harper & Row, p. 69.

11. Peters and Waterman (1982), p. 57.

12. Peters and Waterman (1982), p. 123.

13. A more detailed discussion of punishment in organizations can be found in Arvey, R.D., & Ivancevich, J.M. (1980). Further thoughts on punishment in organizations. *Academy of Management Review, 5,* 133–138. Also see Arvey, R.D., Davis, G.A., & Nelson, S.M. (1984). Use of discipline in an organization: A field study. *Journal of Applied Psychology, 69,* 448–460. And Beyer, J., & Trice, H.M. (1984). A field study of the use and perceived effects of discipline in controlling work performance. *Academy of Management Journal, 27,* 743–764.

14. Wheeler, H.N. (1976). Punishment theory and industrial discipline. *Industrial Relations, 15,* 235–43.

15. Adapted from Peters and Waterman (1982), p. 68.

16. Examples from At Emery Air Freight: Positive reinforcement boosts productivity (1973).

17. Hamner, W.C. (1982). Using reinforcement theory in organizational settings. In H.L. Tosi and W.C. Hamner (Eds.). *Organizational behavior and management* (3rd ed.). (pp. 534–541). New York: Wiley.

18. Skinner, B.F. (1969). *Contingencies of reinforcement.* New York: Appleton-Century-Crofts.

19. Hamner, W.C. (1982). Reinforcement theory. In Tosi and Hamner (pp. 191–208). And Jablonsky, S., & Devries, D. (1972). Operant conditioning principles extrapolated to the theory of management. *Organizational Behavior and Human Performance, 7,* 340–358.

20. Schnake (1986).

21. For more information on vicarious reinforcement, see Manz, C.C., & Sims, H.P., Jr. (1981). Vicarious learning: The influence of modeling on organizational behavior. *Academy of Management Review, 6,* 105–113. And Schnake, M.E. (1986). Vicarious punishment in a work setting. *Journal of Applied Psychology, 71,* 343–345.

22. Based on an example originally presented in Luthans (1981). For additional information about implementing behavior mod programs, see Luthans F., & Kreitner (1985). *Organizational behavior modification and beyond.* Glenview, IL: Scott, Foresman.

23. Skinner, B.F. (1971). *Beyond freedom and dignity.* New York: Knopf.

24. See Fry, F.L. (1974). Operant conditioning in organizational settings: Of mice or men? *Personnel, 51* (4), 17–24. And a series of articles in the *Academy of Management Review* beginning with Locke, E.A. (1977). The myths of behavior mod in organizations (*2,* 543–553). And ending with Parmerlee, M., & Schwenk, C. (1979). Radical behaviorism in organizations: Misconceptions in the Locke-Gray debate (*4,* 601–607). For an interesting debate on organizational behavior mod, see the Luthans-Smith debate in Karmel, B. (1980). *Point and counterpoint in organizational behavior* (pp. 47–93). Hinsdale: Dryden.

25. For a review see Hamner, W.C. (1983). In Tosi and Hamner.

26. Hamner (1983).

27. Hamner (1983), p. 541.

28. For thorough coverage of pay issues see Wallace, M.J., Jr., and Fay, C.H. (1983). *Compensation theory and practice.* Boston: Kent. And Lawler, E.E., III (1981). *Pay and organizational development.* Reading, MA: Addison-Wesley.

29. See Hamner, W.C. (1975). How to ruin motivation with pay. *Compensation Review* (3rd Quarter). And Golberg, M.H. (1977). Another look at merit pay programs. *Compensation Review* (3rd Quarter, 20–28). Also see Latham, G.P. & Wexley, K.N. (1981). *Increasing productivity through performance appraisal.* Reading, MA: Addison-Wesley.

30. For a complete discussion of pay issues, including equity, see Lawler, E.E., III (1971). *Pay and organizational effectiveness: A psychological view.* New York: McGraw-Hill. Also see Martin, J.E. & Peterson, M.E. (1987). Two tier wage structures: Implications for equity theory. *Academy of Management Journal, 30,* 297–315.

31. Hamner (1975) and Golberg (1977) have some suggestions for making merit pay systems work.

32. Bennett, A., (1986, February 28). More managers find salary, bonus are tied directly to performance, *The Wall Street Journal.* And Executive Pay: who got what in '86. *Business Week,* May 4, 1987, 50 cf.

33. Doyle, R.J. (1983). *Gainsharing and productivity: A guide to planning implementation, and development.* New York: AMACOM. For an example, see Schuster, M. (1984). The Scanlon plan: A longitudinal analysis. *Journal of Applied Behavioral Science, 20,* 23–38.

34. Lawler, E.E., III (1986). *High involvement management: Participative strategies for improving organizational performance.* San Francisco: Jossey-Bass.

35. Tosi, H., & Tosi, L. (1986). What managers need to know about knowledge-based pay. *Organizational Dynamics, 14* (Winter), 52–64. Also see Lawler, E.E., III, & Ledford, G.E., Jr. (1985). Skill-based pay: A concept that's catching on. *Personnel,* September.

36. Tosi and Tosi (1986).

37. Tosi and Tosi (1986).

38. See Wallace and Fay (1983). For classic studies showing the effects of piece work, see Whyte, W. (1955). *Money and motivation.* New York: Harper and Row. And Hickson, D. (1961). Motives of people who restrict their output. *Occupational Psychology, 35,* 479–503.

39. Examples and data in this section are taken from Sengoku, T. (1985). *Willing workers: The work ethics in Japan, England, and the United States.* Westport, CT: Quorum Books.

Chapter Seven

JOB DESIGN
AND
GOAL SETTING

PREVIEW

- What makes one job so good that we really like it and another one so bad we cannot stand it?

- How can flexible working hours help enrich almost any job?

- How can a manager actually conduct a job enrichment effort? Learn the steps with the aid of a self-help guide.

- What is a self-managing work group?

- Did you know that the mere presence of goals can result in increased performance?

- Can you write a clear, specific goal? Learn how.

- Which motivation strategy is the most powerful: goals, job enrichment, or money?

MAJOR TOPICS

Preview Case: The Word Processing Center

Job Design

Goal Setting

Choosing a Motivation Strategy

Cross-Cultural OB: Enriching Jobs at Volvo in Sweden

Managerial Applications of Job Design and Goal Setting

Preview Case

THE WORD PROCESSING CENTER

Wendy Maki thought to herself that she had worked hard to get here. And she was pleased. Just think, only six years ago she had been a typist (for another firm). Now she was the new Director of Administration for Sun Island Corp. It had been a lot of work to finish college on a part-time basis, but she had done it and now she was beginning to reap the rewards.

During her interviews Wendy had learned that the past director left because he could not get the Word Processing Center (one of several divisions under her) performance up to the level expected by top management. It seems that all the operators are disgruntled and dissatisfied. They leave the first chance they get. So far it has been relatively easy to find replacements, but each new person must be trained and some just don't work out.

Sun Island seems to be losing money and effectiveness because of the problem. There has even been discussion that the Word Processing Center is nothing but a typing pool and should thus be disbanded, with all operators returning to separate directors. (Perhaps the word processing center *is* the modern-day equivalent of a typing pool, using sophisticated, computer technology.)

Wendy figures that her knowledge of working-level people combined with her academic preparation will yield the key to motivating these people.

Managers are sometimes confronted with complex problems that simultaneously involve poor performance and job dissatisfaction. Sometimes these problems are centered around the very structure of the job itself—its design. In this chapter, we will discuss two major strategies for dealing with structural problems: job design and goal setting. We will see some possible solutions to Wendy's problem and for the problem that Reliance Development Co. was experiencing in Chapter 6—that of framers who were motivated to produce high quality but low quantity.

JOB DESIGN

Every time a manager assigns work, gives instructions, or checks to make sure something is done, job redesign is taking place.[1] Consciously or unconsciously, managers are constantly changing the jobs of their subordinates. Since this type of change is inevitable, it makes sense to plan the structure of jobs deliberately so that they are as motivating as possible. That is what this section is about—systematically redesigning jobs as part of the basic managerial task.

What is Job Design?

Job design is the deliberate, purposeful planning of a job including all its structural and social aspects and their effects on employees. It is a broad concept that can refer to any part or combination of parts of the job. Figure 7.1 provides an overview of job design that highlights its interconnecting, overlapping dimensions. It also indicates that the environment—unions, bosses, technology, working conditions, personnel policies, wages, structure—all affect job design.

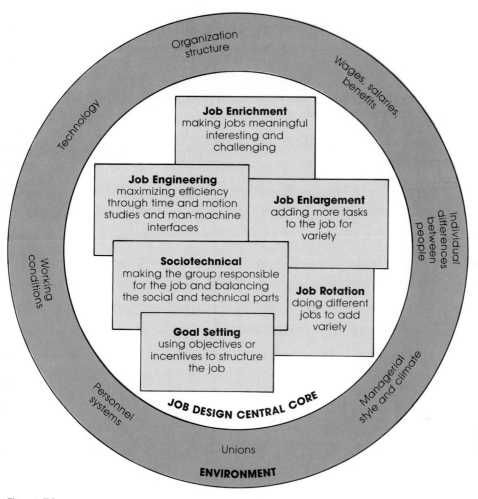

Figure 7.1

THE DIMENSIONS OF JOB DESIGN

SOURCE: From Umstot, D. (1983). Job Design. In D. Hellriegel & J.W. Slocum & R. W. Woodman. *Organizational Behavior* (3rd ed.). Copyright © 1983 by West Publishing Company, St. Paul, Minn. Used with permission.

In this section, we will concentrate most heavily on one aspect of job design—job enrichment. This strategy is aimed at improving employee motivation and work satisfaction.[2] We will also briefly cover the sociotechnical approach to job design that is being used by Volvo and many other companies.

Job Enrichment Concepts

Job Characteristics.   While there are several approaches to job enrichment,[3] the **job characteristics model,** developed by Hackman and Oldham and shown in Figure 7.2, has been selected because it clearly specifies the characteristics that are needed to create an enriching job.[4] Thus, we will define **job enrichment** as the process of making jobs more interesting, meaningful, and challenging by using the proper blend of the following job dimensions or characteristics: [5]

- *Skill variety* —doing different things; using valued skills, abilities, and talents; using complex and high-level skills.

- *Task identity* —doing the entire piece of work from beginning to end; the whole job rather than bits and pieces.

- *Task significance* —the degree to which the job has a meaningful impact on others in the organization; the importance of the job in the broader scheme of things.

- *Autonomy* —chances to use personal initiative and judgment; freedom to do the work; discretion in scheduling, decision making, and means for accomplishing the job.

- *Feedback* —clear and direct information from the job itself about job outcomes and performances. Knowing whether you performed well after completing a job.

Psychological States. The presence of the five job characteristics creates three psychological states: experienced meaningfulness of the work, experienced responsibility for work outcomes, and knowledge of actual results of work actions. When these psychological states are present, a number of positive personal and work outcomes are predicted. People will feel better about themselves and their jobs and will more likely do high quality work. Figure 7.2 shows all of the predicted outcomes.

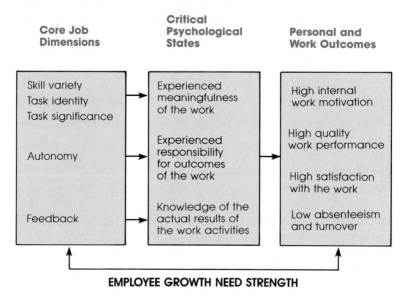

Figure 7.2

JOB CHARACTERISTICS MODEL

SOURCE: From J.R. Hackman and G.R. Oldham (1975). Development of the diagnostic survey, *Journal of Applied Psychology* 60:161. Copyright 1975 by the American Psychological Association. Reprinted/adapted by permission of the authors and publisher.

Growth Need Strength. As we saw in Chapter 5, growth needs are the need to develop, to learn, to experience new skills, and to have a challenge. Growth need strength moderates the relationship between job characteristics and the predicted outcomes. People with high growth need strength respond more favorably to job enrichment than do those with low growth need strength.[6] Apparently, a low growth need strength inhibits the formation of critical psychological states. Thus, for that person, the job may be unenriched in spite of a generous amount of all the necessary job characteristics.

An Enriched Job: The Surgeon. A job that is high on all core job dimensions is that of the surgeon. There is a constant opportunity for using highly varied skills, abilities, and talents in diagnosing and treating illnesses. There is plenty of task identity since the same surgeon normally does the diagnosis, performs the operation, and monitors the convalescence. Task significance is also high, since much of the surgeon's work is life or death to the patient. Autonomy is quite high since the physician is the final authority on the procedures and techniques of the job. Finally, the feedback from the job is excellent because the surgeon can tell almost immediately if the operation was successful. And, of course, a fully recovered patient is powerful feedback.

Social Influences on Job Perceptions

While jobs are certainly affected strongly by the way they are constructed, they also are affected by the social environment.[7] Inputs from coworkers, supervisors, union stewards, consultants, and others can significantly alter our perceptions of job characteristics. Based on our study of perception in Chapter 4, we should not be surprised by this phenomenon—reality is in the mind of the perceiver, not necessarily with the objective situation at hand. For example, a manager may have carefully designed a job to have all the enriching characteristics. However, an alienated core of workers may tell every new person: "This job is the pits. It is boring and uninteresting. You won't like it." With these types

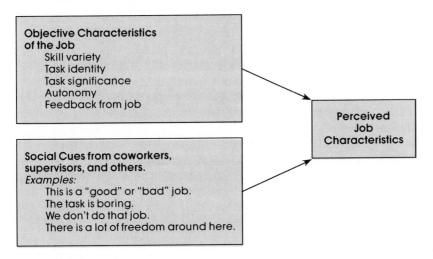

Figure 7.3

HOW SOCIAL CUES AFFECT PERCEIVED JOB CHARACTERISTICS

of information cues, it would not be surprising if the new people found these jobs to be unenriched in spite of the careful design.

In addition, social cues may affect how people weigh the various core job dimensions.[8] If fellow employees say, "Don't let management con you into doing your own quality control—we don't get paid for that", then we would expect the value of autonomy to be perceived as less important. On the other hand, coworkers might say, "It sure is nice to be able to rotate around to different jobs—it makes the time pass a lot faster." In this case skill variety might be more important because of the social cues.

Research results confirm the presence of social cues, although their power is shared with the objective dimensions of the job.[9] People use both objective and social information to form their perceptions about the job, as well as their own personal values and personality orientation. Some evidence even shows that social interaction helps clarify the objective aspects of the task, resulting in more realistic perceptions.[10] Thus, the examples cited in the preceding paragraph may actually be true reflections of the objective job characteristics rather than socially-constructed reality.

Applying the Job Characteristics Model

There are a number of different ways to find out or diagnose job enrichment problems, including observations, interviews, work-flow analysis, and questionnaires.[11] Perhaps the simplest way is just to observe what is going on with a critical eye. For example, go back to the problem faced by Wendy Maki in the introductory case. On a tour of the various functions that report to her, Wendy visits the Word Processing Center.

Ken Asato, the supervisor of the center, says, "The operators just don't seem to be motivated toward anything except avoiding work. Turnover and absence rates are much higher than for other administrative jobs in the company. I've tried everything I can think of, including piped-in music, carpeted floors, special pay, and special attention. Nothing seems to work. I'm really at my wits end. Maybe the best thing for me to do is find another job."

Wendy replies, "Hang in there, Ken. Maybe I can help you solve this problem."

Having recently completed a course in organizational behavior, Wendy is particularly attuned to the possibility of using job enrichment. After Wendy spends some time analyzing the job, she comes up with a number of observations about the word processing jobs. They are listed below using job characteristics terminology:

- *Skill variety*—Moderately low. Once the machines are mastered, the job is basically just different forms of a single skill—typing. Thus, there is little skill variety or challenge.

- *Task identity*—Virtually nonexistent. Jobs are assigned to keep a continuous workload rather than provide whole, identifiable jobs.

- *Task significance*—Low, because the employees do not see the importance of the seemingly endless flow of paperwork.

- *Autonomy* —None. Employees punch in and out on time clocks and breaks are rigidly controlled. The supervisors arrange and direct the daily tasks. Quality control and proofreading are done by another section.

- *Feedback* —Very low. Once the product is sent back to the using department, there is no contact with the typist concerning the quality or acceptability of the product. If retyping or corrections are needed, they are given to the first available typist rather than the person who originally typed the product.

Wendy observes that this is a very unenriched job with particular problems in the area of task identity, autonomy, and feedback. She figures that if she can do something to enrich the job, she can probably cure some of the problems with dissatisfaction and turnover. Table 7.1 shows a number of ways to determine if jobs are unenriched.

How to Enrich Jobs

Although the techniques used for enriching jobs are often specific to the job being redesigned, there are several common **implementing concepts** that are applicable to a wide variety of jobs.[12]

Table 7.1

WHERE ARE THE UNENRICHED JOBS?

Sometimes it is relatively easy to tell if an organization is designed without using enrichment principles. When the structural clues outlined below are present, it is highly likely that the core dimensions will be low as well:

- *Inspectors or checkers.* When inspectors or checkers inspect work rather than the workers themselves, autonomy is usually much lower. Feedback is also less direct and does not come from the job itself.

- *Troubleshooters.* The existence of troubleshooters usually means that all the exciting, challenging parts of a job have been taken from the workers who do not experience a sense of responsibility for work outcomes. Task identity, autonomy, and feedback are usually poor.

- *Communication and customer relations sections.* These sections usually cut the link between the workers who do the job and the customers or clients. Thus, these sections degrade feedback and task identity.

- *Labor pools.* Pools of typists, engineers, computer programmers, and so forth seem appealing because they offer potential efficiency and ability to meet erratic workloads. However, pools almost always destroy the workers' feeling of ownership and, thus, task identity. As we saw in the case study about the word processing center, pools can adversely affect all job characteristics.

- *Narrow span of control.* A supervisor who has only a few subordinates (say three to five) is more likely to become involved in details of the day-to-day operation. Centralization of decision making and over-control often result from too narrow a span of control, and they may seriously affect autonomy.

Based on Whitsett, D.A. (1975, January-February). Where are your unenriched jobs? *Harvard Business Review, 53,* 74–80. From Umstot (1983). In Hellriegel, Slocum & Woodman. *Organizational behavior* (3rd ed.), (p. 292). Copyright © 1983 by West Publishing Company, St. Paul, Minn. Used with permission.

Client Relationships.   One of the most important approaches is to get the worker in touch with the user of the output. Too often, employees wind up working for the boss rather than the customer or client. In the word processing example, Wendy suggested that certain operators be assigned to specific clients or groups of clients, such as sales or engineering, so that when problems arose or peculiarities were present the operator could work directly with the client.

Schedule Own Work.   Most employees are fully capable of scheduling their own work. Deadlines or goals may be set by the supervisor. Within that broad guidance, the individual worker can be allowed to set the pace for meeting the deadline.

Another form of scheduling that is becoming very common is **flexitime,** which allows the employee, within certain limits, to vary arrival and departure times to suit individual needs and desires.[13] Flexitime facilitates self-work scheduling, since the supervisor cannot always be there to breathe down the employee's neck. Wendy knows flexitime is particularly applicable to word processing jobs because the operators do their work independently—they are alone in front of their machines. Thus, it will not make any difference if an op-

---

Perspective 7.1

FLEXITIME

Flexitime is an import from Germany, where it has become extremely popular.[14] The simplest form of flexitime is shown in the example below. Here we find that Connie Young is an early riser. She starts work at 6:30 A.M., works eight hours with one half hour for lunch, and gets off work at 3 P.M. On the other hand, Joe Knapp likes to sleep late so he arrives at work at 9:30 A.M. and works until 6:00 P.M. Their fellow employees arrive at the time or their choice so long as it is before the core hours, which begin at 9:30 A.M.

The idea behind flexitime is that employees can choose from day to day what their work schedules will be without having prior permission from the boss. Even though Connie usually comes in early, she may wish to come in late one morning because of some late event the night before. Often, restrictions are used by management to make sure that certain vital functions are covered during specified times. This can be done without adversely impacting flexitime if the employees themselves are given the responsibility for making sure a function is covered.

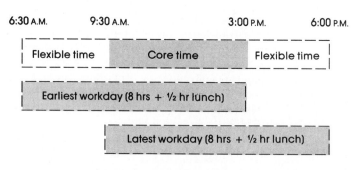

erator works from 6:00 A.M. to 3:00 P.M. or from 9:00 A.M. to 6:00 P.M. *See* Perspective 7.1 for a description of how flexitime works.

Ownership of the Whole Product. An employee who builds an entire television set, assembles an entire washing machine, or types a whole report, feels more identification with the finished product. Allowing employees to perform a whole or complete task cycle helps create a sense of pride and achievement. Another version of this concept is to assign drivers their own vehicle so they can take pride in its upkeep and repair. Ownership can also be created by assigning people total responsibility for a certain geographical area. The Indiana Bell Co. found substantial improvements in performance and satisfaction when telephone directory compilers were assigned a city or part of a city of their very own.[15] In Wendy's case, she made sure that each operator performed the complete task, including all aspects of the work being produced.

Direct Feedback Structures. Most feedback is filtered through the boss, and it often has a negative connotation. This job design strategy focuses attention on getting feedback directly to the worker without management filtering. It may be a simple matter of routing reports or computer outputs directly to employees instead of to their managers. An often-used technique is to let people check their own work so they can catch their own errors.

Direct communication with others may be another way of opening feedback channels. If people in different divisions or companies are allowed to communicate directly by phone and letter, distortions and delays in feedback may be eliminated. In the word processing case, direct contact between the typist and the author was authorized in order to allow both positive and negative feedback to occur between the two directly.

Benefits of Job Enrichment

Job enrichment can lead to improvements in both job performance and job satisfaction.

Performance Improvements. While job enrichment does not always result in increased effort or individual productivity gains,[16] it is related to improved performance most of the time. (The average correlation reported by one literature review was .23.) [17] Motivation changes are often directed more toward improved quality, service, or personnel reductions—all of which are major performance benefits. For example, one common theme of job enrichment is to get rid of inspectors and checkers so that feedback and autonomy can be improved. This action frees up the former inspectors for direct production. Also, the emphasis on quality can result in fewer rejects, lower parts consumption, less waste, and improved customer satisfaction.

Satisfaction Impact. Job enrichment consistently results in improved attitudes and quality of working life.[18] These outcomes are not only socially desir-

Perspective 7.2

A MANAGER'S SELF–HELP GUIDE TO JOB ENRICHMENT[19]

• *Learn all you can about job enrichment.* Read all the references cited in this chapter. Become an expert in enrichment concepts.

• *Is job design a problem?* Look carefully at the jobs. Are they enriched already? Ask people how they feel about the job itself—perhaps they like it the way it is. Do not rock the boat unnecessarily.

• *Is there some other problem besides job enrichment?* Perhaps supervision, communication, or lack of planning are the real problems.

• *Ask the employees if they want job enrichment.* If it looks like job enrichment is appropriate, then teach them what job enrichment is, what it can do for them and you, and see if they are interested in pursuing it. If not, do not begin an effort until they are ready. One aid to overcoming initial resistance is to make the job enrichment program an experiment, done on a trial basis.

• *Establish the goals that you want job enrichment to accomplish.* Be sure they are specific and that the end results desired are measurable and time-phased.

• *Hold a concept workshop with key supervisors and workers away from your office.* Get a room in a local hotel or motel so that you will not be interrupted during the workshop. Be

sure that everyone understands job enrichment theory and the implementing concepts.

• *Brainstorm job enrichment ideas during the workshop.* Allow one hour for brainstorming ideas. The purpose of brainstorming is only to generate ideas, not to evaluate. The rule against any form of evaluation or criticism of any idea should be strictly enforced. Another key rule is to avoid "war stories"—you are looking for ideas, large number of ideas. During a one-hour brainstorming session, you should have between 100 and 200 ideas. (*See* Chapter 13 for details on brainstorming.) Try to use two recorders, preferably people who are not part of the group, to write the ideas on flipcharts and post the completed pages on the wall.

• *Pick out the top ten ideas.* Have each participant pick his top ten ideas and put them on 3 x 5 cards so that a preliminary cut of the important ideas has been made. (Number all the ideas on the flipcharts to make the process easier.)

• *Sort and categorize the ideas into some meaningful sets for discussion and analysis.*

• *Analyze the ideas.* If they have merit, study and implement them. If not, discard them. (Be sure to provide feedback to the participants of the session about the ideas that were discarded or disapproved.)

• *Implement the ideas.*

• *Evaluate the job enrichment effort.* Did the jobs change? Were your goals met? What improvements resulted?

able, but have bottom-line benefits to the organization.[20] People who are satisfied are more likely to come to work (absenteeism declines), and they are more likely to stay in the job (turnover rates are lower). Both of these outcomes have major impact on organizational costs. There are also many less tangible benefits, such as employee goodwill, family support and happiness, and even improved employee health.

Group Approaches to Job Design

An important trend in job design is increasing emphasis on group approaches to structuring jobs. *Business Week* reports that, "Ten years ago, fewer than two dozen manufacturing plants in the U.S. organized work on a team basis. Today teamwork is used in several hundred offices and factories, especially new, highly automated plants with small workforces of 25 to 500 people." [21] When the social structure of the plant is designed in conjunction with the technological system so that both "fit" together and operate to complement one another, this process is called the **sociotechnical systems** approach. In this chapter we will concentrate on the job design aspects of sociotechnical systems. Other concepts relating to this important concept will be discussed in later chapters.

To Use Groups or Individuals?   Some tasks demand that a number of people work to complete it. For example, building a truck requires diverse skills and knowledge. In addition, many sets of hands and muscles may be needed to lift an engine—it might simply be impossible for one individual to build the entire truck. On the other hand, some tasks can only be done by one person, such as conducting an orchestra or taking photographs. Some tasks might be done either way. For example, processing claims at an insurance company might be specialized and divided among a number of individuals. On the other hand, a group of four or five claims processors might work as a team to get the job done. Hence the task itself is the first consideration when deciding between groups and individuals. Group designs work best when several people are needed to complete the task.[22]

Self-Managing Work Groups

When people work together with a high degree of freedom over the task and the interpersonal processes within their group, they are called **self-managing work groups** (often referred to as teams).[23] For example, Tektronix Inc. reorganized its assembly line operations into a teamwork approach where six to twelve workers turn out a product. One group in Tektronix turns out as many defect-free products in three days as did the entire assembly line in fourteen days with twice as many people.[24] Self-managing work groups typically have a great deal of freedom to determine their own pace, conduct their own quality control, schedule their own vacations, have a voice in hiring and firing, purchase necessary supplies and equipment, and decide when members qualify for raises using a knowledge-based pay system (*see* Chapter 6). These groups usually do without a first-level supervisor, although sometimes a group member is appointed or elected as the coordinator. All aspects of the design should reinforce self-management. Figure 7.4 highlights the important aspects of group job design that will be discussed in the following paragraphs.

Designing the Group Task.   Enriched jobs for groups must contain the same job characteristics as do jobs for individuals, but at the *group level* of analysis. For example, a group should be given responsibility for a number of processes or stages of production so that skill variety and task identity are satisfied. When groups are involved in the entire process, task significance should also be clarified and enhanced. Designing in autonomy is obviously a critical element, for without it groups cannot be self-managing; they cannot make important decisions such as the ones illustrated in the previous paragraph. Feedback from the job itself should be high if the group does its own quality

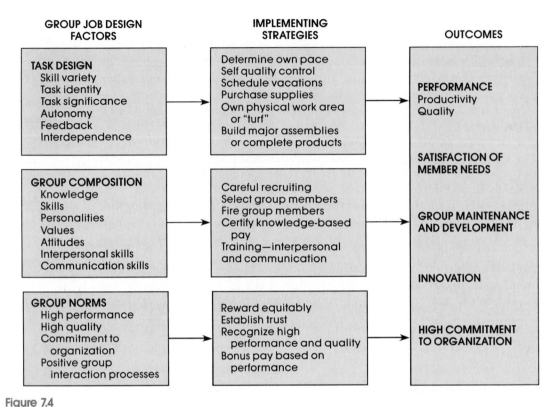

Figure 7.4

DESIGNING SELF–MANAGING WORK GROUPS

control and gets direct feedback on problems that may arise. Thus, all five core job dimensions are also important for group job designs.

Group Composition.   The chemistry of the group must also work if self-management is to succeed. The group must have the knowledge and skills to do the job. If the group does not have the right mix of skills, including interpersonal and communication skills, the chance of failure is high. For example, one life insurance company attempted to redesign the jobs of processing clerks into a group model. However, only one person was really an expert on actuarial projections, a skill that was needed by each team. The newly formed teams kept coming to the one expert who did not have enough time to get her own group's task done. Not surprisingly, everyone was frustrated.

Group Norms.   Every group develops sets of expectations about what is right or wrong and how one should behave in different situations. These expectations are really informal rules called **norms.** (Chapter 9 discusses norms in more detail.) If the group has norms related to high productivity and quality, then we can expect those outcomes. If the norms are the reverse, expect low group performance. A Cummins Engine Co. diesel plant manager, John Read, says the team approach brings out "an entrepreneurial spirit. When this spirit gets wrapped into team efforts to figure out why a machine went down—and if management gets out of the way—it's a tremendously powerful tool." [25] This "spirit" is an example of a positive norm about problem solving.

Perspective 7.3

LOOKING BACK
AT TOPEKA

In January 1971, General Foods opened the Gaines Pet Food plant near Topeka, Kansas.[27] The sociotechnical design of the plant was widely publicized and it was hailed as the plant of the future. Jobs were designed around self-managing groups who had the responsibility for hiring and firing, purchasing their own supplies, and determining when people were qualified for pay increases based on the number of jobs that were mastered. Each group had a team leader whose role was more like a coach than a directive supervisor. Initial results of the experiment showed strong improvements in costs, absenteeism, and quality. Followups in 1974 and 1975 still showed strong performance and satisfaction outcomes. Yet by 1977 a number of rather significant problems had arisen:

- Traditional supervisor-employee behaviors began to return.

- Pay was not always linked with desirable behaviors.

- There was a tendency toward leniency in pay decisions.

- Some of the team jobs were not enriched or challenging.

- Plant-level problem solving was weak because teams focused on their own problems; they did not have an overall perspective.

- Four key managers left the plant, including the plant manager.

- Topeka's originator and protector at corporate headquarters, Lyman Ketchum, was moved to a new job and later left the corporation.

- Managers in General Foods did not share the managerial philosophy of the plan—they were skeptical and lacked understanding.

In spite of all these problems, the Gaines Pet Food plant at Topeka is still using its team approach, although it is no longer owned by General Foods. In 1986, Plant manager Herman R. Simon said, "Topeka produces the same foods as a sister plant in Kankakee, Ill., at 7 percent lower costs." [28]

Results of Team Approaches to Job Design

Empirical research reports of team effort results are scarce, although many case studies support powerful improvements in performance and satisfaction. For a review of one important study, the Topeka Pet Food Project, see Perspective 7–3. Here is a summary of some of the gains cited in a recent review by *Business Week:* [26]

- *Shenandoah Life* found it could process 50 percent more applications with 10 percent fewer employees. Case handling dropped from twenty-seven days to two days and service complaints were practically eliminated.

- *Proctor & Gamble*, which established its first team-based plant in the 1960s, now has eighteen sites. While they refuse to comment publicly for competitive reasons, a senior vice president has said that teamwork plants are "30% to 40% more productive than their traditional counterparts and significantly more able to adapt quickly to the changing needs of the business."

- *Cummins Engines* Vice President, Ted Marsten, says that "this is the most cost-effective way to run plants . . . The people feel a lot better about the work than they did, and we got a much higher-quality product."

GOAL SETTING

Goal setting is one of the most widely used techniques for improving motivation.[29] It is particularly important because many managers tend to focus on *activities* of their subordinates rather than *end results*. Goal setting is a way of focusing attention where it is needed—on performance. **Goal setting** is the process of developing, negotiating, and formalizing targets that an employee is responsible for accomplishing.

Even the most casual observation will reveal that people with indefinite goals often work slowly, perform poorly, lack interest, and accomplish little. On the other hand, people with clearly defined goals appear to be more energetic and more productive—they get things done within a specified time period and move on to other activities (and goals). Goals may be implicit or explicit, vague or clearly defined, self-imposed or externally imposed, but whatever their form, they serve to structure time and activities for people.

Goal-Setting Concepts

A basis for much recent goal-setting research and practice has been Locke's theory of goal setting, which states that clear, moderately difficult goals, if accepted, will result in higher performance.[30] Four factors particularly important in the theory—goal clarity, goal difficulty, feedback, and goal acceptance—will be discussed in the following paragraphs.

Goal Clarity.   Goals must be clear and specific to be effective directors of motivation. A goal such as "do your best to improve production" is not nearly as effective as a specific goal such as, "You are to increase production of motors by 5 percent by the end of March of this year." A goal should specify *what* is to be done (increase production of motors), *who* is to do it (you are), and *when* it is to be accomplished (by the end of March of this year). The goal should also be *measurable*—how will you know when it is done? With motor production, all we have to do is count completed motors. But what about a goal involving customer satisfaction? That is more difficult to measure (perhaps the number of complaints or a questionnaire might be used). Figure 7.5 provides a guide for writing a clear goal.

Fill in the Blanks		Completed Example
To ___(action verb)___	**To** ___increase___
___(end result desired)___	___sales of tractors___
by ___(how much)___	**by** ___25 percent___
within (time)	**within** 3 months (by December 31, 1989)
___(name of person responsible)___	___Deryl Hardwich, sales manager___

Figure 7.5

GUIDE FOR WRITING A CLEAR GOAL

Goal Difficulty.   Setting the level of goal difficulty is an art. You want *moderately difficult* goals that will be challenging and stretching, but not too difficult. If goals are too easy, an employee may procrastinate or attack the goal lackadaisically. If the goals are too difficult, the employee may not accept the goal or attempt to meet it. In addition, a goal that is set unrealistically high may cause frustration and dissatisfaction if the goal is not attained. There can be no sense of achievement if the goal is never reached.

Feedback.   People need to understand how they are progressing toward their goals; they need reinforcement. Feedback fulfills this need. The feedback can come from the supervisor, coworkers, or from the job itself. One example of using feedback is the delivery forms used by United Parcel Service. These forms not only clarify the goals for the person, but provide prompt feedback on goal accomplishment. In addition, the supervisor can examine the forms at the end of the day and positively reinforce desirable behaviors.[31]

Goal Acceptance and Commitment.   If goals are not accepted, then they do not direct behavior or effort and are therefore worthless. Acceptance is a complicated issue that seems to be related to goal difficulty, whether or not the employee participated in setting the goal, and the organizational culture (to be discussed in Chapter 17). Goals must be fair and reasonable, *and* employees must trust management. See Figure 7.6 for an illustration of how the goal setting process works.

Participation in setting goals seems to be an important way to gain acceptance because people are more likely to embrace goals that they have helped set themselves. But it is not always necessary or even desirable to use participative goal setting. Participation takes time and energy, and employees have to be

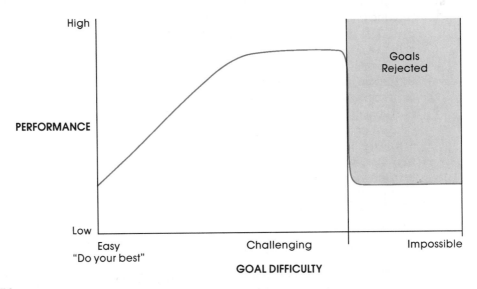

Figure 7.6

THE RELATIONSHIP BETWEEN GOAL DIFFICULTY AND PERFORMANCE

SOURCE: Adapted from Locke, E.A., & Latham, G.P. (1984). *Goal Setting: A Motivational Technique That Works!* Englewood Cliffs, NJ: Prentice-Hall, p. 22.

interested and concerned with the goals. Managers and professional people may perform better using participative strategies. Blue-collar employees may work just as well without participation. (This stereotypic view is beginning to change as values of the blue-collar work force change.) Nevertheless, some people may accept the goals because of their work values, or because they trust the manager and organization. They may also fear for their jobs. However, there is evidence that people who participate in the goal process set higher goals than those who do not.[32]

People can also have negative reactions to goals. Remember when we were discussing piecework pay in the last chapter? We noted that standards or goals seemed to be the key for designing an effective piecework system. If employees think that management is using goals as a way of squeezing out more work or exploiting them, they will be unlikely to accept the goals. A manager who uses goals as a way of clarifying what is expected rather than as a threat is more likely to be successful in obtaining goal commitment.[33]

Goal Setting With Loggers: An Example

There was an immediate problem confronting a large logging company located in the western United States.[34] Its truck drivers, who were unionized and paid by the hour, were underloading their trucks—they averaged only 60 percent of the truck's capacity. This cost the company dearly—extra trips, extra pay, extra trucks. The problem seemed to revolve around state laws that limited the maximum weight for each truck. If the Highway Department found a truck to be overweight, the driver would be fined and might eventually be fired.

The company negotiated with the union to set a goal. The strategy was to set a difficult, but attainable goal of loading a truck to 94 percent of its legal net weight. No monetary rewards or fringe benefits other than verbal praise were provided, and no one was to be reprimanded or criticized for not making the goal. The union felt the idea was too incredible to be taken seriously, so they said O.K.

The very first month, performance increased to 80 percent of capacity, but in the second month performance declined to 70 percent capacity, apparently as a test of management's statement that no punitive steps would be taken. Fortunately, none were. By the third month performance had increased to 90 percent of capacity and remained at this level for the next seven years.

One reason this goal-setting effort worked and the goals were accepted was that informal competition developed between drivers to see who could do the best job of loading his or her truck to maximum capacity. They began to brag about their accomplishments. They viewed goal setting as a challenging game. They said, "It was great to beat the other guy."

Management by Objectives (MBO)

MBO is a widely used technique that employs goal setting as its central thrust.[35] But MBO is a broader concept than just goal setting. It may be closer to a philosophy of management than a specific motivation concept. **MBO** can be defined as a managerial process where superiors and subordinates jointly identify common goals needed to support the organization's purposes, define the specific areas of responsibility in terms of results expected, measure progress toward goals, and assess performance in terms of goal accomplishment.[36]

MBO differs from ordinary goal-setting programs in that it is usually companywide, it usually involves boss-subordinate dialogue about goals, and it is normally an integral part of the organization's appraisal system, perhaps even its incentive pay system. While MBO is usually employed only at managerial levels, goal setting is often employed at the lower levels, as well. MBO often involves complex systems of control that sometimes become its downfall if the MBO system becomes too bureaucratic and loses its original meaning.

Implementing MBO Programs.   Because MBO is usually organizationwide, it requires a great deal of planning and knowledge to implement effectively.[37] Figure 7.7 outlines the basic MBO process. It starts at top management level— the corporate president and board of directors. These people will often meet at some retreat site and, with the aid of a consultant, develop the long-range objectives and plans for the firm; for example, to increase market share by reducing prices and costs.

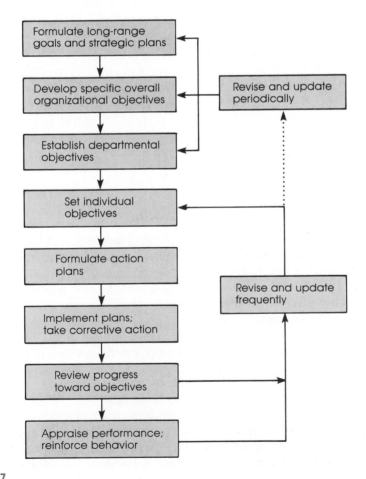

Figure 7.7

THE MBO PROCESS

SOURCE: Adapted from Raia, A.P. (1974). *Managing by Objectives.* Glenview, IL: Scott, Foresman, p. 11.

Perspective 7.4

IS MBO
EFFECTIVE?

There seems to be a great deal of controversy about how well MBO works. One author even titled his article "MBO: An idea whose time has gone?" [38] Apparently, the success of MBO depends a great deal on how it is installed and administered. Perhaps it is only another "gimmick" that is more for show than for action?

A review of the literature would lead to a different conclusion. [39] Many of the 185 studies showed positive results for MBO. In fact, in 141 case studies, the ratio of positive to not-positive results was twelve to one. More sophisticated experimental research designs were three to one in favor of MBO.

MBO tends to be more effective in the short-term, say, less than two years. Apparently, the initial effort generates a lot of interest, but it declines over time. Also, MBO was found to be more effective in the private sector and more effective in organizations that do not have direct customer contact.

Goals are revised frequently. For example, if our goal to reduce energy costs by 10 percent is frustrated by a 50 percent rise in electric rates, then the goal needs to be modified. Finally, the time frame for completing the objective arrives, and the person is evaluated. Was the goal met? If not, why? Is a revised goal needed? There is a continuing cycle of examination, review, and revision. It occurs more frequently at operating levels than at strategic levels.

Next, the specific, overall organizational objectives will be devised; for example, to reduce energy costs by 10 percent during the next year. Then, the objectives "waterfall" down the organizational hierarchy. Each department establishes objectives and individuals are asked to develop objectives that dovetail with corporate objectives. Once objectives are agreed upon, individuals make action plans and are allowed to pursue their objectives with some degree of freedom and discretion. Periodic progress reviews keep control without getting too overbearing.

Goal Setting: A Technique That Works

Goal setting is an effective strategy for changing behavior and improving performance. A review of research found that 90 percent of the studies setting specific, challenging goals led to higher performance. [40] Goals clarify what is expected and provide a framework for action; and they are relatively simple to implement on an individual basis. Goals also mobilize effort, increase persistence, and direct attention.

On the other hand, MBO is considerably more difficult to put into action because it requires many changes in organizational subsystems. There is some evidence that it is an effective strategy, but given the number of research studies completed, its impact has not been as consistent as the results of simple goal-setting efforts (see Perspective 7.4 and Table 7.2).

Goal setting and job enrichment are complementary methods for designing jobs. Job enrichment strategies result in somewhat different outcomes from goal setting, although there are natural interactive effects between the two. A model of job design that shows the various relationships between these two strategies is shown in Figure 7.8.

In the concluding section, we will examine several criteria for selecting a motivation strategy.

Table 7.2

A COMPARISON OF BENEFITS AND PROBLEMS OF MBO

Benefits	Problems
1. Improved communication between superior and subordinate on job content and the relative importance of major duties. 2. Improved utilization of human and material resources. 3. Improved subordinate development. 4. Improved subordinate performance. 5. Improved criteria for evaluating subordinate performance. 6. Improved overall planning.	1. Inadequate top management support. 2. Poorly defined objectives. 3. Inadequate monitoring of progress toward accomplishment of agreed upon objectives. 4. Inability to modify objectives rendered unreasonable by forces within an enterprise or within its external environment. 5. Inadequate evaluation of actual accomplishment of agreed upon objectives. 6. Overemphasis on paperwork. 7. Too time consuming.

SOURCE: Bedeian, A.G. (1986). *Management.* Chicago: Dryden Press, p. 150.

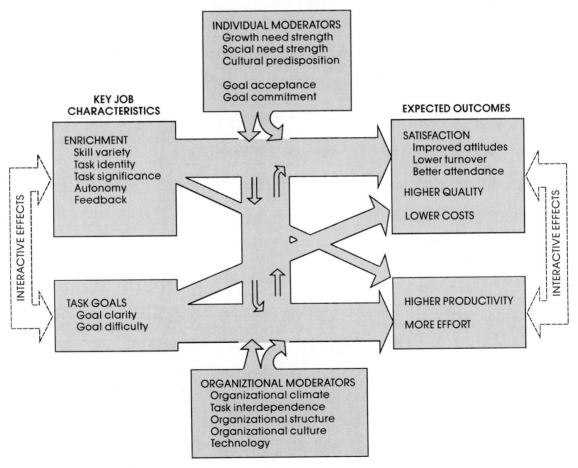

Figure 7.8

INTEGRATIVE MODEL OF JOB DESIGN

SOURCE: Adapted from Umstot, D.D., Mitchell, T.R., & Bell, C.H., Jr. (1978). Goal setting and job enrichment: An integrated approach to job design. *Academy of Management Review, 3,* 877.

CHOOSING A MOTIVATION STRATEGY

In the past chapters we have covered four basic applied motivation techniques: behavior modification, pay, job design, and goal setting. The question is, which technique to use? The answer is not simple, as it will depend on the circumstances or the situation. The information presented in Figure 7.9 should aid in diagnosing motivation problems. Although the Figure is an oversimplification and does not cover all the possibilities, it does provide some guidance for addressing complex motivation problems in work settings.

Before proceeding with an explanation of the Figure, recall that the Reliance Development Co. (the opening case in Chapter 6) was having trouble motivating its framers to complete their jobs on time because the framers were so concerned about doing high quality work. We will use this example to illustrate how to choose and apply motivation techniques.

The Job Itself and the Motivation Strategy

The first step is to ask if the job itself is boring, unenriched, and uninteresting to the people who are doing it. If the answer is "yes," then the next question is, can you do anything about it? If again the answer is "yes," then job redesign is appropriate. In addition, it would be useful to combine job redesign with goal setting to obtain maximum motivational effects.

If the job cannot be changed, and many cannot because of technology or system design, then the best way to motivate may be to combine behavior modification and goal setting. Often, the goals will provide some amount of interest to an otherwise unenriched job, and behavior modification will develop reinforcement strategies to keep the behavior sustained.

In the RDC example with the framers, we note that they already have an enriched job. They have a great deal of autonomy and feedback. They use many skills and see the whole task of building a house unfold in front of them. Thus, the job itself is not the problem.

	Job itself a problem		Job itself not a problem	
	changeable	not changeable	good organizational climate	poor organizational climate
Behavior modification		X	X	X
Pay			X	
Job redesign	X			
Goal setting	X	X	X	

Figure 7.9

APPLICATION OF MOTIVATION TECHNIQUES

Perspective 7.5

MOTIVATION TECHNIQUES: WHICH WORK BEST?

What does research say about which motivation technique works best? A review by Locke and his associates involves an analysis of all the field experimental studies that related motivational strategy with "hard" performance criteria for employees.[41] The researchers did not consider such important additional measures as job satisfaction, absenteeism, or even costs. Thus the results cover only one aspect of total performance.

Four motivational strategies were examined: incentive pay (ten studies), goal setting (seventeen studies), job enrichment (thirteen studies), and employee participation (sixteen studies—*see* Chapter 13 for information on this strategy). Two studies in behavior modification were included within the goal-setting figures.

They found that money (incentives) resulted in the highest increase in performance: 30 percent. Goal setting resulted in improvements of 16 percent, and job enrichment resulted in about 9 percent. Participation resulted in little or no change. When goals and incentives were combined, improvements of over 40 percent resulted.

The authors concluded that money has much more potency as a motivator than other strategies of motivation.

Organizational Climate and Motivation Strategy

If there is nothing wrong with the job's design, then the next consideration is the organizational climate (the degree of trust, open communication, or fairness—to be covered in Chapter 17). If the climate is good, where trust and mutual respect prevail, then goal setting is appropriate, augmented by behavior modification and perhaps an incentive pay scheme (*see* Perspective 7.5). If the climate is poor, then goal setting will be ineffective, and we are left with behavior modification as the only strategy for dealing with the problem.

The framers at RDC work in a good organizational climate. Management has a good reputation with them, and there is mutual trust and respect—they do not feel like management is out to exploit them. Thus, goal setting may be the most effective technique. The framers could be given a goal of so many days to complete a job. The goal could be posted and compared with other framing teams. Positive reinforcement should be used for those teams that complete their jobs on time or early. Pay might be used as an incentive, but in a thin profit-margin business, such as low-cost housing, it is probably better to try other reinforcements first.

CROSS–CULTURAL OB: ENRICHING JOBS AT VOLVO IN SWEDEN[42]

Volvo has also been an innovator in sociotechnical systems.[43] The President of Volvo, Pehr Gyllenhammer, decided on a risky course to improve the quality of working life at Volvo. In 1974, he built an entirely new plant at Kalmar, Sweden, that was designed around **sociotechnical concepts**—an approach that entails balancing both social and technical aspects of the job.[44] To accomplish the job redesign, the conventional auto assembly line that moved through a

Figure 7.10

APPLICATION OF THE SOCIOTECHNICAL APPROACH.
(a) A TRADITIONAL ASSEMBLY LINE AT VOLVO.
(b) VOLVO'S NEW PATENTED CAR CARRIER.

SOURCE: Pehr Gyllenhammar, *People At Work*, © 1977, Addison-Wesley Publishing Company, Inc., Reading, Massachusetts, pp. 57, 97 (photos). Reprinted with permission.

warehouse had to be changed so that the work could remain relatively stationary and the materials be brought to the work station. To accomplish this task, a special car carrier was built that could transport and position an entire car (*see* Figure 7.10).

The basis of the sociotechnical approach is not only technology, such as new carriers and plant layouts, but also work groups organized so as to optimize the social aspects of the system. The Kalmar plant uses twenty-person teams organized to perform all work on certain subsystems, such as electrical systems, instrumentation, steering and controls, and interiors. It takes from twenty to forty minutes to finish each subassembly. Each team has its own area of the shop floor and its own rest area. Each team organizes itself. Responsibilities and work procedures are not dictated by management. Teams may elect to organize so that each member specializes in an individual job, they may organize into subteams to do parts of the job, or they may devise rotation schemes.

The opportunities for self-control are substantial. Teams contract with management to deliver a certain number of items, such as finished brake systems or interiors per day. The pace of work and break times are determined by the groups. Teams conduct their own inspections, and a special computer-based quality control system flashes the results back to the work stations on TV.

At first the results indicated that productivity was about the same as the other Volvo plants, but turnover and absenteeism were about 5 percent lower. By 1983, a Volvo vice president indicated that Kalmar's productivity was "20% higher than the goal set for the plant." [45] However, recently production costs have declined at Kalmar—they are now 25 percent below Volvo's conventional plants.[46] Volvo has built nine additional plants trying new ways of designing work. One of these, the plant at Uddevalla, will be based directly on their Kalmar experience.

In addition to the innovative job design, a performance-oriented gainsharing bonus system was also included. Thus, plant performance may be attributable to a combination of job design and incentive pay.

MANAGERIAL APPLICATIONS OF JOB DESIGN AND GOAL SETTING

Consciously or unconsciously managers are constantly designing their subordinates jobs and setting goals for them. Effective managers will recognize this process and try to make it as motivational as possible. The following pointers may help you recall some of the more important points:

- *Design enriched jobs.* When appropriate, make sure your subordinates' jobs are high on job enrichment characteristics. Autonomy and feedback should be especially emphasized because they give the most powerful effects.

- *Be sure your subordinates want enrichment.* Check the desire for growth to make sure that enrichment is a valued outcome for your subordinates.

- *Manage social pressures.* Try to make sure that people see their jobs in a favorable light. Watch group norms and behaviors to see if they reinforce or detract from job enrichment.

- *Watch for unenriched jobs.* Carefully evaluate each task to make sure it is as enriched as possible before you assign it. Watch out for the clues to unenriched jobs: inspectors, trouble-shooters, customer relations sections, labor pools, or narrow spans of control.

- *Use the enrichment implementing strategies.* Try to include these elements when designing jobs: client relationships, flexible schedules, feelings of ownership of the entire product, and direct feedback structures.

- *Do it yourself!* Job enrichment is amenable to accomplishment without special outside help. All it takes is study and the aid of the self-help guide in Perspective 7.2. Use job enrichment to help solve morale and performance problems.

- *Use groups for interdependent tasks.* Self-managing work groups are an effective strategy for dealing with tasks requiring a combined effort, but team efforts are more complex and difficult than individually-focused strategies.

- *Consider sociotechnical designs for new plants.* Designing factories to take advantage of both advanced technology and advanced social systems can create powerful benefits.

- *Focus on results, not activities.* Let goals guide your subordinates' efforts rather than activities. Examine the results of their efforts, but leave the details of how they accomplish the goal up to them.
- *Set clear, challenging goals.* Specific goals will result in better performance. Goals may be more readily accepted if you use participatory methods for setting them.
- *Know how to write clear goals.* Make sure everyone in your organization knows how to write clear, well constructed, unambiguous goals. Specify who, what, and when.
- *Use MBO for organization-wide goal setting.* However, beware of the tendency to develop an over-rigid system that results in bureaucratic behavior.
- *Carefully evaluate motivation problems.* Avoid premature adoption of some motivation strategy, such as job enrichment. Make sure the job is possible to change and the organizational climate fits the desired design.
- *Combine money with other strategies for maximum motivation.* Whenever possible, an incentive system should be combined with such strategies as MBO and job enrichment to get the most powerful effects.

FOR DISCUSSION

1. How do the five job characteristics relate to job satisfaction? To job performance?

2. Based upon your own work experience, describe either an enriched or an unenriched job using the job characteristics model.

3. Describe the major strategies for enriching jobs. How are these strategies related to the five job characteristics (skill variety, task identity).

4. Explain how flexitime works.

5. How does the sociotechnical approach to job design differ from job enrichment?

6. What elements must be present for group approaches to job design to be successful?

7. What are the four key elements of Locke's theory of goal setting? Which element do you see as most important and least important? Why?

8. Explain why MBO often runs into problems. How could you design an MBO program that would avoid these problems?

9. Using Figure 7.9 as a model, try to think up an example where each of the strategies that are X'd would apply.

10. Are you surprised at the research results presented in Perspective 7.5 about the effectiveness of various motivation strategies? How can you explain the differences between the strategies?

11. Do you think the sociotechnical approach used by Volvo is appropriate for American automakers? Why or why not?

KEY CONCEPTS AND TERMS

job design
job characteristics model
job enrichment
social influence
skill variety
task identity
task significance
autonomy
feedback from the job

growth need strength
psychological states
flexitime
implementing concepts
client relationships
sociotechnical systems
self-managing work groups
team approach to job design
Locke's theory of goal setting

goal clarity
goal difficulty
goal acceptance
participation
management-by-objectives
(MBO)
organizational climate

Cases and Incidents

KEYPUNCH OPERATION

The function of the keypunch division is to transfer written or typed insurance documents on to computer cards. The division consists of ninety-eight keypunch operators and verifiers (both have the same job classification), seven assignment clerks, and seven supervisors. There are two keypunch supervisors (each with about twenty-five keypunch operators), two verification supervisors (again with about twenty-five verifiers each), and an assignment supervisor (with all seven assignment clerks). All the supervisors report to an assistant manager who then reports to the keypunch division manager.

The size of the jobs vary from just a few cards to as many as 2,500 cards. Some jobs are prescheduled while others come in with due dates—often in the form of crash projects that need to be done "right now." All jobs are received by the assignment branch where they are checked for obvious errors, omissions, and legibility. Any problems found are reported to the supervisor who contacts the user department to resolve the problem. If the depart-

mental input is satisfactory, the assignment clerk divides up the work into batches that will take about one hour to complete so that each operator will have an equal workload. These batches are sent to the keypunching branches with the instructions to "Punch only what you see. Don't correct errors, no matter how obvious they look." Operators have no freedom to arrange their schedules or tasks. They also have little knowledge concerning the meaning and use of the data they are punching.

Because of the high cost of computer time, all keypunching is 100 percent verified. The verification process is done by having another operator completely repunch the data to see if the two inputs match. Thus, it takes just as long to verify as it does to punch the data in the first place. After verification, the cards are sent to the supervisor. If errors are detected, they are sent to the first available operator for correction. Next, the cards are sent to the computer division where they are checked for accuracy using a computer program. The cards and the computer output are sent directly to the originating department, which checks the cards and output and returns the cards to the supervisor if any errors are found.

Many motivational problems exist. There are numerous grievances from the operators. Employees frequently display apathy or outright hostility toward their jobs. Rates of work output are low and schedules are frequently missed. Absenteeism is much higher than average, especially on Mondays and Fridays. Supervisors spend most of their time controlling the work and resolving crisis situations. In short, the performance of the keypunch division is marginal at best.

DISCUSSION QUESTIONS

1. What is the most appropriate motivational strategy in this case? Why?

2. Analyze this case in terms of the job characteristics model.

3. How would you enrich the jobs in the keypunch division?

Adapted by D. Umstot from J.R. Hackman, et al., (1975). A new strategy for job enrichment, as published in *Organizational Behavior*, 3rd ed., ed. D. Hellriegel, J.W. Slocum, Jr., and R.W. Woodman. Copyright © 1983 by West Publishing Company, St. Paul, Minn. Used with permission. All rights reserved.

THE RELUCTANT ENTREPRENEURS

In the southern United States, the large multi-million dollar pulpwood processing plants are dependent on independent loggers. These entrepreneurs own their own trucks and hire their own crews. But since these loggers do not work for any single company and, in fact work only for themselves, they set their own schedules. One week they might work two days (the fishing is good), the next week they might work four days, and the third week they might work five, one-half days. The production and reliability of these workers is poor at best, but huge investments in equipment would be needed to develop in-house capability. Even then there might still be the same motivation problem.

DISCUSSION QUESTIONS

1. What is the most appropriate motivational strategy in this case? Why?

2. Develop a plan to motivate the loggers so that they will be motivated to work a full five-day workweek.

GETTING STARTED WITH GOAL SETTING

Sharon Lind, a recent graduate from a respectable business school, has just been appointed as the supervisor of the installation department for residential telephone installations. Her boss told her that she faces a real challenge because productivity of her new workgroup is down and absenteeism is very high. Sharon's boss gave her a free hand to improve the department.

Sharon had learned from her OB class that goal setting is an effective technique for motivation. She decided that she would use it to solve her problems. On her second day on the job she announced to the crew that they would each have a goal for the day to accomplish. These goals were set at 110 percent of the production of each person during the past sixty days. The reception to Sharon's edict was cool, but she was pleased that she was assertive and forceful and had everything under control.

The next day every single person in the department called in sick.

DISCUSSION QUESTIONS

1. What did Sharon do wrong?

2. How could she have used research to assess readiness for goal setting?

3. What research design would she use if she wished to evaluate the effects of her goal-setting program?

REFERENCES

1. Parts of this chapter are abridged and adapted from Umstot, D.D. (1983). Job design. In D. Hellriegel, J.W. Slocum, Jr., & R.W. Woodman. *Organizational behavior* (3rd ed., pp. 280–307). St. Paul, MN: West. Used with permission.

2. For more thorough coverage of job design issues see: Campion, M.A., & Thayer, P.W. (1987). Job design: Approaches, outcomes, and trade-offs. *Organizational Dynamics, 15* (3), 66–79; Hackman, J.R., & Oldham, G.R. (1980). *Work redesign.* Reading, MA: Addison-Wesley. Cummings, T.G., & Srivasta, S. (1977). *Management of work: A socio-technical systems approach.* Kent, IL: Kent State University. Aldag, R.J., & Brief, A.P. (1979). *Task design and employee motivation.* Glenview, IL: Scott, Foresman. And Griffin, R. (1982). *Task design.* Glenview, IL: Scott, Foresman.

3. See Herzberg, F. (1966). *Work and the nature of man.* Cleveland: World. And Herzberg, F. (1976). *The managerial choice.* Homewood, IL: Dow Jones-Irwin.

4. Hackman, J.R., & Oldham, G.R. (1976). Motivation through the design of work: test of a theory. *Organizational behavior and human performance, 16,* 250–279. For a review of this model, see Roberts, K.H., & Glick, W. (1981). The job characteristics approach to task design: A critical review. *Journal of Applied Psychology, 66,* 193–217.

5. Based on Hackman & Oldham (1976). Also Idaszak, J.R., & Drasgow, F. (1987). A revision of the job diagnostic survey: Elimination of a measurement artifact. *Journal of Applied Psychology, 72,* 69–74. For a study of the validity of job characteristics, see Fried, Y., & Ferris, G.R. (1986). The dimensionality of job characteristics: Some neglected issues. *Journal of Applied Psychology, 71,* 419–426.

6. Hackman and Oldham (1980). There has been limited research support for the growth need strength moderator. See Loher, B.T., Noe, R.A., Moeller, N.L., & Fitzgerald, M.P. (1985). A meta-analysis of the relation of job characteristics to job satisfaction. *Journal of Applied Psychology, 70,* 280–289. Also see Roberts & Glick (1981). And Griffin, R.W., Welsh, A., & Moorhead, G. (1981). Perceived task characteristics and employee performance: A literature review. *Academy of Management Review, 6,* 655–664.

7. Salancik, G., & Pfeffer, J. (1978). A social information processing approach to job attitudes and task design. *Administrative Science Quarterly, 23,* 224–253.

8. Pfeffer, J. (1981). Management as symbolic action: The creation and maintenance of organizational paradigms. In L.L. Cummings & B.M. Staw (Eds.). *Research in organizational behavior, Volume 3* (pp. 1–52). Greenwich, CT: JAI Press.

9. Thomas, J., & Griffin, R. (1983). The social information processing model of task design: A review of the literature, *Academy of Management Review, 8,* 672–682.

10. Dean, J.W., Jr., & Brass, D.J. (1985). Social interaction and the perception of job characteristics in an organization. *Human Relations, 6,* 571–582.

11. For more detailed information on implementing job enrichment, see Walters, R.W. (1975). *Job enrichment for results: Strategies for successful implementation.* Reading, MA: Addison-Wesley.

12. For more information on implementing concepts, see Walters (1975). Also Hackman, J.R., Oldham, G.R., Janson, R., & Purdy, K. (1975). A new strategy for job enrichment. *California Management Review, 17,* 51–57. And Herzberg, F. (1974). The wise old turk, *Harvard Business Review, 52,* 70–80.

13. For more information about flexitime, see Cohen, A.R., & Gadon, H. (1978). *Alternative work schedules: Integrating individual and organizational needs.* Reading, MA: Addison-Wesley. And Ronen, S. (1981). *Flexible working hours.* New York: McGraw-Hill. For a review of the effects of flexitime, see Narayanan, V.K., & Nath, R.A. (1982). A field test of some attitudinal and behavioral consequences of flexitime. *Journal of Applied Psychology, 67,* 214–218.

14. Ronen (1981).

15. Ford, R.N. (1973). Job enrichment lessons from AT&T. *Harvard Business Review, 51,* 96–106.

16. Griffin, et al. (1981). A recent study found correlations between both satisfaction and effort; see Glick, W.H., Jenkins, G.D., & Gupta, N. (1986). Method versus substance: How strong are underlying relationships between job characteristics and attitudinal outcomes. *Academy of Management Journal, 29,* 441–464.

17. Berlinger, L.R., Glick, W.H., & Rodgers, R.C. (1986). Job enrichment increases performance: Wishful thinking or a dream come true?: A meta-analysis. Paper presented at the national meeting of the Academy of Management, August.

18. Loher, et al. (1985).

19. Adapted from Umstot, D.D., & Rosenbach, W.E. (1980). From theory to action: Implementing job enrichment in the Air Force. *Air University Review, 31* (3), 74–81. Used with permission.

20. Passmore, W.A. (1982, Spring). Overcoming the roadblocks to work restructuring efforts. *Organizational Dynamics*, pp. 54–67.

21. Management discovers the human side of automation. (1986, September 29). *Business Week*, p. 71. Walton, R.E., & Susman, G.I. (1987). People policies for the new machines. *Harvard Business Review, 65* (2), 98–106.

22. Hackman (1980). Cummings, T.G. (1978). Self-regulating work groups: A socio-technical synthesis. *Academy of Management Review, 3*, 625–634.

23. Hackman 1980.

24. Management discovers . . . (1986, September 29). *Business Week*, pp. 74–75.

25. Management discovers . . . (1986, September 29). *Business Week*, p. 72.

26. Management discovers . . . (1986, September 29). *Business Week*. For an empirical study that supports the positive benefits of autonomous groups, see Wall, T.D., Kemp, N.J., Jackson, P.R., & Clegg, C.W. (1986). Outcomes of autonomous work groups: A long-term field experiment. *Academy of Management Journal, 29*, 280–304.

27. Based on Whitsett, D.A., & Yorks, L. (1983, Summer). Looking back at Topeka: General Foods and the quality-of-work-life experiment. *California Management Review*, Summer, 93–109.

28. Management discovers . . . (1986, September 29). *Business Week*, p. 75.

29. Locke, E.A. (1978). The ubiquity of the technique of goal-setting in theories and approaches to motivation. *Academy of Management Review, 3*, 594–601.

30. Locke, E.A. (1968). Toward a theory of task motivation and incentives. *Organizational Behavior and Human Performance, 3*, 157–189. For reviews supporting Locke's theory, see Tubbs, M.E. (1986). Goal setting: A meta-analytic examination of the empirical evidence. *Journal of Applied Psychology, 71*, 474–483. And Locke, E.A., Shaw, K.N., Sari, L.M., & Latham, G.P. (1981). Goal setting and task performance: 1969–1980. *Psychological Bulletin, 90*, 125–152.

31. Larson, J.R., Jr. (1984). The supervisory feedback process: A preliminary model. *Organizational Behavior and Human Performance, 33*, 42–76. Also see Liden, R.C., & Mitchell, T.R. (1985). Reactions to feedback: The role of attributions. *Academy of Management Journal, 28*, 291–308.

32. Tubbs (1986).

33. See Latham & Locke (1979). For a thorough discussion of goal commitment see Hollenbeck,

J.R., & Klein, H.J. (1987). Goal commitment and the goal-setting process: Problems, prospects, and proposals for future research. *Journal of Applied Psychology, 72*, 212–220.

34. Adapted from Latham & Locke (1979), pp. 72–73.

35. Greenwood, R.G. (1981). Management by objectives: As developed by Peter Drucker, assisted by Harold Smiddy. *Academy of Management Review, 6*, 225–230. Also see Wechrich, H. (1985). *Management excellence: Productivity through MBO.* New York: McGraw-Hill.

36. Based on the definitions of Odiorne, G.S. (1979). *M.B.O. II.* Belmont, CA: Fearon. And McConkie, M.L. (1979). A clarification of the goal-setting and appraisal processes in MBO. *Academy of Management Review, 4*, 29–40.

37. There are a number of good books on MBO that provide implementing guidance, including: Weihrich, H. (1985). *Management excellence: Productivity through MBO.* New York: McGraw-Hill. And Odiorne (1979).

38. Ford, C.H. (1979). MBO: An idea whose time has gone? *Business Horizons, 22* (12), 48–56.

39. For a review see Kondrasuk, J.N. (1981). Studies in MBO effectiveness. *Academy of Management Review, 6*, 419–430.

40. Locke, et al. (1981). Also see Tubbs (1986).

41. Locke, E.A., Feren, D.B., McCaleb, V.M., Shaw, K.N., & Denny, A.T. (1981). The relative effectiveness of four methods of motivating employee performance. In K.D. Duncan, et al. (Eds.). *Changes in working life: Proceedings of the NATO international conference.* London: Wiley.

42. This section is adapted from Umstot (1983). In Hellriegel, et al. (pp. 298–299).

43. Based on Gyllenhammar, P.G. (1977). *People at work.* Reading, MA: Addison-Wesley.

44. Trist, E. (1981). *The evolution of sociotechnical systems.* Toronto: Quality of Working Life Centre. Pava, C. (1986). Redesigning sociotechnical systems design: Concepts and methods for the 1990s. *Journal of Applied Behavioral Science, 22*, 201–221.

45. Interview with Berth Jonsson. (1983). *New Management, 1* (3), pp. 30–33.

46. Macy, B. (1986). Volvo revisited: The new plant decision. In D.D. White & D.A. Bednar. *Organizational behavior: Understanding and managing people at work* (pp. 584–591). Boston: Allyn and Bacon. Also see Management discovers . . . (1986, September 29). *Business Week*.

Part Three

THE INTERACTION BETWEEN PEOPLE

Chapter Eight

COMMUNICATION: THE LINK BETWEEN INDIVIDUALS

PREVIEW

- How do you behave when confronted by an angry boss or coworker? Learn an effective way.

- Why is it that when you tell someone they should do something they often react unfavorably, even if it is to their benefit?

- What is the organizational grapevine?

- How can transactional analysis be used to improve organizational communication?

- Are you a good listener or do you daydream? Find out how to improve your listening skills.

- Do you think managers who spend a great deal of their time just wandering around can be effective?

- Why do managers in Japanese-owned plants often have no office?

MAJOR TOPICS

Preview Case: The Managerial Treadmill

The Communication Process

Interpersonal Communication Dynamics

Listening Behavior

Nonverbal Communication

Cross-Cultural OB: Open Communication in Japanese Organizations

Managerial Applications of Communication Concepts

Preview Case

THE MANAGERIAL TREADMILL

Barbara Lopez is a middle-level manager in charge of the electronics systems for a new series of naval vessels. We are going to see what Barbara does on Tuesday morning between nine and ten in the morning.

9:00 A.M.—She meets with Ray Morse, one of her subordinates who was late this morning for the third time this month. She tells Ray that the late behavior is causing delays in the coordination of important subsystems and could result in a delay in the entire project. Ray is obviously upset; his face shows anxiety and he is nervous and fidgety. She asks him what is causing the late behavior. A discussion ensues revolving around some serious health problems with Ray's wife. Barbara listens attentively and with empathy. At the end of the discussion, Ray resolves to get to work on time in spite of his difficulties at home.

9:12 A.M.—She begins scanning a report that summarizes the progress on the ship. The report highlights any delays or problems with the electronics of a ship.

9:14 A.M.—A telephone call from Louise McIntosh in procurement; there will be a two-week delay in delivery of the cable needed for the radar harnesses.

9:16 A.M.—Barbara calls her chief engineer, Vern Smith, and informs him of the delay. Vern gets quite angry and asks if he can come up and talk to her. Yes, she says.

9:18 A.M.—She continues scanning the report. She jots a short note to one of the project engineers about a possible change in specifications of another electronics subsystem.

9:22 A.M.—Vern bursts into the office. His fists are balled up and his face shows anger. He says,

"Why didn't you let me know sooner that we might be having this delay? I'm the chief engineer here, but it seems that I'm always the last to know." Barbara explains to Vern in a level-headed manner that she did not have any idea that the delay was in the wind and that it was news to her, too. This cools Vern down, and they discuss how they might solve the problem.

9:30 A.M.—Her secretary buzzes on the intercom and says that Leslie Thompson is here for her performance appraisal interview. Barbara almost forgot this rather important appointment in the light of the cable problem. She tells her secretary to delay the appointment for a few minutes so she can get rid of Vern and collect her thoughts.

9:36 A.M.—Leslie enters Barbara's office. Telling someone who is performing at less than expected level is always difficult. Leslie becomes emotionally upset and begins to sob. Barbara handles the emotion as if it were entirely natural. Leslie spends several minutes venting her frustrations and discussing her reasons for her low performance. Barbara gradually develops a set of objectives for Leslie. If they are completed, Leslie's performance will improve. Although still somewhat upset, Leslie departs with positive feelings that she can improve.

9:52 A.M.—Barbara returns the calls of two people who called while she was in conference with Leslie.

9:57 A.M.—Captain York, the project director, calls and asks her what is happening on the cable delay problem. He's worried that it will delay the whole project. She tells him that she is on top of the problem and will let him know as soon as they have an impact statement. The Captain's call puts a lot more pressure on them than she would like.

9:59 A.M.—Her secretary buzzes to remind her of the 10:00 A.M. meeting with other system directors. She grabs the progress report and heads for the conference room.

Barbara Lopez spends most of her time communicating. She must deal with several types of communication, including interpersonal contacts with subordinates, peers, and superiors, the impersonal inputs from computer-generated reports, written memos and reports, and formal oral presentations. While all these aspects of communication are important, the primary focus of this chapter is on the interpersonal aspects of organizational communication.

Barbara's workday is not unusual, for most managers spend a large portion of their time verbally communicating. A study of managerial activities found that managers spend 78 percent of their time in oral communications.[1] Thus, communication is one of the most important skills for a manager to have. Communication can also have a direct effect on organizational performance, satisfaction of employees, and innovation.[2]

In this chapter, we will cover the basic communication process and then turn to transactional analysis as a way of understanding interpersonal communication. We will then study ways to improve listening skills and a strategy for solving various types of communication problems. Finally, we will cover nonverbal communication, a critical and often overlooked aspect of communication.

THE COMMUNICATION PROCESS

A model of the communication process, such as the one presented in Figure 8.1, helps us understand what happens when one person communicates with another.[3] It also shows where the process can break down. Basically, there are four major parts to the communication process: source, message or media, receiver, and feedback.[4] Person *A*, the **source, encodes** the message into words and nonverbal signals. These **messages** are transmitted in oral, written, nonverbal, and other **media** to Person *B*, the **receiver** who **decodes** the message and gives it meaning. Person *B* may transmit **feedback** to Person **A** so that receipt of the message is confirmed.

The Source: Encoding Messages

When you originate a communication, you are the source. Based on your **field of experience,** which is developed from your past experiences, your personal-

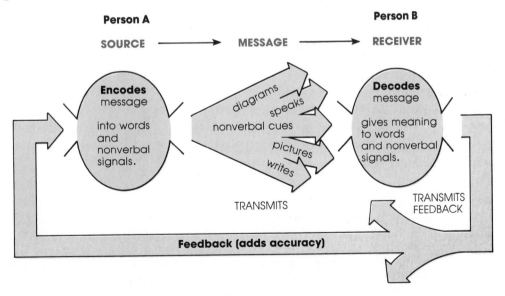

Figure 8.1

THE COMMUNICATION PROCESS

ity, and your self-concept (the topics discussed in Chapters 2, 3, and 4), you use certain words, gestures, facial expressions, posture, and voice to encode your message. You need to be aware of your own field of experience and the receiver's field of experience so that you can properly encode the message. College professors often have problems encoding so that their students understand and receive the message; and many students have experienced the results of such a mismatch.

This same problem is common in all organizations. For example, managers often have a different frame of reference than do hourly employees; engineers have a different one from managers; and marketing people differ from production. Everyone has a somewhat different set of experiences and perceptions that colors their ability to decode the other's messages. If you are dealing with managers from another country and culture, there may be very little common field of experience (*see* Figure 8.2). To communicate effectively, you must use the proper words and **nonverbal signals** (smiles, nods, voice, eye contact), to match the frame of reference of your receiver.

The Message: Transmitting Meaning

Messages can be transmitted in many ways, mediums, or **channels.** They may be written, spoken over the telephone, delivered face-to-face, or transmitted nonverbally, as with a wink.[5] People may react differently to various channels. For example, people may respond much more favorably to a face-to-face request for information than they would to a written memo.[6] Why is this so? Face-to-face provides much better feedback, including nonverbal cues. It also shows the degree of interest and enthusiasm of the sender—in other words, it is

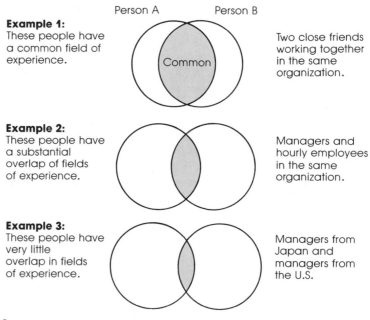

Figure 8.2

FIELDS OF EXPERIENCE

Table 8.1

COMMUNICATION MEDIA AND INFORMATION RICHNESS

Information Medium	Richness of Information Transfer
Face-to-face discussions (one-on-one)	Very high
Discussions in groups	
Oral presentations	
Informal, personal letters and memos (personally addressed)	Moderate
Formal written documents (form letters, bulletins, regulations)	
Formal numeric documents (computer printouts, income statements)	Very low

SOURCE: Adapted from Daft, R.L., & Lengel, R.H. (1984). Information richness: A new approach to managerial behavior and organization design. In B. Staw & L. Cummings (Eds.). *Research in organizational behavior* (p. 196). Greenwich: JAI Press.

a much richer source of information. Table 8.1 shows how different communication media create differing degrees of richness. As expected, face-to-face is at the top of the scale while impersonal, formal numeric documents are at the bottom. People may even react adversely to impersonal, computer-generated messages.[7]

Another problem with the message is that people often send conflicting messages. For example, a salesperson who is doing an excellent job of presenting the product on a verbal level, may be sending a nonverbal signal of apprehension and nervousness that results in conflicting signals.

The Receiver: Decoding the Message

From the study of perception in Chapter 4, we know that we selectively pick up messages from the environment. Communication works the same way—we **selectively receive** messages based on our field of experience, our emotional mood, our reaction to the sender, and the form of the communication. If someone criticizes us or talks down to us, we may cut off the communication and simply "not hear" what is being said. Or, we may react with anger and lash back at the sender (certainly a strong form of feedback for the sender).

To be good receivers we must be good listeners and be able to decode the verbal and nonverbal signals of the sender. Then we must, of course, respond in a way that facilitates communication. The application of these topics will be covered in greater detail later in the chapter.

Feedback

One central part of the communication process is **feedback,** or the information that returns to the sender from the receiver.[8] Feedback is a natural part of most communication transactions although some types of communication, such as face-to-face, offer more opportunities for feedback than others. Feed-

Perspective 8.1

THE GRAPEVINE

The company "grapevine," a term which refers to all informal communication in organizations, is a central part of the informal organization. Ordinarily, communication and authority travel along organizational lines, from supervisor to subordinate or vice versa. However, the grapevine follows the informal organization. It skips levels; it moves laterally; and it moves fast. For example, the wife of the plant supervisor had a baby at 11 P.M. on Tuesday. By 2 P.M. on Wednesday, 46 percent of the management personnel knew of the birth through the grapevine. In another case the wife of the company president knew about a relocation plan on the same day the plan was finalized in secret session. The accompanying chart depicts grapevine communication patterns.[9]

There are a number of managerial uses for the grapevine: [10]

• Leak potentially unwelcome changes to the grapevine to get feedback before they are officially implemented. This allows you to assess the impact of the changes and counter problems.

• Be sure to ask people who are familiar with the grapevine, such as your secretary, "What's new?" This will show interest in the grapevine and allows you to counter problems before they are officially publicized.

• Release good news into the grapevine to improve morale.

• Be careful who you trust with confidential information you do not want transmitted to the grapevine.

An event is known to managers in positions **A** and **B** in a manufacturing company

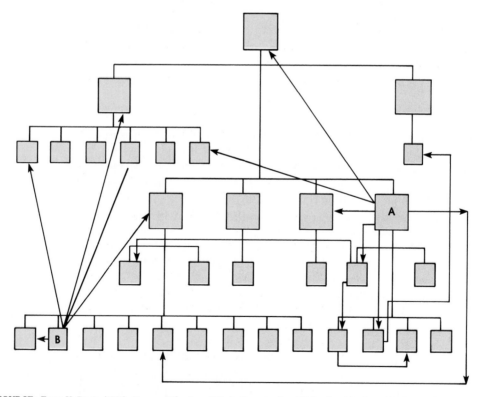

SOURCE: From K. Davis, (1981), *Human Behavior at Work: Organizational Behavior*, 6th ed., p. 336. Copyright © 1981 by McGraw-Hill, New York. Used with permission.

Table 8.2

EXAMPLES OF ORGANIZATIONAL FEEDBACK

Positive feedback from the organization	You receive a formal report of good performance. Your supervisor tells you that you are doing a good job. You are promoted to a more responsible job. You get a raise.
Negative feedback from the organization	The supervisor really lets you have it. Coworkers tell you that you did something wrong. The supervisor makes back-handed comments (like "Have a hard night?") You are demoted to a less responsible job.
Internal feedback from the job	You find better ways of doing the job. Everything goes smoothly. You are able to finish all the work. You have good feelings about how well you did the job.

SOURCE: Adapted from D.M. Herold and M.M. Greller, 1977, Feedback: Definition of a construct, *Academy of Management Journal* 20:144–45. Copyright 1977 by Academy of Management Review. Used with permission.

back may also be a formal process, such as the performance appraisal interview that Barbara was conducting with Leslie in our opening case. Examples of the types of organizational feedback that might be encountered are provided in Table 8.2.

One-way communication, such as a lecture without interaction or a business letter, does not allow corrective feedback from the receiver. If the message is misunderstood, there is no way to rectify it. **Two-way communication,** on the other hand, allows the sender to test the receiver's understanding of the message. A humorous example of the types of distortions that happen when one-way communication prevents feedback is Operation Halley's Comment related below:

A Colonel issued the following directive to his executive officers:	"Tomorrow evening at approximately 2000 hours Halley's Comet will be visible in this area, an event which occurs only once every 75 years. Have the men fall out in the battalion area in fatigues, and I will explain this rare phenomenon to them. In case of rain, we will not be able to see anything, so assemble the men in the theater and I will show them films of it."
Executive officer to company commander:	"By order of the Colonel, tomorrow at 2000 hours, Halley's Comet will appear above the battalion area. If it rains, fall the men out in fatigues, then march to the theater where this rare phenomenon will take place, something which occurs only once every 75 years."
Company commander to lieutenant:	"By order of the Colonel be in fatigues at 2000 hours tomorrow evening. The phenomenal Halley's Comet will appear in the theater. In case of rain, in the battalion area, the Colonel will give another order, something which occurs once every 75 years."

Lieutenant to sergeant:	"Tomorrow at 2000 hours, the Colonel will appear in the theater with Halley's Comet, something which happens every 75 years. If it rains, the Colonel will order the comet into the battalion area."
Sergeant to squad:	"When it rains tomorrow at 2000 hours, the phenomenal 75–year-old General Halley, accompanied by the Colonel, will drive his comet through the battalion area theater in fatigues." [11]

One final concept to keep in mind is that communication is continuous; it is a series of transactions between the sender and the receiver with feedback and reinforcement constantly occurring. Transactions tend to overlap; as one person talks, the other may laugh, smile, frown, nod, or interrupt.

INTERPERSONAL COMMUNICATION DYNAMICS

While it is certainly very important that managers be able to write clearly and to speak well in formal, oral presentations, the majority of all managerial communication is between two people—it is at the interpersonal level. For this reason, we will concentrate our attention on interpersonal communication dynamics.

In the opening case, Barbara had to deal on an interpersonal level with Vern, the angry project engineer; Leslie, the distraught low performer; and Captain York, the worried supervisor. All these interpersonal communications might have caused problems if they had not been understood and resolved. One way of understanding and dealing with interpersonal communication is through transactional analysis, the subject of this section.

Transactional Analysis

One of the best ways to understand and sort out interpersonal communication is by using transactional analysis to identify the underlying structure of interpersonal exchanges. While there is much more to transactional analysis than simply understanding communication patterns, we define **transactional analysis** (TA) as a system for understanding human communication by analyzing transactions and chains of transactions and their associated ego states.[12]

Eric Berne, a psychiatrist, invented TA as a way of getting his patients involved in their own treatment. Thus, he used terms that were understandable and vivid. For some time TA was used only in psychotherapy, but in the past fifteen or twenty years, managers have begun to realize that TA could help them understand and solve organizational problems.[13]

Ego States. An **ego state** is a consistent pattern of feeling, thinking, and experiencing that is related to a corresponding consistent pattern of behavior.[14] Ego states are a reflection of our past experience. They are a natural way of recording and experiencing life. In fact, a common analogy is to say that ego states are videotapes of our past feelings and memories. When a given ego state is aroused, the tape can be replayed and the event may even be re-experienced.

There are three ego states: Parent, Adult, and Child (when these words are capitalized, they refer to ego states rather than actual parents, adults, or children). The ego states have no relation to the age or family status of the person. Young children can have an active Parent ego state (recall how bossy children can be when playing the parent role), just as older people can have an active Child ego state; however, some people will tend to favor one ego state over the others. There is no one single ego state that is more desirable than the others—all are important.

The Parent Ego State.   We develop the **Parent ego state** by observing our parents and other authority figures and by assuming a set of behaviors that seem to be appropriate. The Parent contains "shoulds" and "oughts" or standards of behavior; it contains prejudices and critical behaviors; and it also contains nurturing behaviors and feelings. An impatient, scowling, angry airline passenger who says: "You should not allow this type of foul-up. I'll certainly not fly with this airline again!", is behaving in the Parent ego state. An angry boss who shouts at an employee, "Can't you ever get your reports in on time!", is also acting in the Parent ego state.

The Parent ego state is not always controlling and critical because it also contains our nurturing, encouraging, and supportive behaviors. It is also a Parent behavior when the boss warmly pats you on the back and says, "You're doing fine. Keep up the good work." Certainly, these behaviors are important to organizations. Some of us did not learn them well as children and are not very skillful with this type of Parent behavior.

The Adult Ego State.   The part of a person that seeks knowledge, gathers facts, analyzes data, organizes, and tests reality is known as the **Adult ego state**. This part of the ego, which is not related to a person's age, is computer-like and objective. It deals with problem solving. An example of Adult behavior is when the ticket counter employee says to the irate customer, "I'll check my computer for a connection on another airline." The majority of organizational communication probably takes place in the Adult ego state. This ego state seldom gets us into communication difficulties and may even be used to get ourselves out of a communication predicament, such as the one faced by the ticket counter person.

The Child Ego State.   The impulses and feelings that come naturally to a child are contained in the **Child ego state**. Impulsive and uninhibited release of emotions such as anger, joy, excitement, and fun are part of the Child. The Child is creative and intuitive, and may also be manipulative. Like the other ego states, the child is not related to age.

An example of Child behavior might be this suggestion from a coworker: "Let's go out after work and play tennis. Wow! Wouldn't that be fun on a beautiful day like today?" Another example might be this response to the boss's critical remark about the late report mentioned earlier: (Head and eyes down.) "I'm sorry boss, I'll try not to do it again. I just can't understand why I can't get done on time." (Wipes tears from eyes.)

Table 8.3 shows the behavior associated with each of the ego states and the accompanying body language, expressions, and vocal tone for each.

Table 8.3

EGO STATE IDENTIFIERS

Ego State Behaviors		BODY LANGUAGE	EXPRESSIONS	VOCAL TONE
		Ego State Indicators		
WHAT THE PARENT DOES	Restricts Judges Blames Encourages Nurtures Criticizes	Looking down over rim of glasses. Pointing an accusing finger. Hands on hip.	"You should . . . you ought . . . you must" . . . "Be cool" "Don't tell me . . ." "You disappoint me" "Poor thing" "I'll protect you"	Harsh Judgmental Soothing Indignant Commanding Comforting
WHAT THE ADULT DOES	Processes infor- mation Takes objective action Organizess Plans Solves problems Estimates risks	A straight, relaxed stance Slightly tilted head. Appearance of active listening. Regular eye contact. Confident appearance.	"Aha, I see" "I see your point" "I recognize . . ." "How do you feel about . . ."	Relaxed Assertive Somewhat deliberative Self-assertive
WHAT THE CHILD DOES	Invents Acts on impulse Acts selfishly Loves Imagines Brainstorms Acts belligerently Complains	Forlorn appearance. Drooping shoulders. Withdrawal. Pursed lips. Scowling. Skipping. Hugging. Twinkle in eyes.	"I want" "I wish" "Wow" "I should" "Did I do okay?" "One of these days" "It's not fair" "It's not my fault" "Oh boy!"	Appealing Complaining Nagging Indignant Cheerful Protesting Grumbling

SOURCE: Adapted with permission of the publisher, from *Transactional Analysis*, C. Albano, pp. 7–8, © 1974 AMACOM, a division of American Management Association, New York. All rights reserved.

Analyzing Transactions Between Two People

A **transaction** occurs when one person recognizes another with a verbal or nonverbal transmission, and the other person responds. Each transaction originates in one of the three ego states—Parent, Adult, or Child—and the response also comes from one of the three ego states. There are three types of transactions: complementary, crossed, and ulterior.

A **complementary transaction** occurs when a message that is sent to a specific ego state gets the predicted or expected response. The transaction may involve the same or different ego states. The set of examples illustrated in Figure 8.3 explains and clarifies the nature of complementary transactions. While we can infer that these examples may be actually complementary transactions, we must make several assumptions to do so. We must assume that the transac-

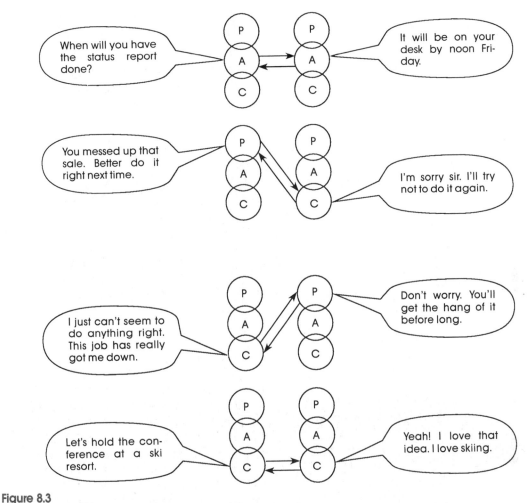

Figure 8.3

EXAMPLES OF COMPLEMENTARY TRANSACTIONS

tion actually originates in the specified ego state and that verbal and nonverbal cues are congruent.

Crossed transactions cause many interpersonal communication failures. In a crossed transaction, people receive a message or behavior that disconfirms their own position, their view of the other person, or both. In other words, an inappropriate ego state is aroused, and the lines of communication between ego states are crossed—an unexpected outcome of the transaction.

However, some crossed transactions do not present problems for communication. An Adult ego state transaction that crosses another may serve to arouse the adult in the other person and change the direction of the transaction from an emotional, angry exchange to a rational, problem-solving one. In fact, intentionally responding to a transaction with an Adult crossing transaction is a major strategy for smoothing conflict and solving communication difficulties. This is the strategy Barbara used in the opening example to cool Vern's anger.

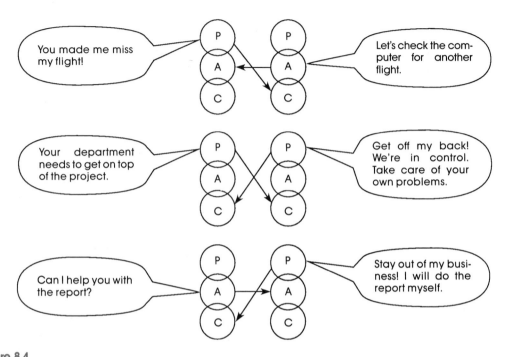

Figure 8.4

EXAMPLES OF CROSSED TRANSACTIONS

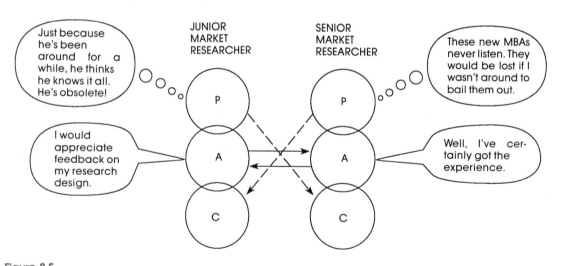

Figure 8.5

EXAMPLE OF AN ULTERIOR TRANSACTION

The examples of crossed transactions in Figure 8.4 illustrate this concept. Note that the example on the left is a desirable use of the crossed transaction because the Adult is used to cross the critical Parent.

Ulterior transactions always involve more than two ego states. There is always a hidden message that is often disguised in some socially acceptable form. For example, when the boss says, "The Morrison case may be a little too tough for you," the real transaction expressed privately as an ulterior one is,

"You're too stupid to do a challenging case like that." Ulterior transactions are also not necessarily bad in themselves. For example, ulterior transactions are almost always involved in courtship behavior. Figure 8.5 presents examples of ulterior transactions.

Using Transactional Analysis

Now that you understand the ego states and how transactions work, you can apply the theory to organizational situations. The key is skillful use of the adult ego state.

Use an Adult Bossing Style.   People often evaluate a comment as good or bad, forming a corresponding opinion about the sender. For example, when a boss tells a subordinate to do something using the critical-Parent ego state, then the subordinate often gets defensive and reacts like an angry, rebellious child. A good way to avoid this is to use the Adult ego state when giving assignments or interacting with subordinates—use an Adult bossing style.[15] Along this same line, a manager who uses a participative style of leadership is probably one that concentrates on using the Adult ego state. On the other hand, an authoritative leader may be likely to use the Parent.[16]

Use the Adult to Cross Undesirable Transactions.   One of the most effective ways of using TA is to defuse undesirable situations by using the Adult to cross the transaction. While this type of cross does tend to stop communication, there is a strong inclination for the other person to respond in the Adult. Since the Adult is problem-solving oriented and nonemotional, it is difficult to remain angry when facing a series of Adult transactions. The key here is to counter each transaction from the critical Parent with an Adult transaction.

An example using airline ticket counter employees is appropriate. When an angry customer berates the person because a flight was cancelled or plane delayed, the best response is to go into an Adult, problem-solving mode. Examine various alternatives, check the computer, check for local hotel availability. A continuous chain of Adult transactions is hard to resist. People are often reinforced for angry behavior when they get the response they want. They want to let off steam at your expense.

Transactional Analysis Applications in Organizations

Transactional analysis has been used by a number of firms:

- Bank of America has used it to train "disadvantaged" people to be more effective and efficient employees. [17]

- AT & T used it to improve communication between employees.[18]

- IBM found it was effective for training sales personnel.[19]

- The U.S. Civil Service found it effective for training women for upwardly mobile careers.[20]

One of the most effective uses of TA is in emotional, high-pressure jobs, such as those with the airlines. One example of how TA helps in these positions is the case of a stewardess working for American Airlines who had been trained in TA: [21]

> I remember one flight between Toronto and Chicago that took three hours because of a snow storm at Chicago. The passengers were mostly business men with connections to make and meetings to attend. My first inclination was to grumble along with them as to how awful the situation was, but then I thought: "Is this the way to make a fun trip?" So I smiled, and smiled, and smiled. I made it a point to chat with each passenger, feeding their Child with the attention it needed and answering their Adult questions. Pretty soon everyone in the first class cabin was chatting with each other. By trying to be happy myself, it brushed off on others who, in turn, infected the whole cabin: A ballooning "I'm OK—You're OK" feeling.

Thus, TA has the potential to improve interpersonal communication substantially in many organizational situations. It can be used by individual managers to improve their everyday effectiveness or it can be used in large-scale organizational improvement efforts, such as the ones cited above. In the next section, we cover how listening affects our communication effectiveness.

LISTENING BEHAVIOR

What aspect of communication do you spend the most time doing—speaking, writing, reading, or listening? If you answered *listening*, you were right. Approximately 45 percent of all time spent communicating involves listening; next comes speaking with 30 percent, reading with 16 percent, and writing with 9 percent.[22]

Listening is one of the most important skills for managers. Not only is much of their time spent listening, but the very performance and satisfaction of the organization may be directly linked with these skills.[23] While much of a manager's listening involves fellow-employees, dealing with customers also requires listening skills. A primary emphasis of today's sales training is on teaching "the salesperson to be a good listener and questioner, sensitive to the needs of others, knowledgeable about his products, more an advisor than a hustler." [24]

The Listening Process

The listening process concentrates on the *receiver* part of our communication model. There are four stages of listening:

1. **Sensing** the message through verbal or nonverbal channels.

2. **Interpreting,** clarifying, and understanding the message.

3. **Evaluating** and appraising it.

4. **Responding** or doing something about the message.

We will discuss two general types of listening: **interpersonal,** which involves interaction between the speaker and the listener, and **informational,** which involves primarily the transmission of information between a listener and a speaker. Both are important in organizations. Interpersonal listening is the

Perspective 8.2

MANAGEMENT BY
WANDERING AROUND[25]

Many of the excellent companies highlighted in the best-selling books, *In Search of Excellence* and *A Passion for Excellence*, use a technique called **"management by wandering around"** or **MBWA.** Managers who practice this technique spend a great deal of time informally wandering about their organization talking with employees and customers. They do a great deal of listening and they ask lots of questions. It is an opportunity to engage in the richest source of communication—direct, face-to-face contact. It enhances two-way communication and provides opportunities to observe nonverbal cues of the work force and customers. The most important part of MBWA is listening, for information gathering and problem sensing are more important than actual problem solving, although inevitably, the two will go together.

The former head of Research and Development at Hewlett-Packard, Barney Oliver, provides an example of how MBWA works: [26]

Barney is a brilliant scientist. He's tough as nails, and intellectually demanding. And yet, he was the personification of effective MBWA at HP Labs . . . the heart of a participative (albeit tough-minded) communication [system].

Barney would wander, we are told, with extraordinary regularity. And he'd stop and chat. And, indeed, you had darn well better have something worthwhile to chat about! He'd look at what you were working on and ask the toughest questions imaginable. He didn't shy away from anything. (MBWA *doesn't* mean, then, that most subjects are *verboten*.) He spoke his mind. But the consensus, among twenty-seven-year-olds and fifty-seven-year-olds alike, was that when Barney had finished with you, (1) you'd learned a heck of a lot, of both lasting and short-term significance, and (2) *the project you were working on was still yours* —Barney had not taken away space, had not in any sense told you what to do or what the next steps should be.

most common type and is illustrated by counseling sessions, informal discussions, and telephone conversations. Informational listening may involve such activities as staff meetings, lectures, and videotape playbacks. The key difference between the two types is the opportunity for interaction. Interpersonal listening involves extensive interaction while informational listening involves little or no interaction.

Interpersonal Listening

Listener Ego States. An important aspect of interpersonal listening is your ego state during the listening. Are you listening with an evaluative tone? Are you conveying approval, disapproval, or opinions? Are you giving advice? These very common organizational behaviors indicate that the Parent ego state is being used. When the Parent ego state is used by the boss, a subordinate may respond in the Child. For example, the subordinate may seem impatient and squirm in the chair and may even withdraw, pout, or giggle. The Adult listening mode is evidenced by a more rational approach to listening. It involves evaluating the situation and then behaving in a manner that is considered to be most effective to solve the problem at hand. Table 8.4 provides examples of nonverbal indicators of various listening ego states.

We will concentrate on the Adult approach to listening because most organizational situations can be handled best with this approach.

Table 8.4

NONVERBAL INDICATORS OF LISTENING EGO STATES

Ego State	Nonverbal Indicators
Parent	Scowl on a tilted head with any amount of side-to-side head rotation indicates parental disciplining or "no!". Head motions, normally evidenced by approving or disapproving nods of the head and often accompanied by tone and words that indicate "It is for your own good" or "the truth is perfectly obvious."
Adult	Level-headed, balanced, straightforward posture with the head slightly turned toward the speaker. Gives the appearance of concentration on what the speaker is saying.
Child	Defiant with head tipped up and to one side, often flat or "stony-faced" with jaw jutting forward. Restless and impatient behavior such as turning toward and then away from the speaker with gross body movements. Pouting and defiantly compliant with face tilted down and gaze averted.

SOURCE: Adapted from Ernst, F.H., Jr. (1968). *Who's listening?* Vallejo, CA: Addressoset.

The Problem-Ownership Model

One way of understanding how to approach various interpersonal listening situations is the **problem-ownership model,** developed by Thomas Gordon.[27] Using this model, you analyze the situation by asking: "Is there a problem?" If there is no problem, then the appropriate ego state can be used to receive the information being transmitted. For example, a foreman might simply listen to a report of one of the workers about a defective machine, noting the fact in memory so it can be reported at the next staff meeting.

However, if there is a problem, ask the question, *"Who owns this problem? The speaker or me?"* If the speaker owns the problem, such as an unhappy marital situation at home, then the listener should use "active listening." If you own the problem—for example, an employee who is not performing up to par—then another approach, called the "I-message," is appropriate. Figure 8.6 diagrams the problem-ownership model.

Active Listening

Whenever the speaker (subordinate) owns the problem and the behaviors of the speaker are acceptable to the listener (boss), then active listening is necessary. **Active listening** means that you concentrate on listening to the other person, on helping him or her to work through the problem. You do it with *empathy* and often using restatements and reflections as a way of checking understanding and showing the speaker that you hear what is being said. You pay particular attention to the emotional tone of the message and respond to it rather than referring only to the verbal content. Active listening takes time, so it should not be attempted unless a substantial amount of time is available to work on the problem.[28]

Examples of Active Listening.   Here are some statements by employees that seem to call for an active listening response:

Machinist named Jack:	"I'm worried that I might not get promoted on time."
Personnel manager named Anne:	"You're concerned about your chances of promotion."
Jack:	"The big layoffs are really frightening. I don't know what will happen if I lose my job."
Anne:	"Sounds like you're worried about being laid off."
Jack:	"I just can't seem to get anything done anymore with all the damn noise from the grinding machine."
Anne:	"You're upset because your performance isn't what it used to be."
Jack:	"My supervisor is always criticizing me. She never has anything positive to say about me."
Anne:	"You're pretty upset with your boss."
Jack:	"This company just doesn't seem to be a good place to work nowadays."
Anne:	"It seems you're disappointed with the company."

Controlling Unacceptable Behavior With I-Messages.   Communications cannot always be nondirective. Sometimes, especially in organizational situations, you have to change behavior even when the other person does not see the need for change. The best way to do this is with an **I-message,** composed of a statement with three major elements: behavior, effects, and feelings.

An I-message to an employee who is late might go like this: "I am afraid that the director will come around at eight o'clock and see that everyone isn't here."

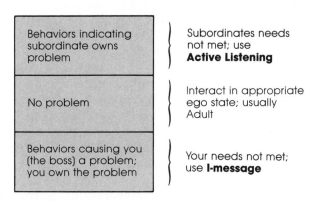

Figure 8.6

PROBLEM–OWNERSHIP MODEL

SOURCE: Adapted from Gordon, T. (1977). *Leader Effectiveness Training L.E.T.* New York: Wyden.

In this case the behavior is implied since the employee was missing at eight o'clock this morning. The effects on you, the boss, are that you might get into a lot of trouble with the director if everyone is not here on time. The feelings reflect your fear that you will be harmed, perhaps reprimanded or passed over for promotion. Other ways you might respond to this same situation might be:

- "I am concerned that others in the office might start coming in late, too."

- "I am really discouraged when I think of all the work we have to do today and I can't get the crew started until you get here."

- "When you come in late, I figure that you don't care about your job and that makes me angry."

Informational Listening

There are a number of important techniques and skills that can improve informational listening.[29] Listening skills can help improve your retention and understanding of information that is presented in briefings, staff meetings, or training films.[30] Improving your informational listening skills can also have payoffs in the college classroom.

There are four strategies for effective listening: clarifying the purpose, concentrating on the speaker, listening for the main ideas, and avoiding premature evaluation. These are discussed in the following paragraphs.

What Is the Purpose?   Perhaps the most important question to ask in an informational listening situation, such as a briefing on a new product or the introduction of a new computer system, is: "Why am I here?" In other words, you should have a purpose for listening. Listen for what you can use.

Work Hard at Listening.   Do not tune out the speaker just because the delivery is boring or inept. Work hard to get the meaning. Avoid daydreaming, for once you go off on a tangent, it is hard to get back on the track. In addition, do not give up just because the material is difficult. Not everything is easy. Many important things in life take discipline and persistence to learn.

Listen for Main Ideas.   Listen for the speaker's main points or themes. The worst thing you could do is take lots of notes about the facts and miss the real meaning of the message. Along this line it is important to take notes, but not necessarily to outline the speaker's presentation. One proven way to take notes is to draw a line down the middle of the page and on one side list facts; on the other principles or themes.

Avoid Premature Evaluation.   Try to avoid making judgments about the presentation or the speaker until the presentation is over. Often, people tend to make up their mind that the speaker is "all wet" because of some early statement or an emotional word that colors all their perception.

Perspective 8.3

KEYS TO EFFECTIVE
INFORMATIONAL LISTENING[31]

Listening Technique	Ineffective Behavior	Effective Behavior
Concentrate on the message.	Faking attention; easily distracted; avoids difficult material.	Actively displays energy and attention; does not become distracted; works hard to understand difficult material.
Listen for ideas.	Tries to remember all the facts.	Searches for ideas or central themes that facts support.
Judge content, not delivery or appearance.	Does not listen if delivery is poor or appearance is unsuitable.	Looks for the content of the message; ignores delivery and appearance problems.
Develop motivation to listen.	Dismisses subject as uninteresting.	Does not prematurely judge interest; searches for reasons to listen.
Avoid premature evaluation.	Tends to think of arguments opposed to speaker's ideas.	Listens with an open mind; does not prematurely decide upon the merits of the arguments.

NONVERBAL COMMUNICATION

Nonverbal communication is so important that it deserves a special section for emphasis. All of us use nonverbal communication, but often we use it unconsciously. We are quite unaware of the signals we are sending. For example, a manager may be trying to communicate the directions for accomplishing a task in a straightforward, Adult way. However, the manager's nonverbal behavior may send different signals. The manager may be sitting behind the desk, arms crossed, and a slight frown on the face. A subordinate may read the nonverbal behavior as a desire for dominance and power, originating from the Parent ego state.[32] The employee may leave the session feeling criticized, attacked, and defensive.

Nonverbal Communication Cues

Nonverbal communication involves vocal cues, facial expressions, posture, hand movements, touch, dress, and spatial relationships. In the previous section, we covered a number of nonverbal behaviors that are associated with listening skills (*see* Table 8.3). In Chapter 4 we discussed impression management, the systematic management of nonverbal behavior to create a favorable image. In this section we will review the major concepts so you will have an awareness of nonverbal communication.

One researcher found that the overall impact of a message depends more on nonverbal behavior than on verbal behavior.[33] Only 7 percent of a message's impact was due to the actual verbal content (the words and grammar). The rest was due to the nonverbal impact—38 percent of the vocal content, and 55 percent for facial content. While not every message would have this same proportion, it is apparent that nonverbal communication is a substantial part of the total message.

When verbal and nonverbal information conflict, nonverbal almost always wins out. For example, "If someone calls you 'honey' in a nasty tone of voice, you are likely to feel disliked; it is also possible to say 'I hate you' in a way that conveys exactly the opposite feeling." [34]

In the following paragraphs, we will cover four elements of nonverbal communication: vocal cues, body position, facial expressions, and physical settings.

Vocal Cues.   The vocal part of a message, sometimes referred to as **paralinguistics,** pertains to how the message is transmitted in terms of range, resonance, rate, control, intensity, pitch, and inflection. Figure 8.7 illustrates the differences in vocal cues that add meaning to our verbal messages.

Facial Expressions.   The face and head are perhaps the most important sources of nonverbal signals. Just by looking at people we can tell, roughly, how old they are, whether they are awake and alert, or if they are listening. We may also be able to tell an individual's sex, race, ethnic origin, status, or occupation. Our cues might include baldness, gray hair, wrinkles, pigmentation of the skin, eye and hair color, and makeup of the person's features. Facial hair (beard or mustache), eyebrows, cleanliness, and makeup are superficial ways of judging how people feel about themselves and how they want to be perceived by others.

Emotional Displays.   People's faces show happiness, sadness, surprise, anger, joy, distress, fear, disgust, and interest. Figure 8.8 shows the exaggerations of the eyes, mouth, forehead, eyebrows, and nose that result in these basic emotional displays. Test your ability to recognize emotional displays by taking the quiz in Figure 8.8.

Emotional display rules are often established by the culture or subculture, even at the organizational level. In organizations, it is important to know which facial behaviors are O.K. or not O.K. for display. For example, some organizational cultures would call for "businesslike" unemotional behavior, while others would value the display of authentic emotions.

Eye behavior is particularly powerful. When you want to be recognized at a staff meeting, you "catch the eye" of the leader. On the other hand, students who do not want to be recognized in class often avoid the eye of the instructor. One of the principal rules of public speaking is to have good eye contact with your audience. In a one-on-one situation, averting another's eyes or a downward gaze indicates lower status. A steady gaze is a **visual dominance** technique. If you want to be treated as an equal, when someone looks at you, look back, maintain eye contact. Loss of eye contact during a conversation may mean that a touchy subject has been encountered.

Figure 8.7

VOCAL CUES

SOURCE: Randall P. Harrison, *Beyond Words: An Introduction to Nonverbal Communication,* © 1974, pp. 106–107. Adapted by permission of Prentice-Hall, Inc., Englewood Cliffs, N.J.

Can you match the above sketches with the correct affects? (1) happy,
(2) sad, (3) surprise, (4) fear, (5) anger, (6) disgust.

Answers: A–5, B–2, C–1, D–3, E–5, F–2, G–6, H–4, I–3.

Figure 8.8

EMOTIONAL DISPLAY QUIZ

SOURCE: Randall P. Harrison, *Beyond Words: An Introduction to Nonverbal Communication,* © 1974, pp.
106–107. Reprinted by permission of Prentice-Hall, Inc., Englewood Cliffs, N.J.

Smiling is another behavior that may have several meanings. It may simply
mean that you are happy. But, it also may mean that you are uncomfortable
and are displaying nervous grinning. Phony smiling puts you in a lower-status
position.

Head position and tilt are another important key. A head tilted too far up
gives an air of superiority, while a head tilted downward shows passiveness and
submission. A level head is more indicative of a confident, neutral style. Head
nods are also important; a nod, up and down, no matter how slight, is seen as
agreement. Whereas, a head shake from side to side indicates disagreement.

Body position is also important. Just as eye contact indicates higher status,
a relaxed body position also indicates high status. When people of unequal
status interact, the higher-status person takes a more relaxed position while the
lower-status person takes the more "at attention" position.[35] Extreme relaxation
is a common behavior with disliked, nonthreatening addressees.[36] In addition,
posture gives an indication of how much a speaker likes another. Leaning
towards another indicates liking, and away, dislike.

If you are making a presentation to the corporate vice-president for finance
for a new system you want to buy, you might adjust your presentation based on
the body language you observe. If the vice-president is slightly relaxed, friendly,
and greets you with a straight gaze, then you may have a receptive person. If,

on the other hand, the VP is leaning back in the chair with folded arms and a wrinkled brow, you may need to be particularly persuasive. If the posture and facial expression change, then you can tailor your presentation to the nonverbal signals.

Physical Environment

A typical chief executive's office is large, carpeted, and well protected by secretaries and assistants. This type of office says: "I'm important. Don't bother me with anything unless it is also important.[37] This nonverbal communication tends to purposely inhibit the flow of information to and from the chief. While executive isolation is typical for American top managers, the Japanese use a more open structure (see the cross-cultural section later in this chapter).

The physical layout of a manager's office also sends important nonverbal signals. Figure 8.9 illustrates how the arrangement can affect communication.

I'm the boss!
I'm in control!

We're equals.
Let's work together.

Let's talk together
informally.

Let's be friendly.

Figure 8.9

OFFICE ARRANGEMENTS SEND NONVERBAL MESSAGES

A traditional layout with the desk centered and the manager firmly behind the desk may send a signal that communication is not wanted. It is almost impossible to practice active listening in this position. The other three positions illustrate more open communication signals that can enhance transmissions.

CROSS–CULTURAL OB: OPEN COMMUNICATION IN JAPANESE–OWNED COMPANIES

Even high-ranking managers in Japanese companies may not have private offices. "In one Japanese-owned TV plant on the West Coast, the top manager's office is next to the receptionist—open and visible to everybody who walks into the building, whether employee, supplier, or customer." [38] Privacy for meetings and conferences is afforded by several small conference rooms and meeting areas. The Japanese encourage this type of office arrangement so face-to-face communication will be easier.

In Japanese companies, the plant manager may also spend at least two hours per day out on the shop floor talking to employees and supervisors. This presence gives a strong nonverbal signal that the manager cares and is interested in everyone's problems.

Foremen (the lowest-level supervisors in the plant) may not have an office at all. They are expected to work with the employees on the shop floor. Thus, there is good communication and less feeling of isolation between supervisors and workers.

An American personnel manager in a Japanese motorcycle plant spends two to four hours per day on the shop floor discussing personnel problems. "We have an open-door policy—but it's their door, not management's (that's open)." [39]

MANAGERIAL APPLICATIONS OF COMMUNICATION

Understanding the communication process (source, message, receiver, and feedback) is vital for managers because a great deal of the managerial task involves communicating effectively. Much of interpersonal communication can be understood by using transactional analysis. The key here is to use the Adult ego state for most management communication.

Listening is also an important managerial skill, whether it be interpersonal listening or informational listening. Interpersonal listening is used to open communication channels and solve problems that are of concern to either the employee or the manager. It helps us learn how to confront problems. Informational listening helps in assimilating and storing information more effectively. Each of these types of listening requires different skills and techniques.

Nonverbal communication permeates everything that we do and is very influential in determining the overall impact of a message. Managers need to

Perspective 8.4

RULES FOR COMMUNICATING IN INTERNATIONAL BUSINESS

• *Rule 1: Know where information flows.*[40] Every culture has its own communication routes. In the U.S., information is expected to be transferred to the manager, who is the center of the communication network. In South America the reverse may be true—the manager may have to solicit information from subordinates.

• *Rule 2: There is no point in getting straight to the point.* Many cultures find that American directness is disconcerting at best. Nigerians say that Americans have an "espionage mentality" because they ask for so much information. Try to approach information gathering in a more conversational mode.

• *Rule 3: Speak simple, but not simpleminded, English to a foreigner.* Talk slowly. Avoid cumbersome words and slang. Be ready to convert all figures to local currency and measures.

• *Rule 4: Don't mistake a courteous answer for the truth.* While Americans like to "tell it like it is" and respect candor, other cultures do not approach communication in such a manner. In the Orient, saving face may be more important than the blunt truth. Remember that "yes" or "no" may not mean the same. In Asia

yes may mean "I heard you," not "yes, I agree." The French often say "no" when they mean "maybe."

• *Rule 5: Silence is a form of speech. Don't interrupt it.* Be patient. Allow the other person to talk.

• *Rule 6: Learn to speak and understand body language.* Nonverbal signals help to communicate, but they can also be misinterpreted. The familiar "thumbs up" sign in the United States is considered vulgar in many parts of the world and roughly equal to raising the middle finger in America. In Yugoslavia people shake their heads from side to side to mean "yes," but we interpret the same behavior as "no." In Japan looking someone in the eye can cause problems. A boss who looks directly in a subordinate's eyes is seen as judgmental and harsh. A subordinate who looks the boss in the eye is seen as hostile and overly aggressive.[41]

• *Rule 7: Learn the language.* Ability to speak the language helps attune you to the local culture and makes an overseas assignment much easier. In addition, it will greatly aid communicating with business associates. Remember that if you are engaged in exporting, the language of international business is that of the customer.

• *Rule 8: Don't trust people just because they speak English.* Ability to speak a language means only that. Don't assume that this ability also means the person is more competent, knowledgable, and intelligent. Also take care not to assume those that cannot speak English are dumb or incompetent.

be attuned to their own and others' nonverbal signals to fully manage the communication process.

Here are some more specific guides for managerial action:

• *Assess others' field of experience.* Good communication means being able to relate to the person or group you are communicating with. Carefully examine the experiences, background, and knowledge of the people whom you are addressing.

• *Use face-to-face communication whenever possible.* This type of communication offers the highest degree of richness and the best opportunities for feedback and clarification.

- *Give and ask for lots of feedback.* Extensive use of feedback helps clarify communication, provide information for correcting work behavior, and is an excellent source of positive reinforcement for good work performance.

- *Use an Adult style for communicating and bossing.* Try to conduct most business communication in the Adult ego state. Use the Adult to cross undesirable communication transactions. Avoid ulterior transactions; they tend to confuse communication.

- *Practice management by wandering around (MBWA).* By getting out and informally communicating with employees and customers, you can greatly enhance the communication process.

- *Use the Problem-Ownership Model to deal with problems of subordinates.* Confront unacceptable behaviors by using I-messages. Use active listening to deal with subordinate-owned problems.

- *Stay attuned to nonverbal signals, both your own and others.* Be particularly aware that nonverbal cues can communicate power, concern, dominance, disinterest, uneasiness, friendliness, liking, status, and many other important indicators.

- *Design your physical environment for effectiveness.* Office layout and other physical nonverbal cues should be used to create the effect you desire. Do you wish an open, easy communication environment or a high power, dominating environment?

- *Be aware of cultural differences in communication.* When communicating across cultures, be aware that there are many differences besides just language. Carefully study the country you are visiting and prepare a plan to insure clear communication.

FOR DISCUSSION

1. Pick an example of communication that you have participated in the past day or two and analyze it using the model shown in Figure 8.1. Was the communication accurate? If distortions were observed, what part of the process do you believe caused it?

2. Is the grapevine something to be encouraged or discouraged? Why?

3. How might a manager design communication systems to stimulate two-way communication rather than one-way?

4. Explain why the ego states are not related to the degree of maturity of the individual.

5. Based upon your own recent experience, give an example of a transaction that originated in each of the three ego states. What was the reaction to each transaction?

6. What is the best way to deal with transactions that are seen as undesirable by the manager, such as one originating from the Child ego state at an inappropriate time?

7. Why is MBWA effective? List the benefits and drawbacks.

8. Explain how the problem-ownership model works.

9. Give an organizational instance for using I-messages and active listening.

10. Observe the nonverbal communication behavior of people for fifteen minutes. What nonverbal behavior did you observe? Did people respond more powerfully to nonverbal or verbal comments?

11. Do you think the open communication used by many Japanese companies is appropriate for American companies? Why or why not?

KEY CONCEPTS AND TERMS

communication process
nonverbal behavior
feedback
field of experience
one-way communication
two-way communication

transactional analysis
ego states
complementary transaction
crossed transaction
ulterior transaction
Adult bossing style

MBWA
Problem-Ownership Model
active listening
I-messages
paralinguistics

Cases and Incidents

LAFAYETTE AERODYNAMICS

Mark Brodstreet is a manager of technical budgets and expenses for LaFayette Aerodynamics. Technical cost analyst Leonardo Schultz reports to him. Communication between these two people is deplorable.

Part of the problem is that Leonardo was originally trained as an engineer and learned his cost accounting in night school. Brodstreet is a CPA with no technical training. He is forever holding forth in Leonardo's presence that engineers are an inferior breed with no conception of cost or profit.

For his part, Leonardo believes in the notion of "the whole man," and he feels that anyone who is monitoring costs should have a basic understanding of design and of the impact of cost cuts on the final product.

Recently, Leonardo supported a group of design engineers who protested Brodstreet's edict that 20 percent of the material cost had to be pruned from a new braking system for jet aircraft. In the middle of a group discussion, Brodstreet lost his temper,

abruptly ended the meeting, and stated that he was going to carry the whole matter to the vice-president of engineering.

Privately, he read the riot act to Leonardo and accused him of being "a frustrated engineer who couldn't make a living at it." He finished the confrontation by questioning Leonardo's "two-bit night-school accounting degree" and reminding him that his first loyalty was to Brodstreet and not to a bunch of spendthrift engineers. They haven't spoken to each other for two weeks now, except to carry on the most essential and rudimentary communication.

DISCUSSION QUESTIONS

1. Describe the transactions between Mark and Leonardo using TA.

2. How might this communication problem be handled more effectively using the problem-ownership model?

From R. D'Aprix. (1972). Why they tune you out. *Machine Design,* December 28 Copyright © 1972 by Penton Industrial Publishing Co., Inc., Cleveland, Ohio. Used with permission.

WHAT IS HAPPENING HERE?

DISCUSSION QUESTIONS

1. Read the nonverbal behavior. What do you see happening here?

2. Describe the specific parts of the nonverbal behavior—face, posture, head position—that caused you to make your conclusions.

Reprinted with permission of Hilton Hotel Corporation, Beverly Hills, California.

RUDOLPH CARTER

Rudolph Carter, a young electrical engineer, three years out of college, received an attractive job offer from the SEMA Co., a major sugar company in the tropics. At the time, Rudolph held a position of junior engineer with the local utility company in a small town. In the three years he had been with the company he had received one "very insignificant salary increase" based essentially on merit, and no promotions. Therefore, for the past year he had been actively looking around the surrounding industrial area for a more attractive job position with an increased salary.

The job offer from SEMA, therefore, came at a very opportune time and, although it represented a "very substantial increase in salary, good promotional promise, plus numerous fringe benefits" (company furnished home and utilities), it did have certain drawbacks. Rudolph was well aware of these as he had been born, reared, and educated through high school on a similar tropical sugar mill plantation where his father had been chief mill engineer until his death five years ago. Having reached manhood in this atmosphere, Rudolph knew well that one of the chief disadvantages was getting to know the local engineers, working with them, winning their acceptance, and coping with other human relations problems.

The position Rudolph had been offered by SEMA was that of assistant chief electrical engineer. He had further been assured that he would be groomed to take over the chief electrical engineer's job when the chief retired in three years and possibly prior to that time, since the chief engineer was in poor health and was considering retiring at an earlier date.

After considerable deliberation and weighing of pros and cons, Rudolph accepted the job and within two months reported for his first assignment.

His first few days on the job proved to be very difficult—not from a professional-technical standpoint, but because of the human relations problems. The chief engineer had suddenly been required to take some sick leave and had flown to the United States for medical treatment. He had left the electrical department in charge of his senior electrical engineer, Señor Jose Gonzales, a national who was a graduate of the technical college on the island. Gonzales was about 45 years old and had 16 years service with the department. The chief engineer had left full written instructions with Gonzales (with a copy for Rudolph) outlining Rudolph's job assignments and responsibilities. The instructions left little doubt that Rudolph was to assume full responsibility and authority for operating the electric plant.

The beginning of the crop-grinding season was two weeks away and Rudolph found himself in a crush of people rushing around trying to put all of the electric plant facilities in final operating condition. The plant force, all locals, numbered about 40, and while most of them could understand English, they could speak it only brokenly. This even applied to Gonzales, the senior electrical engineer.

It was at once apparent to Rudolph that Gonzales was indeed the key man of the entire operations, and that, in fact, he had been running the whole show for a good number of years. His word and directions were law as far as the workers were concerned and they all respected him very highly.

Rudolph quickly noted two things about Gonzales during his first day on the job. First, Gonzales was an extremely competent engineer, completely familiar with the plant operations, and although there was no formal organization procedure, he and his men performed all work very efficiently. Second, Gonzales was highly ambitious, with a strong desire and motivation to become the chief electrical engineer.

Gonzales very quickly and definitely let Rudolph know that his presence was resented; he offered no cooperation, advice, or help. There was only one factor which helped to establish a certain amount of rapport between the two men, and that was Rudolph's ability to speak Spanish. Without this accomplishment, his effectiveness would have been nil.

During Rudolph's second week on his job, and only three days prior to the grinding season, the plant manager requested a detailed report on start-up status of all plant electrical equipment. Being completely unfamiliar with such status reports, Rudolph requested a report from Gonzales, to which Gonzales immediately replied that everything was completely "O.K. and ready to go," and that he had never prepared such a detailed status and it wasn't necessary—the chief engineer always was content with just his word. In a search through the files, which were in a pitiful state, Rudolph was able to locate a status report for the year prior which had been submitted by the chief engineer. It was quite lengthy and in considerable detail, listing all electrical items, and showing everything in a "ready to go" condition. It had been directed to the plant manager with copies to no one.

Rudolph deliberated the problem at length, debating on whether merely to duplicate the prior status report, showing everything on a satisfactory basis and thus relying on Gonzales's verbal say-so, or whether to take the list to him and insist on witnessing the testing and operation of all components. Rudolph realized he was on fairly touchy grounds and that if he were to succeed at his job, one thing was fairly certain: he needed the confidence and cooperation of Gonzales. He surely did not want to antagonize him this early in the game, and yet he wanted to be positive that his first report to the plant manager would be correct and accurate.

He decided to talk to Gonzales, show him the list from the previous year, assure him that he, Rudolph, was willing to accept Gonzales's verbal say-so of equipment fitness, but to ask him to check the list for completeness, since during the past year there might have been some deletions or additions of equipment.

Gonzales was genuinely surprised at seeing the list, and immediately put himself on the defensive. However, after a few minutes of talking, during which time Rudolph emphasized his willingness and confidence to accept Gonzales's assurance that all items were on the "ready-to-go" status and that all he was requesting was a recheck of equipment listing, Gonzales warmed considerably to the situation and cooperated graciously.

During the checking of the list, they did indeed find numerous items which had been physically deleted in the field and a few new installations. Gonzales even pointed out that at least one major piece of equipment had not checked out completely to his satisfaction and that he and his men were having some difficulty in hooking up test instrument equipment for checking it out further. When Rudolph suggested that they put their heads together and see if they could unravel the testing difficulties, Gonzales seemed somewhat relieved.

In reviewing the test hook-up, Rudolph quickly spotted the difficulty but instead of pointing it out directly, he was able to guide Gonzales's analysis to the point where Gonzales himself recognized it on his own, so to speak.

On the face of it, Gonzales's men were most impressed with the fact that their man, and not the new man, had located and corrected the difficulty. Inwardly, Rudolph could tell Gonzales fully realized that he had been very astutely steered toward recognizing the fault and had been allowed to "save face" with his men.

This, then, was the start of a very pleasant and cooperative relationship between Rudolph and Gonzales, with Gonzales recognizing and accepting slowly but surely Rudolph's position and authority over him.

DISCUSSION QUESTIONS

1. What communication problems were faced by Rudolph?

2. What was Rudolph's strategy for dealing with Gonzales? Why did it work?

3. What ego states were used by Rudolph when dealing with Gonzales? What ego states were used by Gonzales? Diagram an example of one of their interactions.

4. Was Rudolph ethical in his relationship with Gonzales?

Written by Leon C. Megginson. In Fisher, D. (1981). *Communication in Organizations.* St. Paul: West, pp. 63–66. Used with permission.

REFERENCES

1. Mintzberg, H. (1975). The manager's job: Folklore and fact. *Harvard Business Review, 53*(4), 49–61.

2. Snyder, R.A., & Morris, J.H. (1984). Organizational communication and performance. *Journal of Applied Psychology, 69,* 461–465. Fidler, L.A., & Johnson, J.D. (1984). Communication and innovation implementation. *Academy of Management Review, 9,* 704–711.

3. For more information on communication theory and processes, see Fischer, D. (1981). *Communication in organizations.* St. Paul, MN: West. Rosenblatt, S.B., Cheatham, T.R., & Watt, J.T. (1982). *Communication in business* (2nd ed.). Englewood Cliffs, NJ: Prentice-Hall. And Porter, L.W., & Roberts, K.H. (1976). Communication in organizations. In M.D. Dunnette (Ed.), *Handbook of industrial and organizational psychology* (pp. 1553–1589). Chicago: Rand-McNally.

4. Axley, S.R. (1984). Managerial and organizational communication in terms of the conduit metaphor. *Academy of Management Review, 9,* 428–437.

5. Daft, R.L., & Wiginton, J.S. (1979). Language and organization. *Academy of Management Review, 4,* 179–191.

6. D'Aprix, R. (1982, September-October). The oldest (and best) way to communicate with employees. *Harvard Business Review,* pp. 30–32.

7. Zuboff, S. (1982, September-October). New worlds of computer-mediated work. *Harvard Business Review,* pp. 142–153.

8. See Herold, D.M., & Greller, M.M. (1977). Feedback: Definition of a construct. *Academy of Management Journal, 20,* 142–147.

9. For more information about the grapevine, see Delaney, W.A. (1983, August). "I heard it through the grapevine." *Management Review.* Davis, K. (1973, July). The care and cultivation of the corporate grapevine. *Dun's Review,* pp. 44–77. And Rowan, R. (1979, August). Where did that rumor come

from? *Fortune*, pp. 130–37. This example is adapted from Davis, K. (1953, September-October). Management communication and the grapevine. *Harvard Business Review*, p. 44.

10. Delaney (1983), p. 5.

11. From a speech by Don Bellus of Bellus & Associates, Santa Monica, CA. In *DS Letter*, 1971, p. 3.

12. Berne, E. (1972). *What do you say after you say hello?* New York: Grove Press.

13. For more coverage of TA, see Villere, M.F. (1981). *Transactional analysis at work*. Englewood Cliffs, NJ: Prentice-Hall. James, M., & Jongeward, D. (1971). *Born to win: Transactional analysis with gestalt experiments*. Reading, MA: Addison-Wesley. And Jongeward, D. (Ed.) (1976). *Everybody wins: Transactional analysis applied to organizations* (rev. ed.) Reading MA: Addison-Wesley.

14. Berne (1972).

15. James, M. (1975). *The OK boss*. Reading, MA: Addison-Wesley.

16. Bowen, D.D., & Nath, R. (1975). Transactions in management. *California Management Review*, *18*(2), 73–85.

17. Harper, M.B. (1976). Banking on people and TA. In Jongeward (pp. 189–196).

18. Tiana, K.O. (1976). Transactional analysis applied to Mountain Bell. In Jongeward (pp. 197–218).

19. Musselwhite, E. (1976). TA in selling. In Jongeward (pp. 219–229).

20. Scott, D. (1976). Using transactional analysis in seminars for career women. In Jongeward (pp. 151–188).

21. Quote from Randall, L.K. (1976). Red, white, and blue TA at 600 MPH. In Jongeward (p. 133).

22. Barker, L.L. (1971). *Listening behavior*. Englewood Cliffs, NJ: Prentice-Hall. And Steil, L.K. (undated). Your listening profile. Sperry Corporation.

23. Snyder, R.A., & Morris, J.H. (1984). Organizational communication and performance. *Journal of Applied Psychology*, *69*, 461–465.

24. Main, J. (1985, February 4). How to sell by listening. *Fortune*, p. 52.

25. Adapted from Peters, T., & Austin, N. (1985). *A passion for excellence*. New York, Random House. And Peters, T.J., & Waterman, R.H. (1982). *In search of excellence*. New York: Harper & Row. Also see Peters, T.J., & Austin, N.K. (1985). Management by walking around. *California Management Review*, *28*, 9–34, for a reprint from their book cited above.

26. Peters and Austin (1985), p. 379.

27. Gordon, T. (1977), *Leader effectiveness training: L.E.T.* New York: Wyden.

28. For further information about active listening, see Brownwell, J. (1986). *Building active listening skills*. Englewood Cliffs, NJ: Prentice-Hall.

29. Brownwell (1986). Nichols, R.G., & Stevens, L.A. (1957). *Are you listening?* New York: McGraw-Hill.

30. Rowe, M.P., & Baker, M. (1984, May-June). Are you hearing enough employee concerns? *Harvard Business Review*, pp. 127–135.

31. Adapted from Nichols and Stevens (1957).

32. Edinger, J.A., & Patterson, M.L. (1983). Nonverbal involvement and social control. *Psychological Bulletin*, *93*, 30–56.

33. Mehrabian, A. (1968). Communication without words. *Psychology Today*, *1*, 53–55. Also see Mehrabian, A. (1971). *Silent Messages*. Belmont, CA: Wadsworth.

34. Mehrabian (1968).

35. LaFrance, M., & Mayo, C. (1978). *Moving bodies: Nonverbal communication in social relationships*. Monterey, CA: Brooks/Cole.

36. Mehrabian (1968).

37. See Goldhaber, G.M. (1983). *Organizational communication* (3rd ed.). Dubuque, IA: William C. Brown.

38. Hatvany, N., & Pucik, V. (1981, Spring). Japanese management practices and productivity. *Organizational Dynamics*, p. 16. Also see Ruch, W.V. (1982). Techniques of communication in U.S. and Japanese corporations: Are they interchangeable? In S.M. Lee & G. Schwendiman (Eds.), *Management by Japanese systems*. New York: Praeger, pp. 287–301. For a discussion of the merits of open communication, see Eisenberg, E.M., & Witten, M.G. (1987). Reconsidering openness in organizational communication. *Academy of Management Review*, *12*, 418–426.

39. Hatvany and Pucik (1981), p. 16.

40. Adapted from Copeland, L., & Griggs, L. (1985). *Going international: How to make friends and deal effectively in the global marketplace*. New York: Random House, pp. 99–118.

41. For additional information see Ekman, P., Friesen, W.V., & Bear, J. (1984, May). The international language of gestures. *Psychology Today*, pp. 64–69.

Chapter Nine

GROUP DYNAMICS: INDIVIDUALS WORKING TOGETHER

PREVIEW

- What factors result in effective groups?
- How can group membership patterns affect how well an organization responds to crisis situations?
- How can task, maintenance, and blocking roles affect the performance of groups?
- When should you avoid a big office with carpets?
- How do the excellent companies use groups for "chunking"?
- What are "schmoozing" and "social loafing"?
- How do you prevent "reality shock" for new employees?
- How can an endurance walk develop teamwork?

MAJOR TOPICS

Preview Case: The Exit Interview

The Nature of Groups

Group Characteristics

Group Development and the Socialization Process

Work Groups: Managing Effective Teams

Cross-Cultural OB: Socializing New Employees in Japan

Guides for Management Action

Preview Case

THE EXIT INTERVIEW

Karen Lopez is a personnel specialist who conducts exit interviews with employees who are leaving to find out why they are quitting. Her ultimate goal is to lower quit rates. There has been a continuing problem with the Machine Department. New people just don't seem to last more than a few months. Karen is interviewing the latest quitter, Roy Zukowski, to see if she can get at the heart of the problem.

Karen: Roy, why are you quitting?

Roy: I just didn't seem to fit in. The group made it rough on me. They all seemed to be mad at me for some reason.

Karen: What did you do that made them mad?

Roy: Well, I'm not sure, but I believe it started my first day of work when I came in fifteen minutes early to get my tools ready so I'd be all set to start at 7:30. One of the guys came over to me and said: "We don't do any work at all before 7:30, so don't get here early. First thing you know the foreman will want all of us here fifteen minutes early." I took his advice and didn't start before 7:30 any more.

Karen: Was that the only thing?

Roy: Oh, no, there were plenty of other incidents. It wasn't long before I was cornered in the washroom and told that I was working too hard. If I didn't watch out I would machine over twenty-five units a day, which is more than the twenty units most others produce. Since I was working pretty easily to produce that many and I wanted to earn the maximum bonus for extra production, I kept making more in spite of what the others said. Besides the foreman, Joe Taylor, told me I was doing a really great job when I made twenty-five or thirty units a day.

Karen: Sounds like you were doing a good job.

Roy: Yeah, but the others started making life miserable for me. They started insulting me and making fun of me whenever they could. I tried to ignore it, but after a while it gets under your skin.

Also, I started to get more than my share of the dirty work. We are supposed to rotate the undesirable jobs, like cleaning the tool dip solution, but somehow I seemed to get saddled with too many of these "scut" jobs. When I complained, it just seemed to make things worse. The foreman called me in and said how disappointed he was that I was getting the reputation of a troublemaker and complainer and that I should just do as I was told. Then I got chewed out because someone in the shop had filed a grievance against me for doing a job they were assigned—it just doesn't pay to have initiative around here!

Karen: Do you have any idea why you weren't accepted by the others?

Roy: Maybe its because I like to dress nice. I always come to work with a clean and neatly pressed set of work clothes. The others are pretty sloppy and dirty. They wear the same pair of jeans all week long.

Another thing might be that I just don't seem to be interested in the same things they are. If you don't like football or baseball, and I don't, then you can't really join in the conversations. So I always felt left out.

I guess the main reason for leaving is that I just couldn't work with the people down there. The company is good, the pay is high, the benefits are terrific, but when you hate to come to work every day because of your coworkers, it's time to change.

Almost everyone in an organization is a member of one or more groups. A typical manager belongs to many groups; for example, a primary workgroup, the strategic planning committee, the social committee, the engineering-change taskforce, a lunchtime jogging group, the department's bowling league. Groups are often useful for getting the job done, but they can cause problems as indicated in the exit interview just described. This chapter is about an extremely important aspect of managing organizations—understanding group dynamics and making effective use of groups to get the job done.

Group dynamics includes a number of concepts that help explain how groups function. We will cover several of these concepts in this chapter, including: The nature of groups, group roles, norms, status, cohesiveness, development and socialization. In addition, we will look at ways of developing effective work teams.

THE NATURE OF GROUPS

Since group behavior is a central concern of organizational behavior, we will begin the chapter with a discussion of some basic issues. Then we will cover why people join groups and problems that happen when people are excluded from groups.

What Is a Group?

A **group** is a collection of individuals who have interactions with one another toward some common goal or purpose.[1] Groups are different from a collection of individuals in several ways.[2] Group members interact with each other and share a set of goals, roles, and norms that give direction to their activities. We will discuss these issues later in the chapter. They also have some common bonds that tend to develop from common likes, dislikes, and interests. Not all interacting sets of people are groups. The engineering department at Boeing Corp. may be too large to be a group. So is the junior class at most universities. In larger conglomerations of people, there will be a number of groups coexisting together, each with its own thread of commonality. People can also be excluded from groups even when they wish they were members, as was Roy in our opening example.

Group Effectiveness

Groups have a number of positive benefits for the organization, provided that their energies are directed toward accomplishing the organization's goals. Throughout the chapter our discussion will focus on the factors relating to making work groups more effective. Figure 9.1 shows a general model for group behavior. As you can see there are many factors that work together to insure an effective group. The group must have the right composition or mixture of people so that a full range of skills and abilities are available. It must also be structured correctly: the size must be right, roles must be clear and balanced, norms must be positive, and leadership must be effective. In addition, the organization must provide the resources needed by the group and rewards for motivating the group. Groups must also be effective in working together. Group process needs to foster good communication, resolution of conflict, and use of effective role behaviors. A final factor that must be considered is the task

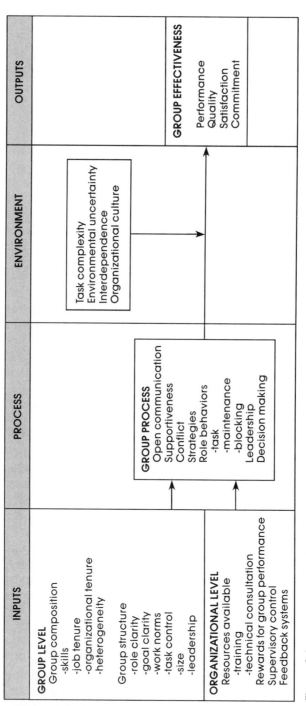

Figure 9.1

GENERAL MODEL OF GROUP BEHAVIOR

SOURCE: Adapted from Gladstein, D.L. (1984). Groups in context: A model of task group effectiveness. *Administrative Science Quarterly, 29,* 502.

itself—its complexity, degree of enrichment, and interdependence have strong influences on effectiveness. (See Chapter 7.)

Group Size: Bigger Is Not Better

A group should be big enough to get the job done, but not too big. Adding people to a group beyond the minimum number required will tend to decrease productivity because of group process losses.[3] **Process losses** are the inevitable inefficiencies that result from people working, interacting, and communicating together. Students working in groups on a class project are a good example—isn't there always someone who is unmotivated or someone who can never come to meetings or fails to get the word? Also, the marginal contribution of adding one more person gets lower as the size of the group gets larger. Adding one person to a two-member group may result in a major improvement in group resources. But adding one more person to a ten-member group will generally add little, if any new resources. The graphs in Figure 9.2 show the relationship between group size and productivity.

Types of Groups

Groups fall into three major categories: **formal work groups,** sometimes called command groups, such as a boss and a set of subordinates, or a board of directors; **ad hoc work groups,** such as committees and task forces; and **informal work groups,** such as people who get together regularly for lunch to discuss common organizational problems. Each of these types of groups serves functions in the organization and contributes to organizational effectiveness.

Formal Work Groups.   Figure 9.3 illustrates how an organization consists of formally structured work groups with supervisors and subordinates. Note that most bosses are members of two groups: the one they supervise and the one that their boss supervises. People who are members of two groups are called **linking pins,** because their task is to link, or coordinate, the two groups together in pursuit of some common goal.[4]

Ad Hoc Work Groups.   Task forces or committees are not only widespread in most organizations, they are essential for effectiveness. Task forces are used to bring together people throughout the organization who have an interest in a topic or problem to make recommendations or take action. Task forces force a broader view of the organization and bring together many diverse viewpoints, perspectives, and interests. This type of group action helps integrate activities throughout the organization.

An illustration of how this strategy works is Lanoga Corp., which has 131 lumber and do-it-yourself stores with about $350 million in annual sales. Lanoga uses four task forces to make decisions concerning marketing, human resource management, management information systems, and finance. Each of Lanoga's three divisions sends a representative to the task force meeting, which is chaired by the corporate representative. For example, when corporate human resource management recommended one companywide pension sys-

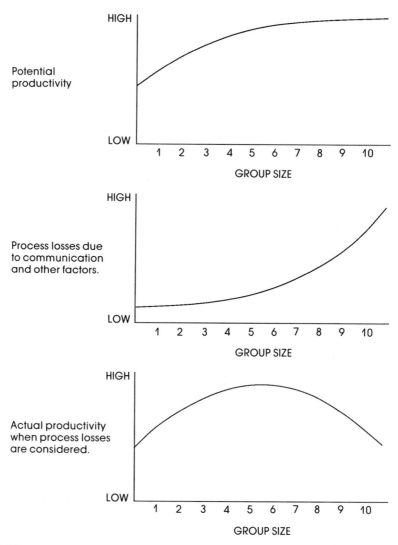

Figure 9.2

THE RELATIONSHIP BETWEEN GROUP SIZE AND PRODUCTIVITY

SOURCE: Adapted from Steiner, I.D. (1972). *Group processes and productivity.* New York: Academic Press, p. 96.

tem to replace the three different pension plans that existed, each division sent its human resource manager to the meeting. The instructions to the group were that all decisions be unanimous and that the corporate member could not vote. At first the group had difficulty making a decision, as unanimous agreement is a difficult goal. However, after considerable discussion the group made the decision to go with a consolidated pension plan. According to Ted Tanase, CEO of Lanoga, these task forces, which have had several years to develop and mature, are quite effective in solving problems and implementing corporatewide changes. This example may be a bit unusual since the group is actually

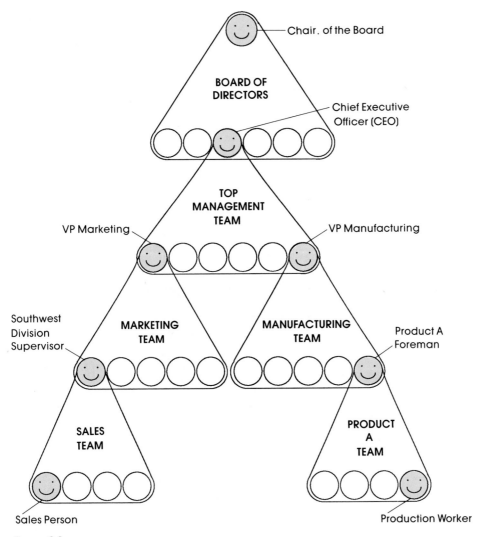

Figure 9.3

EXAMPLES OF FORMAL WORK GROUPS

empowered to *make* the decision rather than merely recommend a course of action.

Informal Groups.   Friendship and common interests or location are usually the basis for these types of groups, sometimes referred to as **friendship cliques.**[5] Most informal groups are formed in subunits, because people are physically close together, and have more opportunities for interaction. These informal groups can contribute or detract from organizational effectiveness. Later in the chapter we will see how negative group norms can create problems. In addition, Perspective 9.1 shows how informal groups can be either positive or negative forces.

FORMAL WORK GROUP

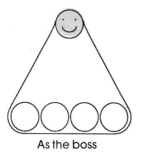

As the boss

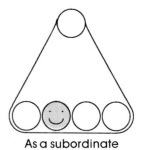

As a subordinate

AD-HOC WORK GROUP

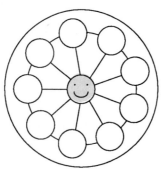

As task force director

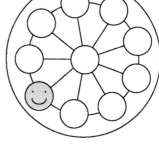

As task force member

INFORMAL GROUPS

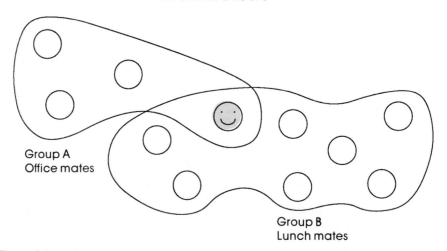

Group A
Office mates

Group B
Lunch mates

Figure 9.4

MANAGERS BELONG TO MANY GROUPS

Perspective 9.1

SOCIAL NETWORKS AND THE MANAGEMENT OF CRISIS[6]

Sometime in the life of most organizations a crisis develops, such as a drastic decline in demand for the firm's products, or the introduction of a revolutionary new product by the competition, or a change in the tax law that will have wide-ranging impact on your organization. **Crisis** can be defined as a situation facing the organization that requires engaging in new untested, unlearned behaviors (within time constraints) to obtain or maintain goals.[7]

In times of crisis it is important that people within the organization cooperate together to meet the demands of the situation. However, since most social networks (informal groups) are centered on the subunit of the group members, there is a tendency to look after one's own unit rather than the good of the organization. In addition, membership in the informal group builds trust, which enhances cooperation. If the informal groups can be structured so that membership exists throughout the organization, then cooperation, trust, and the ability to meet crises situations will be enhanced. Research seems to support this view.[8]

How can more widespread group membership be designed? Extensive use of task forces is one way. People who work in task forces tend to build organizationwide friendships. Company sports and recreational activities will also encourage interaction among different people so that cross-sectional friendships develop.

Why Do People Join Groups?

For thousands of years people have formed groups to get a job done more effectively, whether it be hunting, erecting a home, defending a village, or building a boat. Since groups are generally more effective at solving complex problems than are individuals, organizations are constantly forming task forces and committees to cope with organizational problems. Table 9.1 illustrates some of the benefits of groups to both the organization and the individual.

Table 9.1

POSITIVE IMPACT OF GROUPS ON ORGANIZATIONAL AND INDIVIDUAL EFFECTIVENESS

The impact of groups on organizational effectiveness	The impact of groups on individual employee effectiveness
Accomplishing tasks that could not be done by individual employees	Aiding in learning about the organization and its environment
Bringing a number of skills and talents to bear on complex, difficult tasks	Aiding in learning about one's self
Providing a vehicle for decision making that permits multiple and conflicting views to be aired and considered	Providing help in gaining new skills
Providing an efficient means for organizational control of employee behavior	Obtaining valued rewards that are not accessible by one's self
Increasing organizational stability by transmitting shared beliefs and values to new employees	Satisfying important personal needs, especially needs for social acceptance and affiliation

SOURCE: Adapted from David A. Nadler, J. Richard Hackman, and Edward E. Lawler, III, *Managing Organizational Behavior*, p. 102. Copyright © 1979 by David A. Nadler, J. Richard Hackman, and Edward E. Lawler, III. Used by permission of the publisher, Little, Brown and Company.

Social Interaction and Commitment. Groups provide opportunities for social interaction; they facilitate friendships, companionship, and the satisfaction of our social needs. Groups help develop commitment and loyalty. One of the first things the armed forces do with new recruits is form them into groups. These groups often develop a tremendous esprit de corps during basic training. They serve as a support system, a training vehicle, and a source of obtaining commitment to the goals of the service.

Interpersonal Attraction. If a person finds a group or person in a group particularly attractive, then that will be a strong motivator to join that group. Research has shown that there are several factors that influence attractiveness.[9] The first, close proximity, means that we are usually attracted to those who are near us. It is much more likely that we will join an attractive group in our own office rather than in sales, which is located across the street. In addition, people who have to spend a lot of time interacting are also more likely to form groups. Physical and emotional attractiveness are powerful magnets between people. Finally, we tend to see people as more attractive if they are like us in terms of sex, race, interest, or background.

Problems When People Are Excluded From Groups

While the tendency to include or exclude people from a group based on attractiveness seems normal, it can cause a number of organizational problems, especially for minorities. A recent study of five organizations found that friendship groups for people working in the organizations tended to exclude women and nonwhites.[10] Work group inclusion, on the other hand, seemed to be more influenced by authority position (such as being a director or vice-president) and the education of the group member.

A widely recognized problem of women in managerial positions is the exclusion of women from many of the informal groups to which males belong.[11] In addition, there are often sexual overtones to including women in male friendship groups. Sometimes a woman is too attractive for the male group members' comfort—a difficult situation for both men and women. Dealing with this troublesome issue has been the focus of a number of recent articles and books.[12]

GROUP CHARACTERISTICS

Role Behavior: Doing What's Expected

Just as an actor learns to play a role, organizational participants learn how to play their roles as manager, subordinate, machine operator, popular person, or politician. A **role** is a set of expectations believed by the individual or group to be associated with a person who occupies a given position in the group or organization.[13] Roles are learned in many complex ways.[14] Business schools attempt to develop students into a "managerial role." Organizations attempt to socialize newcomers into their proper role. Group members indoctrinate new

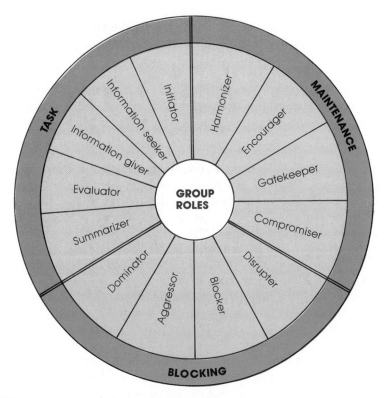

Figure 9.5

ROLES IN GROUPS

SOURCE: Based on Benne, K.D., & Sheats, P. (1948). Functional roles of group members. *Journal of Social Issues, 4,* 41–49.

members into the proper role behavior for that group. One of Roy's problems in the opening incident was the role conflict between what he saw as his role (to produce a high number of units) and what the group saw as his role (to conform to the maximum production specified by the group). While role development processes are important, we will focus primarily on the relationship between role behaviors and group effectiveness.

It takes a number of different roles to make an effective group. The primary ones are **task roles,** which are concerned with getting the job done, and **maintenance roles,** which are concerned with maintaining the interpersonal relationships within the group.[15] In addition, some group roles may oppose the group's goals. These dysfunctional roles are called **blocking roles.** Figure 9.5 visually depicts the roles people play in groups.

Task Roles

While a group can have a variety of tasks or things it is trying to accomplish, a common one is solving problems so that a goal may be reached. The role behaviors in this section relate primarily to groups engaged in some type of group problem-solving activity. In an effectively functioning group, both the members and the leader will play a variety of roles. As you read the descriptions of the roles ask yourself which roles you may play in a group. Then, the next time you observe a group in action, try to pick out which roles lead to more effective group behavior. Task roles include:

Initiator-Contributor.   Proposing new ideas, starting the discussion, or proposing a task, goal, or solution are all initiating activities. While it is often the leader who is the most frequent initiator, any member of the group can play this role.

Information Seeker.   Seeking facts, searching for data, researching sources, asking experts, or asking for clarifications are all information-seeking activities. This is a particularly important role, since many groups tend to act without full information.

Information Giver.   Offering authoritative facts or relevant experience provides the group with more data for their decision. Providing examples to elaborate a suggestion or issue may also be part of this role. Interpreting ideas, defining terms, and clarifying the issues before the group all help the group understand the issues.

Evaluator.   Questioning the practicality, logic or procedures may be a help or hindrance to the group. If the group sees the evaluation as critical and threatening, members may get defensive and interaction may decline or stop. This is especially likely to happen if the leader criticizes the idea. If the evaluation is seen as reality testing, then the reaction may be more positive.

Summarizer.   Pulling together all the related issues, restating positions, and sometimes checking to see if the group is ready to make a decision by proposing alternatives are all parts of the summarizer role.

Maintenance Roles

Role behavior that contributes to building and maintaining the interpersonal relationships of the group is referred to as **maintenance.** If people do not feel good about the group, they may leave it (as Roy did in the opening incident) or be ineffective members. Maintenance roles are considered to be group-centered because they tend to build or keep the group at a given level of energy. Maintenance roles include:

Harmonizer.   This role involves reconciling differences between other members, getting people to explore differences, and minimizing conflicts and reducing tension through humor or other diversionary tactics.

Encourager.   Praising and providing encouragement to other group members encourages them to participate and contribute. Being friendly, warm, and accepting is part of this role. Obviously, Roy did not encounter an encourager in the machine shop.

Gatekeeper. This very important role involves opening and closing the communication "gate" in such a way that gets everyone involved. It means getting people to share their ideas with the group by encouraging quiet people to talk (we haven't heard from Sue yet) or suggesting procedures that let everyone contribute, such as going "round robin" to everyone. Regulating the flow of communication (why not limit the length of our presentations so everyone will have a chance to contribute?) is also part of the gatekeeping role.

Compromiser. Offering to meet someone half way or providing a face-saving way out of a conflict is evidence that the compromiser role is being used.

Blocking Roles

Not all group roles are helpful. Often people try to meet their own needs without regard for the group. This results in a block for the group in accomplishing its goals. Sometimes the group leader is the blocker without realizing it, although just as with task and maintenance roles, anyone can play a blocking role. When blocking roles arise, it is important that group members be trained to recognize them and deal with them with the effective use of task and maintenance roles. The following are examples of blocking roles:

Dominator. This is a role that is easy for the leader to play. The dominator tries to control the group by asserting authority or by appearing superior. In addition, a dominator may try to interrupt or otherwise control the contributions of others. The dominator is best dealt with by another member playing the gatekeeper role, although this may prove difficult if the leader is the problem.

Blocker. Stubbornly opposing the group beyond reason, often for personally oriented reasons, is the main thrust of the blocker's role. Other forms of blocking behavior may involve the use of hidden agendas or attempting to bring back an issue that the group has previously rejected.

Aggressor. The aggressor uses a number of tactics to express disapproval of another's suggestion including attacking the person, group, or problem, joking in a sarcastic or barbed way, or trying to take credit for contributions of others. This behavior is especially destructive and difficult to handle. If the behavior cannot be brought under control, it is often better to remove such people from the group.

Disrupter. This person does not share the group's goals and is not really involved. Cynicism, nonchalance, withdrawal, and irrelevant humor or horseplay are examples of disruptive behavior.

Norms: Governors of Group Behavior

Groups have powerful ways to control group behavior. One of the strongest and most pervasive ways they do is through **norms,** which are rules of behavior

Perspective 9.2

HOW THE EXCELLENT COMPANIES USE TASK FORCES[16]

Small groups or task forces are one of the best ways of "chunking," according to Tom Peters and Robert Waterman, authors of *In Search of Excellence*. By **chunking,** they mean the "ability to get one's arms around almost any problem and knocking it off—now." [17] America's best run companies make effective use of task forces by following these guides:

• Keep the size of task forces at ten or less and make sure that only principal actors, or managers, are members.

• The task force level and member seniority needs to be proportional to the importance of the problem. If it is a big problem, use senior people and have the task force report to the chief executive officer.

• Limit the duration of the task force. Most problems can be solved in four months, rarely do they take more than six.

• Make membership voluntary so that people are motivated to perform.

• Form task forces rapidly with few formalities. The focus should be on solving the problem, not developing a formal bureaucratic charter.

• Make frequent followups. Expect action.

• Don't assign staff to the task force. Avoid permanent "task force directors" or "secretaries."

• Don't expect or demand long reports. Task forces should not be in the business of producing paper, but of producing solutions.

and expected ways of acting, that have been accepted as legitimate by members of the group.[18] Groups expect their members to behave in certain ways, such as not coming to work until 7:30 or not producing over twenty units per day. Members are expected to conform. If they do not, they are considered deviants and pressure is applied to make them conform. Norms and roles are related. Whereas a norm is an expectation applying to all group members, a role is an expectation about behavior that applies to a specific position, such as group leader. A leader who quits leading would encounter much the same kind of pressure to conform as a group member who was producing too much.

The Importance of Norms.   Norms can be positive, neutral, or negative in their effect on organizations. A norm that is negative from the organization's perspective may be quite positive from the employee's perspective. In the following paragraphs, we take an organizational perspective, but the example at the end of the next paragraph shows a different point of view.

Negative Norms.   Norms often make the difference between a high-performing, effective organization and a marginal one. The behavior of management, especially if Theory X values are predominant, may cause negative norms. For example, if the work groups are alienated so that norms develop around production restriction, poor quality, avoiding communications with management, and minimizing the amount of time spent working, then the organization has big problems. The following, rather "earthy" dialogue, is an example of how an experienced worker, Starkey, indoctrinates a new guy, Tennessee, into the norms that apply to dealings with the industrial engineer who does the time and motion studies for their job.[19]

"If you expect to get any kind of a price, you got to outwit that son-of-a-bitch! You got to use your noodle while you're working, and think your work out ahead as you go along! You got to add in movements you know you ain't going to make when you're running the job! Remember, if you don't screw them, they're going to screw you . . . Every movement counts!

"Another thing," said Starkey, "You were running that job too damn fast before they timed you on it! I was watching you yesterday. If you don't run a job slow before you get timed, you won't get a good price. They'll look at the record of what you do before they come around and compare it with the timing speed. Those time study men are sharp!"

"I wasn't going very fast yesterday," exclaimed Tennessee. "Hell, I was going as slow as I could without wearing myself out slowing down."

"Well, maybe it just looked fast because you were going so steady at it," said Starkey.

"I don't see how I could've run it any slower," said Tennessee. "I stood there like I was practically paralyzed!"

"Remember those bastards are paid to screw you," said Starkey. "And that's all they got to think about. They'll stay up half the night figuring how to beat you out of a dime. They figure you're going to try to fool them, so they make allowances for that. They set the prices low enough to allow for what you do."

"Well, then, what chance have I got?" asked Tennessee.

"It's up to you to figure out how to fool them more than they allow for," said Starkey.

"The trouble with me is that I get nervous with that guy standing in back of me, and I can't think," said Tennessee.

"You just haven't had enough experience yet," said Starkey. "Wait until you have been here a couple of years and you'll do your best thinking when those guys are standing behind you."

Positive Norms.   Positive norms contribute to organizational effectiveness. For example, a norm of cost consciousness or positive customer relations can have strong payoffs for the organization. Examples of positive and negative norms are shown in Table 9.2.

How Groups Control Deviance From the Norm

Even though group members generally conform with the norms, groups must deal with the deviate.[20] The first thing a group does when someone steps out of line is apply some type of pressure. Often this is a warning accompanied by a frown or anguished face—in other words, a mild form of punishment. This may be enough to correct the behavior, especially if the group member is new and wants to be a part of the group. If the deviant behavior continues, the group will constantly apply pressure until such time as the group physically or psychologically rejects the deviant. The amount of effort a group will expend trying to correct a deviant will depend on who is deviating. If a long-time, highly valued group member is deviating, this person may be able to get away with more and will be pressured for a much longer time before rejection.

In our opening example, Roy was a new person on the floor. When he deviated from the norms by producing too much, the pressure did not last long before he was rejected from the group. In Roy's case, he seemed to value the extra money more than membership in the group—at least at first. If the group had more powerful rewards and punishments at its disposal, then the chances of bringing Roy into compliance with the norms would have been much better.

Table 9.2

EXAMPLE OF POSITIVE AND NEGATIVE ORGANIZATIONAL NORMS

Examples

Categories	Positive Norms	Negative Norms
Organizational and personal pride	Members speak up for the company when it is criticized unfairly.	Members don't care about company problems.
Performance/Excellence	Members try to improve, even if they are doing well.	Members are satisfied with the minimum level of performance necessary.
Leadership/Supervision	Members ask for help when they need it.	Members hide their problems and avoid their superiors.
Customer/Consumer relations	Members show concern about serving the customers.	Members are indifferent and, when possible, hostile to customers.
Innovation and change	Members are usually looking for better ways of doing their job.	Members stick to the old ways of doing their jobs.

SOURCE: Adapted, by permission of the publisher, from "Confronting the Shadow Organization: How to Detect and Defeat Negative Norms," by R.F. Allen and S. Pilnick, *Organizational Dynamics*, (Spring 1973), pp. 6–9, © 1973 American Management Association, New York. All rights reserved.

In contrast to Roy, an old-timer like Starkey in the time study incident could deviate from group norms and get away with it. Deviations by "old-timers" are tolerated because over a period of time a group member can accrue **idiosyncratic credits** by being a good member of the group, by conforming to group norms and expectations, and by developing a history of working to accomplish group goals.[21] By being a good "group citizen" a positive balance is built up and may be called upon to excuse some deviant behaviors. For example, an executive who has built up idiosyncratic credits might use them to deviate from a norm calling for conservative business attire and wear sports attire to a sales meeting.

Developing and Changing Norms

Norms may be developed in an evolutionary manner—often almost accidentally. For example, one day a highly valued group member might say, "I don't think managers are to be trusted. Look what they did to me." Other group members may say, "Yes, he's right. We just can't trust managers." Thus, a norm is born. The incident that caused the norm may be long forgotten. Even the people may change, but the norm is still there.

The supervisor of the group may be able to set norms by making explicit statements about what is expected. If these are accepted, the group may embrace them as their own.[22] For example, the supervisor may indicate that our members do not drink alcoholic beverages during working hours, or that personal phone calls are not allowed except in emergencies. Setting such expectations is particularly important for new groups, for the first behavior pattern that is encountered by the group is often the one adopted as the norm.[23]

Table 9.3

NORM PROFILE			
Norm	**Negative**	**Neutral**	**Positive**
Cluster		1---2---3---4---5---6---7---8---9---10	
Performance excellence			
Pride in work			
Leadership relations			
Customer relations			
Innovation and change			

SOURCE: Adapted from Andre de la Porte, P.C. (1974, September–October). Group norms: Key to building a winning team. *Personnel.*

Another way for norms to develop is for a group to discuss and consciously decide what its norms should be. Newly formed groups sometimes use this method to develop norms. This strategy is also the key to changing norms. Existing norms can be clearly defined and analyzed and, if needed, changed. Let's say an analysis shows that a norm for customer service is indifference—customers are tolerated but we do not go out of our way to help them. Once this norm has surfaced, we can discuss it as a group and perhaps decide that it is contrary to our group goal of organizational effectiveness. Then we must set a new norm to replace the old one and put emphasis on reinforcing behavior that conforms to the new norm. However, some norms may be very difficult to change regardless of the amount of analysis and effort expended in the change attempt.

A final strategy for changing norms is for the group to determine which categories of norms are important for maintaining the group and for accomplishing the group's task. These might include such items as teamwork, collegial relationships, personal pride in the work, or customer relations. Each norm might then be evaluated in a graphic profile like the one in Table 9.3. Then strong and weak areas could be analyzed and changes implemented where desired. The profile in Table 9.3 shows several areas that may need improvement including pride in work, customer relations, and leadership.

Status: A System of Ranking

Within a group, an individual has a rank or worth that is their **status** within that group. Status is determined by the group, using the behaviors, attributes, characteristics, and possessions that are valued by that group. Status sometimes comes with the position, such as union steward or finance director. Status in the group is also related to status in society. A handsome medical doctor from a well-known family, who drives a Mercedes and heads the local civic club, may have a great deal of status in a group such as the local school board. Most groups are influenced by the overall person; one's overall status in society is just one important input.

Status determines what behaviors are appropriate for group members. A common group norm is for low-status people to defer to high-status people. In Japan, for example, where status is largely determined by age, one always defers to and bows to an elder. In our culture, a high-status person will initiate more conversations with low-status persons. Also, when a high-status person talks, group members pay attention. The high-status person has power and influence and, of course, more idiosyncratic credits. Usually, the group leader is a high-status person, especially if the person has become leader because of personal attributes, effective judgement, and long service to the group.

When a person is high on some valued characteristics, like education, but low on others such as experience, or when talents seem inappropriate for the position, then **status incongruence** exists.[24] One common example is the new college graduate who is placed in charge of a number of experienced production workers. This is often an uncomfortable position for both sets of people. The production group may reconcile their discomfort by finding sufficient reasons to accept the status of their new boss. Or, they may resist by trying to sabotage the boss or by letting him blunder into mistakes. Here is another example of status incongruence:

> An "up-and-coming" young manager had a relatively responsible job with his own office and a private secretary. The trouble was that the manager's office looked drab—small painted desk, common low-backed chair, tiled floor. He decided to fix up his office at his own expense. He built a large walnut top to go over the desk, then bought a piece of carpet, some paintings, and plants. The office was beautiful! Unfortunately, his supervisors were not thrilled. Every time one of them would come in the office, a sarcastic remark or nonverbal cue would be uttered about his "fancy office." The manager did not take the hints; and when his performance evaluation was due, it turned out to be lower than he had expected. While we cannot be certain of the reason for the lower ratings, it is possible that the status incongruence made his supervisors so uncomfortable that it affected his performance rating.

An important part of maintaining and displaying status is the use of possessions, clothes, office, or voice to show our status. These are called **status symbols,** since they are visual or audible indicators of our relative status. Table 9.4 provides examples of high status items.

Table 9.4

EXAMPLES OF HIGH–STATUS ITEMS

Furniture	Large wood desk, couch, high-backed chair.
Interior decorations	Rugs, paintings, plants, draperies.
Location of office	Top floor, corner, good view.
Facilities	Large-sized office, computer terminal, private bathroom, desk water bottle.
Quality of equipment	New Cadillac, Lincoln, or Mercedes for company car.
Type of clothes worn	Expensive suits, silk ties.
Privileges given	Club membership, company jet, car.
Job titles	Director, vice-president, chief.
Employees assigned	Private secretary, executive assistant.

Perspective 9.3

"SCHMOOZING" OR "SOCIAL LOAFING"

Two approaches to understanding group performance offer contrasting approaches to group dynamics.

Schmoozing [25] Groups should be designed so they can **schmooze;** so they can get together in groups of four or five and talk, fool around, or use the telephone. "There is no reason why workers cannot complete their tasks while schmoozing. Anyone who is familiar with factory life knows that workers find informal ways of doing this anyway, by having their 'buddies' cover for them. Why not recognize this basic human need to socialize and build it into the work structure. Given the same level of freedom, a community of workers could organize this informal buddy system to make their work life more humane, and still complete the amount of work expected of them, as they presently do."

Social Loafing [26] The researchers who coined the term **social loafing** believe that groups produce less than individuals because individual group members feel less pressure to perform when they are working with others. This may be because when they are carrying part of the load, no one can tell who is loafing. In addition to avoiding the consequences of slacking off, individuals also may be lost in the crowd and not receive credit for working hard. The researchers cite a number of experiments including a rope-pulling task where individuals are blindfolded and believe they are pulling as part of a group when they are really pulling alone. When they believe they are acting with one other person, they pulled at 90 percent of what they did when alone. When they believed two other people were pulling, they pulled only 85 percent. The researchers conclude that social loafing is "a kind of social disease, with negative consequences for individuals, institutions, and societies."

Cohesiveness: How Tight Is the Group?

When a group has a very strong hold on its members because of the attractiveness of the group, it is a **cohesive** group.[27] Strong loyalty to the group and the desire to remain a group member are indicators of cohesiveness, especially when everyone in the group shares these feelings. Cohesive groups tend to feel good about themselves and evaluate themselves quite favorably. In fact, cohesion often results in distorted perceptions of both group members and the outsiders.

What Makes a Group Cohesive? Cohesiveness is related to attractiveness.[28] If a group is attractive to its members, it is more likely to be cohesive. Groups whose members share background, attitudes, and interests also develop more cohesion than groups that do not. Agreement with the group's goals, leadership, and atmosphere also have an impact on the group's desirability. High entrance requirements are often used for entry into certain groups. The initiation rites into these groups create a common bond of accomplishment that results in cohesion. A final, powerful factor that makes groups cohesive is success: groups that succeed are more desirable.

Is Cohesiveness Desirable? The effectiveness of highly cohesive groups depends on the direction of their efforts and their norms. If they have norms of high performance that agree with organizational goals, then the group probably will be effective. If, on the other hand, their efforts are directed toward restricting production because of negative norms, the group can be a powerful negative force. Research results seem to support this view. One review of thirty-four research studies found twelve positive relationships between cohesion and productivity, eleven negative relationships, and eleven insignificant relationships.[29] Group drive (motivation, enthusiasm, esprit) was a more powerful predictor of performance than cohesion. The key to using cohesive groups is to harness their energy towards positive norms. You must also be careful about decisions made by cohesive groups since they tend to distort inputs. More will be said on this tendency in the chapter on decision making.

GROUP DEVELOPMENT AND THE SOCIALIZATION PROCESS

So far in this chapter we have covered the dynamics that govern group behavior. In this section, we discuss the stages of group development—how they develop over time—and how individuals are integrated into the group through socialization processes. Socialization goes on when a new group is formed or when a new member joins an existing group, thus group development and socialization overlap.[30] First, let's discuss group development.

Group Development

While there are a number of different ways group development can be described, we will use a four-stage model: forming, storming, norming, and performing.[31] At each one of these stages it is possible that the group could run into serious problems that lead to failure or reversion to a more immature level. Figure 9.6 illustrates how this process works.

Forming.   During this stage people begin to establish interpersonal relationships. They feel each other out to see who has the most status, power, and knowledge. At this stage people are friendly and polite. They are trying to size up the benefits and costs to them of belonging to the group. You have probably experienced this stage during your first meeting with a group assigned to some task.

Storming.   Conflicts begin to arise because of disagreements over leadership, goals, norms, roles, task assignments, or other interpersonal behaviors. It is important to work through these problems so that the group can grow and mature. The next chapter on conflict resolution provides ideas for managing this stage. Actual conflict or storming does not always happen, since some groups will be more effective in working through process problems than others. Maintenance roles are particularly important during this stage.

Norming.   By this stage group members have learned to work together. A leader has emerged and the group has developed norms and cohesiveness.

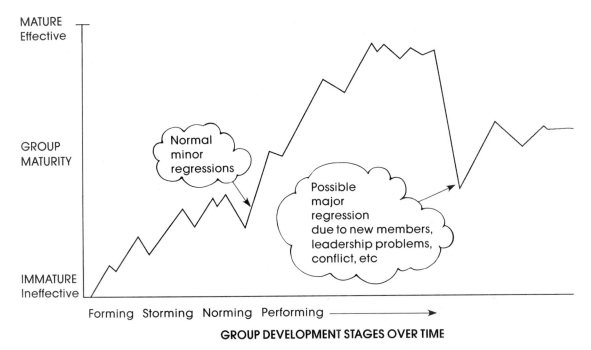

Figure 9.6

STAGES OF GROUP DEVELOPMENT

Based on the ideas of Tuckman, B.W. and Jensen, M.A.C. (1977). Stages of small group development revisited. *Group and Organizational Studies, 2,* 419–427.

Group roles are now fairly well defined with a good mixture of task and maintenance roles. Cooperation and a sense of shared responsibility develops.

Performing.   A natural follow-on to norming is when members actually work together as an effective team to get their task done. Some groups continue to develop and learn beyond this stage, while others may plateau and grow no further or even regress. Eventually the group may finish their task, especially if it is an ad hoc group, and disband.

Organizational Socialization

New members have to learn the goals, the preferred methods for reaching the goals, the expected behaviors for their role, and the norms of the group. They learn these behaviors through **socialization**—the process of learning the norms, values, and behavior patterns of the group and the organization.[32] When a newcomer has high motivation to be a member of the group and has correctly anticipated the norms of the group, then socialization is easy. Under these circumstances, a new person will work hard and adapt easily. However, a complete match in expectations is seldom achieved as Table 9.5 would indicate.

Reality Shock.   When the new group is not what a person expects, he or she may be surprised in either a positive or negative way.[33] If the surprise is positive, then the decision to join the group is positively reinforced, and the person

Table 9.5

EXPECTATION AND REALITY FOR MANAGERIAL JOBS

Expectations	*Reality*
Thoughtful decision making.	Most of the workday is devoted to interaction with other people; getting and exchanging information, persuading and negotiating.
Clearly scheduled and logically planned workday.	Impromptu, sporadic, and unplanned contacts; jumping from issue to issue and among different people.
Efforts devoted to "leading" subordinates, who defer to higher status.	Most of the time with outsiders; even subordinates frequently challenge the manager's authority.
Decisions made by rational judgment of individual in correct position to evaluate all the factors.	Decisions are the product of a complex brokerage and negotiation process, extending over time and involving large numbers of interested parties.
Objectives and goals clear and consistent.	Multiplicity of goals identified with different groups and interests that are conflicting and even contradictory; often-changing priorities.

SOURCE: Reprinted from L.R. Sayles, 1979, *Leadership: What effective managers really do . . . and how they do it*, p. 12. Copyright © 1979 by McGraw-Hill, New York. Used with permission of the publisher and approval of the author.

feels good about the decision. If the surprise is negative, reality shock develops. Expectations are either unmet or are very different than anticipated. Perhaps this is what happened to Roy in the opening incident. He had expectations about how much he could produce and how much money he could make. He also expected management to value his efforts. Reality was that both the group and the organization valued adherence to the group's norms, which differed radically from Roy's. The result of reality shock is often disillusionment and exit from the organization.

Overcoming Reality Shock.   One way to deal with unrealistic expectations is to give potential employees a more realistic and accurate picture of what it is like in the organization. Anyone who has ever been associated with the military knows that the recruiter's picture of what life is like in the service is considerably different from reality. The same thing happens with other organizations.[34] Desirable candidates are given a very rosy picture of the organization. When they are actually hired, they find out that everything is not quite as they expected. To overcome this problem, a strategy is used called **realistic job previews**.[35] The idea is to give job applicants a preview of the positive *and* negative aspects so that expectations are more accurate. This method results in lower quit rates, higher job satisfaction, improved commitment, and higher levels of job performance.[36] Table 9.6 shows how traditional and realistic job previews compare.

Realistic previews are most useful when there are relatively large numbers of people seeking entry level jobs.[37] For example, when recruiting secretarial help, a traditional recruiting videotape might show exciting, challenging work,

Table 9.6

TRADITIONAL AND REALISTIC JOB PREVIEWS

Traditional Procedures	Realistic Procedures
Set initial job expectations too high	Set Job expectations realistically
Job is typically viewed as attractive	Job may or may not be attractive, depending on individual's needs
High rate of job offer acceptance	Some accept, some reject job offer
Work experience contradicts expectations	Work experience confirms expectations
Dissatisfaction and realization that job not matched to needs	Satisfaction, needs matched to job
Low job survival, dissatisfaction, frequent thoughts of quitting	High job survival, satisfaction infrequent thoughts of quitting

SOURCE: Adapted from "Tell It Like It Is at Realistic Job Previews," by J.P. Wanous, *Personnel,* (July/August 1975), p. 54, Copyright © 1975 American Management Association, New York. All rights reserved.

where everyone seems to be smiling and happy. A more realistic view might be that the job is routine and lacking in challenge and that there is close supervision with little opportunity to socialize with coworkers. Here is an example of a realistic preview used in a classified advertisement:

WORKAHOLIC WANTED

As personal aide to tyrannical president and demanding general manager. Will be responsible for representing company in absence of above. Claims, administration, typing, general secretarial work, and coffee-making. Work load from panic to boredom. Applicant should have transportation background. Starting $14,000 PA. Applicants MUST write two page letter explaining why they qualify including resume.[38]

Realistic techniques can also be used by interviewers and in recruiting brochures. Realistic previews have been used in many varied situations, including college recruiting, insurance, nursing, and the armed forces.[39]

Integrating Socialization and Group Development

There are times when socialization and group development happen at the same time.[40] People may enter a group all at once, for example, when students enter together in the fall for a "lock-step" executive MBA program, or for basic military training. Another instance where these two processes work together is when new groups are created within an existing organization, such as when a task force is formed or a reorganized unit is constructed. The overlap between socialization and development is further illustrated in Figure 9.7.

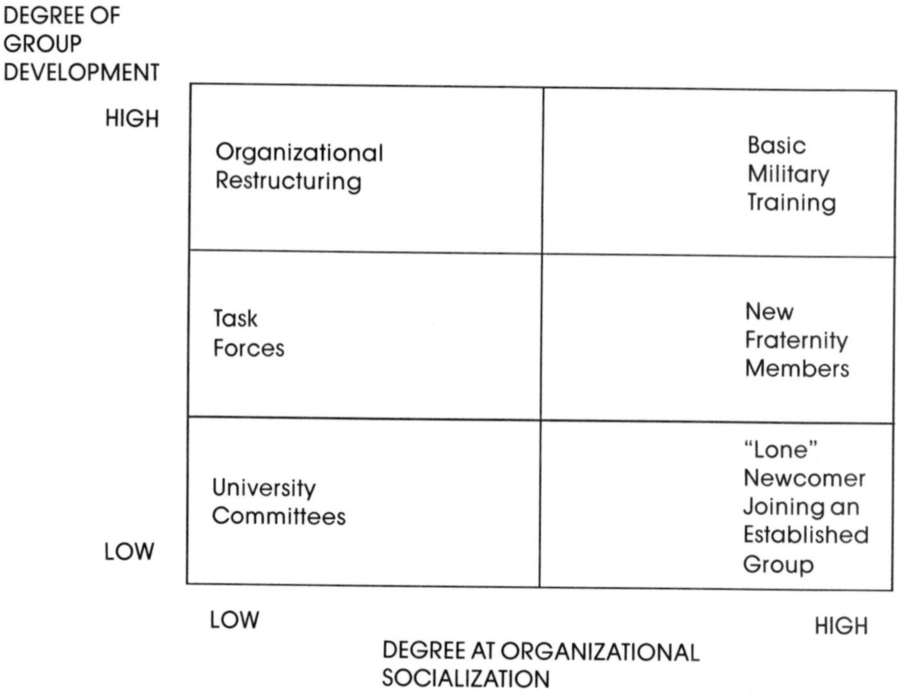

DEGREE OF
GROUP
DEVELOPMENT

HIGH

Organizational Restructuring	Basic Military Training
Task Forces	New Fraternity Members
University Committees	"Lone" Newcomer Joining an Established Group

LOW

LOW   HIGH

DEGREE AT ORGANIZATIONAL
SOCIALIZATION

Figure 9.7

**THE RELATIONSHIP BETWEEN
GROUP DEVELOPMENT AND ORGANIZATIONAL SOCIALIZATION**

SOURCE: Adapted from Wanous, J.P., Rechers, A.E., & Malik, S.D. (1984). Organizational socialization and group development: Toward an integrative perspective. *Academy of Management Review, 9,* 670–683.

WORK GROUPS: MANAGING EFFECTIVE TEAMS

Using the concepts of group dynamics, it is now possible to design high-performing work groups. In this section, we examine teambuilding as an approach to developing effective work teams. Since there are many different types of groups and numerous approaches to developing them, this section provides only a very basic introduction.

Teamwork is Important

A **team** is a group of people who must work together in a collaborative way if individual and group goals are to be achieved.[41] While there are many different types of groups and teams, work teams are particularly important to organizations because many organizational tasks and goals are accomplished through teamwork. Attention to teamwork is an important managerial task. One way to think of teamwork is to use a sports analogy; to compare one type of work team, the management team, with a football team.

> It is obvious that to score touchdowns (and prevent the opponent from scoring) a football team has to play together. It should be just as obvious that a work unit or a management group must also work together to insure success. A football team

---

Perspective 9.4

IDEAL CHARACTERISTICS OF AN EFFECTIVE WORK TEAM[42]

• The group atmosphere is informal, comfortable, and relaxed. When there is criticism, it is constructive and comfortable; there are no personal attacks.

• There is lots of discussion and almost everyone participates. People listen to one another; every position is given a hearing.

• The goals, tasks, and objectives are clearly understood and accepted by everyone in the group.

• Decisions are based on consensus (it is clear that there is general agreement and everyone is willing to go along), but there is certainly discussion of disagreements; there is very little majority voting.

• When action is taken, clear assignments are made and accepted.

• The leader does not dominate the team nor unduly defer to it.

---

practices over and over again how it will execute its plays. The team has "skull" practice—they talk over plans and strategies. They review films of past games, identify mistakes, set up goals for next week. Unfortunately, management groups [seldom] engage in similar types of activities. They do not review their past actions and they do not really plan new strategies. They do not come together to learn from their mistakes, nor do they practice or get coaching in new methods, set new goals, or build up their team "spirit".[43]

Using Teambuilding

Developing teams so they work more effectively, called **teambuilding,** requires some mechanism to review past actions, identify problems, and then develop strategies and skills for coping with the problems. This process is far from simple and often requires an outside consultant to help develop new norms centered around these behaviors.[44] Teambuilding involves trying to find out what problems are keeping the group from being as effective as it might be by collecting data through interviews or questionnaires. The results are fed back to the team, and they work on the problems they believe are most crucial. In the process, they learn skills of communicating and group decision making. The group develops action plans and monitors its progress toward the goals. If the teambuilding effort is a success, and it usually is, the group will more closely approach the ideal one described in Perspective 9.4.

Self-Managing Work Teams

In Chapter 7 we discussed how jobs can be designed for self-managing work groups or teams. In this chapter we will add some additional points pertaining to the group dynamic aspect of self-managing groups. You will recall that these groups are given considerable freedom to design their own jobs, set their own goals, control and reward group members, and sometimes even hire their own members.

Self-managing work groups can only be designed when people must *interact* to get the job done—when they need others to completely reach their goal. An example of an interacting group is the crew of a large commercial airliner. The pilot depends on the engineer and other flight crew members to do their jobs. **Coacting work groups,** in contrast, consist of people who work together, share the same norms, work for the same boss, and interact socially. But, the task of each group member is independent of the other group members. For example, the classified ad clerks in a large newspaper are all members of one work group, but since they may complete their tasks independently of one another, they are members of a coacting group.

Designing self-managing work groups is complex. You have to design not only the task itself, but the group composition, size, goals, norms, and skills. In addition, there may be problems with discipline, conflict resolution, and leadership.[45] The following example shows how self-managing work groups were used at Butler Manufacturing.

> A few years ago the management of Butler Manufacturing Company opened a new plant in Story City, Iowa, for the assembly of two-story high grain driers that sell for about $25,000 each. Assembly of the grain driers is a fairly complicated operation, involving as many as 3,000 parts. Butler management decided to design the work so that teams of workers would have autonomous responsibility for constructing the driers, rather than use a traditional production line.
>
> Members of the Butler work teams work together pretty much as they wish in getting the driers assembled. Employees change their particular job assignments frequently within the teams, both as part of a formal rotational program and informally with the approval of other work-team members. Typically, operators in their first eighteen months on the job master three of five basic tasks: assembly, fabricating, machining, painting, and shipping. At the end of eighteen months, most employees are able to build an entire grain drier by themselves.
>
> There are no quality inspectors at Butler, only two engineers, and very few foremen. As a result, there is substantial team involvement in supervisory functions, including hiring and promotion. Peers help select new team members, and two supervisors were picked by other staff from among the employees.
>
> One supervisor described how his functions are different than those of traditional first-line managers: "It's not the traditional scheduling, pushing people, and taking names. My job is heavily counseling people and behavior modification, and that's more interesting. Meanwhile, every night the conference room is filled with people having their team meetings during working hours and carrying on joint supervision."
>
> There are many kinds of meetings. Probably the most important are the weekly team meetings, in which production, quality, tooling, maintenance, and behavioral problems are considered. Leadership of the meetings rotates weekly. A monthly plantwide meeting is held to discuss financial results and economic trends (productivity data are provided on a daily basis to each team).[46]

Self-managing work groups succeed at Butler Manufacturing Co. for a number of reasons. First, positive group norms encourage members to reinforce the self-managing behavior. In addition, the supervisor's role is perceived to be that of a counselor and behavior modifier (perhaps more emphasis on maintenance roles.) Group members seem to experience a sense of freedom that results in a more enriched job with a heightened sense of responsibility. Another factor that helps foster success is the weekly and monthly meetings to iron out problems and discuss results.

Using self-managing work groups is only one way of making effective use of groups in organizational situations. Managers who consistently use the concepts of group dynamics explained in this chapter will find they are more effective in dealing with a wide range of group-related management problems.

CROSS–CULTURAL OB:
SOCIALIZING NEW EMPLOYEES IN JAPAN

Since Japanese companies expect their new employees to remain with the company throughout their careers, they place considerable emphasis on an intensive socialization program. New college graduates can expect to spend from one to twelve months in intensive training programs. During this time they will typically live in dormitories that are closely supervised by an older company employee. The primary aim of this early orientation is to develop spiritual values, such as pride, self-esteem, sense of duty, and responsibility toward the work and company. Employees are expected to develop values of harmony and teamwork as well.[47] The culmination of this training program is an elaborate "joining-the-company" ceremony that is presided over by the company president, with top company officers and parents in attendance. The newcomers will sing the company song, recite the company principles and the "President's Teachings." Table 9.7 provides examples of the principles and teachings.

Table 9.7

EXAMPLES OF JAPANESE COMPANY PRINCIPLES AND TEACHINGS

Uedagin Bank Principles	"President's Teachings"
Constantly abiding by the ideas of cooperative banking, we will, together with the general populace, advance in our mission to serve as an instrument of small and medium business enterprises.	Harmony (*wa*). The bank is our lifelong place of work, let us make it a pleasant place, starting with our greetings to each other each morning.
Intent in the spirit of service, we will contribute to public welfare and social prosperity. Emphasizing trust and possessing an enterprising spirit we will advance scientific administration.	Sincerity (*seijitsu*). Sincerity is the foundation of trust, let us deal with our customers with a serious and earnest attitude.
With mutual respect and affection, we will work with diligence, employed in maintaining systematic order.	Kindness (*shinsetsu*). Have a warm heart. Be scrupulously kind.
Possessing a spirit of love for Uedagin, we pledge to plan for the prosperity of the bank and for the public welfare and to make the bank the greatest in Japan.	Spirit (*tamashii*). Putting our heart and soul into it, let us work with all our strength.
	Unity (*danketsu*). Strong unity is the source of energy for our business.
	Responsibility (*sekinin*). Responsibility makes rights possible; first let us develop responsibility.
	Originality (*sōi*). In addition, let us think creatively and advance making each day a new day.
	Purity (*seiketsu*). Have a noble character and proper behavior.
	Health (*kenkō*). With ever growing pride let us fulfill the Uedagin dream.

SOURCE: Rohlen, T.P. (1974). *For harmony and strength: Japanese white-collar organization in anthropological perspective* (pp. 36–37). Berkeley, CA: University of Chicago Press.

Instilling Teamwork Values: The Endurance Walk

While many methods are used to develop the values illustrated in Table 9.7, those based on actual experience are considered to be the most powerful. An American anthropologist, Thomas Rohlen, worked in a Japanese bank to gather inside information on how these organizations operate. He participated in the socialization and orientation program along with the other new bank employees. As part of the training all newcomers were required to do the following endurance walk. Here is a description of the walk: [48]

> Ever since the first day [of the new-employee orientation], the trainees had heard about the twenty-five-mile endurance walk held near the end of training. The almost daily mile run and the other climbing and hiking activities had been explained as preparation for this event. On the morning of the event, there seemed to be a high level of anticipation and readiness even among the weaker and less athletic trainees.
>
> The program was simple enough. The trainees were to walk the first nine miles together in a single body. The second nine miles were to be covered with each squad walking as a unit. The last seven miles were to be walked alone and in silence. All twenty-five miles were accomplished by going around and around a large public park in the middle of the city. Each lap was approximately one mile. It was forbidden to take any refreshment. During the second stage each squad was to stay together for the entire nine miles, and competition between squads was discouraged. Finally, it was strictly forbidden to talk with others when walking alone during the last stage.
>
> The training staff walked the twenty-five miles too, going around in the opposite direction, and a dozen or so young men from the bank were stationed along the route to offer the trainees cold drinks which, of course, they had to refuse.
>
> This was the program, and there was no emphasis at all placed on one person finishing ahead of another. Instructions were to take as much time as needed as long as the entire twenty-five miles were completed. The walk began around seven-thirty in the morning and finished around three in the afternoon. There was no time limit, and many had not gone the full twenty-five miles, but the collapse from heat prostration of a few led the instructors to call the event off at a point where most had a lap or two remaining.
>
> On the surface this program was simple enough, but in retrospect it seems to have been skillfully designed to maximize spiritual lessons. When we began, the day was fresh and cool, and it seemed as though we were beginning a pleasant stroll. Walking together in one large group, everyone conversed, joked, and paid little attention to the walk itself. The first nine miles passed quickly and pleasantly, and the severe physical hardship that we had been expecting seemed remote.
>
> Forming up into squad groups at the beginning of the next nine miles, we were reminded again not to compete with other squads. But with squads close before and behind, the pace began escalating and resulted in an uproarious competition. Each time a team would come up from the rear, the team about to be overtaken would quicken its pace, and before long trainees found themselves walking very fast, so fast that those with shorter legs had to run occasionally to keep up. There was much yelling back and forth within each squad—the slower and more tired people crying out for a reduction in speed, the others urging them to greater efforts. A common solution was to put the slowest person at the head, thus slowing down the faster ones and forcing the slow ones to greater effort. By the end of the second nine miles the toll was obvious. Many, besides suffering from stiff legs and blisters, were beginning to have headaches and show evidence of heat prostration.

Some lay under a tree by the finish line sucking salt tablets. It was noon by that time, and the park baked under the full heat of a mid-June sun.

Any gratification the leading squad found in their victory was soon forgotten. At the finish line there were no congratulations and no rest. Squads were instructed to break up and continue walking, this time in single file and in silence. Soon a long line of trainees stretched over the entire circumference of the course. Having already covered eighteen miles, the last nine at a grueling pace, most were very tired.

At that point everything was transformed. The excitement and clamor of competition were gone. Each individual, alone in a quiet world, was confronted by the sweep of his own thoughts as he pushed forward.

My own experience was to become acutely aware of every sort of pain. Great blisters had obviously formed on the soles of my feet; my legs, back, and neck ached; and at times I had a sense of delirium. The thirst I had expected to be so severe seemed insignificant compared to these other afflictions. Upon accomplishing a lap, instead of feeling encouraged I plunged into despair over those remaining. My awareness of the world around me, including the spectators in the park and the bank employees tempting us with refreshments, dropped almost to zero. Each step was literally more painful than the one before, and the temptation to stop and lie down for a while in the lush grass was tremendous. Near the end I could do no more than walk for a minute or two and then rest for much longer. The others around me seemed to be doing the same thing. For some reason it was heartening to discover that six or so of the trainees had fainted. Other moments brought feverish dreams of somehow sneaking away: no one would notice if I slipped out of the park and returned just when the event was closing. Bushes became places to hide. I kept going, I suppose, because I feared discovery.

Though in a feverish state, I was in some sense capable of looking objectively at my response to this new test of endurance. The content of lectures about spiritual strength came back to me. I could see that I was easily tempted and inclined to quit. Under such stress some of my thoughts were obviously not serving my interest in completing the course. Whatever will power I had arose from pride and from an emerging, almost involuntary belief in the spiritual approach. If I was to finish I needed spiritual strength. It angered and amused me to realize how cleverly this exercise had been conceived. I vowed over and over never to get involved in such a situation again, and yet within days, when the memory of the physical pain had dimmed, I was taking great pride in my accomplishment and viewing my completion of the twenty-five miles as proof that I could do anything I set my mind to.

MANAGEMENT APPLICATIONS OF GROUP DYNAMICS

Working with groups is an inevitable part of management since few managerial tasks are done by individuals working alone. There is a lot more complexity in dealing with groups because of the combination of interpersonal and group dynamics. The following guides should help you manage groups more effectively.

- *Keep groups relatively small.* While there is no exact maximum number of people for a group, one rule of thumb is ten. Try to make sure everyone wants to be a part of the group and has something to contribute.

• *Remember that people belong to multiple groups.* Thus, their loyalties may be divided. One group may have different expectations from the other, resulting in conflict and stress.

• *Use task forces to tackle complex problems.* Whenever a problem or issue involves complexity or crosses organizational lines, task forces can help get control and solve problems. Follow the guides for effective task forces used by the excellent companies.

• *Foster organizationwide groups.* Since groups tend to become parochial and committed to their own subunit's goals and values, it is useful to develop companywide groups. This strategy can also make it much easier to deal with crisis situations, should they occur.

• *Be sure groups are trained to use both task and maintenance roles.* While most groups are pretty good at task roles, they often fall short on using maintenance roles. Thus training and formal role prescriptions may be needed to make sure members attend to these vital roles.

• *Carefully foster positive norms.* Be sure to explicitly state expected norms, set the right norms at the founding of the group, and reward behavior consistent with desired norms.

• *Try to change negative norms.* It is far more difficult to change negative norms. The best strategies involve group problem solving, teambuilding, and carefully constructed reward systems.

• *Be aware of the importance of status.* Remember that esteem needs were next to the top on Maslow's hierarchy; people care about their status. Beware of status incongruence situations that can cause friction and resentment.

• *Use schmoozing to improve boring jobs.* Allowing and even encouraging employees to interact socially can increase satisfaction and improve performance if norms are positive.

• *Recognize that groups have a development cycle.* Different management strategies are required for a new group when compared to a mature group.

• *Use realistic job previews.* This socialization strategy improves performance and satisfaction and reduces turnover with low risk and cost to the organization.

• *Carefully socialize new employees.* This is your chance to develop positive work values and norms. Put extra effort into your indoctrination programs.

• *Use self-managing work teams when appropriate.* If your task requires interaction to get it done, try to design self-managing work teams for maximum performance.

FOR DISCUSSION

1. Based on your own experience, give an example of an interacting set of people who are and are not members of a group.

2. What are some of the positive and negative impacts of groups on organizational effectiveness?

3. Give separate examples of when task roles and maintenance roles should be used by the group leader.

4. How do you deal with someone who is exhibiting a blocking role?

5. Describe an example of how norms can influence organizational effectiveness in a positive and a negative way. Why do you think these norms developed?

6. How can norms be changed?

7. When is a highly cohesive group desirable or undesirable?

8. Do you agree with Perspective 9.3 that groups should be allowed to schmooze, or do you believe that social loafing may be the result?

9. Contrast a realistic job preview at a fast-food restaurant with a traditional job preview.

10. Design an ideal orientation program for new employees to instill positive norms and values.

11. Give examples of three jobs where self-managing work groups would be appropriate. Do these jobs all involve interacting rather than coacting work groups?

12. How can an endurance walk help socialize new employees into the company? Would you like to participate in such an event?

KEY CONCEPTS AND TERMS

group
process losses
types of groups
group role
task roles
maintenance roles
blocking roles
chunking

task force
norms
idiosyncratic credits
status
status incongruence
cohesiveness
schmoozing
social loafing

stages of group development
organizational socialization
realistic job previews (RJP)
teambuilding
coacting and interacting groups

Cases and Incidents

DENNIS CALHOUN

"What's wrong with me?" Dennis Calhoun thought to himself on his way home after eight hours at the bank. This was only his second week at work, but he was already disillusioned about his job and was seriously considering quitting once he could find a position that paid at least as much and offered a fairly secure future.

Since the first day on the job, he had experienced nothing but trouble. The trouble was not with the job itself but with the other people working there. Although he thought he got along well with some of the older employees, there was a group of young male employees that seemed to have something against him. He had tried to be friendly and listen to their instructions as they

taught him the various jobs, but they seemed to exclude him from their social activities—such as going to lunch, having a beer after work, and idle chit-chat. Although he didn't know everyone very well, it appeared that this group consisted mostly of the male, part-time college students that worked at the bank during their free time. They didn't seem to be very committed to their job although their work was generally satisfactory as far as Dennis could tell. Most of their conversation was about activities at college, such as football games, fraternity parties, and school work.

In a way, Dennis kind of envied them. After finishing high school he had decided not to go on to college since his high school grades were not that good and his family could not take the financial burden of a college education. After working two years at a local supermarket, then taking a brief fling at selling insurance, he was particularly pleased at being offered a job as a management trainee with the bank. The bank planned to put him on a program which would allow him to rotate through the various departments over a five-year period, after which time he would be in a better position to decide in which area he wished to make his career. He thought this to be an excellent opportunity and was determined to make a good impression on the bank management.

In thinking now about his job, he recalled how unpleasant the last two weeks had been. Not long after he started to work, someone loosened the casters on his chair so that when he sat down, the chair collapsed on to the floor. Later, while on an errand to another bank after banking hours, one of the fellows was supposed to telephone the other bank to inform them that Dennis was on his way; when Dennis arrived, the front door was locked and no one was around, forcing him to pound on the front door until someone inside heard him.

When he came back to the bank, the rear entrance was locked and he had to find a pay telephone to call inside for someone to let him in. And today was the crowning blow. In the middle of trying to balance a deposit containing over two hundred checks, he left briefly to go to the restroom. When he returned and finished the task, his total didn't balance with the deposit slip. When he rechecked his figures, he discovered that someone had added in a few numbers on the calculator while he was out.

DISCUSSION QUESTIONS

1. Why is Dennis having trouble?

2. How do the goals of the group differ from Dennis' goals?

3. What could he do to minimize this uncomfortable situation short of quitting?

From J.L. Gray and F.A. Starke, 1980, *Organizational behavior concepts and applications.* 2nd ed., p. 227 Copyright © 1980 by Charles E. Merrill, Columbus, Ohio.

ACME WHOLESALE DISTRIBUTING COMPANY

In February of 1973, I was hired by the Acme Wholesale Distributing Company, a local firm in Portland. The work group consisted of ten students from the local university. We found the job through the university's placement center.

The group members were approximately the same age, ranging from 18 to 23. The reason for the majority of the workers to seek employment was to earn money for school. The social backgrounds of the group were hard to estimate; however, I believe a middle-class background prevailed. Of the ten, I only knew two, my roommate and a friend of my brother.

The job consisted of about a week's work in the evening from 8:00 P.M. to 2:00 A.M. It involved opening old boxes of a nationally distributed brand of imported, and now moldy, salami; separating the salvageable from the unsalvageable salami; cleaning the salvageable salamis with vinegar and a scrub brush; drying, rewrapping, and reboxing them.

The building was an old, cold, gloomy structure, which was primarily used as a warehouse, with a small office in the front. We worked on the second floor, which was accessible by means of an old open-style elevator used to haul the products. Stairs near the front office also gave access to this floor.

The floor was filled with boxes of various products, with all but one dirty brick wall covered. The few windows were too high to be of any use.

We had one supervisor who was a day employee at the firm. He also had attended the university. His age was around 30. It was his duty to instruct us and see that we did our work. He also made periodic inspections of the finished product to see if it met quality standards. It became apparent at once that he did not like working nights but enjoyed the overtime pay.

On the first night we were divided into two groups, based on where we were standing at the moment. Instructions were given to each person for his specific job, and we started. A diagram of the work area is shown in Exhibit 1.

Bill, the supervisor, stayed with us the whole first night helping at each position. It was also his responsibility to see that a new pallet of 40 boxes was supplied at the same time the old one was finished. This kept an even flow through the line. We had one major break in the evening, which was at 10:30 for half an hour. This time we spent in a nearby tavern, eating and drinking. Bill and one other member who brought a sack lunch did not attend this gathering. Very little conversation took place that night. What did occur was primarily questions directed at Bill. By 2:00 A.M. we had achieved 170 boxes and 10 sore backs. A thorough cleaning of the area at night's end was mandatory. So ended the first night.

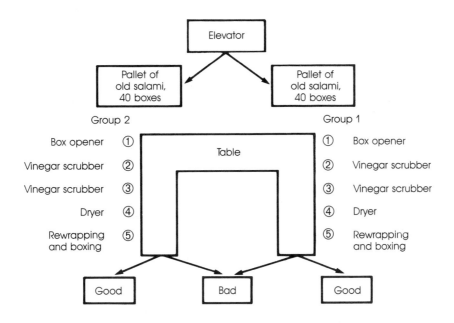

Exhibit 1

DIAGRAM OF WORK AREA

On the second night Bill had been instructed to achieve a production quota of 240 boxes a night, and that we were to produce a higher percentage of good salamis. This meant that we would have to scrub more salamis and scrub them harder to get more mold off.

This, however, produced a conflict of goals between the group and management. We were to work at a rate that seemed impossible and to produce more for the same pay. The incentive was that if we reached this goal early, we were finished for the night and would be paid for the full night. So the work began again, this time with Bill not present but staying in the office, returning only to supply us with more pallets, check our work, and leave again.

Things began slowly, with members changing positions periodically to relieve boredom. Specialization in each job developed, and new methods evolved to increase speed. Rotation slowed when each member found a job he liked best and could do the fastest. If anyone was slow at one position, thus slowing the line and the production, he would give it up for another position. Thus, we all found our optimum spot in the line. On the second night I left group two for group one, in which my roommate and my brother's friend were working. This was the only transfer between the two groups to take place.

We developed a sense of unity which helped our group. Our group talked more, produced faster, and, in general, joked around more. The overall atmosphere changed, with laughter often heard. Someone brought a radio. Individuals were given nicknames, such as "fat man," and so on. Conversations were more within each group, with occasional satirical remarks exchanged between the two groups. It seemed to be our way of communicating to those we didn't know without feeling awkward or leaving anyone open for personal attack. No one spoke of his past. The talk was focused on the strange situation in which we were working. We all decided it was against the law and the health codes. No one seemed to care beyond that point. After all, it was money, which we all needed. Group two spoke little; our group dominated most of what was said. I felt they had less in common with each other. This hampered their overall production, as was demonstrated when short contests between tables took place. One of their members was the individual who didn't go to the tavern with the rest of us. On the fourth day, one of their members left for Washington, D.C., for a protest march.

Members helped out at other positions on their table and at times crossed over to help the other table; this was done to finish faster, both before our break and at the end of the evening. Slacking off was not permitted, and when discovered, immediate verbal attack occurred. By the third night, production reached a surprising 240 boxes in four and a half hours.

The next night, Bill tightened up on his inspections of the finished product and demanded better quality. This, of course, increased the time required to complete 240 boxes per night. Also, he stressed that his boss still wanted more good salamis from the 240 boxes done each night. A good box had a resale value of up to $25, and the rejects about $5.

To make everyone happy, we cheated. Of course the consumer was the ultimate loser, but that was not our concern. We hid the not-so-good salami at the bottom of each box and placed the boxes of ill

repute in the center of the pallet, a hard place for Bill to inspect. So more salamis passed as good ones, thus pleasing Bill; more boxes of good salamis were packed, thus pleasing Bill's boss; all done in less time, pleasing us.

DISCUSSION QUESTIONS

1. Use group dynamics concepts to explain what is happening in this case.
2. How did these groups develop? What factors aided the group's development?
3. Was schmoozing effective in this case?
4. Why didn't the group accept the quality goal?

REFERENCES

1. Definition based on Cartwright, D., & Zander, A. (1968). *Group dynamics: Research and theory* (3rd ed.). New York: Harper and Row, p. 46. And Hare, A.P. (1976). *Handbook of Small Group Research* (2nd ed.). New York: The Free Press, p. 5. For additional information about group dynamics see Napier, R.W., & Gershenfeld, M.K. (1985). *Groups: Theory and experience.* Boston: Houghton Mifflin. And Luft, J. (1984). *Group processes: An introduction to group dynamics.* Palo Alto, CA: Mayfield.

2. Hare (1976).

3. See Hackman, J.R., & Oldham, G.R. (1980). *Work redesign.* Reading, MA: Addison-Wesley. And Hare, A.P. (1981). Group size. *American Behavioral Scientist, 24,* 695–708.

4. Likert, R. (1967). *The human organization.* New York: McGraw-Hill.

5. Krackhardt, D., & Stern, R.N. (1985). The design of social networks and management of crises. *Academy of Management Proceedings '85.*

6. Based on Krackhardt and Stern (1985).

7. Krackhardt and Stern (1985), p. 177.

8. Krackhardt and Stern (1985).

9. For a summary of the research on group attractiveness, see Napier & Gershenfeld (1985). Also Shaw, M.E. (1976). *Group dynamics: The psychology of small group behavior.* New York: McGraw-Hill.

10. Lincoln, J.R., & Miller, J. (1979). Work and friendship ties in organizations: A comparative analysis of relational networks. *Administrative Science Quarterly, 24,* 181–199.

11. Epstein, C.F. (1975). Institutional barriers: What keeps women out of the executive suite? In

F.E. Gordon & M.H. Strober (Eds.). *Bringing women into management* (pp. 7–21). New York, McGraw-Hill.

12. For a review see Crary, M. (1987). Managing attraction and intimacy at work. *Organizational Dynamics, 15*(4), 27–41.

13. Hare (1976), p. 131.

14. For a discussion of role-making processes see Graen, G. (1976). Role making processes within complex organizations. In M.D. Dunnette (Ed.). *Handbook of industrial and organizational psychology* (pp. 1201–1245). Chicago: Rand-McNally.

15. This section is based on the concepts originally developed by Benne, K.D., & Sheats, P. (1948). Functional roles of group members. *Journal of Social Issues, 4,* 41–49.

16. Adapted from Peters, T.J., & Waterman, R.H. (1982). *In search of excellence.* New York: Harper & Row, pp. 127–131.

17. Peters and Waterman (1982), p. 126.

18. Hare (1976), p. 19. Also Feldman, D.C. (1984). The development and enforcement of group norms. *Academy of Management Review, 9,* 47–53.

19. Donald Roy as quoted from page 15 of *Money and Motivation: An Analysis of Incentives* by W.F. Whyte. Copyright © 1955, by Harper and Row Publishers, Inc. Reprinted by permission of the publisher.

20. Hackman, J.R. (1976). Group influences on individuals. In M.D. Dunnette (Ed.). *Handbook of industrial and organizational psychology* (pp. 1455–1525). Chicago: Rand-McNally.

21. Hollander, E.P. (1958). Conformity, status and idiosyncrasy credits. *Psychological Review, 65,*

117–27. And Hollander, E.P. (1964). *Leaders, groups and influence.* New York: Oxford University Press.

22. Feldman (1984).

23. Feldman (1984).

24. Mitchell, T.R. (1987). *People in organizations* (3rd ed.). New York: McGraw-Hill, p. 285.

25. From Schrank, R. (1978). How to relieve worker boredom. *Psychology Today, 12* (2), 79–80. Also see Davis, K. (1980, June). Low productivity? Try improving the social environment. *Business Horizons,* pp. 27–29.

26. From Latane, B., Williams, K., & Harkins, S. (1979). Social loafing. *Psychology Today, 13* (4), 104cf.

27. Jewell, L.N., & Reitz, H.J. (1981). *Group effectiveness in organizations.* Glenview, IL: Scott, Foresman.

28. This section draws heavily from Jewell and Reitz (1981). Also Cartwright, D. (1968). The nature of group cohesiveness. In D. Cartwright and A. Zander (Eds.). *Group dynamics: Research and theory* (3rd ed., pp. 91–109). New York: Harper and Row.

29. Stogdill, R.M. (1972). Group productivity, drive and cohesiveness. *Organizational Behavior and Human Performance, 8,* 26–43. Also see Tziner, A., & Vardi, Y. (1982). Effects of command style and group cohesiveness on performance effectiveness of self-selected tank crews. *Journal of Applied Psychology, 67,* 767–775.

30. Wanous, J.P., Rechers, A.E., & Malik, S.D. (1984). Organizational socialization and group development: Toward an integrative perspective. *Academy of Management Review, 9,* 670–683.

31. Tuckman, B.W., & Jensen, M.A.C. (1977). Stages of group development revisited. *Group and Organizational Studies, 2,* 419–427. See Wanous, et al. (1984) for a comparison of the Tuckman model with other models of group development. For a discussion of how norms are developed see Feldman (1984).

32. Wanous, et al. (1984). Also Van Maanen, J., & Schein, E.H. (1979). Toward a theory of organizational socialization. In B.M. Staw (Ed.). *Research in organizational behavior: Vol. 1* (pp. 209–264). Greenwich, CT: JAI Press. For more in-depth coverage on organizational socialization, see Wanous, J.P. (1977). Organizational entry: newcomers moving from outside to inside. *Psychological Bulletin, 84,* 601–618. And Wanous, J.P. (1980). *Organizational entry: Recruitment, selection, and socialization of newcomers.* Reading: MA: Addison-Wesley.

33. For a much more extensive discussion, see Louis, M.B. (1980). Surprise and sensemaking: What newcomers experience in entering unfamiliar organizational settings. *Administrative Science Quarterly, 25,* 226–251. Also see Reibstein, L. (1987, June 10). Crushed Hopes: When a new job proves to be something different. *The Wall Street Journal.*

34. Hebden, J.E. (1986). Adopting an organization's culture: The socialization of graduate trainees. *Organizational Dynamics, 15* (Summer), 54–72.

35. Breaugh, J.A. (1983). Realistic job previews: A critical appraisal and future directions for research. *Academy of Management Review, 8,* 612–619. Breaugh, J.A., & Billings, R.S. (1986). The realistic job preview: Five key elements and their importance for research and practice. *Academy of Management Proceedings 1986,* 240–244.

36. Premack, S.L., & Wanous, J.P. (1985). A meta analysis of realistic job preview experiments. *Journal of Applied Psychology, 70,* 706–719; McEvoy, G.M., & Cascio, W.F. (1985). Strategies for reducing employee turnover: A meta-analysis. *Journal of Applied Psychology, 70,* 342–353.

37. Wanous (1977).

38. *Seattle Post-Intelligencer* (1983, May 1).

39. Reilly, R.R., Brown, B., Blood, M.R., & Malatesta, C.Z. (1981). The effects of realistic previews: A study and discussion of the literature. *Personnel Psychology, 34,* 823–834. Popovich, P., & Wanous, J.P. (1982). The realistic job preview as a persuasive communication. *Academy of Management Review, 7,* 570–578. Hom, P.W., & Griffeth, R.W. (1985). Psychological processes that mediate the effect of the realistic job preview on nursing turnover. *Academy of Management Proceedings 1985,* 215–219.

40. Wanous, et al. (1984).

41. Dyer, W.G. (1987), *Teambuilding: Issues and alternatives,* 2nd edition, Reading, Mass.: Addison-Wesley. French, W.L., and Bell, C.H., Jr. (1984), *Organization development,* 3rd edition. Englewood Cliffs, NJ: Prentice-Hall.

42. Adapted and abridged from McGregor, D. (1960). *The human side of enterprise.* New York: McGraw-Hill, pp. 232–235.

43. Dyer (1987), p. 4.

44. For a complete discussion of teambuilding techniques, see Dyer (1977). French and Bell (1984). And Bradford, D.L., & Cohen, A.R. (1984). *Managing for excellence.* New York: Wiley.

45. Manz, C.C., & Sims, H.P., Jr. (1987). Leading workers to lead themselves: The external leadership of self-managing work teams. *Administrative Science Quarterly, 32,* 106–128.

46. This is a direct quote from the *World of Work Report* (1977, November). Copyright © 1977 Work in America Institute. As adapted by Hackman, J.R. & Oldham, G.R. (1980). *Work redesign.* Reading, MA: Addison-Wesley, pp. 165–167. Used with permission.

47. Asher, S.M., & Inoue, K. (1985, September). Industrial manpower development in Japan. *Finance and Development*. Sasaki, N. (1981). *Management and industrial structure in Japan*. New York: Pergamon Press.

48. Rohlen, T.P. (1974). *For harmony and strength: Japanese white-collar organization in anthropological perspective* (pp. 205–207). Berkeley, CA: University of California Press.

Chapter Ten

CONFLICT, COMPETITION, AND COOPERATION

PREVIEW

- Why do seemingly minor events trigger major conflicts?

- When is conflict desirable? When do we want to encourage it?

- Which conflict resolution technique works best? When should a particular resolution strategy be used or avoided?

- Have you ever tried to be a mediator of a conflict between two subordinates or friends? This chapter will help you be more effective.

- When can a competitive, win-lose situation deteriorate into a lose-lose situation?

- How would you change your negotiating strategies if you were dealing with the Chinese?

MAJOR TOPICS

Preview Case: Warfare at Advanced Products

Understanding Conflict

Managing Conflict

Competition and Cooperation

Cross-Cultural OB: Negotiating Business Deals with the Chinese

Managerial Applications of Conflict and Cooperation

Preview Case

WARFARE AT ADVANCED PRODUCTS

Advanced Products Inc. is a small office machine manufacturing company with about 400 employees. Herb Thorpe, a long-time employee who came up through the ranks, heads the production department. Liz Rosenberg, who was very successful in the marketing department of Xerox Corp., was hired as the sales manager about two years ago. Both Herb and Liz are on the same organizational level—they report to the president and owner, Mr. Asato.

For the past few months, Herb and Liz have not been getting along. It seems like they butt heads almost all the time; it is almost open warfare between the two. The most recent problem involves a promise that Liz made to one of Advanced's largest customers, Allied Insurance, for early delivery on a shipment of sorting machines. When Liz told Herb about her promise to Allied, he blew his stack. He told her there was no way he could modify his production schedules without costing the firm plenty and making his subordinates mad. His face turned red, the veins in his neck stood out, and he said, "This is a bunch of bull. It's impossible. We can't do it. We'll see who wins this one. Let's go see Mr. Asato."

(*What are Herb's and Liz's private thoughts about this confrontation?*)

Herb: She's done it to me again! After I spent all last week figuring out the most efficient use of our equipment, she comes up with this "hairbrain" promise that I can't possibly fulfill without screwing up everything. And besides, if we don't stay on the production schedule, we won't make our goals and won't get our bonus. Boy, would everyone be mad if that happened! That's money out of our pocket. That woman's a menace to this company. I've had it! I just can't take any more of her."

Liz: "These old-timers like Herb are just too inflexible. How can I get my job done with people like him around? If we can't produce the sorters early, then Allied will probably go to another supplier. We could even lose them permanently. Doesn't that old "has-been" know he's screwing up the company, not to mention our sales record and commissions? If they're going to keep Herb, then maybe I better start looking around for another company where I can work with the people."

Later: Liz and Herb enter the president's office later that day to get a decision. Herb is obviously still agitated and angry. He tells Mr. Asato: "It's either her or me! One of us has got to go!" Liz turns to Mr. Asato and says: "I agree. It's time for obsolete old-timers like Herb to retire! Tomorrow wouldn't be too soon as far as I'm concerned!"

Conflict such as that experienced by Herb and Liz, while not an everyday occurrence, does happen. Almost everyone who manages faces conflict situations on a regular basis, either by being directly involved in the conflict or as a mediator. In fact, research indicates that managers spend about 20 percent of their time dealing with conflict.[1] Research also shows that the most successful managers devote half again as much time to managing conflict as do less successful managers.[2] Thus, conflict management is an extremely important managerial skill.

In this chapter, we will try to understand how conflict works and how to manage it. We will also see how competition relates to conflict, what its effects are, and when it is desirable. Conflict can also cause stress, the subject of the next chapter.

UNDERSTANDING CONFLICT

In this section of the chapter, we will learn about the nature of the conflict process—how it works, its sources, and its desirability.

What Is Conflict?

When two coworkers are having a heated discussion about the nature of the new incentive program, they may or may not be in conflict. If one of the workers perceives that the other is frustrating, or about to frustrate, something that is of concern to him or her, then **conflict** exists.[3] For example, if one worker proposes a change in the rules that will result in a lesser bonus for the other, conflict probably exists. On the other hand, when there is no perceived frustration of an important concern, then there is simply a disagreement, not a conflict. For example, two coworkers may disagree over an interpretation of the bonus plan. Regardless of which interpretation is used there will be little or no long lasting impact on either person.

However, it is sometimes difficult to separate conflict and disagreement unless you know how people perceive the situation. While conflict usually involves disagreements over substantive issues, such as the difference in policies, pay systems, or working hours; it may also arise over seemingly trivial issues such as placement of a desk in a different location. In the opening example, it is obvious that Herb and Liz have built up a great deal of resentment and antagonism between each other because each sees the other as frustrating his or her vital concerns. They are in conflict and not merely having a disagreement.

Levels of Conflict

Conflict can occur at a number of levels. **Intrapersonal conflict** happens entirely within the individual. This often results from feelings of obligation in several competing directions. Later we will discuss role conflict, an important source of intrapersonal conflict. Another type of conflict, illustrated by the opening case, is **interpersonal conflict** or conflict between two people. There can also be two ways of looking at conflict within groups. **Intragroup conflict** exists when there is conflict within the group of an interpersonal nature, perhaps over who will become the group leader. **Intergroup conflict** is possible when two or more groups are involved in a conflict situation, such as a disagreement between the marketing and production departments. Finally, there is **interorganizational conflict,** where two or more organizations are involved in conflict, such as when the union faces off with the organization or when government is involved.[4]

Types of Conflict Issues

There are two general types of conflict issues, substantive and emotional.[5] **Substantive issues** include disagreements over policies and practices, competition for scarce resources, and conflict over roles and responsibilities. **Emotion-**

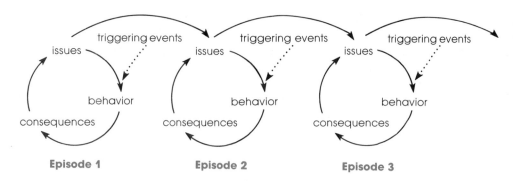

Figure 10.1

THE CONFLICT PROCESS

SOURCE: Richard E. Walton, *Interpersonal Peacemaking: Confrontations and Third Party Consultation*, © 1969. Addison-Wesley Publishing Company Inc., Reading, Massachusetts, Fig. 5–1. Reprinted with permission.

al issues involve negative feelings between people, such as fear, rejection, resentment, anger, and distrust. Conflicts in values, discussed in Chapter 3, are also important emotional issues. Substantive and emotional issues are often mixed, as they were in our opening example where the substantive issue of scheduling the early delivery of goods was combined with the emotional issues of distrust, scorn, and resentment. Emotional issues tend to be more destructive and more difficult to resolve than substantive issues.

How Conflict Works

Conflict in organizations is a cyclical process that often builds through a series of conflict episodes as shown in Figure 10.1. While the process is normally cyclical, it is certainly possible for one powerful incident to provoke extreme conflict. A **conflict episode** occurs when some event, such as the Allied Insurance sale, triggers conflict behaviors. The triggering event causes the conflict to surface and be felt—you get mad and do something (behave) to get it off your chest (an angry outburst, leaving the room, or even quitting). The outcome or consequences of this conflict episode will strongly influence what happens in the future. If the conflict is fully resolved so that the hostility is removed, then there may be no future conflict. If, on the other hand, the conflict is suppressed, then the next time a triggering event occurs there may be an even bigger blowup.

Sources of Conflict

Recognizing the sources of conflict helps us to understand why conflict arises from some situations naturally.[6] Conflict can be stimulated or reduced by changing or eliminating the source. While there are many sources of conflict, including value issues, personality differences, and communication (discussed earlier in the book), several additional ones are noted in the following paragraphs.

Conflict Over Resources. Competition for scarce resources is a very common basis for conflict. Say the equipment budget is being cut by 10 percent, but the research department needs a 20 percent increase. There is a conflict between research, finance, and the other departments over the allocation of these funds. Another type of conflict of interest was illustrated in our opening incident. If the Allied sale were to fall through, Liz would lose the commission. If the production schedule were accelerated, Herb would lose his bonus for meeting his production goals.

Ambiguous Jurisdictions. When responsibilities and roles are clear, people know who must make the decisions, and conflicts seldom arise. However, in a large, complex organization, responsibilities are often unclear—turf is often unspecified and conflicts occur when two groups go after the same responsibilities or try to avoid the responsibility. For example, operations management experts may feel that they should select the type of desk computer to be used for solving problems. Purchasing may disagree. They may believe that their task is to find the lowest cost item that will do the job. Hence, there may be a conflict between operations management and purchasing.[7]

Role Conflicts. A role is a set of expectations that is believed to be associated with a given position in a group or organization. Role conflict occurs when various people, including the person playing the role, have differing expectations about how the role should be acted. The resulting pressure causes psychological conflict, and, as we will see in Chapter 11, stress. Perspective 10.1 gives an example of how role conflict affects the first-line supervisor. Another important type of role conflict happens when there are different role expectations between work roles and family roles; for example, between long hours spent on an important project versus time spent with spouse and children.[8]

Communication Barriers. People or groups who do not communicate are more likely to encounter conflict. Sometimes the barriers are physical, such as

---

Perspective 10.1

THE FIRST–LINE SUPERVISOR: ROLE CONFLICT IN ACTION[9]

A classic example of role conflict is the first-line supervisor, the foreman, the section chief, who is at the lowest level of supervision. Upper managers expect foremen to behave like a manager, to set goals, maintain discipline, maintain schedules, and enforce compliance with company rules. On the other hand, foremen are usually promoted from the shop floor. Subordinates, who were once close friends, expect the role of a friend—to be understanding, lenient, and forgiving. This situation puts the foreman in a bind and creates conflict.

Excessive role conflict results in frustration and strain that affects tension, dissatisfaction, and even health. Often withdrawal from one group or the other by either quitting the job of foreman or isolating oneself from the shop-floor employees, is the only way to resolve the tension. It is no wonder that turnover rates are high for first-line supervisors.

the difference between the day shift and the night shift; and sometimes they are psychological, such as the differences between Liz and Herb's experiences. When people do not communicate, there is more chance for misunderstanding and mistrust, major causes of emotional conflict. The lack of communication serves to perpetuate future conflict cycles.

Dependence of One Party.   When one must rely upon another to get the job done, there will be more conflict. For example, some organizational designs call for functional experts, such as engineers, to be permanently assigned to the engineering department. However, the engineers actually perform tasks for other departments, such as the J–81 engine project manager. Thus, the project manager is dependent upon engineers who are under someone else's control. The engineers, in turn, are dependent upon the project manager for performance feedback.

Domination.   When one or more persons or groups are trying to control the behavior of others, they are trying to dominate.[10] This produces conflict because most people do not want to be controlled by others. A boss who overly controls employees may create conflict. A committee chair who tries to control and direct the meeting too tightly may generate conflict.

Is Conflict Good or Bad?

A moderate level of conflict is usually constructive. If there is no conflict, the organization may be complacent and stagnant; it may lose much of the energizing force and tension that conflict creates. Change and innovation, two ingredients of healthy organizations, normally mean conflict. As illustrated in Figure 10.2, conflict can be thought of as a continuum of intensities ranging from no conflict to extreme conflict.[11] A manager can plot the "conflict temperature" to see if the level is about where it should be and then take action either to reduce or stimulate conflict—in other words, manage the conflict.

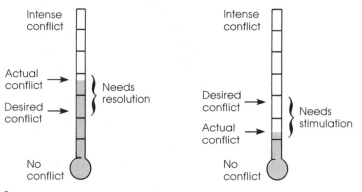

Figure 10.2

CONFLICT INTENSITY SCALES

SOURCE: Adapted from Robbins, S.P. (1974). *Managing organizational conflict: A nontraditional approach* (pp. 96–97). Englewood Cliffs, NJ: Prentice-Hall.

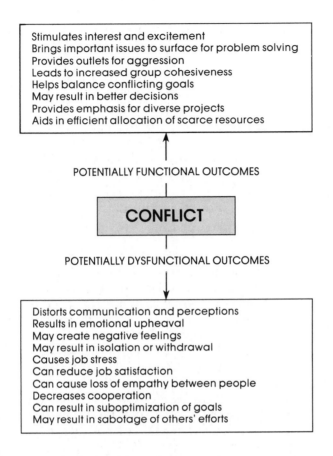

Figure 10.3

POTENTIAL OUTCOMES FROM CONFLICT

An important consideration when determining if conflict is desirable is the nature of the conflict itself. Conflicts that serve to raise important organizational issues, such as customer deliveries, or to focus on equitable division of scarce resources between two parts of the organization, such as domestic and international operations, are usually desirable types of conflict. On the other hand, conflicts that do not help resolve organizational problems, but only create hard feelings and tension, such as the confrontation between Herb and Liz, are usually undesirable. Most emotional conflicts over values, personality issues, or communication, are dysfunctional. Figure 10.3 illustrates the potential outcomes of conflict, both positive and negative.

An example of when conflict is desirable or good might be when production and sales disagree over how fast an item can be delivered to a customer, as was illustrated in our opening example. If such conflicts do not arise, then important sales may be lost. Let's say that there was no conflict between sales and production. If production says they cannot deliver when the customer wants the product, then the customer is simply told to "take it or leave it." Do you think a customer, such as Allied Insurance, would go elsewhere? Most probably. Of course, the emotionally draining type of conflict illustrated in our opening example between Herb and Liz was not a desirable form of conflict.

The key here is to recognize that some conflicts can be beneficial while others need to be eliminated. We must develop strategies for dealing with or managing conflict, the topic of our next section.

MANAGING CONFLICT

If there is some optimal level of conflict as we have just implied, then conflict must be managed so we can reach it. This means increasing or decreasing the conflict level.

Raising Conflict Levels

There are a number of reasons why you might want to increase the level of conflict. For example, a smoldering quarrel between two subordinates that is disrupting your efforts to build an effective work team would demand action to resolve it.[12] Raising the level of this type of conflict can force the parties to confront the issues, air their differences, and resolve the festering problem. Another instance for increasing conflict could be when two goals are desirable but competing with one another. This can happen when a company is interested in marketing a product in two countries, each with differing requirements and goals. If conflict is avoided, one of the countries will probably be unduly emphasized at the expense of the other. However, forcing these conflicts out in the open may result in optimal coverage for both countries. Later, in the chapter on organizational design, we will see how a matrix structure can actually encourage such conflicts.

Conflict can be raised by structuring the organization so that relationships are ambiguous and people are competing for scarce resources (discussed under sources of conflict). Another way to heighten conflict is to structure the organization so that there are opposing interest groups; for example, one department might be concerned with the success of its product, such as toothpaste, and another department might be responsible for making sure that costs are kept as low as possible. Competition, discussed later in this chapter, is another way to heighten conflict. Table 10.1 shows how language can either raise or lower conflict levels.

Lowering Conflict Levels

Most of the literature on conflict management deals with reducing conflict levels.[13] In this section, we will cover five methods for dealing with undesirable conflict: avoiding, accommodating, forcing, compromising, and collaborating. When choosing a conflict-resolution strategy, the first decision is whether to confront or avoid the conflict.[14] There are times when conflict arises that you will want to put off acting upon it even though it is a problem.

Avoidance and Diffusion.   Any strategy that avoids a major confrontation or conflict is called **avoidance.** For example, say the research and development manager knows that a major conflict exists over funds allocated for new prod-

Perspective 10.2

ENCOURAGING CONFLICT AND CONFRONTATION AT INTEL CORPORATION

The President of Intel Corp., Andrew S. Grove, encourages conflict and its "constructive confrontation." He believes that dealing with conflict lies at the very heart of managing any business. Every organization faces problems that can result in conflicts. These must be resolved if the organization is to go forward. He also believes that conflict puts people's aggressive energy to work *for* the organization. Intel's method focuses on an attack on the problem, not the person, in a polite and businesslike way. Say, "I disagree with your proposed solution," rather than "You're out of your mind to suggest such a thing." The following incident, which actually took place at Intel, shows how they encourage conflict: [15]

"I just don't understand how your new way of measuring things around here will help us at all," the plant manager said, grimacing. Others at the meeting merely looked puzzled. The vice president of manufacturing, the plant manager's direct superior, had just finished vigorously urging the use of a particular statistical indicator to determine whether the company's plants were delivering products on time. Faced with the plant manager's incredulity, the vice president redoubled his efforts, trying again to win over everyone in the room.

The plant manager remained unconvinced. His colleagues then jumped into the fray. Arguments generated rebuttals, numbers collided with other numbers. New ideas began to surface, most of them to be immediately rejected, until eventually the heated exchanges dissipated. The still-animated group of people in the room suddenly realized, with considerable satisfaction, that they had now come up with the right statistical measure.

As the meeting ended, the vice president shook his head in mock dismay. "It's too bad," he said, "that you people are so reticent." He put away his papers somewhat ruefully—his hours of preparation for the meeting had not resulted in his proposal being adopted. But he also knew that what had finally been agreed upon was better than his original idea.

Table 10.1

THE LANGUAGE OF CONFLICT

Certain words and phrases serve to intensify or defuse conflict. Careful use or avoidance of this language can help resolve or prevent conflict. Some examples are given below:

Words that intensify conflict	Words that help resolve conflict
You . . .	I . . .
You performed poorly.	Performance was 10 percent lower compared to last month.
The way you talk makes me angry.	When you interrupted me just now, you seemed uninterested in what I was saying.
I am right and you are wrong.	How can we find a solution that will satisfy both of us?
You make me mad.	I get angry when you belittle me in front of others.
You said . . .	What I heard you say was . . .

SOURCE: Filley, A.C. (1975). *Interpersonal conflict resolution* (chap. 3). Glenview, IL: Scott, Foresman.

uct development. However, the manager does not want to confront the conflict at this time because there are some important market research studies that have not been completed. The manager takes great care to avoid issues that might trigger the conflict. While avoidance is sometimes useful as a delaying tactic, it can also cause problems. If Mr. Asato had avoided the conflict between Liz and Herb, it might have been disastrous for Advanced Products.

Table 10.2 illustrates situations when chief executives think avoidance or other resolution techniques are appropriate. The reasons cited may help clarify the five styles.

Accommodation.   A strategy that gives in to others, lets them have their own way, or appeases them is called **accomodation.** While this strategy appears weak, there may be reasons for generosity and self-sacrifice. Perhaps you wish to maintain a good relationship with a valued colleague. If you confront the conflict so that your position is properly presented, it may lead to loss of friendship or other undesirable outcomes. You may also elect to "lose" on this confrontation with the hopes of "winning" on another, perhaps more important, conflict.

Table 10.2

CEO RECOMMENDATIONS FOR CONFLICT RESOLUTION

Avoiding	1. When an issue is trivial, or more important issues are pressing.
	2. When you perceive no chance of satisfying your concerns.
	3. When potential disruption outweighs the benefits of resolution.
	4. To let people cool down and gain perspective.
	5. When gathering information supercedes immediate decision.
Forcing	1. When quick, decisive action is vital—e.g., emergencies.
	2. On important issues where unpopular actions need implementing—e.g., cost cutting, enforcing unpopular rules, discipline.
	3. On issues vital to company welfare when you know you're right.
	4. Against people who take advantage of noncompetitive behavior.
Compromising	1. When goals are important, but not worth the effort or potential disruption of more assertive modes.
	2. When opponents with equal power are committed to mutually exclusive goals.
	3. To achieve temporary settlements to complex issues.
	4. To arrive at expedient solutions under time pressure.
	5. As a backup when collaboration or competition is unsuccessful.
Problem solving	1. To find an integrative solution when both sets of concerns are too important to be compromised.
	2. When your objective is to learn.
	3. To merge insights from people with different perspectives.
	4. To gain commitment by incorporating concerns into a concensus.
	5. To work through feelings which have interfered with a relationship.
Accommodating	1. When you find you are wrong. To allow another position to be heard, to learn, and to show your reasonableness.
	2. When issues are more important to others than to yourself. To satisfy others and maintain cooperation.
	3. To minimize losses when you are outmatched and losing.
	4. When harmony and stability are especially important.
	5. To allow subordinates to develop by learning from mistakes.

SOURCE: From K.W. Thomas, 1977, Toward multidimensional values in teaching: The example of conflict behavior, *Academy of Management Review* 2:487. Copyright © 1977 by Academy of Management. Reprinted with permission of the publisher and author.

Forcing.   Using power, coercion, or force to resolve conflict results in an imposed or forced solution. **Forcing** may involve the use of institutional authority and power, rewards and punishments, bribery, or even physical force. In an emergency or under other circumstances shown in Table 10.2, forcing may be the appropriate resolution method. In our opening case, forcing could be used by the president to resolve the conflict. Depending upon the nature of the forced solution, a number of outcomes are possible. If the president were to make a decision in favor of either Liz or Herb, then problems would be likely to arise. The solution would most probably be only a temporary fix for the problem. Liz and Herb would still have lingering resentment and hostility. Another problem with this approach is that the loser, say Herb (if the decision were made in favor of Liz), may get angry and quit, or at the very least be demotivated and dissatisfied. Forcing does not seem to be the best solution for our case.

Compromising.   A solution that involves give and take, bargaining, and negotiations is called **compromising**. This is the standard method of resolving labor relations conflicts. Compromise is used when there is a relatively equal balance of power between the parties. They negotiate a sharing of limited resources. Bargaining is commonly used when there is some fixed amount of resources to divide, such as new authorizations for personnel or travel funds. During negotiations, each party tries to control and distort information in its favor. There is little concern for the overall good of the organization. The focus is on achieving a beneficial solution or minimizing losses.[16] Compromising does not seem to be a good approach for the solution of Herb and Liz's conflict.

Collaboration.   The problem-solving or **collaborative** approach means that all parties work together to find a mutually acceptable solution to their conflict. The idea is to work together so that the conflict is resolved permanently and there is shared commitment to the solution. There are a number of problem-solving techniques that work, including the negotiation strategy, "getting to yes," highlighted in Perspective 10.4. Another useful and simple approach involves the following steps: [17]

1. *Define and clarify the problem.* What are the tangible issues in the conflict? Where does each party stand? It is helpful to write down this information on newsprint so that it will be visible.

2. *Search for solutions.* Generate a range of solutions without being judgmental. One way to do this is to use brainstorming (*see* Chapter 13 for details).

3. *Evaluate the solutions.* Each party works to achieve a consensus decision (a solution to which both can generally agree) on the best solution for both parties.

4. *Implement the decision.*

5. *Follow up,* if appropriate, to make sure everything is working out as planned.

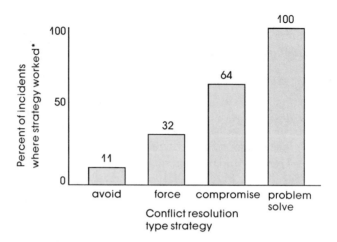

*Based on research results from two different studies comparing four conflict-resolution techniques over 153 incidents. The resolution technique is categorized as "not working" if the respondents felt particularly bad about the way the conflict was handled. In reality, the results of the research do not tell us if the strategy worked, but only how the respondents felt about the outcome to the technique.

Figure 10.4

CONFLICT RESOLUTION: WHAT WORKS?

SOURCE: Based on the combined results of Burke, R.J. (1970). Methods of resolving superior-subordinate conflict: The constructive use of subordinate differences and disagreements. *Organizational Behavior and Human Performance, 5,* 403; and Phillips, E., & Cheston, R. (1979). Conflict resolution: What works? *California Management Review, 21* (4), 79.

Which Resolution Strategy Should You Use? As you can see from Figure 10.4, it is hard to go wrong with collaboration and problem solving. However, this strategy takes time. Thus, in some cases forcing or compromising may be more apropos.

The conflict experienced by Liz and Herb might best be resolved through problem solving. In fact, this is the strategy Mr. Asato used to resolve the conflict. He began by asking both Liz and Herb to state separately their concerns that resulted in the conflict. From these two statements, it was apparent that a problem existed—how to satisfy Allied Insurance without disrupting the production schedule. Mr. Asato led a discussion of ways that the problem might be resolved. They wrote all the potential solutions on the blackboard in the conference room. Next, the three of them sat back and evaluated the possible solutions (by this time Liz and Herb had cooled off and were actually cooperating). Jointly, they decided that it would be possible to delay a shipment to another company whose needs were not so pressing and still keep their delivery schedule with Allied. In this case, the conflict was resolved, and Herb and Liz were at least communicating more freely than before.

Using Third Parties for Conflict Resolution

Third parties are often used to help resolve conflict. A third party can be a co-worker, boss, or a conflict-resolution specialist. Almost everyone acts as a third

Perspective 10.3

HOW TO BE AN EFFECTIVE THIRD PARTY

Since almost everyone is a third party at one time or another, we need to review some techniques that will make that job easier and more effective. The following list contains some useful and practical hints for improving your conflict-resolution skills.[18]

• Talk to each conflicting person or group alone and find out where they are coming from. While you are doing this try to establish norms of openness and confrontation.

• Find an appropriate neutral setting. Go to a location that is neutral, such as a conference room. Stay away from offices. They are perceived as another's turf and inhibit the process.

• Unless the conflict is minor, be sure to establish a large, open-ended block of time to resolve the conflict. One way to do this is to have the session begin at 3:00 P.M., with the un-derstanding that it will continue until it is resolved, even if it takes until midnight.

• Avoid getting the parties defensive. Avoid crossed transactions, except from the Adult ego state (*see* Chapter 8). Avoid the critical Parent state. Use the right language for problem solving (*see* Table 10.1).

• Focus on behavior and the tangible effects of the behavior. It is often useful to have both parties separately write out the conflict's cause and the tangible effects on them, then share their results. Use I–messages (*see* Chapter 8).

• Listen carefully. Use active-listening techniques (Chapter 8).

• The third party may restate the issues and concerns of each party.

• Be prepared with a problem-solving procedure such as the one we discussed earlier in this chapter. Suggest its use at an appropriate time if the use seems warranted by the type of conflict.

• Try to avoid proposing or imposing solutions.

party at one time or another. The major reason for using a third party is to make concessions easier without the loss of face, thus promoting easier and quicker conflict resolution.[19] The third party may absorb some of the responsibility for the concession.

Examples of third parties abound. As related above, Mr. Asato acted as the third party to resolve Herb and Liz's conflict. Mediators or arbitrators are often used to resolve labor contract disputes. Counselors are used to resolve interpersonal disputes between employees or between family members.

There are a number of skills and techniques that are important for an effective third party. Perspective 10.3 provides an overview of how to conduct third-party conflict resolution.

COOPERATION AND COMPETITION

Competition and win-lose dynamics can create a number of organizational problems including conflict. Cooperation, on the other hand, can aid in solving problems and developing teamwork. In this section, we will look at the process of competition and cooperation in organizations.

Deutsch's Theory of Cooperation

Deutsch's Theory of Cooperation states that the fundamental process underlying cooperation and competition is the type of goal interdependence.[20] **Cooperation** means that people's goals are positively related; that movement toward your own goals helps others reach their goals. It means working together toward mutual goals. **Competition,** in contrast, means that people's goals are negatively linked; movement toward your goals interferes with someone else's goal attainment. In other words, competition is involved when two or more people or groups are seeking to gain the same thing that others are seeking— when one wins the other loses. For example, take the funds allocation process between two departments. People within the marketing department may cooperate to help the department obtain the maximum funds allocation. However, the marketing department is in competition with the production department for the monies. Thus competition exists because whatever funds are won by marketing are lost to production.

Competition is certainly a cornerstone of United States culture. People are taught to be competitive at an early age. Sports and organizational policies often encourage competition. Obviously, competition can be an energizing force, but it can also be quite destructive for organizations that need teamwork to get the job done. Table 10.3 illustrates the outcomes of competition and cooperation. As you can see, the organizational implications of competition are generally unfavorable. We will discuss this topic further in the section on win-lose dynamics.

Competition and Conflict Compared

How does competition differ from conflict? The main difference is whether one party is trying to frustrate or block another. If this blocking is present, then

Table 10.3

OUTCOMES OF COOPERATION AND COMPETITION

Behavior	Expected outcomes from COOPERATION	Expected outcomes from COMPETITION
Assistance	People help each other to reach goals or to exchange resources.	People suspect others; unwilling to help others to achieve goals.
Communication	Active seeking and giving of accurate information.	Distortion and withholding information; suspicious; ulterior messages.
Task orientation	Division of tasks; cooperation to reach goals.	No task division; may attempt to undercut others.
Friendliness and support	Positive attitudes towards others.	Tend to dislike or derogate others.
Reaction speed	Slower to respond.	Faster to respond.
Productivity	Higher for most complex tasks.	Lower for most tasks except simple tasks.
Job satisfaction	Generally higher	Generally lower.

SOURCE: Based on the literature review in Tjosvold, D. (1984). Cooperation theory and organizations. *Human Relations, 37,* 743–767. Also see Johnson, D.W., Maruyama, G., Johnson, R., Nelson, D., & Skon, L. (1981). Effects of cooperative, competitive, and individualistic goal structures on achievement: A meta-analysis. *Psychological Bulletin, 89,* 56–57.

competition and conflict coexist. For example, if all departments are competing with one another for the lowest absentee rate, then competition exists, but not conflict. If all departments are competing for a limited amount of office improvement funds and each is doing its best to win at the expense of the others, then conflict exists.

It is also possible to have conflict without competition when the parties are not seeking to gain over each other. For example, a manager who presents a proposal to the staff to find loopholes, inconsistencies, and problems, is encouraging conflict, but there is no competition.

The Win-Lose Model: Outcomes of Competition and Cooperation

When people are striving to attain the same thing, three outcomes are possible: one can win and the other can lose (**win-lose**), they both can lose (**lose-lose**), or they both can win (**win-win**). This way of looking at outcomes, called the **win-lose model,** is a great help in interpreting what happens in competitive situations.[21] Figure 10.5 illustrates win-lose dynamics.

Win-Lose. Our opening example was a good one for win-lose, since either way the decision went—with Liz or with Herb—the other perceived a loss. In this case, the loss was not only psychological but financial, since the system was designed to reward sales differently from production. Sales were rewarded by commissions for sales made. Production was rewarded for making the production schedule on time. If a client, such as Allied Insurance, wanted early delivery, then the system would force a win-lose confrontation.

Lose-Lose. Win-lose can often deteriorate into lose-lose because of the effects of the conflict on the organization. Let's say that the Advanced Products' president had decided in favor of Herb, as a result Liz quit, and Allied Insurance went to another supplier. In this case, the organization would have lost. Even Herb might have lost in the long run if the effects of the loss of the largest client caused production layoffs.

Win-Win. The key strategy of a win-win approach is to seek a way of satisfying the needs of both parties so that both get rewarded and win. A win-win strategy attempts to make the pie (total reward pool) bigger rather than slicing up a pie (giving a fixed pool of rewards to the parties). This is usually done by problem solving or collaborative approaches. When Mr. Asato used a problem-solving approach to resolve the conflict between Liz and Herb, it resulted in a solution that was good for everyone concerned. It was a win-win situation.

Effects of Win-Lose Competition

Suppose the president of your firm decides to use the same techniques that professional sports teams use to improve organizational productivity. Each major department (marketing, production, personnel) will make up a team. These teams then compete against each other to see who can be the most productive. The team that wins will get a major bonus, while the losers get nothing.

WIN-WIN

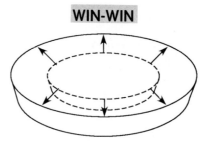

Expand pie; everybody WINS

WIN-LOSE

Split fixed pie, or winner takes all

LOSE-LOSE

Pie gets smaller, or disappears

Figure 10.5

WIN–LOSE DYNAMICS

There is a strong possibility that this win-lose strategy will create problems. Production and marketing will be looking out for their own interests rather than those of the firm. They may even withhold information from each other so the other will look bad and have a greater chance of losing. After a while, they may not even be communicating. Such a competitive climate may result in incidents like our opening one where marketing commits the firm to an impossible delivery schedule. When the delivery fails, both sides may lose if the customer is lost. If marketing perceives itself to be the loser, it will be looking for ways to make those "dunderheads" in production look bad. Instead of a spirit of working together that may have once existed, every department will be out for itself.

Then, is competition always bad? Win-lose situations almost always create conflict since the loser's goals are frustrated. As we discussed earlier, there may be times when such conflict and competition are desirable. The next section addresses this issue.

Perspective 10.4

GETTING TO YES: A WIN–WIN NEGOTIATION STRATEGY[22]

The Harvard Negotiation Project has been researching negotiation and conflict resolution methods for many years. The directors of the project, Roger Fisher and William Ury, have written a book, *Getting to Yes*, that describes their recommended method. The five major parts of their strategy are summarized below:

1. *Don't bargain over positions.* When people take positions, they tend to get locked into them and defend them from attack. It can often result in win-lose or lose-lose outcomes. The longer the negotiation goes on, the more committed they become. Since position taking usually means taking rather extreme positions at the start of negotiations, it is usually quite inefficient. Moving from one position to another takes lots of time and energy.

2. *Separate the people from the problem.* Every negotiation involves both the substance being negotiated and the people involved. The key here is to pay attention to the "people" side of negotiation. Recognize that perceptual differences exist; try to empathize. Be sure that both parties participate fully in any decisions made about the negotiation process. Look for "face-saving" solutions that will allow the other party to keep a high level of self-esteem. Recognize that emotions are a natural part of the process; treat them as legitimate. Be sure to listen actively and keep communication channels open. Use "I-messages" rather than "you messages."

For example, say "I feel let down," rather than "You broke your word." The thrust of separating the people from the problem is to develop a "side-by-side" collaborative strategy rather than a conflictual strategy.

3. *Focus on interests, not positions.* Interests are the underlying outcomes that motivate people. Interests differ from positions in that positions are something you decide upon while interests are the underlying cause of the decision. There are often several positions that can satisfy a given interest. To identify interests, ask *"why?"* . . . What is your basic concern? Most interests can be tied to basic human needs: physiological, security, social, esteem, or self-actualization. A discussion of mutual interests helps show that you are concentrating on solving the problem, not attacking the other person.

4. *Invent options for mutual gain.* Try to develop options where both sides will gain a win-win solution. Strategies to accomplish this goal include separating idea generation from decision making by using techniques such as brainstorming (*see* Chapter 13). You should try to identify shared interests where there are possibilities for mutual gain.

5. *Use objective criteria.* For each issue, try to find criteria, such as efficiency, cost, market value, professional standards, fairness, or scientific merit to use for evaluating decisions. For example, if you were buying a building, you might say: "I know that you would like to get a high price for this office building, while I would like to pay a low one. Let's figure out what a *fair* price would be." This strategy would result in a mutual search for fair criteria, rather than haggling over positions.

When to Use Competition

The preceding example may give the impression that competition is bad. This is not always the case. We all know of situations wherein people or groups have achieved and performed at very high levels because of competition—in the Olympics, for example. Competition in itself is not necessarily bad. If cooperation is not needed and if tasks are independent, then competition can work well. An organizational example illustrating when competition might work is one where a company is organized into autonomous product divisions (such as soap, shampoo, toothpaste). In this case, competition between divisions could be an energizing force that makes the overall organization more productive. However, if the competition groups must cooperate to accomplish the organization's mission, then establishing intergroup competition is undesirable.

The key rule for using competition is to avoid it when individuals or groups are interdependent and must cooperate to reach the organization's goals. Use it if they are independent and cooperation is not needed to reach the goals. The following conditions are favorable for the use of competition: [23]

- *When the competitors are from different organizations that do not need to cooperate to get the job done.* An example might be top salesperson at the south branch versus top salesperson at the north branch.

- *When each party has a relatively equal chance to win.* No one wants to compete if they are destined to lose; if they have no chance. If absentee rates are the basis for competition and the research department has always had a much lower rate, then production will not be motivated to compete.

- *When later cooperation between the parties is not needed.* Since the loser is unlikely to help the winner, people better be independent of one another.

- *Winning must be a rewarding experience.* If a pieceworker wins a production competition only to be isolated from the group, then competition will be ineffective.

Managing Competition

Since research has shown competition to be generally less effective than cooperation in most organizational situations, here are some ways of reducing and managing competition.[24]

- *Establish superordinate goals.* By establishing a **superordinate** or overall goal that everyone in all groups can work towards, competition will be directed toward goal accomplishment rather than against other groups. For example, if marketing and production were assigned the superordinate goal of developing a new product, then there would be pressures toward cooperation rather than competition.

- *Concentrate on total organizational effectiveness.* This is another way of implementing superordinate goals. Everyone should be measured and rewarded based on their contribution to the total effort rather than their individual effectiveness.

- *Increase communication between competitors.* Ways can be structured so that people have to get together and communicate. Frequent meetings, joint task forces, geographical relocation, and team-building workshops are all ways to get people talking to each other.

- *Avoid win-lose situations.* Design organizational systems on a win-win basis. For example, a bonus for reduced costs should be allocated equally between all people in the company rather than just to a few. In fact, many bonus plans are designed in a win-win fashion, such as gainsharing, discussed in Chapter 6.[25]

- *Rotate people between departments.* When people rotate to other parts of the company, they get a different perspective; they gain empathy.

- *Reward cooperation.* Design reward systems, bonuses, recognition, performance appraisals—so they positively reinforce cooperation. Gainsharing plans, such as those discussed in Chapter 6, are appropriate. Bonuses based on team performance are also desirable.

CROSS–CULTURAL OB: NEGOTIATING BUSINESS DEALS WITH THE CHINESE

Doing business with the People's Republic of China makes many a manager's pulse quicken. The thought of a one-billion person market for their products is quite exciting. Many have jumped aboard an airplane and attempted to sell their products to the Chinese. Unfortunately, many have failed. Major reasons for failure are: communication breakdowns, differences in business practices, and differences in negotiating styles.[26] The problems boil down to an inability to negotiate with the Chinese, who have spent centuries honing this subtle art.

A Comparison of American and Chinese Negotiating Strategies

This section compares American and Chinese negotiating strategies and recommends ways of improving the process.[27]

American Strategies	Chinese Strategies
There is a tendency to be clear and open about priorities; to be overenthusiastic.	Priorities are kept hidden. Enthusiasm is very restrained.
Americans try to reduce misunderstandings by getting a detailed agreement. They perceive the letter of agreement as a "warm up," not to be taken too seriously.	Chinese negotiators try to get Americans to agree to a very broad letter of agreement that can later be used for leverage by citing failure to follow the guides.
Contracts are seen as legal, binding agreements to be followed to the letter.	Contracts are seen as a commercial document that defines the desired outcomes of the parties. The long-term relationship is what is really important.
American firms like to be seen as strong and influential. They tend to brag about their capabilities. They have an upbeat, outgoing, enthusiastic style.	The Chinese try to get the other side to exaggerate its capabilities so that they can easily ask for more from the "stronger" partner. They see Americans as easily flattered, and thus readily manipulated.
Americans may be willing to offer a low price to get into the market, with hopes of later profitability.	Chinese press for early price concessions and then behave like they were locked in concrete during later negotiations.
There is a tendency to be overly honest and self-critical about past mistakes.	An important strategy is to make the other party feel that they are doing or have done something wrong and thus should make amends.

Perspective 10.5

CONSTRUCTIVE

CONFRONTATION IN JAPAN

Earlier in this chapter (Perspective 10.2), we discussed how Intel Corp. encouraged conflict and confrontation. However, when they tried to apply their technique in a Japanese subsidiary problems arose: [28]

Some cultures do seem to better prepare people to use [constructive confrontation]. I was once asked to teach [the technique] to a group of managers at our subsidiary in Japan. The Japanese readily grasped the rea-

sons for the practice, and we sailed along merrily until we came to the role playing. So that I could follow it, they began by doing this in English. It went well. Gradually their role playing switched into Japanese. While I could not follow the dialogue, I noted growing amusement among the Japanese managers who were watching. When I asked them to explain their mirth, it turned out that while the role players had a fairly easy time practicing their confrontational roles in English, they absolutely froze when they tried to do it in Japanese. The ingrained habits of nonconfrontational behavior so strongly established in Japanese upbringing effectively inhibited them from bringing off a confrontation in their native language.

As guests, Americans must adjust to Chinese norms and practices without seeming rude. They must be amenable to the host's suggestions.

Americans are anxious to reach agreement and return home to other pressing problems. They may agree to an "eleventh hour" contract just be achieve a sense of accomplishment.

Being the host allows control over the agenda, pace, team size, and entertainment. Chinese always ask the Americans to open the session, thus showing their hand first for later attack.

Time is on the side of the Chinese since the Americans have to go home on a deadline. They often seem passive and wait until the last minute before truly negotiating.

In summary, there are vast differences in the negotiating strategies of these two countries. Americans believe in a give-and-take process that results in both sides optimizing their positions. The Chinese see the agreement as the beginning of a long-term relationship; as more like a pledge to do business.

While this section illustrates how negotiation strategies differ between the U.S. and China, every country has its own cultural factors that make negotiation difficult. [29]

How to Negotiate With the Chinese

The first step is awareness of Chinese negotiating strategies, such as those discussed above. However, do not expect that you can ever master Chinese ways—be sensitive, but be yourself. Accept that the very nature of the contract will differ from the norm; relationships will shape the actual nature of the business interaction. One of the most important behaviors is patience during all phases of the negotiation. Many problems can be minimized or avoided by hiring a good translator who understands Chinese negotiating tactics and is willing to share the knowledge with you. Another tactic is to manage time. Clearly specify when you will be leaving and then do it on schedule. These are only a few of the many tactics that may help create a more successful negotiation experience. [30]

MANAGERIAL APPLICATIONS OF CONFLICT AND COOPERATION

Our discussions have shown that some level of conflict may be useful for energizing or developing "creative tension" in organizations. The key is the basic nature of the conflict. If it centers around resolving important organizational problems and issues, then it is probably functional conflict. If it only serves to stir up interpersonal animosity, it is probably a dysfunctional conflict.

Competition in organizations also needs careful attention. Managers often create win-lose situations when win-win is just as easily developed. Cooperation helps people work together as a team and prevents the divisions that result from win-lose situations. Here are some specific guides for managers:

- *Be prepared for conflict episodes.* Expect conflict to happen and devise your strategies for dealing with it in advance.

- *Take action to avoid undesirable conflicts.* Ways to avoid conflict include: creating an open communication environment, avoiding ambiguous assignments, watching out for role conflicts, and trying to build in as much autonomy and control into the job as possible.

- *When conflict is functional, encourage it.* When extra energy is needed or careful attention to scarce resources and special projects is required, encourage conflict by making it a norm of the organization, creating ambiguous jurisdictions, or purposely setting up two or more units to compete with each other. However, be ready to resolve the conflict if it gets out of hand.

- *Use the appropriate conflict resolution strategy.* Each strategy has its own advantages and disadvantages. Use avoidance when you do not have time for confrontation or cooling off is needed. Use accommodation when harmony is important or when the issues are more important to others than to you. Use forcing when fast decisions are needed or when the conflict resolution strategy will be unpopular, but necessary. Use compromising when powerful people are equally committed to opposing interests, or to achieve a solution to a complex problem. Use collaboration whenever possible, since the potential for win-win exists when you focus on problem solving.

- *Recognize the benefits of third parties.* Since third parties help defuse conflicts and make resolution both easier and faster, use them whenever possible. Be prepared to act as a third party yourself by using the guides in Perspective 10.3.

- *Encourage cooperation.* Since you can expect many positive outcomes from cooperation, try to design jobs, groups, and reward systems to encourage this approach. You may also use superordinate goals, job rotation, and concentration on the total organization as ways to encourage cooperation.

- *Be wary of competition.* As a general rule competition causes problems, creates win-lose dynamics, and lowers organizational performance. Unless you have an unusual situation where people work quite independently from one another, avoid the strategy. Even when competition is theoretically appropriate, it may create communication difficulties and derogation of others.

● *Design reward systems so that everyone wins.* Take care to avoid win-lose strategies that may deteriorate into lose-lose. Establish structures where there is no upper limit to rewards and no exclusion of certain people or groups. Make sure everybody wins.

● *Use the Getting to Yes, win-win negotiation strategy.* Avoid bargaining over positions by separating the people from the problem, focusing on mutual interests, inventing options for mutual gain, and using objective criteria to evaluate the options.

● *International negotiation requires careful attention to cultural differences.* Whether you are negotiating with China, Japan, Mexico, or Germany, cultural differences will cause the negotiation process and tactics to change. Be aware of these possible differences before entering into a negotiation.

FOR DISCUSSION

1. How does conflict differ from disagreement? From competition?

2. Give an example of each of the five levels of conflict, starting with intrapersonal conflict.

3. Based on your experience, explain how a conflict episode might occur.

4. Explain the difference between substantive and emotional conflict.

5. The job of the first-level supervisor is described in Perspective 10.1. What are the sources of conflict for a person in this position?

6. When is conflict desirable and undesirable?

7. Discuss the pros and cons of each conflict resolution technique.

8. When should competition be encouraged or discouraged in organizations?

9. Why do win-lose situations often result in lose-lose outcomes?

10. Compare and contrast the methods for managing conflict with those for managing competition. How do they differ? How are they similar?

11. Based on your knowledge of Chinese negotiating strategies, how would you prepare to negotiate a contract to sell toilet tissue to the Chinese?

KEY CONCEPTS AND TERMS

conflict	substantive issues	accommodation
interpersonal conflict	compromising	role conflict
intrapersonal conflict	collaboration	avoidance
intergroup conflict	third parties	forcing
intragroup conflict	competition	win-lose model
interorganizational conflict	cooperation	superordinate goals
Deutsch's Theory of Cooperation	emotional issues	

Cases and Incidents

JAMES FARRIS

James Farris was a college student who, during the summer, worked in the Denver plant of Western Gypsum Company, a manufacturer of drywall material, various ready-mix patching compounds, and other assorted home-improvement products. The plant was a small one and employed only twenty-five people. Farris worked on the second floor and mixed raw materials (diatomaceous earth, dolomite, limestone, sand, etc.) together in specified proportions to make the ready-mix compounds. Consumers needed only to add water in the right amount to use the product. Because of this, quality control was a key function in the production process.

Farris hated his job but felt it was necessary to pay his way through college. On several occasions he had argued with his foreman about the level of work demanded, but to no avail. One hot afternoon the foreman approached Farris and the following discussion took place:

Foreman: Farris, you've got to be more careful when mixing the compound. Walters (the quality control inspector) tells me that six of the last eight batches you mixed were no good. All that stuff has to be remixed and that's going to cost the company a lot of money. We're paying you to mix those batches right! And another thing, you're not mixing the required seventeen batches a day. What's the problem?

Farris: I'm making mistakes because you're too demanding. I'm doing only fourteen batches a day instead of seventeen because I physically can't do seventeen. I'm not about to kill myself

running around up here in this heat just so I can mix seventeen batches a day. Look, I'm the fifth guy to have this job in the last seven months, right?

Foreman: Right.

Farris: Doesn't that tell you something?

Foreman: Yeah, it tells me that most people today don't want to do an honest day's work!

Farris: Don't give me that! To do this job right, I can only do eleven batches a day. Besides, I'm not so sure those batches were actually bad. I've heard that Walters is very picky when checking batches because it gives him a sense of power over the other workers. Besides, he's just trying to get me because he thinks I scraped his new car in the parking lot the other day.

Foreman: You college guys are all alike! I used to do this job and I never had any trouble. You're just too lazy. And stop blaming Walters; he's been here for twenty-three years and knows a lot more about ready-mix compounds than you'll ever know! Now get back to work and start pulling your weight around here.

One week later, the foreman was told by the personnel manager that Farris had quit.

DISCUSSION QUESTIONS

1. What are the sources of this conflict?

2. What strategies would you use to resolve it?

INFLATED PERFORMANCE APPRAISALS

The General in charge of Air Force Personnel was worried. Officer effectiveness report (an annual performance appraisal) ratings were getting so inflated that almost all officers were rated "outstand-

ing." He decided to cure the problem by implementing a forced-distribution performance appraisal system. From now on only 22 percent of the officers could be "1's" or outstanding, 28 percent could be "2's" or excellent, and the remaining half of the officers would be "3's" or typically effective. All the senior staff endorsed this new system as a solution to the inflated ratings problem.

The new system worked as planned. Tight controls insured that the distribution was maintained. However, some alarming side effects arose. It seems that many people who had considered themselves to be outstanding, were now getting "3's," which indicated that they were in the lower half of all officers rated; they felt like they had lost and would never be promoted with such ratings. As a result, many of these people were either leaving the service or losing their motivation.

Worse yet was the lack of cooperation and teamwork among the officers. If there were ten captains in an office, then only two could get 1's, three 2's, and the rest 3's. Teamwork began to disappear. Why should you help someone else look good; they might get the 1! Unit effectiveness suffered. Friendships dissolved. Backbiting and political tactics arose.

After several years of denying the problems, it became clear to the General that he had made a mistake. The forced distribution system was replaced with one much like the earlier one. Morale improved and turnover declined.

DISCUSSION QUESTIONS

1. Explain what happened using the win-lose model. Explain how win-win, win-lose, and lose-lose apply.
2. Was competition appropriate in this case? Why or why not?

REFERENCES

1. Thomas, K.W., & Schmidt, W.H. (1976). A survey of managerial interests with respect to conflict. *Academy of Management Journal, 19,* 315–318.

2. Luthans, F., Rosenkrantz, S.A., & Hennessey, H.W. (1985). What do successful managers really do? An observation study of managerial activities. *Journal of Applied Behavioral Science, 21,* 255–270.

3. Thomas, K. (1976). Conflict and conflict management. In M.D. Dunnette (Ed.). *Handbook of industrial and organizational psychology* (p. 891). Chicago: Rand-McNally. Also see Likert, J.G. (1976). *New ways of managing conflict.* New York: McGraw-Hill. And Blake, R.R., Shepard, H.A., & Mouton, J.S. (1964). *Managing intergroup conflict in industry.* Houston: Gulf.

4. DiStefano, T. (1984). Interorganizational conflict: A review of an emerging field. *Human Relations, 37,* 351–366.

5. Walton, R.E. (1987). *Managing Conflict* (2nd ed.). Reading, MA: Addison-Wesley.

6. See Filley, A.C. (1975). *Interpersonal conflict resolution* (pp. 9–12). Glenview, IL: Scott, Foresman. And Fraser, N.M., & Hipel, K.W. (1984). *Conflict analysis: Models and resolutions.* New York: North-Holland.

7. For an in-depth look at this issue see Pearce, J.L. (1981). Bringing some clarity to role ambiguity research. *Academy of Management Review, 6,* 665–674.

8. Greenhaus, J.H., & Beutell, N.J. (1985). Sources of conflict between work and family roles. *Academy of Management Review, 10,* 76–88. Also see Stead, B.A. (1985). *Women in management* (2nd ed.). Englewood Cliffs, NJ: Prentice-Hall.

9. Kahn, R.L., Wolfe, D.M., Quinn, R.P., & Snoek, J.D. (1964). *Organizational stress: Studies in role conflict and ambiguity.* New York: Wiley.

10. Nye, R.D. (1973). *Conflict among humans* (pp. 82–84). New York: Springer.

11. Robbins, S.P. (1974). *Managing organizational conflict: A nontraditional approach.* Englewood Cliffs, NJ: Prentice-Hall.

12. van de Vliert, E. (1985). Escalative intervention in small-group conflicts. *Journal of Applied Behavioral Science, 21,* 19–36.

13. Blake, R.R., & Mouton, J.S. (1984). *Solving costly organizational conflicts.* San Francisco: Josey-Bass. Fraser & Hipel (1984). Filley (1975).

14. Also see Thomas (1976).

15. Reprinted from Grove, A.S. *Fortune,* Copyright © 1984 Time Inc. All rights reserved.

16. For more thorough coverage of this topic see Lewicki, R.J., & Litterer, J.A. (1985). *Negotiation.* Homewood, IL: Richard D. Irwin.

17. For detailed presentations on problem solving as it applies to conflict resolution see Blake & Mouton (1984). Also Brown, D.L. (1983). *Managing conflict at organizational interfaces.* Reading, MA: Addison-Wesley.

18. See Walton (1987). Filley (1975). Fisher, R.J. (1983). Third party consultation as a method of intergroup conflict resolution. *Journal of Conflict Resolution, 27,* 301–334. And Sheppard, B.H. (1984). Third party conflict intervention: A procedural framework. In B.M. Staw & L.L. Cummings (Eds.). *Research in organizational behavior: Vol. 6,* Greenwich, CT: JAI Press. For I–messges and active lis-

tening see Gordon, T. (1977). *Leader effectiveness training L.E.T.,* New York: Wyden.

19. This discussion is based on Ruben, J.Z. (1980). Experimental research on third-party intervention in conflict: Toward some generalizations. *Psychological Bulletin, 87,* 379–391.

20. Deutsch, M. (1973). *The resolution of conflict,* New Haven CT: Yale University Press. Deutch, M. (1980). Over fifty years of conflict research. In L. Festinger (Ed.). *Four decades of social psychology* (pp. 46–77). New York: Oxford University Press.

21. For more information on win-lose dynamics see Schein, E.H. (1980). *Organizational psychology* (3rd ed.). Englewood Cliffs, NJ: Prentice-Hall. And Blake & Mouton (1984). For another view of how conflict relates to competition, see Cosier, R.A., & Ruble, T.L. (1981). Research on conflict-handling behavior: An experimental approach. *Academy of Management Journal, 24,* 816–831.

22. Adapted from Fisher, R., & Ury, W. (1983). *Getting to yes: Negotiating agreement without giving in.* New York: Penquin.

23. Based on Gray, J.L., & Starke, F.A. (1980). *Organizational behavior concepts and applications* (2nd ed.). Columbus, OH: Charles E. Merrill.

24. Schein (1980).

25. For an example of a win-win bonus plan, see Schuster, M. (1984). The scanlon plan: A longitudinal analysis. *Journal of Applied Behavioral Science, 20,* 23–38.

26. Tung, R.L. (1982). U.S.–China trade negotiations: Practices, procedures, and outcomes. *Journal of International Business Studies, 13* (Fall), 25–37. Pye, L.W. (1986, July-August). The China trade: Making the deal. *Harvard Business Review, 64,* 74 cf.

27. Based on Pye (1986). Also Kapp, R.A. (1983). *Communicating with China.* Chicago: Intercultural Press.

28. Reprinted from Grove, A.S., *Fortune,* Copyright © 1984 Time Inc. All rights reserved.

29. For a comparison of American, Mexican, French, and Japanese negotiation styles, see Fisher, G. (1980). *International negotiation: A cross-cultural perspective.* Chicago: Intercultural Press.

30. For more information see Pye, L.W. (1986). *Chinese commercial negotiating styles.* Boston, MA: Oelgeschlager, Gunn, & Hain.

Chapter Eleven

MANAGEMENT OF STRESS

PREVIEW

- What are the impacts of stress on physical and mental health?
- How does the fight-or-flight response work?
- What is job burnout and how do you prevent it?
- How much stress is enough? Too much? Too little?
- Are you an aggressive, hard-charging achiever? Then you may be a Type A person. What does this mean to you?
- Does stress affect women differently than men?
- What are the major causes of stress, and what can you do about them?
- How is shift work like jet lag? What causes the reaction?
- Is the United States a high-stress culture?

MAJOR TOPICS

Preview Case: People Uptight!

The Nature of Stress

Burnout: A Special Form of Stress

Sources of Stress

Managing Stress

Cross-Cultural OB: Executive Stress Goes Global

Managerial Applications of Stress Management

Preview Case

PEOPLE UPTIGHT!

Liz Rosenberg: Liz thought to herself, "My job here at Advanced Products hasn't worked out as well as I planned and it's all Herb Thorpe's fault. If it wasn't for him, I could get my job done easily. But every direction I turn Herb seems to be butting heads with me.

"In fact, I've been really uptight for about a month. I can't sleep at night; I'm not interested in food; I feel my neck muscles tense up, and then I have a whale of a headache. I'm jittery and anxious and it seems that I am constantly annoyed. I won-

der if I need to see a psychologist. Am I having a nervous breakdown?"

Herb Thorpe: Herb's feelings were not unlike those of Liz: "I'm fed up with that woman! Ever since she arrived I've felt there's a big heavy chain around my neck. It seems she does everything she can to screw me up.

"But I need to forget Liz for the moment and make an appointment with the doctor because something's wrong with me. My heart beats rapidly, I have constant indigestion, and my hands aren't steady anymore. Maybe I have heart disease or something? I feel so bad it's hard to get up the motivation to come to work, much less put in the kind of effort this job takes. Maybe I should be thinking of an early retirement."

Liz and Herb are experiencing a number of symptoms of stress that may have resulted from their long-standing conflict (*see* the Preview Case for Chapter 10). While some stress may be beneficial for energizing the organization, too much stress can have a powerful, negative impact on people and on organizational effectiveness. Thus, stress management is becoming a major managerial task.

An additional reason for being concerned about stress is the potential legal liabilities, as courts find organizations responsible for job-related stress problems. Take the following examples: [1]

* Helen J. Kelly, a Raytheon Co. employee with 22 years seniority, suffered a nervous breakdown when told she would be transferred to another department. The Massachusetts Supreme Judicial Court ruled 4 to 3 that she was entitled to workers' comp benefits [amounting to $40,000]. Her breakdown was a "personal injury arising out of and in the course of . . . employment," the court explained.

* Gary Pearl, a white sanitation supervisor in Louisville, blamed his depression on the stress of being forced to work with blacks. The Kentucky Workers' Compensation Board awarded him the maximum benefits [of $241 per week] and ordered the city to return him to an all-white setting. The ruling is under appeal.

* Harry A. McGarrah, an Oregon deputy sheriff, blamed his depression on the belief that his supervisor was persecuting him. The Oregon Supreme Court upheld his claim for [$20,000 in] workers' comp benefits.

Thus everyday personnel actions that result in stress can wind up costing the organization plenty. Managers need to be aware of causes of stress in the work environment and take actions to do something to reduce the effects of stress.

In this chapter, we will discuss the nature of stress, its sources, and how to manage it.

THE NATURE OF STRESS

Stress is a natural way of coping with changes in our environment. In this section, we will examine the nature of the stress process, the impact of stress on health and organizational performance, and the individual differences that people experience in their response to stress.

How Does Stress Develop?

Stress is some type of response, physical or psychological, to an external event or situation that places special physical or psychological demands on a person and causes a deviation from his or her normal functioning.[2] A **stressor** is a stimulus condition that results in the response of stress. For example, a stressor (stimulus) in the environment, such as Herb's hostility, results in stress (a response) within Liz, such as increased heart rate with a jolt of adrenalin, that prepares her to cope with the threat.[3] Figure 11.1 presents a simplified model of the stress process. Notice that people react to stress differently depending on individual characteristics. In Liz's case, the problem with Herb (stressor) coupled with her high need for achievement, resulted in a loss of appetite and irritability.

Fight-or-Flight Response.   Our reactions to stress are a product of evolution. Our cave-dwelling ancestors needed to react to threats in the environment, such as an attacking hairy mammoth, by either fighting or fleeing. When such an attack occurred, the body prepared itself by pumping adrenalin, increasing heart and respiration rates, higher blood pressure, and sharpened senses. These physiological reactions, called the **fight-or-flight** response, helped primitive people to cope with the emergency.

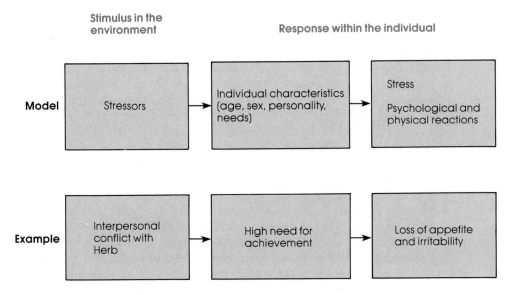

Figure 11.1
THE STRESS PROCESS

Table 11.1
_____
SOME SYMPTOMS OF JOB STRESS
_____
1. Rapid pulse or pounding heart.
2. Increased perspiration from hands, underarms, and forehead.
3. Tightening of the forehead and jaw.
4. Inability to sit still or keep your feet still while you are sitting.
5. Tensing of shoulder and neck muscles.
_____
SOURCE: Collected from Ivancevich, J.M., & Matteson, M.T. (1980). *Stress and work: A managerial perspective.* Glenview, IL: Scott, Foresman. And Manuso, J. (1980). Manage your stress. *CRM Multimedia Module,* New York: McGraw-Hill.

Although mammoths are gone, we still react as if they were here. When Liz told Herb of her deal with Allied Insurance for early delivery of machines, Herb felt under attack, and his body reacted as if Liz were a modern-day mammoth. But Herb cannot fight Liz, at least not physically; and he cannot flee from the situation. The problem is that the physiological response to a threat is not as appropriate in work situations in the 1980s as it was in prehistoric times, and stress results.[4] Some of the common symptoms of stress can be seen in Table 11.1.

Types of Stress and the Impact on Health

Some amount of stress is useful for coping with emergencies and everyday management problems, but stress effects seem to build upon one another in a cumulative fashion.[5] The duration and number of stress experiences is important for determining the long-term effects of stress.[6] Single or isolated stress situations probably have little effect on health. However, when a stress situation results in a relatively constant state of agitation, such as the conflict between Liz and Herb, there may be a negative impact on health.

Stress situations can be divided into short-term or low-level, moderate, and severe categories.[7] Short-term situations involve a brief event, such as being caught in traffic or being bawled out by your boss. As long as these situations do not become too frequent, they usually pose no threat to your health.

Moderate stress situations may last a few hours or several days. Examples might be an unresolved disagreement with the boss, new job responsibilities, or making a presentation to a large group. The disagreement between Liz and Herb probably falls in the upper range of this category. Individuals who have predispositions to certain diseases, such as heart problems, may experience health difficulties at this stage.

Severe stress involves chronic situations that may last weeks, months, or years. Prolonged financial difficulties, extremely heavy job demands, or the death of a loved one are examples of such stress. Table 11.2 shows the relative importance of selected stressful events. The death of a spouse with a score of 100 represents twice as much stress as marriage with a score of 50. Even pleasant events such as vacations or graduation from college cause stress.

There seems to be a relationship between stress and many physical illnesses, such as hypertension, ulcers, diabetes, headaches, coronary heart disease, cancer, and a number of other diseases.[8]

Table 11.2

RELATIVE IMPACT OF STRESSFUL EVENTS

Life event	Scale value
1. Death of spouse	100
2. Divorce	73
3. Marital separation	65
4. Jail term	63
5. Death of close family member	63
6. Personal injury or illness	53
7. Marriage	50
8. Fired at work	47
9. Marital reconciliation	45
10. Retirement	45
11. Change in health of family member	44
12. Pregnancy	40
13. Sex difficulties	39
14. Gain of new family member	39
15. Business readjustment	39
16. Change in financial state	38
17. Death of close friend	37
18. Change to different line of work	36
19. Change in number of arguments with spouse	35
20. Mortgage or loan for major purchase (home, etc.)	31
21. Foreclosure of mortgage or loan	30
22. Change in responsibilities at work	29
23. Son or daughter leaving home	29
24. Trouble with in-laws	29
25. Outstanding personal achievement	28
26. Wife begin or stop work	26
27. Begin or end school	26
28. Change in living conditions	25
29. Revision of personal habits	24
30. Trouble with boss	23
31. Change in work hours or conditions	20
32. Change in residence	20
33. Change in schools	20
34. Change in recreation	19
35. Change in church activities	19
36. Change in social activities	18
37. Mortgage or loan for lesser purchase (car, TV, etc.)	17
38. Change in sleeping habits	16
39. Change in number of family get-togethers	15
40. Change in eating habits	15
41. Vacation	13
42. Christmas	12
43. Minor violations of the law	11

SOURCE: Reprinted with permission from *Journal of Psychosomatic Research 11*, 213–18, T.H. Holmes and R.H. Rahe, The social readjustment rating scale. Copyright © 1967, Pergamon Press, Ltd.

Stress and Organizational Performance

Excessive levels of stress can cause a number of problems for organizations.[9] If employees become physically ill, their attendance and performance will suffer. People under severe stress often seem to care less about their jobs and their organization. Their commitment is low and the possibility of quitting is quite high. If the conflict between Liz and Herb continues, we may predict that the stress will become severe and will affect organizational performance. See Figure 11.2 for a summary of the impacts of stress.

A study of the relationship between stress and performance among nurses found that high levels of stress resulted in anxiety, hostility, and depression.[10] These states then led to declines in tolerance for frustration, clerical accuracy, and interpersonal sensitivity. Highly stressed nurses were less able to cope with uncooperative patients, difficulties with physicians, or lack of support from supervisors. They were less sensitive to others and had less warmth and consideration. Stress also seemed to affect ability to concentrate, composure, perseverance, and adaptability. In other words nurses who experienced high levels of stress performed at lower levels.

While there are many undesirable side effects from severe stress, some stress can be quite beneficial for energizing behavior. While there are a number of examples we might use, two strategies for raising stress are goal setting and job

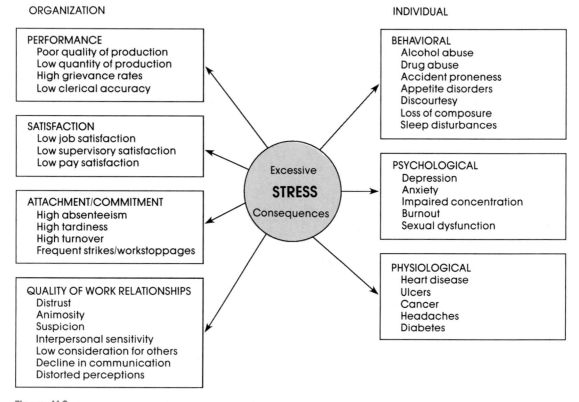

Figure 11.2

CONSEQUENCES OF EXCESSIVE STRESS

SOURCE: Based in part on Quick, J.C., & Quick, J.D. (1984). *Organizational stress and preventive management* (pp. 44, 76). New York: McGraw-Hill.

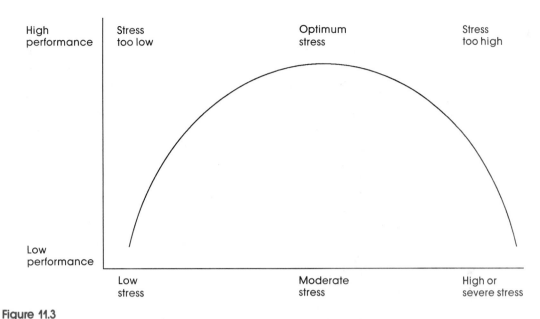

Figure 11.3

THE RELATIONSHIP BETWEEN PERFORMANCE AND STRESS

processes. If goals and performance standards are set too high, people may become overstressed and performance may suffer. Another way to increase stress is through job design. When a job is enriched, there is an attempt to instill more responsibility in the job and responsibility becomes quite stressful. If we increase it too much, we may exceed the optimum level of stress and performance may decline. The key is to balance stress so that an optimum level is reached. Figure 11.3 illustrates the relationship between stress and performance.[11]

Individual Differences and Stress

Reactions to stress are also a function of the individual. There are numerous individual differences that may help explain why people react differently to similar levels of stress. These include age, education, occupation, needs, values, abilities, sex, and personality.[12] While space limits our coverage of these differences, one aspect of personality that is often researched is the relationship between Type A behavior, stress, and health. Before we discuss Type A and Type B behavior, you can gain insight into your own behavior pattern by completing the quiz in Table 11.3.

As you may guess from the quiz, the **Type A** pattern applies to people who are involved in a chronic, incessant struggle to achieve more and more in less and less time. In addition, Type A people exhibit patterns of aggressiveness, easily aroused hostility and anger, a sense of time urgency, a high need for power, an achievement orientation, and high levels of organizational commitment.[13] A **Type B** behavior pattern applies when none of the Type A behaviors are present. People who exhibit a Type A behavior pattern are more susceptible to coronary heart disease.[14] The exact relationship between Type A behavior and stress is unclear, although it seems that Type A behaviors may, in the long-

Perspective 11.1

HELP! MY COMPANY HAS JUST BEEN TAKEN OVER

Corporate mergers are creating a new source of stress. Staff consolidations result in loss of jobs.[15] People have to start all over again. Even if they keep their jobs, demotion is possible or promotions may evaporate. At a very minimum bosses will change, and the corporate culture will be jolted into a different form. These outcomes can be very threatening. For example:

"Don't go down to the cellar," Chris Donahue's suicide note warned his family. That's where the 38-year-old economist hanged himself recently, four days after he lost his $63,000-a-year job at Heublein Inc. following a takeover by R.J. Reynolds Industries. A

week earlier he thought he'd been promised an auspicious Reynolds headquarters job. Instead he got 11 weeks severance pay. "Tell someone at RJR that I loved their generosity and compassion," his note continued. "They owed me more—the first-class f——ers. I know you will think I failed, and maybe I did . . . I didn't have the strength to endure the pain that was coming." [16]

Organizations need to attend to the human problems associated with mergers. Certainly the people who lose their jobs are the most seriously affected, but even people who are retained will experience considerable stress. Clear communication is imperative—tell people as soon as possible what their fate is to be. In addition, counseling and outplacement services should be established to ease the transition. Careful planning and handling of the human side of the merger may have much to do with its eventual success.

Table 11.3

TYPE A BEHAVIOR QUIZ

To find out which type you are, circle the number on the scale below that best characterizes your behavior for each trait.

1. Casual about appointments	1---2---3---4---5	Never late, sense of time urgency
2. Not competitive	1---2---3---4---5	Very competitive
3. Never feel rushed even under pressure	1---2---3---4---5	Always pressured for time
4. Take things one at a time	1---2---3---4---5	Try to do many things at once, think about what I am going to do next.
5. Slow doing things	1---2---3---4---5	Fast (eating, walking, etc.)
6. Easy-going reaction to frustrations	1---2---3---4---5	React to frustration with hostility
7. Do not perform at full capacity	1---2---3---4---5	Push myself to capacity

Scoring: Add your score for each question; then convert it to Type A or Type B behavior using the table below:

Number of Points	Type of Behavior
20 or Less	B
21–24	A
25 or More	A+

SOURCE: Adapted from Bortner, R.W. (1966). A short rating scale as a potential measure of Type A behavior. *Journal of Chronic Diseases, 22*, 87–91; and Friedman, M., & Rosenman, R.H. (1974). *Type A behavior and your heart.* New York: Knopf.

run, create stress.[17] In any event, it is probably desirable for people who are high on the Type A scale to move more down the continuum toward Type B. This may be done by reestablishing priorities, by allowing more time for activities, and by reducing the total number of activities.[18]

BURNOUT: A SPECIAL FORM OF STRESS

There are a number of factors that result in **burnout,** a state of mental, emotional, and physical exhaustion that results from working with people and complex organizations over an extended period of time in emotionally draining situations.[19] Burnout seems to take place when people become exhausted due to the existence of unavoidable pressures with little or no corresponding sources of satisfaction for coping with these pressures. Burnout results from chronic daily stresses rather than some unique, critical life event.[20]

For example, a high-performing vice-president was transferred from a subsidiary to corporate headquarters. While he had been recruited to revamp the control system, he was immediately sucked into a major corporate reorganization because he was a newcomer who could be trusted. Here is what happened:

> . . . His task was arduous. Not only did the long hours and unremitting pressure of walking a tightrope among conflicting interests exhaust him, but also they made it impossible for him to get control of problems that needed attention. Furthermore, because his family could not move for six months until the school year was over, he commuted on weekends to his previous home 800 miles away. As he tried to perform the unwanted job that had been thrust on him and support the CEO who was counting heavily on his competence, he felt lonely, harassed, and burdened. Now that his task was coming to an end, he was in no psychological shape to take on his formal duties. In short, he had "burned out." [21]

While burnout can happen in any type of job, it is most common in professions where dealing with people is the central task. This includes such jobs as manager, social worker, teacher, and police officer. Causes of burnout are associated with the person, the nature of organizational interactions, and the nature of the work itself. Research shows that women and single persons of either sex experience a higher incidence of burnout. New employees also seem to be particularly vulnerable during their first year or two. In addition, the degree of supervisory support and group cohesion seems to be related to this form of exhaustion. Finally, the task itself is a key factor. Enriched tasks (high on the core job dimensions described in Chapter 7) are less likely to lead to burnout.[22]

Burnout often results in withdrawal, low performance, or psychological disorders. Prevention is the best cure for burnout. Here are some steps that may be used to prevent burnout.[23]

1. Recognize burnout situations and rotate people out of potentially exhausting positions.

2. Put time constraints on the job. Do not allow people to work twelve to sixteen hours a day over an extended period.

3. Avoid using the same people as "rescuers" or "trouble-shooters" in problem situations time after time.

4. Take an entire work group on nominal business trips to a recreational site.

5. Make sure the organization has a systematic way to recognize people, to provide feedback, to show them how important they are.

SOURCES OF STRESS

Practically any event or situation in an organization that puts abnormal physical or psychological demands on people is a potential source of stress. We will cover four major sources of stress: Personal interfaces with the organization, job characteristics, role characteristics, and organizational characteristics and processes.[24] Figure 11.4 provides a summary of the major sources of job stress.

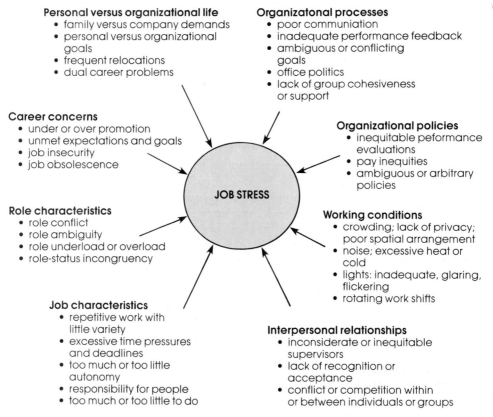

Figure 11.4

MAJOR SOURCES OF JOB STRESS

SOURCE: Developed in part from the categories proposed by Brief, A.P., Schuler, R.S., & Van Sell, M. (1981). *Managing Job Stress.* Boston: Little Brown and Cooper, C.L., & Marshall, J. (1975). The management of stress. *Personnel Review, 4* (4).

Perspective 11.2

STRESS AND
WOMEN MANAGERS

A study of 135 top female executives in the United Kingdom found that managerial women face the same stressors as men plus some additional ones that make their overall stress level even higher than that of men.[25] The strongest reason for stress seemed to be lack of control over the work environment and extreme pressure in the work environment. Women experienced migraine headaches, high blood pressure, tiredness, irritation, anxiety, and other symptoms of stress. The authors of the study conclude that higher stress levels may deter women from seeking advancement, enhance Type A behavior patterns in women, and have adverse effects on the physical and mental health of women.

Other studies of stress among women managers has found that they experience a unique set of added stressors not faced by men.[26] These stressors include discrimination, stereotyping, marriage/work interfaces, and social isolation. Discrimination takes many forms, including opportunities for promotion (less than 2 percent of higher level managers are women[27], inequities in pay (women earn 57 to 86 percent of a comparable male's salary)[28], and exclusion from male-dominated informal organization.

Women must also overcome negative sex-role stereotypes such as: women are too emotional, women are terrible bosses, women managers lose their femininity, or women's place is in the home. The marriage-work interface is a formidable problem for dual-career families. There are problems concerning whose career takes priority and child-care responsibilities. In addition, there may be unusually high stresses placed on the husband of a successful managerial woman, resulting in mental health problems.[29] Social isolation can result from withdrawal due to fear of sexual involvement,[30] or because leadership roles are perceived to isolate the managerial woman.[31] Thus there are formidable added stressors for women managers.

Are these stress-related problems an inevitable result for professional women? An analysis of the research on stress found that while women do face additional sources of stress in the managerial world, they can do something about it by developing strong mentor relationships and working to increase self-confidence and self-awareness.[32]

Interfaces of the Individual With the Organization

Personal Versus Organizational Life.   There are numerous opportunities for conflict between family and personal desires and organizational demands. An example is Brian, a college professor, who is married to a middle manager in a large corporation. His wife, Ellen, has been offered a promotion to vice-president if she will agree to move to corporate headquarters in San Francisco. Her boss implies that if she does not move, she should not expect another chance at a major promotion. Brian is a full professor with tenure and perceives that it will be difficult, if not impossible, to find a faculty position in San Francisco. This decision is causing a great deal of stress in their relationship.

Career Concerns.   Unfulfilled career expectations are a major source of stress. If peoples' advancement in the organization keeps up with their expectations, then they are likely to be more satisfied and stress free. On the other hand, a person who feels prematurely plateaued or "topped out" on the advancement ladder may encounter severe stress.

A good illustration is Bob Lyons, the highly successful executive described in the case at the end of Chapter 2.[33] Bob appeared to be a Type A person; he worked hard and drove himself relentlessly. After about ten years with the company, he perceived that his career was plateauing. He was being assigned to jobs where little action was required. Bob began to lose his motivation and became embroiled in conflicts with other executives. Bob's bosses were afraid he was having some type of mental breakdown, so they agreed when the doctor said all Bob needed was some time off. When Bob decided he was ready to come back to work, the president again suggested that he take another week of vacation. A few days later, Bob Lyons committed suicide. While there were a number of complex factors at work here, one important one—Bob's perceived lack of further career opportunities—resulted in severe stress. Bob was not ready to sit back and be a dreamer; he was a doer.

Job Characteristics

The Demands of the Job Itself.   There are a variety of stressors that fall in this category. Job design, discussed in Chapter 7, can foster or inhibit stress in several ways. If the work is repetitive with little variety, it may be too boring and stressful for some people. If the job contains too little or too much autonomy, it may also be stressful. Certainly too many tight deadlines and high standards can cause job stress (*see* Perspective 11.3). In addition to the structural aspects of the job, another important issue is the degree to which the job entails responsibility for people. For example, managers must balance conflict and hostility between subordinates, such as the situation of Liz and Herb. They must make hard, disagreeable decisions about their subordinates and appraise their performance. Many of these tasks can be emotionally draining. In addition, managers often find that the demands of the job in terms of heavy workloads and extremely difficult tasks take a heavy toll. Over long periods of time these stressors may cause burnout or other stress-related outcomes.

Role Characteristics

Role conflicts, ambiguity, and overload can be stressors.[34] In the last chapter, we saw that **role conflicts** occur when people disagree about how a role should be performed. The first-line supervisor was singled out as someone who experiences a great deal of role conflict that results in stress. Another example might be a salesperson who is directed to sell something that the customer does not want or need just to meet the company's quota. Table 11.4 shows examples of this concept.

   Role ambiguity occurs when job responsibilities and duties are ambiguous and unclear.[35] A therapist in a hospital may be unclear about the role to be played. What is expected? To treat and cure patients? To keep accurate records? To supervise other newer therapists? In short, the therapist does not know what is expected and thus experiences frustration and stress. Table 11.4 illustrates several dimensions of role ambiguity.[36]

   Role overload is expecting someone to perform too many jobs or roles at one time. Even though the roles may be compatible, there is just too much to do. **Role and status incongruence,** described in Chapter 9, results when someone is performing a role that is at a lower or higher status level than they are comfortable with. An example might be a new assistant professor who is asked to chair the university's curriculum committee.

Perspective 11.3

STRESS AND THE
AIR TRAFFIC CONTROLLER

The following is an excerpt from an article describing air traffic controllers at Chicago's O'Hare Airport.[37]

"HELP WANTED: World's busiest airport seeks jockies for unusually stimulating, high intensity environment. Must be able to direct at least twelve aircraft at one time and make instant decisions affecting the safety of thousands. No degree required, but prior experience as traffic cop, seeing eye dog, or God helpful. Severe stress will jeopardize sanity and result in early termination from job, but employer will absorb cost of medical and psychiatric care."

The ad above never appeared, but it could have. The pressures air traffic controllers feel in the control tower have been likened to what pilots experience in combat. Nowhere is that stress more acute than at Chicago's O'Hare Airport, better known to controllers as the ulcer factory.

The herculean task of coping with 1,900 flights a day rests squarely on the O'Hare controllers' shoulders. For some, it is a burden they can't endure. In the last year, at least seven men have been carried out of the O'Hare control tower on stretchers, victims of acute hypertension. Most controllers have already succumbed to one or more by-products of prolonged stress: ulcers, high blood pressure, arthritis, colitis, skin disorders, headaches, allergies, and upset stomachs. Other controllers struggle with more severe

problems, such as alcoholism, depression, horrifying nightmares, and acute anxiety.

This journalistic introduction gives a little feel for the type of stress experienced by air traffic controllers. Studies of stress among controllers have reached conflicting conclusions. One review of the literature, conducted by the FAA, found that the demands of the controller's job do not appear to place unusual stress on the controllers.[38] Another more recent study found that the job involved what is termed **acute episodic stress,** or stress caused by intense, relatively infrequent events with relatively brief physiological effects, but long-lasting psychological effects.[39] The differences in findings may be due to the two types of stress being measured. The controller's job may indeed be of rather moderate stress in terms of the day-to-day task. Their **chronic stress** (stress associated with a normal workload and pressure) level is moderate. But, over a period of years the acute stress episodes may accumulate and cause burnout.

Part of the analysis of the newer study was to find out which controllers were high in a burnout scale and then try to determine what factors seem to account for the burnout. They found that the burnout sample averaged 41.3 years of age with 19.1 years of service, whereas the sample as a whole averaged 34.4 years of age and had 13.6 years of service. In addition, burnouts accounted for only 21 percent of those who were 41.0 or older, but 69 percent of those with 19.0 or more years of service. They conclude that burnout seems to be more a function of length of service than any other factor. They also speculate that the acute episodic stress events accumulate to cause the eventual burnout.

Organizational Characteristics and Processes

Interpersonal Relations.   As our opening case involving Liz and Herb illustrates, conflicts over interpersonal relationships can cause severe stress. This type of stress often takes the form of problems between supervisor and subordinate. A supervisor who does not listen or seem to care, or who treats subordinates inequitably, can cause a great deal of stress in the subordinate. An example of this stressor happened in a large hospital. The chief of nursing was professionally competent, but did not know how to manage people. Whenever a subordinate did anything that offended her (and one never quite knew what the offense was), she would completely cut off communication with that

Table 11.4

ROLE CONFLICT AND ROLE AMBIGUITY ITEMS

Role Conflict Items	I receive incompatible requests from two or more people. I work on unnecessary things. I work with two or more groups who operate quite differently. I have to buck a rule or policy in order to carry out an assignment.
Role Ambiguity Items	I know that I have divided my time properly. I know exactly what is expected of me. I feel certain about how much authority I have on this job. I have clear, planned goals and objectives for my job.

SOURCE: Adapted from J.R. Rizzo, R.J. House, and S.I. Lirtzman, 1970, Role conflict and role ambiguity measures. *Administrative Science Quarterly, 15,* 150–63. Copyright © 1970 by *Administrative Science Quarterly,* Ithaca, New York. Used with permission.

subordinate for days or even weeks. This behavior resulted in a great deal of stress, low job satisfaction, and a high turnover rate for nurses under her supervision.

Organizational Processes. Almost all organizational processes—motivation, communication, goal setting, group dynamics, conflict or competition, politics, performance appraisal, controlling—can cause stress. Throughout the book, we discuss problems and issues surrounding various processes. An important point to remember is that most problems cause stress as well as other outcomes.

Organizational Policies. Perhaps the central stressor that results from organizational policies is when rules or systems are perceived to be inequitable or unfair. A policy that the best performance ratings will go only to the production division populated solely by men will cause considerable stress among those who are not assigned to production or who are women. Another example is when two managers do exactly the same job but one is paid more than the other because of being hired more recently at a higher starting salary level.

Working Conditions. While most stressors seem to occur in the psychological environment,[40] there are a number of stressors in the physical environment, particularly for blue-collar jobs.[41] Loud and distracting noise, poor or flickering lighting, crowded conditions, and temperatures that are too hot or too cold, have been experienced by most of us. Another important aspect of working conditions is shift work. Perspective 11.4 shows how shift work can affect people and cause stress.

MANAGING STRESS

The goal of stress management is not to eliminate stress but to keep it at optimum levels so that performance is high and the dysfunctional symptoms of stress are minimized. In practice, the most common problem is that stress levels are too high rather than too low. Therefore, the thrust of this section is on reducing stress. We will highlight several individual and organizational strategies for dealing with stress.

Perspective 11.4

SHIFT WORK

AND STRESS[42]

Anyone who has ever crossed a number of time zones has experienced "jet lag" because of the interruption of the body's cyclical rhythm. Shift work can also cause the same type of physiological reaction. In either case, it takes several days for the body to adjust. These adjustments are necessary because of the twenty-four hour rhythm of the body called **circadian rhythm.** Body temperatures, urine flow, heart-rate, metabolism, sleep cycles, and other changes keep pace with this regular schedule. Shift work, like jet lag, interrupts this rhythm. In addition, those people who work the night shift (11 P.M.–7 A.M.) are cut off from the activities of our daytime-oriented society. The impact of shift work on the family and other social relationships may be so strong that severe stress results.

Individual Methods for Coping With Stress

Start with an example of how stress affects a young attorney:[43]

Jim Gardner, an aggressive and successful attorney, was feeling frightened and angry as he drove home through the heavy rush hour traffic. The doctor's report that afternoon had scared Jim: either he slowed down, stopped smoking, lost weight, drank less, got more exercise, and—above all—stopped driving himself so hard, or the chest pain would turn into a heart attack before he was forty.

The traffic light turned green, and Jim's car charged into the intersection, narrowly missing a blue sedan. "Idiot!" Jim exploded at the driver. "How can I slow down? I've got four new cases coming to trial next month. Relax! How can I relax when I'm responsible for those briefs? What am I suppose to do, retire at age thirty-six?"

Soberly, Jim recalled the doctor's final words: "Jim, right now you have a choice. But if you keep pushing yourself and neglecting your health, you won't live to see your kids grow up."

"Damn it all!" The light changed. "Hey you!" Jim yelled at the driver of the car ahead. "Get moving! I don't have time to waste!"

Jim, who appears to be a Type A individual, needs help to cope with a severe stress problem. He might turn first to one of the most effective individual approaches to stress reduction: meditation or the **relaxation response.**[44] The relaxation response is the opposite of the fight-or-flight response discussed earlier. The body's metabolism and heartrate slow down, and the rate of breathing declines. The relaxation response has four elements: a quiet environment, a mental device, (a single-syllable sound or word), a passive attitude, and a comfortable position.

How might Jim use relaxation to reduce his stress? He should set aside about twenty minutes once or twice a day to meditate. He should find a quiet environment, sit in a comfortable position (shoes off, clothing loosened), close his eyes, breathe deeply, and relax all muscles. Each time he breathes out through the nose, he should use his mental device (repeat his word, such as "one"). He should maintain a passive attitude and push distracting thoughts from his mind. For the next twenty minutes he repeats: breathe in . . . breathe out . . . "one" . . . breathe in . . . breathe out . . . "one".[45]

There are two other alternatives Jim might consider: exercise and biofeedback.[46] Exercise seems to reduce tension and stress and to strengthen the cardiovascular system.[47] Jim might gradually begin a jogging or other exercise program after checking with his doctor for advice on the best way to proceed. A second strategy is to use **biofeedback** to monitor bodily processes like pulse, breathing rate, and blood pressure. Various relaxation techniques are then tried with accurate feedback about their effectiveness. Biofeedback is not as commonly used in organizations because complex and expensive equipment is often necessary.

Organizational Methods of Coping With Stress

There are a host of organizational methods for dealing with stress, including those we studied in earlier chapters: job enrichment, goal setting, and positive reinforcement. Another strategy, changing the organizational climate or culture, will be discussed in a later chapter. In this section, we will discuss reducing job stress by using stress recognition techniques, management training, and role clarification techniques.[48]

Recognizing Stress. It is not always easy to recognize someone who is experiencing excessive stress. Careful observation of behavior may reveal a number of behavior patterns that indicate stress overload.[49]

- Working late more than usual or the opposite; increased tardiness or absenteeism.

- Difficulty in making decisions.

- Increase in the number of careless mistakes.

- Missing deadlines or forgetting appointments.

- Problems interacting and getting along with others.

- Focusing on mistakes and personal failures.

Management Training.   Teaching people to recognize stressful situations and then use coping strategies is an effective and widespread method for reducing stress.[50] In addition, management skills training—focusing on instruction in goal setting, time management, conflict resolution, and dealing with people—can also reduce stress.[51] Apparently, people who understand how to manage and deal with people are better able to cope with stress.

Role Clarification.   Many organizational stressors relate to how an employee perceives the job. The role an employee plays provides the focus of the job and a potential source of stress if that focus is unclear or if two or more roles conflict. Roles get mixed up with expectations, responsibilities, and reporting relationships. In our opening case regarding Liz and Herb, there was a role conflict brought about when each had differing expectations about what role behaviors would foster organizational effectiveness.

The most common strategy for clarifying roles is **role analysis technique.** This method involves open discussion of role expectations by addressing such questions as: [53]

1. What do you think is expected of you?

2. What do you expect of me (your boss)?

3. What information do you need to do your job well?

4. What areas, if any, trouble you about the nature and scope of your job?

In addition, it may be useful to ask a question such as, "If (*name of focal person*) were operating in an optimally effective way, what would he or she be doing?" The answer to this question can be recorded on a blackboard or on newsprint. Then the person who answered the question discusses the response with the focal person. This process helps clarify roles and reduce role-related stress.

CROSS–CULTURAL OB: EXECUTIVE STRESS GOES GLOBAL

A research study, sponsored by *International Management,* measured a number of aspects of stress in ten countries: Britain, Sweden, Germany, Japan, Singapore, the United States, Nigeria, South Africa, Brazil, and Egypt.[54] A questionnaire was sent to 2,800 executives who subscribe to the journal and 1,065 responded for a 38 percent return rate. They measured various symptoms of stress, including depression, anxiety, and psychosomatic tendencies. In addition, they measured a number of sources of stress to see how causes of stress vary across cultures.

Stress Levels across Cultures

Figure 11.5 shows the relative overall stress levels based on reported levels of depression, anxiety, and psychosomatic tendencies. Germany, Sweden, and the United States are considerably lower than average while Brazil and Egypt are substantially above average. Britain, Japan, Singapore, Nigeria, and South Africa all hover around the mean. Why are stress levels so high in Brazil and Egypt? Both are developing countries where management skills and experience are at relatively low levels. In Egypt the government rules, regulations, and bureaucracy make the manager's day-to-day job more difficult. Both countries have experienced a number of major financial crises that may have "echo effects" on the business community. The high rates of inflation experienced in

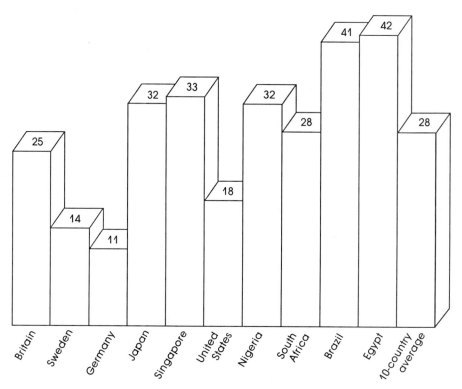

Percentage of respondents who expressed high stress levels.

Figure 11.5

STRESS LEVELS ACROSS CULTURES

SOURCE: Adapted from Cooper & Arbose (1984, May). Executive stress goes global. *International Management,* p. 46.

Brazil make the manager's job more difficult and stressful. Figure 11.5 indicates that other sources of high stress levels may include incompetent or poorly trained subordinates.

Another interesting result is the relatively high levels of stress in Japan. Of the industrialized countries, Japanese executives experienced the highest levels of stress. Those who are familiar with Japan will not be surprised at this result. There are strong pressures exerted by the company, the workgroup, and even society to work hard and achieve perfection. Figure 11.6 shows that Japan, along with Brazil, are the only counties where interpersonal relations are a substantial contributor to stress. The Japanese value harmony and thus put great pressure on maintaining harmonious interpersonal relationships even in the face of interpersonal conflict.

Sources of Stress in Different Cultures

Figure 11.6 also shows that the major stress creators for managers everywhere are time pressures, deadlines, work overload, and long working hours. However, there are also a number of major sources of stress that vary across cultures. For example, inadequately trained subordinates is a major source of stress in

Over 45%

36-45%

25-35%

Blank cells show less than 25%.

Which of the following are a source of pressure for you at work?

	Britain	Sweden	Germany	Japan	Singapore	United States	Nigeria	South Africa	Brazil	Egypt
Time pressures & deadlines	62	54	65	42	55	46	54	59	62	45
Work overload	57	56	59	42	45	54	50	48	38	77
Inadequately trained subordinates			36		47	26	57	36	41	65
Long working hours	26	34	27	26		30	40	34		
Attending meetings					26		25	28	28	
Demands of work on my private and social life		32					31			
Demands of work on my relationship with my family		27	25				30	29		25
Keeping up with new technology	26			33						
My beliefs conflicting with those of the organization						30	26			
Taking my work home		30				28				30
Lack of power & influence						46				
Interpersonal relations				30			30		26	
The amount of travel required by my work										
Incompetent boss						30				
Number of respondents	143	145	110	134	85	43	111	137	97	60

Figure 11.6

SOURCES OF STRESS IN VARIOUS CULTURES

SOURCE: Adapted from Cooper, C. & Arbose, J. (1984, May). Executive stress goes global. *International Management*, p. 48.

seven of the ten countries. Only in Great Britain, Sweden, and Japan was this source relatively minor. In developing countries, such as Nigeria and Singapore, where there are major shortages in skilled professional people and workers, this is a crucial source of stress. However, even in the United States one quarter of the executives indicated problems with their subordinates.

One of the more surprising results was that lack of power and influence caused stress for over 46 percent of the U.S. managers, while it was relatively unimportant for managers in other countries. Perhaps American managers want more say in major decisions and actions. Or, it could be the need for power is higher among this group of managers. This result could also indicate that American leaders are more autocratic than managers in other countries and are reluctant to share power. Further research will be needed to determine the causes of this difference.

Another place where American managers varied from others was that 30 percent felt the conflict between their beliefs and those of the organization was a source of stress. Does this mean that there is more value conflict in the United States? The result certainly points in this direction.

Over 30 percent of U.S. executives also indicated that an incompetent boss was a source of stress—by far the highest number of any country. Do American subordinates have higher expectations about their boss' performance, or are American bosses less competent? Again, the research only brings up the question; it does not give us the answer.

While this cross-cultural research on stress raises many questions, it does show how culture can affect both the sources of stress and the reactions of managers to stressful situations.

MANAGERIAL APPLICATIONS OF STRESS MANAGEMENT

Almost all organizational processes cause stress for someone, manager or subordinate. Since stress cannot and should not be entirely eliminated, it should be kept at moderate levels where performance and satisfaction are high. Particular care should be exercised by managers to observe stress levels of individual subordinates and, when they are too high, to attempt to lower the stress using some of the strategies that have been discussed. Here are some additional guidelines for action:

- *Try to head off burnout situations.* Use job rotation, careful communication, strong social support, and lots of positive reinforcement as strategies to reduce the likelihood of burnout.

- *Recognize Type A people.* Be aware of the behavior patterns that indicate possible Type A personalities in yourself and others. Whenever you think someone is a Type A, provide extra opportunities for the person to learn about stress reduction techniques.

- *Design jobs for optimum stress.* Jobs that are extremely difficult or involve very heavy workloads should not always be assigned to the same "workhorse." Try to spread such jobs around. Try to enrich subordinate's jobs to provide an optimum level of stress.

- *Pay special attention to reducing stress for professional women.* Since women experience even more stress than men, it is important that coping strategies be developed, such as establishing mentors and developing training programs to build self-confidence and self-awareness.

- *Train and develop effective managers.* Since effective, competent management is one of the best ways to reduce stress, careful attention to training and development is a must. This strategy has many other positive paybacks for the organization as well.

- *Encourage stress reduction techniques.* Provide opportunities for employees to use the relaxation response, exercise, or other stress reduction techniques by constructing facilities and making time available.

- *Clarify role expectations.* Use the role analysis technique to help resolve role conflicts and ambiguities.

- *Involve people in decisions.* Participation in decision making often reduces stress and may provide a number of other benefits which we will discuss in Chapter 13.

FOR DISCUSSION

1. Explain how the fight-or-flight process works. Give an example from your personal experience.

2. How can a manager recognize that a subordinate is experiencing too much stress?

3. What types of jobs seem most subject to burnout? Why?

4. If the research reported in Perspective 11.2 is correct in finding that women executives experience even more stress than men, what are the personal and organizational implications?

5. Figure 11.4 indicates eight major sources of stress. Based on your own experience, provide one example of each of these sources.

6. What is the difference between acute episodic stress and chronic stress? Explain the implications of these two types of stress for organizations.

7. Give an example of how role ambiguity, role conflict, and role overload can cause stress.

8. Weigh the advantages and disadvantages of the various methods for coping with stress.

9. Examine the sources of stress shown in Figure 11.6. Choose one of the countries, other than the United States, and analyze what special preparation might be needed before reporting for a management job in that country.

KEY CONCEPTS AND TERMS

stress
stressor
fight-or-flight response
burnout
Type A behavior

Type B behavior
acute episodic stress
chronic stress
role ambiguity
role overload

circadian rhythm
relaxation response
role analysis technique

Cases and Incidents

THE FINANCE PROFESSOR

Dr. Olivia Shipla, professor of finance, looked up angrily from the budget report she was trying to read before the committee meeting just twenty minutes away. "Come in!" she said, and Ms. Anne Stevens, the department secretary, edged nervously into the room. "Excuse me, Dr. Shipla," she began. Her voice was interrupted by the phone's jangling. Dr. Shipla grabbed it. "No, Mr. Carlson, I have not graded your capital budgeting paper yet. Check back on Monday." She replaced the phone receiver and raised an eyebrow at the waiting secretary. "What is it?"

"Dr. Shipla, perhaps I had trouble reading the note you left with this book on my desk." Ms. Stevens held a thick, faded green book in her hand. "Did you want fifteen copies of one of the chapters by tomorrow morning?"

"Ms. Stevens, can't you read?" Dr. Shipla inquired sarcastically. "I quite clearly asked for fifteen copies of the book. The whole book!"

Anne Steven's jaw jutted forward almost imperceptibly. "I'm sorry, Dr. Shipla, but that's not possible. As you know, the new cost cutting directives,

which I *did* read, require that a job of this size have at least five days' notice so that we can send it through the Central Printing Service. It's cheaper. I'm afraid I have to obey those rules."

Ms. Stevens opened the office door, then turned before closing the door deliberately to say, "I will send it out this afternoon, but I'm afraid it will be at least a week."

Back in her own office, Anne Stevens set the book on her desk and took several deep breaths to calm her anger, then sat down to resume her typing chores. Seeing that Olivia Shipla's "rush job" manuscript was on the top of her stack of typing, she paused a moment, then slid it under the stack and smiled as she began typing a letter.

DISCUSSION QUESTIONS

1. What are the sources of stress for Dr. Shipla? For Anne Stevens?

2. What are the effects of stress on performance in this case?

3. How would you recommend that this stress situation be managed?

From Arthur P. Brief, Randall S. Schuler, and Mary Van Sell, *Managing Job Stress*, pp. 64–65. Copyright © 1981 by Arthur P. Brief, Randall S. Schuler, and Mary Van Sell. Reprinted by permission of the publisher, Little, Brown and Company.

TOP EXECUTIVES THRIVE ON STRESS

Some stress experts claim that many high-powered executives thrive on stress; that they are adrenalin freaks. To support this position they cite a report by Metropolitan Life Insurance Co. that found top executives in the Fortune 500 firms had 40 percent fewer fatal heart attacks than middle managers in the same companies. The study concluded that stress ranked only tenth out of fourteen factors predicting coronary risk.

Interviews with top managers also support the notion that many top executives can take stress in stride:

John H. Vogel, chairman of the National Bank of North America, for example, starts his business day at 6 A.M. and does not stop until after a dinner engagement. "The hours are tough on a typical person," he says, but quickly adds, "I don't think you can get to the top unless

you can handle stress." Roy A. Anderson, chairman of Lockheed Corp., says he does "not particularly enjoy stress," but he adds: "Some degree of stress is a motivator. If the job's too soft, you lose your mental acuity." And John H. Zimmerman, vice-president of employee relations for Firestone Tire & Rubber Co., who faces an Apr. 21 contract deadline with the United Rubber Workers, declares: "Stress is what you make of it, and that can be the difference between coping and collapsing."

DISCUSSION QUESTIONS

1. How do you account for the ability of top executives to cope with stress?

2. Would you predict a difference in stress levels between top, middle, and lower level management? How would they differ? Why?

3. Do you think these top executives display Type A behavior patterns?

Executive stress may not be all bad. (1979, April 20). *Business Week*, p. 96.

WHAT KILLED BOB LYONS?

Refer to the case, "What killed Bob Lyons?" at the end of Chapter 2.

DISCUSSION QUESTIONS

1. What sources of stress were having an impact on Bob Lyons?

2. What could Bob have done to reduce the stress?

3. What should have been done by Bob's supervisors to reduce or eliminate the stress?

REFERENCES

1. *Business Week* (1985, October 14), p. 152.

2. Beehr, T.A., & J.E. Newman (1978). Job stress, employee health, and organizational effectiveness: A facet analysis, model, and literature review. *Personnel Psychology, 31,* 665–699. Ivancevich, J.M., & Matteson, M.T. (1980). *Stress and work: A managerial perspective.* Glenview, IL: Scott, Foresman. Also, Schuler, R.S. (1980). Definition and conceptualization of stress in organizations. *Organizational behavior and human performance, 25,* 184–215.

3. Seyle, H. (1976). *The stress of life* (2nd ed.). New York: McGraw-Hill.

4. For more on the fight-or-flight process see Seyle (1976). Also Benson, H. (1974). Your innate asset for combating stress. *Harvard Business Review, 52* (4), 49–60.

5. Schuler (1980).

6. Ivancevich & Matteson (1980), Chapter 4.

7. Ivancevich & Matteson (1980), pp. 78–79.

8. Quick, J.C., & Quick, J.D. (1984). *Organizational stress and preventive management.* New York: McGraw-Hill. Jenkins, C.D. (1976). Recent evidence supporting psychological and social risk factors in coronary heart disease. *New England Journal of Medicine, 294,* 1033–1038. Ivancevich, J.M., Matteson, M.T., & Preston, C. (1982). Occupational stress, Type A behavior, and physical well being. *Academy of Management Journal, 25,* 373–391. And Ivancevich & Matteson (1980), pp. 90–92.

9. See Jamal, M. (1985). Relationship of job stress to job performance: A study of managers and blue-collar workers. *Human Relations, 38,* 409–424. Schuler (1980). And Allen, R.D., Hitt, M.A., & Greer, C.R. (1982). Occupational stress and perceived organizational effectiveness in formal groups: An examination of stress level and stress type. *Personnel Psychology, 35* (2), 359–370.

10. Motowidlo, S.J., Packard, J.S., & Manning, M.R. (1986). Occupational stress: Its causes and consequences for job performance. *Journal of Applied Psychology, 71,* 618–629.

11. For a discussion of these issues see Quick & Quick (1984). And McGrath, J.E. (1976). Stress and behavior in organizations. In M.D. Dunnette (Ed.). *Handbook of industrial and organizational psychology* (pp. 1351–1395). Chicago: Rand-McNally.

12. For reviews see Schuler (1980). Also Ivancevich & Matteson (1980).

13. Friedman & Rosenman, *Type A behavior and your heart.* Hood, J.N., & Chusmir, L.H. (1986). Factors determining Type A behavior among employed women and men. *Academy of Management Proceedings 1986,* 332–336. For a review see Matthews, K.A. (1982). Psychological perspectives on Type A behavior pattern. *Psychological Bulletin, 91,* 293–323. For the role of anger and hostility in Type A behavior, see Diamond, E.L. (1982). The role of anger and hostility in essential hypertension and coronary heart disease. *Psychological Bulletin, 92,* 410–433.

14. Matthews (1982).

15. Title from Magne, M. (1984, July 9). Help! My company has just been taken over. *Fortune,* pp. 44–48.

16. Magne, M. (1984), p. 44.

17. Fischman, J. (1987). Type A on trial. *Psychology Today, 21* (2), 42–44.

18. Pittner, M.S., & Houston, B.K. (1980). Response to stress, cognitive coping strategies, and Type A behavior pattern. *Journal of Personality of Social Psychology, 39,* 147–157.

19. For a complete discussion of the concept of burnout, see Meier, S.T. (1983). Toward a theory of burnout. *Human Relations, 10,* 899–910. Also see Levinson, H. (1981, May-June). When executives burn out. *Harvard Business Review,* pp. 73–81. Perlman, B., & Hartman, E.A. (1982). Burnout: Summary and future research. *Human Relations, 35,* 283–305. Moss, L. (1981). *Management stress.* Reading, MA: Addison-Wesley.

20. Etzion, D. (1984). Moderating effect of social support on the stress-burnout relationship. *Journal of Applied Psychology, 69,* 615–622.

21. Levinson (1981), pp. 73–74.

22. Gaines, J., & Jermier, J.M. (1983). Emotional exhaustion in a high stress organization. *Academy of Management Journal, 26,* 567–586.

23. Levinson (1980).

24. For a more complete discussion of the sources of stress, see Quick & Quick (1984). Ivancevich & Matteson (1980). Parasuraman, S., & Alutto, J.A. (1981). An examination of the organizational antecedents of stressors at work. *Academy of Management Journal, 24*, 48–67. Parks, K.R. (1982). Occupational stress among student nurses: A natural experiment. *Journal of Applied Psychology, 67*, 784–796. And Braum, A., Singer, J.E., & Baum, C.S. (1981). Stress and the environment. *Journal of Social Issues, 37*, 4–35.

25. Cooper, C.L., & Davidson, M.J. (1982). The high cost of stress on women managers. *Organizational Dynamics, Spring*, 44–53. For more information about women and stress, see Brief, A.P., Schuler, R.S., & Van Sell, M. (1981). *Managing job stress*. Boston: Little, Brown.

26. Nelson, D.L., & Quick, J.C. (1985). Professional women: Are distress and disease inevitable? *Academy of Management Review, 10*, 206–218.

27. Forbes, J.B., & Piercy, J.E. (1983). Rising to the top: Executive women in 1983 and beyond. *Business Horizons, 26* (5), 38–47.

28. Rubin, D.K. (1984). Fifth annual salary survey: Who makes what, where? *Working Woman, 9* (1), 59–63.

29. Staines, G.L., Pottick, K.L., & Fudge, D.A. (1986). Wives' employment and husbands' attitudes toward work and life. *Journal of Applied Psychology, 71*, 118–128.

30. Hemming, H. (1985). Women in a man's world: Sexual harassment. *Human Relations, 38*, 67–79.

31. Shaver, P., & Buhrmester, D. (1984). Loneliness, sex-role orientation and group life: A social needs perspective. In P.B. Paulus (Ed.). *Basic group processes* (pp. 259–288). New York: Springer-Verlag.

32. Nelson, D.L., & Quick, J.C. (1985). Stead, B.A. (1985). *Women in management* (2nd ed.). Englewood Cliffs, NJ: Prentice-Hall.

33. Levinson, H. (1981, March-April). What killed Bob Lyons? *Harvard Business Review*, pp. 144–162.

34. A classic study in this area is Kahn, R.L., Wolfe, D.M., Quinn, R.P., Snoek, J.D., & Rosenthal, R.A. (1964). *Organizational stress: Studies in role conflict and ambiguity*. New York: Wiley.

35. For more complete information on role ambiguity, see Howard, J.H., Cunningham, D.A. (1986). Role ambiguity, Type A behavior, and job satisfaction: Moderating effects on cardiovascular and biochemical responses associated with coronary risk. *Journal of Applied Psychology, 71*, 95–101.

36. For a validation of the scale, see Schuler, R.S., Aldag, R.J., & Brief, A.P. (1977). Role conflict and ambiguity: A scale analysis. *Organizational Behavior and Human Performance, 20*, 111–129.

37. Reprinted with permission from *Psychology Today Magazine*, copyright © 1977, American Psychological Association.

38. Smith, R. (1980). *Stress, anxiety, and the air traffic control specialist: Some conclusions from a decade of research*. FAA Civil Aeromedical Institute.

39. Bowers, D.B. (1983). What would make 11,500 people quit their jobs? *Organizational Dynamics, Winter*, 5–19.

40. Ivancevich & Matteson (1980), p. 105.

41. Stostak, A.B. (1980). *Blue-collar stress*. Reading, MA: Addison-Wesley.

42. Ivancevich & Matteson (1980), pp. 136–138.

43. Brief, et al. (1981), p. 64.

44. Benson (1974). Peters, R.K., & Benson, H. (1978). Time out for tension. *Harvard Business Review, 56* (1), 120–124. Goleman, D. (1976). Meditation helps break the stress spiral. *Psychology Today, 9* (9), 82cf.

45. See Benson (1974). For do-it-yourself relaxation techniques. For research showing how relaxation works, see Ganster, D.C., Mayes, B.T., Sime, W.E., & Tharp, G.D. (1982). Managing organizational stress: A field experiment. *Journal of Applied Psychology, 67*, 533–542.

46. Ivancevich & Matteson (1980).

47. Falkenberg, L.E. (1987). Employee fitness programs: Their impact on the employee and the organization. *Academy of Management Review, 12*, 511–522.

48. For details see French, W.L., & Bell, C.H., Jr. (1984). *Organization development* (3rd ed.) (pp. 146–149). Englewood Cliffs, NJ: Prentice-Hall, pp. 146–149. And Ivancevich & Matteson (1980), pp. 210–211.

49. Ivancevich & Matteson (1980), p. 208.

50. Ganster, et al. (1982).

51. Bruning, N.S., & Frew, D.R. (1985). The impact of various stress management training strategies: A longitudinal field experiment. *Academy of Management Proceedings, '85*, 192–196.

52. Jackson, S.E. (1983). Participation in decision making as a strategy for reducing job-related strain. *Journal of Applied Psychology, 68*, 3–19.

53. Ivancevich & Matteson (1980), p. 210.

54. Cooper, C., & Arbose, J. (1984, May). Executive stress goes global. *International Management*, 42–48.

Chapter Twelve

POWER AND POLITICS IN ORGANIZATIONS

PREVIEW

- Should managers use power or political tactics?

- How can you use expert power to further your career?

- Why does the boss' secretary often have more power than many managers?

- What kinds of power tactics are used in large corporations?

- Did you know that putting your arm around someone may be a sign of superior power?

- How do you know when people are playing organizational politics?

- Are organizational political tactics always unethical?

MAJOR TOPICS

Preview Case: The Powerless Ones

Power, Authority, and Influence: Getting Things Done

Sources of Power

Using Power and Influence

Political Strategies and Tactics

The Ethics of Power and Politics

Cross-Cultural OB: Power Dynamics in China

Managerial Applications of Power and Politics

Preview Case

THE POWERLESS ONES

Karen Jennings, Frank Eason, and Stan Sullivan are unhappy executives.[1] All three began new jobs recently, but things aren't working out, and each is afraid of being fired.

The problem is not that Karen, Frank, and Stan are incapable of doing their jobs. The big complaint of all three is identical: each feels powerless to do the work he or she was hired to do, and all three feel frustrated at not being able to accomplish the objectives of their basic assignments.

Karen is the first woman to attain a vice-presidency in her company, an architectural firm. Discriminated against, underpaid, and underutilized for years, she was finally promoted to a responsible position six months ago, thanks to affirmative-action legislation. Success in the job is important not only to Karen but to other women in her highly competitive and male-dominated field. But so far she has been blocked by her male colleagues in every attempt at creativity. Her efforts to be "nice" lead only to being shunted aside again; when she tries to be firm and outspoken, she becomes the target of more hostility and derision. She feels helpless and angry, and her work is deteriorating.

Frank was hired to install a new accounting and computer procedure to control the worldwide shipping activities of an international company. The company has needed up-to-date control procedures for some time, and the president hired Frank virtually on the spot after hearing him speak at a computer-systems convention. Unfortunately, the president's enthusiasm for Frank is not shared by other company officers who perceive him as uninformed about the shipping industry, an invader of their territories, and thus a threat to their jobs. They do nothing to help Frank and, in fact, do everything possible to impede him. When Frank reported these problems to the president, he was told that one of the marks of a successful executive is the ability to handle people.

Stan, who was instrumental in developing a new product line for his company, has been assigned to direct test-marketing of the product in one section of the country. The budget for the project was added to the budget of the division manager, but the manager wants nothing to do with the endeavor, much less with someone assigned by the home office. As a result, Stan receives no cooperation on the new product work and has felt extreme pressure to do other assignments. In addition to battling frustration at not being able to proceed with his assignment, Stan worries because the hostile manager will evaluate him and report on his performance to headquarters.

Karen, Frank, and Stan are all having trouble getting their jobs done—they feel powerless in light of the obstacles they face. This chapter is about power and politics. Everyone who manages needs to understand how power and politics work and, to be effective, managers must be able to use the strategies and tactics of power. Since power is concerned with our ability to get things done, it is at the very core of managerial work.[2]

In this chapter we will define the concepts of power and politics, examine the sources of power, and discuss the tactics and strategies of power and politics. We will also look at some ethical issues since these concepts often make people uncomfortable. Many managers might say: "Who me? Use power or political tactics? Not on your life. I'm not that kind of person!" What kind of person are you? Would you use power and politics to get your job done?

POWER, AUTHORITY, AND INFLUENCE: GETTING THINGS DONE

Before we can learn how to use power to get things done, we need to understand the meaning and interrelationship of power, authority, and influence.

What Is Power?

While there are a number of ways that one might define **power,** we will use it to mean the ability to bring about outcomes that are desired by using influence.[3] Often, this involves getting people to do something they might not otherwise do. It also means the ability to resist others who are trying to get you to do something you do not want to do. You don't have power in a vacuum, but only in relation to other people or groups. For example, you might have power over your secretary, but the controller may have power over you. In addition, your power over another is seldom absolute. The secretary also has power over you; especially if you need something done in a hurry.

Power and Influence

Another term that is used in conjunction with power is influence. These terms are so interrelated that they are often used interchangeably. We will use **influence** to mean the process of producing intended effects in individuals, groups, and organizations.[4] Power differs from influence in that power is the capacity or potential for influence.[5] Your capacity to influence your secretary is great because you have power. However, when you try to get your secretary to work overtime on Saturday you will use influence tactics to obtain the desired behavior.

Power and Authority

Authority is the right to order or ask others to do what you want them to do. It is usually associated with some legal or institutionalized sanctions: it is legitimized power. One might think of authority as downward influence.[6] Some of the power you have over your secretary is authority. You have the right to assign tasks, set goals, or rate performance. On the other hand, you might not have the authority to order Saturday work. If you want your secretary to work on Saturday, you may need to use a different source of power. It is possible to have authority without power. In the opening case in this chapter, Karen, Frank, and Stan have authority, but not enough power to get their jobs done— an extremely frustrating and stressful situation.

SOURCES OF POWER

There are a large number of bases or sources of power.[7] Anything that enhances your ability to get others to do what you want them to do is a source of

Table 12.1

EXAMPLES SHOWING SOURCES OF POWER

Sources of power	Organizational example
Reward	Telling a subordinate, "Well done!" after an oral briefing to a customer group.
Coercive	Advising a peer in another department to "Help me get the information I want or I'll report you for incompetence."
Expert	Including an accountant in all meetings and decisions because of in-depth knowledge of accounting systems.
Legitimate	Initiating a person's transfer to another department.
Referent	Emulating a senior professor who is widely respected.

power and influence. The following section covers several important sources. Table 12.1 summarizes these sources and provides an example of each.

Interdependence: An Underlying Basis for Power

When you have control over what others want, they are dependent on you and you have power over them. It happens the other way around too. When you are dependent on others, such as people from other departments, then they have power over you. Dependence and interdependence are a normal and natural part of the manager's job. Two factors make interdependence inherent: Limited resources and the division of labor.[8] There are never enough scarce resources (funds, people, materials, space, time) to go around. In addition, tasks are divided into specialized subtasks. Bob Goldberg, controller at Ace Freight Co. has accountants, financial analysts, payroll, and benefits people all reporting to him. These people rely upon Bob for career advice and performance appraisals.

The more others are dependent on you, the greater your power. The more you are dependent on others, the less your power. In the opening case Karen, Frank, and Stan are dependent on others in the organization, and few people are dependent on them.

Another example of how interdependence works in managerial situations is the story of John Correa who is manager of environmental engineering planning for a large corporation. Correa is dependent on his boss and some ten other top managers for information and rewards. Except for his boss, most of the other managers are not dependent on him. Correa is dependent on his subordinates and even the people who work for his subordinates, since the work is technical and they would be difficult to replace. In addition, he is dependent on two other department managers in his division—he simply could not do his job without them. The situation is not mutual since they do not need Correa's department. The dependencies go on and on. There is a union of engineers that can shut down his department, and there is a sole outside supplier who does not really care about his department because the size of the orders are so small. Since Correa's department has so little natural power, due to its dependence on so many others, he has to carefully develop and nurture the power he does have.

Perspective 12.1

POWER IS ALSO
A GREAT MOTIVATOR

David McClelland has spent several decades working on the power motive. One of his more recent studies concludes that power is the strongest motivator for managers.[9]

In examining the motive scores for over fifty managers of both high and low morale units in all sections of the same large company, we found that most of the managers—over 70 percent—were high in power motivation compared with men in general. This finding confirms the fact that power motivation is important for management. (Remember that as we use the term "power motivation," it refers not to dictatorial behavior, but to a desire to have impact, to be strong and influential.) The better managers . . . tended to score even higher in power motivation.

The most important determining factor [for determining managerial effectiveness] turned out not to be how [sales managers'] power motive compared to their need to achieve but whether it was higher than their need to be liked. This relationship existed for 80 percent of the better sales managers as compared to only 10 percent of the poorer managers. And the same held true for managers in nearly all parts of the company.

[In summary,] the better managers we studied are high in power motivation, low in affiliation motivation, and high in self-control. They care about institutional power and use it to stimulate their employees to be more productive.

From McClelland's research we might conclude that since effective managers have a high need for power, they will be motivated to develop sources of power. Exercising this power to get things done can result in higher performance and even more power.

Reward Power

One important form of dependence is control over rewards, a very scarce and important resource. Anytime you are in a position to reward people with money, recognition, promotion, status, and similar outcomes, you have **reward power.**[10] When you offer someone extra pay to do some task that the person might not otherwise do, you are using this power. If you can offer the secretaries double-time pay for working on Saturday, you may be able to influence their decision favorably, even though their decision to work overtime may be entirely voluntary. However, managers are most often limited in their reward power. They may not have the authority to offer such financial rewards. But on the other hand, a smile, a good performance rating, or a few hours off may be even more effective rewards than money.

Coercive Power

When you are able to order someone to do something and back up the order with force or punishments, then **coercive power** exists. When someone has legitimate authority over another then coercive power is often, but not always, present. Coercion power can, of course, exist without authority. An armed robber has coercive power when he points a gun at you and tells you to lie down. When your boss tells you to fly to Chicago to see a client (even though you had other plans and did not want to go), it is also coercion. The difference between the two types of coercion is that your boss has the legitimate right to order you to do things you do not wish to do (with the threat of losing your job), while the robber is using brute force.

Expert Power

When you build a reputation as an expert, people become dependent upon you for advice within your area of expertise; you have **expert power.** You tend to be able to control the information in some specialized area. This type of power is normally developed through achievements and performance. You have to establish a "track record" and a "professional reputation." An example of expert power is Betty Roll, a statistical clerk in a large public sector organization. While her job was only rated a G–7 (relatively low ranking), she exerted more power than most GS–12's in the organization because she was an expert in data collection and retrieval. If you wanted an answer to any question, you knew you could turn to Betty and she would find it. Thus, many high-ranking managers became dependent on Betty to answer their queries. Betty had power. She could pretty much call the shots on anything she wanted.

A variant of expert power is making yourself irreplaceable. In a French tobacco plant,[11] maintenance workers were quite successful in keeping all maintenance procedures and techniques secret. They were able to get rid of all manuals, blueprints, and directions. New people were trained by word of mouth during long apprenticeships. Neither production workers nor management understood anything about maintaining the complex production equipment. Thus, the maintenance workers through their monopoly on knowledge, had tremendous power to control the operation of the plant.

Legitimate Power

While dependence is certainly a central issue in most power relationships, power can also be viewed as the right to direct and control behavior because of one's position or role.[12] Subordinates usually accept supervisors' rights to direct them because the supervisor holds a position in the organizational hierarchy. For example the director of marketing may be authorized to hire and fire employees and determine pay raises. The right to command or direct subordinates may stem from authority granted by stockholders or it may be created by law in the cases of military supervisors or judges.

In the opening case in this chapter, we found three managers, Karen, Frank, and Stan, who were powerless in spite of apparent legitimate power to get the job done. These three examples illustrate the importance of the *acceptance* of power. Unless others are willing to accept the direction of the person who is vested with the right to direct, then the person will be powerless.

Referent Power

Another important source of power is the manager or leader's personality or charisma. People have **referent power** when others admire them and want to be like them; they identify with the person. Many young managers identify with Lee Iacocca, the charismatic CEO of Chrysler Corp. They want to be like Iacocca; they follow his advice and thus, he has referent power over them. You do not have to be famous to have referent power and you do not have to be a manager. A particularly admired production worker, such as Norma Rae—a union organizer in a Southern textile mill made famous in the movie by the same name—achieved referent power because she was admired for her outspokenness and courage.

Referent power can also be developed by fostering friendships with others so that there is a reciprocal identification, or mutual admiration.[13] Common interests, values, viewpoints, and preferences help lead to mutual attraction and referent power.

USING POWER AND INFLUENCE

While we have been discussing the sources of power, you have probably thought of a few ways to acquire and use power, such as making yourself an expert or obtaining an influential position of authority. In this section, we turn to a more specific discussion of power and influence strategies and tactics—how to use power effectively. Figure 12.1 highlights the various approaches to using power.

Assessing Power Relationships

Perhaps the first step in dealing with any power situation is to analyze what power you have and what powers the other people in the organization have. This may be as simple as sitting back and thinking about the power situation or as complex as doing a detailed power analysis of your entire organization.[14] If Karen, Frank, and Stan, in our opening incident, had assessed their power, they would have found they had more power than they thought. Karen has the power of equal opportunity under law in back of her, plus the increased emphasis on opportunity for women in organizations. Frank's power lies in his ex-

Figure 12.1

POWER STRATEGIES AND TACTICS

pertise in a complex, new area and his relationship with the boss. Stan's task is directly related to the future of the company. Each needs to assess his or her own power and the power of the people with whom they work. Then, strategies can be devised to improve a low-power situation.

Creating a Sense of Obligation

A good way to create IOU's is to do favors for people to create a sense of reciprocity. The strategy here is that when you help others, they will come to your aid when you need them. This is especially powerful if you do the favor for someone who is in a position to help you later. An example of how this tactic might be used is the case of Barney.[15]

> Barney worked as a dispatcher in a national moving and storage company. After spending most of his life in Minneapolis, Barney and his wife longed for the chance to live in a southern climate. One day a unique opportunity presented itself, and Barney had the foresight to recognize the opportunity. An executive in Barney's company wanted a friend's belongings shipped in a hurry. A telephone call to Barney (whom the executive knew only slightly) was all the executive needed to make the necessary arrangements for his friend. Thanking Barney for his quick action, the executive stated, "Let me know if I can ever help you out of a jam."
>
> Six months later Barney telephoned the executive with a request. "Mr. Higgins, do you remember me? I'm Barney Weatherbee, the dispatcher in charge of routing the moving vans. My wife and I have a little problem that needs your help. Her arteries are beginning to harden a little, making cold weather in Minneapolis insufferable to her. We're wondering if I could be given favorable consideration for a transfer to our Miami or Tampa office. We would both be grateful to you for the rest of our lives if the transfer did come through."
>
> The executive replied, "I'll see what I can do." Within one year, Barney, who had extended himself for the executive (slightly bending company regulations in the process), was transferred to a comparable position in Tampa. His IOU had been reimbursed.

Identifying with Powerful People

While knowing the right (powerful) people is important, it is even more important to be known. One of the most effective ways to the executive suite is through a powerful sponsor or **mentor.**[16] Having a mentor who is powerful puts you in a powerful position. This person is often someone who was your boss at one time in your career, but has now rapidly advanced to a high-level position. Getting a mentor is sometimes a matter of luck, although shrewd, upward-bound junior managers will usually make an effort to link up with upwardly mobile senior managers. They accomplish this by joining task forces headed by the mentor or by getting themselves transferred into the mentor's department. Once they are connected with the mentor, they use a combination of high performance and favorable impression management (discussed in Chapter 4) to establish their reputations. Several of the power games related in Perspective 12.2 illustrate this tactic.

Association with powerful people may increase your power. A classic example of power through association is the secretary to the chief executive officer

Perspective 12.2

POWER GAMES
IN A LARGE CORPORATION[17]

A study of men and women in a large corporation called INDSCO (not its real name) found the following power tactics were used:

• *Extraordinary job performance* Performance that is extraordinary, visible, relevant—and identified with a solution to a pressing organizational problem—results in increased power.

• *Reorganization to increase power* "Empire building," as it is sometimes termed, by creating new and seemingly more influential organizations, is a way to increase power. A side benefit is that your own "chosen" people can fill the new positions.

• *Risk taking* Few people dare to take extraordinary risks, but those who pull them off become very powerful, for both social and organizational reasons. Organizationally, they have proved they can perform in most difficult circumstances. Socially, they have developed a charisma in the eyes of those who are less willing to take risks.

• *Power positions* Jobs on the boundaries between organizational units or between the company and the outside world often have good visibility and become power positions because of it.

• *Social connections and sponsors* Long-term, stable social connections outside your own work group—with powerful peers, superiors, and subordinates—are a source of power. Sponsors, called "godfathers" at INDSCO, are in a position to fight for protégés, to stand up for them in meetings, and to promote them into promising positions. The sponsor helps distinguish the person from the crowd.

• *Peer alliances* Powerful people build a strong network of peer alliances. They have team spirit. They help others.

(CEO) in a large organization. The secretary may not have much formal authority, but there are numerous other ways to gain power because of the position. The secretary knows all the secrets; knows all the people; controls information flow to the CEO; develops meeting agendas, and performs many other crucial tasks that result in the possession of high power.

Controlling Scarce Resources

When you control something that is valued by others, you have power. A controller who approves the budget and allocates funds has power. A personnel director who approves requests for manpower has power. Other scarce resources include control of information, control over supplies, and control over the interpretation of rules and regulations.

Controlling Information. Without timely and accurate information, it is impossible for a manager to perform effectively.[18] Thus, anyone who is in a position to control the information is in a powerful position. This may be an expert, like Betty Roll who was mentioned earlier, or it may be someone who controls access to a top manager, such as an executive secretary.

An unusual example of how control of information is used to gain power is the case of Shirley Olsen, who is the personnel director for a medium-sized industrial firm. Shirley suggested to the president that more information was needed about the effectiveness of human resource management. Shirley proposed a quarterly questionnaire of the employees. The president agreed, and before long the survey results became a very important part of the evaluation of manager effectiveness. While Shirley did not create or "doctor" the data, she was in a position to determine what questions would be asked and how the data would be collected and presented. Thus, she could make managers look good or bad by the way she designed the data collection and feedback system. Shirley became a very powerful person in the firm as a result of this information-gathering task.

Controlling Supplies. While a supply supervisor's job does not sound glamorous, there is often a great deal of power associated with it. If people are forced to order all their supplies through a central source, then the supply person is in a good position to control this resource by doing special rush orders, by releasing back orders to certain people first, and by assuring that a higher-quality item be ordered than is normally authorized. These are only a few of the ways a supply person can garner power.

Interpreting Rules. While staff lawyers are an obvious example of this type of power, there are often other people in the organization whose task it is to interpret rules and thus to make powerful decisions. Corporate auditors make many decisions that affect managers, thus making them quite powerful. Some organizations have a procedure department whose job it is to write, revise, and control procedures. These people have power because they can affect a manager's discretion about how to do the job.

The 10 Percent Rule.[19] When you have discretionary control over an organization's resources, you have power. "A relatively small amount of resources, if utilized in a strategically appropriate fashion," can create resource dependence. This is referred to as the **10 percent rule,** which states that "organizations can be taken over by discretionary control over not more (and frequently less) than 10 percent of the organization's total budget." This is possible because such a large portion of an organization's funds are nondiscretionary and fixed (salaries, interest, and leases).

Establishing Power Relationships

There are many opportunities for you to improve your odds of finding or developing a situation where you become powerful. The most crucial factor is to seek jobs that are associated with powerful people, tasks, or departments (see Table 12.2 for ideas about the kinds of content such a job should have.) If you want to be a senior executive of General Motors, you do not want to start in personnel or marketing because that is not where the power lies. Seven of the last nine chairmen of General Motors had finance backgrounds, while the remaining ones were engineers.[20] An obvious choice in that organization is finance or engineering. Other organizations will differ. You have to analyze every organization, every job and promotion opportunity, to see what effect it will have on your power.

Table 12.2

FACTORS THAT CONTRIBUTE TO POWER OR POWERLESSNESS

Organizational factors contribute to whether you have power or do not have power. The following list indicates factors that result in high or low power.

Factors	Generates power when factor is:	Generates powerlessness when factor is:
Rules inherent in the job	few	many
Predecessors in the job	few	many
Rewards for performance	many	few
Flexibility in using people	high	low
Approvals needed for decisions	few	many
Physical location	central	distant
Publicity about job activities	high	low
Interpersonal contact on job	high	low
Contact with senior officials	high	low
Participation in conferences	high	low

SOURCE: Reprinted with permission of the *Harvard Business Review.* Exhibit from "Power Failure in Management Circuits," by Rosabeth Moss Kanter (July/August 1979). Copyright © 1979 by The President and Fellows of Harvard College; all rights reserved.

Making Power Work

Even when you have power and have decided on a good approach to applying the power, your power moves may not work. Three additional factors need to be considered: the zone of acceptance, power balancing, and possible undesirable side effects.

Zone of Acceptance.   People do not always accept your decision even if it is based on formal authority.[21] For every possible use of power there is a **zone of acceptance** in which the power move will be successful. Power users must assess this zone before they take action. Even a direct order may fall outside the zone of acceptance. For example, a manager may use legitimate power to order a speedup of an assembly line only to have the union call a "wildcat" (unauthorized) strike resulting in trouble with the president and costing the firm dearly. There are also more subtle ways to avoid an order, like working strictly by the rules, which causes a slowdown rather than a speedup.

Power Balancing.   Every use of power tends to be offset by a counter use of power. Power is normally in a balanced state of equilibrium. When someone uses power, this state becomes unbalanced and the natural tendency is to seek balance again. Skill in exercising power is important here. A blatant use of power, such as an appeal to the president to reorganize to make you more powerful, is likely to be offset by a counter power move. For instance, your opponent might use personal contacts and influence to discredit the proposed reorganization, thus neutralizing your power.

Another way that power can get out of balance is through organizational romances.[22] Resources are often exchanged between the two romantic partners

Perspective 12.3

NONVERBAL SIGNALS OF POWER[23]

• *Shoulder hold* A corporation president can put his or her arm around the shoulder of a lower-ranking employee, but the reverse is unthinkable. [The] one-way shoulder hold is also found between teachers and students, coaches and athletes, and parents and children.

• *Interruption license* One excellent sign of power is the "interruption license." In almost any conversation, interruptions usually involve a more powerful person interrupting a less powerful person. This part of the power script [may be] largely unconscious, but it appears to be extremely consistent. In an organization, the interruption license appears to follow the organization hierarchy. Presidents do not hesitate to interrupt vice-presidents, vice-presidents interrupt assistant vice-presidents, and so on down the hierarchy.

• *Spatial signs* There are also spatial signs of power. People tend to stand further away from people who are high in status or rank. For example, on the night John F. Kennedy was elected president, his friends and advisors were watching the election returns, and they suddenly realized that their friend had just become the president of the United States. At that moment, according to one advisor, their spatial interaction with Kennedy changed dramatically—the advisors moved back a "respectful" distance and formed a sort of circle around Kennedy. This formal distance was in response to the tremendous power Kennedy had just acquired. Another spatial aspect of the power script involves seating position. At a rectangular table, the most powerful person is almost always seated at one end of the table, while less powerful persons are seated along the sides of the table.

• *Visual attention* Powerful people may listen to other people without looking at them. By contrast, less powerful people usually pay close "visual attention" when listening to a powerful person. Visual attention seems to be a gesture of respect in our culture, and powerful people may feel free to make this gesture or not.

• *Eyebrows* Elevated eyebrows indicate deference, while lowered eyebrows reflect power . . . A face with raised eyebrows looks meek and submissive in comparison to the more aggressive, determined, or "powerful" expression conveyed by lowered eyebrows.

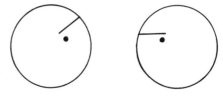

at a much higher level than among others in the work group. Rewards are likely to be more frequent and inequitably distributed. The "good jobs" are more likely to go to the romantic partner.

Reactions to Power.   People may react to some types of power, such as coercion and control, much as they would to punishment. They will comply because they have to, but they will try to get even later through sabotage or some other way. They may also be angry and leave the organization. Coercive power must be used cautiously.

Power of Lower-Level Participants

Most power studies concern uses by managers, but lower-level organizational participants (rank and file workers, lower-level clerks and foremen, technicians) are also powerful.[24]

A summary of the methods of upward-oriented power tactics that are used by lower-level participants is provided in Table 12.3. While several of these tactics have already been discussed, some new ones appear, including the most of-

Table 12.3

THE MOST-OFTEN USED METHODS OF UPWARD INFLUENCE FROM THE SUBORDINATE'S PERSPECTIVE

Method	Total events	Success ratio*
Logically presenting ideas	143	52%
Using repetition, persistence	51	41
Trading job-related benefits	39	59
Using organizational rules	33	48
Going over supervisor's head	29	62
Using group or peer support	18	67
Threatening to resign	18	17

* The success ratio is the successful events divided by total events (successful plus unsuccessful).

SOURCE: Adapted from W.K. Schilit and E.A. Locke, 1982, A study of upward influence in organizations, *Administrative Science Quarterly* 27:310. Copyright © 1982 by Administrative Science Quarterly, Ithaca, New York. Used with permission.

ten-used one—logically presenting ideas. The second highest one, using persistence or repetition to "wear the boss down" is surprising. Another unexpected result is the power of going over the boss' head. One would think that would be a dangerous strategy indeed.

The Power Process: An Overview

Figure 12.2 shows how the dynamics of power fit together. It begins with the manager. One who has a high need for power will be motivated and interested

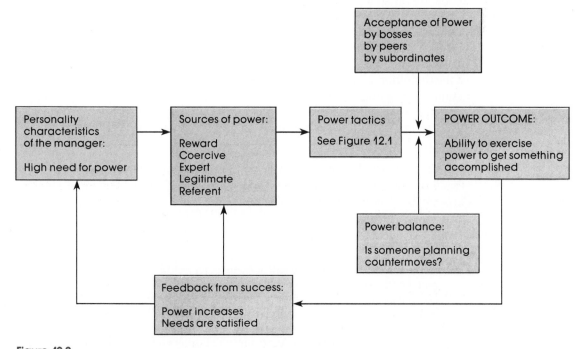

Figure 12.2

MANAGERIAL POWER: A MODEL OF THE PROCESS

in developing power. Such a manager would carefully evaluate all the various sources of power and power tactics to see which ones best fit the situation at hand. A person familiar with power knows that acceptance of a power act by bosses, subordinates, or peers is critical for success. The person also knows that failure will decrease power; thus, success is highly valued. Another consideration is the power balance. Will others attempt to counter your moves? In the final stage the power event takes place and, if successful, feeds back additional power to the instigator and satisfies the need for power.

POLITICAL STRATEGIES AND TACTICS

Have you heard about people "playing politics" in some organizations? Most people have because it is certainly a widespread and important influence strategy in most organizations. But few people understand what organizational politics is and how it works. This section may help provide some illumination by defining organizational politics and reviewing some political strategies and tactics. We will also discuss the ethics of organizational politics.

What Is Organizational Politics?

Although **organizational politics** is an elusive quality to define,[25] an emerging definition seems to be "intentional acts of influence undertaken by individuals or groups to enhance or protect their self-interest when conflicting courses of action are possible." [26] There are several important parts to the definition. First, politics are an intentional behavior; people choose whether or not to engage in political behavior. The second aspect of the definition is that political behavior centers around the self-interest of the individual, group, or organization; people are interested in satisfying their own needs and goals. The final aspect of the definition centers around protecting oneself when conflicting courses of action are possible. In other words, trying to obtain the best possible outcome consistent with self-interest is the goal.

An example of how organizational politics works may help clarify the definition.[27]

> Lee, 61, has been Director of Engineering for American Semiconductor for fourteen years. He is very bright and a fine supervisor but has not kept abreast of new developments in technology.
>
> American Semiconductor's manufacturing process creates substantial quantities of toxic materials. Lee's rather casual attitude toward the deposit of these chemicals has resulted in a number of environmental citations. The firm is now tied up in court on two cases and will probably be forced to pay a substantial amount of damages. Yet, Lee still does not perceive the disposal problem as urgent. For three years, Charlie, the executive vice-president, has tried to persuade Lee to make this a priority issue but has failed. Charley has reluctantly concluded that Lee must be taken out of his position as Director of Engineering.
>
> Charlie recognizes that it would demoralize other managers if he were to fire Lee outright. So, Charlie decides that he will begin to tell selected individuals that he is dissatisfied with Lee's work. When there is open support for Lee, Charlie qui-

Perspective 12.4

DEVELOPING
POSITIVE POLITICAL SKILLS

Peter Block, a veteran consultant, has written a book, *The Empowered Manager: Positive Political Skills at Work.*[28] He believes that while much political activity in organizations is negative and manipulative, it need not be so. He proposes that we focus on enlightened self-interest as a way of concentrating energy in a positive direction:

- *Enlightened self-interest No. 1: Meaning.* Focus on activities and goals that have personal meaning to us and are genuinely needed by the organization.

- *Enlightened self-interest No. 2: Contribution and service.* Try to make important and

genuine contributions to the organization. Share information rather than hoard it. Focus on service and giving. In other words, treat the business as if it were our own.

- *Enlightened self-interest No. 3: Integrity.* Many people fear that if they tell the truth they will be punished or even fired. However, this fear is often overemphasized. A crucial self-interest is telling it like it really is; being honest.

- *Enlightened self-interest No. 4: Positive impact on others' lives.* It is in our own self-interest to treat others well and to care about what happens to them. This means we should avoid unjust criticism, talking behind others' backs, and control policies that hurt people.

- *Enlightened self-interest No. 5: Mastery.* Take pride in being the expert; being the high performer; knowing as much as you can about the job.

etly sides with Lee's opposition. He casually lets Lee's peers know that he thinks Lee may have outlived his usefulness to the firm. He even exaggerates Lee's deficiencies and failures when speaking to Lee's coworkers. Discouraged with the waning support from his colleagues, Lee decides to take an early retirement.

Comparing Politics With Power

Most political acts involve power. However, since power does not have to be directed toward self-interest, it can involve altruistic use of rewards, such as praise or giving one's expertise to help others without expectations of rewards. An example of a nonpolitical use of power is a supervisor who uses power to get competent subordinates promoted even though the promotion will mean a transfer and will be against his or her self-interest. On the other hand, this very same act might be political if the supervisor merely wanted a "crony" in a position to collect advance information about funding in order to have an advantage over other managers. However, it is not always easy to determine if people are pursuing selfish ends.

To test your knowledge of the amount of organizational politics involved in various business functions, you may wish to take the quiz shown in Table 12.4. Then, check your answers with the research results reported at the end of the chapter. Are you surprised by the results? Why do you think the top-ranked functions are so political?

There are more politics involved in some organizational processes than in others. Table 12.5 shows that managers perceive politics much more in promotion decisions than in hiring decisions.

Table 12.4

HOW POLITICAL ARE BUSINESS FUNCTIONS?

Test your prediction of how much politics exists in various business functions with the results of a research study reported at the end of this chapter. Rank order the amount of organizational politics that you estimate exists in each area beginning with 1 as the most political and 9 as the least political.

Functional area	Rank for level of politics
Sales	_____
Personnel	_____
Marketing staff	_____
Purchasing	_____
Production	_____
Research and development	_____
Accounting and finance	_____
Board of directors	_____
Manufacturing staff	_____

SOURCE: Adapted from Madison, D.L., Allen, R.W., Porter, L.W., Lenwick, P.A., & Mayes, B.T. (1980). Organizational politics: An exploration of managers' perceptions. *Human Relations, 33,* 88.

Political Tactics

To understand organizational politics, we must also understand political tactics. In this section, we will cover five tactics: use of information, creating a favorable image, forming coalitions, coopting opponents, and blaming or attacking others.[29] Most of these tactics can be used in either a negative or positive way. It all depends on what self-interests are paramount. If interests such as those shown in Perspective 12.4 are the primary goal, then tactics will take a positive direction. If self-interest is gained at the expense of others or the organization, then tactics will be negative.

Use of Information. Information can be withheld, distorted, used to inundate your opponent with the "facts," or to make a situation so complex that only you can interpret it. You may also use the "your opinion versus the facts" approach,[30] especially when you are in control of the information sources. Say you are faced with a disagreement in a staff meeting that would make you look bad. When your rival provides information contrary to your position, you simply state, "Thank you for your opinion. Now I have the facts here that show a different position." Your opponent is in no condition to question your facts and loses that round.

Another, more subtle use of information is selective use of objective criteria. When you use criteria that are favorable to your position and omit unfavorable criteria, a decision is more likely to be made in your favor. An example of this tactic is a district sales manager who has made sure that the primary criteria for division of this year's budget is the geographical dispersion of customers. This was done because the sales manager knows it will result in a larger travel budget than is actually needed; thus there may be enough "slack" for some really good trips.

Table 12.5

POLITICS IN ORGANIZATIONAL PROCESSES

Process	Percent coded always or frequently
Interdepartmental coordination	68
Promotions and transfers	60
Delegation of authority	59
Facilities, equipment allocation	49
Performance appraisals	42
Budget allocation	38
Pay	33
Grievances and complaints	32
Hiring	23
Disciplinary penalties	21

SOURCE: Adapted from Gantz, J., & Murray, V.V. (1980). The experience of work place politics. *Academy of Management Journal, 23,* 242.

Creating and Maintaining a Favorable Image. Is impression management (discussed in Chapter 4) a political tactic? Yes, when it is directed toward self-interest. People who manage their image to create the impression of success, prestige, or belonging to a certain group may be engaging in political behavior. For example, people who carefully cultivate their reputations and images so that they will be candidates for promotion may be exhibiting political behavior.

Taking credit for another's accomplishments is another form of impression management that is particularly harmful. Most of us have encountered the person or even a boss who says, "I've worked hard to accomplish this task and I'm proud of what I've done," when, in fact, the task was done by someone else in part or completely. For example, Kim Chuong, a production worker in the Advanced Products plant, developed a process that makes circuit boards much more reliable and will result in saving the company lots of money. But Kim's boss takes credit for the idea and has been promoted because of the favorable attention generated by the improved process. How do you think this political act will affect Kim's motivation? It seems quite likely to decline.

Coalitions. A **coalition** is an alliance or union between two or more people or groups.[31] Because organizations are interdependent—tasks are divided and specialized—coalitions form to further cooperation and get things done. They also form to defeat opponents by outvoting them or to protect the self-interest of the people in the coalition. For example, engineers and maintenance technicians might form a coalition to lobby against the purchase of new equipment that is desired by production. The new equipment is a threat to their self-interest because it takes less maintenance and engineering, thus creating a threat to their jobs. The corporate coup d'état, related in Perspective 12.5, shows a dramatic use of coalitions.

Building External Constituencies. Coalitions are not limited to those formed within the organization. Allies can be recruited from outside sources: government, other organizations, consultants, customers, or clients. A good

Perspective 12.5

CORPORATE
COUP D'ÉTAT[32]

An unsuspecting Marion Harper, Jr., presided over what was to be his last board of directors meeting in a nineteen-year career as chairman and chief executive officer of the Interpublic Group, the world's largest advertising business. Harper was interrupted by one of his hand-picked directors before he could even bring the first item on his prepared agenda before the board. It was moved that the first order of business be replacement of the chief executive officer. The motion was immediately seconded, and carried with six "ayes" and one abstention.

An organization coup can be defined as the infiltration of a small but critical segment of the organization's structure (board of directors) to displace the CEO from control of the organization by an unexpected succession. The plotters are usually some combination of inside and outside directors, often including members of the CEO's palace guard. The term "infiltration" is used to underline the fact that the group's action must be secret if it is to succeed. And, although goals involving change of policy may be significant, the primary goal is succession: a new man at the top.

The corporate coup contrasts in a number of ways with more routine successions to power— replacements resulting from mandatory retirement policies or sudden successions following the illness or death of the CEO. When the succession is expected, the process of choosing a new CEO is conducted with considerable awareness on the part of other employees and relevant stockholders and directors. When the CEO dies, the succession is unexpected, but once the initial shock wears off, replacement activities follow regular institutionalized procedures.

Corporate coups, on the other hand, are unexpected and deviate sharply from routinized replacement procedures. They are engineered in secrecy, without the knowledge of the public or most other employees and, most important, without the knowledge of the CEO who is the coup's target. "Going public" before the coup is a *fait accompli* that is almost invariably fatal (to the dissidents) since it allows the CEO time to muster his own considerable resources to put down the coup.

---

example of this is accounting groups in business schools. They often get more resources and higher faculty salaries due at least in part to their strong connections with the professional accounting community. Many accounting departments have become so powerful that they have split from the business school and formed their own school of accounting.

Cooptation. Another way to build support and create alliances is **cooptation.** This strategy involves making people whose support is desired members of the group, with the expectation that they will adopt the group's norms and goals and support the group's goals. The most common form of cooptation in organizations is the board of directors. People are selected because they can support the firm in some way. For example, bankers are popular board members. They can provide financial advice and perhaps financial support.

However, cooptation is not reserved for the boardroom. Whenever you have a task to do that requires broad organizational support, a typical way to do it is to form a taskforce or committee. The membership of the taskforce is designed to include those people who are needed to get the idea approved, even though they may be opposed to the idea. The theory here is that when people become part of a problem-solving group, they will be much more easily persuaded to go along with the goals of the group.

Blaming or Attacking Others. People who use this tactic try to avoid association with something that has gone wrong. They do not want to be associated with failure. "Scapegoating" is trying to find someone else to blame for a negative outcome; trying to find a scapegoat so you can "get off the hook." Another version of this tactic is to make your rivals look bad by asserting or implying that they made a mistake, have poor judgment, are only lucky, or are behaving in a self-serving way.

THE ETHICS OF POWER AND POLITICS

Earlier in the chapter you were asked whether you would be willing to engage in the power of political tactics. What is your answer now? Can you avoid it even if you want to? When, then, is it ethical? In this section, we will take a brief look at some of the ethical issues and their managerial implications.

Tests for Ethical Behavior

To provide some guidelines for testing ethical political and power tactics, we will pose four tests or questions.[33] For behavior to be ethical, it must meet *all four* tests.

1. *Does the behavior support organizational and societal goals?* Behaviors that are self-serving and result in ends that are unfavorable or dysfunctional for the organization are unethical. A person who tries to discredit the boss so that he or she can get the boss' job is behaving in an unethical manner. An act may also be unethical if its aims are in conflict with societal goals (such as blaming another firm for dumping chemicals into a stream when it is really your firm that is dumping them).

2. *Does the behavior result in optimizing the results?* If the outcome of a political behavior is the greatest good for the greatest number of people, then it is ethical. For example, if you have figured out a way to distort information to force your opponent to withdraw from a contract that is unfavorable to your firm and its stockholders, then the behavior might meet this test for ethics. But remember that this is not simply a restatement of "the end justifies the means," for this is only one of four tests the behavior must meet. Certainly the behavior must support organizational and societal goals as well as result in the greatest good.

3. *Does the behavior violate the rights of the parties?* There are a number of basic human rights, including the right to privacy, freedom of conscience, (you do not have to do something you consider immoral), due process (fair and impartial hearings), free consent (right to be treated only as you knowingly consent to be), and freedom of speech.[34] The notion here is that if any of these basic rights are violated, then the behavior is unethical. An example of unethical behavior is the case used at the opening of this section, where Charlie wanted Lee to leave because his careless handling of toxic waste disposal was costing the company money. Although Charlie engaged in political behavior that was good for society and the company, Lee's rights were clearly violated. Charlie's attempt to discredit him behind his back violated his right of consent—his right to be treated honestly and forthrightly.

4. *Does the behavior violate the rules of justice?* The rules of justice say that people must not be treated arbitrarily but that differences in treatment must be fairly distributed. Individuals who are similar should be treated similarly and those who are different should be treated accordingly. For example, a job evaluation system that assigns points for various job skills and responsibilities, and is then tied to pay, differentiates accurately and fairly between individuals and is thus fair and ethical. If the system were based more on knowing the right people, then it would be unethical. Another aspect of the rules of justice is that the rules should be clearly stated, well published, and consistently enforced. When Al gets a verbal warning for violating the same rule that Bob was suspended for, then the judgement is not consistent and impartial.

Ethics, Power, Politics, and Management

There are no simple answers to the ethics of power and politics. The decision-free method provided in Figure 12.3 can only be a rough guide. Each manager

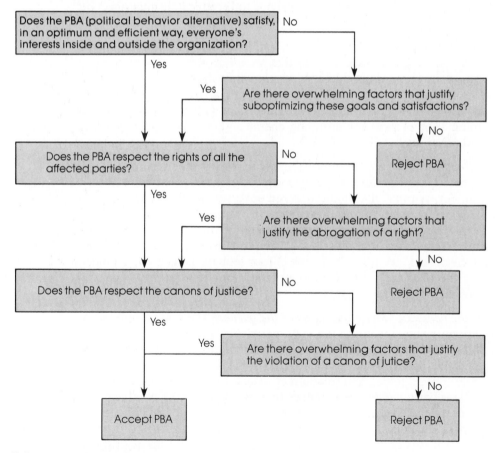

Figure 12.3

DECISION–TREE APPROACH TO RESOLVING ETHICS DECISIONS

SOURCE: Adapted from G.F. Cavanagh, D.J. Moberg, and M. Velasques, (1981). The ethics of organizational politics, *Academy of Management Review* 6:368. Copyright © 1981 by Academy of Management. Used with permission of publisher and authors.

must personally struggle with ethical questions and conflicts of self-interest versus the interests of the organization or others. In spite of the ethical problems, power and politics are an ever-present part of organizational life. They represent the leverage that allows managers to get the job done. Without power it would be difficult, if not impossible, to lead, motivate, or control organizational behavior.

CROSS-CULTURAL OB: POWER DYNAMICS IN CHINA

Two Americans, who developed and taught a management course in Bejing, China, found that classroom behavior of their Chinese students told them a lot about the power relationships in Chinese organizations. After the 30–week course was over, students were asked to rank each group members' contribution to their group study efforts. Group leaders had been appointed at random at the beginning of the course. Students were asked to work together to arrive at the ranking decision. The trainers observed the group processes and decision making. Here is what happened in the words of the trainers: [35]

> Every group began their meetings with each member offering to be ranked last. This struggle for last place continued feverishly for approximately 15 minutes, which was one-half of the allotted meeting time. The student who had protested loudest and offered the most convincing argument for being the worst "won the honor" of lowest rank. Pleased with this victory, the lowest-ranked student relaxed into a quiet contentment.
>
> Each group then nominated and ratified the assigned group leader as first in the ranking. Each group member offered support and evidence for the rightful designation of the group leader as deserving the highest rank. The group leader declined the nomination several times before modestly accepting. This procedure took about 15 minutes, using up the remaining discussion time. Students then either hurriedly drew lots for middle rankings or declined to attempt ranking the remaining members.
>
> We were surprised by this process. We were also surprised that every group had behaved in the same manner. After asking the students to analyze this for us, we began to see the reasons behind the consistent use of the process.
>
> The fight for last place was a face-saving ritual performed for the benefit of the lowest group member. Everyone's admission of her or his own shortcomings created an atmosphere in which the worst member could feel comfortable. Moreover, the competition for last place allowed the worst member to "win" the title of lowest rank. By framing a defeat as a victory, the defeated person could feel satisfied with "winning" last place.
>
> Leaders were awarded first place in deference to their formal authority. Deference to authority is integral to traditional Chinese society. Early family relationships with elders set the tone for later adult relationships with authority. Indeed, one could "lose face" by failing to show proper rituals of "submission/dependency" and deference to the authority figure.[36] The appropriate behaviors in the presence of authority influenced more than just deference to the appointed group leader. We also saw evidence of deference to the authority of the trainers.
>
> One group discussion was interrupted by a ruckus in the courtyard outside. The scuffle sounded serious enough that we ran to the courtyard to intervene. When we arrived, members of a group whose meeting we had just observed scat-

Perspective 12.6

POWER DISTANCE
IN VARIOUS CULTURES[37]

A large study of one major international firm with offices in 40 countries resulted in 116,000 questionnaire responses. While many different aspects of organizational behavior were examined (*see* Chapter 5 for another part of the study), one salient point was the study of power distance across cultures. The index of power distance reflects "the extent to which a society accepts the fact that power in institutions and organizations is distributed unequally."[38] Examples of large power distance include such items as:[39]

- Powerholders are entitled to privileges.

- Superiors consider subordinates to be a different kind of people.

- The way to change a system is to dethrone those in power.

- Superiors are inaccessible.

- A few people should be independent; most should be dependent.

- Latent conflict exists between the powerful and powerless.

Examples of small power distance include such items as:

- All should have equal rights.

- Superiors consider subordinates to be "people like me."

- The way to change a system is to redistribute power.

- Superiors are accessible.

- Latent harmony exists between the powerful and the powerless.

Figure 12.4 shows the results of the research. Note that while the United States ranks below average on power distance, it is still much higher than a number of other Western countries. The authority-oriented countries of Latin and South America show high power distance scores, as do most Asian countries. What implications for managers does this data have for operating in areas where power-distance differs from that of the United States?

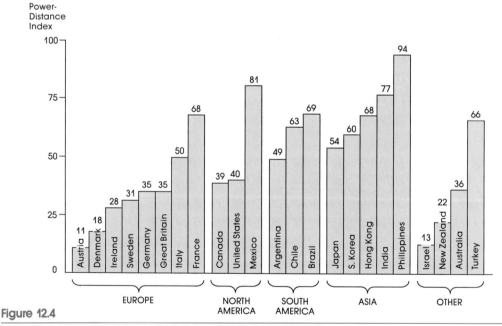

Figure 12.4

POWER DISTANCE INDICES FOR VARIOUS COUNTRIES

SOURCE: Based on data from Hofstede, G. (1983). The cultural relativity of organizational practices and theories. *Journal of International Business Studies, 14*, 84. Also, data from Hofstede, personal correspondence June 12, 1987.

tered. No one at the scene would explain what had taken place. Later we pieced together the story with the aid of volunteer, but secretive, informants. The appointed leader had actually contributed very little to the group, and the other members, who had done his work for him, felt a personal antagonism and dislike toward the leader. During the group exercise these group members exhibited what they considered to be the proper behavior of electing the leader to the highest rank. As soon as the group was not in the presence of the teacher-authorities, however, they showed their dislike for the leader.

MANAGERIAL APPLICATIONS OF POWER AND POLITICS

Recognizing and using power is at the very core of a manager's job. To get things done you must have and use power. However, you must also recognize that power often results because those you are trying to influence accept your power. Thus, every action should consider the effects of your behavior on your subordinates, superiors, and peers. Here are some additional guides for action:

- *Evaluate your own need for power.* Are you interested in wielding power? Do you have a desire to give orders and control? Are you interested in getting things done through others? If you answered "yes", you may have a high need for power and may thus be well suited to managerial work. If you answered "no," perhaps you should reevaluate your career goals.

- *Choose jobs that have the greatest power potential.* Carefully evaluate positions to see if they have legitimate power or offer good opportunities to build expertise, make powerful connections in the organization, or control resources. Choose a career track, such as marketing, production, or finance, based upon its potential for power.

- *Develop interdependancies with others.* Make friends and alliances with others by helping them out and creating feelings of obligation.

    Use reward and expert power whenever possible. These two sources of power are particularly good for new managers. Positive reinforcement is always a good source of power; use it. Build your expertise in some relevant area where you will be the "person to ask."

- *Perform extraordinarily well, take risks, and reorganize to enhance power.* Research has shown that these three power tactics are often successful in large organizations.

- *Recognize and use nonverbal signals of power.* Shoulder holds, interruptions, spatial signals, visual attention, and eyebrows can all be important indicators of power. In addition, office location, layout, and furnishings can create powerful impressions.

- *Develop enlightened self-interest.* Since self-interest and political behavior are inevitable in organizations, try to develop that which is congruent with the organization's and society's self-interest.

- *Carefully evaluate others' self-interest.* Since not everyone will have enlightened self-interest, try to identify what others are striving for. It will help predict their behavior and the types of tactics they will employ.

- *Recognize and be ready to use or counter political tactics.* Using information, creating favorable images, forming coalitions and alliances, building external constituencies, cooptation, and blaming others are tactics to be concerned about.

- *Make sure your use of political strategies is ethical.* Test political behaviors or actions to make sure they do not interfere with the rights of others and that they are directed toward the optimization of organizational goals.

- *Manage power relationships differently in other cultures.* Evaluate the power-distance orientation of people in another culture that you must deal with. For example, in Europe power sharing is appropriate while in much of Latin America and Asia a more centralized, hierarchical approach seems warranted. Be aware of the importance of "face" in dealing with Asians.

FOR DISCUSSION

1. How does power differ from influence? From politics?

2. Give an example of how you might create power through dependence. Would your example be ethical?

3. When the tactic of "identifying with powerful people" is used, what sources of power (reward, coercive, expert, referent, or legitimate) are involved?

4. How do the power games described in Perspective 12.2 relate to power tactics?

5. Explain why the use of coercive power may cause problems for the manager.

6. Table 12.3 gives a number of methods used for upward influence by subordinates. Which of these methods do you recommend using or avoiding? Why?

7. Analyze the reasons for the degree of political activity in various business functions indicated by the answers to the quiz in Table 12.4.

8. Using the four tests for ethical behavior, make an ethical determination for each of the political tactics (for example, blaming or attacking others, use of information).

9. How does the use of power apply to other topics in organizational behavior, such as motivation, decision making, and leadership?

10. Assume you are taking a management position with a firm that manufactures electronics parts in Mexico. What changes in managerial behavior will be needed to operate in that culture?

KEY CONCEPTS AND TERMS

power	expert power	power tactics
influence	referent power	political tactics
authority	legitimate power	coalitions
dependence	zone of acceptance	cooptation
interdependence	power balancing	enlightened self-interest
reward power	nonverbal signals of power	power distance
coercive power	organizational politics	

Cases and Incidents

RESEARCH AND DEVELOPMENT AT GENERAL RUBBER

Sam and Bob are highly motivated research scientists who work in the new-product development lab at General Rubber. Sam is by far the most technically competent scientist in the lab, and he has been responsible for several patents that have netted the company nearly six million dollars in the past decade. He is quiet, serious, and socially reserved. In contrast, Bob is outgoing and demonstrative. While Bob lacks the technical track record Sam has, his work has been solid though unimaginative. Rumor has it that Bob will be moved into an administrative position in the lab in the next few years.

According to lab policy, a $300,000 fund is available every year for the best new-product development idea proposed by a lab scientist in the form of a competitive bid. Accordingly, Sam and Bob both prepare proposals. Each proposal is carefully constructed to detail the benefits to the company and to society if the proposal is accepted, and it is the consensus of other scientists from blind reviews that both proposals are equally meritorious. Both proposals require the entire $300,000 to realize any significant results. Moreover, the proposed line of

research in each requires significant mastery of the technical issues involved and minimal need to supervise the work of others.

After submitting his proposal, Sam takes no further action aside from periodically inquiring about the outcome of the bidding process. In contrast, Bob begins to wage what might be termed an open campaign in support of his proposal. After freely admitting his intentions to Sam and others, Bob seizes every opportunity he can to point out the relative advantages of his proposal to individuals who might have some influence over the decision. So effective is this open campaign that considerable informal pressure is placed on those authorized to make the decision on behalf of Bob's proposal. Bob's proposal is funded and Sam's is not.

DISCUSSION QUESTIONS

1. What political tactics are used?
2. In your opinion, are the tactics ethical? Why or why not?
3. Use the decision tree (Fig. 12.3) to sort out an ethics decision. Was the decision different from your personal one? How?

From G.F. Cavanagh, D.J. Moberg, and M. Velasques (1981). The ethics of organizational politics. *Academy of Management Review* 6:369. Copyright © 1981 by Academy of Management. Used with permission of publisher and authors.

THE SHOWDOWN: HOW HENRY FORD FIRED LEE IACOCCA by *Lee Iacocca*

At the beginning of 1977, Henry declared war. He brought in McKinsey & Company, the management-consultant people, to reorganize our top administration. When the project was over, an executive high in the company left a little note on my desk that said, in effect: "Hang in there, Lee. But it won't be easy. Your boss is an absolute total dictator and I don't know how you guys put up with it."

After months of study and a couple of million dollars in fees, McKinsey issued its recommendation. The plan called for a troika—a three-member office of the chief executive—to replace the standard structure of chairman and president.

The new arrangement was formally established in April. Henry, of course, remained as chairman and chief executive officer. Phil Caldwell was named vice-chairman, while I continued as president.

We each had our own areas of responsibility, but the key change—and the obvious reason for the new arrangement—was spelled out in a memo issued by Henry, which specified that "The Vice Chairman is the Chief Executive Officer in the absence of the Chairman." In other words, if Henry was first among equals, Phil Caldwell was now second.

Making Caldwell number two brought my fight with Henry out in the open. Until then, it had been guerrilla tactics. But now Henry was getting bolder. The entire management shift was no more than an ornate and expensive way to defuse my power in a socially acceptable manner. Without having to confront me directly, Henry had succeeded in installing Caldwell above me.

It was a real crack in the face. Every time there was a dinner, Henry hosted table one, Caldwell hosted table two, and I was shoved down to three. It was public humiliation, like the guy in the stockade in the center of town.

He tore me up inside. He tore up my wife and my kids. They knew I was under great pressure, but I didn't tell them all the details. I didn't want them to go crazy. I was killing myself but I wouldn't yield. It might have been pride, it might have been stupidity, but I was not going to crawl out of there with my tail between my legs.

The office of the chief executive was a three-headed monster. It was ridiculous that Caldwell, who used to work for me, was suddenly above me for no apparent reason except malice. Privately, I told Henry that his new plan was a big mistake. But in typical fashion, he tried to reassure me with platitudes. "Don't worry," he said. "It will all work out in the end."

Although I was boiling inside, in public I defended the new structure. I reassured all the people who worked for me that the new arrangement was perfectly fine.

Not surprisingly, the office of the chief executive didn't last very long. In June of 1978, fourteen months after it was established, Henry announced another shift in top management. Instead of three members, our little team would now have four. The new arrival was William Clay Ford, Henry's younger brother. Bill was brought in to maintain a Ford family presence in the event of Henry's illness or death.

Now I had dropped to fourth in the pecking order. Moreover, I was reporting not to Henry but to Phil Caldwell, who was named deputy chief executive officer. To make the humiliation complete, Henry didn't even bother to tell me about this new restructuring until the day before it was announced.

When he finally gave me the news, I said: "I think you're making a mistake."

"That's my decision and the board's," he snapped.

It was salami-slicing time—one slice at a time. I was getting cut up. Each day I found another part of my body missing. I put out the word that I wasn't going to take it.

Four days later, on June 12, Henry met with our nine outside board members and told them he was about to fire me. This time the board drew the line. They said: "No, Henry, you're doing this wrong, let's

cool it. We'll talk to Lee. We'll work things out. You go in and apologize to him."

"I lost my board today," he told Franklin Murphy.

The next day Henry came to my office for only the third time in eight years. "Let's bury the hatchet," he said.

The board had decided that I should get together with some of its members to try to iron out the problems. Over the next couple of weeks, I met separately with Joseph Cullman, chairman of Philip Morris in New York, and George Bennett, president of the State Street Investment Corporation in Boston. There was nothing secret about these meetings. It was their idea. I flew to see each of them on the company plane and I submitted expense accounts, so they were all a matter of record.

The false peace lasted one month. On the evening of July 12, 1978, Henry had dinner with the outside board members, as he did every month on the eve of the board meeting. Again he announced that he was going to fire me. Now he claimed I was ganging up on him by going to the outside directors behind his back—even though they had asked for the meeting with me. He also said that the personal chemistry between the two of us had never been right. It seems to have taken Henry Ford thirty-two years to decide he didn't get along with me.

This time, too, several of the board members challenged him. They cited my loyalty and my value to the company. They asked Henry to reinstate me to my former position as number two man.

Henry was livid. He wasn't used to backtalk from the board. "It's him or me," he growled. "You have twenty minutes to make up your minds." Then he stormed out of the room.

Until this point he had not dared to fire the guy who was making him all this money, who was the father of the Mustang and the Mark and the Fiesta, and who was so popular in the company. I think he had doubts as to whether he could get away with it.

But finally, in frustration, he just blew his stack. "It's taken three whole years," he must have been thinking, "and this bastard's still here!" When he couldn't get me to quit, he finally decided to move in and occupy the land. He could always justify it later.

That same night I received a telephone call from Keith Crain. Crain was the publisher of *Automotive News*, the trade weekly of the car industry. "Say it isn't so," he said.

I had no doubt as to what he meant. Crain was a close friend of Henry's son, Edsel, and my guess is that Henry had instructed Edsel to leak the story to him. That way, I could learn about my own firing indirectly, through the press.

It was classic Henry. He wanted the news of my firing to reach me through a third party. Henry was a pro at turning the screws. This move also ensured that the king wouldn't have to get his hands dirty with messy affairs of state.

DISCUSSION QUESTIONS

1. What power tactics did Henry Ford use to decrease Iacocca's power? Did they work?

2. What were Ford's sources of power?

3. What political tactics were used by Ford to remove Iacocca? Were the behaviors ethical?

4. What strategies were used by Iacocca to counter Ford's power and political tactics? How successful were they? What other tactics did Iacocca overlook?

From Iacocca, L. (1984). *Iacocca: An autobiography.* New York: Bantam Books, pp. 124–126. Used with permission.

REFERENCES

1. From Reichman, W., & Ley, M. (1977). Personal power enhancement: A way to executive success. *Management Review, 66*(3), pp. 28–29.

2. Kotter, J.P. (1986). Why power and influence issues are at the very core of executive work. In Srivasta and Associates (Eds.). *Executive Power* (pp. 20–32). San Francisco: Jossey-Bass.

3. For discussions of definitions of power, see the following references. Pfeffer, J. (1981). *Power in organizations.* Boston: Pittman. Cobb, A.T. (1984). An episodic model of power: Toward an integration of theory and research. *Academy of Management Review, 9,* 482–493. Grimes, A.J. (1978). Authority, power, influence, and social control: A theoretical synthesis. *Academy of Management Review, 3,* 723–735. Kakabadse, A., & Parker, C. (Eds.). (1984). *Power, politics, and organizations: A behavioural science view.* Chinchester, England: Wiley.

4. This definition follows that used by Allen, R.W., & Porter, L.W. (1983). *Organizational influence processes* (p. 3). Glenview, IL: Scott, Foresman. Also see Kipnis, D., Schmidt, S.M., & Wilkinson, I. (1980). Intraorganizational influence tactics: Explorations in getting one's way. *Journal of Applied Psychology, 65,* 440–442. And Schilit, W.K., & Locke, E.A. (1982). A study of upward influence in organizations. *Administrative Science Quarterly, 27,* 304–316.

5. Allen & Porter (1983), p. 3.

6. Allen & Porter (1983), pp. 124–25.

7. This discussion is heavily influenced by the classic works of French, J.R.P., Jr., & Raven, B. (1959). The bases of social power. In D. Cartwright (Ed.). *Studies in social power* (pp. 150–167). Ann Arbor: University of Michigan ISR. For a recent review see Podsakoff, P., & Schriesheim, C. (1985). Field studies of French and Raven's bases of power.

Psychological Bulletin, 97, 387–411. Also see Pfeffer (1981).

8. See Kotter, J.P. (1985). *Power and influence.* New York: Free Press. Kotter, J.P. (1977). Power, dependence, and effective management. *Harvard Business Review, 55*(4), 125–36. And Pfeffer (1981).

9. McClelland, D.C., & Burnham, D.H. (1976, March-April). Power is the great motivator. *Harvard Business Review,* pp. 102–103.

10. The importance of rewarding behavior is reviewed in Kerr, S. (1975). On the folly of rewarding A, while hoping for B. *Academy of Management Journal, 18,* 769–782.

11. Crozier, M. (1964). *The bureaucratic phenomenon.* Chicago: University of Chicago Press.

12. Astley, W.G., & Sachdeva, P.S. (1984). Structural sources of intraorganizational power: A theoretical synthesis. *Academy of Management Review, 9,* 104–113.

13. Benfari, R.C., Wikinson, H.E., & Orth, C.D. (1986, May-June). The effective use of power. *Business Horizons, 29,* 12–16.

14. Pfeffer (1981) has a complete discussion on assessing power.

15. From *Survival in the office,* by Anthony DuBrin. Copyright © 1977 by Mason/Charter Publishers. Reprinted by permission of Van Nostrand Reinhold Company.

16. For a thorough discussion of mentors, see Jennings, E.E. (1971). *Routes to the executive suite.* New York: McGraw-Hill. And Schein, E.H. (1978). *Career dynamics: Matching individual and organizational needs.* Reading, MA: Addison-Wesley.

17. Adapted from Kantor, R.M. (1977, July). Power games in the corporation. *Psychology Today,* p. 48 cf.

18. Zand, D.E. (1981). *Information, organization, and power.* New York: McGraw-Hill.

19. Pfeffer (1981), p. 106.

20. Pfeffer (1981), p. 97.

21. Chester I. Barnard talked about the zone of acceptance way back in 1938 in *The functions of the executive.* Cambridge, MA: Harvard University Press.

22. Mainiero, L.A. (1986). A review and analysis of power dynamics in organizational romances. *Academy of Management Review, 11,* 750–762.

23. Archer, D. (1980). *How to expand your social IQ* (pp. 130–131). New York: M. Evans & Co. Used with permission. Also see Fast, J. (1980). *Body politics: How to get power with class.* Norfolk, CT: Tower Books.

24. See Schilit & Locke (1982). Mowday, R.T. (1978). The exercise of upward influence in organizations. *Administrative Science Quarterly, 23,* 137–156. Porter, L.W., Allen, R.W., & Angle, H.L. (1981). The politics of upward influence in organizations. In B. Shaw and L.L. Cummings (Eds.). *Research in organizational behavior* (Vol. 3). Greenwich, CT: JAI Press.

25. For a full discussion of the definitional issues see Gray, B., & Ariss, S.S. (1985). Politics and strategic change across organizational life cycles. *Academy of Management Review, 10,* 707–723. Mayes, B.T., & Allen, R.W. (1977). Toward a definition of organizational politics. *Academy of Management Review, 2,* 627–677. Vredenburgh, D.J., & Maurer, J.G. (1984). A process framework of organizational politics. *Human Relations, 37,* 47–66. And Pfeffer (1981).

26. Gray and Ariss (1985), p. 707.

27. Cavanagh, G.F., Moberg, D.J., & Velasques, M. (1981). The ethics of organizations politics. *Academy of Management Review, 6,* 369–370.

28. Block, P. (1987). *The empowered manager: Positive political skills at work.* San Francisco: Jossey-Bass.

29. This section based in part on Allen, R.W., Madison, D.L., Porter, L.W., Renwick, P.A., & Mayes, B.T. (1979). Organizational politics: Tasks and characteristics of its actors. *California Management Review, 22*(1), 77–83. And Pfeffer (1981), Chapter 5. For additional tactics, see Kipnis, D., Schmidt, S.M., & Wilkinson, I. (1980). Intraorganizational influence tactics: Explorations in getting one's way. *Journal of Applied Psychology, 65,* 440–52.

30. Korda, M. (1975). *Power! how to get it, how to use it* (p. 151). New York: Ballantine.

31. See Pfeffer (1981) for a complete discussion of these issues.

32. Excerpted from Zald, M.N. & Berger, M. (1978, Summer). Corporate coup d'état. *The Wharton Magazine.* University of Pennsylvania Press. Reprinted by permission of the authors.

33. This section is based primarily on Cavanagh et al. (1981).

34. Cavanagh (1981), p. 366.

35. Linsay, C.P., & Dempsey, B.L. (1985). Experiences in training Chinese business people to use U.S. management techniques. *Journal of Applied Behavioral Science, 21,* 75. Reprinted with permission of publisher. Also see Easterby-Smith, M., & Boot, R. (1987). Between cultures: Issues in transferring Western management education methods to China. *The Organizational Behavior Teaching Review, 11*(3), 95–103.

36. Solomon, R.H. (1971). *Mao's revolution and the Chinese political culture.* Berkeley: University of California Press.

37. This perspective is based on data from Hofstede, G. (1980, Summer). Motivation, leadership, and organization: Do American theories apply abroad? *Organizational Dynamics, 9,* 42–63.

38. Hofstede (1980), p. 45.

39. Hofstede (1980), p. 46.

Answers to the level of politics in business functional areas posed in Table 12.4.

Function	Rank
Sales	3
Personnel	5
Marketing staff	1
Purchasing	6
Production	9
Research and development	7
Accounting and finance	8
Board of directors	2
Manufacturing staff	4

Chapter Thirteen

PROBLEM SOLVING AND DECISION MAKING

PREVIEW

- Why do people and organizations make less than optimal decisions to solve their problems?

- Why must some managerial decisions be made intuitively?

- Why use groups for decision making when one exceptional person often makes more accurate decisions than a group?

- When should you involve your subordinates in participative decision making?

- Why do people seem to stick to a decision even when it is obviously a poor one?

- How do you actually use decision-making techniques such as consensus, brainstorming, nominal groups, and delphi?

MAJOR TOPICS

Preview Case: Metro Publishing's New Plant

The Decision Process: How Decisions Get Made

Using Groups for Decision Making

Participation and Delegation in Decision Making

Group Decision-Making Techniques

Cross-Cultural OB: Arab Decision Making

Managerial Applications of Decision Making

Preview Case

METRO PUBLISHING'S NEW PLANT

March 16, 1983: Leigh McManus, CEO of Metro Publishing, located in Boston, had a right to be pleased with the way things were going under her leadership. Sales had quadrupled over the past three years. Profits were up over 200 percent and would be even higher if Metro had enough production capacity to do everything in-house.

Leigh thought to herself: "We've got to build a new production plant. These subcontractors are bleeding us to death. I'm not sure where we should locate the new plant, so rather than go through all the anxiety and hassle of trying to make the decision myself, I'm going to commission a task force. I'll appoint all the experts, and we should get a more accurate and better decision than if I made it myself."

March 17, 1983: A letter signed by Leigh McManus appointed a seven-person task force to decide on the location for the new plant. They were given three months to complete the task and a generous budget for travel, hiring consultants, and other expenses. The task force was made up of all the interested functions—finance, production, marketing, and personnel. It also included an expert in law, real estate, transportation.

March through May 1983: The task force, chaired by Kevin Schultz, worked hard on its task. They visited a number of potential sites. They analyzed relative costs, advantages in transportation, and availability of the kind of manpower they would need to run the plant. Of course there was no easy agreement on the relative importance of various criteria; in fact, there was considerable disagreement and conflict. At one time they even hired a management consultant to help resolve their conflict and aid them in making a decision.

Early June, 1983: They finally resolved their differences and made their decision in favor of Peoria, Illinois. It offered a central location, reasonably priced real estate, and a good labor pool. It was by far the most cost-effective place to locate.

June 21, 1983: Leigh was pleased with the briefing she had just received from the task force. She thought to herself, "I'm pleased with the result. They did an excellent job of analysis and their decision looks good." Leigh decided that her next step would be to appoint the manager for the new plant. She wanted someone who had experience with Metro; someone she knew and trusted. The only logical choice was Lloyd Webb, the present assistant production manager at the Boston plant. She called him into her office to break the good news.

"Lloyd, are you interested in heading up our new plant in Peoria? You would not only become a plant manager but would get the salary of one—almost double what you're now making with lots of opportunities for bonuses." Lloyd had a surprised look on his face. He replied, "Sure, it would be a great promotion, and we could sure use the money, but in Peoria? (with a slight grimace) Let me think about it and check with my wife. I'll let you know tomorrow."

June 22, 1983: Lloyd tells Leigh: "My wife is not in the least interested in moving to the Midwest or Peoria even at double the salary. My kids are also rebelling. The oldest will be a junior in high school this fall. She says she would die if she had to move and leave her friends; from the intensity of her reaction I kind of half-way believe her. To keep peace in my family, I'm going to have to turn down the offer. Now if the new plant were on the East Coast or even the West Coast, I might be able to talk my family into it."

Later: Leigh thinks to herself, "What am I going to do do now? The only logical choice for the job has turned it down. There's nobody else I feel comfortable with. Maybe we should go back to the drawing board and find another, more acceptable location?"

A large part of a manager's job centers around decision making.[1] Managers face many types of decisions, such as:

- Where to locate a new plant.

- Whether to introduce a new product, such as "New Coke."

- Who should be hired to fill a new research job.

- What offer to make in a labor negotiation.

- Whether to accept a promotion in an undesirable location.

- How to implement a change like flexitime.

- How to divide up the travel budget.

- Ways to resolve conflicts between subordinates.

- How to motivate people to produce higher quality products.

These are only a few examples of the many varied types of decisions managers must make. In this chapter we will examine the decision-making process with the aim of improving and sharpening our decision-making capability. We will also look at some common group decision-making strategies and techniques that will help us make better decisions. We will study when to delegate and seek participation in the decision process. Even with all this knowledge, making the right decision is often difficult because of incomplete information, perceptual difficulties, or group pressures. The more complete your understanding of decision processes, the greater your chances of making high-quality decisions.

THE DECISION PROCESS: HOW DECISIONS GET MADE

In this section, we will discuss a basic model of the problem solving and decision process, which involves identifying a problem or goal, developing alternatives, judging the alternatives, and making a choice. We will also find why the process does not always work well. Figure 13.1 illustrates this basic process.

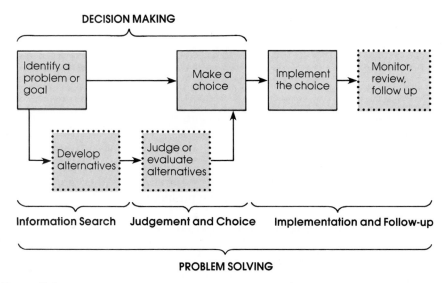

Figure 13.1

THE DECISION–MAKING AND PROBLEM–SOLVING PROCESS

Table 13.1

PROBLEM–SOLVING STEPS

There are a number of good problem-solving models such as the one below. (Note the similarity to the model shown in Figure 13.1.)

- Recognize that a problem exists.

- Define the problem.

- Generate possible solutions to the problem.

- Evaluate alternative solutions (make judgements).

- Choose a course of action (the decision).

- Take action to implement.

- Establish controls and follow up to make sure the problem is solved.

Decision Making and Problem Solving

Decision making is the process of thought and action that results in choice behavior.[2] Decision making differs somewhat from **problem solving**, which involves a systematic process of defining the problem, gathering data, generating alternatives, making a choice between alternatives, implementing the solution, and following up as necessary (*see* Table 13.1).[3] Although the term *problem solving* is often used interchangeably with *decision making,* we will use it to mean a more systematic, rational process that encompasses the decision-making process but adds additional steps (illustrated in Figure 13.1 and Table 13.1). For example, some people make "spur-of-the-moment" decisions such as, "Let's go to the beach," without resorting to the problem-solving process. On the other hand, Kevin Schultz and the task force used a problem-solving approach to generate their recommendation in the opening case.

Identifying Problems or Goals

Perhaps the weakest link in the decision process is identifying and defining the problem. It is easy to misdiagnose or misinterpret the true nature of a problem. In Chapter 4, we learned how perceptions can influence and distort our view of reality. This is particularly true when it comes to problem recognition. One reason why auditors are important for organizations is that they see problems from another perspective and become good at problem identification. Values and attitudes, discussed in Chapter 3, are also important. Since attitudes are a predisposition to respond in some way to an object or event, we may find ourselves responding to a problem because of our attitude rather than the existing facts. Two additional blocks to adequate problem exploration follow.[4]

Defining the Problem in Terms of a Proposed Solution. An example might be: "The problem is that we need a bigger computer." This problem definition states a proposed solution—to get a bigger computer. The real problem might be response time for customer service for which there are a number of possible solutions other than buying a bigger computer.

<table>
<tr><td>

Perspective 13.1

DEFINING PROBLEMS
USING THE
KEPNER–TREGOE APPROACH

A widely employed approach to problem solving, the Kepner-Tregoe method, states that there are several steps to recognizing and defining a problem.[5]

• To find a problem, a manager must be alert; surveillance and inspection are needed.

• The manager must know what the level of performance *should* be so that actual performance can be compared with it and deviations noted. This method defines a problem as a deviation from a standard of performance.

</td><td>

• If the problem is complex, it needs to be separated into subproblems, and priorities are set based upon the problem's urgency, seriousness, and growth trend.

• The problem should be specified in terms of: [6]

What is the deviation, and what is the thing or object on which the deviation is observed?

Where is the deviation on the thing or object, and where are objects with the deviation observed?

When does the deviation appear on the thing or object, and when are objects with deviations observed?

How big are the deviations, and how many objects with deviations are observed?

</td></tr>
</table>

Diagnosing a Problem in Terms of Its Symptoms. We often tend to oversimplify a problem by dealing only with its symptoms. For example, a vice-president notes in a staff meeting that there is a turnover and absentee problem. As we learned in Chapter 3, these behaviors are usually symptoms of some other organizational problem that is causing dissatisfaction, such as supervisory style or job design.

Searching for Alternatives

A perfect problem-solving approach would entail a detailed and complete search for relevant alternatives that might solve the problem. In most cases, however, this search for alternatives may be severely limited or nonexistent due to several processes that will be discussed in this section.

Bounded Rationality. This concept means that although people may seek the best solution, they normally settle for less than the best, because they do not have the capacity to acquire and process the complex information that would be needed for reaching the best solution.[7] People seek to bound or limit the rationality of their search process. For example, if you were in the market for a home computer, your search will probably be limited to two or three models. To gather data about the hundreds of home computers that are available would be a complex, full-time job; thus, you will probably set bounds on your decision process.

Satisficing. One form of bounded rationality is **satisficing,** which means that most decisions, whether individual or organizational are concerned with the selection and discovery of satisfactory alternatives rather than optimal alterna-

Perspective 13.2

KNEE–DEEP IN BIG MUDDY: ESCALATING COMMITMENT TO A COURSE OF ACTION[8]

Some people or organizations seem to get locked into a costly course of action in spite of the potential losses. Instead of cutting our losses when we find ourselves in a losing situation, we often invest more resources; we increase our commitment to a course of action. The classic example is purchasing stock. Say you paid $100 per share, but the price has now declined to $70 per share. Since you are still convinced the stock is a good buy, you invest more money at the $70 bargain price. Then, when the price declines to $50, you are faced with another decision. Often, the choice is to buy again. Here's an additional example: [9]

A company overestimates its capability to build an airplane brake that will meet certain technical specifications at a given cost. Because it wins the government contract, the company is forced to invest greater and greater effort into meeting the contract terms. As a result of increasing pressure to meet specifications and deadlines, records and tests of the brake are misrepresented to government officials. Corporate careers and company credibility are increasingly staked to the airbrake contract, although many in the firm know the brake will not work effectively. At the conclusion of the construction period, the government test pilot flies the plane; it skids off the runway and narrowly misses injuring the pilot.

While the reasons for this phenomenon are not fully known, it appears that there is a strong motivation to justify previous decisions because we want to be seen as competent decision makers and do not want threats to our self-esteem. In addition, there are strong societal norms toward consistency. Thus, we rationalize our commitment to a course of action in light of our past decisions and felt pressures from within ourselves to conform. Another possible explanation centers around whether we have experienced success or failure in previous decisions. A history of successes will result in a choice between gains and will be risk aversive. In contrast, a history of failures will result in choice between losses and will be risk seeking. Thus, escalation to either a positive or negative decision can result, but the negative one carries that greatest chance of loss.[10]

---

tives.[11] The process works something like this: "John, you don't like Applicant *A*, Mary thinks *B* doesn't have enough experience, and I don't think that *C* would fit in. Since no one has any strong feelings one way or the other about *D*, let's offer *D* the job." This decision process could result in hiring a very mediocre performer who is marginally acceptable to everyone. While satisficing and bounded rationality result in less than optimal decisions, they do serve the useful purpose of simplifying the search process. However, a manager should take care to recognize this phenomenon and try to avoid overlooking a particularly good alternative. Has Metro Publishing looked at all the possible new plant locations so that an optimal decision can be made? Probably not.

The Anarchic or "Garbage Can Model". The decision process can also be conceptualized as a garbage can where organizational members deposit problems, preferences, and solutions which get all mixed up in the can. Decisions are then inferred from various combinations of problems and solutions. This way of explaining the process is more formally called **anarchic** decision making.[12] The organization is, in effect, a collection of problems, issues, and feelings looking for decision situations. In other words, any part of the decision process may be able to generate action. A "wonderful solution" may be used to seek out a problem to which it can be applied. The model describes how decisions *are* made rather than how they *should be* made. In most cases the garbage-can model can be avoided by carefully following the sequence of problem solving—beginning with problem identification and definition.

Implicit Favorite Model. It appears that many people who use problem solving pick an implicitly favored solution early in the decision process.[13] Even though the search may be continued, decision rules and perception distortions are used that guarantee the implicit favorite selection. This approach rests heavily on the concept of cognitive dissonance discussed in Chapter 3—once a favorite is chosen, reasons are found to discount the others. An example might be choice of a job. Early in the process, you may develop an implicit favorite. All other possibilities are then ruled out by criteria that insure only the favorite will win.

Evaluating Alternatives

If we have complete information about all the alternatives, know their value, and know the probability that various alternatives will work, evaluating the decision will be easy. But, we know that bounded rationality means we will be working with less than complete information and that through satisficing we will probably settle for less than the best.

Judgment. When we weigh alternatives, we must make a judgment about the acceptability of the possible courses of action, then make our decision. There are two aspects of judgment: expressing preferences and making predictions.[14] In the opening case, Lloyd expressed a preference not to go to Peoria as the main reason for declining the position. The task force made a predictive judgment since they tried to predict an uncertain future. They tried to predict construction costs, labor availability, and transportation advantages, among others.

Using Probabilities to Evaluate Alternatives. Most people in business fields have taken a course in statistics that included the study of probability. Whenever we make predictions, we are consciously or unconsciously predicting the chances of various outcomes. When we discussed motivation theory in Chapter 5, we noted that people may evaluate various outcomes and have certain expectancies (probabilities) about attaining the outcomes. They are motivated (make a decision to behave) based upon these assessments. In the opening case, the task force should have gathered probabilities of getting a plant manager to relocate. Of course, bounded rationality may have prevented them from considering this important data.

An example of the rational use of probabilities would be a business relocation problem. If you were a business owner making a decision about opening a new outlet in the west side versus the east side of the city, you might have different probability assessments for each location alternative. If you locate on

Perspective 13.3

INTUITIVE DECISION MAKING: USING THE RIGHT–BRAIN

Recent evidence suggests that there are differences in the way people make decisions based on whether they are oriented toward the right side of the brain (intuition, feeling, visual-spatial) or the left side of the brain (sequential, fact-seeking, calculating).[15] This raises some controversial issues for managers. Analytic, rational problem solvers, dominated by the left brain, have been accused of causing problems for organizations by overlooking unmeasurable, but important, subtleties and redefining real problems into forms that miss the point.[16] The creative, more humanistic approach to problem solving, exhibited by people with right-brain skills, has often been de-emphasized by managers. Thus, managers need to distinguish between those problems that need analytic, left-brain skills and those that need intuitive, right-brain skills.

Examples of decisions where intuition is important include: [17]

- When a high level of uncertainty exists.

- When little previous precedent exists.

- When variables are less scientifically predictable.

- When "facts" are limited or do not clearly point the way to go.

- When analytical data are of little use.

- When several plausible alternative solutions exist to choose from, with good arguments for each.

- When time is limited and there is pressure to come up with the right decision.

Examples of intuitive decisions include refusing to pull a drug off the market in the face of FDA tests showing adverse reactions in animal tests or supporting the regional decentralization of a mental health department in spite of strong objections.[18]

The value of intuitive decision making is becoming more widely recognized. A study of over 2,000 managers in both private and public-sector organizations found that top managers were better able to use intuition in making key decisions than were lower-level managers.[19] A follow-up study of seventy top executives who scored in the top 10 percent of the intuition scale found that they actually used intuition to guide their major decisions. However, over half the intuition-based decision makers were unwilling to share the fact that they used intuition to guide their most important decisions.[20] It appears that many are embarrassed to admit that they use intuition rather than pure logic.

Another part of the research was to find out what techniques and exercises were used by executives to help activate intuitive decision making. Table 13.2 presents the results.

the east side you estimate that there is a 40 percent chance that the outlet would succeed, but the potential profit is $100,000. On the west side there is a 70 percent chance of success, but the potential profit is only $60,000. Which do you choose?

	Ultimate Value	Probability	Expected Value
East location	$100,000 profit	.4	$40,000 profit
West location	$60,000 profit	.7	$42,000 profit

Choosing Alternatives

The outcome of problem solving and judgment is the actual choice of a course to follow. The choice will be more likely to satisfice rather than maximize the

Table 13.2

HOW TOP EXECUTIVES ACTIVATE INTUITIVE DECISION MAKING

Relaxation Techniques
Clear mind mentally.

Seek quiet times.

Seek solitude.

Listen to classical music.

Sleep on problem.

Fast.

Meditate.

Pray.

Drop problem and return to it later.

Exercise.

Joke.

Mental Exercises
Play freely with ideas without a specific goal in mind.

Practice guided imagery.

Practice tolerating ambiguity and accepting lack of control.

Practice flexibility and openness to unknowns as they appear.

Practice concentration.

Try to think of unique solutions.

Be willing to follow up on points that have no factual justification.

Analytical Exercises
Discuss problem with many colleagues who have different perspectives as well as with respected friends.

Concentrate on listening not only to what but also to how one expresses oneself.

Immerse self totally in the issue at hand.

Identify pros and cons; then assess feeling about each option.

Consider problem only when most alert.

Tune into internal reactions to outside stimuli.

Analyze dreams.

Insist on creative pause before reaching decision.

Ask, "What do I want to do, and what is 'right' to do?"

SOURCE: Adapted from "The Logic of Intuition: How Top Executives Make Important Decisions," by W.H. Agor, *Organizational Dynamics*, (Winter 1986), p. 13. Copyright © 1986 American Management Association, New York. All rights reserved.

outcomes of the problem-solving process. In our opening case, the actual choice of the task force was to relocate to Peoria while Lloyd's choice was to remain in Boston.

Intuitive Decision Making

Few decisions are made based on a careful problem solving and analysis process. In addition to the processes of satificing, choosing implicit favorites, and using a garbage-can model described earlier, many decisions are made instinctively using **programmed decision-making** process. For example, when you are driving a car, the decision to apply the brakes is intuitive since it comes almost automatically and without reasoning. Programmed decisions are based on our past experiences and the reinforcement associated with these experiences. Years of driving experience has taught us precisely when to put on the brakes. The same type of programs often guide an experienced manager's decisions. The decision to discipline an employee, to buy an item for inventory, to sell a stock—all these may be quite intuitive for the manager.

Henry Mintzberg's classic study of managerial behavior found that managers worked at a fast, action-oriented pace.[21] Half of the activities of CEOs lasted less than nine minutes and only 10 percent exceeded an hour. He concluded that executives are action oriented and do not like reflective activities. These data support our observation that much decision making is intuitive. The fast and hectic pace of managerial jobs makes use of programmed decision making almost a necessity.

USING GROUPS FOR DECISION MAKING

Group decision making permeates our lives. We are all part of some group whether it be a family group or a work group. Sometimes there is a choice of whether to use a group, such as Leigh's decision in the opening incident. At other times there may be no choice—we must work in a group; for example, a labor-management negotiating committee. In this section we will discuss the advantages and disadvantages of groups versus individuals. In the next section, we will be discussing when groups should participate in decisions.[22]

Why Use Groups for Decision Making?

Greater Sum Total of Knowledge.   If the problem is complex, then the resources offered by a number of people can all contribute to the solution. Gaps in knowledge of one person can be filled by another. The wide variety of skills and technical expertise, with the potential for cross-checking and verification, make groups more powerful than individuals in this case. An example might be selecting the location for a new plant, such as Metro Publishing did in the opening case. By having representatives from key areas of the company, more expertise and resources were available to help develop a better decision. Another example might be the introduction of a new piece of machinery. Engineers would provide technical input, machinists would see the problem from a more practical perspective, and a production worker could provide information about how well the new machine would be accepted from the operator's perspective.

Greater Number of Approaches to the Problem.   Individuals tend to have tunnel vision. That is, they see only one way of solving the problem. When several people approach a problem, each brings new insights that may result in a better solution. An engineer may see redesign as the answer, while the machinist sees that tolerances need to be changed. In addition, a comment by one person may trigger a new idea or approach from another person.

Group Decisions Are Easier to Implement.   We tend to accept and support decisions that we make rather than those others make. Thus, anytime you anticipate difficulty in getting a decision accepted, group participation in the decision can be an aid. For example, if you want to introduce a new computer into your firm, it may be easier to do so if you involve the key people who have to work with the computer—programmers, operators, data input clerks, managers. Once these people have hashed over the advantages and disadvantages of various alternatives and reached agreement on which computer to buy, it will make it easier to implement the decision. We will discuss participation later in this chapter.

Disadvantages of Groups for Decision Making

Social Pressure Toward Conformity.   This disadvantage has received considerable attention (*see* Perspective 13.4). When we studied group dynamics, we saw that there were pressures toward conformity in the group because of norms and desires for cohesiveness. Group pressures are stronger in groups that have developed a powerful sense of cohesiveness. An example might be the top-management group of an advertising firm who have worked together for years. They know each other well and feel like they are a part of an effective, cohesive team. They are effective, but they have to be careful to make sure that

---

Perspective 13.4

GROUPTHINK

Irving Janis has coined the term **groupthink**, which means a deterioration in mental efficiency, reality testing, and judgment that results from in-group pressures. When a work group or policy group displays most or all of the symptoms related below, its effectiveness will be impaired and decisions will not be of good quality. The eight symptoms of groupthink are:[23]

1. An illusion of invulnerability; shared by most or all the members which creates excessive optimism and encourages taking extreme risks.
2. Collective efforts to rationalize in order to discount warnings which might lead the members to reconsider their assumptions before they recommit themselves to their past policy decisions.
3. An unquestioned belief in the group's inherent morality, inclining the members to ignore the ethical or moral consequences of their decisions.
4. Stereotyped views of enemy leaders as too evil to warrant genuine attempts to negotiate, or as too weak and stupid to counter whatever risky attempts are made to defeat their purposes.
5. Direct pressure on any member who expresses strong arguments against any of the group's stereotypes, illusions, or commitments, making clear that this type of dissent is contrary to what is expected of all loyal members.
6. Self-censorship of deviations from the apparent group consensus, reflecting each member's inclination to minimize to himself the importance of his doubts and counterarguments.
7. A shared illusion of unanimity concerning judgments conforming to the majority view (partly resulting from self-censorship of deviations, augmented by the false assumption that silence means consent).
8. The emergence of self-appointed mindguards—members who protect the group from adverse information that might shatter their shared complacency about the effectiveness and morality of their decisions.

excessive conformity does not result in groupthink and a poor decision. One way to avoid such problems is to establish the role of **devil's advocate,** someone whose task is to question decisions, to take the other side of an issue, or to cast doubt on the decision.[24] It is also a good idea for the group leader to avoid taking a position early in the discussion of a problem.

Individual Domination. A critical aspect of group decision making is the leader. Regardless of whether the leader is appointed or emerges informally, he or she will tend to dominate the decision-making process. If the leader happens to be an effective problem solver, then it makes little difference. If the leader tends to block others or to stubbornly persist, then the group may be ineffective. An example of this type of problem is a hard-charging junior manager at Metro Publishing, Jack Slater. Whenever Jack joins any group without a formal leader, he feels that he should be the leader. By stubborn persistence, he usually wears down his opposition. Once elected leader, he carefully prevents or puts down inputs from people who disagree with him. Thus, the decision is usually Jack's. Needless to say, the decision may not be the same one that would have been chosen with another leader. From this line of reasoning it follows that a manager should be careful who is appointed to decision-making groups; do not appoint the "Jacks" just because they volunteer every time.

Costs. It is costly to use groups for decision making. They are slower than individuals because of all the give and take that is needed to reach a decision. There are lost manhours involved, especially if production workers are used and overtime must be paid. Most of you have experienced a group-decision situation where the discussion and haggling seemed to be endless. However, this extensive discussion is often useful in the long run to resolve conflicts and make sure that all dissenting opinions are heard.

Group Decision Effectiveness

The process of evaluating the overall effectiveness of groups is summarized in Figure 13.2. Research has shown that group decision-making performance is

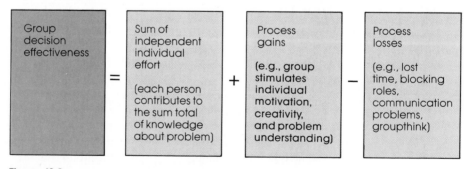

Figure 13.2

GROUP DECISION EFFECTIVENESS

SOURCE: Based on Hill, G.W. (1982), Group versus individual performance: Are N + 1 heads better than one? *Psychological Bulletin, 91,* 517–539.

generally quantitatively superior to the performance of the average individual in the group.[25] However, the best individual in the group is often superior to the group's performance. Thus, groups that contain a number of low-ability individuals may not perform as well as the exceptional individuals in that group.

In addition, the process gains and losses must be weighed to see if group decision making is worth the cost and effort. **Process gains** may include the energizing force of working with other people, a stimulation to creativity when many different ideas are discussed, and a more careful weighing of the pros and cons of a given decision. **Process losses** involve the time and energy that must be expended to reach a decision; communications difficulties that may arise from the group's activities; and the ineffective use of group task, maintenance, and blocking roles.

PARTICIPATION AND DELEGATION IN DECISION MAKING

There are three basic ways that a manager can handle decision making: make the decision alone, allow subordinates to participate in the decision, or delegate the decision entirely to subordinates. This aspect of decision making also involves leadership style and thus serves as an introduction to the leadership process that will be covered in Chapter 14. A continuum of manager decision behaviors is shown in Figure 13.3.

Participation in Decision Making

Participation in decision making has been a subject for organizational writers and researchers for many years.[26] While one can define **participation** in

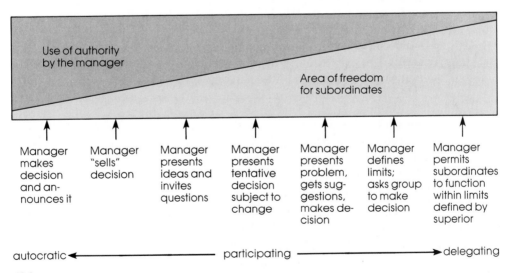

Figure 13.3

A CONTINUUM OF DECISION–MAKING BEHAVIOR

SOURCE: Reprinted and adapted by permission of the *Harvard Business Review.* Figure from "How to choose a leadership pattern," by Robert Tannenbaum and Warren Schmidt (March/April 1958). Copyright © 1958 by the President and Fellows of Harvard College; all rights reserved.

decision making in many ways, we will use it to mean the process of joint decision making by two or more parties.[27] This definition implies that all involved people contribute in some way to the decision. For example, let's say you are a manager and you want your subordinates to participate in the decision to buy a new office copier. Participation here means that you would form a group of interested employees to address the goal (purchase of a copier). You might or might not be a member of the group. If you are not a member, you would probably reserve the right to make the final decision after listening to the group's position. If you actually let the group make the decision, you are delegating—the subject of the next section. The degree of participation can range from almost none to a great deal as illustrated by Figure 13.3.

Research has shown that participation is related to productivity, satisfaction, and other important organizational outcomes.[28] A review of the literature found that there was a mean correlation of .15 between participation and productivity across twenty-five studies.[29] While this effect is far from strong, it does provide some limited link between participation and productivity. Later in the chapter we will discuss the reasons why participation does not always have a positive outcome. Participation is more strongly related to job satisfaction with a mean correlation of .34 for forty-one studies.[30] Participation in decision making can add satisfaction to the job in many ways. It can provide better feedback, increased task significance, and help instill a sense of responsibility for work outcomes. It can open up communication channels between bosses and subordinates. And it results in better utilization of employees' skills and abilities.

Delegating Decisions

When you **delegate** a decision, you allow a subordinate or group to actually make the decision. You transfer authority to a subordinate and give that person the freedom to make the decision.[31] Delegation is the way managers get more done and avoid being bogged down in details and minor decisions. This skill is a difficult one for many managers to master. Many managers want to be involved in everything; however, this means that they often pay the price of long working hours and little personal time.

Most top executives find delegation strategies are crucial for their success. For example, Ronald Reagan says: "Surround yourself with the best people you can find, delegate authority, and don't interfere as long as the policy you've decided upon is being carried out." [32] Mark McCormack, successful CEO and author of *What They Don't Teach You at Harvard Business School*, gives his views on delegation:

> People will often delegate—or fail to delegate—for all the wrong reasons. They hold on to a task because they like doing it, or want to do it, or are afraid of not doing it, and they will pass down some task because they find it distasteful or "beneath them" or have rationalized that it is not the best use of their time.[33]

Of course, not all decisions are candidates for delegation. For example, if Leigh McManus, the CEO in our opening case, had told the task force that their decision was final on site selection, she would have been delegating the decision. In fact, Leigh would not delegate such a decision because the ultimate responsibility for a correct decision of such magnitude is hers. Thus, she will listen to the task force, and quite probably follow their advice, but she would still share in the decision. Thus, the task force was working under participative decision making, not delegation.

When to Use Participation and Delegation

In this section, we will briefly cover the key issues involved in deciding when to use participation and delegation. There are a number of keys to using participation and delegation effectively. One way of systematizing the issues is the **Vroom-Yetton Model.**[34] There are two major parts to this model: decision-making options and rules for deciding on the options. Remember that these decisions are also related to leadership styles, ranging from autocratic to democratic decision-making behavior.

Decision-Making Options: The Vroom-Yetton Model

The Vroom-Yetton Model uses six decision-making options that are developed from and closely related to those described in Figure 13.3. The six options are:

1. Make the decision yourself based upon available information (called *Autocratic I,* or AI).

2. Obtain the information from subordinates, but make the decision yourself (called *Autocratic II,* or AII).

3. Get ideas and suggestions from your subordinates on an individual basis and then make your decision, which may or may not reflect subordinates' inputs (called *Consultative I,* or CI).

4. Share the problem with your subordinates as a group to get their collective inputs and ideas. Again, the decision may or may not reflect subordinates' inputs (called *Consultative II,* or CII).

5. Share the problem with your subordinates as a group and jointly develop a decision which reflects the consensus of everyone in the group. Your role in this case is like a "chair" rather than a "boss"; you try not to influence the group towards a solution (called *Group,* or G).

6. Delegate the decision to the individual or group with full authority for making the decision. (This option is not shown in Figure 13.4 because that model refers primarily to group participation.)

Rules for Participative Decision Making

There are several key factors or rules that determine whether or not to use participation. Vroom and Yetton have arranged them into a decision tree. Each decision point shown in Figure 13.4 is explained below. Use the letters to cross-reference between the figure and the text.

A: Does It Make a Difference Which Course of Action Is Adopted?   Some decisions, such as which delivery driver gets a new truck, may make little or no

difference to the manager so long as the decision is accepted by all the drivers. However, the decision to get rid of one of the trucks may make a difference since the one that is in the worst mechanical condition or that has been fully depreciated might be chosen so the overall costs are lowered.

B: How Important Is the Quality of the Decision?   If the outcome of the decision, such as the plant location, is crucial, then the decision should not be delegated although participation may be used with final approval reserved for the manager.

C: Who Has the Knowledge to Make the Decision?   If you do not have the knowledge that is needed, it is difficult to make a good decision. This goes both ways. Sometimes subordinates have knowledge of actual processes that makes them the experts. Then, participation or delegation would be appropriate. On the other hand, if the manager or the electrical engineer is the only one with the knowledge to make the decision, then participation may not be warranted unless there is some other reason to use it, such as getting the idea accepted. If a problem needs an expert to solve it, then a group should not be used. For example, a firm might have a complex problem concerning the issue of corporate bonds. It would not make sense to use representatives from throughout the firm to participate in the decision because most of them would not have the expertise needed. What is needed is a financial expert.

D: Is the Problem Structured?   If the problem is one where the decision is relatively structured or programmed, then its solution means that adequate research is the key to the solution. This normally does not require a group effort. If, on the other hand, the problem is very complex and unstructured, a group can bring varied knowledge and insights that can result in a more accurate decision. An example of such a complex, unstructured decision might be the introduction of a new product, such as New Coke.

E: Is Acceptance of the Decision Critical for Implementing It?   People are often more committed to decisions they help make. For example, if you want to change to a new management information system, it is crucial that people who must use the system support the change. If they do not, it may be extremely difficult, time consuming, and costly to implement the system because of overt or covert resistance.

F: If You Make the Decision Yourself, Is it Reasonably Certain That It Will Be Accepted by Your Subordinates?   This question follows directly from E. If subordinates do not accept the decision, it may be very difficult, if not impossible, to implement it. As we have seen in the last chapter, subordinates often have a great deal of power that can frustrate implementing even the best decision.

G: Do Subordinates Share the Goals Associated With the Decision?   Let's say that your goal is improved organizational effectiveness, especially in terms

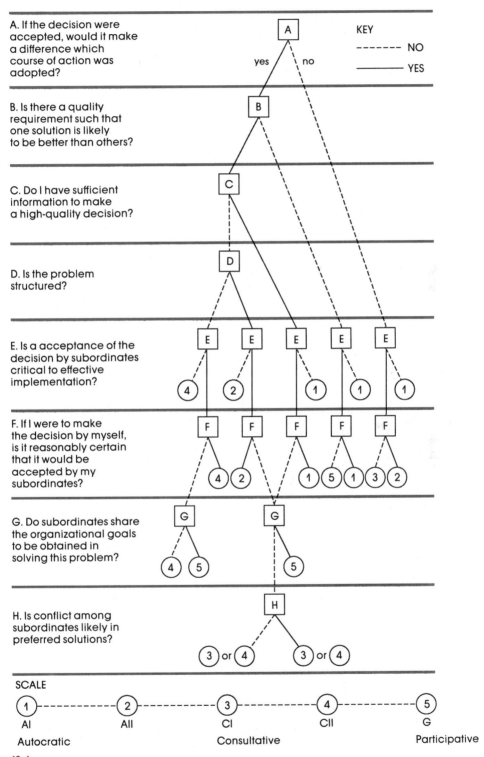

A. If the decision were accepted, would it make a difference which course of action was adopted?

KEY
------- NO
———— YES

B. Is there a quality requirement such that one solution is likely to be better than others?

C. Do I have sufficient information to make a high-quality decision?

D. Is the problem structured?

E. Is a acceptance of the decision by subordinates critical to effective implementation?

F. If I were to make the decision by myself, is it reasonably certain that it would be accepted by my subordinates?

G. Do subordinates share the organizational goals to be obtained in solving this problem?

H. Is conflict among subordinates likely in preferred solutions?

SCALE

1 — AI — Autocratic
2 — AII
3 — CI — Consultative
4 — CII
5 — G — Participative

Figure 13.4

THE VROOM–YETTON MODEL OF THE GROUP DECISION PROCESS

SOURCE: Adapted from *Leadership and Decision-Making* by Victor H. Vroom and Philip W. Yetton by permission of the University of Pittsburgh Press. © 1973 by University of Pittsburgh Press.

of lower production costs. If your subordinates have a different goal, such as preserving work standards and maintaining social relationships with their co-workers, then participation or delegation would be futile.

H: Are Subordinates Likely to Agree on a Position?   If positions are polarized between two or more groups so that a joint solution is unlikely, then participation should not be used. Say one group of employees is interested in getting more overtime while another is more interested in preventing overtime. These opposing positions create conflict which may be intensified by participative decision making.

I: Do Subordinates Have Sufficient Information to Make a High Quality Decision?   This question relates to delegation. If a subordinate does not have the knowledge to solve the problem and make the decision, then delegation should be avoided. While delegation is not illustrated in Figure 13.4, this question may be asked as a final branch on the decision tree to determine whether delegation is appropriate.[35]

Examples Using the Vroom-Yetton Model

Overseas Assignment.   Jane Flores, director of engineering, has just heard from her boss that another division of the company, located in the Middle East, has placed an emergency request for four engineers to help with a high-priority project. Jane agrees that their help is needed and that she has the resources to meet the requirement. There is no reason why one engineer should be chosen over another. Using the Vroom-Yetton model, Jane would answer *no* to question *A*, since it makes little difference to her how the problem is solved so long as four engineers are chosen. The next question *E*, "Is acceptance of the decision important?" must be answered *yes*. If the wrong people are chosen, morale will be affected and key engineers may be alienated and could even quit. Question *F*, "If I make the decision alone, will subordinates accept it?" must be answered *no*. No matter how she decides, it is impossible to consider all the personal and professional motivations of the engineers to go or to stay home. Thus, the only reasonable way to handle this decision is to use *CI:* participative, group decision making. Let the engineers work out a consensus for solving the problem of who will go.

Factory Construction.   In this case assume that you are the project supervisor for building a new factory. You have seven engineers and three architects working for you, each of them specializing in some subsystem of the factory. You are the only one with a business management background and detailed financial knowledge of the entire project. The question is: Should you involve your staff in the decision of whether or not to ask for more money to cover anticipated cost overruns? Work out the answer on your own using the decision tree. Would you involve the group? How?

GROUP DECISION–MAKING TECHNIQUES

While there are many decision-making techniques, we will emphasize four: group consensus, brainstorming, nominal groups, and Delphi.[36] Consensus and brainstorming use interacting groups comprised of people who are actively working together on a face-to-face basis with open discussion and communication. The nominal technique mixes interactive and noninteractive strategies, and Delphi does not involve the direct interaction of group members.

Group Consensus

When committees or task forces work together to solve some problem or make some decision, they often use a technique called **group consensus,** which means that a decision should be acceptable to all group members even though some members may not completely agree with it.[37] While complete unanimity is not the goal of consensus, each individual should be given an opportunity to express dissent. Each must be able to agree, at least in part, with the decision. Group members should not acquiesce until they feel relatively comfortable about the decision. Listed below and in Figure 13.5 are some guidelines for reaching consensus:

- Avoid arguing for your own position until you have carefully listened to the position of others. You should state your position clearly and listen carefully to others' comments about it. Try to be rational and avoid arguing for your position just because it is yours.

- Do not change your mind simply to avoid conflict and confrontation. If you cannot support a decision, state your case—stand up for what you believe. However, you should carefully explore your reasons for taking a position. Are they sound? Do others agree with them? On the other hand, you should yield to the arguments of others when they are sound and reasonable.

- Try to avoid win-lose dynamics. When the discussion reaches a stalemate, carefully evaluate each position; try to search for other alternatives; or perhaps turn to brainstorming.

- Avoid conflict-reducing techniques. Majority vote or coin-tosses should be avoided, although there is some evidence that a majority vote *prior* to a group discussion may result in better decisions.[38]

- View differences of opinion as helpful. Try to establish a norm of speaking up if you differ. Since one of the major advantages of groups is the varied resources and points of view that others bring to the decision, it only makes sense to try to take advantage of this diversity.

Consensus is probably the most widely used group-decision strategy. Whenever a task force is created, such as the Metro Publishing site selection group in the opening example, it normally uses consensus as the primary method for arriving at decisions. Most corporate staff meetings rely on consensus as their primary strategy. Even though consensus is widely used, it is often less effective than it might be because the guidelines cited above are not followed or because of political and power tactics of the decision makers.[39]

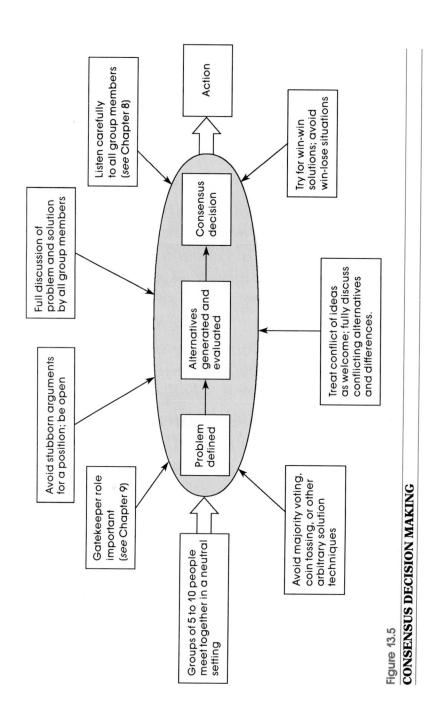

Figure 13.5
CONSENSUS DECISION MAKING

Creativity Through Brainstorming

This technique, developed by Alec Osborne, has been around for over forty years.[40] **Brainstorming** is a system for creatively generating alternatives. Evaluate your own attitudes toward ideation by completing the questionnaire in Table 13.3 before reading the remaining discussion.

Brainstorming's strong point is that **ideation** is separated from **evaluation.** There is a natural tendency for people to evaluate a proposed solution immediately. Often, people get so bogged down criticizing and evaluating ideas that many excellent ones are overlooked. Thus, the principle of **deferred judgment** is a key element of the process.[41]

As an idea-generation technique, brainstorming may not be any more effective than the pooled effort of a number of people generating ideas on their own.[42] However, the technique is simple, widely used, easy to do, and fun. Here are the general procedures for brainstorming.

The central problem to be addressed needs to be clearly stated, in writing, on a piece of paper or a blackboard. The problem should be

---

Table 13.3

IDEATION QUESTIONNAIRE

Instructions: The following is a series of questions designed to increase understanding of how people approach ideas and problem solving. None of these questions are meant to *evaluate* you in any way. There are no right or wrong answers. Please answer each question as naturally and honestly as you can.

Listed below are several statements concerning various situations. Indicate whether you agree or disagree with each statement by writing the number beside each question.

1	2	3	4	5
Strongly disagree	Disagree	Neither agree nor disagree	Agree	Strongly agree

_____ 1. I feel that people at work ought to be encouraged to share *all* their ideas, because you never know when a crazy-sounding one might turn out to be the best.

_____ 2. One new idea is worth ten old ones.

_____ 3. I think people should say whatever pops into their heads whenever possible.

_____ 4. I like to listen to other people's crazy ideas since even the wackiest often leads to the best solution.

_____ 5. I feel that all ideas should be given equal time and listened to with an open mind regardless of how zany they seem to be.

_____ 6. The best way to generate new ideas is to listen to others, then tailgate or add on.

Scoring: Add the scores for all the questions. This is your *preference for ideation* score. If you scored 22 or over, you have a high preference for ideation groups. If you scored 16 or below, you have a low preference for ideation groups.

Adapted from Basadur, M., & Finkbeiner, C.T. (1985). Measuring preference for ideation in creative problem-solving training. *Journal of Applied Behavioral Science, 21,* 42–43. Reprinted with permission of publisher.

narrowed to some manageable level. For example, brainstorming, "How can we increase profitability?" is perhaps too broad a question. A more focused question might be, "In what ways might we decrease costs on the new brake assemblies?"

Rules of Brainstorming.   Carefully enforcing the rules is the key to successful outcomes because it forces deferred judgment and encourages large quantities of ideas. Post the rules on flip-chart paper so you can merely point them out to get compliance. There are four rules:

1. Absolutely no evaluation, verbal or nonverbal. Criticism is not allowed.

2. Freewheeling is welcome. The wilder the ideas, the better. No idea is too wild. An unusual idea may trigger some more feasible idea in another participant's mind.

3. Quantity is welcome and desired. The greater the number of ideas, the greater the useful ideas after evaluation.

4. Piggybacking is encouraged. Try to combine, embellish, or improve on an idea. No one should feel individual ownership for an idea.

Nominal Group Technique

The **nominal group technique,** or NGT, involves people working together with little verbal interaction to solve problems and make decisions.[43]

How NGT Works.   The group members, say seven or eight people, sit around a table in full view of each other, but they do not talk to each other at all. Instead, they spend five to ten minutes jotting down ideas on a piece of paper. After this first silent stage is completed, people go around the table and share one of their ideas at a time. The ideas are recorded on a flip chart in full view of everyone. Members continue to share their private ideas in this round-robin fashion until all ideas are reported. When sharing is completed, ideas are discussed and votes are taken to determine their importance. After the first vote, there is more discussion and then a final vote to make the decision. Table 13.4 provides a more detailed summary of what happens during the NGT process.

Advantages of NGT Over Interacting Groups.   The major advantages of nominal techniques are ensuring that ideation is kept separate from evaluation, ensuring balanced participation of all members, and providing a systematic way of aggregating votes for decision selection. Research results show NGT to be superior to interacting groups, such as a brainstorming group, in terms of generating relevant solutions, more creative solutions (because of less premature evaluation), and more broadly focused solutions.[44] Interacting groups tend to pursue one train of discussion for long periods of time; sometimes even to the exclusion of others.

Table 13.4

PROCEDURES FOR NOMINAL GROUP TECHNIQUE

Five to nine people should make up an NGT group. A flip chart at the front of the room is used to record ideas. The six steps in the NGT process are summarized below:

1. Silently generate ideas in writing	Five to ten minutes is usually enough time for this phase. The question is posted on a flip chart at the front of the room. Participants are asked to answer the question on the chart. They are cautioned not to talk to other members or look at the work sheets of others.
2. Round-robin recording of the ideas	The leader goes around the room asking for one idea from each participant and recording it on the flip chart. This goes on, round-robin fashion, until all ideas are exhausted. The chief goal of this step is to get an accurate list of ideas in front of the group to serve as a mapping of the ideas of the entire group.
3. Serially discuss the ideas	Each idea on the chart is discussed in the order it appears on the chart (serially). The leader reads each item and asks the group if there are any questions, needs for clarification, agreement or disagreement.
4. Preliminary vote on item importance	Each group member makes an independent judgment about the alternatives by rank ordering them secretly on 3″ × 5″ cards. The mean or average of these judgments is used as the group's decision. The NGT process may end here or the decision may be further refined through discussion and revoting.
5. Additional discussion after the first vote	The voting patterns are analyzed and reasons examined to see if a more accurate decision can be made.
6. Final vote	The final voting occurs in the same fashion as the original vote, by secret rankings. This action completes the decision process and provides closure.

SOURCE: Summarized from *Group techniques for program planning: A guide to nominal groups and Delphi techniques* by Delbecq, A.L., Van de Ven, A.H., & Gustafson, D.H. Copyright © 1975 by Scott, Foresman and Company. Reprinted by permission.

The Delphi Technique

The **Delphi technique** can be used when people cannot get together physically to make a group decision. It is a method for systematically gathering written judgments from individuals by using sequential questionnaires interspersed with summaries of results from previous responses. Delphi was developed by Rand Corp. as a way of forecasting future events.[45] It takes a considerable amount of time and effort to administer; it is more costly than other group methods. The technique is particularly useful when the experts in solving a problem or making a decision cannot get together because of geography, time, or other constraints.

How the Delphi Process Works. Delphi uses a series of questionnaires that begin with a rather broad question focusing on whatever needs a solution or decision. Each subsequent questionnaire uses the responses from earlier ones as its basis. The process is complete when consensus is reached or when enough information has been gathered. Delphi takes lots of time, participant skills in writing, and motivation to complete the questionnaires and participate in the process. However, the widespread use of desktop computers with modern capability provides the mechanism for expediting and simplifying the Del-

Table 13.5

PROCESS OUTLINE AND SCHEDULE FOR DELPHI

Activities	Estimated Minimum Time for Accomplishment
1. Develop the Delphi question	½ day
2. Select and contact respondents	2 days
3. Select sample size	½ day
4. Develop Questionnaire # 1 and test	1 day
a. Type and send out	1 day
b. Response time	5 days
c. Reminder time (if used)	3 days
5. Analysis of Questionnaire # 1	½ day
6. Develop Questionnaire # 2 and test	2 days
a. Type and send out	1 day
b. Response time	5 days
c. Reminder time (if used)	3 days
7. Analysis of Questionnaire # 2	1 day
8. Develop Questionnaire # 3 and test	2 days
a. Type and send out	1 day
b. Response time	5 days
c. Reminder time (if used)	3 days
9. Analysis of Questionnaire # 3	1 day
10. Prepare a final report	4 days
a. Type report and send out	1 day
b. Prepare respondents' report	1 day
c. Type report and send out	1 day
Total estimated minimum time	44½ days

SOURCE: From *Group Techniques for Program Planning* by A.L. Delbecq, A.H. Van de Ven, and D.H. Gustafson. Copyright © 1975 Scott, Foresman and Company. Reprinted by permission.

phi process. The process outline in Table 13.5 gives you some indication of the amount of time and effort needed to conduct Delphi.

An Example of How Delphi Is Used.   A large computer manufacturer wanted to develop a "leading-edge" laptop portable computer that would be better than any of its competitors and become the industry standard. The product development manager made up a questionnaire to probe the views of key people throughout the marketing, engineering, and production forces. The first iteration of the questionnaire contained many open-ended questions. The experts' responses were used to construct yet another questionnaire that was more finely tuned. This process of successive improvements to the questionnaire continued through two more iterations until a convergence of direction was found and a decision became apparent. Finally, a report was sent to the participants that provided feedback on the results of their efforts. In this case Delphi resulted in a product-prototype plan that promised major improvements over the original proposals of the research and development division.

Which Technique to Use?

There are no easy answers to this question. Interacting groups, especially consensus, allow for much more attention to the needs of the group and its members—it is a teambuilding experience. Brainstorming is a quick and easy way to get a number of ideas out for consideration and to avoid premature judgment. Nominal group technique helps get better quality decisions, but takes a bit more preparation and structure. Delphi technique is most useful when people cannot get together to make a decision or when there are too many people to use one of the other techniques.[46]

CROSS–CULTURAL OB: ARAB DECISION MAKING

Forty-two Arab top executives in six countries were interviewed by Farid Muna to determine their management styles and techniques.[47] One part of his research concerned decision-making. He found that throughout the Middle East the predominant style was consultative (equivalent to Vroom and Yetton's CI or CII options). Fifty-five percent of the executives indicated this strategy would be used for most decisions. Only 22 percent indicated that autocratic decision making would be used and these were mostly older executives. Group decision making (Vroom and Yetton's Option G) was used only 13 percent of the time and delegation was used even less often, at 10 percent. Thus, group decision making, so widely employed in the United States, Japan, and other countries, seems to have little relevance for Arab managers. Why?

• *Consultation is expected.* Senior managers, partners, friends, and relatives expect to be consulted on organizational decisions. "One executive described it as 'a tradition, a custom . . . there are always some people whose opinion you must seek, or else they will be hurt and angry.' The same executive reminded [Mr. Muna] that this 'custom' applies not only in business organizations, but at the higher levels of family, clan, tribe, or nation." [48] We should note here that while key people expect to be consulted they do not actually expect to help make the decision. Subordinates and others might perceive lack of decisiveness as a sign of weakness.

• *Consultation is used as a human relations strategy.* By consulting others conflict can be avoided. In addition, people who are consulted feel important because of the attention and are less likely to oppose the executive in the future—it is one way of coopting people. In addition, it serves as a face-saving device since the consulted person can always say "yes" to the question: Were you consulted about the decision?

• *Arab executives and subordinates do not like teamwork.* Arabs are uncomfortable working in committees, task forces, or other group settings. They are much more at home in one-on-one, individually oriented sessions. Therefore, most group decision-making strategies would not be appropriate, while consultative decision making seems right on target.

- *Delegation is difficult because of the top-man syndrome.* In the Arab world clients, suppliers, and government officials insist on doing business only with the head of the organization. The reason for this is that trust is placed in personal relationships, not in impersonal organizational linkages. "One president of a large company (over 10,000 employees) put it: 'They [clients] insist on my presence during negotiations . . . They are offended if I am not personally involved . . . I am unable to delegate these things to my specialized subordinates.' Another executive complained: 'People with a problem come here and demand to see me; they start from the top instead of starting from where the problem eventually gets solved.'" [49]

MANAGERIAL APPLICATIONS OF DECISION MAKING

There are many fundamental considerations in the decision-making process. You must carefully define the problem before proceeding to generating and evaluating alternatives. There are many pitfalls along the way, such as satisficing, selecting implicit favorites, or using a garbage can method. It is also easy to become overly committed to some course of action. In addition, as a manager and leader you must decide on the level of participation and group involvement you will employ. These are fundamental decisions that can affect your success. The following guides provide additional application advice:

- *Take great care in defining the problem.* Carefully evaluate goals and standards so that you can determine deviations. Ask questions like: Who? What? Where? When? and How much? Separate huge problems into smaller parts so they are manageable.

- *Avoid the pitfalls of alternative generation.* Recognize that it is inevitable that decisions will be satisfactory rather than optimal, but be careful to evaluate enough alternatives that you feel you are at least approaching optimal. You can use some of the intuitive decision methods cited in Table 13.2 as aids, or you can use brainstorming or NGT.

- *Use intuitive decision making when appropriate.* Do not be afraid of your intuition. When you encounter decisions where uncertainty is high, you have little previous experience, and there is little or no objective data available, rely on your intuition to aid the decision process.

- *Use group decision making when needed.* Groups are appropriate when you have a complex problem and where the combined knowledge of group members will create a synergistic solution. Groups are also quite useful when commitment to the solution is needed or when political tactics show that an alliance is required. Take care to appoint people to groups who have good interpersonal and group dynamics skills.

- *Avoid groupthink.* Cohesive groups, such as a boss and subordinates, are particularly subject to groupthink. Avoid it by using a devil's advocate approach and by waiting for powerful inputs, such as the boss', until last.

- *Use participation in decision making to improve organizational effectiveness.* Participation has a strong effect on satisfaction and job design and some effect on productivity. It can help create a very positive and innovative organizational culture. Determine when to use participation by following the Vroom-Yetton guidelines.

- *Learn how to delegate.* A major key to managerial success is the ability to delegate. As you go up the organizational ladder there will be less and less time to do everything yourself—you must learn to delegate.

- *Use group consensus for most group decisions.* Consensus is simple and works well when you follow the guidelines. Take care to make sure that everyone is heard.

- *Use brainstorming to get fresh ideas.* The power of this technique is that it structures the process so that judgment is deferred. Be sure to follow the rules carefully and have a good method for recording the ideas.

- *Use NGT when a more powerful ideation structure is needed.* NGT not only ensures that everyone will contribute ideas, but it also helps participants avoid getting locked into one mindset because of the group process. It is somewhat more effective than brainstorming, but requires more effort to implement.

- *Use Delphi when people cannot get together or there are too many people.* This technique is so time consuming that it is only appropriate for major problems.

- *Culture is important for determining appropriate decision style.* The Arab countries demand attention to consultative decision process, but not group decision making. In Japan, group decision making and consensus are critical. In the United States we have a mixture with participation as an important positive strategy. Study each country carefully; develop a strategy in advance.

FOR DISCUSSION

1. How does decision making differ from problem solving?

2. Define a problem with which you are familiar using the Kepner-Tregoe approach.

3. Explain why managers do not always make optimal decisions. What impact does this have on an organization? How do these limits to rationality affect decisions such as the one to launch the *Challenger* space shuttle?

4. What are the major advantages and disadvantages to using groups for decision making?

5. Using the Vroom-Yetton model shown in Figure 13.4, outline the circumstances where participation should be used or avoided.

6. Compare and contrast group consensus, brainstorming, and the nominal group technique.

7. What are some examples of the types of decisions that would be appropriate for Delphi?

8. Should a manager be an autocratic or democratic decision maker? How does culture affect your answer?

9. If you were in charge of a project in the Middle East that required decision inputs from several business and government organizations, how would you go about organizing the decision-making process?

KEY CONCEPTS AND TERMS

decision making
problem solving
bounded rationality
satisficing
escalating commitment
delegation
intuitive decisions
consultative option
unprogrammed decisions

implicit favorite model
deferred judgment
devil's advocate
ideation
groupthink
participation
process gains and losses
autocratic option

programmed decisions
anarchic or garbage can model
Vroom-Yetton model
group decision option
group consensus
brainstorming
nominal group technique
Delphi

Cases and Incidents

PARTICIPATION AT MOONLIGHT COSMETICS

Eva Gibbs, President of Moonlight Cosmetics Corp., just finished reading an article about participation in decision making in a news magazine. She thought it sounded like a good idea and decided that participation was just what Moonlight Cosmetics needed. The next day she dictated a memo:

Participation in decision making can make a substantial improvement in our operations. Effective at once, each supervisor will include all employees who are affected by a decision in the decision-making process. Let me know if you have any problems.

Signed, Eva Gibbs

Within three months, eight of her twenty-five supervisors quit. She figured, "Good riddance. They were probably ones who couldn't adapt to a participative style."

DISCUSSION QUESTIONS

1. What decision-making process did Eva use?

2. Brainstorm some reasons why the supervisors may have left the company?

3. Evaluate the ideas you came up with in brainstorming.

4. How might Eva have handled this change differently?

THE ENGINEERING CHANGE

The Inverse Corp. is a diversified manufacturer of component assemblies for a variety of industries. A major Inverse product line consists of passenger seat constructions for the trucking industry. Federal safety standards (FMVSS) effective in August required several major engineering changes to be incorporated into currently produced assemblies by that date. A meeting was called in June to discuss the effects of these changes.

The Meeting Manufacturing and Production Control agreed that the changes would not cause their areas any major problems. Process and Project engineering concluded that the changes were compatible with present manufacturing facilities and

would pose no appreciable obstacles. Top management assessed the changes and concluded that they would primarily affect tooling.

The tool division, represented by its chief engineer, W. Track, and his two assistant superintendents, were divided in their opinions of the situation. Track, recently obtained from outside the corporation to head the tool division, believed the changes were compatible with present tooling and could be accomplished for the start of product in August. His two assistants, however, disagreed and predicted a November completion date as being more realistic. They based their opinions on past tooling practices and procedures.

Sales reiterated that a November date was impossible. L. Stanley, sales chief, pointed out that competitors, who have the same type of tooling as

Inverse, have committed themselves to the August date and Inverse should be able to do the same. The meeting adjourned with Inverse committed to the August completion schedule. All were in favor of the decision except the two assistant tool superintendents, H. Jones and A. Smith. The following conversation between Jones and Smith occurred directly after the meeting.

Smith: "That young hot shot said he could do it but we're the ones who are actually going to do the work!"

Jones: "Did you hear him knuckle under to sales?"

Smith: "No one paid any attention to our arguments or suggestions. They acted as if we didn't know what we are talking about. We've been doing most of the work

around here for the past twenty years and look who they listen to, a young outsider!"

Jones: "He thinks he's going to change the way we do things around here. Come August we'll see who is right, him or us, and believe you me it's going to be us."

After leaving the meeting Track knew he had a problem and pondered his possible solutions.

DISCUSSION QUESTIONS

1. How might Track solve this problem?
2. Which decision-making techniques would be most appropriate here and why?

From J.V. Murray and T.J. Von der Embse (1973), *Organizational behavior: Critical incidents and analysis,* pp. 304–05. Copyright © 1973 by Charles E. Merrill, Columbus, Ohio. Reprinted with permission of publisher.

THE *CHALLENGER* LAUNCH DECISION

In three months of intensive investigation after an explosion destroyed the space shuttle *Challenger,* it has become clear that the disaster represents a managerial failure even greater than has been suspected up till now . . . The tragically flawed decision to launch was no fluke. It was the almost predictable result of a pattern of mismanagement that has spread throughout the agency since the glory days of the Apollo moon landings. The people at the top ended up isolated, a grimly instructive example of a problem that can overtake any organization, governmental or corporate.

The agency's leaders have been preoccupied with raising money for NASA from Congress. To win over the politicians, they have set goals for the shuttle program totally out of sync with the resources at their command. Organizational components that were supposed to work closely together—the Marshall, Kennedy, and Johnson space centers—have behaved like quasi-independent baronies, uncommunicative with one another and with the top. Watching the agency's fortunes decline, employees have tended to act like cowed bureaucrats. The result: an organization in which the flow of vital information up and down was as flawed as the now notorious O-rings—the large synthetic rubber rings that were supposed to seal the joints between the stacked sections of the solid-fueled booster rockets.

It was a failure of NASA's command system, a system supposedly honed for years in the proper handling of last-minute "go/no go" choices. At virtually every NASA launch, engineers have raised last-minute technical questions. The *Challenger* launch was delayed twice; the previous launch of *Columbia* was delayed seven times. But NASA insiders up to the highest levels of the organization say that the refusal by Alan McDonald, the senior engineer present at the launch site for Morton Thiokol, the manufacturer of the booster rocket, to sign off on the launch even after lengthy argument, was not just another case of an engineer's last-minute nerves. It was unprecedented in the history of the 24 previous shuttle launches. McDonald's refusal forced the conference call in which the managers of the Marshall Space Center persuaded or, depending on one's view, pressured Thiokol executives to override the company's engineers.

At the very least, say insiders, the fact that an unprecedented argument had taken place should have been passed up the chain of command. Managers from the Marshall Center, in trying to explain to the presidential commission why they had not relayed to the top the vehement objections of Thiokol's engineers, presented their judgment as a matter of routine decision-making at the appropriate level of the organization: the question of the O-rings' safety had been dealt with at Level III—that is, at Marshall, which supposedly had the technical expertise—rather than being referred upstairs to the executives at Levels I and II.

It would have been easy to pass word of the debate upward. Jesse Moore, associate administrator for space flight and the man who had the last word on the space shot, was at Cape Kennedy. Arnold Aldrich, head of the space shuttle program, was at Houston mission control. Both were plugged into a communications network that allows everyone at a console to listen in on discussions and arguments taking place about the launch all through the 48–hour countdown.

Both Marshall and NASA headquarters were constrained by their budgets in what they could do about design problems like those of the O-rings. Richard Cook, the budget analyst who warned NASA's top executives in a memo last July of engineers' fears about the O-rings, points out that his report focused both on the O-ring safety issue and on the fact that the O-rings "posed a major *budget* threat. If a design change had to be made," he says, "you could be talking about shutting the program down for a year"—and spending what NASA now estimates at around $350 million to fix the problem. Cook elaborates: "There were several major design issues outstanding, and there was not enough money to pay for fixing them."

In effect, the O-rings were seen by NASA managers, both at Marshall and at headquarters, simply as one of many long-term problems for which immediate fixes weren't available. So-called flight readiness reviews take place two weeks or so before each shuttle launch. Past and present NASA managers who have been among the upwards of 100 people participating in each review say that so many minor but immediate problems are brought up that it is easy to lose track of long-term issues like the O-rings.

DISCUSSION QUESTIONS

1. How was NASA's decision process flawed?

2. Do you think groupthink applies to this case?

3. Is this an example of the "escalating commitment" phenomenon?

4. Would use of the Vroom-Yetton model have helped make a better decision?

5. How could this be prevented in the future?

REFERENCES

1. Mintzberg, H. (1973). *The nature of managerial work*. New York: Harper & Row.

2. Maccrimmon, K.R., & Taylor, R.N. (1976). Decision making and problem solving. In M.D. Dunnette (Ed.). *Handbook of industrial and organizational psychology* (pp. 1397–1453). Chicago: Rand-McNally.

3. This usage of the term is similar to that of Huber, G.P. (1980). *Managerial decision making*. Glenview, IL: Scott, Foresman. Maccrimmon and Taylor (1976) do not differentiate between decision making and problem solving; they note that one may be considered to be a subset of the other depending upon usage.

4. Huber (1980), pp. 13–15. For a complete discussion of problem formulation, see Kepner, C.H., & Tregoe, B.B. (1976). *The rational manager* (2nd ed.). Princeton, NJ: Kepner-Tregoe.

5. Kepner & Tregoe (1976). Also see Cowan, D.A. (1986). Developing a process model of problem recognition. *Academy of Management Review, 11,* 763–776.

6. Kepner and Tregoe (1976), p. 76.

7. Simon, H.A. (1957). *Administrative behavior* (2nd ed.). New York: The Free Press.

8. The title is based on Staw, B.M. (1976). Knee-deep in the big muddy: A study of escalating commitment to a chosen course of action. *Organizational Behavior and Human Performance, 16,* 27–44. This section is based on Staw, B.M. (1981). The escalation of commitment to a course of action. *Academy of Management Review, 6,* 577–87. Ross, J., & Staw, B.M. (1986). Expo 86: An escalation prototype. *Administrative Science Quarterly, 31,* 274–297. Brockner, J., Houser, R., Birnbaum, G., Lloyd, K., Dietcher, J., Nathanson, S., & Rubin, J.Z. (1986). Escalation of commitment to an ineffective course of action: The effect of feedback having negative implications for self-identity. *Administrative Science Quarterly, 31,* 109–126.

9. From Staw (1981), p. 577. Based on Vandiver, K. (1972). Why should my conscience bother me? In A. Heilbroner (Ed.). *In the name of profit.* Garden City, NY: Doubleday.

10. Whyte, G. (1986). Escalating commitment to a course of action: A reinterpretation. *Academy of Management Review, 11,* 311–321.

11. March, J.G., & Simon, H.A. (1958). *Organizations* (pp. 140–141). New York: Wiley.

12. Pinfield, L.T. (1986). A field evaluation of perspectives on organizational decision making. *Ad-*

ministrative Science Quarterly, 31, 365–388. Cohen, D., March, J.G., & Olsen, J.P. (1972). A garbage can model of organizational choice. *Administrative Science Quarterly, 17,* 1–25. And Martin, J. (1981, November-December). A garbage can model of the psychological research process. *American Behavioral Scientist,* pp. 131–151.

13. Soelberg, P.O. (1967). Unprogrammed decision making. *Industrial Management Review, 8,* 19–29.

14. Hogarth, R.M. (1980). *Judgment and choice,* New York: Wiley. Also see Ulvila, J.W., & Brown, R.V. (1982, September-October). Decision analysis comes of age. *Harvard Business Review,* pp. 130–141.

15. Simon, H.A. (1987). Making management decisions: The role of intuition and emotion. *Academy of Management Executive, 1,* 57–64. Taggart, W., & Robey, D. (1981). Minds and managers: The dual nature of human information processing and management. *Academy of Management Review, 6,* 187–195. For a nontechnical explanation of the left-brain, right-brain concept, see Mintzberg, H. (1976, July-August). Planning on the left side, managing on the right. *Harvard Business Review,* pp. 49–58. Also see Ornstein, R.E. (1977). *The psychology of consciousness* (2nd ed.). New York: Harcourt, Brace, Jovanovich.

16. Peters, T.J., & Waterman, R.H. (1984). *In search of excellence.* New York: Harper & Row. Leavitt, H.J. (1975). Beyond the analytic manager. *California Management Review, 17*(3), 5–12. And Leavitt, H.J. (1975). Beyond the analytic manager: Part II. *California Management Review, 17*(4), 11–21.

17. Agor, W.H. (1986). The logic of intuition: How top executives make important decisions. *Organizational Dynamics, 14* (Winter), 9.

18. Agor, W.H. (1986), p. 9.

19. Agor, W.H. (1986).

20. Agor, W.H. (1986).

21. Mintzberg, H. (1975). The manager's job: Folklore and fact. *Harvard Business Review, 53*(4), 49–61.

22. This section is based primarily on Maier, N.F. (1967). Assets and liabilities in group problem solving: The need for an integrative function. *Psychological Review, 74,* 239–249. And Hill, G.W. (1982). Group versus individual performance: Are N + 1 heads better than one? *Psychological Bulletin, 91,* 517–539.

23. Abridged from Janis, I (1982). *Groupthink: Psychological Studies of Policy Decisions and Fiascoes,* 2nd edition pp. 256–259. Copyright © by Houghton Mifflin Company.

24. See Herbert, T.T., & Estes, R.W. (1977). Improving executive decisions by formalizing dissent: The corporate devil's advocate. *Academy of Management Review, 2,* 662–667.

25. Based on Hill (1982).

26. Sashkin, M. (1984). Participative management is an ethical imperative. *Organizational Dynamics, 12* (Spring), 4–22.

27. For a complete discussion of these issues see Locke, E.A., & Schweiger, D.M. (1979). Participation in decision making: One more look. In B.M. Staw (Ed.). *Research in organizational behavior, Vol. 1* (pp. 265–339). Greenwich, CT: JAI Press. And Miller, K.I., & Monge, P.R. (1986). Participation, satisfaction, and productivity: A meta-analytic review. *Academy of Management Journal, 29,* 727–753. For a discussion of various modes of participation, see Hinckley, S.R., Jr. (1985). A closer look at participation. *Organizational Dynamics, 13* (Winter), 57–67.

28. For literature reviews, see Locke, E.A., Schweiger, D.M., & Latham, G.P. (1986). Participation in decision making: When should it be used? *Organizational Dynamics, 14* (Winter), 65–79. Leana, C.R. (1987). Power relinquishment versus power sharing: Theoretical clarification and empirical comparison of delegation and participation. *Journal of Applied Psychology, 72,* 228–233. And Miller & Monge, P.R. (1986).

29. Miller and Monge (1986).

30. Miller and Monge (1986).

31. Leana, C.R. (1986). Predictors and consequences of delegation. *Academy of Management Journal, 29,* 754–774. Leana (1987). For practical applications of delegation, see Taylor, T.O., Friedman, D.J., & Couture, D. (1987) Operating without supervisors. *Organizational Dynamics, 15*(3), 26–38.

32. Dowd, A.R. (1986, September 15). What managers can learn from manager Reagan. *Fortune,* p. 33.

33. McCormack, M.H. (1984). *What they don't teach you at Harvard Business School* (p. 187). New York: Bantam.

34. This discussion is based on Vroom, V.H., & Yetton, P.W. (1973). *Leadership and decision making* (p. 12). Pittsburgh, PA: University of Pittsburgh Press. Also see Vroom, V.H., & Jago, A.G. (1978). On the validity of the Vroom-Yetton Model. *Journal of Applied Psychology, 63,* 151–162. Also see Leana (1987).

35. For a more complete version of the decision tree that includes delegation, see Vroom and Yetton (1973) p. 194.

36. For additional decision-making strategies, see Schweiger, D.M., Sandberg, W.R., & Ragan, J.W. (1986). Group approaches for improving strategic decision making: A comparative analysis of dialectical inquiry, devil's advocacy, and consensus. *Academy of Management Journal, 29,* 51–71.

37. This section based on Hall, J. (1971, November). Decisions. *Psychology Today,* 51 cf.

38. Holliman, C.R., & Henrick, H.W. (1972). Adequacy of group decisions as a function of decision making process. *Academy of Management Journal, 15,* 175–184.

39. Gray, B., & Hay, T.M. (1986). Political limits to interorganizational consensus and change. *Journal of Applied Behavioral Science, 22,* 95–112.

40. Osborne, A.F. (1941). *Applied Imagination: Principles and procedures for creative thinking.* New York: Scribner's. (There are many later editions of this classic book.) Also see Parnes, S.J., Noller, R.B., & Biondi, A.M. (1977). *Guide to creative action.* New York: Charles Scribner's Sons. For a summary of strategies for creativity, see Rice, B. (1984, May). Imagination to go. *Psychology Today,* 48 cf. Gilbert, S. (1986, March). Profiting from creativity. *Science Digest,* 36 cf. And Are you creative? (1985, September 30). *Business Week.*

41. See Basadur, M., & Finkbeiner, C.T. (1985). Measuring preference for ideation in creative problem-solving training. *Journal of Applied Behavioral Science, 21,* 42–43.

42. For a review see Maccrimmon & Taylor (1976), p. 1407.

43. NGT was developed in 1968 by Andre L. Delbecq and Andrew H. Van de Ven. See their article (1971). A group process model for problem identification and program planning. *Journal of Applied Behavioral Science, 7,* 466–492.

44. See Delbecq, et al. (1975), Chapter 2.

45. Dalky, N.C. (1967). *Delphi.* Rand Corporation.

46. Van de Ven, A.H., & Delbecq, A.L. (1974). The effectiveness of nominal, delphi, and interacting-group decision-making processes. *Academy of Management Journal, 17,* 618.

47. Muna, F.M. (1980). *The Arab executive.* New York: St. Martin's Press. For additional information about Arab management see Al-Jafary, A., & Hollingsworth, A.T. (1983). An exploratory study of managerial practices in the Arabian Gulf region. *Journal of International Business Studies, 14* (Fall), 143–152.

48. Muna (1980), p. 59.

49. Muna (1980), p. 31.

Chapter Fourteen

LEADERSHIP

PREVIEW

- Why aren't managers always leaders?
- Are taller, smarter, more active people better leaders?
- What is your leadership style? People-oriented or task-oriented? Find out by filling out a questionnaire.
- How can the maturity of subordinates affect leader behavior?
- Should leaders change their style to fit the situation, use "one best style," or find situations that fit their style?
- Are there built-in barriers that make organizational leadership more difficult for women?

MAJOR TOPICS

Preview Case: The Second Lieutenant

In Search of Leadership

Traits and Behaviors of Leaders

Social Exchange and Leadership

Behavior of Leaders

Situational Approaches to Leadership

Leadership: Summarizing What We Do Know

Cross-Cultural OB: How Does Leadership Differ?

Managerial Applications of Leadership

Preview Case

THE SECOND LIEUTENANT

Roy Kern, Second Lieutenant, United States Air Force, sat up straight at his desk and rotated 360 degrees in his government-issue executive chair, his hands firmly grasping the armrest. It was his first morning on the job as Manager of War Readiness Spares at Hunter Air Force Base. He thought to himself, "Well, you finally made it. Now's the time to put all the education to work. It's not every twenty-two year old who has sixteen people working for him; man, that's power. And, it sure is a lot of responsibility. But I know I can do it. . . ."

The telephone interrupted his thoughts. It was his boss, Lt. Col. Rosenberg, an eighteen-year veteran who seemed to know everything. Col. Rosenberg said, "Roy, I know today's your first day, but we need to get going on the warehouse beautification program. I just got a call from headquarters alerting us that the inspector general (IG) will be here next month. I want us to look good so we'll get a good rating. Why don't you talk to your NCO's (noncommissioned officers) and decide what you're going to do."

After Col. Rosenberg hung up Roy considered what to do. "Now's my chance to show the colonel what I can do. Earlier this morning, when I toured the facilities with the NCOIC (NCO in charge), Se-

nior Master Sergeant Juanita Rogers, I noticed some good ways to spruce things up. We can paint the floors grey, with bright yellow lines. We can repaint the walls and ceilings from that awful green to a light blue. Boy, will things look better!"

Lt. Kern called a meeting at 11:00 o'clock for all the people who worked for him. Here's what he told them: "I just got the word from Col. Rosenberg that the IG is coming, and we have to get busy on the warehouse beautification program. Our warehouse really looks cruddy, but we can do something about it. I've decided that the best way to beautify it is to paint it. We'll paint the floors, walls, ceilings—the whole works. It will look fantastic. Since we still have to get our normal work done, I've decided that we'll do the painting over the next two weekends. Now, let's get busy and get all the supplies ready."

By the end of the week, things had gone sour for Lt. Kern. First, there had been a complaint lodged against him by a black warehouseman for violating affirmative action rules. Then, the base safety officer came by and told him that he could not paint the floors. One airman, who told him he had a prior engagement for the weekend, had gone to the chaplain and complained. To top it all off, Col. Rosenberg had called him in and told him to talk to his NCO's before he did anything. His "troops" now treated him with distaste and loathing.

He said to himself, "I thought I was a leader. Where did I go wrong?"

Where did Lt. Kern go wrong? What could he have done to be a more effective leader? Does he have the right traits, characteristics, and education to be a leader? Did he behave appropriately? Does the situation demand a different approach to leadership? Many managers in both the public and private sector experience leadership problems. We will attempt to address these problems and their solutions in this chapter.

The plan of the chapter is to cover a number of major concepts of leadership, with the goal of improving our understanding of the leadership process and thus making ourselves better leaders. We will try to understand the nature of leadership. Then we will turn to a discussion of the traits or characteristics that are associated with effective leaders. Next, we will look at the social process of leadership and the behaviors used by effective leaders. Finally, we will look at the influence of situations on leadership and then sum up what we do know about leadership.

IN SEARCH OF LEADERSHIP

Does this title, "In Search of Leadership," seem strange? No topic in organizational behavior has been so thoroughly researched. There seem to be more major theories for leadership than for any other organizational topic. But, in spite of all this theorizing and research, we still have no generally accepted comprehensive theory of leadership.[1] Thus, we are still in search of leadership.

On the other hand, all this effort has given us some insights. Each theory provides partial answers. When considered as a whole and carefully analyzed for convergence, we find that we do know something of leadership, even though we might wish for more. In this chapter, we will sift through the theories to find those aspects that are useful for managers.

The Nature of Leadership

Leaders excite the imagination of almost everyone. Most movie themes involve some type of leader. When we think of organizational leaders, we conjure up images of powerful chief executive officers at the top of large corporations, of generals in the military, of bishops in the church, and of senators in politics. Most of us aspire to be leaders. We, like Lt. Kern, want people to follow us, to respect us, to be influenced by us. The following excerpt illustrates our fascination with leadership.[2]

> Leadership is a subject that has long excited interest among scholars and laymen alike. The term connotes images of powerful, dynamic persons who command victorious armies, direct corporate empires from atop gleaming skyscrapers, or shape the course of nations. Much of our conception of history is the story of military, political, religious, and social leaders. The exploits of brave and clever leaders are the essence of many legends and myths. The widespread fascination with leadership may be because it is such a mysterious process, as well as one that touches everyone's life. Why do certain leaders (Gandhi, Mohammed, Mao Tse-tung) inspire such intense fervor and dedication? How did certain leaders (Julius Caesar, Charlemagne, Alexander the Great) build great empires? Why were certain leaders (Winston Churchill, Indira Ghandi, the Shah of Iran) suddenly deposed, despite their apparent power and record of successful accomplishments? How did certain, rather undistinguished persons (Adolf Hitler, Claudius Caesar) rise to positions of great power? Why do some leaders have loyal followers who are willing to sacrifice their lives for their leader, and why are some other leaders so despised that their followers conspire to murder them (e.g., as occurred with the "fragging" of some military officers by enlisted men in Viet Nam)?

This romanticized view of leadership is an important part of our culture and social reality. We often attribute variations in performance of organizations to leadership, even if external factors in the environment are the major contributors.[3] This process is another way of applying attribution theory, discussed in Chapter 4.[4] We like to believe that people can control what happens in organizations. Thus, we are likely to attribute many organizational outcomes to leaders, even though other factors are the true cause. Of course, this process makes it difficult to fully understand leadership.

Perspective 14.1

LEADERS VERSUS MANAGERS: IS THERE A DIFFERENCE?

How do leaders differ from managers? Or do they? Some assert that leaders, at least "great leaders" are quite different from great managers.[5] **Management** is the process of coordinating human and material resources toward objective accomplishments.[6] This definition is usually followed by a description of tasks involving planning, organizing, controlling, and motivating. It seems clear that management involves a lot of things that are not leadership.

But even when tasks are the same, there is speculation that managers may be different from leaders.[7] For example, managers are often impersonal about goals while leaders get quite emotionally involved in their goals. Managers also tend to act rationally to structure activities and limit choices whereas leaders go in the opposite direction by inspiring creativity and developing fresh approaches. Managers tend to work rather impersonally with others—they are good team players. Leaders, in contrast, are more emotionally oriented—and people have strong emotion feelings toward them. In the opening example, Lt. Kern might be a competent manager, but he failed as a leader.

Does this mean that if you aspire to be a manager, you cannot be a leader? Certainly not. Ideally, you would combine the two roles by striving to be both a strong manager and a strong leader. Throughout the rest of the chapter we will not make a major distinction between managers and leaders. We will assume that one of the goals of a good manager is also to be a good leader. We will also assume that not all good leaders are "great leaders," but that all managers of people need to be at least competent leaders.

While leaders may have less impact than our romanticized notions attribute to them, there is general agreement that leadership does contribute significantly to organizational performance and effectiveness.[8] In this chapter we will examine various ways that leaders can be successful in improving organizations.

What is Leadership?

Since researchers have had trouble understanding leadership, it is not surprising that it is also difficult to define. Often the definition depends more on the situation or the purpose of research than on some universal truth. It makes a difference whether you are training leaders, identifying them, or finding which behaviors are more or less effective.[9] For our purposes, we will define **leadership** as the process of influencing others toward goals.[10]

The concepts of leadership and power (discussed in Chapter 12) are closely related, since both power and leadership are concerned with the ability to bring about desired goals by influencing others. Leadership might be considered as a special case of power, where we are concerned with the relationship between leader, follower, situation, and the individual characteristics of the people involved.

Approaches to Understanding Leadership

There are four major approaches to understanding leadership: finding out what individual traits and behaviors successful leaders possess, understanding the social exchange process between leaders and followers, observing the behaviors of effective leaders, and analyzing the situations in which various types of leadership are successful. We will discuss all four, for each offers a different insight into the leadership process.

TRAITS AND BEHAVIORS OF LEADERS

Are leaders born? Are certain people predestined to be leaders? Are there certain **traits** (individual characteristics, such as physical or mental characteristics, personality, social background, intellectual ability) and **skills** (learned behaviors, such as social skills, task skills, communication skills) that all successful leaders must have? Several decades of leadership research has yielded little evidence to support these positions; however, recent analysis suggests that the results may have been misinterpreted and that leadership traits are more important than we once thought.[11] It appears that while the possession or absence of specific traits does not guarantee success or failure as a leader, some traits and skills affect the way people perceive leaders and can thus affect a leader's performance.[12]

Traits of Leaders Compared With Nonleaders

Early research into leadership traits focused on comparing leaders with nonleaders. Low-level relationships were found in many different areas. The research suggested that leaders possessed a number of traits and skills, although the presence of a given trait seemed to vary across situations. Some of these traits and skills are highlighted below.[13]

- Intelligence
- Alertness to the needs of others
- Understanding of the task
- Initiative and persistence in dealing with problems
- Desire to accept responsibility
- Tend to be taller, heavier, and more athletic
- Present a good appearance
- Ability to speak fluently
- Self-confident

If Lt. Kern had possessed all the above traits, do you think he would have been successful? He appears to have most of them except alertness to the needs of others and an understanding of the task. Perhaps these two traits are crucial in this instance. One of the problems with trait research is that we do not know which traits are needed in a given situation. Many leadership traits and skills seem to be related to the ability to perform in a group or to attain group objectives—thus, certain traits will help a leader get things done in the group.

Table 14.1

TRAITS AND SKILLS ASSOCIATED WITH SUCCESSFUL LEADERS

Traits	Skills
Adaptable to situations	Clever (intelligent)
Alert to social environment	Conceptually skilled
Ambitious and achievement-oriented	Creative
Assertive	Diplomatic and tactful
Cooperative	Fluent in speaking
Decisive	Knowledgeable about group task
Dependable	Organized (administrative ability)
Dominant (desire to influence others)	Persuasive
Energetic (high activity level)	Socially skilled
Persistent	
Self-confident	
Tolerant of stress	
Willing to assume responsibility	

SOURCE: Gary A. Yukl, *Leadership in Organizations,* © 1981, p. 70. Reprinted by permission of Prentice-Hall, Inc., Englewood Cliffs, N.J.

But more than just the traits seem necessary; they must form a combination that helps the leader cope with the situation at hand.

Traits of Effective Leaders

More recent trait research is being conducted in a different way. Rather than comparing leaders versus nonleaders across a number of situations, we compare effective versus ineffective leaders in the same situation, or we compare the relationship between traits and leadership effectiveness. The results of these studies show stronger, more consistent results than the earlier trait studies.[14] Many of the traits and skills, illustrated in Table 14.1, are similar to those found in the earlier studies.[15]

Assessment Centers: Using Traits and Skills to Select Leaders

Assessment Center Design.   Much recent research has focused on using traits and skills to select leaders. At the core of this movement is the **assessment center,** a technique that uses a number of traits and skills (behaviors) to assess a person's suitability for being hired or promoted.[16] Assessment centers use a number of methods including objective tests (skills, knowledge, interests), projective tests (to measure motivation or other personality traits), interviews (to probe areas of interests), situational exercises (individual or group activities that call for behaviors similar to those in the situation), and peer ratings (how well can the candidate evaluate others). Several assessors judge the performance of each candidate and make an overall selection decision.

Perspective 14.2

HISTORY OF THE
ASSESSMENT CENTER[17]

The U.S. pioneer of the assessment method was the U.S. Office of Strategic Services [OSS], forerunner of the CIA. On the assumption that it takes dirty men to do dirty work, early in World War II the OSS reportedly tried recruiting some agents directly from the ranks of gangland mobs. When a number of missions were bungled, OSS officials laid part of the blame on their selection procedures. Searching for something better, they turned to the assessment method. First developed in the early 1900s by German psychologists, it had been picked up by the German military high command in the 1930s for use in choosing officers, and then borrowed by the British War Office for the same purpose.

The OSS organized the first U.S. assessment center in 1943, at a secret estate called Station S, about 18 miles from Washington, D.C. The program for that first center was developed principally by Henry Murray, the famous Harvard psychologist. By then, the service had specified somewhat more precisely the personality traits and behavioral skills it thought an effective secret agent needed. To test for them, Murray and his colleagues designed a series of simulated cloak-and-dagger situations. One required prospective spies to assume quickly and use convincingly a false identity or "cover," even under intense interrogation. By war's end, more than 5,000 recruits were processed through Station S, although no one ever really found out for sure whether the method worked.

The assessment method was essentially abandoned as a wartime relic until the mid 1950s, when American Telephone and Telegraph launched its ambitious Management Progress Study of the careers of more than 400 young executives. In order to establish a baseline measure of their abilities, AT & T industrial psychologist Douglas Bray and some colleagues developed a series of management exercises that have survived remarkably well as the core of what goes on at most of today's assessment centers. Bray [later became] director of human resources at AT & T, and under his supervision, the company put nearly 200,000 employees through various assessment programs. It currently tests more than 20,000 a year at seventy different centers throughout the Bell system.

Do Assessment Centers Work? The assessment center has become extremely popular since its first corporate use at American Telephone and Telegraph (AT & T) in the 1950s.[18] Currently, over 1,000 organizations are using assessment centers and over 200,000 people have participated.[19] Assessment centers are good, long-run predictors of future performance.[20] Thus, it seems that many organizations have found a good way to predict managerial success.

One of the top predictors of success in assessment center studies is human relations skill, in terms of the person's ability to lead a group to accomplish a task without arousing hostility (*see* Table 14.2). Thus, it seems logical that a social-interaction approach might help explain leadership. This is the topic of the next section.

SOCIAL EXCHANGE AND LEADERSHIP

Leadership is fundamentally a social process that involves perceptions and interactions between leaders and followers. This view stresses that people tend to allow others to lead them when their behaviors and traits match what the

Table 14.2

PREDICTORS OF ADVANCEMENT IN AT&T MANAGEMENT PROGRESS STUDY

Trait or skill

1.	Oral communication skill	How good this person would be in presenting an oral report to a small conference group on a well-known subject.
2.	Human relations skill	How effectively this person can lead a group to accomplish a task without arousing hostility.
3.	Need for advancement	How much this person wants to be promoted significantly earlier than his or her peers.
4.	Resistance to stress	How well this person's work performance will stand up in the face of personal stress.
5.	Tolerance of uncertainty	How well this person;s work performance will stand up under uncertain or unstructured conditions.

SOURCE: From D.W. Bray, R.J. Campbell, and D.L. Grant (1974), Formative years in business: *A long term AT&T study of managerial lives.* Copyright © 1974 by J. Wiley & Sons, New York. Reprinted with permission.

followers think they should be.[21] In addition, there is an exchange that takes place between leaders and followers, called the social exchange process, or **transactional leadership.**[22] Interactions and activities (called transactions) are exchanged between followers and leaders that provide rewards for both parties.

Balancing Rewards and Benefits of an Exchange

Since the exchange process involves weighing the perceived costs and benefits of a transaction to see if the net result is advantageous, the relative contributions of each party are important. For example, leaders contribute their intelligence, communication skills, and power to help accomplish the group's goal. They also coordinate the group's activities, and they reward group members. Followers, on the other hand, provide status, esteem, influence, and loyalty to their leader. If the group is successful, then the leader will maintain influence. If the group fails, it is a different story. If the failure appears to be the leader's fault, the leader will lose influence. If the fault does not seem to lie with the leader, then the leader may maintain influence or power.

The opening incident might be explained by social exchange theory. Lt. Kern is new. The group does not see the benefits of supporting him when the goal is negative for them, painting the warehouse. Lt. Kern has not contributed to the group's operation and welfare—there is no positive exchange of rewards between him and the group. Thus, the lieutenant is in a poor power position, but he does not recognize it and gets himself into trouble.

Social Exchange and Power

A social exchange approach to leadership involves the use of power and influence (discussed in Chapter 12). The leader convinces the follower that some benefit will accrue if the follower behaves as the leader wishes.[23] Because

Perspective 14.3

CHARISMATIC LEADERSHIP[24]

Charisma is a characteristic that describes leaders who by the force of their personality and abilities (a special source of power) are able to have a profound and extraordinarily strong effect on their followers. The leader and followers almost always share some common value system, ideology, or religion. Inspired, enthusiastic obedience, loyalty, and commitment are characteristics of the followers of charismatic leaders. There is a mysterious, magnetic quality of the relationship between charismatic leaders and followers.

Characteristics of charismatic leaders that distinguish them from noncharismatic leaders are dominance, self-confidence, the need for influence, and a strong conviction of the moral righteousness of their beliefs.[25] Charismatic leaders behave in the following ways:

- **Role modeling.** The leader "role models" a value system of the followers. Often, it is a self-sacrificing behavior. Thus, followers perceive the leader as competent, attractive, and successful.

- **Image building.** Charismatic leaders actively build their images so they are viewed favorably by others. They prove their extraordinary powers to their followers.

- **Transcendent goals.** Ideological goals with moral overtones often characterize the charismatic leader. There is a vision of what the future could be.

- **High expectations.** By showing confidence in subordinates and having high expectations, leaders enhance a follower's self-esteem and solidify their charismatic position.

- **Motivation.** The charismatic leader is able to arouse the motivation of followers toward accomplishing some mission. They get people involved emotionally.

exchange theory is based on trading between parties, both should incur benefits from the exercise of power. If Lt. Kern had shown the warehouse crew how they would benefit from painting (and they believed him), he might have been more successful in exercising leadership and power.

BEHAVIOR OF LEADERS

Another way of understanding leadership is to compare the *behaviors* of effective and ineffective leaders to see how good leaders behave. The implication here is that if we find out what behaviors effective leaders use, then all we have to do is emulate them to be successful ourselves. Before proceeding in this section, you might wish to fill out the Leadership Questionnaire in Table 14.3.

Ohio State Leadership Studies

The origin of the behavioral approach to leadership is the Ohio State University research program that began in the late 1940s.[26] The researchers developed a questionnaire, called the Leader Behavior Description Questionnaire (containing questions similar to the ones in Table 14.3), to measure leadership behavior. It includes items on organization, communication, recognition, integration, and coordination. Analysis of the questionnaire responses found two general

Table 14.3

LEADERSHIP QUESTIONNAIRE

Directions: The following items describe aspects of leadership behavior. Respond to each item according to the way you would if you were the leader of a work group. Circle whether you would most likely behave in the way described: always (**A**), frequently (**F**), occasionally (**O**), seldom (**S**), or never (**N**):

A F O S N	1.	I allow members complete freedom in their work.
A F O S N	2.	I would stress being ahead of competing groups.
A F O S N	3.	I would turn members loose on the job and let them go to it.
A F O S N	4.	I would decide what should be done and when it should be done.
A F O S N	5.	I would be willing to make changes.
A F O S N	6.	I would ask the members to work harder.
A F O S N	7.	I would trust group members to exercise good judgment.
A F O S N	8.	I would schedule the work to be done.
A F O S N	9.	I would consult my group before acting.
A F O S N	10.	I would urge the group to beat its previous record.

Scoring: Count the number of always (A) or frequently (F) responses for the odd questions (1, 3, 5, 7, 9). Multiply this number by two and call it your P score; $P = $ _____. Now count the number of always or frequently for the even questions (2, 4, 6, 8, 10), multiply this number by two and call it your T score; $T = $ _____. Save these numbers for later interpretation.

Abridged and adapted from the T–P Leadership Questionnaire: Seigiovanni, T.J., Metzcus, R., & Burden, L. (1969). Toward a pluralistic approach to leadership style. *American Educational Research Journal*, pp. 62–79.

factors, called consideration and initiating structure. **Consideration** includes such items as openness of communication, friendliness, supportiveness, consulting with subordinates, recognition of subordinates. **Initiating structure** includes items dealing with role clarification, directing, planning, controlling, problem solving, criticizing, efficient use of resources.

You may now want to plot your scores from the questionnaire in Table 14.3 on the scale provided in Figure 14.1. Note that the P score equates roughly with consideration or concern for people and the T score corresponds with initiating structure or concern for task.

Consideration, Initiating Structure, and Performance. Generally, leaders who are high on *both* consideration and initiating structure will have more satisfied and productive subordinates than leaders who are low on these dimensions.[27] The desirability of consideration or initiating structure behaviors also varies with the situation.[28] Successful leaders are flexible in their behavior. They can recognize when a given situation calls for a particular behavior. A description of several different situations is provided in Table 14.4. Later in the chapter we will discuss theories that consider situational effects as a major aspect of the theory.

In our opening incident, Lt. Kern was probably quite high on initiating structure and relatively low on consideration. His imbalanced behavior caused problems.

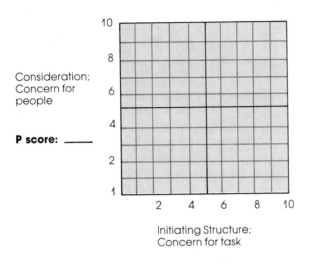

Directions: Plot your *P* score on the vertical axis and your *T* score on the horizontal axis.

Consideration; Concern for people

P score: _____

Initiating Structure; Concern for task

T score: _____

Figure 14.1

CONSIDERATION AND INITIATING STRUCTURE

Table 14.4

SELECTING APPROPRIATE LEADER BEHAVIORS

- The greater the pressure (deadlines, goals, controls, etc.), the more tolerance subordinates have for initiating structure.

- When the task is enriched, consideration is not as important to subordinate's satisfaction, and initiating structure has a less negative effect on satisfaction.

- When the tasks are routine and specified, there is a stronger relationship between consideration and satisfaction.

- When subordinates need a lot of information and expertise from the leader, they are more tolerant and satisfied with initiating structure.

SOURCE: Partial list adapted from Kerr, S., Schriesheim, C.A., Murphy, C.J., & Stogdill, R.M. (1974). Toward a contingency theory of leadership based on the consideration and initiating structure literature. *Organizational Behavior and Human Performance, 12,* 62–84.

The Managerial Grid®

Closely related to, but independent of, the Ohio State studies is the **Managerial Grid** (*see* Figure 14.2), a widely used training strategy in industry.[29] The Grid is based on two factors: concern for production (bottom line, profits, results) and concern for people (friendly, thoughtful, comfortable, people-oriented climate). The "concern for" does not relate directly to the amount of behavior, but to the strength of assumptions behind the leader's style. The two dimensions interact together; they are not independent. Managers are referred to as 9,1; 9,9;

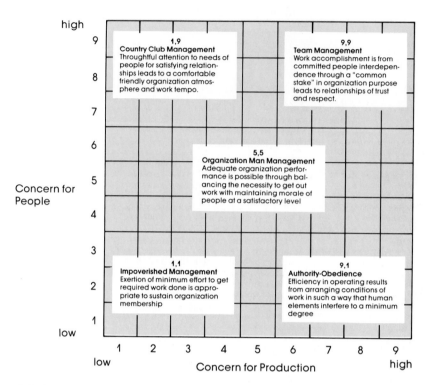

9,1 In the lower right-hand corner of the Grid, a maximum concern for production (9) is combined with a minimum concern for people (1). A manager acting under these assumptions concentrates on maximizing production by exercising power and authority and achieving control over people through compliance. This is a 9,1 orientation.

1,9 The 1,9-oriented leadership style is in the top left corner. Here a minimum concern for production (1) is coupled with a maximum concern for people (9). Primary attention is placed on promoting good feelings among colleagues and subordinates even at the expense of achieving results.

1,1 A minimum concern for both production and people is represented by 1,1 in the lower left corner. The 1,1-oriented manager does only the minimum required to remain within the organization.

5,5 The center depicts the 5,5 orientation. This is the "middle of the road" theory or the "to-go-along-to-get-along" assumptions which are revealed in conformity to the status quo.

9,9 Represented in the upper right corner of the Grid, this style integrates production and people concerns. It is a goal-centered, team approach that seeks to gain optimum results through participation, involvement, commitment, and conflict solving of everyone who can contribute.

Figure 14.2

THE MANAGERIAL GRID®

SOURCE: From *The Managerial Grid III: The Key to Leadership Excellence*, by Robert R. Blake and Jane Srygley Mouton. Houston: Gulf Publishing Company, Copyright © 1985, pages 12, 13. Reproduced by permission.

1,9; 1,1. The 9,9 team manager is the ideal, while the 1,1 impoverished manager is to be avoided.

Here are some examples of how a 9,9 or team manager, would handle various managerial tasks: [30]

> *Planning:* "I get the people who have relevant facts and/or stakes in the outcome together to review the whole picture. We formulate a sound model of an entire project from start to completion. I get their reactions and ideas. I establish goals and flexible schedules with them."
>
> *Organizing:* "We determine individual responsibilities, procedures, and ground rules."
>
> *Directing:* "I keep informed of progress and influence subordinates by identifying problems and revising goals or action steps *with* them. I assist when needed by helping to remove barriers."
>
> *Controlling:* "In addition to critiques to keep projects on schedule, I conduct a wrap-up with those responsible. We evaluate the way things went to see what we learned and how we can apply it to future projects. I give recognition on a team basis as well as for outstanding individual contributions."
>
> *Staffing:* "Work requirements are matched with personnel capabilities or needs in deciding who is to do what."

The Managerial Grid offers a relatively simple way to view leadership that is intuitively appealing. It offers the "one most effective style" approach to leadership, the 9,9 style.[31] In the next section, we will add to the power of the behavioral approach by examining how situational approaches to leadership can add to our understanding of the leadership process.

SITUATIONAL APPROACHES TO LEADERSHIP

So far we have seen that certain behaviors and traits seem to relate to leadership or managerial effectiveness, but that none of these approaches presents a comprehensive picture of leadership. A **situational** approach seeks to remedy this problem by identifying situations or conditions wherein a particular leadership behavior or style is more effective. We will cover three major situational approaches to leadership: Fiedler's contingency model, situational leadership theory, and path-goal theory.

Fiedler's Contingency Model

Perhaps the most widely researched leadership theory is the approach developed by Fiedler, called the **contingency model.**[32] This model tries to predict leadership effectiveness by considering the style of the leader in combination with the favorableness of the situation. Three aspects of the situation are considered: leader-member relations, position power, and task structure.

Leadership Style. Fiedler believes that leadership style is a relatively stable personality trait. He measures style in a rather unusual way by using the Least Preferred Coworker Scale (LPC). The LPC asks people to "Think of all the people with whom you have ever worked, and then think of the person with whom you could work *least well.* This does not have to be the person you liked least well, but should be the person with whom you had the most difficulty getting the job done, the *one* individual with whom you could work *least well.*" [33] People are then asked to respond to a number of bipolar adjectives such as "friendly-unfriendly, tense-relaxed, cold-warm, backbiting-loyal, nasty-nice, and agreeable-disagreeable." If a person responds in a relatively positive way toward his or her least preferred coworker, then the leadership style is people-motivated. If the person responds negatively, the leader is considered task-motivated.

People-motivated leaders are sensitive to others. Good interpersonal relations are very important to them; their self-esteem is affected by how others relate to them. Task-motivated people, on the other hand, are more concerned about getting things done. They need tangible evidence of achievement for their sources of self-esteem. They are likely to take charge and not be overly concerned about their followers' feelings. Lt. Kern in the opening case is probably a task-motivated leader.

Situational Characteristics.   After figuring the LPC, three situational characteristics are considered:

- *Leader-member relations.* These relations are good when followers support the leader with loyalty and commitment. The leader and the followers get along well and have good feelings about each other. Poor leader-member relations might be illustrated by Lt. Kern—a new person without much experience who had not built good relations with his followers. There was no commitment or loyalty. In fact the followers seemed to be doing everything they could to frustrate and undercut Lt. Kern.

- *Task structure.* Tasks may be either structured and routine, or unstructured and nonroutine. Structured tasks, such as an airline baggage-handler or a parts assembler on a television assembly line, have clearly defined steps and work procedures. Unstructured tasks, such as the job of manager or of a market researcher, have multiple ways that the task can be done. Innovation and initiative are needed for successful task accomplishment.

- *Position power.* As we learned in Chapter 12, power is crucial for getting things done. Leaders with strong position power have legitimate, reward, coercive, or expert power because of the position they hold. A leader with high position power might be the CEO of a large organization. Someone with low position power might be the chair of a university committee.

Applying the Contingency Model.   Figure 14.3 illustrates contingency model predictions. The most favorable situation on the far left-hand side of the figure is when leader-member relations are good, the task is structured, and when the leader possesses considerable power. The most unfavorable situation for the leader is when leader-member relations are poor, the task is unstructured, and the power position is weak. Interestingly enough, the task-motivated leader is best for each of these extremes. As you can see from the figure, relationship-motivated leaders do better in moderately favorable or moderately unfavorable situations.

Situational Characteristics

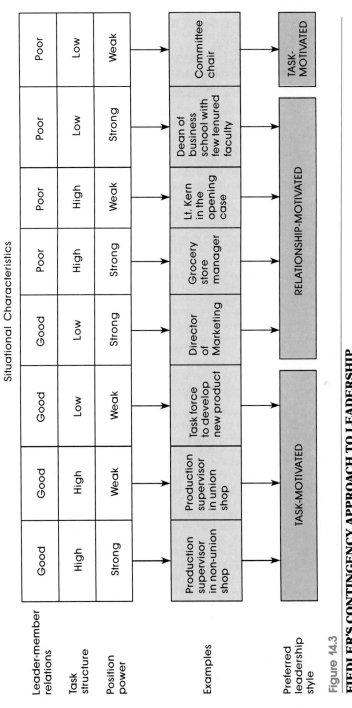

Leader-member relations	Good	Good	Good	Good	Poor	Poor	Poor	Poor
Task structure	High	High	Low	Low	High	High	Low	Low
Position power	Strong	Weak	Weak	Strong	Strong	Weak	Strong	Weak
Examples	Production supervisor in non-union shop	Production supervisor in union shop	Task force to develop new product	Director of Marketing	Grocery store manager	Lt. Kern in the opening case	Dean of business school with few tenured faculty	Committee chair
Preferred leadership style	TASK-MOTIVATED			RELATIONSHIP-MOTIVATED				TASK-MOTIVATED

Figure 14.3

FIEDLER'S CONTINGENCY APPROACH TO LEADERSHIP

None of the examples shown in Figure 14.3 are locked in concrete—conditions can and do change. A production supervisor who has good leader-member relations may find that a decision regarding forced overtime has caused relations to deteriorate, with the result that a union is voted in. The new situation might then be poor leader-member relations, high task structure, and weak position power. This combination would call for a relationship-motivated leader rather than a task-motivated leader. Fiedler's model predicts that a new leader would be needed to match the new situation.

Another implication of Fiedler's model is for promotion. An outstanding manager may be promoted to a new position at a higher organizational level. Unfortunately, the situation may be quite different at the new level and the manager may fail. There may be less position power or the task may be quite unstructured compared to the previous job. In other words a person who performs well in one job may not perform well in another because the situation may be different. Thus, the contingency model boils down to matching the leader with the situation.

A formal training program has been developed using the contingency model, called **LEADER MATCH**.[34] It has been used by over 40,000 managers to improve their leadership effectiveness. LEADER MATCH training recognizes that classifying situations into the categories shown in Figure 14.3 is merely a guideline, not an ironclad rule. They indicate that leaders must use judgment in categorizing and analyzing situations. For example, it is entirely possible that leader-member relations could be so poor it could overwhelm high position power and task structure. Sometimes position power may be so high that other factors mean little, such as when the CEO directly chairs a task force of market researchers. Even the task structure can sometimes dominate; for example, the launch officer of a space mission.

Evaluating Fiedler's Model. The model has been found to do a very good job of predicting group performance.[35] However, there are a number of criticisms centering around LPC.[36] Critics argue that LPC implies people are either task-motivated or relationship-motivated. As we saw earlier in the chapter, other approaches see leaders as possessing both characteristics. Leaders can also change the situation—relations with followers can be improved; task structure can be changed through job enrichment; power can be enhanced by using power tactics, as described in Chapter 12. In other words, leaders can change the characteristics of the situation if they so desire. Leaders may also be able to change their behavior from task-oriented to relationship-oriented and vice versa.

Situational Leadership Theory

One of the most popular leadership theories among practitioners is **Situational Leadership,** developed by Hersey and Blanchard.[37]

Situational Leadership and the Ohio State Studies. Situational Leadership starts with the Ohio State leadership studies, which we discussed earlier in this chapter. Leader behaviors involve a combination of task and relationship behaviors (similar to the initiating structure and consideration, or task and people, shown in Figure 14.2). Leadership style is the behavior pattern (high task, low relationship; high relationship, low task) that someone uses when attempting to influence the activities of others. Leadership style and behavior are evaluated by the leader's followers, superiors, or colleagues—not by the leader. As we saw in Chapter 4, people's perceptions of themselves are often inaccurate reflections of their true behavior.

The key difference between Situational Leadership and the Ohio State studies and the Managerial Grid is that no single style of leadership, such as 9,9, is seen as effective, but that the effectiveness of leadership will depend upon the situation or environment. For example, in a fire department, the appropriate style in an emergency would be high task, low relationship. The time pressures do not permit discussions and attention to member feelings. However, once the crisis is over, a different style will probably be appropriate.

The Situational Key: Maturity of Followers.   While many environmental or situational issues are important, Situational Leadership focuses on the relationship between the leader's behavior and the maturity of the followers. Two types of maturity are seen as particularly important: job maturity and psychological maturity.

Job maturity includes the extent and relevance of past job experience, job knowledge, and the degree of understanding of the job's requirements. For example, a machinist or forklift driver who has been on the job for many years and is thoroughly competent in all aspects of the job would be rated high on job maturity.

Psychological maturity involves the willingness or motivation to do something. Psychologically mature people are eager to accept responsibility, have a strong desire to achieve, and high commitment to their jobs. They have a positive self-concept and feel good about themselves and their jobs. An exam-

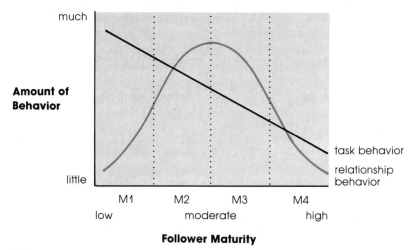

Figure 14.4

BEHAVIOR PRESCRIPTIONS OF SITUATIONAL LEADERSHIP

SOURCE: Gary A. Yukl, *Leadership in Organizations,* © 1981, p. 142. Reprinted by permission of Prentice-Hall, Inc., Englewood Cliffs, N.J.

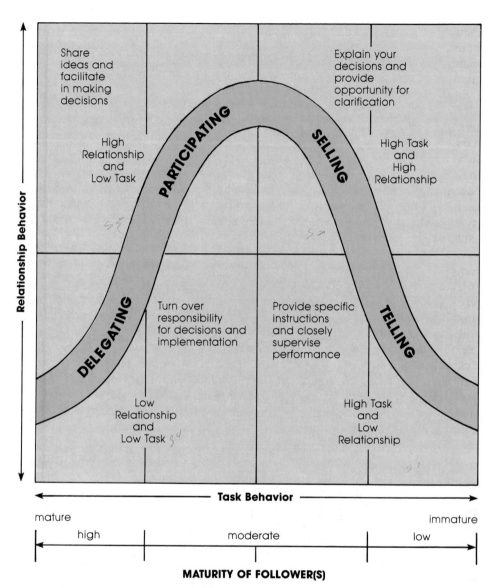

Figure 14.5

SITUATIONAL LEADERSHIP AND DECISION MAKING

Adapted from Paul Hersey, Kenneth H. Blanchard, *Management of Organizational Behavior: Utilizing Human Resources*, 4th ed., © 1982, p. 152. Reprinted by permission of Prentice-Hall, Inc., Englewood Cliffs, N.J.

ple might be a scientist who works independently and feels a strong internal sense of responsibility toward the task.

Subordinate Maturity and Leader Behavior.   Depending upon the maturity level of subordinates, the leader will have to behave differently. For example, in a situation where the followers have low maturity, such as a newly formed crew of manual workers who are generally not motivated and alienated from their jobs, the appropriate style is high task, low relationship (*see* Figure 14.4). In our opening incident, Lt. Kern's followers probably had a high degree of task maturity and a moderate degree of psychological maturity. Thus, the best leadership style would have been high relationship and moderate to low task.

Situational Leadership and Decision Making.   One important form of leader behavior, discussed in Chapter 13, was the degree of subordinate involvement in the decision-making process. Leaders can *delegate*, or allow subordinates to make the decision; they can use *participation*, or joint decision making; they can *sell* their decisions to subordinates even though the decision has already been made; or they can be completely autocratic, make the decision, and *tell* the subordinate what to do.[38] These four decision-making styles—delegating, participating, selling, and telling—are related to situational leadership, as shown in Figure 14.5.

Evaluating Situational Leadership.   The theory makes several important contributions.[39] It focuses attention on the need for behavioral flexibility in different situations. It also recognizes the subordinate as the most important situational factor—we must treat subordinates differently, depending on their abilities and motivation. In addition, the implication is that people may be trained and motivated so that a leadership style may evolve over time from one style to another. The final positive for the model is its relative simplicity and clear link with real, practical, everyday organizational leadership problems.

On the negative side, the theory probably ignores other important situational factors, such as the position power of the leader and task structure. In addition, there is relatively little validation research to support the theory.[40]

Path-Goal Theory

Path-goal theory is concerned with how leaders influence subordinates' perceptions of their work goals and the paths for attaining those goals.[41] Effective leaders help their followers achieve their goals. Examples of goals might include more pay, a promotion, a transfer to a better job, or more free time away from work.

Path-goal theory is based on the expectancy theory of motivation discussed in Chapter 5. Leaders have influence over the subordinate's ability to reach goals, the rewards associated with reaching goals, and the importance of the goals.

Leader Behaviors.   There are four categories of leadership behavior: supportive, directive, participative, and achievement-oriented.[42] The first three are similar to the ones we have already discussed. **Supportive** is similar to people-oriented; **directive** is similar to task-oriented; and **participative** means that subordinates are consulted about decisions. The fourth category, **achievement-oriented** leadership, means setting challenging goals for subordinates, showing confidence in them, and continuously seeking improvement in the performance of subordinates. Whether or not each of these behaviors will be effective depends on the situation.

Situational Factors. Two major groups of situational factors are considered: [43]

• **Subordinate characteristics,** which are similar to those used in the Situational Leadership theory, are needs (for achievement, power, affiliation, and autonomy), the ability to do the job (skills, knowledge, and ability), and a person's personality traits (self-esteem, locus of control, authoritarianism). These personal characteristics of subordinates determine how well they will respond to various leadership behaviors. For example, someone who is high in need for achievement would work best for an achievement-oriented leader; while someone who is low in need for achievement would do best under a directive leader.

• **Environmental pressures** are concerned with any force in the environment with which the subordinate must cope to get the job done. Three major aspects of the environment are the task (*see* Chapter 7), the formal authority system (*see* Chapters 12 and 15), and work group dynamics (*see* Chapter 9). For example, when the task is clear, people need less supervision, and participative or supportive behavior is indicated. On the other hand, if tasks are ambiguous, directive leadership may be more appropriate. These factors bear a close resemblance to Fiedler's situational variables of leader-member relations, task structure, and position power.

Since the situational factors are more numerous and complex than either situational leadership theory or Fiedler's model, more factors must be bal-

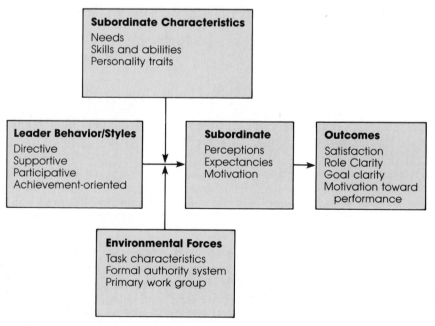

Figure 14.6

THE PATH–GOAL THEORY OF LEADERSHIP

Adapted from Luthans, F. (1981). *Organizational behavior,* 3rd ed., p. 428. Copyright © 1981 by McGraw-Hill, New York. Used with permission.

Perspective 14.4

BARRIERS TO
FEMALE LEADERSHIP[44]

Do women make poor leaders? Are effective female leaders more masculine? Some might answer *yes* to these myths. While more women are reaching leadership positions, there are some serious barriers to female leadership. Jean Lipman-Blumen reviewed the issue of female and male leadership in mixed-sex groups and found that:

1. "Men talk more than women." Apparently, "women, in the company of men, often feel inhibited about talking." Other leadership research shows that "those group members who are most active—including verbally active—are most likely to be perceived as leaders by other group members."

2. "Men's opinions are more likely than women's to influence the opinions of both male and female group members. . . . The resistance women encounter when offering their analyses of problems presents a serious obstacle to female leadership."

3. "Males are more task-oriented, while females are more socio-emotionally oriented." Her research analysis concludes:

Despite the many areas of conflict among the research results to date, some useful insights still may be gained from juxtaposing certain findings that have emerged:

If, in mixed-sex situations (as in day-to-day organizational life), the more active members are seen as leaders;

men are given more opportunities to talk and act;

men actually do talk more than women;

men's opinions are more likely to influence the group positively and women's opinions are more likely to evoke negative or resistant reactions;

male subordinates are more likely than female subordinates to express dissatisfaction with their leader, regardless of the leader's sex; and

the most important informal groups consist of men,

then the current structure of organizations serves as a serious barrier to the acceptance of female leadership.[45]

Other researchers are not as pessimistic as Lipman-Blumen. A recent literature review found no differences between male and female leaders in initiating structure, consideration, or in satisfaction of subordinates.[46] Other reviews have found no differences in performance of male versus female leaders.[47] We should note that while there are many differences in attributes associated with leadership emergence, as pointed out by Lipman-Blumen, the differences seem to blur or evaporate after women have achieved the status of leaders. In other words, "Once legitimized as a leader, women actually do not behave differently from men." [48]

---

anced, compared, and judged before a prescription can be made. The model in Figure 14.6 shows how the factors fit together in the full path-goal model.

Evaluating Path-Goal Theory.   While much research and testing remains, it appears that path-goal theory does explain the leadership process reasonably well.[49] There are many variables involved, and it is difficult to test the model simultaneously. Most research to date has involved partial tests, such as the effects of task structure.[50] Another issue is that the leader's role is seen as a relatively passive one of providing guidance, assistance, and coaching. This role is certainly an important one, but there seem to be many leaders who are much more active and are still quite effective. The path-goal theory, while interesting and promising, needs much more research.

LEADERSHIP: SUMMARIZING WHAT WE DO KNOW

By now you have been exposed to a sample of the bewildering array of leadership theories. Rather than examining the weaknesses of leadership theories—and there are many—let's summarize what we do know about leadership.[51]

Task-Relevant Expertise

The leader's expertise in matters that are important to the group gives an important source of power. It is difficult for a leader who does not know what is going on to have influence. Leaders need skills in group process and in the technical aspects of the task. Effective leaders are able to organize and structure group activities; they plan, coordinate, clarify, set goals, train, summarize, and solve problems. In short, an effective leader needs to understand the group's processes and the technical aspects relating to the group's task.

Relationship With Subordinates

Many theories point out the importance of a leader's ability to get along with people, and particularly with subordinates. Most effective leaders treat subordinates fairly and are concerned for their needs; leaders are considerate. Feelings of trust, mutual loyalty, and increased subordinate satisfaction result. However, while some level of concern is always needed, some situations may call for leaders who emphasize the task much more than the people.

Decision-Making Participation

While we covered participation in decision making in Chapter 13, it is also an important leadership factor. Subordinate commitment in both the decision and the leader improve when participation is used. Effective leaders use a variety of task and maintenance roles (discussed in the chapter on group dynamics) to aid in the decision-making process.

The Influence of the Leader

An effective leader has "clout" in all organizational directions. The leader has the ability to get things done and to influence superiors and peers to help the group. In other words, the effective leader is powerful and is thus an effective link with the world outside the group.

Motivation to Lead

Leaders want to lead. They enjoy the power and achievement that comes from leading. Trait research and assessment centers have shown that the desire for power and advancement are important predictors of leadership success.

CROSS–CULTURAL OB:
HOW DOES LEADERSHIP DIFFER?

While leadership is a universal phenomenon, there are vast differences in style and behavior across cultures.

Cross-Cultural Leadership Differences

Leadership tends to vary a great deal within and between cultures. The following examples from Margaret Mead's anthropological studies help illustrate these differences: [52]

- In central Africa, the Bachiga were characterized by individualism, lack of political integration, and noncompliance with their leaders. The Bathonga, on the other hand, emphasized obedience, respect for the chief, and cooperative effort, with little room for rivalry.

- Among traditional Eskimos, one person's importance in relation to others was not emphasized. The Samoans, however, ranked individuals in clear hierarchy and enforced conformity to these ranks.

- Among Native Americans, the Iroquois achieved leadership through behavior that was socially rewarding to others, such as generosity, cooperation, and hospitality. In contrast, among the Kwakiutl, the ideal chief was one who could successfully compete financially against the other chiefs.

- The Arapesh of New Guinea did not consider ownership of land as a basis for leadership; however, the Ifugao of the Philippines considered the landowner the ideal of success.

Studies have also been conducted to compare similarities and differences of leadership across cultures. The results of one of these studies are shown in Figure 14.7.[53]

Cultural Factors That Affect Leadership

There are many cultural factors that influence leadership behavior. Several of them are summarized below: [54]

Traditionalism versus modernism. Traditionalism places emphasis on family, class, reverence for the past, and status. It is strong in India or Afghanistan. The traditional leader will most likely be the oldest male. This leader is in a powerful position and thus may find leadership relatively easy. **Modernism** emphasizes merit, rationality, and progress. It is strongest in the United States or Sweden. Relations with followers and position power are important here. The following story illustrates how leaders with a different cultural background can get into trouble: [55]

> A U.S. firm in Spain had a different kind of "American" problem. The home office had a tradition of holding company picnics where management and workers mingled with ease in a comfortable environment. The firm tried to import its compa-

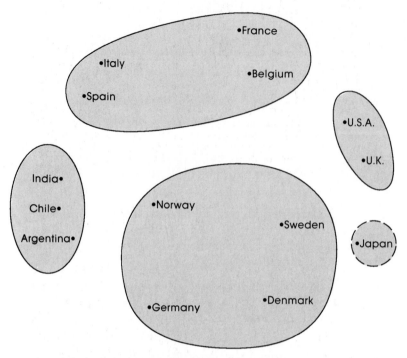

(Cluster analysis based on the degree of intercorrelation between various leadership attitudes.)

Figure 14.7

LEADERSHIP CLUSTERS AMONG SELECTED COUNTRIES

SOURCE: S. Ronen and A. Krant (1977). Similarities among countries based on employee work values and attitudes. *Columbia Journal of World Business,* *12* (2), p. 92. Used with permission.

ny picnic to Spain, and to highlight management's "democratic" belief, the U.S. executives dressed as chefs and served the food. However, the picnic failed to help elicit the desired rapport between U.S. managers and the Spanish workers. In fact it was a most awkward affair, as the lower staff clung together and did not want to be served by their superiors. When an executive approached their table, everyone stood up. Spanish attitudes of class distinction and social groups prohibit casual mixing and socializing of workers with executives.

Particularism versus universalism. Particularism implies allegiance to friends and stresses the importance of interpersonal relations. It is very important in Mexico and Latin America. **Universalism** emphasizes obligations to society and organization. It is more common in the Anglo-American world.

Pragmatism versus idealism. Pragmatists are opportunistic; they are interested in what works. **Idealists,** on the other hand, seek the truth. While there is a great deal of variation, managers throughout the world tend to be more pragmatic. Their behaviors and values emphasize productivity, profitability, and achievement.

Autocratic versus democratic leadership. Democratic leadership, which uses participation in decision making as a common strategy, is much more common in the West than in Latin America or India, where **autocratic leadership** is the norm. For example, paternalism, featuring an autocratic patron and compliant followers, is a common feature of Latin organizations.

MANAGERIAL APPLICATIONS OF LEADERSHIP

Leadership is a crucial skill for getting things done. Managers who supervise others must be able to influence and motivate them to achieve goals; to perform. Leadership is complex. It involves almost every concept we have studied or will study in this book—leaders must have clear values; they must be able to motivate behavior; they must be able to communicate and work successfully within a group. They must be able to make decisions and, when appropriate, involve their followers in decisions. Leaders must be able to balance all organizational behavior skills to accomplish the goal. They establish the culture of the organization.

- *Develop leadership skills.* There is much you can do to improve your leadership ability. Develop skills in working with people and communicating. Learn as much about the task as possible—become the expert. Develop self-confidence, take the initiative, and be persistent in solving important problems.

- *Recognize that leadership is transactional.* As a leader you contribute skills, knowledge, and power for accomplishing the goal. Your followers provide you with loyalty, status, esteem, and power. Remember that leadership is a mutual influence process based on trust. Followers are just as important as leaders.

- *Use both task and people behaviors.* Leadership involves using both initiating structure and consideration to be effective. Take care to properly balance these approaches. Use a 9,9 team approach when appropriate.

- *Consider the situation in deciding how to lead.* The contingency model indicates that task-motivated leadership is most effective in either favorable or unfavorable situations while relationship-motivated leadership works best in moderately favorable or unfavorable situations.

- *Match the leader to the situation.* If you believe that a leader's orientation toward task or relationship is relatively unchangeable, as does Fiedler, then you should be careful to choose people who will be leaders in a given situation. Use the model for hiring, promotions, and transfers.

- *Consider your followers' maturity.* Mature followers demand more consideration and participation in decision making while immature followers should be led in a more task-oriented style with little participation.

- *Help clarify paths to your followers' goals.* Use supportive, directive, participative, or achievement-oriented leadership as ways to help subordinates achieve their valued outcomes and goals.

- *Help overcome barriers to female leadership.* Encourage women to actively participate and lead mixed-group sessions to develop their leadership potential.

- *Recognize differences in leadership across cultures.* Be particularly alert to traditionalism and particularism. These cultural factors will have great influence on decision making, goal orientation, and relations with subordinates.

FOR DISCUSSION

1. Perspective 14.1 points out a number of differences between managers and leaders. Do you agree with these differences? Support your position.

2. What traits or skills seem to be associated with effective leaders? How powerful are these traits or skills?

3. How is power related to the social exchange approach to leadership?

4. Compare and contrast the Managerial Grid with Situational Leadership. Which do you think more accurately portrays effective leader behavior?

5. Which approach to leadership do you support—matching leaders to situations or training leaders to change their leadership styles for different situations? Defend your position. Can you think of an instance where one leader has been successful in a number of different types of situations?

6. What other variables besides follower maturity do you think are important for explaining leader behavior?

7. Explain how the path-goal theory of leadership works. What are its major weaknesses?

8. List all the situational variables used in the contingency model, situational model, and path-goal model. Which of these seem to overlap? Do you believe they are all needed?

9. Summarize what we do know about leadership by listing those behaviors and traits that you think are important for a leader to possess.

10. Based upon your personal experience, do you agree with the barriers to female leadership highlighted in Perspective 14.4?

11. Assume you are being transferred to Mexico as the manager of an auto parts manufacturing plant. How will you need to change your leadership style? Will these changes be comfortable for you, or will they create discomfort or conflict?

KEY CONCEPTS AND TERMS

leadership
traits
skills
assessment center
social-exchange process
transactional leadership
charismatic leadership
Ohio State leadership studies
consideration
initiating structure

Managerial Grid
Fiedler's contingency model
leader-member relations
position power
task structure
situational leadership theory
job maturity
psychological maturity
environmental pressures
path-goal theory

supportive leadership
directive leadership
participative leadership
achievement-oriented leadership
LEADER–MATCH
traditionalism
modernism
particularism
universalism

Cases and Incidents

THE ANTILEADERSHIP VACCINE

(The following excerpt from an article by John W. Gardner provides an interesting perspective on leadership.)
Indeed, it is my belief that we are immunizing a high proportion of our most gifted young people

against any tendencies to leadership. It will be worth our time to examine how the antileadership vaccine is administered.

The process is initiated by the society itself. The conditions of life in a modern, complex society are not conducive to the emergence of leaders. The young person today is acutely aware of the fact that he is an anonymous member of a mass society, an individual lost among millions of others. The processes by which leadership is exercised are not visible to him, and he is bound to believe that they are exceedingly intricate. Very little in his experience encourages him to think that he might some day exercise a role of leadership.

This unfocused discouragement is of little consequence compared with the expert dissuasion the young person will encounter if he is sufficiently bright to attend a college or university. In those institutions today, the best students are carefully schooled to avoid leadership responsibilities.

Most of our intellectually gifted young people go from college directly into graduate school or into one of the older and more prestigious professional schools. There they are introduced to—or, more correctly, powerfully indoctrinated in—a set of attitudes appropriate to scholars, scientists, and professional men. This is all to the good. The students learn to identify themselves strongly with their calling and its ideals. They acquire a conception of what a good scholar, scientist, or professional man (sic) is like.

As things stand now, however, that conception leaves little room for leadership in the normal sense; the only kind of leadership encouraged is that which follows from the performing of purely professional tasks in a superior manner. Entry into what most of us would regard as the leadership roles in the society at large is discouraged.

In the early stages of a career, there is a good reason for this: becoming a first-class scholar, scientist, or professional requires single-minded dedication. Unfortunately, by the time the individual is sufficiently far along in his career to afford a broadening of interests, he often finds himself irrevocably set in a narrow mold.

The antileadership vaccine has other more subtle and powerful ingredients. The image of the corporation president, politician, or college president that is current among most intellectuals and professionals today has some decidedly unattractive features. It is said that such men (sic) compromise their convictions almost daily, if not hourly. It is said that they have tasted the corrupting experience of power. They must be status seekers, the argument goes, or they would not be where they are.

Needless to say, the student picks up such attitudes. It is not that professors propound these views and students learn them. Rather, they are in the air and students absorb them. The resulting unfavorable image contrasts dramatically with the image these young people are given of the professional who is almost by definition dedicated to his field, pure in his motives, and unencumbered by worldly ambition.

My own extensive acquaintance with scholars and professionals on the one hand and administrators and managers on the other does not confirm this contrast in character. In my experience, each category has its share of opportunists. Nevertheless, the negative attitudes persist.

As a result the academic world appears to be approaching a point at which everyone will want to educate the technical expert who advises the leader, or the intellectual who stands off and criticizes the leader, but no one will want to educate the leader himself.

DISCUSSION QUESTIONS

1. Do you agree that most people are vaccinated against leadership?

2. What can be done to change the situation?

3. What can you do to keep yourself from being vaccinated? How can you enhance your own leadership potential?

From Gardner, J.W. (1965). The antileadership vaccine. Carnegie Corporation of New York annual report essay. For a reprint see W.E. Rosenbach and R.L. Taylor (Eds.) (1984). *Contemporary issues in leadership*. Boulder CO: Westview Press, pp. 323–324.

BILL KADOTA'S PROBLEM

The years of single-minded dedication to his education and then to his work were beginning to pay off for Bill Kadota. He had become a first-line supervisor and believed that if he performed well, a career in management would be open to him. Arriving in this country in the 1970s with very little money, Bill had worked his way to a masters degree in engineering (with several business courses as part of his program). He was promoted to a supervisory position after three years of work in the electronics industry, the last 18 months at Dandy Electronics, a medium-sized firm in the Southwest. Bill was proud of his achievements both at the university and in his work life.

Bill Kadota was anxious to show that he could be a good supervisor. He saw his promotion as a challenging opportunity to find out how well he could handle supervisory responsibilities. Yet he wondered whether the people whom he would be supervising would work well for him, and he felt he would have to prove himself quickly, because he believed that opportunities for promotion in management were limited and the company didn't give people long to show how well they could perform. Bill was anxious to please his new boss, John Davidson, and he wondered how much cooperation he would get from him. In talking with Bill about his new position, Davidson had emphasized the importance of meeting production deadlines. Bill formed the impression that Davidson might be personally supportive, but he was not sure.

Bill was taking over the Production Control (PC) section, which had responsibility for some aspects of product testing, evaluation, and shipping. The section included nine non-exempt technicians, in addition to the supervisor. The previous supervisor, Tom Brown, had left the company before Bill was notified of his promotion. For the six weeks before Bill took over the section, John Davidson (the department manager) had directly supervised the PC section.

Before moving into his new position, Bill talked with two people who had previously worked in the PC section in order to get information about the quality of the employees now in the section. According to the former members of the section, most of the current employees were at least reasonably conscientious and regular in their work. They told Bill that one of the workers, Joe Calonico, had been a "buddy" of the previous supervisor, had exercised a lot of freedom to come and go pretty much as he pleased, and hardly put in more than four or five hours a day of real working time. Bill felt that Calonico might be a problem.

On hearing of Tom Brown's resignation, Joe Calonico had approached John Davidson to ask for promotion to section supervisor. Davidson denied his request and gave the following reasons: (1) Calonico was not qualified for the position, because he had neither a university degree nor the six years of experience required as a substitute for the degree; (2) he lacked experience in one of the section's work areas and in coordinating work with other departments; and (3) he had no supervisory experience that would demonstrate his ability to work under pressure in performing high-priority tasks.

Calonico was unhappy with this decision. He told Davidson that he was a top performer as a technician. He also reminded Davidson that he had been promoted to "engineer" (an exempt but non-supervisory position) two years earlier, and had held that position for ten months until he and many other employees were demoted to their previous positions during one of the quite frequent periods of company cutbacks (a characteristic of many firms in the electronics industry). Calonico

retained his engineer's salary despite his demotion to special technician. He had also been put through several technical and a few "human relations" courses in house training programs.

When Bill took over as supervisor of the PC section he discussed work tasks, work flow relationships, and task priorities with each employee in the section individually. By doing this he hoped to learn much about each employee's abilities and to establish good relations with all employees from the start. He left task assignments and work flow much as they had been, although he changed some output priorities in line with some new directives from the department manager.

Bill was satisfied with the performance of most of the section employees but he immediately sensed an attitude of personal hostility on the part of Joe Calonico, who also seemed apathetic toward his own work. Calonico would accept a task assignment, then either fail to perform it or take what Bill felt to be an unduly long time to complete it. He would give no reason to Bill, or he stated that he simply hadn't had enough time, or gave what Bill felt were vague excuses.

Bill thought that perhaps Calonico felt he could get away with this behavior because he expected to get a job in another department for which he was bidding. Calonico was unsuccessful in securing this other job. Bill never found out why; he thought that perhaps the manager who had advertised the opening didn't really have such an opening immediately available but was simply scouting for good candidates for the time when such an opening should become available. Calonico was upset about his lack of success in getting that job. Bill noted that Calonico became even more careless about completing his tasks. He sometimes reported late for work. Bill observed him sitting idly or talking with employees from other sections for long periods. On a few days, Calonico stayed away from work without notifying Bill, who felt that he must be looking for a job outside the company. Although other employees in the section sometimes depended on Calonico to help accomplish their tasks, they exerted no informal pressure on him. Bill felt this was because Calonico had been around longer than most of the other employees and had a forceful personality. Calonico sometimes argued with Bill about job assignments and work methods in the presence of other employees.

Trying to find out more about Calonico, Bill discovered that his predecessor had given Calonico favorable performance appraisals, although Bill noticed that most of the supervisor's comments were of a very general nature. These appraisals indicated that Calonico had done the job well, had done good work, and had put in the effort required to solve some special problems. Bill didn't know what to make of these appraisals. He thought that perhaps they had been influenced by personal friendship between Tom Brown and Calonico, or that Brown had simply wanted to be sure he kept Calonico in light of the company cost control practice of not replacing people who were transferred or fired.

Calonico's behavior puzzled and disturbed Bill because he felt Calonico lacked the qualifications to perform the supervisory job. Yet it was not unusual, in Bill's experience, to find technicians who felt they could do jobs that require real engineering know-how. It seemed to Bill that there were many people like that in the electronics industry. Bill felt that Calonico should recognize that he lacked such qualifications and get on with doing good work in his present position (which he felt Calonico had the ability to do). Bill never felt that he understood why Calonico behaved as he did. The section's workload was heavy, output was in continuous danger of falling behind schedule, and Bill had to meet a succession of output objectives to meet company deadlines and pressure from Davidson. He frequently told Calonico that he was too indifferent to his work, was working inefficiently, and was weak on punctuality. Bill also indicated that Calonico should improve in each of these areas. Bill's actions had little effect but, having wanted to establish good relations right from the start he kept hoping Calonico would improve.

Bill had talked with John Davidson about Calonico's behavior. Davidson made no proposals about how to solve the problem but indicated that Bill must solve it. "You're the manager of the PC section," Davidson said. He would quickly shift discussion to technical and output issues. Bill felt he had inherited the problem of Calonico, and whereas it should have been solved earlier, it was now his own responsibility. He worried about it a great deal at work and during his leisure time.

After two months on the job, Bill felt that pointing out Calonico's performance inadequacies was not having much effect, and that Calonico had had enough time to show improvement. He then decided to try to motivate Calonico to perform more effectively. He did not want to take a hard line and desired to maintain good relations in the section. Especially because he was still quite new, he did not wish to appear to be domineering or to put on too much pressure in the section. He wished "to be

employee-oriented" and to avoid "close supervision." These approaches seemed consistent with ideas emphasized by instructors in his college business courses and in a human relations course taken at Dandy Electronics. He also felt that Calonico might be personally hostile because Bill had obtained the job that Calonico had badly wanted. While continuing to point out Calonico's performance problems and the necessity to improve, Bill tried to establish favorable relations with him by socializing during coffee and lunch breaks. Bill felt that this would help make Calonico "feel part of the group" and show him that Bill would treat him objectively and fairly. As Bill saw it, he was trying to "turn him on by way of motivation . . . to win him over."

Calonico's job performance did not improve and Bill felt his efforts had been in vain; nothing would work, Calonico just didn't care and would never accept Bill as his supervisor. After two weeks of trying to be friendly with Calonico, Bill felt he had to take a firm stand. At this point another department requested early resolution of a quality control problem that had been sitting on Calonico's desk for two weeks. Bill told him to solve the problem and provide recommendations within two days. Calonico agreed. On the afternoon of the second day, the following discussion took place:

Kadota: Do you have the results and recommendations on the Production department problem?

Calonico: No. I haven't gotten around to it yet.

Kadota: Joe, what have you been doing in the past week?

Calonico: Some of those customer requirement projects.

Kadota: Which customer projects?

Calonico: Oh . . . you know, some of those we have had around.

Kadota: You aren't even working at half speed, even though you're the highest-paid special technician in the division.

Calonico: I get as much done in four hours as anyone else does in eight.

Bill broke off the discussion. He decided to take a very firm stand to settle the Calonico problem once and for all. Because he wasn't sure just how to accomplish this, he called the Organization Development specialist for advice. He had heard about MBO, Managerial Grid, and related programs run by the OD specialist, and felt that the OD man— whom everyone in the company was authorized to contact directly and informally—should be able to help in a problem of this type. The OD specialist's secretary told Bill to call back after two weeks because the OD man was attending an important OD conference in New York.

Bill wanted to act right away. It occurred to him that maybe it was just as well that the OD specialist was out of town; now that he thought more about it, he remembered that the OD man concentrated on helping to solve problems related to output and productivity failures of work groups. Bill decided to go to the Personnel Department, even though he wasn't sure how much help he could get from that department in solving problems in his section. He did know that the Personnel Department had a formal responsibility to help resolve differences between employees and to act as a sort of "mediator," whatever that meant.

Bill described the Calonico issue to a personnel specialist who suggested that Bill give Calonico a formal written warning, putting him on probation and indicating that failure to improve in all areas would lead to dismissal. To Bill, this sounded like the kind of tough action that was needed. It would represent a formal recognition of the problem and lead to formal involvement of John Davidson, whose endorsement of the formal warning would be required. Davidson approved of this approach when Bill told him what he intended to do.

In his formal letter to Calonico, Bill criticized (1) his failures to complete assignments on time; (2) the adverse impact of his attitude on achievement of section output objectives; and (3) his irresponsibility. Bill cited examples of failures to perform specific tasks and of tardiness. He told Calonico that he would be dismissed after one month if he did not improve his productivity, show a greater sense of responsibility and a more positive attitude, and get to work on time. Bill also told Calonico to provide a daily report on tasks completed, progress in ongoing tasks, and problems being met in completing tasks.

After Calonico read the letter he threw it at Bill and made abusive comments to the effect that the letter was "ridiculous," "stupid," and "a lot of nonsense." Calonico accused Bill of incompetence. Calonico also refused to sign the letter (which would be a formal acknowledgment that he had received it). Calonico then went off to complain to the personnel manager. The next day Bill took Calonico into the department manager's office, where Calonico repeated his criticisms, accused Bill of being incompetent and of having failed to provide enough direction in the section, and attempted to refute each item in the letter. Davidson replied that he be-

lieved everything in the letter. When Calonico continued to refuse to sign it, Davidson signed the letter himself, to formally witness that refusal. Davidson also told Calonico that he had the right to file a reply to the probationary letter.

Bill now felt that Calonico "would have to toe the line" or get out. Bill's experience was that employees at Dandy Electronics couldn't challenge their bosses and get away with it. As with many companies in the electronics industry, Dandy Electronics experienced periodic sales downturns—sometimes due to poor product or market decisions—that resulted in periodic layoffs. Bill felt the company kept an eye out for "troublemakers" and that layoff times were used as occasions to get rid of them. He felt that Calonico would now be scared of losing his job. Bill felt rather sorry for Calonico.

Later that week the personnel manager called in Bill to talk about Calonico's probation, and reviewed in detail the probationary letter. The personnel manager then asked Bill to withdraw the probationary letter. Bill was upset and told the personnel manager that he was responsible to the company for the efficient and profitable operation of his section, and could not tolerate an ineffective and disrespectful employee. Bill refused to withdraw the letter, and the meeting ended. Bill felt that his stand was "adamant, but rational," and that he had to treat his subordinates "within the boundaries set by my own boss." Bill also felt he had persuaded the personnel manager of the correctness of his position. Since the Personnel Department did not have the formal authority to reverse Bill's position, he felt his decision would stand.

The following week Calonico again met with John Davidson to find out exactly how he was to remove his probationary status. When Davidson reviewed the situation with Bill, Bill told him that Calonico's work behavior had not improved and that the sooner he was fired, the sooner a replacement might be hired to deal with the backlog of work. Davidson told Bill that he agreed with this perspective. Later that day Davidson called Bill and Calonico together. Davidson said, "I believe that a personality conflict exists between you two and that it might well be impossible to resolve this conflict. Maybe you fellows can never work together." Davidson then presented the following options and told Calonico to select one of them:

1. Stay in his present job, improve his performance, and show the proper respect toward Bill Kadota.

2. Write a formal rebuttal letter to Bill's formal charges, which Davidson would then evaluate.

3. Find a job in another department.

4. Resign.

5. Accept a transfer into another section within Davidson's department and, in order to remove his probationary status, show that he could perform effectively in that section.

Calonico chose the fifth alternative.

A few days later—three months into his supervisory job—Bill Kadota expressed some feelings while he shared a few beers at a local bar. "I'm pleased that Calonico is gone from the section. The problem seems finally over. But I'm uneasy about the way things have gone. So much seemed to go wrong along the way. Things have been pretty unpleasant. There's a lot of pressure, and I don't seem to get much cooperation. You know, Dandy seems a cruel place sometimes. It's tough to manage. Why won't people just get on with their work, do what they're paid to do?"

DISCUSSION QUESTIONS

1. What leadership style does Bill Kadota employ?

2. Describe the situation using Fiedler's model as your guide.

3. What conflict resolution strategy seems appropriate here?

4. What might have Bill Kadota done differently to resolve the problem?

Reprinted by permission of the publisher from Bill Kadota's problem, by J.M. Walker, *Journal of Management Case Studies, 2,* 70–75. Copyright © 1986 by Elsevier Science Publishing Co., Inc.

REFERENCES

1. Yukl, G.A. (1981). *Leadership in organizations.* Englewood Cliffs, NJ: Prentice-Hall. Bass, B.M. (1981). *Stogdill's handbook of leadership: A survey of theory and research.* New York: The Free Press. Miner, J.B. (1982). The uncertain future of the leadership concept: Revisions and clarifications. *Journal of Applied Behavioral Science, 18,* 293–307.

2. Gary A. Yukl (1981), p. 1. Reprinted by permission of Prentice-Hall, Inc., Englewood Cliffs, N.J.

3. Meindl, J.R., Ehrlich, S.B., & Dukerich, J.M. (1985). The romance of leadership. *Administrative Science Quarterly, 30,* 78–102. Meindl, J.R., & Ehrlich, S.B. (1987). The romance of leadership and the evaluation of organizational performance. *Academy of Management Journal, 30,* 91–109.

4. Lord, R.G., & Smith, J.E. (1983). Theoretical, information processing, and situational factors affecting attribution theory models in organizational behavior. *Academy of Management Review, 8,* 50–60. Pfeffer, J. (1977). The ambiguity of leadership. *Academy of Management Review, 2,* 104–112.

5. Zaleznik, A. (1977). Managers and leaders: Are they different? *Harvard Business Review, 55* (3), 67–78.

6. Kast, F.E., & Rosenzweig, J.E. (1985). *Organization and management,* (4th ed., p. 5). New York: McGraw-Hill.

7. Zaleznik (1977).

8. Smith, J.E., Carson, K.P., & Alexander, R.A. (1984). Leadership: It can make a difference. *Academy of Management Journal, 27,* 765–776. House, R.J., & Baetz, M.L. (1979). Leadership: Some empirical generalizations and new research directions. In B.M. Staw, (Ed.). *Research in organizational behavior, vol. 1* (pp. 341–423). Greenwich, CT: JAI Press.

9. See Bass (1981). And Karmel, B. (1978). A challenge to traditional research methods and assumptions. *Academy of Management Review, 3,* 475–482.

10. This definition is similar to the one used in Barrow, J.C. (1977). The variables of leadership: A review and conceptual framework. *Academy of Management Review, 2,* 232–251.

11. Lord, R.G., De Vader, C.L., and Alliger, G.M. (1986), A meta-analysis of the relation between personality traits and leadership perceptions: An application of validity generalizations procedures. *Journal of Applied Psychology, 71,* 402–410.

12. Lord, et al. (1986). Yukl (1981).

13. Stogdill, R.M. (1974). *Handbook of leadership* (p. 63). New York: The Free Press.

14. Stogdill (1974).

15. Yukl (1981), p. 70. Also see Campbell, J.P., Dunnette, M.D., Lawler, E.E., III, & Weick, K.E., Jr. (1970). *Managerial behavior, performance and effectiveness.* New York: McGraw-Hill.

16. Thornton, G.C., & Byham, W.C. (1982). *Assessment centers and managerial performance.* New York: Academic Press. Finkle, R.B. (1976). Managerial assessment centers. In M.D. Dunnette (Ed.). *Handbook of industrial and organizational psychology,* (pp. 861–888). Chicago: Rand-McNally.

17. Rice, B. (1978). Measuring executive muscle. *Psychology Today, 12* (7), 99. Reprinted with permission from *Psychology Today* Magazine. Copyright © 1977 American Psychological Association.

18. Bray, D.W., Campbell, R.J., & Grant, D.L. (1974). *Formative years in business: A long-term AT & T study of managerial lives.* New York: Wiley.

19. Cascio, W.F., & Sibey, V. (1979). Utility of the assessment center as a selection device. *Journal of Applied Psychology, 64,* 107–118.

20. Cascio & Sibey (1979). Klimoski, R.S., & Stricktland, W. (1977). Assessment centers: Valid or merely prescient. *Personnel Psychology, 30,* 353–363. Russell, C.J. (1985). Individual decision processes in an assessment center. *Journal of Applied Psychology, 70,* 737–746.

21. Lord, R.G. (1985). An information processing approach to social perceptions. In L.L. Cummings & B.M. Staw (Eds.). *Research in organizational behavior, vol. 7* (pp. 87–128). Greenwich, CT: JAI Press. Another way to examine the leader-member exchange process is summarized in Dienesch, R.M., & Liden, R.C. (1986). Leader-member exchange model of leadership: A critique and further development. *Academy of Management Review, 11,* 618–634.

22. Exchange theory was developed by Homans, G.C. (1958). Social behavior as exchange. *American Journal of Sociology, 63,* 597–606. For the use of exchange theory in leadership, see Jacobs, T.O. (1971). *Leadership and exchange in formal organizations.* Alexandria, VA: Human Resources Research Organization. Transactional leadership was developed by Hollander, E.A. (1978). *Leadership dynamics: A practical guide to effective relationships.* New York: The Free Press. Also see Bass, B.M. (1985). *Leadership and performance beyond expectations.* New York: Free Press. And Bass, B.M. (1985). Leadership: Good, better, best. *Organizational Dynamics, Winter,* 26–40.

23. Jacobs (1971), p. 339.

24. Based on House, R.J. (1977). A 1976 theory of charismatic leadership. In J.G. Hunt & L.L. Larson, (Eds.). *Leadership: The cutting edge* (pp. 189–207). Carbondale, IL: Southern Illinois University Press.

25. House (1977), pp. 193–194.

26. Stogdill (1974).

27. Kerr, S., Schriesheim, C.A., Murphy, C.J., & Stogdill, R.M. (1974). Toward a contingency theory of leadership based on the consideration and initiating structure literature. *Organizational Behavior and Human Performance, 12,* 62–84.

28. Kerr, et al. (1974).

29. Managerial Grid is the registered trademark of R.R. Blake & J.S. Mouton. See Blake, R.R., & Mouton, J.S. (1985). *The Managerial Grid III: The key to leadership excellence.* Houston: Gulf. For a discussion of the Grid and a comparison with the Situational Leadership theory, see Blake, R.R., & Mouton, J.S. (1982). A comparative analysis of situationalism and 9,9 management by principle. *Organizational Dynamics, 10* (4), 20–43.

30. From Robert R. Blake and Jane Srygley Mouton. *The Managerial Grid III: The key to leadership excellence,* p. 94. Copyright 1985 by Gulf Publishing Company, Houston. Reproduced by permission.

31. Blake & Mouton (1985). Also, see Hornstein, H.A., Heilman, M.E., Mone, E., & Tartell, R. (1987). Responding to contingent leadership. *Organizational Dynamics, 15*(4), 56–65.

32. Fiedler, F.E. (1967). *A theory of leadership effectiveness.* New York: McGraw-Hill. Fiedler, F.E., & Chemers, M.M. (1974). *Leadership and effective management.* Glenview, IL: Scott, Foresman. Fiedler, F., Chemers, M., & Mahr, L. (1976). *Improving leadership effectiveness.* New York: John Wiley and Sons.

33. Fiedler, et al. (1976), p. 7.

34. Fiedler, F.E., Chemers, M.M. (1984). *Improving leadership effectiveness: The LEADER MATCH concept* (rev. ed.). New York: Wiley. For a critical review, see Jago, A.G., & Ragan, J.W. (1986). The trouble with LEADER MATCH is that it doesn't match Fielder's contingency model. *Journal of Applied Psychology, 71,* 555–559. Other arguments against the LEADER–MATCH concept are presented in the book review of *Improving leadership effectiveness,* written by Hosking, D., & Schriesheim, C. (1978). *Administrative Science Quarterly, 23,* 496–505. For a practical view of leadership similar to Fiedler's, see Herbert, T.T., & Deresky, H. (1987). Should general managers match their business strategies. *Organizational Dynamics, 15*(3), 40–51.

35. For reviews see Strube, M.J., & Garcia, J.E. (1981). A meta-analytic investigation of Fiedler's contingency model of leadership effectiveness. *Psychological Bulletin, 90,* 307–321. And Vecchio, R.P. (1983). Assessing the validity of Fiedler's contingency model of leadership effectiveness: A closer look at Strube and Garcia. *Psychological Bulletin, 93,* 404–408.

36. Singh, R. (1983). Leadership style and reward allocation: Does Least Preferred Coworker Scale measure task and relation orientation? *Organizational Behavior and Human Performance, 32,* 178–197.

37. Hersey, P., & Blanchard, K.H. (1982). *Management of organizational behavior: Utilizing human resources* (4th ed.). Englewood Cliffs, NJ: Prentice-Hall.

38. See Tannenbaum, R., & Schmidt, W.H. (1958, March-April). How to choose a leadership pattern. *Harvard Business Review.* Also see the discussion of Vroom and Yetton's model of decision making discussed in Chapter 13.

39. This critique is based on Graeff, C.L. (1983). The Situational Leadership theory: A critical view. *Academy of Management Review, 8,* 285–291. And Yukl (1981).

40. For a study supporting Situational Leadership theory, see Hambelton, R.K., & Gumpert, R. (1982). The validity of Hersey and Blanchard's theory of leader effectiveness. *Group and Organizational Studies, 7* (2), 225–242. Also see Blake, R.R., & Mouton, J.S. (1981). Management by Grid principles or situationalism: Which? *Group and Organizational Studies, 6,* 439–455. And Hersey, P., & Blanchard, K.H. (1982). Grid principles and situationalism: Both! A response to Blake and Mouton. *Group and Organizational Studies, 7,* 207–210.

41. House, R.J. (1971). A path-goal theory of leader effectiveness. *Administrative Science Quarterly, 16,* 321–339. Actually, the first path-goal theory, a non-contingency version, was developed by Evans, M.G. (1970). The effects of supervisory behavior on the path-goal relationship. *Organizational Behavior and Human Performance, 5,* 177–298.

42. House, R.J., & Mitchell, T.R. (1974). Path-goal theory of leadership. *Journal of Contemporary Business, Autumn,* 81–89.

43. Based on House & Mitchell (1974). And Yukl (1981).

44. From Lipman-Blumen, J. (1980). Female leadership in formal organizations: Must the female leader go formal? In H.J. Leavitt, L.R. Pondy, & D.M. Boje (Eds.). *Readings in managerial psychology* (3rd ed., pp. 341–362). Chicago: University of Chicago Press. Also see Donnell, S.M., & Hall, J. (1980). Men and women as managers: A significant case of no significant differences. *Organizational Dynamics, 8,* 60–77. And Bass (1981).

45. Lipman-Blumen (1980), p. 344.

46. Dobbins, G.H., & Platz, S.J. (1986). Sex differences in leadership: How real are they? *Academy of Management Review, 11,* 118–127.

47. Bass (1981).

48. Bass (1981).

49. Indvik, J. (1986). Path-goal theory of leadership: A meta-analysis. *Best papers proceedings; Academy of Management,* 189–192.

50. Indvik, J. (1986). Path-goal theory of leadership: A meta-analysis. *Best papers proceedings; Academy of Management,* 189–192. Fulk, J., & Wendler, E. (1982). Dimensionality of leader-subordinate interactions: A path-goal approach. *Organizational Behavior and Human Performance, 30,* 241–64. Schriesheim, J., & Schriesheim, C.A. (1980). A test of the path-goal theory of leadership and some suggested directions for future research. *Personnel Psychology, 33,* 349–370.

51. Yukl (1981).

52. From Ronen, S. (1986). *Comparative and multinational management* (p. 191). New York: Wiley.

53. This study is also cited by Bass (1981), p. 524, as an international comparison of leadership styles. For a more complete discussion of cross-cultural clusters, see Ronen, S. (1986). *Comparative and multinational management.* New York: Wiley.

54. This section is based on Bass (1981), pp. 491–507.

55. Ricks, D.A., Fu, M.Y.C., & Arpan, S. (1974). *International business blunders* (p. 44). Ohio: Orid.

Part Four

THE TOTAL
ORGANIZATION

Chapter Fifteen

ORGANIZATIONAL DESIGN AND BEHAVIOR

PREVIEW

- How do you design an effective organization?
- Why should the manager ask the questions: "What is our business?" and "Who is our customer?"
- When is it better for a manager to supervise a large number of people?
- What is a "skunkworks"?
- Why is decentralization used by so many large corporations? What are the benefits?
- Are bureaucratic organizations to be avoided?
- When might you purposely structure an organization so that people can have two bosses?
- Can organizations be structured to help women succeed?

MAJOR TOPICS

Preview Case: Synergistic Advertising Systems

Organizational Purpose and Objectives

The Organization's Environment

Designing the Organizational Structure

Types of Organizational Structures

Cross-Cultural OB: Japanese Organizational Structure

Managerial Applications Relating to Organizational Design

Preview Case

SYNERGISTIC ADVERTISING SYSTEMS

Adam O'Brien, President of Synergistic Advertising Systems (SYNAD), pondered the report in front of him from Reorganization Consultants, Inc.[1] He thought, "Perhaps a reorganization is just what we need to put new vitality into SYNAD. We're really hurting now that two of our largest clients have moved to other agencies. There must be something wrong to cause clients to leave. The consultant's recommendation will certainly tighten things up and clarify responsibilities."

Adam turned to the pages marked "current organization." The organizational chart (Figure 15.1) was the one SYNAD had used for the last five years since Adam had arrived. He was intimately familiar with it.

The next page gave the consultant's summary of the problems with the organization, which he already knew quite well:

1. Communication between specialists is poor.

2. Conflict exists between different account managers who compete for the specialists' time.

3. Coordination takes too much effort and energy.

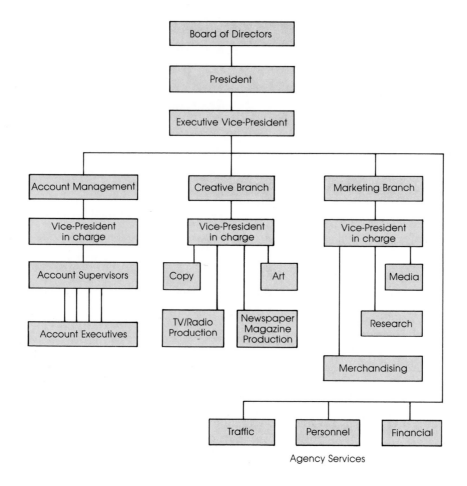

Figure 15.1

THE CURRENT ORGANIZATION OF SYNAD

SOURCE: Arthur J. Kover, (1963) Reorganization of an advertising agency, *Human Organizations, 22*(4):252–259. Reproduced by permission of the Society for Applied Anthropology.

4. Some clients feel they are not getting the attention they deserve. They are likely to move to another agency.

Adam then turned to the pages marked "proposed organization for SYNAD." He liked what he saw (Figure 15.2).

The Creative Branch and the Marketing Branch would be reorganized into a number of composite creative groups and marketing groups, each with a set of specialists in each area. The consultants listed the benefits as:

1. More tightly integrated client service.

2. Clearer lines of responsibility.

3. Less shifting of people between clients.

4. Better coordination.

5. Faster service for clients.

The consultant's conclusion: "The net effect of the reorganization will be to create a number of small, semiautonomous agencies under the umbrella of SYNAD with significantly improved responsiveness to clients and increased organizational effectiveness."

One year later Adam sat in his office and stared at the New York City skyline. He turned to his executive vice-president, Mary McCulley, and said, "Mary, this reorganization just hasn't worked out as well as we thought it would."

She replied, "I certainly agree. We have a lot better control of communication between the staff and clients, but professional communications have declined sharply and communication between members of different composite groups is almost nil. I'm afraid the result has been less challenging jobs. People feel they are being controlled. Some of our best creative people are moving to other agencies."

Adam nodded his head in agreement and continued, "The other day, I was talking to Milo Greco, our top market researcher, who said, 'Mr. O'Brien, it's getting mighty lonely since we reorganized and

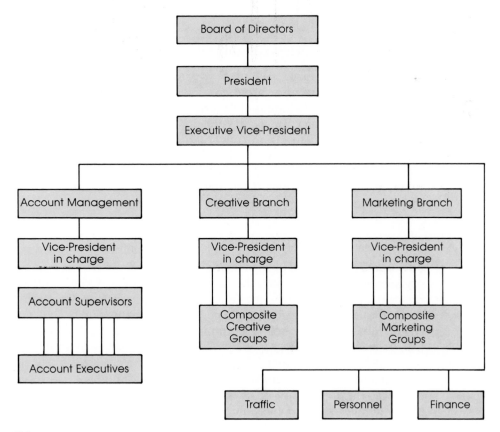

Figure 15.2

THE RECOMMENDED ORGANIZATION FOR SYNAD

I moved out of our research department. There's nobody to talk to about research. Before the reorganization, we used to talk over all sorts of things, and each one could learn from what the other was doing. Now, I don't get a chance to talk to other professional researchers; all we talk about is sales.

If we don't go back to the old way, I may have to start looking for another job.' "

Mary turned to Adam and said, "Well, shall we bite the bullet and go back to the old organization? While it had its problems, it may be the lesser of two evils."

Adam O'Brien, President of SYNAD, made a rational decision to reorganize, but there were side effects on people that produced unexpected and unintended results. In this chapter, we learn some of the basics of organizational design and some of the impacts of these designs on behavior. We will also cover the environment within which organizations must work since it can have a profound effect on the organization and its people.

Designing organizations involves many factors other than organizational structure. Additional important considerations include designing jobs and motivation systems, communication and leadership processes, group dynamics and decision making. The systems model discussed in Chapter 1 is particularly apropos for understanding structure since the structural subsystem interacts strongly with all the other subsystems and the environment (Figure 15.3). This chapter provides a basic introduction to organizational design concepts.[2]

Organizational Purpose and Objectives

Organizational purpose and objectives are the overall guidelines that give meaning and direction for organizing; they provide the web that holds the organization together. Critiques of American management have highlighted problems in this area, especially when compared with Japanese firms.[3] Organizational structure and functioning should be "vision-led" rather than "problem-driven."[4] This means that rather than waiting for some calamity to force changes in the organization, managers need to clearly identify their purposes, directions, and goals. Then, they should use this vision for restructuring the organization.

Organizational Purpose

The **organizational purpose** is the fundamental reason for the existence of the organization. Peter Drucker, the famous management writer and consultant, points out that two crucial questions must be asked before we can understand the purpose of an organization.[5] The first is, "What is our business and what should it be?" The answer is seldom as obvious as it seems. For example, American Telephone and Telegraph Co. (AT&T) determined early in its history (between 1905 and 1915) that "Our business is service." They knew that for a regulated monopoly to survive, they needed public goodwill. However, in 1984 it appears the answer was different. AT&T divested itself from all the Bell telephone companies so they could expand into applications of computer and communications technology.

The second basic question is, "Who is the customer?" The answer to this question will have strong influence over objectives and goals. There may be

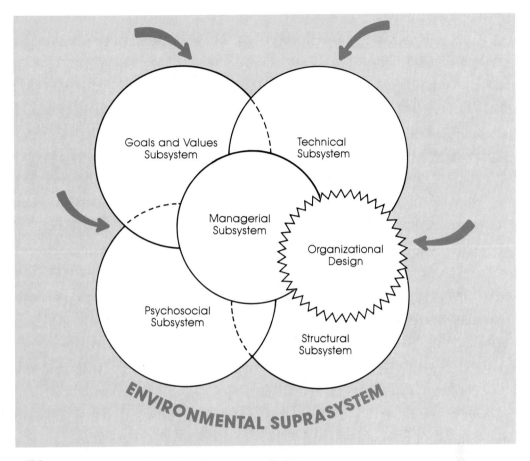

Figure 15.3

THE SYSTEMS PERSPECTIVE AND ORGANIZATIONAL DESIGN

SOURCE: Adapted from Kast, F.E., and Rosenzweig, J.E. (1979). *Organization and Management* (3rd ed.), p. 19. Copyright © 1979 by McGraw-Hill, New York. Used with permission.

many answers to the question, each deserving separate emphasis. For example, Boeing Aircraft Corp. sells to commercial airline companies, foreign governments, and the defense department. These three customers require different approaches and perhaps different organizational structures. This was certainly one of the issues facing SYNAD in our opening case.

Organizational Objectives

Once the basic purpose of the organization has been determined, the next step is to translate it into objectives. An **objective** is a broad statement of a desired future condition that provides direction. An example might be "to achieve sufficient profit to finance growth and provide a reasonable rate of return to our stockholders." Although the terms *objective* and *goal* are often used interchangeably, we will define **goals** more narrowly as specific, measurable targets that we are trying to reach within a given time. For example, a goal in support of the above objective might read "to increase profit during the next fiscal year, ending in July 1985, by 10 percent." (*See* Chapter 7 for more details on goal setting.)

Table 15.1

AN EXAMPLE OF CORPORATE OBJECTIVES: HEWLETT–PACKARD CO.

Profit	*Objective:* To achieve sufficient profit to finance our company growth and to provide the resources we need to achieve our other corporate objectives.
Customers	*Objective:* To provide products and services of the highest quality and the greatest possible value to our customers, thereby gaining and holding their respect and loyalty.
Fields of Interest	*Objective:* To participate in those fields of interest that build upon our technology and customer base, that offer opportunities for continuing growth, and that enable us to make a needed and profitable contribution.
Growth	*Objective:* To let our growth be limited only by our profits and our ability to develop and produce innovative products that satisfy real customers needs.
Our People	*Objective:* To help HP people share in the company's success which they make possible; to provide employment security based on their performance; to ensure them a safe and pleasant work environment; to recognize their individual achievements; and to help them gain a sense of satisfaction and accomplishment from their work.
Management	*Objective:* To foster initiative and creativity by allowing the individual great freedom of action in attaining well-defined objectives.
Citizenship	*Objective:* To honor our obligations to society by being an economic, intellectual and social asset to each nation and each community in which we operate.

SOURCE: Used with permission of Hewlett-Packard, Palo Alto, California.

While objectives can vary from firm to firm, there are eight key areas where objectives are usually needed.[6] (Table 15.1 provides an example of the corporate objectives for Hewlett-Packard).

1. Marketing Knowing who your customer is and designing the organization to serve that customer.

2. Financial resources Almost all organizations rely on financing from various sources such as bank loans or the sale of bonds.

3. Physical resources Plant and facilities, raw materials, and space utilization are important physical resources.

4. Human resources Being able to attract and keep qualified people is an important objective.

5. Productivity Effective management of resources is needed to insure productivity.

6. Innovation Creating new approaches and ideas keeps a firm from becoming obsolete.

7. Social responsibility Organizations exist within a social and political environment, thus businesses must discharge their social responsibilities.

8. Profit requirements All of the other objectives depend on profits, for profit provides the financing to pursue all other objectives.

PURPOSE, OBJECTIVES, AND STRUCTURE

An organization's structure should grow naturally from its purpose and objectives. If one of an organization's objectives is to encourage a creative environment where innovation will flourish, the structure must be compatible. A militarylike organization with tight supervision and control would be quite inappropriate. If a human resource objective is to insure the personal satisfaction that comes from a sense of accomplishment, then the organization needs to develop structures that help reach this goal.

THE ORGANIZATION'S ENVIRONMENT

All organizations operate in some external environment. The **environment** consists of "all elements or factors outside the boundary of the organization that have potential to affect all or part of the organization." [7] Pressure from the environment is an important reason for reorganization. One of the reasons that SYNAD reorganized was the loss of customers (an important environmental factor.)

The importance of different aspects of the environment will vary with the purpose or task of the organization. There are six components of the environment that we will consider: technology, customers, suppliers, competitors, socio-political, and economic. [8] The interaction of these components may create an environment with varying degrees of uncertainty. Figure 15.4 shows the impact of the environment on organizations.

In this section we will first discuss the issue of environmental uncertainty and then go over the components of the environment. To help integrate these concepts, we will take a look at how one corporation, Boeing Aircraft, might view its environment.

Environmental Uncertainty

When managers lack information about the environment, they experience **environmental uncertainty.** This increases the risks associated with a decision. Two elements of uncertainty are environmental complexity and the degree of environmental change. [9]

Environmental complexity refers to the number, variety, and diversity of external forces experienced by the organization. We would expect a large aircraft manufacturer to experience many complex environmental forces and thus be quite high in complexity. On the other hand, an auto parts store in a large suburban community would experience low environmental complexity.

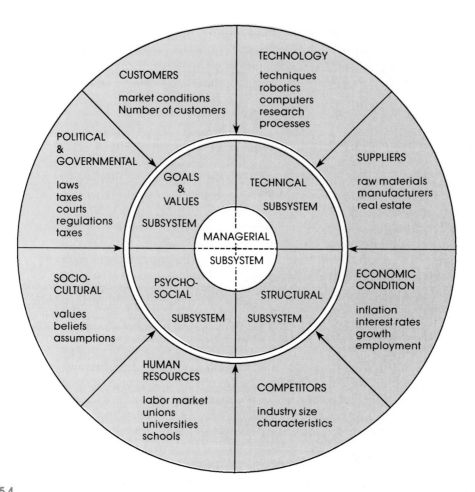

Figure 15.4

**THE IMPACT OF ENVIRONMENTAL FACTORS
ON ORGANIZATIONAL SYSTEMS**

Environmental change refers to the stability or instability of the environment. Does the environment remain stable over a period of months or years or does it change almost constantly? Unexpected changes in the environment, such as an increase in the price of fuel or a change in interest rates, can cause major repercussions for Boeing. An example of a relatively stable environment might be a supermarket. The environment usually changes slowly, thus there is time to plan and redesign organizational systems.

What Makes Up the Organization's Environment?

Technology.   A crucial part of the environment is **technology,** or the types and patterns of activity, equipment, knowledge, and experience used to get the job done.[10] Technology includes methods, designs, machines, equipment, information, managerial techniques, and procedures.[11] Boeing's production technology is extremely complex, using both large batch and assembly line techniques. In addition, their technology is constantly changing. New fuel-saving designs in airframes and engines are being developed. Computer technology allows aircraft to take off and land in zero-visibility conditions. Organizing to harness technology is a major problem for Boeing. The corporation needs to be able to develop and respond to technological changes and yet maintain some stability in its internal organization.

Customers.   When we discussed organizational purpose, we noted that a crucial issue is "Who is the customer?" All users of your product or service are customers, including distributors and wholesalers. SYNAD was very concerned about client service—the heart of its business. Boeing has a much more complex set of customers, including major airline corporations, foreign governments, and the defense departments of the United States and other countries. These customers are just as important to Boeing as SYNAD's are to it. Without buyers, an organization cannot sell its product or exist.

Suppliers.   Few organizations are completely independent. Most must rely on some type of supplier, whether it involves supplies, equipment, raw materials, or people. A large corporation like Boeing is dependent on its suppliers for subassemblies, electronic equipment, or engineering information. It is also dependent on the supply of highly qualified engineers and technicians—without them the firm could not function. A new dimension in supplier relationships is the linkages with overseas suppliers. Boeing has supplier relationships with Japan, China, Great Britain, and many other countries. Often, a sale can only be closed by agreeing to have parts of the aircraft built in the purchasing country.

Competitors.   Knowledge of your competition is extremely important. What deals are they offering? What new products are they developing? What are their sales approaches? How does their product or service differ from yours? How is it superior or inferior? Boeing is conscious of its competitors. If the European airbus is too successful, it might seriously threaten Boeing's success. This aspect of the environment is particularly crucial for Boeing since the European aircraft consortium that builds the airbus is supported and financed by Great Britain and France. Boeing is in effect competing with these nations.

Political-Social Environment.   This dimension has to do with government regulation, political attitudes toward the industry and product, and relations with trade unions. All organizations have some dealings with the government—it is unavoidable. Boeing, being a major government contractor, has to abide by a number of additional regulations and laws. Furthermore, all the airline safety regulations have to be interpreted and implemented. Relations with Congress are particularly important to Boeing. When such sensitive decisions as the Boeing 747 versus the Lockheed C–5 are discussed and voted on in Congress, Boeing needs all the good will it can muster.

Economic Environment.   The general state of the economy—interest rates, inflation, unemployment, growth—all have a major impact on organizations. The recession of 1981–83 caused numerous cancellations of new aircraft for Boeing. However, deregulation and mergers of many airlines in the mid–1980s resulted in record orders for Boeing. But Boeing is aware that these orders are fragile. A major business downturn could mean cancellations and layoffs.

The Environment and Structure. There is no simple answer to the question: "How do I best organize to cope with the environment?" SYNAD reorganized for the prime purpose of better relations with their clients; yet, they ran into difficulties. Perhaps the major way to cope with environmental turbulence is to establish buffers.

Environmental Buffers

Buffers are departments that deal with various aspects of the environment. They prevent the environment from interfering with the primary task of the organization, such as building aircraft. (The departments that perform this primary task are referred to as the **technical core**.) Buffer departments deal di-

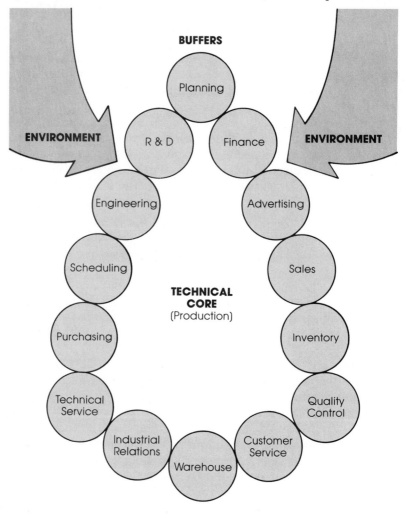

Figure 15.5

**BUFFER DEPARTMENTS FOR COPING
WITH ENVIRONMENT UNCERTAINTY**

SOURCE: From R.L. Daft, (1983), *Organizational theory and design,* p. 57. Copyright © 1983 by West Publishing Company, St. Paul, Minn. Used with permission.

rectly with the environment and prevent turbulence from reaching the people who have to do the production or service—the technical core.[12] Examples of buffer departments are shown in Figure 15.5.

　Stability of the environment is an important consideration when organizing. Generally, the more turbulent the environment, the more flexible and responsive the organization must be to deal effectively with the turbulence. This often requires departments and people who act as buffers or specialists in various environmental concerns.

DESIGNING THE ORGANIZATIONAL STRUCTURE

The **organizational structure** represents formal patterns and relationships that exist among work units or positions.[13] Organizational structure can be viewed in a number of ways: it is the framework that divides up tasks and activities; it is the formalized network of interactions for coordination; and it establishes formal authority and reporting relationships.[14] The organizational structure is usually enduring and persistent. It is published in the form of an organizational chart that is widely disseminated.

Inputs into the design process	Design Elements	Strategic aspects of the functioning organization	Valued outcomes
Management philosophy	Structure	Upward influence	Quality
Organizational purpose	Divison of labor	Downward communication	Cost superiority
Organizational values	Span of management	Development of skills	Innovation
Assumptions about workers' skills, attitudes and values	Staff size and function	Clarity of priorities	Flexibility
	Functional versus product departments	Employee competence	Delivery
Business strategy	Integrative mechanisms	Employee commitment	Quality of work life
Organizational objectives and goals	**Systems**	Union-management cooperation	Development and growth
Evolving technology	Rewards		job satisfaction
	Information and computer systems		
Environmental Conditions	Controls		
	Personnel		
	Selection		
	Training		

Figure 15.6

FACTORS TO CONSIDER WHEN DESIGNING AN ORGANIZATION

SOURCE: Adopted by permission of the publisher from "A Vision-Led Approach to Management Restructuring" by R.E. Walton. Organizational Dynamics (Spring) p. 8. Copyright © 1986 American Management Association All rights reserved

The organizational structure is more than just a chart on the wall—it strongly influences the behavior of the organization. For example, should roles of people be narrowly specialized or broad? Should control be centralized or decentralized? Should access to managers be easy because of few organizational layers or difficult because of multiple layers? These and other questions affect decision making, group dynamics, communication, motivation, and other important organizational behaviors. Figure 15.6 illustrates many of the factors that must be considered when designing an organization.

In this section we will see what design elements are needed to make up an organizational structure. We will cover the division of labor, span of management, line and staff, departmentation, centralization and decentralization, and coordination and integration. Then in the following section, we will see how these concepts are used in various organizational structures.

Vertical Division of Labor

In all but the smallest organizations, there must be a division of labor since one person cannot do everything. There are two major ways of dividing labor: vertically, and horizontally.

Vertical division refers to how authority, responsibility, and decision making are divided from highest levels, such as the president, to lowest levels, such as a laborer or clerk. When an organization has more vertical levels, each level of management usually makes fewer decisions since the total number of decisions must be divided among more people. For example, SYNAD's original organization had at least five levels between the president and a copywriter. If the executive vice-president were to be eliminated, the number of levels would be reduced by one, or 20 percent. Figure 15.7 shows the vertical division of labor at SYNAD.

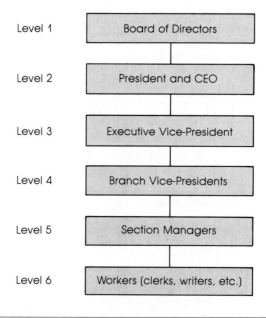

Figure 15.7

THE VERTICAL DIVISION OF LABOR AT SYNAD

Perspective 15.1

THE INFORMAL ORGANIZATION

While this chapter concentrates on structuring the formal organization, every organization also has an **informal organization:** a "network of personal and social relationships not established or required by formal authority but arising spontaneously as people associate with one another." [15] Informal organizations may be stable or constantly changing. They rely upon social relationships that are established within and between work groups. Power and politics are often the basis for the informal organization. The following organizational chart is a humorous representation of the informal organization. [16]

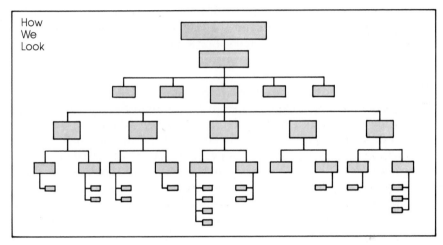

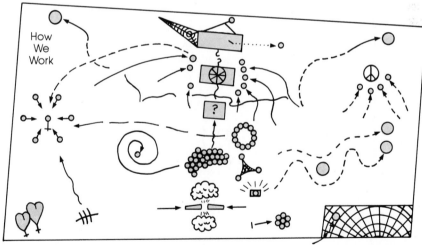

SOURCE: From J.L. Gray and F.A. Starke, (1977), *Organizational behavior concepts and applications*, p. 137. Copyright © 1977 by Charles E. Merrill, Columbus, Ohio. Reprinted with permission.

Span of Management

One important factor to consider when dividing management up vertically is the number of subordinates that report to a supervisor. It would be impossible for one person to supervise everyone in a large or even medium-sized organization. The number of subordinates supervised by a given supervisor is called the **span of management,** or span of control. Adam O'Brien, President of SYNAD, has only one subordinate, Mary McCulley, the Executive Vice-President. Thus, he has a narrow span of management. (However, in practice, many presidents share supervision with an executive vice-president, both of them giving orders to the various divisions of the company.) Mary, in turn, has six subordinates: account management, creative branch, marketing, traffic, personnel, and finance—a moderately wide span of management. An organization where supervisors have few subordinates is a **tall** organization; whereas an organization where supervisors have many subordinates is a **flat** organization (Figure 15.8), provided that the organizations are the same size.

What Is an Ideal Span of Management?   Early theorists believed that one person could not directly supervise more than five or six persons because of the complexity of relationships that develop when more people are supervised.[17] However, in more recent years, this proposition has been disproved. In fact, one expert recommends developing spans at least twice as wide as any good rule of thumb—perhaps ten to twelve in the above case.[18] In many situations it is quite effective for a supervisor to have many more subordinates than six and there are some real psychological benefits, too. Subordinates have a

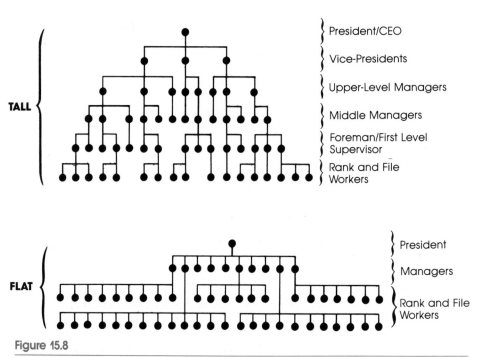

Figure 15.8

TALL VERSUS FLAT ORGANIZATIONAL STRUCTURE

Table 15.2

FACTORS THAT DETERMINE THE SPAN OF MANAGEMENT

Similarity of functions	The more dissimilar the tasks and functions, the more supervisory effort needed, and hence the narrower the span.
Geographic location	The more geographically dispersed, the narrower the span.
Complexity of functions	Highly varied and complex jobs require more supervision and a narrower span.
Nature of the personnel	The motivation and orientation of the personnel. Professional researchers will require less supervision than clerks because they are usually more committed and qualified to do the job.
Coordination and planning	The more complex the coordination and planning systems are between people, the narrower the span.

SOURCE: From Koontz, H. (1966). Making theory operational: The span of management. *The Journal of Management Studies, 3*, 229–243.

greater sense of autonomy and responsibility.[19] Spans also tend to vary with organizational level. The higher the level, the wider the span.[20] Table 15.2 shows some of the factors that need to be considered when designing the span of management.

Impact of the Span of Management. If the span is too narrow, say one manager supervising three to five subordinates, then it tends to result in overcontrol. Subordinates' initiative and morale may be low because the supervisor spends too much time reviewing and checking their work. Narrow spans discourage delegation and participative decision making—when a boss is so close to the operation, it is all too easy for the boss to make all the decisions. In addition, narrow spans cost money by adding additional layers of supervision and delaying decisions as they move through numerous organizational levels (as illustrated in Figure 15.8).[21]

Wide spans, in contrast, force you to delegate. When a boss has many people to supervise, there simply are not enough hours in the day to make all the decisions for subordinates. Thus, a wide span of control and flat organizational structure build commitment and ownership.[22]

Line and Staff

The line-staff concept of organization goes back thousands of years, for it originates probably with early military organizations. As it applies to business, **line** refers to those people who are involved in direct production and sales, while **staff** refers to all others (personnel, legal, administrative, public relations, finance, plans.)

There are also two kinds of authority called line authority and functional authority (associated with staffs because they have functional expertise.) **Line authority** is the ability to give orders because of a superior position in the organizational hierarchy. **Functional authority** is exercised by the staff when they issue orders that are concerned with their area of expertise. For example,

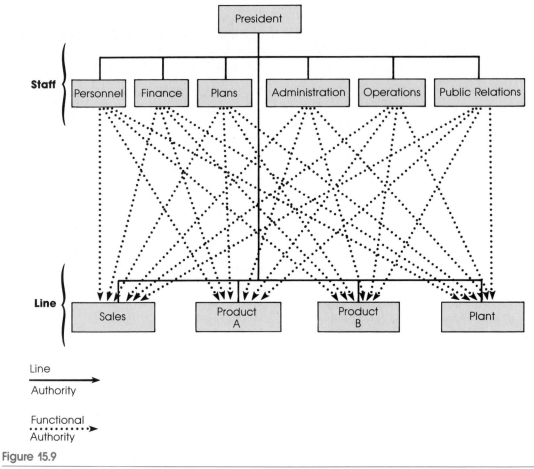

Figure 15.9

LINE AND STAFF ORGANIZATION

personnel might issue an order that all job position forms must be rewritten. Even though personnel does not have a straight-line authority to direct the various divisions of the company, its word is law concerning personnel matters. Figure 15.9 graphically portrays the staff relationship.

Staffs have traditionally been formed to handle specialized problems. They contain experts in finance, marketing, production, personnel, and so forth. Their task is to give advice and provide policy guidance to line managers. There is a tendency for staffs to grow and assume more and more authority. Recent trends show organizations cutting staffs to save money and operate more effectively. See Perspective 15.2 for more discussion of this point.

Horizontal Division of Labor and Departmentation

The **horizontal division of labor** refers to breaking the organization down into tasks, function areas, or products. For example, the creative branch of SYNAD

Perspective 15.2

ACHIEVE EXCELLENCE BY HAVING A LEAN STAFF

According to Tom Peters, coauthor of *In Search of Excellence* and *A Passion for Excellence,* the excellent companies keep staff levels to an absolute minimum. A large staff generates complexity and more work. Staff people are often among the best in the company. They ask good, intelligent questions that take a lot of time to answer. One division manager noted that, "Smart staff guys ask smart questions. Smart questions can tie us up for days, if not months. And if it were just one request, that would be fine, but it's multiple staffs, with multiple centers of intelligence, asking multiple series of smart questions that really keep us from getting the job done." [23]

Peters and Waterman have coined what they call the "**rule of 100,**" which means that with rare exceptions total staff should be limited to 100 regardless of the organization's size. [24] For example, Schlumberger, a six-billion dollar diversified oil company has a staff of ninety. Dana reduced its staff from 600 to 150 even though it grew from $1 billion to $3 billion in annual sales. [25] Outboard Marine cut over 2,000 people—25 percent of its white collar work force—and has since been able to compete with Japanese imports of outboard motors. [26]

What do managers say about all these cuts? The most notable difference appeared to be better staff work and, of course, reduced costs. One manager noted: "We find that we're living a lot better—and more effectively as well as efficiently—without seventy-five percent of [our previous staff]." [27]

(shown in Figure 15.10) is divided into four functions or divisions: copy, art, TV/radio, and newspaper/magazine. The process of horizontally dividing an organization is often referred to as **departmentation,** which refers to the way organizations are broken down into various departments. Departmentation is the central issue with the SYNAD reorganization. Should they keep the original four divisions based on function (copy, art) or should they develop composite creative groups with functional experts in each group?

The SYNAD reorganization developed around the issue of how to departmentalize, by function or goal. **Functional** departments have all the people concerned with one area of expertise in the same department; for example, all art people would work in the same department. A **product** approach means that instead of being organized around the expertise of the labor, you organize around the output of that department; such as product, product group, service, markets, customer, or programs. [28] An example of product approach is Boeing Co., which includes divisions that make commercial aircraft, military aircraft, aerospace vehicles, and marine systems.

Functional departments are usually more efficient because there is less duplication of effort and there is a greater depth of expertise when problems arise. The functional approach also gives specialists a sense of belonging to people of their own kind and the knowledge that their work is evaluated and controlled by other specialists. But functional departments are more likely to pursue professional or specialist objectives than the organization's central purpose. Product departments, on the other hand, are usually more sensitive to the needs of the product, customer, or region. They may also be easier to man-

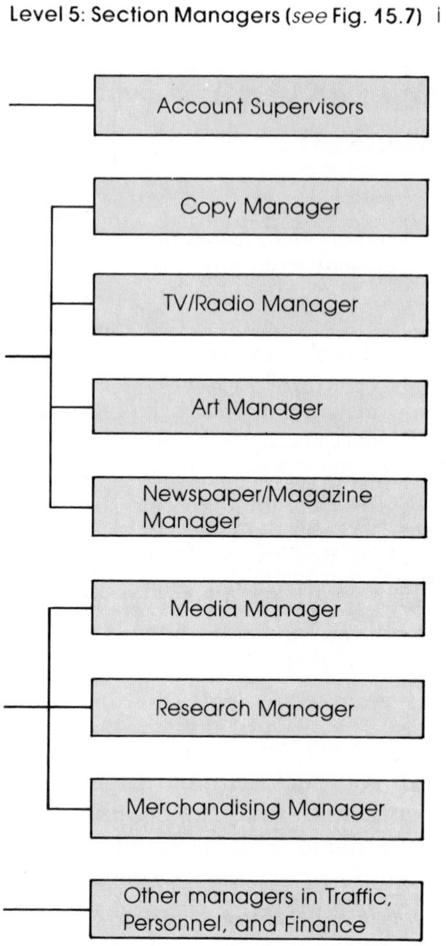

Level 5: Section Managers (*see* Fig. 15.7)

Account Supervisors

Copy Manager

TV/Radio Manager

Art Manager

Newspaper/Magazine Manager

Media Manager

Research Manager

Merchandising Manager

Other managers in Traffic, Personnel, and Finance

Figure 15.10

THE HORIZONTAL DIVISION OF LABOR AT SYNAD

age because they experience a common, unified purpose and objectives, and they are more easily held accountable for results.[29]

Our opening case involving SYNAD is a good example of the problems arising from the functions versus product dilemma. Putting the specialists (researchers, copywriters), into composite groups created a product organization, where customer service and creativity were paramount. But the specialists were unhappy because there was no one to talk to; they felt isolated. They were also concerned that their bosses did not understand their work and did not recognize good work when they saw it. Of course, SYNAD's problems might not occur in a larger organization like the Boeing 747 division, for it could be subdivided into functions, too.

Centralization and Decentralization

The concept of **decentralization** refers to the delegation or dispersion of decision making to lower organizational levels.[30] Decentralization is not simply a

Perspective 15.3

REORGANIZATION AT GENERAL MOTORS

General Motors was one of the first and most famous examples of decentralization. Alfred P. Sloan, Jr., President of General Motors (GM) in the 1920s, found a number of serious problems when he took over, including excessive time being consumed by administrative details and problems. Sloan described his concept as:

> . . . to divide the organization into as many parts as consistently as can be done, place in charge of each part the most capable executive that can be found, develop a system of coordination so that each part may strengthen and support each other part; thus not only welding all parts together in the common interest of a joint enterprise, but importantly developing the ability and initiative through the instrumentalities of responsibility and ambition—developing men [sic] and giving them an opportunity to exercise their talents, both in their own interests as well as in that of the business.[31]

Over the years GM has become much more centralized. Ross Perot has indicated that "GM has lost sight of Sloan's original intent—to create a more responsive, flexible organization, and instead has developed a cumbersome bureaucracy that has turned away from the needs and desires of customers."[32]

Recently, GM has reorganized in an attempt to overcome some of these problems.[33] In 1984, it consolidated its five car divisions into two groups—a large car group and a small car group. All the staffs were combined, except for marketing. Chevrolet, Pontiac, and the Canadian divisions went into the small car group. Buick, Oldsmobile, and Cadillac went into the large car group. There have been problems with the reorganization. For example, it took eighteen months to consolidate the engineering departments. The staff size has been trimmed slightly—it is down almost 12 percent since 1979. However, sales have also declined since 1979. In contrast, Ford is 20 percent leaner and Chrysler is 50 percent leaner in white-collar staff. Needless to say, GM's costs are the highest in the industry. By 1987 Ford had taken over first place in both car and truck sales from Chevrolet.

function of organizational structure, it is more a function of the decision-making policies and norms of an organization. For example, we normally think of a flat organization as being more likely to be decentralized. While this may be true, it is also possible for it to be centralized. The inverse can happen when an organization uses decentralized decision making.

In theory, a decentralized organization could use a wider span of management since the supervisor would not have to spend as much time making decisions. We already know from Chapter 13 that participation in decisions often results in higher levels of employee satisfaction. Decentralization can provide a sense of autonomy that enriches jobs. It can also provide a focal point for responsibility and performance. On the other hand, coordination and integration may be more difficult in decentralized organizations.

The overall effects of decentralization are generally positive.[34] Employees are more satisfied; there is often higher performance, particularly for sales personnel.[35] There is also likely to be greater communication between coworkers and higher satisfaction with supervision.

Coordination and Integration

As organizations become increasingly complex and are organized into more and more departments, the task of coordinating and integrating becomes much more important and difficult. In some particularly complex industries, such as plastics manufacturing, up to 22 percent of management personnel are involved in integrating roles.[36] An **integrator** is someone who is responsible for linking and coordinating the activities of two or more departments. Integration and coordination are important in both a vertical and a horizontal direction.[37]

Vertical coordination is usually accomplished by structuring positions with the primary task of linking together people who work at different organizational levels. This is often done by setting up "assistants to" (the president, the vice-president, the director) or by setting up "deputies to" (the director, the general manager, the department head). These people may have no formal line authority, but their task is to gather and disseminate information, coordinate goals, and insure everyone is headed in the direction their boss wants. Figure 15.11 shows how the chart for SYNAD might look with the addition of several vertical integration positions.

Horizontal coordination, linking together people who work at the same organizational level, is accomplished through several structures. Formal integrators or liaison departments may be created to coordinate effort across functional department lines to insure that all work is directed toward the best interests of the company. Teams, committees, and task forces are also commonly used strategies for improving horizontal integration.

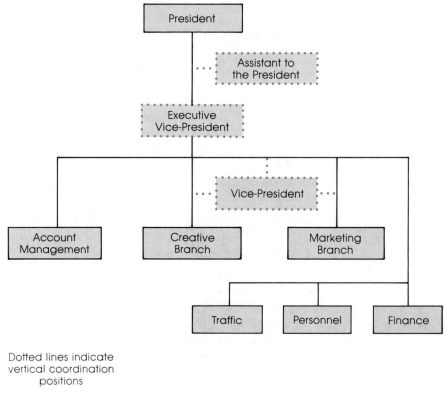

Dotted lines indicate
vertical coordination
positions

Figure 15.11

POSSIBLE VERTICAL INTEGRATION POSITIONS FOR SYNAD

A good example of horizontal integration is often found in schools of business administration. There are a number of functional departments, like accounting, management, and marketing. There is also someone who integrates and coordinates the programs for undergraduates, graduates, and research. For example, the undergraduate director (coordinator) would be concerned with the needs and problems of undergraduate business students. Some of the concerns might be: Are there sufficient numbers of course offerings? Do schedules meet the needs of students? Is the workload appropriate? Is the sequencing of courses correct? Figure 15.12 diagrams this type of organizational structure.

Behavior of Integrators.   Anyone assigned to an integrating role must have considerable behavioral skills to succeed. Integrators have little authority. They must use persuasion, expert power and logic to accomplish their task. They must be able to communicate well, confront problems, resolve conflicts, avoid dysfunctional politics, and build organizational trust. The integrator must be able to get things done without alienating the functional departments.[38]

Linking Arrangements and Socio-technical Designs.   As we have seen in earlier chapters, more and more new plants are using innovative structural designs, with emphasis on autonomous work groups and multiskilled team approaches to getting the job done.[39] These new designs require new strategies for integrating and coordinating between work teams and management. Team leaders are often given the coordination role. In addition, multiteam membership is often used. Committees may also be established to insure coordination and integration. These and other new linking arrangements require different organizational structures than the traditional ones discussed above.[40]

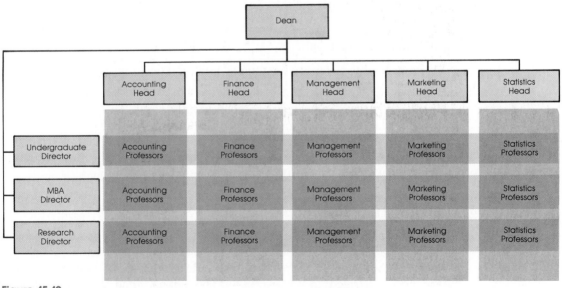

Figure 15.12

FULL-TIME INTEGRATING ROLES IN A BUSINESS SCHOOL

SOURCE: From R.L. Daft, (1983), *Organizational theory and design*, p. 219. Copyright © 1983 by West Publishing Company, St. Paul, Minn. Used with permission.

TYPES OF ORGANIZATIONAL STRUCTURES

This section of the chapter provides insight into a variety of organizational structures. We will first discuss bureaucracies as a general model for large organizations. Then, we will cover examples of functional, product, and matrix organizations. An important issue to remember throughout this section is that most organizations are a blend of several structures.

Bureaucratic Organizations

Bureaucracy is not a type of organizational structure, but a set of characteristics that were needed for an ideal organization. Max Weber, who developed the concept of bureaucracy, felt that if the characteristics listed below were present, a more efficient and effective organization would result. Here are Weber's features of **bureaucracy:**[41]

- An organization that functions by the rules. It is impersonal and treats all clients alike.

- A systematic sphere of competence for each individual with the authority to accomplish the task.

- The organizational structure follows the principle of hierarchy in that compliance is not left to chance—every office has a superior one that checks on it.

- Rules are applied quite rationally and by people with adequate technical training. Where rules do not exist, norms become quite important.

- Members of the organization should be separated from the owners of the organization. Personal lives and official lives should be kept separate.

- Resources, including job positions, must be allocated without outside control. Favoritism is out.

- Administrative acts are formulated and recorded in writing, thus providing a systematic record of rule or norm enforcement.

Almost all organizations have some elements of bureaucracy. In fact, it would be hard to envision an organization that did not rely upon some rules or where favoritism is not frowned upon. In most cases, effective, larger organizations will have more bureaucracy because it is needed for coordination and control.[42] Figure 15.13 shows the results of research on this topic.

Functional Organizations

Since functional organizations revolve around the use of functional specialists who are organized into homogeneous units, it is not surprising to see the proliferation of functional departments in a large, complex organization such as the one illustrated in Figure 15.14. The dotted lines show the impact computer systems have on this organization. Note how information from lower-level parts of the organization is processed, summarized, and fed to top managers.[47] This process facilitates coordination and control.

Perspective 15.4

"SKUNKWORKS"

Perhaps the opposite of a bureaucracy is the **skunkworks,** a small group of people who are formally or informally set off from the rest of the organization and are working on some problem or innovation.[43] One skunkworks group for a $5 billion survey company is headed by a technical genius with only a high school degree (even though the company has thousands of Ph.D. scientists). This skunkworks has about ten people and is located in a dingy second-floor loft about six miles from corporate headquarters. It has developed three of the last five new products and has solved a number of other product problems. Another example of a skunkworks, this time at IBM, is the use of six competing teams to develop a personal computer. The winning team "initially consisted of twelve somewhat discredited people working in a run-down facility in Boca Raton, Florida."[44] They developed one of the most successful computers of all time!

A skunkworks can emerge or be officially appointed. It should consist of from five to twenty-five full-time members. The leader should be a "tinkerer" with an urge to act, not a "blue-sky" person. Keep rules and restrictions to a minimum—you want these people to innovate. The skunkworks must have its own purchasing authority; nothing will kill an idea faster than having to wait two weeks for a requisition to be filled. While you do not have to develop monetary incentives for the skunkworks, other types of rewards, such as the opportunity to participate in future projects, are a must. Finally, don't expect every project to be a success; most will not. Make sure there are positions for members to go to and that failure is not punished.[45]

Skunkworks become necessary because organizations get too large, bureaucratic, and cumbersome. Innovation and entrepreneurship are difficult in such organizations. Tom Peters believes that the only way to achieve excellence is to keep your organization small. Only in a small organization can a true sense of ownership and commitment be achieved.[46] Larger organizations can use the skunkworks as a strategy for creating smallness within bigness.

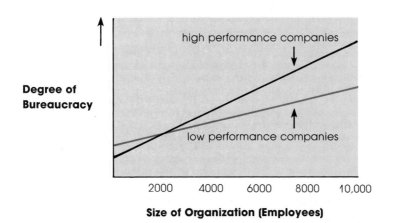

Figure 15.13

SIZE OF THE ORGANIZATION, BUREAUCRACY, AND PERFORMANCE

SOURCE: Adapted by R.L. Daft from J. Child (1975), Managerial factors associated with company performance analysis, *Journal of Management Studies* 12:12–27. Copyright © 1975 by Basil Blackwell Publishing Ltd., Oxford, England.

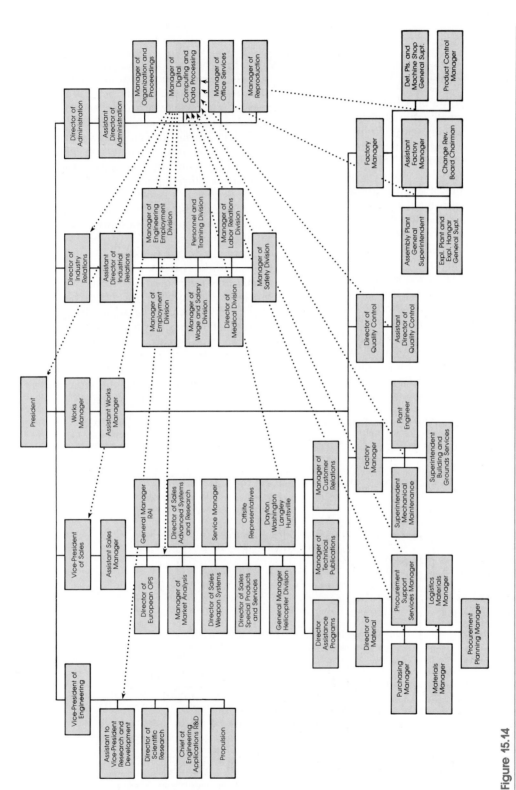

Figure 15.14

A FUNCTIONALLY ORGANIZED AEROSPACE COMPANY SHOWING THE FLOW OF INFORMATION TO AND FROM THE COMPUTER DEPARTMENT

SOURCE: From R.L. Daft, (1983), *Organizational theory and design*, p. 337. Copyright © 1983 by West Publishing Company, St. Paul, Minn. Used with permission.

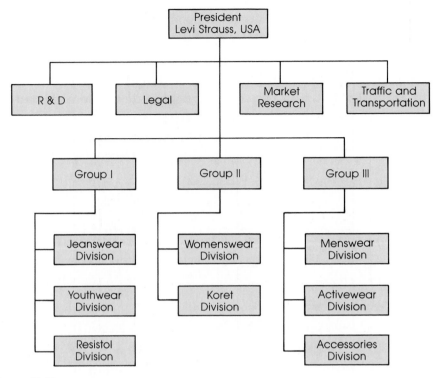

Figure 15.15

THE PRODUCT ORGANIZATION OF LEVI STRAUSS, USA

SOURCE: From R.L. Daft, (1983), *Organizational theory and design*, p. 235. Copyright © 1983 by West Publishing Company, St. Paul, Minn. Used with permission.

Product Organizations

Product structures are organized around the product, product group, service, market, customer, or programs of the organization. There are almost no pure types of product organization. Most combine at least function and product. The organization for Levi Strauss, USA, illustrated in Figure 15.15, shows this tendency. Note that there are two levels of product departmentation, one at the individual product level (Jeanswear Division) and one combining several products into a group (Group 1).

Hybrid Organizations

We noted above that it is rare to find a pure goal-oriented or product organization. Most large corporations show a variety of structures, although one may dominate. The organizational structure for the corporate headquarters of Boeing Co., illustrated in Figure 15.16, shows a hybrid structure. There are some traditional functional areas, mostly at the staff level, such as public affairs, industrial relations, finance, and product development. There are also product divisions, such as Boeing Commercial Airplane Co., Boeing Computer Services, and Boeing Marine Services. There are even a few geographic departments, such as Seattle Services Division, and the Washington, D.C. office.

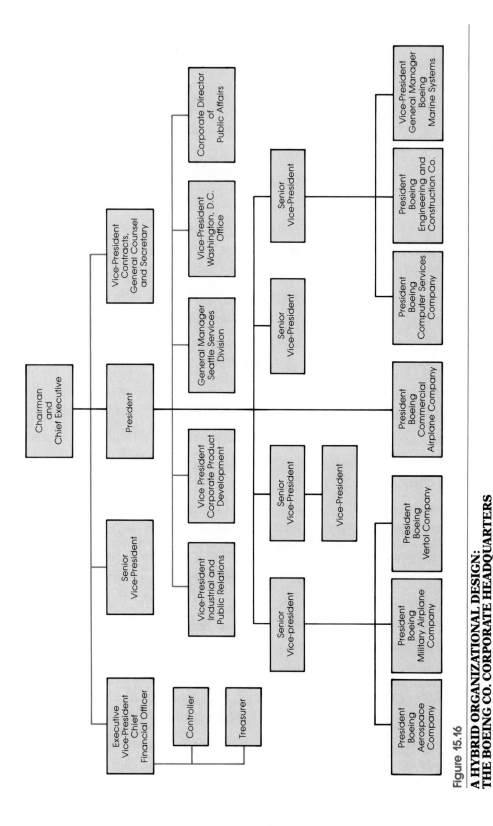

Figure 15.16

A HYBRID ORGANIZATIONAL DESIGN:
THE BOEING CO. CORPORATE HEADQUARTERS

SOURCE: Used with permission of The Boeing Company, Seattle, Washington.

Matrix Organizations

What Is a Matrix Organization?   A **matrix** organization has two reporting
channels so that the same manager has two bosses. For example, an engineer
may report to the chief of engineering and to the radar project manager (see
Figure 15.17). Thus, the matrix organization combines into one organization
both functional divisions that concentrate on specialized, in-house resources,
and on product divisions that concentrate on the output. Companies turn to the
matrix design when: [48]

- It is absolutely essential that they be highly responsive to two sectors
simultaneously, such as markets and technology.

- They face uncertainties that generate high information processing
requirements.

- They must deal with strong constraints on financial and/or human
resources.

Problems With Matrix.   There is a great deal of duplication in a matrix
structure. There must be dual reporting, control, reward, and evaluation systems. In addition, the role of the top manager is crucial for balancing the
inevitable conflicts that result from the dual-reporting structure of a matrix
organization. When one boss tells you to do one thing and the other gives
conflicting orders, you are torn—what do you do? The bosses of the person in
the matrix must also use special skills. For example, individuals who work in a
geographically isolated location from their function may find that they are like-

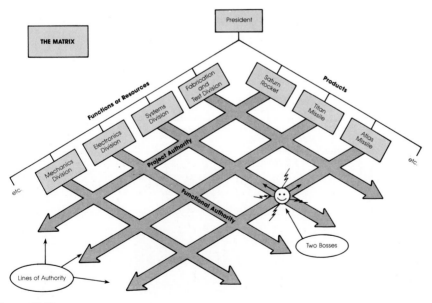

Figure 15.17

HOW THE MATRIX ORGANIZATION WORKS

Perspective 15.5

STRUCTURES TO ENCOURAGE MANAGERIAL PROGRESSION OF WOMEN

In the last chapter, we discussed some of the problems women face in leadership positions, including research that shows men talk more in mixed male-female groups; men's opinions are more likely to influence both males and females; and males are more task-oriented. In addition, women generally find it more difficult to become members of the informal managerial organization. While these problems are formidable, there are structural methods for dealing with them, including: [49]

• Decentralize the organization into smaller, relatively autonomous units to give women and men a better chance to show what they can do—to perform and be measured.

• Since women have more difficulty establishing credibility when they enter organizations, they might be given more powerful symbols (corner offices) and resources (budgets).

• Women can establish their own informal organizational networks and ties so they are more involved in the organizational mainstream.

• Groups can be structured so that there is a slight preponderance of women, thus, giving women a chance to perform in a more favorable situation and build a reputation before tackling mostly male groups.

• Structure opportunities for women to talk more, perhaps by making oral presentations and serving as team leaders.

ly to be forgotten unless the boss makes an effort to provide regular feedback and recognition. Power struggles and the tendencies toward anarchy are also two frequent problems associated with matrix organizations.[50] Even though communication quantity may increase, quality of communication tends to be lower. Other negative effects on work attitudes and coordination are sometimes found.[51] With the many problems associated with matrix, it is probably a structure to avoid unless it seems absolutely necessary.

An example of matrix for Pittsburgh Steel Co. is shown in Figure 15.18. Note that the matrix does not include Field Sales or Industrial Relations.

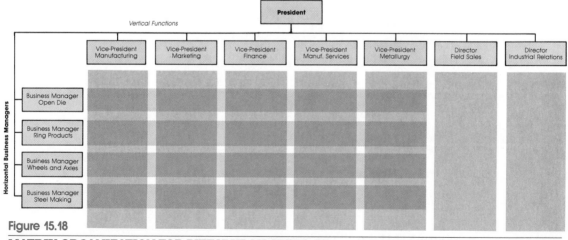

Figure 15.18

MATRIX ORGANIZATION FOR PITTSBURGH STEEL CO.

SOURCE: From R.L. Daft, (1983), *Organizational theory and design*, p. 249. Copyright © 1983 by West Publishing Company, St. Paul, Minn. Used with permission.

CROSS–CULTURAL OB: JAPANESE ORGANIZATIONAL STRUCTURE

At first glance the naive observer would think that a Japanese organization's structure looks almost exactly like an American structure (*see* Figure 15.19). However, there are some important differences.

Top Management

The chairman of the board of directors may be only an honorary title awarded to a semi-retired president or some other person with relatively little power.[52] However, there is movement toward the U.S. model of a chairman who is the chief executive officer. How do you know? One certain clue is if the business card or letter uses the title "representative director." By law this person is the only person who has authority to represent the organization legally. He or she is equivalent to our chairman and CEO.

The title of "vice-president" also has different meaning in Japan since there can only be one vice-president in a Japanese company. In the United States

Model Strata of Japanese Corporations

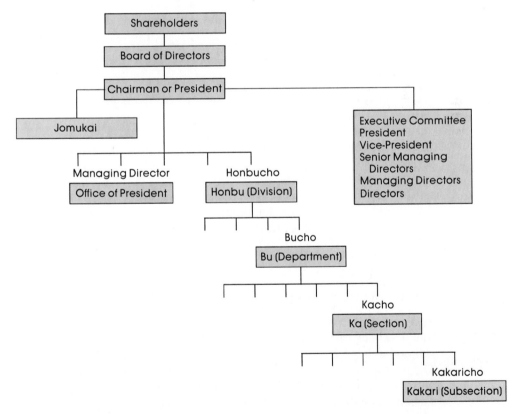

Figure 15.19

ORGANIZATIONAL STRUCTURE OF A TYPICAL JAPANESE COMPANY

SOURCE: Copyright © 1986 by the Regents of the University of California. Reprint from Otsubo, M. (1986). A guide to Japanese business practices. *California Management Review*, Vol. 28, No. 3. By permission of The Regents.

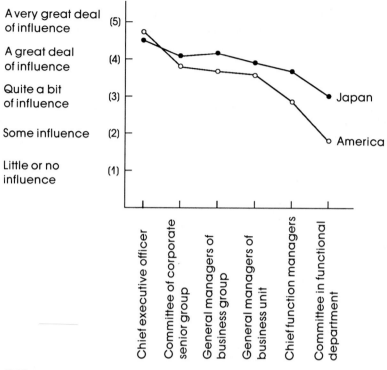

Figure 15.20

**DISTRIBUTION OF INFLUENCE
IN JAPANESE AND AMERICAN ORGANIZATIONS**

SOURCE: The figure is adapted from Nonaka, I. & Okumura, A. (1984, Spring) *Management Japan,* vol. 17, no. 1,
published by the International Management Association of Japan, Inc.

there are often many vice-presidents headed by an executive vice-president or
senior vice-president.

"Director" is a tricky title since many members of the board of directors also
perform operating-level functions. Employees are elected as directors; you will
rarely find an outside director on a Japanese board. Being elected director is
considered to be an important step toward top management. The title of "director" is not used in other organizational contexts, such as director of personnel
or director of finance.

Middle Management

Middle-management titles are extremely important in Japan. There are at least
four levels of middle managers. The lowest manager, called a *kararicho,* or
subsection head, is roughly equivalent to our supervisor or first-line supervisor.
The next level is the *kacho,* or section head who is in charge of several subsec-
tions. Then follows the *bucho,* or department head, who is in charge of several
sections. Finally, there is the *honbucho,* or general manager, who is in charge
of several departments. At each of these supervisory levels, job position becomes part of the person's name. For example, suppose you work for Mr. Ichiro
Nakayama, the marketing department head. You would never call him "Ichiro"
or "Mr. Nakayama." He should be addressed as "Manager Mr. Nakayama" (*Na-*

kayama bucho in Japanese), or simply "Manager" (*bucho*). Thus all Japanese are very aware and concerned about their titles. You should take great care to use the proper one.

Summary of Other Structural Differences

A study comparing Japanese and American management polled 291 Japanese companies and 227 American companies.[53] Part of the study compared the two countries on structural issues. Their research concludes that American firms are more centralized, formalized, have elaborate horizontal relationships, and give greater weight to their financial divisions. Figure 15.20 shows the differences in centralization between the U.S. and Japan.

MANAGERIAL APPLICATIONS RELATING TO ORGANIZATIONAL DESIGN

As we have seen throughout the chapter, an organization's design can have a profound influence on the behavior of its members. Design affects decision-making patterns, reward systems, status, group dynamics, communication, power, and other important processes. Organizational behavior is often a product of the structure. There are a number of important managerial applications of organizational design:

- *Clarify the organization's purpose.* Be sure to ask: "What is our business?" and "What should it be?" Before any organization can be designed, we must have a clear ideal of its philosophy, purpose, and mission. While this may seem obvious, many organizations do not experience such clarity. Make sure your structure fits your organization's purpose and objectives.

- *Stay close to your customers.* Customers are often the most important elements in business decision making. If the organization gets out of touch with its customers, it is in grave danger.

- *Minimize environmental threats.* Organizations should not allow themselves to become hostage to a single customer, supplier, or other environmental threat. Diversification is one way to spread this risk.

- *Watch for changes in technology.* Careful observation of technological changes may prevent your company from being overtaken by competitors or from technological obsolescence.

- *Keep it simple and lean.* Organizations should not overorganize. They need to adopt enough division of labor and bureaucratic characteristics to get the job done, but they should avoid going overboard. Keep staffs small; follow the "rule of 100." Remember that staff people can tie up an organization in unproductive endeavors.

- *Use a wide span of control.* Relatively wide spans of control will save people and result in more challenge for supervisors while at the same time increasing autonomy and commitment of subordinates. They force delegation.

- *Establish responsibility centers.* Large corporations can be divided into smaller product or geographic divisions and thus behave as if they were a small or medium-sized corporation. This same concept can be carried to much lower levels. Whenever an autonomous unit can be structured and its performance isolated from the total organization, there will be improved creativity, better performance, and clearer control of such units.

- *Decentralize decision making.* Decentralization generally results in higher performance, satisfaction, communication, and commitment. It also encourages development of managerial talent.

- *Recognize the importance of linking roles.* Be sure to develop structures, such as coordinators or task forces, to facilitate cross-organizational communication and coordination.

- *Design skunkworks when innovation is needed.* These small, informal, relatively autonomous structures can be an effective anecdote to bureaucracy and bigness.

- *Avoid complex matrix structures.* Use this form of organization only when you must simultaneously respond to two different sectors and you do not have the resources to create independent organizations.

- *Carefully analyze foreign organizational structures.* Even though structures may appear similar to yours, be aware that there may be major differences that impact people's behavior in quite different ways.

FOR DISCUSSION

1. Why is the answer not obvious to the question, "What is our business and what should it be?" Give an example of an organization that has not properly answered this question.

2. What is the difference between objectives and goals?

3. Explain how the span of management may be related to leadership and decision-making behaviors.

4. Give an example of a line and a staff position in a university organization.

5. Weigh the advantages and disadvantages of the various ways to divide up labor horizontally.

6. What is decentralization? How is it related to decision making? To power? To leadership style?

7. Explain the structures that are often used to attain coordination and integration.

8. Why is the environment so important for structuring organizations?

9. Under what circumstances might the bureaucratic organization be the most effective structure?

10. What special organizational behavior problems are created by the matrix organization?

11. Figure 15.20 illustrates the distribution of influence in Japanese and American firms. Assuming that your company does extensive business with Japanese firms, what are the implications of these findings for you?

KEY CONCEPTS AND TERMS

organizational structure	horizontal division of labor	line and staff
organizational purpose	span of management	line authority
objectives	tall organizational structures	functional authority
vertical division of labor	flat organizational structure	technical core

departmentation

functional organization

product organization

centralization

decentralization

informal organization

vertical integration

horizontal integration

environment

environmental uncertainty

buffers

technical core

bureaucracy

"skunkworks"

matrix organization

hybrid organization

responsibility center

rule of 100

Cases and Incidents

THE ADVANCED AEROSPACE RESEARCH LABORATORY

Dr. Hans Engstrom, the newly appointed head of the Advanced Aerospace Research Laboratory (AARL), was delighted with the job. He had worked at several labs as a scientist before being selected to head the AARL. Long ago he decided that if he ever got to be a lab director he would run a "tighter" ship than the directors he had observed.

During his second week he announced two major management changes:

- *Reorganization.* Instead of having the three assistant lab directors, each supervising ten to twelve scientists, he announced that henceforth a supervisor would not have more than four subordinates. This created another level of supervision with a number of scientists gaining the title of "Supervisory Scientist." He figured

the new organization would not only result in better control, but would give added prestige to the supervisory jobs.

- *Time and activities reporting system.* The second managerial innovation was a detailed reporting system to describe how time was spent on each task. This, he thought, will result in much better records so we can more easily justify our existence in the event of budget cuts.

DISCUSSION QUESTIONS

1. What effects do you predict from the managerial innovations in terms of satisfaction, performance, and retention?

2. What organizational structure is most appropriate for a research lab? Why?

3. What impact might you expect from the control system? Is there a better way to control and coordinate activities?

LEE IACOCCA REORGANIZES CHRYSLER

It turned out that my worries were justified. I soon stumbled upon my first major revelation: Chrysler didn't really function like a company at all. Chrysler in 1978 was like Italy in the 1860s—the company consisted of a cluster of little duchies, each one run by a prima donna. It was a bunch of mini-empires, with nobody giving a damn about what anyone else was doing.

What I found at Chrysler were thirty-five vice-presidents, each with his own turf. There was no real committee setup, no cement in the organizational chart, no system of meetings to get people talking to each other. I couldn't believe, for example, that the guy running the engineering department wasn't in constant touch with his counterpart

in manufacturing. But that's how it was. Everybody worked independently. I took one look at that system and I almost threw up. That's when I knew I was in really deep trouble.

Apparently these guys didn't believe in Newton's third law of motion—that for every action there's an equal and opposite reaction. Instead, they were all working in a vacuum. It was so bad that even this description doesn't begin to do it justice.

I'd call in a guy from engineering, and he'd stand there dumbfounded when I'd explain to him that we had a design problem or some other hitch in the engineering-manufacturing relationship. He might have the ability to invent a brilliant piece of engineering that would save us a lot of money. He might come up with a terrific new design. There was only one problem: he didn't know that the manufacturing people couldn't build it. Why? Because he had never talked to them about it.

Nobody at Chrysler seemed to understand that interaction among the different functions in a company is absolutely critical. People in engineering and manufacturing almost have to be sleeping together. These guys weren't even flirting!

Another example: sales and manufacturing were under the same vice-president. This was inconceivable to me because these were huge and primarily separate functions. To make matters worse, there was virtually no contact between the two areas. The manufacturing guys would build cars without ever checking with the sales guys. They just built them, stuck them in a yard, and then hoped that somebody would take them out of there. We ended up with a huge inventory and a financial nightmare.

The contrast between Chrysler's structure and Ford's was simply amazing. Nobody at Chrysler seemed to realize that you just can't run a big corporation without calling some pregame sessions to do blackboard work. Every member of the team has to understand what his job is and exactly how it fits in with every other job.

One of the luxuries we had to eliminate was a large staff. Ever since Alfred P. Sloan took over the presidency of General Motors, all management functions in our industry have been divided into staff and line positions—just like the Army. Line guys are in operations. They have hands-on involvement and specific responsibilities, whether it's in engineering, manufacturing, or purchasing.

The staff guys are the overall planners. They're the ones who integrate the work of the line guys into a workable system. Virtually the only way that a staff guy can be effective is if he's come up through the line. Yet the tendency, especially at a place like Ford, is to take a Harvard Business School graduate who may not know his ass from his elbow and make him staff. He's never run anything, but now he's telling the line guy, who's been doing his job for thirty years, that he's doing it all wrong. I've spent too much time in my career refereeing staff/line disputes that should never have come up in the first place.

You do need a staff—so long as you don't overdo it. At Ford, when Henry was trying to get rid of me, he brought in the consulting firm of McKinsey & Company. In addition to forming the office of the chairman, McKinsey also set up a superstaff of about eighty people. Its purpose was to check all the other staff and line people to make sure everybody was doing his job. Over the years, this group has become like a sovereign power at Ford—a company unto itself.

When Chrysler got hit, I had to let most of the staff go. I've been a line guy all my life, which might have made it easier. But my thinking was simple: I needed somebody to build the cars and sell the cars. I couldn't afford to have a guy who says that if we had done this or that, we could have built that car a little better. Even if he was right, we didn't have the luxury to consider it. When the bullets start to fly, the staff is always first out the door.

With all the firings, we ended up stripping out several levels of management. We cut down the number of people who needed to be involved in important decisions. Initially we did it out of the sheer necessity to survive. But over time we found that running a large company with fewer people actually made things easier. With hindsight it's clear that Chrysler had been top-heavy, far beyond what was good for us. That's a lesson our competitors have yet to learn—and I hope they never do!

DISCUSSION QUESTIONS

1. What organizational design structures were weak or missing when Iacocca took over Chrysler?

2. How could these deficiencies be resolved?

3. What benefits did Chrysler derive from cuts in staff?

From Iacocca, L. (1984). *Iacocca: An autobiography* (pp. 152–153, 190–191). New York: Bantam Books.

REFERENCES

1. Adapted from a case presented in Kover, A.J. (1963). Reorganization in an advertising agency: A case study in integration. *Human Organization, 22,* 252–259.

2. For extensive coverage of organizational design see Daft, R.L. (1986). *Organizational theory and design* (2nd ed.). St. Paul, MN: West. Robey, D. (1986). *Designing organizations* (2nd ed.). Homewood, IL: Irwin. Mintzberg, H. (1983). *Structure in Fives: Designing effective organizations.* Englewood Cliffs, NJ: Prentice-Hall. And Nystrom, P.C., & Starbuck, W.H. (Eds.). (1981). *Handbook of organizational design.* New York: Oxford University Press.

3. See Abegglen, J.C., & Stalk, G., Jr. (1985). *Kaisha, the Japanese corporation.* New York: Basic Books. Pascale, R.T., & Athos, A.G. (1981). *The art*

of Japanese management: Applications for American executives. New York: Simon and Schuster. And Ouchi, W. (1981). *Theory Z: How American business can meet the Japanese challenge.* Reading, MA: Addison-Wesley.

4. Walton, R.E. (1986). A vision-led approach to management restructuring. *Organizational Dynamics, 14* (Spring), 4–16. Also see Pearce, J.A. II, & David, F. (1987). Corporate mission statements: The bottom line, *Academy of Management Executive, 1,* 109–116.

5. Drucker, P.F. (1974). *Management: Tasks, responsibilities, practices.* New York: Harper and Row. Also, *see* Drucker, P.F. (1982). *The changing world of the executive.* New York: Truman Talley/Times Books. And, Drucker, P.F. (1986). *Frontiers of management.* New York: E.P. Dutton.

6. Drucker (1974), p. 100.

7. Daft, R.L. (1986). *Organizational theory and design* (p. 9). St. Paul: West. For reviews see Dess, G.G., & Beard, D.W. (1984). Dimensions of organizational task environments. *Administrative Science Quarterly, 29,* 52–73. And Tung, R.L. (1979). Dimensions of organizational environments: An exploratory study of their impact on organization structure. *Academy of Management Journal, 22,* 672–693.

8. Duncan, R.B. (1972). Characteristics of organizational environments and perceived uncertainty. *Administrative Science Quarterly, 17,* 313–327.

9. Jurkovich, R. (1974). A core topology of organizational environments. *Administrative Science Quarterly, 19,* 380–394. And Thompson, J.D. (1967). *Organizations in action.* New York: McGraw-Hill.

10. Gillespie, D.F., & Mileti, D.S. (1977). Technology and the study of organizations. *Academy of Management Review, 2,* 8. Also, *see* Gerstein, M.S. (1987). *The technology connection: Strategy and change in the information age.* Reading, MA: Addison-Wesley.

11. Randolph, W.A. (1981). Matching technology and design of organizational units. *California Management Review, 23,* 39–48.

12. Thompson (1967). Jemison, D.B. (1984). The importance of boundary-spanning roles in strategic decision making. *Journal of Management Studies, 21,* 131–152.

13. This definition is similar to one posed by Blackburn, R.S. (1982). Dimensions of structure: A review and reappraisal. *Academy of Management Review, 7,* 59–66.

14. Ranson, S., Hinings, B., & Greenwood, R. (1980). The structuring of organizational structures. *Administrative Science Quarterly, 25,* 1–17.

15. Davis, K. (1981). *Human behavior at work: Organizational behavior* (6th ed., p. 329) New York: McGraw-Hill.

16. Gray, J.L., & Starke, F.A. (1977). *Organizational behavior concepts and applications* (p. 137). Columbus, OH: Charles E. Merrill.

17. See Urwick, L.F. (1956). The manager's span of control. *Harvard Business Review, 34*(3), 39–47.

18. Peters, T., & Austin, N. (1985). *A Passion for excellence.* New York: Random House.

19. See Koontz, H. (1966). Making theory operational: The span of management. *The Journal of Management Studies, 3,* 229–243.

20. Dewar, R.D. (1981). A level of specific prediction of spans of control examining the effects of size, technology, and specialization. *Academy of Management Journal, 24,* 5–24. And Van Fleet, D.D. (1983). Span of management research and issues. *Academy of Management Journal, 26,* 546–552.

21. For reviews see Dalton, D.R., Todor, W.D., Spendolini, M.J., Fielding, G.J., & Porter, L.W. (1980). Organizational structure and performance: A critical review. *Academy of Management Review, 5,* 49–64. Oldham G.R., & Hackman, J.R. (1981). Relationships between organizational structure and employee reactions: Comparing alternative frameworks. *Administrative Science Quarterly, 26,* 66–82. And Cummings, L.L., & Berger, C.J. (1976). Organizational structure: How does it influence attitudes and performance? *Organizational Dynamics, 5* (2), 34–49.

22. Peters, T., & Austin, N. (1985). *A Passion for excellence* (p. 317). New York: Random House.

23. Peters & Austin (1985).

24. Peters, T.J., & Waterman, R.H., Jr. (1982). *In search of excellence* (p. 311). New York: Harper & Row.

25. Peters and Austin (1985).

26. Sease, D.R. (1986, September 16). How U.S. companies devise ways to meet challenge from Japan. *The Wall Street Journal.*

27. Peters & Austin (1985), p. 317.

28. Jelinek, M., Litterer, J.A., & Miles, R.E., (Eds.). (1981). *Organizations by design: Theory and practice.* Plano, TX: Business Publications.

29. See McCann, J., & Galbraith, J.R. (1981). Interdepartmental relations. In P.C. Nystrom & W.H. Starbuck (Eds.). *Handbook of organizational design.* New York: Oxford University Press. Also see a classic article discussing these issues: Walker, A.H., & Lorsch, J.W. (1968, November–December). Organizational choice: Product versus function. *Harvard Business Review.*

30. For a more complete discussion of decentralization, see Vancil, R.F. (1980). *Decentralization: Managerial ambiguity by design.* New York: Financial Executives Research Foundation.

31. Curtice, H.H. (1972). General Motors organization, philosophy, and structure. In H. Koontz & C. O'Donnell (Eds.). *Management: A book of readings* (3rd ed., p. 343). New York: McGraw-Hill.

32. Ross Perot's crusade. (1986, October 6). *Business Week*, p. 61.

33. This discussion is based on: Ross Perot's crusade. (1986, October 6). *Business Week*, p. 61. Also see: Peace for a price at GM. (1986, December 15). *Time.* And Levin, D.P., & Buss, D.D. (1986). GM plans offer to pay $700 million to buy out its critic H. Ross Perot. (1986, December 1) *The Wall Street Journal.*

34. For a review see Cummings & Berger (1976). See also Duncan (1979).

35. Govindarajan, V. (1986). Decentralization, strategy, and effectiveness of strategic business units in multibusiness organizations. *Academy of Management Review, 11,* 844–856. Ivancevich, J.M., & Donnelly, J.H., Jr. (1975). Relation of organizational structure to job satisfaction, anxiety-stress, and performance. *Administrative Science Quarterly, 20,* 272–280.

36. Lorsch, J.W., & Lawrence, P.R. (1972). Environmental factors and organizational integration. In P.W. Lorsch & P.R. Lawrence (Eds.). *Organizational planning: Cases and concepts.* Homewood, IL: Irwin and Dorsey.

37. For a more complete discussion of vertical and horizontal integrating roles see Daft (1986).

38. Lawrence, P.R., & Lorsch, J.W. (1967, November–December). The new managerial job: The integrator. *Harvard Business Review*, pp. 42–51.

39. Management discovers the human side of automation. (1986, September 29). *Business Week.* See Chapters 7 and 9 for more on socio-technical systems. Also, *see* Manz, C.C., & Sims, H.P., Jr. (1987). Leading workers to lead themselves: The external leadership of self-managing work teams. *Administrative Science Quarterly, 32,* 106–128.

40. Kolodny, H.F., & Dresner, B. (1986). Linking arrangements and new work designs. *Organizational Dynamics, 14* (Winter), 33–51.

41. Adapted from Weber, M. (1947). *The theory of social and economic organization.* New York: Oxford University Press.

42. Child, J. (1977). *Organizations.* New York: Harper & Row.

43. Peters & Waterman (1982). Peters & Austin (1985).

44. Peters & Austin (1985), pp. 137–138.

45. Peters & Austin (1985), pp. 143–144.

46. Speech by Tom Peters as reported in *The News Tribune* (1986, October 3). Think small: Author preaches on how business should change. (Tacoma, WA.)

47. See Daft (1986) for a discussion of the impact of computers on organizational structure.

48. Summary from Davis, S.M., Lawrence, P.R. (1978). Problems of matrix organizations. *Harvard Business Review, 56,* 134. Also see Davis, S.M., & Lawrence, P.R. (1977). *Matrix.* Reading, MA: Addison-Wesley.

49. Based on Lipman-Blumen, J. (1980). Female leadership in formal organizations: Must the female leader go formal? In H.J. Leavitt, L.R. Pondy, & D.M. Boje (Eds.). *Readings in managerial psychology* (3rd ed., pp. 354–355). Chicago: University of Chicago Press.

50. Davis & Lawrence (1977). Kolodny, H.F. (1981, March–April). Managing in a matrix. *Business Horizons*, pp. 17–35.

51. Joyce, W.F. (1986). Matrix organization: A social experiment. *Academy of Management Journal, 29,* 536–561.

52. This section is based on Otsubo, M. (1986). A guide to Japanese business practices. *California Management Review, 28* (3), 34.

53. Nonaka, I., & Okumura, A. (1984). A comparison of management in American, Japanese, and European firms. *Management Japan, 17* (Spring), 23–40.

Chapter Sixteen

ORGANIZATION CHANGE AND DEVELOPMENT

PREVIEW

- Why is it that even chief executives sometimes have trouble changing their organizations?

- When is creating dissatisfaction desirable?

- Which change factor do you think is more powerful: a manager's expectations or the nature of the change innovation itself?

- Why do people sometimes revert back to their original behaviors in spite of all your efforts to change them?

- What is organization development? Why is it so popular with companies? Does it really work?

MAJOR TOPICS

Preview Case: Great Pacific Shipbuilding

The Change Process

Unfreezing: Getting Ready for Change

Moving: The Change Itself

Refreezing: Making the Change Stick

Organization Development

Cross-Cultural OB: Fitting OD to National Culture

Managerial Applications of Change and OD

Preview Case

GREAT PACIFIC SHIPBUILDING

Mallory Webb was the third chief executive of Great Pacific Shipbuilding in the past four years.[1] Great Pacific was such a big money loser that the President of Meganational Conglomerates, owner of Great Pacific, told him this was going to be the last chance for the corporation. If it could not be turned around by the end of next year, then Meganational would cut its losses and liquidate it.

Great Pacific was poorly managed. It had plenty of business but was plagued by duplication of effort and lack of responsiveness to its customers. Previous CEOs had known these problems and tried to "shake up" and reorganize the company. Somehow nothing ever seemed to change—there was always some reason why change could not be done.

Mallory, a successful manager with a good track record, had also tried to make changes. He ran into the same roadblocks and became frustrated, knowing that if he could not succeed at Great Pacific, his career as a chief executive would be over. He decided to seek the aid of Douglas Nelson, a Northwest University professor, who is an expert in organizational change and development.

After several lengthy discussions, they decided on a strategy using a systematic change process. Here's what they did:

• **Getting ready.** They worked together to figure out who the "stakeholders" were—those key people who might have a stake in the success or failure of the change. The group included most of the major line and staff executives, about sixteen people. Mallory appointed them to a planning team and asked them to join himself and the consultant at a three-day offsite workshop at the Meganational Retreat Center at Lake Wilderness. Doug interviewed each of these executives in preparation for the workshop to find out how they felt about the performance of Great Pacific.

• **The Offsite Workshop.** Mallory began the meeting by "laying it on the line." Performance was low and there was a threat to the very existence of Great Pacific. He stated his objective of figuring out how to turn around the business and make it profitable again. Then Doug fed back recurring themes from the interviews, which centered around widespread dissatisfaction with organizational performance.

During the three days, the group worked to analyze the organization. They considered the basic purpose and mission of Great Pacific. They asked, "What is our business and what should it be?" They asked, "Who is the customer?" After extensive problem-solving sessions using a technique called Force-Field Analysis (to be discussed later in the chapter), they decided on reorganization as their major change strategy. A transition team was appointed (one person from each major line and staff division) to help implement the planning group's ideas.

• **Organizing the Transition.** The day after they returned, Mallory wrote a memo to all division chiefs summarizing the results of the workshop, announcing the transition team, and setting the date for a companywide management meeting to discuss the new organizational structure. The transition team put the finishing touches on the new design, including detailed statements of strategy and purpose for the new structure. They developed a detailed transition plan outlining time schedules, responsibilities, and methods. The transition team met frequently with the planning group, including several, one-day offsite meetings.

• **Top Management Support.** Mallory continued his involvement and strong support for the changes the planning group had developed, for he agreed with the plan and had been a major influence in its formulation. He attended transition group meetings from time to time to find out what was happening and to show support and concern. In private, he confronted several people who were resisting and sought their support. He was also careful to insure that rewards, such as promotions, went to people who were enthusiastic supporters of the change.

• **Executing the Plan.** During the next four months, the reorganization took place just as the transition team had planned. Several times during the period, questionnaires were used to find out how things were going and whether the employees saw any problems. When problems were uncovered, they were addressed, and the new structure fine-tuned.

• **Results.** The change was effective. Performance improved and both managers and employees were more satisfied with Great Pacific. Profits were in the black within six months, assuring the survival of Great Pacific and enhancing Mallory's record as a chief executive.

Managing the change process is one of the most important aspects of a manager's task. Effective change management often makes the difference between a highly successful manager and a mediocre or poor one. Mallory's predecessors had all failed to change Great Pacific and as a result faded into managerial obscurity. Mallory's success will lead to other challenging positions.

Even the largest corporations find change is difficult. General Motors has experienced considerable difficulty in building "the factory of the future" at Hammtramck, Michigan. "A fleet of robotic vehicles built to carry materials through the factory sat idle for months while GM workers tried to figure out the software needed to make them go. Problems with programming the robots in the paint shop . . . forced GM to truck some cars to an older plant for painting. An expensive vision-inspection system was erected in the wrong spot on the assembly line to catch defective parts in time; it has now been relocated."[2]

Ross Perot, founder of Electronic Data Systems (EDS) (EDS was bought by GM, making Ross Perot GM's largest single stockholder until GM bought out its outspoken critic in 1987), has complained that GM is not very good at implementing change. He believes part of the reason is its study-it-to-death bureaucracy. "'The first EDSer to see a snake kills it,' Perot tells reporters. 'At GM, first thing you do is organize a committee on snakes. Then you bring in a consultant who knows a lot about snakes. Third thing you do is talk about it for a year.'"[3]

Obviously, change is not as easy as it appears. In this chapter, we will provide some of the keys to understanding and managing the change process. We will also discuss organization development, an effective change strategy concentrating on organizational behavior issues.[4]

THE CHANGE PROCESS

To **change** is to move from one state or condition to another state or condition. While change is constant and inevitable, it does not always occur in the direction a manager wants it to go. Every CEO at Great Pacific wanted a positive change in organizational performance; only Mallory was successful in achieving this goal. The key reason for his success was an understanding of the change process. Change was carefully managed and directed toward the desired goals using a total systems perspective.

There are many pressures on managers to change. Thus, planning and executing change is one of the major tasks of managers who are working in the managerial subsystem. Some of the pressures toward change and resistance to change are shown in Figure 16.1.

A Systems Perspective of Change

Since organizations are systems made up of a number of subsystems existing within the environmental suprasystem, we would expect the change process to affect all systems.[5] For example, Mallory's predecessors at Great Pacific thought all they had to do to change the organization was to change the structure by managerial edict. They failed. Mallory's approach considered the entire system,

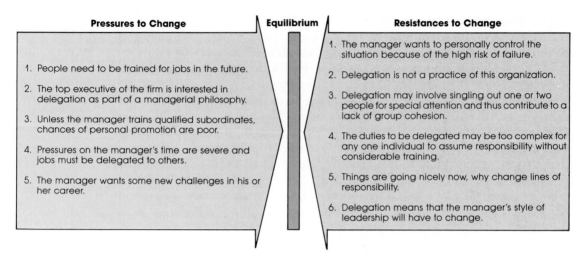

Pressures to Change	Equilibrium	Resistances to Change

Pressures to Change

1. People need to be trained for jobs in the future.

2. The top executive of the firm is interested in delegation as part of a managerial philosophy.

3. Unless the manager trains qualified subordinates, chances of personal promotion are poor.

4. Pressures on the manager's time are severe and jobs must be delegated to others.

5. The manager wants some new challenges in his or her career.

Resistances to Change

1. The manager wants to personally control the situation because of the high risk of failure.

2. Delegation is not a practice of this organization.

3. Delegation may involve singling out one or two people for special attention and thus contribute to a lack of group cohesion.

4. The duties to be delegated may be too complex for any one individual to assume responsibility without considerable training.

5. Things are going nicely now, why change lines of responsibility.

6. Delegation means that the manager's style of leadership will have to change.

Figure 16.1

CHANGE AND THE MANAGER: PRESSURES AND RESISTANCES

SOURCE: From D. Hellriegel and J.W. Slocum, Jr., (1979). *Organizational behavior,* 2nd ed., p. 557. Copyright © 1979 by West Publishing Company, St. Paul, Minn. Used with permission.

with particular attention to the psycho-social subsystem including power relationships, communication, group dynamics, and motivation. By structuring the groups into planning groups and task forces, Mallory was able to get people involved, motivated, and directed towards the change.

Changing pay systems, computer systems, performance appraisal procedures, structures, supervisors, or working hours, all have an impact on the organization. For example, a new appraisal system designed to get more accurate records for assignments and promotions will affect motivation, conflict, group dynamics, and other aspects of the organization.

Equilibrium and Change

Since change involves moving from one state to another, change means the **equilibrium** of the system is affected—the forces acting upon the system have become imbalanced and **disequilibrium** has been created. Before Mallory's arrival at Great Pacific, previous CEOs had been unable to break the equilibrium; no matter what they tried, things remained the same. Thus, an important part of the change process is recognizing that the force of inertia is great and that something may be needed to force the system into disequilibrium before change can happen. Thus, we will envision a three-part change process: unfreezing, changing, and then refreezing in the desired state.[6] The idea is to move from one equilibrium state to another in an orderly way. Figure 16.2 graphically depicts the change process.

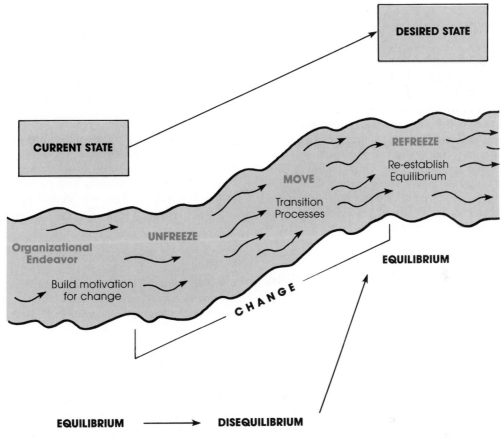

Figure 16.2

THE CHANGE PROCESS

SOURCE: Model adapted from the ideas of Lewin, K. (1947). Frontiers of group dynamics. *Human Relations, 1,* 5–41.

Overview of the Change Process

Organizations move along in a state of equilibrium, transforming inputs into outputs (organizational endeavor). Then someone or something comes along and creates the motivation to change because of dissatisfaction with the current state. This process of creating a need for change is called **unfreezing.** Once the system is unfrozen, it can be changed—hopefully in the direction planned by the manager—into a new and desired state. This part of the process is called **moving** or changing. It involves a number of processes that make the change more effective. Finally, when the desired state is reached, the system must be **refrozen** at this new level; equilibrium must be reestablished. Perspective 16.1 illustrates how the change process works in the case of managerial succession.

Now that we have covered an overview of the change process, we will discuss each aspect of the process: unfreezing, changing or moving, and refreezing.

Perspective 16.1

WHEN A NEW MANAGER TAKES CHARGE[7]

John Gabarro, a Harvard professor, conducted a study of fourteen managers (division presidents, general managers, and functional department heads) who had assumed new jobs. He wanted to study the change process over time. The three-year study evaluated the number of changes made and the operation of the change process. Figure 16.3 shows how changes clustered into five stages. These are described below:

• *Taking hold.* The first three to six months is a period of intense learning. The manager grapples with the new situation, people, and problems. Both manager and organization are unfrozen—the equilibrium has been disrupted.

• *Immersion.* Managers now know more about their organizations and begin to make many more changes. Fundamental underlying problems are more likely to surface. Resistances to changes are identified and overcome.

• *Reshaping.* This stage contains the greatest number of actual changes. Problems that were identified and studied in the immersion phase can now be acted upon. This period contains high levels of energy, activity, and action.

• *Consolidation.* This stage is primarily a follow-through and evaluation stage. The manager wants to make sure the changes are refrozen.

• *Refinement.* This is the new equilibrium. Few changes are made. Managers look for opportunities in the marketplace or technology.

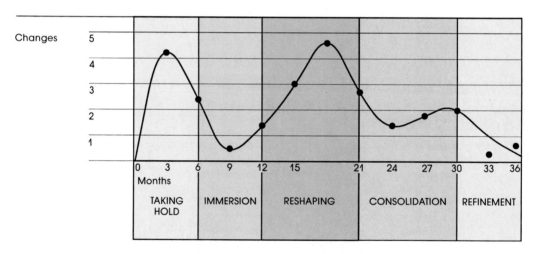

Figure 16.3

AVERAGE NUMBER OF CHANGES PER THREE–MONTH PERIOD FOLLOWING SUCCESSION

UNFREEZING: GETTING READY FOR CHANGE

Many of the problems associated with change concern the forces against unfreezing; the forces for maintaining the equilibrium or status quo. We will discuss two major problems, resistance to change and power and political dynamics. Table 16.1 provides an instrument to assess readiness and potential success of a change effort. If you have some change in mind, why not fill out the questionnaire before reading the rest of the chapter.

Resistance to Change

Perhaps the overriding cause of resistance is fear; fear of the unknown; fear that our needs will not be met. People resist change for a number of reasons.[8]

Interference With Need Fulfillment. If people's security, social, esteem, or other needs are threatened, resistance will be great. Even such relatively minor changes as relocating people may disrupt social relations or status relationships and arouse great resistance.

New Learning May Be Needed. It takes a lot of effort to find new and different ways to manage the environment when the status quo changes. For example, if the change is a new boss, an employee must learn the new boss' idiosyncracies and desires. A new organizational structure means you have to learn who to go to with a problem; where to go to get things done.

Vested Interests. People who have power have a vested interest in the status quo. A manager whose department is threatened with merger into another will resist to maintain the current position.

Comfort With the Status Quo. People like stability and may have invested a great deal of effort in the current system. The present system may be rewarding, easy, and certain. Change often creates anxiety and at least temporary discomfort. People generally prefer the positive reinforcement of the present system over the punishment—even though it might be short-term—resulting from a change to a new system.

Impaired Feeling of Self-Control. Change, especially if imposed by management, often reduces feelings of self-control and autonomy. These feelings may be de-enriching, dissatisfying, or even threatening. A faculty member who has been writing textbooks is told that writing texts is not sufficient to get promoted; articles must also be published in professional journals. This results in an experienced loss of autonomy.

Group Norms. As we noted in Chapter 9, norms are powerful determinants of behavior. Norms generally support the status quo. For example, a change in work standards may result in a violent reaction from the members of the involved work groups.

Ideological Objections. The person may be against the change for ideological reasons, such as the change's relationship to human rights, war, or status of women. For example, a manager may resign rather than support a planned acquisition of a subsidiary in South Africa because of opposition to apartheid.

Table 16.1

PREDICTING SUCCESS OF A CHANGE PROGRAM

Predicting Success of a Change Program

How ready and able are you to achieve an organizational change you have in mind? The following questions will help you see your strengths and short-comings.

1. Are you able to clearly describe the change you desire and the benefits that will be achieved?

   1---------2--------3--------4--------5--------6--------7

   Not too able.   I can describe
                                   this to anyone.

2. How committed are *you* to achieving the desired change?

   1---------2--------3--------4--------5--------6--------7

   Not too   Highly
   committed.   committed—my
                                   highest priority.

3. How committed to the change are *other people* who will be affected by the change?

   1---------2--------3--------4--------5--------6--------7

   Not too   Highly
   committed.   committed—it is
                                   their highest
                                   priority concern.

4. Are you willing to stand up to your boss and go to bat for the change project?

   1---------2--------3--------4--------5--------6--------7

   Not too willing.   Very willing to
                                   stand up to boss.

5. Are you able to get the necessary time, people, or resources needed to achieve the change?

   1---------2--------3--------4--------5--------6--------7

   Not too able.   I can get all I
                                   need.

6. How supportive of the change are the key people who must support the change if it is to be successful?

   1---------2--------3--------4--------5--------6--------7

   Not very   All of the key
   supportive.   people are very
                                   supportive.

7. How sure are you that you have all the necessary skills needed to move the project ahead?

   1---------2--------3--------4--------5--------6--------7

   Not too sure.   Absolutely
                                   confident I have
                                   the skills.

8. How easily are you discouraged if success does not come right away?

   1---------2--------3--------4--------5--------6--------7

   Very easily.   Almost never.

9. Do you feel you know how to get the support you need to achieve this change?

   1---------2--------3--------4--------5--------6--------7

   Not sure I know   I am very sure I
   how.   know exactly
                                   what must be
                                   done to get
                                   support.

10. Do people trust you and feel willing to work with you in this change project?

    1---------2--------3--------4--------5--------6--------7

    Trust level is low.   People trust me
                                   implicitly and
                                   will work with
                                   me.

11. Will you and others who support you get appropriate rewards and recognition if your change succeeds?

    1---------2--------3--------4--------5--------6--------7

    Not sure we will   The organization
    get rewards.   will give us all
                                   the rewards
                                   needed.

12. If you run into snags or resistance, do you feel you will be able to cope with them—to know what to do and how to do it?

    1---------2--------3--------4--------5--------6--------7

    Not very sure I   I feel confident I
    know how to   will know what
    cope.   to do and how to
                                   do it.

Add up your score for all the items. If you have a score between 65 and 84, you should feel confident you can move ahead with your change program. If your score is between 40 and 64, you should probably get more training or consulting help before you begin the change. If your score is below 40, your chances of achieving the change are poor.

SOURCE: Predicting success of a change program by W.G. Dyer. Reprinted from Academy of Management OD Newsletter, Summer 1986.

Power and Politics

Power and politics are particularly important when it comes to change. Whenever you unfreeze a situation, you are, in fact, tearing down or destroying the old system and creating a new one. The increased ambiguity that results is likely to increase political and power-oriented behavior as people jockey for position in the new state.[9] If the change is opposed by powerful factions, as it was at Great Pacific, then there is little likelihood of successful unfreezing without some strategy to motivate those factions to action. When Mallory created the planning group that included all the important "stakeholders," he was forcing the power coalitions to join in designing the change; thus, they were unfrozen.

Strategies for Unfreezing

Arouse Dissatisfaction With the Current State. Sometimes dissatisfaction already exists and this step is not needed. But if the organization is complacent and content, as Great Pacific may have been before Mallory's arrival, some act is needed to jolt the organizational members into a dissatisfied state. Mallory did this by telling them Great Pacific would be closed if they could not improve organizational performance. This strategy of highlighting deficiencies in organizational performance or functioning is the most common way of unfreezing. Since data is particularly useful for justifying discrepancies, it is an important aid in creating a belief that the present state is unsatisfactory and in need of correction.[10]

Activate and Strengthen Top Management Support. If top managers are not supporting the change or just giving it "lip service," then unfreezing is unlikely.[11] Lack of top management support means middle management is also unlikely to be firmly committed to the change. Top management pressure may be enough in itself to unfreeze the organization, especially if the CEO has considerable power. A top manager's expectations can have a powerful influence (*see* Perspective 16.3). But in many cases, top management support is not sufficient, as was the case at Great Pacific where various organizational power centers were resisting change.[12]

Use Participation in Decision Making. Perhaps the single most powerful technique for aiding the change process is participation in planning and decisions surrounding the change. People tend to support what they have developed. If some outside group or person tries to introduce change, people resist—the "not invented here" syndrome is at work. Participation builds ownership for the change and heightens motivation to make the change work.[13] Participation also helps communicate what the change is about and provides information about the circumstances surrounding the change.

In the preview case, Mallory used participation by having both a planning group and a transition team. Each involved different levels of the organization and built ownership and commitment to the change. Perspective 16.2 shows

Perspective 16.2

OVERCOMING RESISTANCE
TO CHANGE:
A CLASSIC EXPERIMENT[14]

Just after World War II, the Harwood Manufacturing Corp., which employed mostly women
who made pajamas, was having trouble implementing a change related to increasing production. There was a strong norm that production
should not exceed sixty units per hour. There
was also considerable resistance to changing
jobs because of the time needed to get fully up
to speed on a new task.

To help unfreeze the workers, an experiment
was set up in which total participation (all
group members) was used in two groups: representative participation (elected or appointed
person represents the group) in one group, and
no participation for a control group. Participation took the form of explaining the need for
change in terms of costs, and having the group
approve a plan to achieve the objective and take
the action to effect the change.

Immediate improvements were seen in the
groups using total participation and somewhat
slower improvements in the group that used
representative participation. Learning new
techniques occurred much more rapidly in the
participation groups and efficiency improved
more rapidly in the participation groups. In
addition, the quit rates were much lower for
these groups. The control group production remained low during the whole time of the experiment. Thus, participation greatly facilitated
the change.

A follow-on experiment used participation
in the control group with the same improved
results. The researchers concluded that by using group participation, resistance to change
could be reduced or eliminated.

how one of the earliest organizational experiments links participation with
change.

Build in Rewards. Since people are motivated to behave in ways that are
rewarding, a key to unfreezing is to tie rewards to the change. For example, use
recognition, praise, status symbols, or even bonuses to get people involved in
the change. In addition, if you can show how the outcome of the change will
create long-term rewards, be sure to make these linkages clear. Mallory used
both rewards and punishments (private verbal reprimands) to help with the
change at Great Pacific. He also made it clear the change was necessary to
insure permanent employment.

Use Force-field Analysis. One useful technique for identifying resistance to
change is called **force-field analysis,** or FFA.[15] The notion here is that there are
both driving and resisting forces that tend to keep the situation in equilibrium.
If these forces can be clearly identified, then a manager or task force can work
on the resisting forces to try to get the equilibrium to move to a new level. The
length of the arrows represents the power of each force, just as if it were a
mathematical vector. Increasing driving forces, while sometimes effective, is
usually much weaker than removing restraining forces because increased drive
often tends to be offset by increased resistance. (*See* Figure 16.4 for an example
of this technique.)

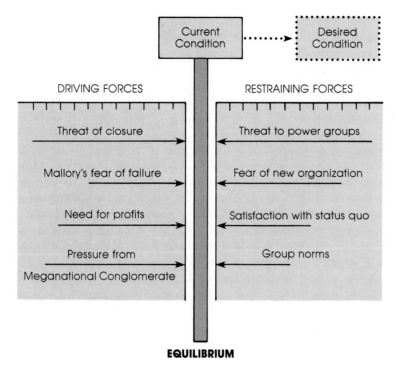

Notes

1. Length of the arrow indicates the strength of that vector—driving or restraining.

2. Always try to remove restraining forces rather than increasing driving forces.

Figure 16.4

FORCE–FIELD ANALYSIS FOR GREAT PACIFIC SHIPBUILDING

MOVING: THE CHANGE ITSELF

Once resistance has been overcome, we move into the change itself—the **transition** or movement from one state or condition to another.[16] Some changes are instantaneous, like a new parking plan effective on Monday. Others take much longer, like the conversion of an accounting system from manual to computer records or introducing robotics into a manufacturing plant. Regardless of how long the transition lasts, it must be managed. We will discuss four aspects of the moving phase: establishing goals, using leverage points, structuring the transition, and maintaining communication.

Establish Clear Goals

Once people are unfrozen, they want to know where to move. Goals provide a clear picture of what you want. They provide the blueprint for action, and they communicate what you want the future condition to look like. A written state-ment explaining the goals and purposes of the change should be widely disseminated to all who are involved in the change.[17] A statement developed through participation is desirable. In the Great Pacific example, Mallory made sure everyone knew the goal of the change: to make the business profitable by the end of next year.

Use Leverage Points

Our systems perspective says that change has a multiple impact—it permeates many organizational systems. Every possible point in the system that will help create the change must be utilized. That is where **leverage points** come in because this term refers to any point in the organization serving to reinforce and support the change. For example, the change at Great Pacific involved changing procedures and rules, job descriptions, and reporting relationships. Training is also an effective leverage point for clarifying what needs to be done and why it needs to be done, thus creating a smooth transition.

Develop Management Structures for Change

Someone or some group needs to be the focal point for the change. This **transition manager** or **transition task force** develops a transition plan specify-ing the resources for the transition, the timetable, transition management strat-egies (pilot projects, consultants), and control mechanisms to insure the change is proceeding as planned. The transition is often easier if the transac-tion manager is not closely identified with either the present state or the future state. This means the manager will be perceived as impartial and without a high personal stake in either the new or the old state. In addition, the transition manager should be selected because he or she has the clout to mobilize the re-sources needed, has the respect of top management, and has effective interper-sonal skills.[18]

The types of structures that may be used for transition management are shown in Table 16.2

Maintain Open, Two-Way Communication

The last major step in a transition is to make sure communication channels are open. Problems and concerns can then be resolved with haste and feedback re-ceived about the progress of change. Data can be collected through interviews, observations, open forums, reports, company records, or other sources. With-out communication and followup, the CEO, or other person implementing the change, may be surprised, or even horrified, that an important change has not been completed. One reason for these "unexpected surprises" is that "bad news" is often avoided, especially when there is no reporting system forcing people to bring it to the surface, or when people are punished for presenting unfavorable reports.[19]

Perspective 16.3

EXPECTATIONS

AND CHANGE[20]

An important element in the success or failure of any change effort is the expectations of the parties. If the manager who is making the change expects success and the other participants believe it will succeed, then it seems plausible and even likely that the change will be successful. This raises an interesting question about the effect of any innovative organizational change: Are the results due to the manager's expectations that the innovation will succeed? A field experiment was designed to test this issue.

The study involved four plants of a large, nonunionized clothing patterns manufacturer. Management was implementing a job enrichment plan to improve productivity and to help ward off a union organizing campaign. The research was designed to find out the relative effects of the innovation and the effects of the top manager's expectations about the results of change efforts.

Managers at two of the plants were told job redesign would result in higher productivity while the managers of the other two plants were told the aim was to improve employee relations. Results showed that the manager's expectations were a more powerful predictor of outcomes than the form of innovation itself. When managers expected higher productivity, it happened. When they expected better employee relations, improvements actually took place.

Thus, managerial expectations surrounding a change may be more powerful in explaining the results than the innovation itself. Thus, expectations may result in a self-fulfilling prophecy.[21]

Table 16.2

TRANSITION MANAGEMENT STRUCTURES

- **CEO as the transition manager.** If the change is very important and is not so time consuming that it becomes unmanageable, then the CEO may elect to be the transition manager. In the early unfreezing states of change, the CEO often takes personal charge as Mallory did in the opening example.

- **Appoint a transition manager.** Someone may be appointed as the temporary project person for the change. This person serves a role that is very similar to a product person's role in the matrix organization we studied in the last chapter. The transition manager's job is to keep all activities oriented toward the change goals and to bring to the surface problems that need resolving. The person that is appointed may be either a functional expert, a line manager, or someone who is a charismatic leader who can marshal considerable confidence and trust of colleagues participating in the change. An example of this later category is when a university president selects one of the most esteemed and respected professors to effect a change in the university's calendar.

- **Appoint a task force.** This is one of the most popular and effective transition structures because you involve all the constituencies that are concerned with the change on the transition team. This is the approach used by Mallory in our preview case. The reason this approach works so well is that it allows participation of all concerned parties in the change.

- **Normal hierarchy.** Managers are given the additional task of carrying out the change. This approach has the advantages of the task force, and it involves management personnel in the change itself. This is often a good strategy since the managers will have to live with the change and should have a hand in designing it.

SOURCE: Based on Beckhard, R., & Harris, R.T. (1987). *Organizational transitions: Managing complex change* (2nd ed.). Reading, MA: Addison-Wesley.

REFREEZING: MAKING THE CHANGE STICK

If the change has been properly managed, refreezing in the new state of equilibrium should be relatively easy. People will be motivated to adopt the new state and management mechanisms will insure it is easy to do. However, there are still a few key points to consider when refreezing: building success experiences, rewarding desired behaviors, building social bonds, and developing structures for institutionalizing the change.

Build Success Experiences

Success is a very powerful positive reinforcer. If the new system works well, people will be motivated to adopt it. This means care must be taken to make sure the change will actually work as planned, without major defects or problems. A good strategy for extremely difficult and complex changes is a piece-by-piece or incremental implementation so one small success can build on another.

For instance, assume a firm has decided to use quality circles to improve its quality and productivity (*see* Perspective 16.4). The circle facilitator ensures that the first problems tackled by the circle have a good chance of success. Positive outcomes will reinforce the behavior and help refreeze the experience of participating in quality circles.[22]

A success experience can sometimes be created by using **pilot projects,** trying out a change in one section or division where the change has a high probability of success. Let's say the manager of a large division believes job redesign is a good strategy for improving the organization. The manager knows that while six different sections have volunteered to try the job redesign, there is a much greater probability of success in two of them. The change strategy is to use these two sections as a pilot project. The success of the pilot efforts may encourage job redesign throughout the division. But pilot projects do not always work as planned. The rest of the division may see the pilot groups receiving special attention while they do not, resulting in increased resistance to change.

Reward Desired Behavior

Refreezing the change should employ good behavior management techniques discussed in Chapter 6. Desired behaviors should be positively reinforced and undesirable behaviors—usually those associated with the old situation—should be ignored (extinguished) or punished. While this strategy seems obvious, many organizational changes keep on rewarding people for the old behaviors rather than the new behaviors.

For example, a supply manager was inadvertently guilty of such behavior. A large, complex supply activity was being converted from manual records to computer files. But, there were numerous problems in the computer records causing out-of-stock conditions. When this happened on some items, like typing paper or pens, it was quite embarrassing to the supply manager. Several of the manager's subordinates, who had been supply clerks under the old system, continued to keep manual records on these "hot" items in their desk

Perspective 16.4

QUALITY CIRCLES[23]

Quality circles are small groups of volunteers who meet periodically to identify, analyze, and solve problems related to product quality or other issues.[24] These meetings normally involve about one hour per week. Circles investigate problems, recommend solutions, and take action when they have the authority.

The concept of quality circles originated in Japan in the 1950s, based on American quality control techniques. However, they emphasized the involvement of workers in the entire quality process rather than using quality control techniques as is commonly practiced in the United States. Quality circles have been enormously successful in Japan with over a million workers participating.

The strategy of quality circles is to make every member a quality control technician so he or she can analyze problems using a number of problem-solving techniques.[25] The first step in the process is extensive training for circle leaders who, in turn, train the circle members. The leader is normally the work group supervisor of the circle. In fact, the circle process is designed to use the regular and normal chain of command; the hierarchy is not bypassed.[26]

Once their training is complete, circles may select or be assigned a problem to solve. They use various techniques to identify the problem, such as a cause and effect diagram, which graphically identifies all possible causes that may result in the target effect (i.e., a defective part). Once the problem is clearly identified, they develop solutions and present these solutions to management through normal channels. The presentation process itself is emphasized as a way of providing recognition and perhaps job enrichment for circle members. Rewards may or may not be given for implemented ideas.

drawers. Whenever the manager needed to know something about a hot item, they would be consulted and then praised for their good work. The manager did not realize the old system was being positively reinforced and thus the change was not being refrozen.

Build Social Bonds

While building social bonds is not applicable to all types of change, it certainly is whenever group dynamics are disrupted. Organizational structure changes, physical location changes, or shift changes, all have the potential for disrupting established social and group relations. During this time it is often good strategy to get the group to work together on some common problem—to do team-building.[27] Social interactions, such as office parties, may also facilitate building social bonds.

Develop Structures to Institutionalize

Often a structure that helps solidify the change can make the difference between success and failure. To illustrate, two companies send their employees to training on quality circles. Upon their return, one company relies on individual managers to develop and support the quality circles, while the other company establishes a quality circle section, headed by a full-time facilitator. Needless to say, the first company's program never gets off the ground while the second company's efforts are quite successful because they established a structure to institutionalize the change.

Making Change Work

The problems, processes, structures, and dynamics we have discussed all interrelate within the organizational system. All must be considered if change is to be effective. At each step, unfreezing, moving, or refreezing, it is possible to "blow it" and revert back to the original state. Thus, vigilance must be constant until the change is firmly refrozen. In the next section, we will see how the change process is often systematized using the concept of organization development.

ORGANIZATION DEVELOPMENT

The roots of organization development (OD) go back over thirty years to such people as Kurt Lewin (who developed the notions of unfreezing, changing, and refreezing), Douglas McGregor (of Theory Y fame), and Robert Blake (one of the developers of the Managerial Grid).[28] These people and others developed OD as a way of applying behavioral theories to solve organizational problems. Over the years, OD has continued its growth and its orientation toward solving organizational problems. It is certainly an important way of changing and improving organizations, involving many of the change strategies we have already discussed.

What Is Organization Development?

While there is no definition everyone agrees upon, we will define **organization development** (OD) as a process of planned organizational improvement, sustained for a relatively long period and employing behavioral science technology.[29] This definition is quite broad. It includes almost everything relating to applied behavioral science, including quality of work life strategies, transactional analysis, quality circles, teambuilding, and weekend sensitivity training.

While people generally agree on some aspects of the definition, many go further in limiting the definition of OD. The following dimensions are often considered essential or at least important to defining OD:

- *Organizationwide.* Some feel OD should focus on the entire organization, not just part of it. In practice, most organizations are too big to tackle all at once, so one part is often the focus. However, the systems perspective would say that change in one part may affect the others so an organization-wide perspective is needed.

- *Managed from the top.* Others feel OD must have the total commitment, involvement, and support of top management. While this is certainly desirable, it may be possible to conduct OD in lower levels of the organization where top management is not involved at all.[30]

- *Using action research.* Action research, which we will discuss in detail later in the chapter, involves gathering data on organizational problems and then taking action based on the data to solve the problems. One could argue that there are some OD strategies, such as transactional analysis or goal setting, that may not involve action research. However, many consider action research to be an essential element of the OD process.

It is difficult to capture the essence of OD in a definition for there are many important aspects of the OD process but they are not universally applicable. For instance, many OD activities (often called interventions) focus on working with and developing intact, formal work groups. In addition, OD practitioners are often tied to a set of humanistic assumptions and values, like collaborative management, the importance of individuals, congruence between individual and organizational goals, and the desirability of authentic, open, interpersonal relations. Another way to get the flavor of OD by highlighting how it differs from other techniques is provided in Table 16.3.

Action Research

Action research is the process of gathering data, feeding data back to the clients, problem solving or dealing with issues that arise from the data, developing action plans to resolve problems, and following up to see if the action has worked as planned (*see* Figure 16.5).[31] Action research is a way of finding out what problems exist and then dealing effectively with any changes needed to solve them. Consultants are often involved in action research because an impartial third party is more likely to get accurate data than an insider with an "axe to grind." However, there are strategies, such as the confrontation meeting (*see* Perspective 16.5), or brainstorming (*see* Chapter 13), that can generate data without a consultant.

Table 16.3

HOW OD DIFFERS FROM OTHER TECHNIQUES

- An emphasis, although not exclusively so, on group and organizational processes in contrast to substantive content.

- An emphasis on the work team as the key unit for learning more effective modes of organizational behavior.

- An emphasis on the collaborative management of work-team culture.

- An emphasis on the management of the culture of the total system.

- Attention to the management of system ramifications.

- The use of the action research model.

- The use of a behavioral scientist-change agent, sometimes referred to as a "catalyst" or "facilitator."

- A view of the change effort as an ongoing process.

Wendell L. French, Cecil H. Bell, Jr., *Organization Development: Behavioral Science Interventions for Organization Improvement*, 2nd ed., © 1978, p. 18. Reprinted by permission of Prentice-Hall, Inc., Englewood Cliffs, N.J.

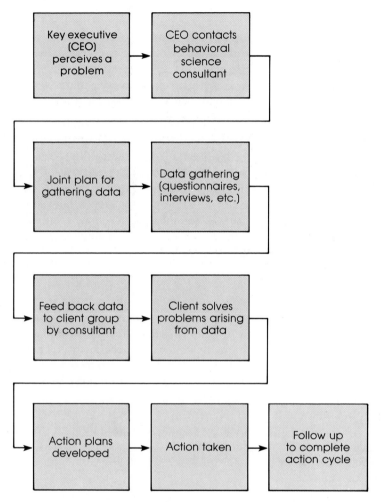

Figure 16.5

THE ACTION–RESEARCH PROCESS FOR OD

Gather Data for Diagnosis. The first step in action research is to find out what is going on so that a situation can be diagnosed or defined. Gathering data can be done in a number of informal and formal ways. Simply observing what happens is the first step. Are people cheerful? Efficient? Helpful? Watch for nonverbal cues that might indicate problems. The next step, covered earlier in Chapter 8, is to listen carefully and objectively. Listen for meaning. Probe when needed. Obviously, an outsider can elicit freer responses than someone inside the organization. Formal ways of gathering data include polling, sensing, questionnaires, and interviews. Each is briefly discussed in Table 16.4.[32]

Feedback Data to Clients. The next step in the action-research process is to summarize the data in some usable form for clients. Incidentally, we have not addressed who is the client, an important issue. While there is disagreement here, many feel the client is the workshop or entire group from which the data

Table 16.4

DATA–GATHERING TECHNIQUES

- **Polling.** This technique simply floats a question and provides some scale to respond to. For example, a manager may say, "How optimistic are you that we can complete the contract on time? Use a scale where 1 is very pessimistic and 10 is very optimistic." The manager then counts the poll, posts the results on a blackboard or chart, and discusses what they mean.

- **Sensing.** This technique is a little more structured. The manager may or may not be present depending on how threatening that presence might be. Groups of five to seven respond to an open-ended question such as, "What kinds of things are getting in the way of you doing your job more effectively?" A recorder captures the responses on flip-chart paper for later consolidation and review.

- **Questionnaires.** Questionnaires are widely used to measure such things as job satisfaction. They can also be used effectively if they are tailored to the situation and have open-ended questions. The trouble with questionnaires is that they can cover only a limited number of topics, and it is difficult to decipher the relative importance of different problems. Nevertheless, they are cheap and when you have a large number of people to cover, perhaps the only feasible way.

- **Interviews.** Whenever feasible, this is probably the favorite data-gathering method of OD consultants because it is possible to get a better feeling for problems, and it is more likely that some unexpected problem may surface. However, interviews cost more, both in consultant time and in time of the interviewee.

was gathered. The data is normally summarized into themes or problems that come up during data collection. These are displayed on flipcharts or some other method so the entire group can see them.

Problem Solve, Action Plan, and Follow Up. The clients absorb the data and review it to more clearly define their problems. Once the problems are clearly defined, they are often placed in priority order. Then one is chosen for solving; one where there is a reasonable chance of success. The group goes through the process of weighing alternatives, generating solutions, and evaluating data before finally reaching a consensus on the problem's solution. Next follows the **action plan**—spelling out who will do what and when. It sets responsibilities for action. A follow-up meeting is scheduled for a few weeks or months hence to see if actions are proceeding as planned.

Great Pacific Shipbuilding as an OD Example

Can our preview case be used as an example of OD? Let's see how well it fits the OD and action-research model. It began when the CEO contacted a consultant who was an expert in organizational change (and probably OD). Together they developed a strategy for involving the right people (the stakeholders) and gathering data about performance through interviews. The next step, in what you will recognize as an action-research process, was an offsite, three-day retreat. The consultant fed back the data he had gathered, and the group spent the rest of the retreat working on important issues that were raised. The problem-

Perspective 16.5

THE CONFRONTATION MEETING

A confrontation meeting is an OD design that can be accomplished in one day. It is usually conducted by the senior manager (CEO) of the target organization. It has seven phases.[33]

- **Phase 1: Climate setting.** The CEO sets the climate for the meeting by stating the objectives and making it clear that people are free to express their concerns openly. This phase will take about one hour.

- **Phase 2: Data gathering.** The total group is divided into heterogeneous groups of seven to eight people each. No boss and subordinate should be together and each group should contain people from every functional area. Top managers usually meet in a separate group so they will not inhibit communication. The group is given some question to address such as "What obstacles are getting in the way of achieving higher productivity?" or "What is the single most important problem facing you as a manager?" Each group elects a recorder and presents its results to the entire group one hour later.

- **Phase 3: Information sharing.** Each reporter writes the group's data on newsprint and tapes it to the wall. The reporter then orally presents the results to the group. After all the

data has been reported, the leader or members suggest themes or categories that seem to summarize the major issues. This process usually takes at least one hour.

- **Phase 4: Priority setting and action planning.** The group decides which theme or problem it will work on. Then the entire group divides into subgroups based upon their formal work group assignment (i.e., all salespeople would be in one group headed by the sales manager). These functional groups discuss the problem and decide what action they are willing to take to correct the problem. In addition, they highlight problems that must go to the top management team for resolution. This phase takes about an hour and fifteen minutes.

- **Phase 5: Organization-level action planning.** When the total group reconvenes, each functional unit reports its commitment to action to the total group. In addition, the groups indicate which items they believe should be addressed first. Top management reacts to the recommendations and makes commitments and decisions (setting targets, assigning task forces, providing resources). This phase will take one to two hours.

- **Phase 6: Top management team follow up.** Immediately after the confrontation meeting, top management decides when it will follow up on the actions that were agreed upon.

- **Phase 7: Progress review.** A two-hour follow-up meeting is held with the total group four to six weeks later.

solving process resulted in an action plan for reorganizing the company and creating a transition team. Actions were taken by the CEO and the transition team to make sure the action plan was proceeding as desired. Follow-up was accomplished by several offsite, one-day workshops. The Great Pacific case is, indeed, a good example of OD in action.

Effectiveness of OD

OD has been widely used in industry, hospitals, churches, military organizations, city governments, Indian tribes, and many other types of organizations. But has it been valid in improving organizational effectiveness? The research evidence has not been encouraging, but it is muddied by the very nature of OD—a broadly focused organizational change strategy. The sheer number of processes and outcomes that may be affected by OD is staggering. Since almost everything in an organization is potentially affected by the OD process, it is not surprising that the outcomes are difficult to capture with normal experimental procedures that rely on measuring two or three variables and hoping the remaining ones are constant. Perhaps a more optimistic view would be that OD has been growing over the past generation to a point where most major corporations have some type of internal OD effort.[34]

CROSS–CULTURAL OB: FITTING OD TO NATIONAL CULTURE

Organization development has been widely applied in other cultures, with uneven success.[35] For example, OD has been less successful in the United Kingdom because of a clash between OD strategies and cultural norms.[36] British norms that are counter to OD's include: avoiding "unsuitable topics," "not rocking the boat," a sense of fatalism, and feelings of class structure that prevent more egalitarian strategies. Thus action-research strategies may uncover uncomfortable issues and "boat-rocking" action just does not seem to fit.

The Japanese avoid assertive OD interventions because if the OD effort is successful, it would make the Japanese person a deviant from societal values, which state "The nail which sticks up gets pounded down." [37] Thus, this type of OD effort would be counterproductive in Japanese culture.

Two cultural factors seem to be strongly related to the success of an OD effort in another culture: power-distance and uncertainty-avoidance.[38] As you will recall from Chapter 12, **power-distance** reflects the degree to which power is distributed equally among members of the organization. **Uncertainty-avoidance** reflects the degree to which a society feels threatened by uncertain and ambiguous situations. Uncertainty can be created by a lack of rules, action research strategies, and deviant ideas or behavior.

To analyze how these two factors apply to an OD intervention, take the confrontation meeting described in Perspective 16.5. It requires a very low uncertainty-avoidance because a lot of unforeseen and unexpected information will be generated. In addition, relatively low power-distance is needed because people must feel free to speak up in the presence of supervisors, or even the CEO. In high power-distance, high uncertainty-avoidance countries, the confrontation meeting will probably fail. Countries falling into this category include Latin American and Mediterranean countries, as well as Belgium, Japan, Iran, Thailand, and Taiwan. Countries with lower power-distance and uncertainty-avoidance, such as the United States, Canada, Australia, New Zealand, the Netherlands, and the Scandinavian countries, have a good shot at a successful intervention.

Thus, like most organizational behavior strategies we have studied, care must be taken to consider cultural difference that may require modifications to our techniques and strategies. While the basic model of the change process works across many cultures, specific methods may not. Perspective 16.6 describes Soviet problems with change in information technology and computers. Does the basic change process of unfreezing, changing, and refreezing apply here?

Perspective 16.6

THE GREAT SOVIET COMPUTER SCREW-UP

Soviet industry is in big trouble with computers. Its hardware isn't modern. Breakdowns occur endlessly. The telecommunications are terrible. And Soviet managers have lots of sneaky reasons for not wanting effective information systems.

With some kicking and screaming along the way, the business managers of the Western world have long since adapted to computers. No sizable capitalist enterprise could be competitive nowadays without computer-driven management information systems—what the data-processing department calls MIS. A problem that Mikhail Gorbachev must find maddening these days, as he looks around for ways to cure the sick Soviet economy, is his country's broad failure in MIS. With every year that goes by, it is increasingly apparent that Soviet industry has fundamental problems with computers. Russian managers aren't exactly kicking and screaming, but they also aren't adapting very well.

Computers present several challenges to the Soviet leadership. Presumably it worries about the military implications of the U.S.S.R.'s inferiority in computer hardware. Gorbachev must also be concerned about the computer's implicit threat to the official Communist monopoly on ideas: a few Apple II computers hooked up to printers could make instant best-sellers out of dissident literature. So just about all computers in the Soviet Union are closely guarded in state-run institutions. Americans worry about hackers electronically breaking into institutions and gaining access to various business and military secrets. In the Soviet Union, things are reversed: the state's problem is to prevent any computer users from *breaking out* of the institutions.

Thus far, at least, the regime seems to have dealt effectively with these widely publicized problems. It has been reasonably successful in stealing and otherwise acquiring Western technologies with military applications. And the KGB seems to have had little difficulty in preventing dissidents from getting their hands on printers and other duplicating devices. But the problem posed by computers for Soviet enterprises—the state-owned counterparts of Western corporations—is another matter. At the enterprise level, the Russians have generally failed to exploit the fantastic efficiencies made possible by the new electronic technology, and this failure is a major reason for expecting the gap between the Soviet and Western economies to keep widening.

Among those who have been most closely tracking the record at the enterprise level is a team at the University of Arizona's College of Business and Public Administration, under the direction of Seymour E. Goodman. The team's members have worked hard at interviewing the occasional Soviet emigré who is knowledgeable about information systems; most of their data, however, are based on exhaustive analysis of Soviet technical journals. Professor Goodman, who was recently in Brussels briefing NATO officials on Soviet computers, believes the Russians are deeply distressed by their shortcomings. "They sit there and watch this competition between Japan and the West over development of a fifth generation of computers," he observed recently. "They know they can't just sit out the contest. They know they have to at least look as though they're doing the same kinds of things, but that's not easy."

Most Soviet enterprises still lack mainframes of any kind. William K. McHenry, a colleague of Goodman's and author of a recent prodigious Ph.D. dissertation on management information systems in the Soviet Union, estimates that only 7.5% of the country's industrial enterprises—3,300 out of 44,000—had mainframes in 1984. To be sure, this minority includes a disproportionate number of large, high-priority enterprises. Even so, the evidence suggests that most sizable plants in the Soviet Union are still getting by without mainframes. McHenry, who will be an assistant professor at Georgetown's School of Business Administration beginning this fall, has assembled data showing that only one-third of large plants ("large" meaning at least 500 employees) had mainframes in 1984. With or maybe even without rounding, the comparable figure for the U.S. would be 100%.

The systems in use in the U.S. typically enable managers to instantly call up an infinity of data about payrolls, inventories, production, sales, and anything else useful. American managers take it for granted that they can function more effectively if these data are accurate and timely. But Soviet managers are frequently under pressures to falsify data, and so they are understandably nervous about computerized systems for keeping track of what's happening.

Soviet managers have many perverse incentives to misuse computers. One that nullifies productivity gains in many sectors of the economy is the regime's guarantee of employment to all workers. This means that the manager who acquires a mainframe can't easily use it to replace all the workers with abacuses who are now on his payroll—and his plant might literally have hundreds of them. Soviet enterprises typically consist of numerous small fiefdoms, each with its own statistical department, and the evidence thus far suggests that management information systems have not really dented these fiefdoms. Their survival is additionally ensured by the organizational rigidity of Soviet enterprises: an enterprise of a given size in a given industry is ordinarily required to have certain well-defined line and staff relationships. These requirements are intended to make it easier for the ministries to supervise the many enterprises under their jurisdiction, but, of course, the effect is to prevent managers from devising new organizational arrangements suitable to the computer age.

As you might assume, the overriding obstacle to rational use of computers in the enterprises is the managers' recurring need to falsify much of their data. The garbage-in, garbage-out phenomenon is pervasive, and there is little the ministries can do about it. Soviet managers frequently have to make purchases in various black markets to get needed supplies. Knowing that such illegal purchases are often necessary, they may set up a slush fund by diverting money from, say, the payroll account; to make this possible they might overstate the number of workers at the enterprise, which would enable them to get extra wages from the ministry in charge. Meanwhile, their computers would inevitably be spitting out garbage.

The pressures that drive managers to cook the books are clear enough. The economic system in which they operate features unrealistic planning targets, causing chronic shortages of resources—so they hoard resources, doing their best to conceal from the ministries the true state of inventories and the true number of production workers. The system provides bonuses for fulfillment of the plan but also tends to raise required norms for anyone who overfulfills it—so the managers suppress any data that might suggest they were capable of increased output. On the other hand, they tend to overstate performance when norms are not being met.

The Soviet economy's failure to assimilate computers is not only an economic disaster. The failure also has a symbolic dimension. Communism is, after all, an idea claiming to stand for progress, and computers are the quintessential symbol of progress. The performance of Soviet managers in the face of the new technology can be taken as another threat to the legitimacy of the regime.[39]

MANAGERIAL APPLICATIONS OF CHANGE AND OD

As our opening case illustrated, effective management of change often makes the difference between success and failure for a manager. Understanding the process so you can make change work for you is a must. Here are some recommendations that can help make you more effective as a changemaster:

- *Always use a systems perspective of change.* Remember that when one thing is changed it will often affect other parts of the system. Thus, your first step toward success is to analyze how your proposed change will affect other organizational systems.

- *Analyze resistance to your change.* Figure out where the resistance to your change lies, and formulate plans for removing the resistances. Pay careful attention to power changes and try to offer incentives for people to change.

- *Take actions to unfreeze the organization.* Arouse dissatisfaction with the current condition through use of information, action research, outside consultants, or other strategies. Be sure to get strong top-management commitment and support.

- *Use participation.* Involving those who are the target of the change is the most effective way to change.

- *Use force-field analysis as a tool for analyzing change.* This technique helps sort through the many factors that are driving or resisting change. It systematically evaluates the current equilibrium and gives ideas for unfreezing.

- *Establish clear goals and communicate.* Open two-way communication processes along with clear goals relating to the change. This will help insure success.

- *Build expectations of success.* Positive expectations about the success of your change may become a self-fulfilling prophecy.

- *Refreeze the change.* Build in rewards, success experiences, organizational structures, and social bonds that reinforce the new equilibrium. Remove rewards or structures that encourage return to the old equilibrium.

- *Use quality circles to involve people in change.* The QC process is a good method of getting shop-floor or clerical people involved in ways to improve work processes and quality.

- *Use OD as a major organizational improvement strategy.* Attack major issues, goals, and problems using the organization development method. Use it to improve teamwork and group processes; to gain participation and to share power.

- *Use action research to take your organization's pulse.* Every organization needs time to do some introspection; to find out how well it is doing and what problems it may be having. Action research is good strategy for this purpose. Try the confrontation meeting if you want a "do-it-yourself" effort.

- *Be aware of cultural differences.* Many factors related to national or organizational culture can cause changes to the specific parts of the change or OD process. Be especially aware of power-distance, uncertainty-avoidance, norms, and values.

FOR DISCUSSION

1. Explain why the change manager must consider the systems ramifications of change.

2. Why do people resist change and what can be done to reduce this resistance?

3. How do expectations and the self-fulfilling prophecy relate to the change process?

4. Explain why even powerful managers must pay careful attention to strategies for unfreezing resistance to change.

5. Pick a problem in implementing change with which you are familiar and make up a Force-Field Analysis chart similar to the one shown in Figure 16.4.

6. What are transition structures and how are they used?

7. Describe the major strategies for refreezing a change.

8. Using the example of implementing quality circles (Perspective 16.4), indicate which actions are needed to carry out the entire change process in terms of unfreezing, changing, and refreezing.

9. What makes organization development different from other organizational change activities such as management development?

10. Explain how the action-research process works.

11. Using the change process, identify why Soviet managers may be resisting the computer revolution.

KEY CONCEPTS AND TERMS

change process	transition manager	action research
equilibrium	quality circles	diagnosis
disequilibrium	pilot project	data-gathering techniques
transition	institutionalize	confrontation meeting
force-field analysis	organization development	power distance
leverage point	collaborative management	uncertainty avoidance

Cases and Incidents

SHIFT CHANGE

There are eight employees in the Reliability Test Laboratory. The laboratory performs a quality control function by testing random samples of daily production for physical characteristics. Until January of this year, the employees had worked from 6:30 A.M. to 3:00 P.M. each day. Don Kuntz, a Reliability engineer, was in charge of the major product line tested in the lab and held the secondary responsibility of managing the lab. As a result, the lab employees were relatively unsupervised.

In mid-December, when it became evident to top management that Kuntz was overworked in this dual capacity, David Barnes was advised that he would become foreman of the lab effective January 1. Barnes had previously worked in an office adjoining the lab as a non-supervisory member of the Reliability Engineering Department.

When Harry Boyles, supervisor of Reliability Engineering, advised Barnes of his new assignment he also cautioned him that employees were not working between 6:30 A.M. and 8:00 A.M. Don Kuntz had worked from 8:00 A.M. until 4:45 P.M. in order to handle his engineering responsibilities, and as a result, the lab had been unsupervised early in the shift. To combat this, Boyles had decided to change the hours for all lab employees to 8:00 A.M. through 4:30 P.M. effective January 1. Boyle also in-

formed Barnes that the lab employees had already been informed of the change.

On January 1, when Barnes was introduced as the foreman of the lab, reporting directly to Kuntz, the change in working hours became effective. The change in working hours met with drastic reaction. The men had worked the same shift (as in all the production areas) for an average of twenty-three years each, and immediately began requesting consultation with their union representatives in order to fight the shift change. They were told that such action was legitimate, according to the labor agreement. Next, the group began a work slowdown in protest. After approximately two weeks, Charles Turner approached Kuntz with the comment, "We know that the shift was changed because we weren't working before 8:00 A.M. If you will return the shift to the original time, we will promise to begin work promptly each morning." Kuntz told him that management was pleased with the new arrangement and had no changes in mind.

One of the policies of the company was that safety glasses were to be worn at all times in the lab area; however, Kuntz had been quite lax in enforcement of this rule and Barnes had been told by Boyles to remedy the situation. He relayed this message to the group and everyone wore their glasses the first day until about 4:00 P.M. The group had gathered around a table to the rear of the lab, and Barnes noticed the absence of the glasses as he approached the table. He reminded the group to wear the glasses and they all responded except for Turner who replied, "Why doesn't Kuntz wear his safety glasses over there in his office;" Barnes replied that it was necessary to wear the glasses only around the moving machinery in the lab. Turner responded, "I won't wear my glasses unless Kuntz does." With this, several other employees removed their glasses. Barnes then told Turner, "You are suspended for the balance of this shift and one day, with no pay."

The next day there were five employees absent from work.

DISCUSSION QUESTIONS

1. What factors seem to cause this resistance to change?

2. How might the change process be better designed for success?

3. What should Barnes do now?

From D.W. Borger. (1973), Shift change case in J.V. Murray and T.J. Von der Embse, *Organizational behavior: Critical incidents and analysis*, pp. 288–89. Copyright © 1973 by Charles E. Merrill, Columbus, Ohio. Reprinted with permission.

A NEW PLANT MANAGER

Several years ago a new plant manager arrived at a continuous process facility (a plant where there is a continuous shaping of raw materials into finished products, as, for example, in a steel-making plant or an oil refinery). He surveyed the scene and found the following characteristics: the plant had over 2,000 employees, there were several layers of managers arranged in functional departments (production, maintenance, technical research, purchasing and stores, engineering, etc.); the plant performed fairly well in terms of productivity and profitability. The new manager's predecessor had been an energetic and autocratic man who had made all the operational and administrative decisions at the plant. The rest of the upper and middle management were called "superintendents"—they superintended their bailiwicks, supplied information to the plant manager, and received orders from the manager about what should be done in their departments and divisions, as the plant was run on a day-to-day basis.

The new manager had a different managerial philosophy and a different leadership style: he believed in delegating as much responsibility to his subordinates as possible; he believed in allowing wide participation in the important decisions affecting the works and the work force; he believed that better information and decisions would come from involved, committed "managers"; he wanted to develop subordinates so that they would move to higher positions of responsibility; and, as he told the managers at one of his first meetings with them, he wanted them to "share in the work and share in the fun." The new manager knew that he needed to build strong individual managers, an effective "management team," and that he needed to change the managerial culture and climate in the plant. He knew that this change in the way things were done would require new skills and a new management climate in the plant. And that would require training; the habits of 10 years could not be changed just by his issuing an order. He called in several consultants, told them his desires, and solicited their aid.

As things evolved, there turned out to be six goals of the change project: (1) to increase the abilities and skills of the individual managers; (2) to build an effective top management team; (3) to build stronger division and department teams; (4) to improve the relations between work groups, such as between production and maintenance, and thus reduce the level of energy spent in competition; (5) to change the managerial culture from one in which one person made all the decisions to one in which all managers made or participated in decisions that affected them; and (6) to improve the long-range planning and decision-making abilities of managers at all levels. These change goals and the ideas of the new plant manager were public knowledge.

DISCUSSION QUESTIONS

1. What resistances to change would you predict?

2. What strategies would you use to overcome them?

3. Which OD strategies would be appropriate for changing this organization?

Wendell L. French and Cecil H. Bell, Jr. (1984) *Organization Development: Behavioral Science Interventions for Organization Improvement*, 3rd ed. Copyright © 1984 pp. 11–14. Reprinted by permission of Prentice-Hall, Englewood Cliffs, New Jersey.

REFERENCES

1. Adapted from a situation presented by Nadler, D.A. (1981). Managing organizational change: An integrative perspective. *Journal of Applied Behavioral Science, 17,* 191–211. Names, places, and events have been changed.

2. Detroit stumbles on its way to the future. (1986, June 16). *Business Week,* p. 104. Also see Petre, P. (1985, November 11). How GE bobbled the factory of the future. *Fortune.*

3. Ross Perot's Crusade. (1986, October 6). *Business Week,* p. 61.

4. For more information on change see; Lippit, G.L., Langseth, P., & Mossop, J. (1985). *Implementing organizational change.* San Francisco: Jossey-Bass. McCaskey, M.B. (1982). *The executive challenge: Managing change and ambiguity.* Boston: Pitman. And Levy, A. (1986). Second-order planned change: Definition and conceptualization. *Organizational Dynamics, Summer,* 4–23.

5. For complete coverage of systems theory in relation to change, see Katz, D., & Kahn, R.L. (1978). *The social psychology of organizations* (2d ed.). New York: Wiley. And Alderfer, C.P. (1976). Change processes in organizations. In M.D. Dunnette (Ed.). *Handbook of industrial and organizational psychology* (pp. 1591–1638). Chicago: Rand-McNally.

6. Based in part on the ideas of Lewin, K. (1947). Frontiers of group dynamics. *Human Relations, 1,* 5–41. For a contemporary view of the change process, see Beer, M. (1987). Revitalizing organizations: Change process and the emergent model. *Academy of Management Executive, 1,* 51–55.

7. Based on Gabarro, J.J. (1985, May–June). When a new manager takes charge. *Harvard Business Review,* pp. 110–123.

8. Many of the ideas in this section come from Zaltman, G., & Duncan, R. (1977). *Strategies for planned change.* New York: Willey. Also Nadler (1981). Also see Odiorne, G.S. (1981). *The change resisters.* Englewood Cliffs, NJ: Prentice-Hall.

9. Nadler (1981). Tichy, N.M. (1982). Managing change strategically: The technical, political, and cultural keys. *Organization Dynamics, 11,* 59–80. And Gray, B., & Hay, T.M. (1986). Political limits to interorganizational consensus and change. *Journal of Applied Behavioral Science, 22,* 95–112.

10. Nadler, D.A. (1977). *Feedback and organization development: Using data-based methods.* Reading, MA: Addison-Wesley.

11. Zand, D.E., & Sorenson, R.E. (1975). Theory of change and the effective use of management science. *Administrative Science Quarterly, 20,* 532–545.

12. Lee, J.A. (1977). Leader power and managing change. *Academy of Management Review, 2,* 73–80.

13. Nutt, P.C. (1986). Tactics of implementation. *Academy of Management Journal, 29,* 230–261. Kanter, R.M. (1982). Dilemmas of managing participation. *Organizational Dynamics, Summer,* 5–27.

14. Coch, L., & French, J.R.P., Jr. (1948). Overcoming resistance to change. *Human Relations, 1,* 512–532.

15. The origin of this technique is Lewin, K. (1951). *Field theory in social science.* New York: Harper & Row. It is widely used by organization development consultants. See Fordyce, J.K., & Weil, R. (1979). *Managing with people: A manager's handbook of OD methods* (2nd ed.). Reading, MA: Addison-Wesley.

16. Kimberly, J.R., & Quinn, R.E. (Eds.). (1984). *Managing organizational transitions.* Homewood, IL: Richard D. Irwin. Bridges, W. (1986). Managing organizational transitions. *Organizational Dynamics, Summer,* 24–33.

17. Nadler (1981).

18. Kimberly, J.R., & Quinn, R.E. (1984). *Managing organizational transitions.* Homewood, IL: Irwin. Beckhard, R., & Harris, R.T. (1987). *Organizational transitions: Managing complex change* (2nd ed.). Reading, MA: Addison-Wesley. Ackerman, L.S. (1982). Transition management: An in-depth look at managing complex change. *Organizational Dynamics, Summer,* 46–67.

19. Nadler (1981).

20. King, A.S. (1974). Expectation effects and organizational change. *Administrative Science Quarterly, 19,* 221–230.

21. For more information on expectation effects, see Eden, D. (1986). OD and self-fulfilling prophecy: Boosting productivity and raising expectations. *Journal of Applied Behavioral Science, 22,* 1–13. And Eden, D. (1984). The self-fulfilling prophecy as a management tool: Harnessing Pygmalion. *Academy of Management Review, 9,* 64–73.

22. For a review of some of the problems with change, see Saporito, B. (1986, July 21). The revolt against 'working smarter'. *Fortune,* 58cf.

23. For details on quality circles, see Lawler, E.E. III, & Mohrman, S.A. (1985, January–February). Quality circles after the fad. *Harvard Business Review,* 65–71. Lawler, E.E. III & Mohrman, S.A. (1987). Quality circles: After the honeymoon. *Orga-*

nizational Dynamics, 15(4), 42–54. Ingle, S. (1982). *Quality circles master guide: Increasing productivity with people power.* Englewood Cliffs, NJ: Prentice-Hall. For a research review see Wood, R., Hull, F., & Azumi, K. (1983). Evaluating quality circles: The American application. *California Management Review, 26,* 37–53.

24. Munchus, G. III (1983). Employer-employee based quality circles in Japan: Human resource policy implications for American firms. *Academy of Management Review, 8,* 255–261.

25. For information about reasons for joining quality circles, see Dean, J.W., Jr. (1985). The decision to participate in quality circles. *Journal of Applied Behavioral Science, 21,* 317–327.

26. For further information on organizational impacts, see Goldstein, S.G. (1985). Organizational dualism and quality circles. *Academy of Management Review, 10,* 504–517.

27. See Chapter 9 for a discussion of teambuilding. Dyer, W.G. (1987). *Teambuilding: Issues and alternatives* (2nd ed.). Reading, MA: Addison-Wesley. Liebowitz, S.J., & Meuse, K.P. (1982). The application of team building, *Human Relations, 35,* 1–18.

28. French, W.L., & Bell, C.H., Jr. (1984). *Organization development* (3rd ed.). Englewood Cliffs, NJ: Prentice-Hall.

29. For a discussion of definitional issues see Huse, E.F., & Cummings, T.G. (1985). *Organizational development and change* (3rd ed.). St. Paul, MN: West. French, W.L., & Bell, C.H., Jr. (1984). *Organization development* (3rd ed.). Englewood Cliffs, NJ: Prentice-Hall. French, W.L., Bell, C.H., Jr., & Zawacki, R.A. (Eds.) (1987). *Organization development: Theory, practice, and research* (3rd ed.). Dallas: BPI. Burke, W.W. (1982). *Organization development.* Boston: Little, Brown. And Beer, M. (1980). *Organizational change and development: A systems view.* Santa Monica: Goodyear.

30. Beckhard, R. (1969). *Organization development: Strategies and models.* Reading, MA: Addison-Wesley.

31. This definition is similar to the one used by French & Bell (1984), pp. 107–108. Also see Peters, M., & Robinson, V. (1984). The origins and status of action research. *Journal of Applied Behavioral Science, 20,* 113–124. And Frohman, M.A., Sashkin, M., & Kavanagh, M.J. (1976). Action-research as applied to organization development. *Organization and Administrative Sciences, 7,* 129–142.

32. For more information about data collection techniques, see Fordyce & Weil (1979). Kilmann, R., & Thomas, K. (Eds.). (1983). *Producing useful knowledge for organizations,* New York: Praeger. And Nadler, D. (1977). *Feedback and organization development: Using data-based methods.* Reading, MA: Addison-Wesley.

33. Beckhard, R. (1967). The confrontation meeting. *Harvard Business Review, 45,* 153–154.

34. For reviews see Nicholas, J.M. (1982). The comparative impact of organization development interventions on hard criteria measures. *Academy of Management Review, 7,* 531–542. Armenakis, A.A., Bedeian, A.G., & Ponds, S.B., III (1983). Research issues in OD evaluation: Past, present, and future. *Academy of Management Review, 8,* 320–328. Porras, J.I., & Berg, P.O. (1978). The impact of organization development. *Academy of Management Review, 3,* 240–266. Leitko, T.A., & Szczerbacki, D. (1987). Why traditional OD strategies fail in professional bureaucracies. *Organizational Dynamics, 15* (3), 52–65.

35. Jaeger, A.M. (1986). Organization development and national culture: Where's the fit? *Academy of Management Review, 11,* 178–190. And Heenan, D.A., & Perlmutter, H.V. (1977). *Multinational organization development.* Reading, MA: Addison-Wesley.

36. Steel, F. (1977). Is culture hostile to organization development?: The UK example. In P.H. Mirvis & D.N. Berg (Eds.). *Failures in organization development and change* (pp. 23–31). New York: Wiley.

37. Jaeger, A.M. (1986).

38. Hofstede, G. (1980). *Culture's consequences.* Beverly Hills, CA: Sage. Jaeger, A.M. (1986).

39. From Seligman, D. The great soviet computer screw-up. *Fortune,* pp. 32–36. Copyright © 1985 Time Inc. All rights reserved.

Chapter Seventeen

ORGANIZATIONAL CULTURE AND THE QUALITY OF WORK LIFE

PREVIEW

- Why is it that some organizations seem to be vibrant and alive while others stagnate?

- How can corporate heroes help instill values and improve performance?

- What is the climate of your organization? Fill out a questionnaire to find out.

- Can organizational culture be changed?

- What factors make up a good quality of work life?

- What kinds of culture shocks are experienced by foreign managers who come to the United States to work?

MAJOR TOPICS

Preview Case: Delta Airlines

Organizational Culture

Organizational Climate

Type Z Organizational Cultures

Quality of Work Life

Organizations of the Future

Cross-Cultural OB: The Cultural Relativity of the QWL Concept

Managerial Applications of Organizational Culture and QWL

Preview Case

DELTA AIR LINES

Delta is called the "family airline." It is noted for its excellent employee relations, its open communication patterns, and its unique esprit de corps. Delta Airlines was founded in 1929 by Collett E. Woolman with a dozen employees and three six-passenger, 90–mph Travel Air planes. It has grown into a 38,500-employee company—one of the largest airlines in the world. It has managed to maintain the "family feeling", or what they refer to as the "Delta spirit," in spite of the growth.[1]

Delta maintains its culture in a variety of ways. It promotes from within, pays well, and goes to extraordinary lengths to keep people on the payroll in spite of recessions or business downturns. Perhaps even more importantly, Delta listens to its employees and truly cares. Ex-president, William Beebe explains how an open-door policy sets the tone: [2]

> "My rug has to be cleaned once a month. Mechanics, pilots, flight attendants—they all come in to see me. If they really want to tell us something—we'll give them the time. They don't have to go through somebody. The chairman, president, vice president—none of us has a single 'administrative assistant' to screen people out, no intermediaries."

Of course, this system only works because something *happens* when the open door is used; action is taken on employees suggestions, comments, or complaints.

One important Delta value is a "can-do" attitude. A Delta executive with twenty-five years' experience says: [3]

> "If I have a request that I make of somebody here—as I did recently for information from the Technical Operations Center [Delta's vast maintenance facility]—I never call back twice to see whether the job's gotten done. I know it's going to be done.

> "On the other hand, if somebody calls here with something they want us to do, we'll stay up until 2:00 in the morning if necessary to get it done."

This organizational culture has certainly paid off for Delta. They have very high job satisfaction and productivity. Delta's last strike was in 1942. Its last union vote was in 1955. One of the most visible signs of the family bond was an extraordinary gift from the employees to the company—a $30 million Boeing 767! In 1981–1983, there was a recession in the airline industry that was having a significant impact on Delta. The employees banded together and bought the new airplane.[4]

Tom Peters [author of *A Passion for Excellence*] asked Beebe about it, a little unbelievingly to tell the truth: "What is all this about your people buying you a plane?" Beebe began to describe what had happened, in particular the rolling out of the plane onto the tarmac in Atlanta, with a bright red ribbon wrapped around it. There was wonder in his voice. His eyes misted over. Beebe was sixty-eight then, had been forty years in the industry—and he was not jaded one iota. Only moments later he introduced Delta's recently retired chief pilot. Upon retirement the fellow had taken full-page ads in the morning and evening Atlanta papers to thank Delta management for a great career!

Unquestionably, Delta has a strong and successful organizational culture. Perhaps the paramount reason for Delta's success is shared organizational values, beliefs, goals, and philosophy. Everyone believes in what the company is doing and provides strong support for the direction it is moving.

While every aspect of managing people in organizations is important, when combined, they make up the organizational culture—perhaps the major determinant of effectiveness and quality of working life for organizational members. Culture is the force that drives, or fails to drive, the organization. Most of what happens in organizations is guided by shared cultural meanings, rules, and behaviors.[5] Delta Airlines, IBM, Dana, McDonalds, and many other successful enterprises, have cultures that reinforce the organization's goals.

In this concluding chapter, we will see what elements make up the organizational culture and examine the nature of quality of working life. Then we will speculate about future forms of organization that may be an outgrowth of environmental and cultural change.

ORGANIZATIONAL CULTURE

Organizational culture consists of all the shared assumptions, beliefs, values, behaviors, expectations, and symbols (including language) that are characteristic of an organization at a given time.[6] These dimensions often operate at an unconscious level and are "taken-for-granted" by organizational members.[7] The concept of culture is broad and encompasses all of the organizational subsystems we have covered so far in this text. Culture describes how everything meshes together to form the organization's essence—its personality.

In the first part of this chapter, we will discuss the major dimensions of culture and then turn to the interrelationship between culture and organizational climate. Finally, we will discuss the Type Z culture that is displayed by many successful American companies.

While culture encompasses the entire organizational milieu, there are four aspects that seem particularly important: basic assumptions, values, rites and rituals, and heroes.[8]

Basic Assumptions

The foundation for culture is the underlying **basic assumptions** about human nature, the nature of human activity and relationships, and the organizational-environmental interaction.[9]

Assumptions About Human Nature. For example, do your basic assumptions about human nature correspond more closely to Theory X or to Theory Y (*see* Chapter 3)? If you feel that people are lazy and must be closely supervised and driven, you will behave quite differently than if your assumptions say people are competent, motivated, and will do a good job if left on their own.

Assumptions About the Nature of Human Relationships. These assumptions have strong links with group and organizational dynamics. For example, most people in the United States culture see themselves as individuals first and group members second. In the Japanese culture, individual-oriented assumptions may be weak—behavior will be centered on group satisfaction and performance. The concept of power-distance, discussed in Chapter 12, relates to group membership and interaction. In high power-distance cultures, such as the Philippines, Mexico, or Venezuela, managers would expect to have much stronger control over their work groups and organizations.

These power-distance assumptions also vary across organizational cultures. For example, a low power-distance organization, such as Action Products, may assume that good ideas can come from anyone at any time and that: "Senior managers are always available and willing to talk to anyone about any issue,

Perspective 17.1

THE CULTURE OF EXCELLENCE

Peters and Waterman's best-selling book, *In Search of Excellence,* has been cited a number of times throughout this book. They found that excellent companies display eight general characteristics, reflecting a culture of excellence: [10]

- *A bias for action* This characteristic means a preference for getting things done rather than spending endless time analyzing the problem in committees or task forces. Delta's "can-do" attitude illustrates one way of approaching the action orientation.

- *Close to the customer* Learning the customer's problems, preferences, and needs is a crucial element of excellence. Some companies literally go to work for a few days for their customer as a way of finding out what products and services are really needed. IBM sales personnel are expected to act as if they were on the customer's payroll.

- *Autonomy and entrepreneurship* The idea here is to create relatively small organizational units so that managers and employees feel a sense of ownership and control. In a relatively small, autonomous unit people feel that their efforts are essential for organizational performance. It encourages independent thinking and competitiveness. The "skunkworks" discussed in Chapter 15 illustrates this characteristic. In another instance, Mountain Bell successfully operated a 100–person unionized unit with no direct supervisors. [11]

- *Productivity through people* Involve people so they realize that their best efforts are essential. Reward people for doing a good job.

Wal-Mart refers to all of its employees as "associates." Sam Walton, the CEO of Wal-Mart, believes that the best ideas come from clerks and "checkboys." Thus, it is crucial to get out in the stores and listen. [12]

- *Hands-on, value driven* The key here is for managers to keep in touch with the firm's purpose, philosophy, and values and to live by them on a day-to-day basis. Values reflect what the organization wants to be about. In Delta, it is the family spirit. At Dana, it is keeping things simple and getting the job done without too much control. At Johnson & Johnson, it is product quality.

- *Stick to the knitting* Determine what your business is and then remain with it by avoiding acquisitions of dissimilar businesses or producing divergent products. Boeing has concentrated most of its efforts in the commercial airplane business, and has continued to dominate the world market.

- *Simple form, lean staff* By holding down administrative layers and top-level managers, the organization can function better. Boeing has been systematically eliminating layers of supervision to reduce costs and improve responsiveness. The "rule of 100," discussed in Chapter 15, relating to maximum staff size, also illustrates this characteristic.

- *Simultaneous loose-tight* The "tight" part of this characteristic is a common set of organizational values that are widely understood and used to guide action. The "loose" part means giving people a great deal of freedom to operate, providing they adhere to the values. For example, 3M allows a great deal of freedom to develop new products, but maintains tight control because of strong values about market potential and profit margins.

constrained only by the practicalities of time. A senior manager in R & D recently left the organization for a bigger and better job [at Multi Products], only to return three months later with the comment: 'In the new company, I had an idea for a new product and was told that I would have to talk first to my boss, then to the director of R & D, and then to the senior vice-president. In Action if I have an idea, I go straight to the president and we kick it around. This is the kind of place I want to work.' " [13] The assumptions at Multi revolve around formality, hierarchy, and protocol—one does not interact informally.

Assumptions About Human Activity. Organizations can also vary in their assumptions about human activity. At one extreme is the "can-do" orientation that is focused on performance and achievement. One of Peters and Waterman's characteristics of excellence, highlighted in Perspective 17.1, is, "A bias for action." In contrast, another assumption might be that the organization is primarily a place to achieve growth, self-development, and self-actualization— a focus on what a person *is* rather than what a person can *accomplish*. Other important assumptions in this area revolve around the relationship between work, leisure, family, and personal concerns. The later part of this chapter on quality of working life addresses some of these issues.

Assumptions About the Organization's Relation to the Environment. Does the organization control the environment, or vice versa? What is the organization's primary task? Its core mission? Several of these assumptions are covered in Perspective 17.1, which discusses the excellent companies. For example, "close-to-the-customer" means the organization feels this aspect of the environment is crucial for success. Careful attention to customer satisfaction, communication, and needs are all emphasized.

Organizational Values

In Chapter 3, we defined values as broad, general beliefs about some way of behaving or some end state that is preferred by the individual.[14] **Organizational values** are defined in the same way except that the end states are those that are preferred by the organization and shared by organizational members rather than those held by a single individual. Cultures of successful organizations see a good match between individual and organizational values.

An organization's values provide its philosophical direction. Slogans often reflect these shared values. For example, Delta Airlines is called "the family airline" to signify its concern for its employees and caring attitude toward customers. Other examples of these shared values might be Caterpillar's "Twenty-four hour parts service anywhere in the world," which indicates a great concern for prompt worldwide customer service; and Dupont's "Better things for better living through chemistry," which reflects a commitment to innovation as a prime value.[15]

Many authors attribute Japan's success to the shared values held by everyone in the organization.[16] Japanese organizations spend a great deal of time and effort socializing and instilling values in their employees (remember the endurance walk described in Chapter 3).

Rites, Rituals, and Ceremonies

Organizations have rather formal, standardized ways of dealing with organizational events. These **rites and ceremonies** involve relatively elaborate, planned sets of activities, that are carried out through social interactions. They normally are for the benefit of the audience and often have many social consequences.[17] Rites and ceremonies include such activities as fraternity or sorority initiations, Mary Kay seminars for sales people, collective bargaining with unions, college graduation, and so forth. Table 17.1 illustrates six types of rites

Table 17.1

EXAMPLES OF RITES AND THEIR CONSEQUENCES

Types of Rites	Example	Visible Consequences	Hidden Consequences
Rites of passage	Induction and basic training, U.S. Army	Facilitate transition of persons into social roles and statuses that are new for them.	Maintain stable Army social roles. Maintain equilibrium in ongoing social relations (e.g., officer-enlisted relations).
Rites of degradation	Firing and replacing top executive	Dissolve social identities and their power.	Publicly acknowledge that problems exist and discuss their details. Defend group boundaries by redefining who belongs and doesn't.
Rites of enhancement	Mary Kay seminars	Enhance social identities and their power.	Spread good news about the organization. Provide public recognition of individuals for their accomplishments; motivate others to similar efforts. Enable organizations to take some credit for individual accomplishments.
Rites of renewal	Organizational development activities	Refurbish social structures and improve their functioning.	Reassure members that something is being done about problems. Focus attention toward some problem and away from others.
Rites of conflict reduction	Collective bargaining	Reduce conflict and aggression.	Compartmentalize conflict and its disruptive effects. Reestablish equilibrium in disturbed social relations.
Rites of integration	Office Christmas party	Encourage and revive common feelings that bind members together and commit them to a social system	Permit venting of emotion and temporary loosening of various norms.

SOURCE Adapted from Trice, H.M., & Beyer, J.M. (1984). Studying organizational cultures through rites and ceremonies. *Academy of Management Review, 9,* 657. Copyright © 1984 by the Academy of Management Review. Reprinted by permission.

that have powerful organizational effects. We will describe one of them more fully in the next paragraph.

One example of the **rite of enhancement** is Mary Kay Cosmetics Co.'s elaborate "Mary Kay seminar"—a real extravaganza attended by some 30,000 enthusiastic Mary Kay "consultants." [18] Countless awards are given including gold and diamond bee-shaped pins and fur stoles. Top performers are given pink Cadillacs, the ultimate Mary Kay status symbol. "The awards are presented in a setting reminiscent of the Miss America Pageant—in a large auditorium, on a stage in front of a large cheering audience, and with all participants dressed in glamorous evening clothes. Underlying this impressive and dramatic rite is the saga of Mary Kay and how her personal determination and optimism enabled her to support herself and her children after her husband left her, and later to use those experiences as a basis on which to found her own company. The bee-shaped pin [that is so often used as a reward] is a symbol of the founder's ideology that with help and encouragement, everyone can 'find their wings and . . . fly.' " [19] These elaborate rites serve to motivate and energize people. They also enhance the social identities of all organizational members. Numerous other benefits, such as spreading the good news about the organization, also accrue.

Another important aspect of organizational culture is the nature of its **rituals,** which include many different types of actions such as shared leisure and play and habitual behavior patterns. For example, the people who work for one of the Delta divisions get together on the first Saturday of each month for a beer bust. Practically everybody attends and has a good time. In a university, members of the math department get together for jogging every day at lunch, rain or shine. Staff meetings are another example of ritualistic activities. The number of meetings held, the time, the setting, the seating arrangement, the attendees, and the conduct of the meeting all are influenced by rituals.[20]

Heroes

Most successful organizations have their **heroes.**[21] The hero may be someone who is living, such as Lee Iacocca of Chrysler, or it may be a historical person like C.E. Woolman, founder of Delta Airlines, who established the airline and its values. Heroes reinforce the organization's cultural values by making success seem human and attainable, providing role models, symbolizing the company to the outside world, and setting a performance standard that motivates achievement.

There are two types of heroes, visionary heroes and situational heroes. **Visionary heroes** have a broad philosophical influence on the organization; they light the way for all employees. In contrast, **situational heroes** inspire people with an example of their day-to-day success.

A visionary corporate hero is driven by the ethic of creativity. The hero inspires employees throughout the firm. Visionary heroes often differ from managers, who are driven by the ethic of competition, or a desire to win the game. However, it is certainly possible for a hero also to be a manager. Thomas Watson, the head of IBM for many years, is an example of a visionary hero-manager. Mary Kay Ash is certainly an example of a visionary hero. She provides a role model for others to emulate. At General Electric, the visionary hero is Thomas Edison, an inspiring role model for engineers and scientists.

There are three characteristics of visionary heroes. First, they are right about something, such as a new product, marketing strategy, or organizational strategy—they succeeded in a big way. Second, they are persistent; they do not give up easily even in the face of considerable resistance. Third, they have a sense of personal responsibility for the continuing success of the organization.

Situational heroes are made because of some interaction between personal characteristics, motivation, and organizational goals that creates a winner. An example might be the article in IBM's corporate magazine, *Think,* which features a salesperson in Seattle who has just completed thirty years of membership in IBM's Hundred Percent Club (those people who sold 100 percent of their quota for the month).

Situational heroes serve to humanize success by publicizing the results obtained by high-performing organizational members. For example, a million-dollar club may be formed with membership linked to generating $1 million worth of sales within a given period. People who make this goal are rewarded with bonuses or a trip to the South Pacific or Europe. These people are then seen as heroes by other organizational members. Their exceptional performance sets high standards for organizational members and thus motivates performance.

In this section, we have covered only four dimensions of culture—basic assumptions, organizational values, rites and rituals, and heroes. There are many other organizational processes that have a significant impact on culture, including: communication, group dynamics, decision making, power, leadership, organizational design, design of physical spaces and buildings, and organizational change methods.[22] Several of these dimensions are included within the concept of organizational climate, the topic of the next section.

ORGANIZATIONAL CLIMATE

One way to measure the organizational culture, at least in part, is by evaluating its **organizational climate,** which consists of the way people perceive their organizational environment.[23] As with culture, so many different factors make up the organization's climate that no single, universally applicable list of factors may be possible.[24] What is important in one organization or even one part of an organization may not be important in another.[25] To aid you in understanding climate, you may wish to complete the questionnaire in Table 17.2.

From the questionnaire you will note that there are a number of factors that seem to be important determinants of organizational climate across many different organizations.[26] These factors correspond to the five factor scores in the Organizational Climate Questionnaire.

1. *Individual autonomy.* The amount of individual freedom, initiative, and responsibility that a person possesses.

2. *The degree of structure imposed upon the position.* The amount of direction, supervision, rules and procedures, and objectives associated with the job.

3. *Reward orientation.* The promotions, praise, pay, and other rewards including the fairness of the rewards.

4. *Consideration, warmth, and support.* The degree of care for employees evidenced by the organization and supervisors.

5. *Trust.* The degree to which employees feel they can make themselves vulnerable to the organization without having that vulnerability abused.[27]

An organization such as Delta Airways will probably have a supportive organizational climate. We already know from the introductory case that the

Table 17.2

ORGANIZATIONAL CLIMATE QUESTIONNAIRE

Directions: The following are types of behaviors that may occur in organizations. Using the scale below, mark the number that corresponds to the way you perceive your organization behaves in each situation.

1	2	3	4	5
It makes a great effort to do this	It tends do this	I do not know what it would do	It tends to avoid doing this	It makes a great effort to avoid this

_____ 1. This organization allows people a great deal of freedom to determine how to do the job.
_____ 2. The pay here is fair and equitable.
_____ 3. This organization will "screw you" if you are not careful.
_____ 4. There are many rules and regulations in this organization.
_____ 5. This organization really cares about its employees.
_____ 6. Innovation and initiative are encouraged around here.
_____ 7. Promotions in this organization are based on politics.
_____ 8. There are detailed standards for most tasks in this organization.
_____ 9. Employees are often asked to participate in important decisions in this organization.
_____ 10. There is a great deal of criticism in this organization.

Scoring: The first scoring step is to correct several reverse-scored items. For Questions 3, 4, 7, 8 and 10 the score must be converted using the following table:

Your Score	Corrected Score
1	5
2	4
3	3
4	2
5	1

Now add the scores as indicated below:

1. Autonomy, question 1 + 6 _____ (range 2 to 10)
2. Structure, question 4 + 8 _____ (range 2 to 10)
3. Rewards, question 2 + 7 _____ (range 2 to 10)
4. Caring, question 5 + 10 _____ (range 2 to 10)
5. Trust, question 3 + 9 _____ (range 2 to 10)
6. Total Organizational
   Climate Score _____ (range 10 to 50)

A low score (10 to 25) indicates a very supportive organizational climate. A high score (35 to 50) indicates a hostile climate.

organization seems to really care about its employees; they express consideration and warmth. We might also surmise from the data that an atmosphere of trust prevails because of the way layoffs are avoided even under adverse business conditions. As you might expect, Delta also has an excellent reward program where people are paid fairly and equitably with bonuses for outstanding performance. One aspect of Delta that runs somewhat counter to their otherwise supportive climate is that there are many rules and regulations required by the government that take away some of the autonomy in the job. However, this is not a serious problem since most employees feel that it is simply a "fact of life" for the airline industry.

TYPE Z ORGANIZATIONAL CULTURES

During the past decade there has been considerable concern about the ability of American organizations to compete with the Japanese. Analysis of Japanese management generally concludes that there are a number of cultural reasons for Japan's success.[28] William Ouchi has studied this process and asserts that there are also a number of American firms that operate in much the same fashion as Japanese firms—he calls these Type Z organizations.

Ouchi classifies organizations into three types shown in Table 17.3. **Type A** organizations display the typical pattern of most American firms: high rates of mobility, self-reliance, and individual responsibility. Because of high turnover of employees, there is little long-term concern for employees. **Type J** organizations are typical Japanese companies with life-time commitment to employees, consensus decision making, slow promotion, and high concern for employees. **Type Z** organizations are American organizations that share some of the same types of concern for people and commitment to long-term goals as do Japanese organizations.

A model of Theory Z, such as the one shown in Figure 17.1, predicts such outcomes as cooperation, intimacy, closeness, trust, autonomy—all aspects of organizational climate. In addition, both Type J and Type Z organizations have a strong sense of corporate values, goals, and culture; there is a cohesion and sense of togetherness.[29] This cultural combination is predicted to result in improved satisfaction, a heightened sense of autonomy, and increased production.

When we look for examples of Type Z organizations we find many of them already exist, including Delta Airlines, IBM, Hewlett-Packard, Rockwell, Eli Lilly, and Intel.[30] Note that all these organizations also have a reputation for excellent performance.

Table 17.3

TYPE A, TYPE J, AND TYPE Z ORGANIZATIONS

Type A (American)	Type J (Japanese)	Type Z (Modified American)
Short-term employment	Lifetime employment	Long-term employment
Individual decision making	Consensual decision making	Consensual decision making
Individual responsibility	Collective responsibility	Individual responsibility
Rapid evaluation and promotion	Slow evaluation and promotion	Slow evaluation and promotion
Explicit, formalized control	Implicit, informal control	Implicit, informal control with explicit, formalized measures
Specialized career path	Nonspecialized career path	Moderately specialized career path
Segmented concern	Holistic concern	Holistic concern, including family

SOURCE: From W.G. Ouchi and A.M. Jaeger (1978), Type Z organization stability in the midst of mobility, *Academy of Management Review* 3:308, 311. Copyright 1978 by the Academy of Management Review. Reprinted by permission.

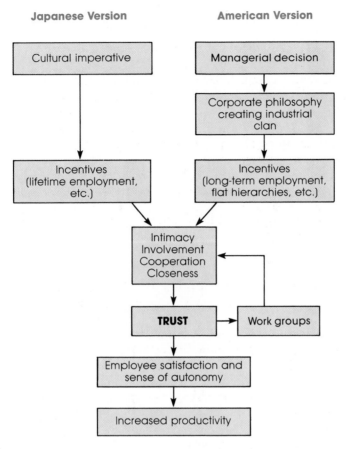

Figure 17.1

MODEL OF THEORY Z

SOURCE: From J.J. Sullivan (1983), A critique of Theory Z, *Academy of Management Review* 8:133. Copyright © 1983 by Academy of Management. Reprinted by permission of publisher and author.

A Critique of Theory Z

Since Theory Z is relatively new, it is not surprising that little research has been done to test it. There is some research support for the notion that Type J organizations have flourished in Japan.[31] Problems with Theory Z seem to center around whether or not it can be widely employed in modern American society with our individualistic values.

There is also the question of whether American workers would tolerate slow evaluation and promotion and less specialized career paths. These parts of Theory Z are certainly quite different from the actual practices of many organizations, including some that have been categorized as Type Z.

Another concern centers around our ability to change organizational cultures. Ouchi suggests a strategy for going from Type A to Type Z (*see* Figure 17.2).[32] We know from our discussion of change in the last chapter that

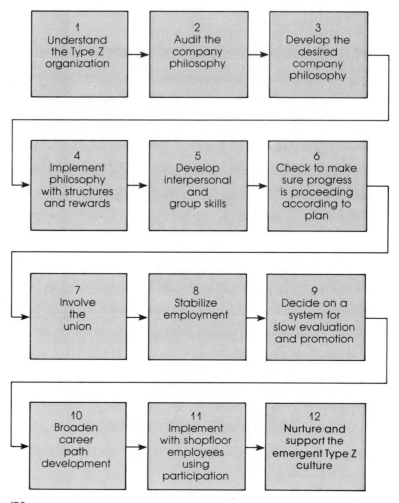

Figure 17.2

GOING FROM TYPE A TO TYPE Z

Adapted from Ouchi (1981), *Theory Z: How American business can meet the Japanese challenge.* Reading, MA: Addison-Wesley Publishing Co.

unfreezing is often difficult. This is especially true for the organization's culture.[33]

QUALITY OF WORK LIFE

Quality of work life (QWL), a concept that developed around 1970, is a reflection of the organization's culture.[34] In this section, we will review the meaning of QWL, examine the criteria that result in high QWL, and discuss how to successfully implement QWL innovations.

What Is Quality of Work Life?

The meaning of QWL is quite vague. Numerous organizational improvements bear the QWL label including: incentives plans, job enrichment, socio-technical systems, and quality circles. Since all of these strategies aim at improving the individual employee's well-being, perhaps they are all concerned with improving QWL. We will define **quality of work life** as a concern for the impact of work on an individual's well-being as well as a concern for improving organizational effectiveness.[35] The focus of QWL is on outcomes for the individual—how work can cause people to be better rather than how people can do better work.[36]

What Makes Up Quality of Work Life?

Another way to define QWL is to review the criteria that make QWL good or poor. Five criteria are particularly important: adequate and fair compensation, opportunity to use human capacity and to grow, social integration in the work place, constitutionalism in the work organization, and the relationship of work to the total lifespace.[37] These are explained in the following paragraphs.

Adequate and Fair Compensation. While there are no clear standards for adequate pay, it is nevertheless quite an important influence over QWL and quality of life in general. Without sufficient pay, it is difficult to go beyond physiological and safety needs to achieve esteem, growth, and self-actualization. Equitable and fair pay are important determinants of motivation and job satisfaction (*see* Chapter 5). People who are inequitably treated are generally dissatisfied with their jobs and experience low QWL.

Opportunities to Use Human Capacities and Grow. This criterion has to do with the design of work so that it is an enriching experience. The work itself needs to provide opportunities for autonomy, responsibility, and feedback (*see* the discussion of the Hackman-Oldham model in Chapter 7). People want to be able to use valued skills and abilities and learn new ones. People are also interested in opportunities for promotion and growth coupled with reasonable job security.

Social Integration in the Workplace. The nature of interpersonal and group relationships is quite important. People need to belong, to fulfill their social needs. An organization offers the opportunity to form supportive social relationships and friendships. It offers the potential for a sense of community. It is also important that the organization be relatively free of prejudice and sexual harassment.

Constitutionalism in the Work Organization. High QWL organizations are concerned about the rights of employees. The right to privacy, due process, equity, and free speech are all important. Individuals want to be respected.

APPLICATIONS OF
QWL STRATEGIES

"An important minority of the Fortune '500' companies are attempting some significant work improvement projects," says Richard Walton, an QWL expert who closely follows what industry is doing towards changing QWL.[38] Some of the leaders include General Motors, Proctor and Gamble, Exxon, General Foods, TRW, Cummins Engine, and Citibank.[39] In Sweden, Volvo has also been a leader in QWL efforts centered around socio-technical improvements.[40]

An example of how one of these firms, General Motors, has used QWL is illustrated by its project at Tarrytown, New York, which focused upon management-labor cooperation to improve both plant effectiveness and QWL.[41] Most of the 3,800 employees were involved in planning and problem-solving processes with a heavy emphasis on participative management. Costs of the QWL program of about $1.6 million were offset by gains in productivity and quality. For example, Tarrytown went from one of the poorest plants in terms of quality to one of the best. In addition, absenteeism was reduced from over 7 percent to between 2 and 3 percent. Grievances declined from over 2,000 to thirty-two. The conclusion at Tarrytown is that QWL worked.

Work and the Total Lifespace.   The interaction of work with family, friends, and geographical location are also important. Does the work demand so much that it interferes with family and leisure activities? Is there so much stress and pressure that health suffers (*see* Chapter 11)? The interaction between the organization, the family, and the community are increasingly important concerns of QWL.

Quality of Work Life Activities

There are four general types of QWL activities: participative problem solving, work restructuring, innovative reward systems, and improved work environments.[42] These activities are discussed in the following paragraphs.

Participative Problem Solving.   Participation in decision making (discussed in Chapter 13) has often taken the form of some type of labor-management cooperative groups.[43] More recently, quality circles (work group level people who solve problems relating to quality and other issues; *see* Chapter 16) have become a popular strategy.[44]

Work Restructuring.   The strategy here is to change the nature of work by redesigning the task to be more interesting, challenging, and growth-related. Such changes as job enrichment and socio-technical system designs (discussed in Chapter 7) apply here.[45]

Innovative Reward Systems.   Pay systems that stimulate creativity, innovation, and improved sharing of rewards are another key approach. Perhaps the best example here is use of the Scanlon Plan, which entails tying financial incentives to organizationwide productivity.[46] A committee of workers and managers is formed to stimulate increased productivity, and a philosophy of participative management is the central focus. Monthly bonuses are paid to everyone in the plant based on increased labor productivity that is obtained through problem-solving approaches to improving production.

Improving the Work Environment. The strategy here is to improve the tangible working conditions by changing working hours, physical conditions, or rules. Such innovations as flexitime (described in Chapter 7) are often used.[47] Another way to rearrange working schedules is **job sharing,** a strategy where two people share the same job.[48] Each fully qualified person works part-time, and the people divide the responsibilities and benefits of one full-time job. This allows individuals who want to work, but do not wish to work a full work week, to be meaningfully employed.

Another strategy for improving the work environment involves redesigning the physical facilities of the workplace to be more pleasing, safe, and comfortable.[49] Many companies are responding to this aspect of QWL—witness the beautiful surroundings of Weyerhaeuser's corporate headquarters shown in Figure 17.3.

Figure 17.3

WEYERHAEUSER HEADQUARTERS, FEDERAL WAY, WASHINGTON

Courtesy of Weyerheuser Company.

Making QWL Innovations Work

Unfortunately, QWL efforts do not always work. One recent study examined the long-term effects of QWL projects that had been initially successful. They found that at the end of five years "only *one third of the change programs* exhibited some reasonable level of persistence." [50] The others either no longer existed or they were declining in importance. One reason for the demise of these efforts is that they were never institutionalized, which means that patterns of behavior did not become part of the daily, persistent functioning of the organization.[51]

Fortunately, there are some strategies that may help institutionalize the innovations (*see* Chapter 16 for other suggestions). The following paragraphs cover some of them.

Thoroughly Train People.   While initial training efforts are usually good, follow-on training may be dropped and new organizational members ignored. Where inadequate training exists, the innovations are less likely to be institutionalized.[52] The key is to conduct regular training sessions to make sure everyone knows what behaviors are associated with the QWL efforts.

Seek Commitment by Using Volunteers and Participative Decision Making. People who are committed are motivated to continue the behaviors associated with the QWL innovation. People seem to have a stronger commitment if they voluntarily choose to participate in the program.[53] They also are more committed if they perceive a need for the program.[54]

Make Rewards an Integral Part of the Change.   When improvements in productivity, quality, or other tangible benefits accrue, rewards need to be shared equitably. It is unwise to assume that employees will be satisfied solely with intrinsic rewards.[55] Another issue is whether rewards are linked to performance. Based upon our knowledge of motivation (Chapter 5), we would expect that rewards will be more motivating and will cause more persistent interest in the QWL effort if they are tied to performance.

Insure Diffusion by Involving Key People.   The issue here is how widespread or **diffused** the QWL innovation is. If it applies only to a small portion of the organization, it is less likely to persist because "we-they" relationships develop that result in intergroup conflict and competition.[56] If lower-level managers are involved (such as in a job enrichment project), but middle-level managers are left out, they will likely resist the innovation and "sandbag" it at the first opportunity. In addition, QWL innovations are sometimes more punishing than rewarding for middle managers who are already maintaining a hectic workplace. More attention needs to be directed toward removing this resistance to change by structuring rewards and improving the QWL for the middle-managers themselves.[57]

The preceding recommendations give ideas for how QWL efforts can be institutionalized. However, it is not easy to accomplish such changes, for QWL efforts often involve a basic change in the organization's culture. For example,

Perspective 17.3

CONSIDERATIONS FOR REINVENTING THE CORPORATION

John Naisbitt, author of the best seller *Megatrends,* has teamed up with Patricia Aburdene to write another best seller, *Reinventing the Corporation.* They recommend that ten factors be considered when attempting to change an organization or plan your career. They believe you should use these guidelines to measure where you are and where you want to go. Here are their factors to consider:[58]

1. The best and brightest people will gravitate toward those corporations that foster growth.
2. The manager's new role is that of coach, teacher, and mentor.
3. The best people want ownership—psychic and literal—in a company; the best companies are providing it.
4. Companies will increasingly turn to third-party contractors, shifting from hired labor to contract labor.
5. Authoritarian management has yielded to a networking, people style of management.
6. Entrepreneurship within corporations—**intrapreneurship**—is creating new products and markets and revitalizing companies inside out.
7. Quality will be paramount.
8. Intuition and creativity are challenging the "it's all in the numbers" business-school philosophy.
9. Large corporations are emulating the positive and productive qualities of small business.
10. The dawn of the information economy has fostered a massive shift from infrastructure to quality of life.

participative management strategies abound within QWL techniques. An organization with an authoritarian culture will find it extremely difficult to implement them. In spite of these difficulties, organizations of the future must cope with an increasingly complex environment and much stiffer international competition. Thus, an organizational culture that harnesses the creativity of its members may be the key to organizational effectiveness and survival.

ORGANIZATIONS OF THE FUTURE

Effective management of an organization's culture is certainly one of the critical elements for coping with the rapidly changing environment of the 1980s and 1990s. It may even be necessary to re-invent the corporation (*see* Perspective 17.3) to meet these dynamic environmental changes.

The following are some predictions drawn from a variety of sources about the future nature of organizations:

- The Type Z culture will become more widespread.

- Managers will become even more concerned with managing human resources and finding ways to improve participation in decision making.[59]

- New ways of working with unions will develop so that more collaborative cultures emerge.[60]

Perspective 17.4

THE CONTRACTUAL ORGANIZATION: FOR FEES, NOT WAGES[65]

Charles Handy foresees major changes in organizations of the future. People may work more like contractors with greater self-control and less alienation. Here is how he describes the "contractual organization":

Wages are paid for time spent, input. Fees are paid for work done, output. The professional gets the fee; the worker a wage. Fees are more liberating for the individual, avoiding the hierarchical relationships detested by the Greeks and allowing work to be done at a person's own pace in his or her own way. More and more organizations are realizing that they can contract out a lot of the work to be done without forfeiting control. No longer, with electronic controls, do you have to bring everyone into one shed in order to control their work. The controls can go on line. Minielectronics puts the factory in the bedroom, with an automatic sewing machine, or at least in a community workshop where sophisticated equipment could be on hire. The new businesses that are springing up increasingly rely on high-technology contracted work. If Marks and Spencer can contract out their manufacturing and still control it, why not others? If hamburger chains can franchise distribution, why not others?

- Organizations will realize that high performance and high QWL can go "hand-in-hand." Thus, more collaborative, participative cultures will be the norm.

- Organizations of the future will place more emphasis on developing a clear sense of organizational purpose and philosophy.[61] But they will also need to develop better systems for maintaining these key aspects of culture during the transition from one chief executive to the next.[62]

- There will also be a major shift in the way work is organized. More emphasis may be placed on team approaches, where people work together in relatively autonomous groups to accomplish the task.[63]

- It is possible that teams may become so autonomous that they are treated like independent subcontractors (see Perspective 17.4).[64]

In conclusion, there will be many changes in organizations that help to cope with environmental change and the competition created by the increasing internationalization of business activity. Emphasis on quality will become increasingly important. We may also expect employees to demand that organizations place more emphasis on QWL issues. This changing world of work is certainly an exciting place for the manager of tomorrow.

CROSS–CULTURAL OB: THE CULTURAL RELATIVITY OF QWL CONCEPT

How culturally bound is our quality of work life concept? Does it apply in Japan, Hong Kong, Spain, Germany, Saudi Arabia, or the Philippines? How central is work to the quality of life? These questions raise issues that can be addressed by examining cross-cultural research.[66]

American culture stresses challenge, achievement, growth, and satisfaction of intrinsic needs. Work is seen as central to our quality of life. The famous industrialist and inventor, Charles F. Kettering illustrates this point:

> I often tell my people that I don't want any fellow [sic] who has a job working for me. What I want is a fellow whom a job has. I want the job to get the fellow and not the fellow to get the job. And I want that job to get hold of this young man [sic] so hard that no matter where he is, the job has got him for keeps. I want that job to have him in its clutches when he goes to bed at night, and in the morning I want that same job to be sitting on the foot of his bed telling him it's time to get up and go to work. And when a job gets a fellow that way, he's sure to amount to something.[67]

In other cultures people may feel quite differently toward their work. For example a high quality job may be one that allows individuals to fulfill family obligations rather than seek achievement and challenge.

Power-Distance and Individualism as Cultural Determinants of QWL

To find out if QWL is culturally determined, we will again use the concept of power-distance, discussed in Chapter 12 and earlier in this chapter. **Power-distance** is: "The extent to which the less powerful person in a society accepts inequality in power and considers it normal."[68] Another key concept is **individualism,** or the degree to which people look after themselves and their immediate families as opposed to a more collectivist culture where the good of the group and society is paramount. The combination of these two factors can be plotted as shown in Figure 17.4.

In an individualistic culture (lower half of Figure 17.4), such as the United States or Australia, high quality of work life means success, achievement, self-actualization, and respect. The task is seen as more important than relationships. People will often choose a transfer that offers a promotion rather than staying with friends and relatives. Intrinsic rewards, such as satisfaction with a job well done, are individually-oriented. In addition, job life and private life are quite separate.

In contrast, a collectivistic culture (upper half of Figure 17.4), such as Guatemala or Korea, is much more oriented toward family and group. It is a "we" culture rather than an "I" culture. Status is much more important than individual achievement. Recognition from the group is extremely important. Preserving face and avoiding shame within the reference group dominates behavior and motivation. A collectivist culture also has an "us-them" orientation—others are either part of our family grouping or they are not. It takes much time and effort to build relationships with a new group or person.

In a low power-distance culture (left side of Figure 17.4), such as Austria or Denmark, exerting power over others is seen as undesirable. Status differences are viewed with suspicion and democratic consultation is required. Ideal leaders are those who faithfully execute the will of their groups. Note the United States and Canada are in the middle. Participative management, initiat-

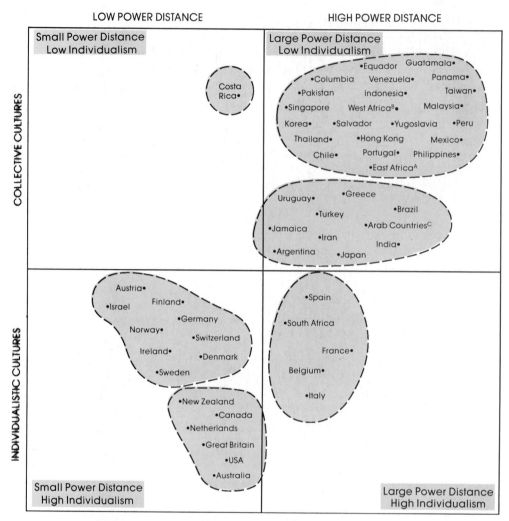

Figure 17.4

POWER DISTANCE AND INDIVIDUALISM—COLLECTIVISM FOR FIFTY COUNTRIES

SOURCE: Adapted from Hofstede, G. (1984). The cultural relativity of the quality of life concept. *Academy of Management Review, 9,* 391–392. Copyright © 1984 by the Academy of Management Review. Reprinted by permission.

ed by the leader, is desirable but not imperative. Moderate differences in status, power, authority, and privileges are expected.

In large power-distance cultures (right side of Figure 17.4), such as Malaysia or Saudi Arabia, subordinates expect leaders to make decisions themselves. There are major differences in status and privileges. There may even be different laws that apply to the elite. Status symbols are widely used. A high power-distance society is a more vertical society.

Perspective 17.5

AMERICAN CULTURE: A SHOCK FOR FOREIGN MANAGERS

Direct foreign investment in the United States has increased tremendously over the past ten years. In 1985, 65,349 foreign managers entered the United States to work.[69] Many of them are encountering culture shock when they try to use their management skills in their U.S. company. Here are some examples:

• "Transferees [from other cultures] find that behavior suitable at home may irritate co-workers here. 'Living in the U.S.A.,' a recent training film, portrays a Japanese employee angering an American colleague by repeatedly apologizing for a late report; the American expects explanations and solutions. 'In America, if you talk around things people get frustrated with you,' says Lennie Copeland, who helped produce the film."[70]

• Jose Carlos Villates, a manager from Puerto Rico, is used to starting business meet-

ings with relaxed chit-chat. At the headquarters of American Cyanamid Co., where he works, he picks up signals or body language that Americans find such sociability as time wasting. Even after fifteen months in the United States, Mr. Villates still feels uncomfortable plunging abruptly into business. "It strikes me as cold-blooded," he said.[71]

• Friction built up between a Swiss parent company and its American subsidiary because of centralized decision making practiced by the Swiss. The Americans wanted more autonomy; they wanted to be in charge. A Swiss executive explains: " 'There's more of a macho, cowboy, I'm-in-charge style of operating' here in contrast to the collegial approach prevalent in Europe and Asia."[72]

• During a role-playing session designed to train Japanese managers to deal with their American subordinates, a Japanese manager was told to criticize an American employee's performance. It took five runs through the same situation before the Japanese manager was direct enough so that the American subordinate realized he was being criticized.

Applicability of QWL Concepts

Even the definition of QWL may be suspect when exported to other cultures. For example, opportunities to use human capacities and grow are not strong goals in a collectivist culture; this goal may not be valued as improving QWL. Constitutionalism in the work organization, such as the right to privacy, due process, and free speech do not apply well in a high power-distance culture.

In terms of QWL activities, participative problem solving would be very uncomfortable—and probably unsuccessful—in a high power-distance society. In a very low power-distance culture, it would be seen as the norm; it would be expected. The applicability of work restructuring and socio-technical activities are also limited by culture. In a collectivist culture, traditional job enrichment strategies, such as those discussed in Chapter 7, would not be appropriate. Socio-technical approaches would require considerable modification because the "socio" part of the system may be defined quite differently. Thus a design that works in Sweden may not fit in Korea. Reward systems would also require careful review. Individually-oriented rewards would, of course, be inappropriate in collectivist cultures. The work environment is also a problem. Flexible working hours may work fine in an individualistic society, but how appropriate are they for a Japanese subsidiary? Thus, all aspects of QWL are affected by culture. Great care must be taken when exporting QWL activities to other parts of the world.

MANAGERIAL APPLICATIONS OF
ORGANIZATIONAL CULTURE AND QWL

One factor that always seems to be associated with well-run companies is an effective organizational culture.[73] A distinctive culture exerts a powerful influence on managerial behavior and on the strategies of the organization. It provides the sense of direction and values for all members of the organization. In addition, an organization with a supportive organizational climate has a culture that should enhance the quality of work life of organizational participants. Thus, culture and quality of work life are central to organizational and managerial effectiveness.

● *Recognize that much of organizational culture is at the subconscious level.* It resides in assumptions and values, which serve as perceptual filters for feelings, thoughts, and behaviors.

● *Do not assume that culture can be easily manipulated.* Culture controls the manager more than the manager controls the culture.[74] There is no good or bad culture. What is important is the match between culture and environment so an effective organization is created.

● *Learn the eight characteristics of excellence.* Apply them when developing your organization's purpose and goals. Use them as guides for change. Emulate them when they fit with your organizational culture and environment.

● *Try for a match between organizational and individual values.* By carefully selecting and socializing employees, value congruence can be obtained that will make management easier and improve organizational effectiveness.

● *Use rites, ceremonies, and rituals.* These seemingly unproductive activities serve many social purposes. They help clarify and reinforce the organization's culture.

● *Develop and nurture heroes.* They serve as role models, exemplify high performance, and inspire motivation.

● *Recognize the benefits of Type Z organizations.* If feasible, use Theory Z as a guide for changing your organizational culture.

● *Use quality of work life criteria for organizational effectiveness.* Pay people equitably, provide opportunities for growth and development, provide social integration opportunities, and insure constitutionalism is followed. Work life also needs to be balanced with total lifespace to insure quality of life.

● *Design organizational systems to improve QWL.* When changes are considered, try to use QWL strategies, such as: socio-technical systems, job enrichment, flexitime, job sharing, participative decision making, and the Scanlon plan. However, be sure the QWL strategy fits your organization's culture and that you pay careful attention to the change process.

- *Stay current with the environment.* Read about organizations of the future. Scan the environment to see how you may adapt your organization to be more effective. Read books and journals. Stay current.

- *Recognize the cultural basis for organizational behavior.* Cross-cultural examples show how managers can go astray with their own cultural backgrounds as filters. Remember that cultural differences also exist *within* countries, regions, industries, and even within companies.

FOR DISCUSSION

1. Describe the factors that make up an organization's culture. Based on your experience, give two contrasting examples of organizational culture.

2. Give an example of an organizational hero. Was this person a visionary or situational hero?

3. Compare and contrast organizational climate with organizational culture.

4. Explain the difference between Type A, Type J, and Type Z organizations. Which one would you prefer? Why?

5. Using the model for going from Type A to Type Z shown in Figure 17.2, explain how it fits with Lewin's model of the change process (unfreezing, changing, refreezing) discussed in Chapter 16. Do you see problems? Explain.

6. Describe an organization with a high quality of work life and a low quality of work life.

7. Do you agree that the organization of the future must be reinvented as proposed in Perspective 17.3?

8. Choose some organization that you are familiar with and redesign it as a contractual organization like the description in Perspective 17.4.

9. Do you think flexitime would work in a Japanese company? Why or why not?

KEY CONCEPTS AND TERMS

organizational culture
basic cultural assumptions
organizational values
rites
rituals
visionary hero

situational hero
organizational climate
Type A, J, Z organization
characteristics of excellent
   companies
individualism-collectivism

Theory Z
quality of work life
job sharing
diffusion
intrapreneurship
contractual organization

Cases and Incidents

THE CONSOLIDATED LIFE CASE: CAUGHT BETWEEN CORPORATE CULTURES

PART I

It all started so positively. Three days after graduating with his degree in business administration,

Mike Wilson started his first day at a prestigious insurance company—Consolidated Life. He worked in the Policy Issue Department. The work of the department was mostly clerical and did not require a high degree of technical knowledge. Given the repetitive and mundane nature of the work, the successful worker had to be consistent and willing to grind out paperwork.

Rick Belkner was the division's vice-president, "the man in charge" at the time. Rick was an actuary by training, a technical professional whose leadership style was laissez-faire. He was described in the division as "the mirror of whomever was the strongest personality around him." It was also common knowledge that Rick made $60,000 a year while he spent his time doing crossword puzzles.

Mike was hired as a management trainee and promised a supervisory assignment within a year. However, because of a management reorganization, it was only six weeks before he was placed in charge of an eight-person unit.

The reorganization was intended to streamline workflow, upgrade and combine the clerical jobs, and make greater use of the computer system. It was a drastic departure from the old way of doing things and created a great deal of animosity and anxiety among the clerical staff.

Management realized that a flexible supervisory style was necessary to pull off the reorganization without immense turnover, so they gave their supervisors a free hand to run their units as they saw fit. Mike used this latitude to implement group meetings and training classes in his unit. In addition he assured all members raises if they worked hard to attain them. By working long hours, participating in the mundane tasks with his unit, and being flexible in his management style, he was able to increase productivity, reduce errors, and reduce lost time. Things improved so dramatically that he was noticed by upper management and earned a reputation as a "superstar" despite being viewed as free spirited and unorthodox. The feeling was that his loose, people-oriented management style could be tolerated because his results were excellent.

A Chance for Advancement. After a year, Mike received an offer from a different Consolidated Life division located across town. Mike was asked to manage an office in the marketing area. The pay was excellent and it offered an opportunity to turn around an office in disarray. The reorganization in his present division at Consolidated was almost complete and most of his mentors and friends in management had moved on to other jobs. Mike decided to accept the offer.

In his exit interview he was assured that if he ever wanted to return, a position would be made for him. It was clear that he was held in high regard by management and staff alike. A huge party was thrown to send him off.

The new job was satisfying for a short time but it became apparent to Mike that it did not have the long-term potential he was promised. After bringing on a new staff, computerizing the office, and auditing the books, he began looking for a position that would both challenge him and give him the autonomy he needed to be successful.

Eventually word got back to his former vice-president, Rick Belkner, at Consolidated Life that Mike was looking for another job. Rick offered Mike a position with the same pay he was now receiving and control over a 14–person unit in his old division. After considering other options, Mike decided to return to his old division feeling that he would be able to progress steadily over the next several years.

Enter Jack Greely; Return Mike Wilson. Upon his return to Consolidated Life, Mike became aware of several changes that had taken place in the six months since his departure. The most important change was the hiring of a new divisional senior vice-president, Jack Greely. Jack had been given total authority to run the division. Rick Belkner now reported to Jack.

Jack's reputation was that he was tough but fair. It was necessary for people in Jack's division to do things his way and "get the work out."

Mike also found himself reporting to one of his former peers, Kathy Miller, who had been promoted to manager during the reorganization. Mike had always "hit it off" with Kathy and foresaw no problems in working with her.

After a week Mike realized the extent of the changes that had occurred. Gone was the loose, casual atmosphere that had marked his first tour in the division. Now, a stricter, task-oriented management doctrine was practiced. Morale of the supervisory staff had decreased to an alarming level. Jack Greely was the major topic of conversation in and around the division. People joked that MBO now meant "management by oppression."

Mike was greeted back with comments like "Welcome to prison" and "Why would you come back here? You must be desperate!" It seemed like everyone was looking for new jobs or transfers. Their lack of desire was reflected in the poor quality of work being done.

Mike's Idea: Supervisor's Forum. Mike felt that a change in the management style of his boss was necessary in order to improve a frustrating situation. Realizing that it would be difficult to affect his style directly, Mike requested permission from Rick Belkner to form a Supervisor's Forum for all the managers on Mike's level in the division. Mike explained that the purpose would be to enhance the existing management-training program. The Forum would include weekly meetings, guest speakers, and discussions of topics relevant to the division and the industry. Mike thought the forum would show Greely that he was serious about both his job and improving morale in the division. Rick gave the O.K. for an initial meeting.

The meeting took place and ten supervisors who were Mike's peers in the company eagerly took the opportunity to "Blue Sky" it. There was a euphoric attitude about the group as they drafted their statement of intent. It read as follows:

To: Rick Belkner
From: New Issue Services Supervisors
Subject: Supervisors' Forum

On Thursday, June 11, the Supervisors' Forum held its first meeting. The objective of the meeting was to identify common areas of concern among us and to determine topics that we might be interested in pursuing.

The first area addressed was the void that we perceive exists in the management-training program. As a result of conditions beyond anyone's control, many of us over the past year have held supervisory duties without the benefit of formal training or proper experience. Therefore, what we propose is that we utilize the Supervisors' Forum as a vehicle with which to enhance the existing management-training program. The areas that we hope to affect with this supplemental training are: a) morale/job satisfaction; b) quality of work and service; c) productivity; and d) management expertise as it relates to the life insurance industry. With these objectives in mind, we have outlined below a list of possible activities that we would like to pursue.

1. Further utilization of the existing "in-house" training programs provided for manager trainees and supervisors, i.e., Introduction to Supervision, E.E.O., and Coaching and Counseling.

2. A series of speakers from various sections in the company. This would help expose us to the technical aspects of their departments and their managerial style.

3. Invitations to outside speakers to address the Forum on management topics such as managerial development, organizational structure and behavior, business policy, and the insurance industry. Suggested speakers could be area college professors, consultants, and state insurance officials.

4. Outside training and visits to the field. This could include attendance at seminars concerning management theory and development relative to the insurance industry. Attached is a representative sample of a program we would like to have considered in the future.

In conclusion, we hope that this memo clearly illustrates what we are attempting to accomplish with this program. It is our hope that the above outline will be able to give the Forum credibility and establish it as an effective tool for all levels of management within New Issue. By supplementing our on-the-job training with a series of speakers and classes, we aim to develop prospective management personnel with a broad perspective of both the life insurance industry and management's role in it. Also, we would like to extend an invitation to the underwriters to attend any programs at which the topic of the speaker might be of interest to them.

cc: J. Greely
    Managers

The group felt the memo accurately and diplomatically stated their dissatisfaction with the current situation. However, they pondered what the results of their actions would be and what else they could have done.

PART II

An emergency management meeting was called by Rick Belkner at Jack Greely's request to address the "union" being formed by the supervisors. Four general managers, Rick Belkner, and Jack Greely were at that meeting. During the meeting it was suggested the Forum be disbanded to "put them in their place." However, Rick Belkner felt that if "guided" in the proper direction the Forum could die from lack of interest. His stance was adopted but it was common knowledge that Jack Greely was strongly opposed to the group and wanted its founders dealt with. His comment was "It's not a democracy and they're not a union. If they don't like it here, then they can leave." A campaign was directed by the managers to determine who the main authors of the memo were so they could be dealt with.

About this time, Mike's unit had made a mistake on a case, which Jack Greely was embarrassed to admit to his boss. This embarrassment was more than Jack Greely cared to take from Mike Wilson. At the managers staff meeting that day Jack stormed in and declared that the next supervisor to "screw up" was out the door. He would permit no more embarrassments of his division and repeated his earlier statement about "people leaving if they didn't like it here." It was clear to Mike and everyone else present that Mike Wilson was a marked man.

Mike had always been a loose, amiable supervisor. The major reason his units had been successful was the attention he paid to each individual and how they interacted with the group. He had a reputation for fairness, was seen as an excellent judge of personnel for new positions, and was noted for his ability to turn around people who had been in trouble. He motivated people through a dynamic, personable style and was noted for his general lack of regard for rules. He treated rules as obstacles to management and usually used his own discretion as to what was important. His office had a sign saying "Any fool can manage by rules. It takes an uncommon man to manage without any." It was an approach that flew in the face of company policy, but it had been overlooked in the past because of his results. However, because of Mike's actions with the Supervisor's Forum, he was now regarded as a thorn in the side, not a superstar, and his oddball style only made things worse.

Faced with the fact that he was rumored to be out the door, Mike sat down to appraise the situation.

PART III

Mike decided on the following course of action:

1. Keep the Forum alive but moderate its tone so it didn't step on Jack Greely's toes.

2. Don't panic. Simply outwork and outsmart the rest of the division. This plan included a massive retraining and remotivation of his personnel. He implemented weekly meetings, cross training with other divisions, and a lot of interpersonal "stroking" to motivate the group.

3. Evoke praise from vendors and customers through excellent service and direct that praise to Jack Greely.

The results after eight months were impressive. Mike's unit improved the speed of processing 60% and lowered errors 75%. His staff became the most highly trained in the division. Mike had a file of several letters to Jack Greely that praised the units

excellent service. In addition, the Supervisor's Forum had grudgingly attained credibility, although the scope of activity was restricted. Mike had even improved to the point of submitting reports on time as a concession to management.

Mike was confident that the results would speak for themselves. However, one month before his scheduled promotion and one month after an excellent merit raise in recognition of his exceptional work record, he was called into his supervisor's, Kathy Miller's, office. She informed his [sic] that after long and careful consideration the decision had been made to deny his promotion because of his lack of attention to detail. This did not mean he was not a good supervisor, just that he needed to follow more instead of taking the lead. Mike was stunned and said so. But, before he said anything else, he asked to see Rick Belkner and Jack Greely the next day.

The Showdown. Sitting face to face with Rick and Jack, Mike asked if they agreed with the appraisal Kathy had discussed with him. They both said they did. When asked if any other supervisor surpassed his ability and results, each stated Mike was one of the best, if not *the* best they had. Then why, Mike asked, would they deny him a promotion when others of less ability were approved. The answer came from Jack: "It's nothing personal, but we just don't like you. We don't like your management style. You're an oddball. We can't run a division with ten supervisors all doing different things. What kind of a business do you think we're running here? We need people who conform to our style and methods so we can measure their results objectively. There is no room for subjective interpretation. It's our feeling that if you really put your mind to it, you can be an excellent manager. It's just that you now create trouble and rock the boat. We don't need that. It doesn't matter if you're the best now, sooner or later as you go up the ladder, you will be forced to pay more attention to administrative duties and you won't handle them well. If we correct your bad habits now, we think you can go far."

Mike was shocked. He turned to face Rick and blurted out nervously, "You mean it doesn't matter what my results are? All that matters is how I do things?" Rick leaned back in his chair and said in a casual tone, "In so many words, Yes."

Mike left the office knowing that his career at Consolidated was over and immediately started looking for a new job. What had gone wrong?

EPILOGUE

After leaving Consolidated Life, Mike Wilson started his own insurance, sales and consulting firm, which specialized in providing corporate-risk managers with insurance protection and claims-settlement strategies. He works with a staff assistant and one other associate. After three years, sales averaged over $7 million annually, netting approximately $125,000 to $175,000 before taxes to Mike Wilson.

During a return visit to Consolidated Life, three years after his departure, Mike found Rick Belkner and Jack Greely still in charge of the division in which Mike had worked. The division's size had shrunk by 50 percent. All of the members of the old Supervisor's Forum had left. The reason for the decrease in the division's size was that computerization had removed many of the peoples' tasks.

DISCUSSION QUESTIONS

1. Describe the culture of Consolidated Life under Jack Greely.

2. What value conflicts existed between Wilson and Greely? Could these have been resolved?

3. Compare the leadership styles of Wilson and Greely. Which was most appropriate for the situation?

4. How could group dynamics help explain what happened in this case?

5. What were the power relationships between the major parties?

Reprinted by permission of the publisher from J. Weiss, M. Wahlstrom, and E. Marshall, "The consolidated life case: Caught between corporate cultures." *Journal of Management Case Studies, 2,* 238–243. Copyright © 1986 by Elsevier Science Publishing Co., Inc.

REFERENCES

1. Moss, P. (1986, April). What it's like to work for Delta Air Lines. *Business Week Guide to Careers,* p. 43cf.

2. Peters, T.J., & Waterman, R.H., Jr. (1982). *In search of excellence* (p. 253). New York: Harper & Row.

3. Moss, P. (1986), p. 49.

4. Peters, T., & Austin, N. (1985). *A passion for excellence* (p. 204). New York: Random House.

5. Kilmann, R.H., Saxton, M.J., & Serpa, R. (1986). Issues in understanding and changing culture. *California Management Review, 28* (Winter), 87–94.

6. This definition is similar to the ones used by Barney, J.B. (1986). Organizational culture: Can it be a source of sustained competitive advantage? *Academy of Management Review, 11,* 656–665. Harris, P.R., & Moran, R.T. (1987). *Managing cultural differences* (2nd ed.). Houston: Grid. Sathe, V. (1983). Implications of corporate culture: A manager's guide to action. *Organizational Dynamics, 12* (2), 5–23. And Pettigew, A.W. (1979). On studying organizational cultures. *Administrative Science Quarterly, 24,* 570–581.

7. Schein, E.H. (1985). *Organizational culture and leadership.* San Francisco: Jossey-Bass.

8. Schein (1985). Trice, H.M., & Beyer, J.M. (1984). Studying organizational cultures through rites and ceremonials. *Academy of Management*

Review, 9, 653–669. Deal, T.E., & Kennedy, A.A. (1982). *Corporate culture.* Reading, MA: Addison-Wesley.

9. This section on assumptions is based on Schein, E.H. (1985).

10. Adapted from Peters, T.J., & Waterman, R.H., Jr. (1982). *In search of excellence.* New York: Harper & Row. For a critical review of their research, see Hitt, M.A., & Ireland, R.D. (1987). Peters and Waterman revisited: The unended quest for excellence. *Academy of Management Executive, 1,* 91–98.

11. Taylor, T.O., Friedman, D.J., & Couture, D. (1987). Operating without supervisors: An experiment. *Organizational Dynamics, 15* (3), 26–38.

12. Peters & Waterman (1982), p. 247.

13. Schein (1985), pp. 105–106.

14. Based on Rokeach, M. (1968). *Beliefs, attitudes, and values.* San Francisco: Jossey-Bass.

15. Deal & Kennedy (1982).

16. Pascale, R.T., & Athos, A.G. (1981). *The art of Japanese management.* New York: Simon and Schuster. Ouchi, W.G. (1981). *Theory Z.* Reading, MA: Addison-Wesley.

17. Trice, H.M. & Beyer, J.M. (1984). Studying organizational cultures through rites and ceremonials. *Academy of Management Review, 9,* 655. Beyer, J.M., & Trice, H.M. (1987). How an organization's

rites reveal its culture. *Organizational Dynamics, 15*(4), 5–24.

18. Peters & Austin (1985), p. 361.

19. Trice & Beyer (1984), p. 660.

20. Deal & Kennedy (1982).

21. Based on Deal & Kennedy (1982). Also see Reich, R.B. (1987). Entrepreneurship reconsidered: The team as hero. *Harvard Business Review, 65* (3), 77–83.

22. For further discussion of the dimensions of culture, see Schein (1985). And Harris & Moran (1987). For a discussion of how rewards affect culture, see Kerr, J., & Slocum, J.W., Jr. (1987). Managing corporate culture through reward systems. *Academy of Management Executive, 1,* 99–108.

23. Schneider, B., Parkington, J.J., & Buxton, V.M. (1980). Employee and customer perceptions of service in banks. *Administrative Science Quarterly, 25,* 252–267.

24. See Jones, A.P., & James, L.R. (1979). Psychological climate: Dimensions and relationships of individual and aggregated work environment perceptions. *Organizational Behavior and Human Performance, 23,* 201–250.

25. See Powell, G.N., & Butterfield, D.A. (1978). The case for subsystem climates in work organizations. *Academy of Management Review, 3,* 151–157. And Drexler, J.A. (1977). Organizational climate: Its homogeneity within organizations. *Journal of Applied Psychology, 62,* 38–42.

26. Organizational climate factors originally from Campbell, J.P., Dunnette, M.D., Lawler, E.E., III, & Weick, K.E. (1970). *Managerial behavior, performance, and effectiveness.* New York: McGraw-Hill. For recent reviews, see Ashforth, B.E. (1985). Climate formation: Issues and extensions. *Academy of Management Review, 10,* 837–847. And Schneider, B., & Reichers, A.E. (1983). On the etiology of climates. *Personnel Psychology, 36,* 19–39.

27. See Zand, D.E. (1972). Trust and managerial problem solving. *Administrative Science Quarterly, 17,* 229–239. And Barnes, L.B. (1981, March–April). Managing the paradox of organizational trust. *Harvard Business Review,* pp. 107–116.

28. Ouchi, W.G., & Jaeger, A.M. (1978). Type Z organization: Stability in the midst of mobility. *Academy of Management Review, 3,* 305–314. Ouchi, G. (1981). *Theory Z: How American business can meet the Japanese challenge.* Reading, MA: Addison-Wesley Publishing Co.

29. Marshland, S., & Beer, M. (1983). An evaluation of Japanese management: Lessons for U.S. managers. *Organizational Dynamics,* (Winter), 49–67.

30. Ouchi (1981), p. 31.

31. Sullivan, J.J. (1983). A critique of Theory Z. *Academy of Management Review, 8,* 132–142.

32. Also see Joiner, C.W. (1985). Making the "Z" concept work. *Sloan Management Review, Spring,* 57–63.

33. For changing an organization's culture refer to the works of Schein (1985) and Ouchi (1981). Also see Allen, R.F. (1985). Four phases for bringing about cultural change. In R.H. Kilmann, M.J. Saxton & R. Serpa (Eds.). *Gaining control of the corporate culture* (pp. 332–350). San Francisco: Jossey-Bass. For creating a new organizational culture, see Perkins, D.N.T., & Lawler, E.E., III (1983). *Managing creation: The challenge of building a new organization.* New York: Wiley.

34. For a review of the origins of QWL, see Nadler, D.A., & Lawler, E.E., III (1983). Quality of work life: Perspectives and directions. *Organizational Dynamics,* Winter, 20–30. Also see (1973) *Work in America.* Cambridge, MA: MIT Press. Davis, L.E., & Cherns, A.B. (Eds.) (1975). *The quality of working life.* New York: The Free Press. And Hackman, J.R., & Suttle, J.L. (1977). *Improving life at work.* Santa Monica: Goodyear.

35. This definition is based on Lawler, E.E., III (1982). Strategies for improving the quality of work life. *American Psychologist, 37,* 486–493. And Nadler & Lawler (1983).

36. Nadler & Lawler (1983), p. 26.

37. This section is adapted from Walton, R.E. (1973). Quality of working life: What is it? *Sloan Management Review,* (Fall), 11–21. Empirical support for Walton's categories can be found in Levine, M.F., Taylor, J.C., & Davis, L.E. (1984). Defining quality of working life. *Human Relations, 37,* 81–104.

38. Walton, R.E. (1979). Work innovations in the United States. *Harvard Business Review, 57,* 91.

39. Walton (1979). Also see Mares, W.J., & Simmons, J. (1983). *Working together: From shopfloor to boardroom.* New York: Knopf.

40. Kolodny, H., & Stjernberg, T. (1986). The change process of innovative work designs: New design and redesign in Sweden, Canada, and the U.S. *Journal of Applied Behavioral Science, 22,* 287–301. Gyllenhammer, P.G. (1977). *People at work,* Reading, MA: Addison-Wesley.

41. Guest, R.H. (1979). Quality of work life—learning from Tarrytown. *Harvard Business Review, 57.*

42. The categories and the discussion are based on Nadler & Lawler (1983).

43. See Fuller, S.J. (1980, July). How quality-of-work life projects work for General Motors. *Monthly Labor Review,* pp. 37–39. Bluestone, I. (1980). How quality-of-work life projects work for the

United Auto Workers. *Monthly Labor Review*, 39–41.

44. Marks, M.L., Mirvis, P.H., Hackett, E.J., & Grady, J.F., Jr. (1986). Employee participation in a quality circle program: Impact on quality of work life, productivity, and absenteeism. *Journal of Applied Psychology, 71*, 61–69. Yeager, E.G. (1981, April). The quality control circle explosion. *Training and Development Journal*, pp. 98–105. And Wood, R., Hull, F., & Azumi, K. (1983). Evaluating quality circles: The American application. *California Management Review, 26* (Fall), 37–53.

45. Pava, C. (1986). Redesigning sociotechnical systems design: Concepts and methods for the 1990s. *Journal of Applied Behavioral Science, 22*, 201–221.

46. Schuster, M. (1984). The Scanlon Plan: A longitudinal analysis. *Journal of Applied Behavioral Science, 20*, 23–38. And Driscoll, J.W. (1979). Working creatively with a union: Lessons from the Scanlon Plan. *Organizational Dynamics*, (Summer), 61.

47. Ronen, S. (1981). *Flexible working hours.* New York: McGraw-Hill.

48. Frease, M., & Zawacki, R.A. (1979, October). Job sharing: An answer to productivity problems? *Personnel Administrator.*

49. Peponis, J. (1985). The spatial culture of factories. *Human Relations, 38*, 357–390. Steele, F.I. (1973). *Physical settings and organization development.* Reading, Mass.: Addison-Wesley. And Holahan, C.J. (1978). *Environment and behavior.* New York: Plenum.

50. Goodman, P.S., & Dean, J.W., Jr. (1983). Why productivity efforts fail. In W.L. French, C.H. Bell, Jr., & R.A. Zawacki, *Organization development: Theory, practice, and research* (rev. ed.). Plano, TX: Business Publications.

51. This definition is similar to the one used by Goodman & Dean (1983).

52. Goodman & Dean (1983). Nadler & Lawler (1983).

53. Goodman & Dean (1983).

54. Nadler & Lawler (1983).

55. Walton, R.E. (1980). Establishing and maintaining high commitment in work systems. In J.R. Kimberly & R.H. Miles (Eds.). *The organizational life cycle.* San Francisco: Jossey-Bass.

56. Goodman & Dean (1983). Nadler & Lawler (1983). Also see Walton, R.E. (1975). The diffusion of new work structures: Explaining why success didn't take. *Organizational Dynamics*, (Winter), 3–21. And Walton, R.E. (1977). Successful strategies for diffusing work innovations. *Journal of Contemporary Business*, (Spring), 1–22.

57. Schlesinger, L.A., & Oshry, B. (1984). Quality of work life and the manager: Muddle in the middle. *Organizational Dynamics, 13* (Summer), 4–19.

58. From Naisbitt, J., and Aburdene, P. (1985), *Reinventing the corporation.* New York: Warner, p. 53. For examples of companies that may have already been reinvented, see O'Toole, J. (1985), *Vanguard management.* New York: Doubleday.

59. Miles, R.E., & Rosenberg, H.R. (1982). The human-resource approach to management: Second-generation issues. *Organizational Dynamics, Winter*, 26–41. Saskin, M. (1986). Participative management remains an ethical imperative. *Organizational Dynamics, 14* (Spring), 62–75.

60. Greensburg, P.D., & Glaser, E.M. (1981). Viewpoints of labor leaders regarding quality of work-life improvement programs. *International Journal of Applied Psychology, 30*, 157–175.

61. Walton, R.E. (1986). A vision led approach to management restructuring. *Organizational Dynamics, 14* (Spring), 4–16. Vaill, P.B. (1982). The purposing of high performing systems. *Organizational Dynamics*, (Autumn), 23–39.

62. Pickhardt, C.E. (1981). Problems posed by changing organizational membership. *Organizational Dynamics, 13* (Summer), 69–80.

63. Miles & Rosenberg (1982). Pava (1986). Reich (1987).

64. For a further extension of this concept involving networks and brokers, see Miles, R.E., & Snow, C.C. (1986). Organizations: New concepts and new forms. *California Management Review, 28* (Spring), 62–73.

65. Handy, C. (1980). The changing shape of work. *Organizational Dynamics, 9*, 31.

66. This section is based on Hofstede, G. (1984). The cultural relativity of the quality of life concept. *Academy of Management Review, 9*, 389–398.

67. Whyte, W.F. (1969). Culture and work. In R.A. Webber (Ed.). *Culture and management* (p. 31). Homewood, IL: Irwin.

68. Hofstede, G. (1984), p. 390.

69. Bennett, A. (1986, February 12). American culture is often a puzzle for foreign managers in the U.S. *Wall Street Journal.*

70. From Bennett (1986).

71. Bennett (1986).

72. Bennett (1986).

73. Swartz, H., & Davis, S.M. (1981). Matching corporate culture and business strategy. *Organizational Dynamics*, (Summer), 30–48.

74. Schein (1985), p. 314.

GLOSSARY

ability The skills and knowledge that make it possible for a motivated person to perform.

absenteeism The number and duration of absences from work of an employee or group of employees. Often expressed as a percentage of total available working hours.

accommodation Reducing conflict by giving in to others.

achievement motive Concern with pursuit of excellence, accomplishing unique goals, and achieving high levels of performance and efficiency.

achievement-oriented leadership Behavior that encourages subordinates to set challenging goals, shows confidence in subordinates, and continuously seeks improvement in subordinates' performance.

action-research The process of gathering data, feeding back the data to a client group, problem-solving issues that arise from the data, developing action plans to resolve problems, and following up to see that actions have worked out as planned.

active listening Empathic listening used when someone else owns a problem and needs to work through its solution.

acute episodic stress Stress caused by intense, relatively infrequent events, with relatively brief physiological effects but long-lasting psychological effects.

ad hoc work group A work group that is brought together for a limited time, such as a task force.

Adult ego state That part of a person that seeks knowledge, gathers facts, analyzes data, and organizes and tests reality.

Adult-bossing style A managerial style that is problem-solving oriented and nonemotional.

affiliation motive Concern for social relationships, such as friendship, love, and approval.

assessment center A technique that uses a number of traits and behaviors to assess a person's suitability for being hired or promoted.

attitude Tendency to react in a favorable or unfavorable way toward some object, person, group, or idea.

attribution To consider something, someone, or some idea as belonging to or being caused by another. Interpreting or attributing behavior because of these inferred causes.

attribution theory A model that attempts to understand causes of events, assess responsibility for outcomes of the event, and assess personal qualities of the people involved in an event.

authority The right to order or ask others to do what you want them to do.

autocratic decision making The manager makes decisions without consulting subordinates.

autocratic management A management style in which a domineering manager makes decisions without consulting employees.

autonomous workshops   Another term for self-managing work groups.

autonomy   The degree of freedom surrounding the work.

aversive   Unpleasant, repugnant, or disgusting.

avoidance   (1) In behavior modification: behavior associated with escaping or avoiding some aversive situation or outcome. Also called negative reinforcement or escape conditioning. (2) A strategy of conflict resolution that relies upon avoiding a confrontation with the hope that the conflict will defuse itself.

behavior modification   The process of changing behavior by managing the consequences that follow some behaviors.

behavior   An observable, tangible act done by someone.

belief   A personal conclusion about what is true or not true or what is beautiful or not beautiful about the world.

biofeedback   Using information about pulse, breathing rate, and blood pressure to provide feedback for enhancing relaxation.

blocking roles   Roles played by group members that oppose or obstruct the group's roles.

bounded rationality   The ability to seek and choose rational decisions is limited or bounded by our capacity to acquire and process complex information.

brainstorming   A technique for creatively generating and evaluating ideas.

buffers   Departments or people whose task is to deal with the environment and thus shield and protect the technical core of the organization.

bureaucracy   A form of organization that is oriented toward impersonal rule enforcement, systematic spheres of competence for members, fair allocation of resources, and written records.

burnout   A state of mental, emotional, and physical exhaustion that results from working with people and complex organizations over an extended period of time in emotionally draining situations.

centralization   Decision making and control that is concentrated at the top levels of the organization.

change   To move from one state or condition to another state or condition.

charismatic leadership   Leadership by force of personality and abilities that has a profound and extraordinary effect on followers.

charting   The use of some type of graph or chart to monitor behavior over time.

chief executive officer (CEO)   The senior manager in the firm who is responsible for the overall operation of the organization; usually, the CEO is also the president.

Child ego state   That part of personality that is concerned with impulses, feelings, and uninhibited release of emotions; not related to age.

chronic stress   Stress that is encountered relatively frequently as part of the day-to-day workload and tasks.

chunking   Structuring a problem so that it can be tackled and solved, often by a task force.

circadian rhythm   The twenty-four hour cycle of the body involving changes in heart rate, metabolism, sleep cycles, and urine flow.

client relationships   Direct contact between the person doing the job or task and the person for whom it is being done.

coacting work groups   People who work together as a group but whose tasks are relatively independent from one another.

coalition   An alliance or union between two or more people.

coercive power   The ability to order someone to do something backed up by force or punishment.

cognitive dissonance   When two attitudes, beliefs, or behaviors conflict or are inconsistent with each other.

cohesiveness The attractiveness and hold that a group has for its members. The strength of the members' desire to remain in the group and be committed to the group.

collaborative management A management style that obtains the involvement of employees in the management of the organization.

collectivism The tendency to look after the needs of the group, organization, and society rather than one's own needs; as contrasted with individualism.

competition Two or more people or groups seeking to gain the same thing that others are seeking.

complementary transaction When a message is sent to a specific ego state and it gets the predicted or expected response.

compromising A strategy of conflict resolution that involves bargaining and negotiations.

compulsive neurotic style Preoccupation with perfectionism and attention to details.

conflict The perception that one's needs, concerns, or desires are being frustrated or are about to be frustrated.

conformity The degree of adherence to the group's norms.

confrontation meeting An OD strategy that is designed to diagnose organizational problems and take action to resolve them.

consensus (1) In decision making, see group consensus. (2) In attribution theory: the way others behave in a similar fashion in the same situation.

consequence The outcome that follows some behavior, such as a reward or punishment.

consideration The concern of a leader for the followers, including friendliness, supportiveness, open communication, recognition.

consistency (1) The degree to which a person behaves in the same way in a variety of situations or with different tasks. (2) Reliability.

consultative decision making Conferring and consulting with subordinates before the leader makes a decision. Information is collected either individually or from the group as a whole.

contingencies of reinforcement The systematic management of the S–O–B–C model of behavior modification so the behavior changes in the desired direction.

contingency approach An approach to management that is based upon using situational effects to explain and predict behavior.

contractual organization An organization that is structured so that employees are treated as independent contractors with fees being paid for work done.

contrast People or things who stand out because they are distinct; they diverge from other things or people around them.

control group A group in an experiment that is not exposed to the experimental treatment.

cooperation Working together to achieve mutual goals.

cooptation Offering group or organizational membership to people whose support is needed so that they will embrace the group or organization's norms, values, and goals.

correlation A statistical method of showing a relationship between two variables. Correlation coefficients range from -1.0 to $+1.0$. Zero correlation means no relationship while a positive or negative number of 1.0 means perfect correlation.

crossed transaction A message that is addressed to one ego state but receives an unexpected response from another ego state and disconfirms the person's position.

decentralization The delegation or dispersion of decision making to lower organizational levels.

decision making The process of thought and action that culminates in making a choice.

defense mechanisms Strategies and techniques that are used by an individual to reduce anxiety and frustration and to protect self-esteem.

deferred judgment Delaying any evaluation or judgment of ideas until a later time. A major principle of brainstorming.

delegation Allowing subordinates or groups to make a decision on their own.

Delphi technique A method for systematically gathering written judgments from individuals by using sequential questionnaires interspersed with summaries of results from previous responses.

departmentation The process of breaking down the organization into units or departments.

dependent variable A measurement of an end result that is caused by some prior action or event (independent variable); an outcome that is dependent on some other event, action, or variable.

depressive neurotic style Feelings of depression; hopelessness, guilt, self-reproach, and inadequacy.

devil's advocate Someone whose role is to question decisions and take the opposing view on a decision.

diagnosis Determining what the problem is using data gathering or analysis techniques.

differentiation The degree to which departments differ from one another, both structurally and emotionally.

diffusion The spreading of innovation; particularly QWL projects.

directive leadership Leaders who are more concerned with the task; with initiating structure.

disequilibrium A condition that results from the disruption of the current state or equilibrium.

displacement Transferring an emotional feeling from one person or thing to another person or thing.

distinctiveness In attribution theory: the degree to which a person behaves in the same way over a variety of situations.

division of labor The way that tasks are divided among organizational members.

dramatic neurotic style Seeking attention and trying to impress people.

efficiency Accomplishing the job with a minimum expenditure of effort and materials.

ego state A consistent pattern of feeling, thinking, and experience that is related to a corresponding consistent pattern of behavior. The three ego states are Parent, Adult, and Child.

employee citizenship Behaviors which fit the organization's goals, values, and rules; such as, helping coworkers, accepting assignments without complaint, making constructive statements about the work environment, and promoting a positive organizational climate.

encoding The process of making the message of the sender into a form that can be recognized by the receiver.

environment The environment consists of all the elements or factors outside the boundary of the organization; such as customers, suppliers, politics, economic conditions, and national culture.

equilibrium A state of balance created when opposing forces are of equal strength.

equity theory The process of explaining how individuals compare their rewards and efforts with others and perceive fair and equal treatment.

E.R.G. theory A theory of motivation that builds upon Maslow's hierarchy of needs. It involves only three needs: existence, relatedness, and growth.

expectancy An anticipatory belief or desire.

expectancy theory A theory of motivation that attempts to explain why people choose various paths that will lead to need satisfaction.

expectations Anticipation that an event or behavior will lead to outcomes.

experimental research A researcher manipulates the situation or events and controls the research environment to establish causality between the experimental treatment and the results.

expert power Power derived from expertise on a subject. Others are influenced because they perceive superior knowledge on the part of another.

external attribution Blaming behavior on factors outside the person being evaluated.

extinction (1) A strategy of ignoring or doing nothing following some behavior. (2) The effect on behavior of doing nothing.

extrinsic rewards   Rewards that come from sources outside the individual; rewards from others.

feedback   Any kind of returned information from a source; a response to a sender's message; clear and direct information about job outcomes and job performance.

feedback from the job   Information that comes directly from doing the job rather than from bosses, coworkers, or others.

Fiedler's Contingency Model   A situational approach to leadership that considers the leader's personality interacting with leader-member relations, position power, and task structure.

field of experience   The totality of one's past experiences, personality, and self-concept.

fight-or-flight response   A reaction to a stressor that prepares the body for fighting or fleeing by increasing the heart rate or pumping adrenalin into the body.

fixed ratio schedules   A reward is given after a fixed or specified number of responses.

fixed interval schedule   A fixed amount of time passes between rewards.

flat organizational structure   An organization with few levels between the highest and lowest person in the organizational hierarchy; wide spans of control.

flexitime   A system where employees can choose their own work schedules—especially arrival and departure times—within certain limits.

force-field analysis   A technique for identifying the driving and restraining or resisting forces associated with a given change.

forcing   A method of conflict resolution that involves the use of power or coercion to resolve a conflict.

formal work group   A formally constituted group with a supervisor and subordinates.

frustration-regression   That part of E.R.G. theory which states that people who are continually frustrated in satisfying a need will regress to seeking satisfaction of a lower need.

functional departments   Structuring based on placing people with the same expertise in the same department.

functional authority   The ability of a staff to give orders relating to their functional expertise.

fundamental attribution error   The tendency to blame behavior on factors within the individual rather than on environmental factors.

gainsharing   An incentive pay system based on sharing the gains from improvements in productivity or reduction in costs; with employee involvement.

garbage-can model   A way of looking at decision making where organizational members deposit problems, solutions, and preferences in a "garbage can" where they all get mixed up.

goal clarity   The degree of specificity and clarity possessed by the goals.

goal difficulty   The level of challenge or difficulty of the goals.

goal setting   The process of developing, negotiating, and formalizing targets that an employee is responsible for accomplishing.

goal acceptance   Whether or not goals are accepted by the employee.

goals and values subsystem   That part of the organizational system that is concerned with beliefs, attitudes, goals, and values of the organization and its members.

grapevine   All informal communication within the organization.

group   A collection of individuals who have interaction with one another toward some common goal or purpose.

group consensus   A decision process wherein all group members can accept the decision even though they may not completely agree with it.

group decision making   (1) Any time a group is used as part of the decision-making process. (2) A jointly developed decision between the manager and the subordinates.

group roles   Sets of behaviors associated with working in groups, including: task, maintenance, and blocking types of roles.

groupthink   The tendency for a group to have reduced reality testing, mental efficiency, and judgment because of in-group pressures.

growth-need-strength   A moderator of the job enrichment process; the need to develop, grow, experience new skills, and be challenged.

halo effect   A general impression that causes one or more characteristics to be used to evaluate a person on other characteristics.

heroes   People that are held in high regard by members of an organization. They may be visionary heroes, who have broad philosophical impact on the organization, or they may be situational heroes, who inspire others through day-to-day success.

hierarchy   A system that ranks one person, organization, or thing above another.

horizontal division of labor   Breaking down and organizing into tasks, functions, products, or areas; departmentation.

horizontal integration   People, groups, or departments whose purpose is to coordinate the activities of functional departments.

hygiene factors   Factors that are similar to extrinsic rewards: pay, supervision, rules and regulations, working conditions.

I-message   A way of confronting problems that involves making a statement composed of three elements: behavior, tangible effects, and feelings.

idealism   Emphasis is placed on seeking the truth, as opposed to being pragmatic.

ideation   The process of generating ideas without evaluating them. A major strategy of brainstorming.

idiosyncratic credits   Deviance that is tolerated because an individual has accumulated credits for being a good group member and conforming to group norms over a long period of time.

implicit favorite model   The decision model which states that people pick an early favorite in the decision process and even though they continue to evaluate alternatives they have already chosen an implicit favorite solution.

impression management   The process of controlling the images and perceptions that others form about us.

incentive pay   Pay that provides motivation to produce or perform.

independent variable   The causal factor in research.

individualism   The tendency to look after one's self rather than the group, organization, or society; as contrasted with collectivism.

inequity   The ratio of outcomes to inputs is perceived to be unfair when compared with those of some other person or group.

influence   The process of producing intended effects in individuals, groups, and organizations.

informal organization   A network of personal and social relationships that arise spontaneously as people associate with one another.

informal listening   A listening process that consists primarily of the transmission of information from a speaker to a listener.

informal group   People who join together as a group for friendship or other reasons.

ingratiation   A process by which people make a conscious effort to increase another's liking of them.

initiating structure   The concern of the leader for tasks; such as directing, planning, controlling, problem solving.

institutionalize   To make a new condition part of the normal day-to-day, persistent operation of the organization.

integration   The process of coordinating and integrating diverse activities that are created by the division of labor.

integrators   People whose job involves coordination and linking together people and groups.

interacting group   A work group in which all members must complete the task before the product is done. Also, a group that communicates openly during the group process.

interdependence   Mutual dependence of one person or group on other people or groups.

intergroup conflict   Conflict between two groups.

internal attribution   Blaming behavior on factors within the person being evaluated.

interpersonal conflict   Conflict between two people.

interpersonal listening   A listening process that involves an interaction between the speaker and the listener.

interpersonal attraction   The desire to be close to another.

intervention   Any action that intervenes in an organizational process; a term often used by OD practitioners.

intragroup conflict   Conflict within a group.

intrapersonal conflict   Conflict within an individual.

intrinsic rewards   Rewards that come from within the person or from the job itself.

intuitive decisions   (1) Decisions that are habitual and automatic; programmed decisions. (2) Decisions based on the creative and holistic orientation of the right brain; "gut" or "seat of the pants" decisions.

job characteristics   Those characteristics that are needed for an enriched job; including skill variety, task identity, task significance, autonomy, and feedback.

job characteristics model   A model of the enrichment process that predicts certain outcomes if the jobs are enriched.

job design   The deliberate, purposeful planning of the job, including all its structural and social aspects and their effect on the employee.

job engineering   Maximizing the efficiency of the job through time and motion studies and man-machine interfaces.

job enlargement   Adding more tasks to the job for variety.

job enrichment   The process of making jobs more interesting, meaningful, and challenging by using the proper blend of job characteristics.

job maturity   The extent and relevance of past job experience.

job rotation   Doing different jobs to add variety, or for training.

job satisfaction   The degree of pleasurable or unpleasurable feelings that one has toward a job or job experiences.

knowledge-based-pay   A pay system where compensation is determined by the number of skills the employee can competently perform.

leader-match approach   An approach to leadership which states that leaders should be matched to the situation or that situations should be redesigned to fit the leader.

leadership   The process of influencing others toward goals.

Least-Preferred-Coworker Scale   An instrument used to measure the personality of a leader using Fiedler's Contingency Model.

left-brain functions   The left brain (of a right-handed person) controls the analytic, systematic, sequential, and verbal functions.

legitimate power   A source of power emanating from formal authority relationships or laws.

leverage point   Any point in an organization that serves to support and reinforce a change.

lifetime employment   An employment system where people work for only one company during their entire career.

line authority   The ability to give direct orders to people because of a superior organizational position.

line activities   Activities that affect the direct production and sales of an organization.

linking   Structures that bring two or more organizational subunits together, such as a liaison position.

locus of control   The degree to which a person feels that his or her life is controlled by the self (internally) versus by the environment, fate, or chance (externally).

maintenance roles   Those roles performed by an individual or group that are concerned with maintaining the interpersonal relationships of the group.

management   The process of planning, organizing, controlling, and leading the efforts of organizational members toward goals.

management by objectives (MBO)   A managerial process where superiors and subordinates jointly identify common goals, define areas of responsibility, measure progress, and assess results.

management-by-walking-around   A management technique involving wandering around the workplace and informally communicating with employees and customers.

Managerial Grid®   A model of leadership that considers the interaction of concern for people and concern for production on a grid and classifies leaders according to their location.

managerial subsystem   That part of the organizational system that is concerned with coordinating, planning, controlling, and leading.

Maslow's hierarchy of needs   A theory of motivation that states that needs are arranged in a hierarchy. When a given need predominates, it will motivate until satisfied; then another higher-level need will take over.

matrix organization   An organizational structure with dual reporting channels so that the same person has two bosses, a functional one and a project or product one.

mentor   A senior organizational member who looks after the career of a junior person.

merit pay   Pay that is tied to performance appraisals.

messages   The thoughts, images, feelings, ideas, and facts that are transmitted from one person to another.

modernism   Emphasis placed on merit, rationalism, and progress; as contrasted with traditionalism.

motivation   The process that causes behavior to be energized, directed, and sustained.

Motivation-Hygiene Theory   A motivation theory developed by Herzberg that states that the causes of satisfaction (motivation) and dissatisfaction (hygiene) are not the same; they can be managed separately.

motivator factors   Those factors in Motivation-Hygiene Theory that are linked with satisfaction; such as, achievement, recognition, the work itself, responsibility, and advancement.

motive   The state of tension within an individual that arouses behavior directed toward satisfying some goal; see need.

need   A tension created by some psychological or physiological deficiency that arouses an individual to try to satisfy that need.

negative reinforcement   Avoidance; the removal of an unpleasant or aversive stimulus that results in increased behavior.

negativism   Active resistance, passive resistance, or aggression.

neurotic organizations   Suffering from mental and behavioral disorders, such as the dramatic, depressive, paranoid, compulsive, schizoid styles.

nominal group technique (NGT)   A decision-making system using a structured group meeting where people work in the presence of others but without interaction with them.

nonverbal communication   Any conscious or unconscious signal other than a verbal one, that communicates. Typically, nonverbal signals include eyes, face, body posture, hand movements, dress, and spatial relationships.

norming   Part of the group development process when norms are formed and roles are established.

norms   Rules of behavior and expected ways of behaving that have been accepted as legitimate by members of the group.

novelty   Something that is different and therefore stands out and is perceived more easily.

object factors in perception   The part of the perceptual process focusing on the thing or object being perceived.

objective   A broad statement of a desired future condition that provides direction.

operant conditioning   The management of behavior by altering environmental events and the consequences that follow behavior.

organization   A system that coordinates people, jobs, technology, and management practices to achieve goals.

organizational behavior   The study of the human aspects of organizations, including individual behavior, group behavior, and their interaction with organizational structure, culture, and processes; with the goal of improving organizational effectiveness.

organizational behavior modification   The application of behavior modification strategies to organizational situations.

organizational climate   The way people perceive their organizational environment; including such aspects as autonomy, structure, rewards, consideration, and trust.

organizational commitment   Belief in the organization's goals and values; willingness to expend extra effort; desire to stay with the organization; loyalty to the organization.

organizational culture   The shared beliefs, philosophies, values, behaviors, and symbols (including language) that characterize an organization at a given time.

organizational politics   Seeking selfish ends to enhance or protect the self-interest of individuals or groups.

organizational purpose   The fundamental reason for the existence of the organization.

organizational socialization   The process of learning the norms, values, and behavior patterns of a group or organization.

organizational structure   The formal patterns of relationships that exist among work units or positions, the way tasks are divided between organizational members, the rules and procedures for accomplishing these tasks, and the authority and responsibility relationships that exist between people in the organization.

organization development (OD)   A process of planned organizational improvement that is sustained for a relatively long period of time and employs behavioral science technology.

paralinguistics   The study of the vocal part of a message, including such aspects as range, resonance, tempo, control, intensity, and pitch.

paranoid neurotic style   Suspicion and mistrust guide attitudes and behaviors.

Parent ego state   That part of the personality that is concerned with limits of behavior, prejudices, critical behaviors, and nurturing, concern for what should and ought to be done. Developed from observing parents and other authority figures.

participant observer   An academic researcher who becomes a member of an organization so that behavior can be observed in a natural way.

participation in decision making   The process of joint decision making between two or more parties.

participative leadership   Leaders who allow subordinates to participate in decision making.

particularism   Emphasis placed on obligations to friends and relatives; as contrasted with universalism.

paternalism   Managing an organization as if the employees were the children and management the parents.

path-goal theory   A model of leadership that considers the leader's ability to influence the subordinate's goal attainment. The model considers both leader behaviors and situational factors.

perception   The process of organizing and interpreting environmental inputs that are obtained through our senses.

perceptual organization   Fitting diverse perceptions into a structure that makes sense to one's self.

person factors in perception   That part of the perception process focusing on the person who is perceiving. Factors include: self-concept, values, attitudes, past experience, habits, nonverbal cues, and expectations.

personality   A set of relatively stable personal characteristics and tendencies that determine our thoughts, feelings, and actions in combination with the social and biological pressures of the moment.

piece-rate pay   Paying on the basis of the number of units that are produced.

pilot project   Trying out a change by implementing it in only part of the organization.

position power   The amount of power possessed by a leader because of the position that is held.

positive reinforcement   The application of a pleasant or desirable outcome following some behavior that results in an increase in future behavior.

power   The ability to bring about outcomes that are desired through the use of influence.

power balancing   Each use of power tends to be offset by a counter use of power; power is normally in a state of equilibrium.

power motive   Concern with controlling and influencing others.

power distance   The degree to which a society believes that power should be unequally distributed.

powerlessness   Perceived feelings of a lack of power.

pragmatism   Emphasis is placed on what works; what is practical; as contrasted with idealism.

preparatory set   A mental set for perceiving something; see expectancy.

problem-ownership model   A strategy for approaching interpersonal problem solving by using active listening or I-messages depending upon who owns the problem.

problem solving   A systematic method of defining the problem, gathering and evaluating data, generating alternatives, implementing the solution, and following up as needed.

process   The study of how and why activities, results, or states happen; procedures for carrying out a sequence of activities within a system.

process gains   Additional information obtained through communication and synergy of people working together.

process losses   Decreases in effectiveness because of losses in communication and decision making; usually caused by group size.

product form of organization   An organization that is structured around the output, product, product group, service, market, customer, or program.

productivity   The output of goods or service per worker.

programmed decisions   Decisions that are habitual and automatic; intuitive decisions.

projection   Projecting one's own shortcomings on others without admitting that they are true of yourself.

proximity   Perceptual effects caused by closeness or nearness of a person, event, or thing.

psychological maturity   Willingness of subordinates to accept responsibility; their motivation; their positive orientation toward task accomplishment.

psychosocial subsystem   That part of the organizational system that is concerned with individual and group behavior of people working together.

punishment   The application of an unpleasant or aversive outcome that causes a decrease in behavior.

qualitative research   Research that is based upon observation or authoritative opinion.

quality   The average number of defects per unit produced; high quality means low numbers of defects.

quality circles   Small groups of volunteers who meet periodically to identify, analyze, and solve problems related to product quality or other issues.

quality of work life (QWL)   Concern for the impact of work on individuals' well-being as well as improving organizational effectiveness.

rationalization   Self-satisfying explanations for behavior.

realistic job preview   Giving prospective employees a realistic picture of the positive and negative aspects of the job.

reality shock   Surprise experienced by a new employee when the reality of organizational life is much different than expected.

referent power   A source of power depending on others' liking the person or wanting to be like him or her.

refreezing   Making sure that an equilibrium is established for the new condition after change.

relaxation response   The slowdown of the body's heart rate, metabolism, breathing; opposite of the fight-or-flight response.

reliability   The degree to which the research instrument or design yields consistent results time after time or question after question.

repression   Excluding a feeling, experience, or event from one's consciousness.

responsibility centers   Autonomous subparts of the organization that have more or less total responsibility for their product or function.

reward power   Influence obtained by the ability to reward people with money, recognition, promotion, status, and other similar outcomes.

right-brain functions   The right hemisphere (for right-handed people) controls the intuitive, visual-spatial, sensuous, and holistic functions.

rites   Relatively elaborate, planned sets of activities that are carried out through social interactions.

rituals   Part of an organization's culture consisting of symbolic actions; such as ceremonies, leisure and play, and other behavior patterns.

role   Set of behaviors that are expected when a person occupies a certain position in an organization or in life.

role ambiguity   Uncertainty and lack of clarity surrounding the role to be performed.

role clarification   Open discussion of role expectations to clarify roles and reduce stress.

role conflict   Incompatible messages and expectations concerning the roles to be played.

role overload   Expecting someone to perform too many jobs or roles at one time.

S–O–B–C model   A model for understanding the behavior modification process, which involves the stimulus (S), the person (O), the behavior (B), and the consequences (C).

salience   The degree of prominence or conspicuousness.

satisficing   The process of seeking acceptable alternatives rather than optimal ones.

Scanlon Plan   A financial incentive plan that involves sharing cost savings and using participative management techniques.

schedules of reinforcement   The timing of rewards or other outcomes following behavior. Ratio schedules involve a certain number of desirable responses, while interval schedules are concerned with the time interval.

schizoid neurotic style   Withdrawn and uninvolved; daydreaming; not in touch with reality.

schmoozing   Allowing groups to socialize, to talk, use the telephone, and fool around.

selection   (1) Part of the perceptual process having to do with paying attention to things and people we feel comfortable with and filtering out those we do not feel comfortable with. (2) Choosing a person to join the organization, be promoted, or receive an assignment.

selective perception   The process by which our minds select or allow certain inputs to predominate.

self-actualization   A need that indicates desire for self-fulfillment and reaching potential.

self-concept   The totality of an individual's thoughts and actions with reference to himself or herself as an object.

self-fulfilling stereotype   Generalized beliefs and attitudes that form stereotypes reinforce our own behavior in such a way that the behavior or outcomes associated with the stereotypes actually comes true.

self-fulfilling prophecy   When expectations about ourselves or others result in behavior that causes the expectation to come true.

self-managing work groups   Groups who are given autonomy over many aspects of their jobs; including, job design, goal setting, rewards, and member selection.

shaping   Using behavior modification techniques to gradually change behavior as desired.

similarity   Part of the perceptual process dealing with grouping people or things together because they are from similar backgrounds, live in similar places, and so forth.

situation factors in perception   That part of the perceptual process dealing with the circumstances or situation, including: selection, similarity, and organization.

situational leadership theory   An approach to leadership that combines relationship behavior and task behavior and their interaction with the maturity of followers.

skills   Learned behaviors; such as social skills, task skills, and communication skills.

skill variety   Doing a number of different things; using valued skills and abilities.

skunkworks   A small group of people who are formally or informally set off from the main part of the organization with the goal of innovation, usually in product development.

social exchange process   The interaction or exchanges between people who are members of a group, including those between a leader and the follower.

social influences   The effects of the social environment on perceptions and behavior; including inputs from coworkers, supervisors, subordinates, and other people.

social loafing   The possible tendency of individuals to produce less when working in the presence of others because they feel less pressure to perform.

social network   The communication network that links informal groups together.

sociotechnical systems   Designing the jobs and organization so as to optimize the relationship between the technical system and the social system.

span of management   The number of subordinates that report directly to a supervisor.

sponsor   A form of mentorship which involves a senior person who attempts to further the career of a junior person.

staff activities   Activities that support the primary purpose of the organization, such as personnel and legal.

status   An individual's rank or worth within a group as determined by the individual's behaviors, attributes, characteristics, and possessions that are valued by the group.

status incongruence   When status characteristics are inappropriate for the position in the group.

status symbols   The possessions—clothes, office, position—that reflects a person's relative status in a group.

stereotype   A generalization about a class or group of people.

stimulus   An environmental cue that elicits behavior.

stress   A response, physical or psychological, to an external event that places special physical and psychological demands on a person and causes a deviation from their normal functioning.

stressor   A stimulus condition that results in the response of stress.

structural subsystem   That part of the organizational system that is concerned with rules, procedures, structures, reporting relationships, authority and responsibility.

superordinate goal   An overall goal that transcends all others.

supportive leadership   Leaders who show a great deal of consideration for their followers; leaders who are people-oriented.

survey research   Using questionnaires to gather data about some issue that is of concern to the manager.

system   An organized, unitary whole made up of interdependent subsystems and delineated by identifiable boundaries.

tall organizational structure   An organization with many levels of hierarchy between the highest and lowest person; narrow spans of control.

task identity   Doing the whole task or job from beginning to end.

task force   An ad hoc work group with a limited lifespan set up to accomplish a limited objective.

task roles   Roles performed by an individual or group that are concerned with getting the job done.

task significance   The meaningful impact of the task on the organization and other people.

team   A group of people who must work together in a collaborative way to achieve the group's goals.

teambuilding   A strategy for improving the ability of teams to work together in an effective way, with a heavy focus on identifying and solving problems.

technical core   The primary task of the organization, such as production.

technical subsystem   That part of the organizational system concerned with the knowledge, processes, techniques, and facilities used to transfer inputs to the organizational system into outputs.

technology   Types and patterns of activities, equipment, materials, knowledge, and expertise needed to accomplish the task.

theory   A way of relating how concepts, variables, or things relate to one another.

Theory X   An assumption that people are essentially lazy, dislike work, and must be coerced and controlled to be motivated to perform.

Theory Y   An assumption that people are self-directed, have the capacity for imagination and innovation, and that they seek responsibility.

Theory Z   A model that predicts that the proper corporate philosophy and human resource management systems will create a climate of intimacy, involvement, cooperation, and trust with long-term positive effects on satisfaction and performance.

third party   A person who acts as a facilitator to resolve problems or conflicts between two other people.

traditionalism   Emphasis placed on the past, on family, class, and status; as contrasted with modernism.

traits   Individual characteristics of a person; such as physical characteristics, personality, and intellectual ability.

transactional leadership   A process of mutual influence based on the rewards and punishments exchanged between leader and followers. See social exchange approach to leadership.

Transactional Analysis (TA)   A theory of personality and human behavior that focuses on psychological positions, games, and transactions between people. It may also refer to that aspect of TA that is concerned with analyzing transactions and chains of transactions and their associated ego states.

transition   Movement from one state of equilibrium to another.

transition manager   A person, group, or unit that is responsible for planning and executing a change.

turnover   The proportion of employees who leave or quit.

Type A behavior   Behaviors that exhibit a chronic, incessant struggle to achieve more and more in less and less time. Often involves aggressiveness, hostility, anger, a sense of time urgency, and an achievement orientation.

Type B behavior   Behavior that does not include Type A behavior. Easy-going, nonaggressive, with little sense of time urgency or achievement orientation.

Type Z organization   An American organization that shares some of the same concerns for people and commitment to long-term goals as do Japanese organizations.

ulterior transaction   A hidden message that always involves more than two ego states.

uncertainty avoidance   The degree to which a society tends to feel threatened and avoid ambiguous situations and uncertainty.

universalism   Emphasis placed on obligations to organization and society; as contrasted with particularism.

unprogrammed decisions   Decisions made after careful problem solving and analysis.

valence   The desirability of a given outcome for a specific individual.

validity   The degree to which the research design, data, collection method, and instrument measure what they are supposed to measure.

value   A broad, general belief about some way of behaving or some end state that is preferable to the individual.

value programming   The process by which values are formed.

variable interval schedule   A variable amount of time passes (based on some average) between rewards.

variable ratio schedule   Rewards are given after a person performs the behavior a variable number of times.

vertical division of labor   The way authority, responsibility, and decision making are divided between the highest and lowest levels of the organization.

vertical integration   People, groups, or departments whose purpose is to coordinate between different levels in the organization.

vicarious reinforcement   Experiencing the rewards of others as if they were your own.

Vroom-Yetton model   A systematic decision-tree approach for evaluating when to use participative decision making.

win-lose model   The outcomes that result from competition and cooperation; including, win-win, win-lose, and lose-lose.

withdrawal   Leaving the situation either physically or psychologically.

zone of acceptance   The area of behavior in which people will be likely to accept the use of power.

TOPIC INDEX

Accommodation 272
Achievement motive 48
Achievement orientation 128–129
Action plan 463
Action research 461–463
Active listening 210–211
Adult bossing style 207
Affiliation motive 48
Air traffic controllers 301
Alderfer's ERG theory 115–116
American Airlines 208
American Can 64
AT&T 49, 207, 379, 380, 412
Anarchic model of decision making 346–347
Apple Computer 5, 20, 32
Arab
   decision making 365–366
   time perceptions 103
Assessment center 378–379
Atari Corp. 91
Attitudes 68–74
   behavior 72
   change 73–74
   cognitive dissonance 73–74
   job satisfaction 70–71
   management of 77–78
   measurement of 69
   perception 88
   surveys 69–70
Attribution theory 92–94
Authority
   defined 315
   functional 423

Authority-obedience management 384
Automotive News 338
Avoidance
   behavior modification 145–146
   conflict reduction strategy 270–272

Bank of America 207
Behavior
   attitudes 72
   leadership 381–385
   managerial 7–9
   personality 47–51
Behavior modification 139–157
   (see organizational behavior modification)
Beliefs 61
Bell Labs 7
Best companies to work for 7
Boeing Company 20, 32, 433–434
Bonuses 154–155
Bounded rationality 345
Brain-hemisphere dominance 40
Brainstorming 361–362
Brazil, time perceptions 103
Bureaucracy 430
Burnout 297–298
Business Week 174, 177
Butler Manufacturing Co. 252

Centralization 426–427
Challenger launch decision 369–370
Change, organizational 447–460
   (see organizational change)

Characteristics of general managers 49
Charismatic leadership 381
Charting 142–143
Chemical Bank 64
China
   negotiation with 281–282
   power dynamics 333, 335
Chrysler Corp. 4, 5, 15, 155, 441–442
Climate, organizational 480–481
Coalitions 329
Coercive power 317
Cognitive dissonance theory 73–74
Cohesiveness, of groups 245–246
Collaboration 272–273
Commission pay 156–157
Commitment, organizational 72
Communication 196–220
   active listening 210–211
   and change 456
   feedback 199–202
   grapevine 200
   international 219
   interpersonal 202–208
   Japan 218
   listening 208–213
   management of 219–220
   nonverbal 213–218
   problem-ownership model 210
   process 197–204
   selective perception 85–86
   transactional analysis 202–208
Compensation 154–157

Competition 275–281
  compared with conflict 276–277
  Deutsch's theory of cooperation 276
  effects of 277–278
  management of 280–281, 283–284
  negotiation 279, 281–282
  when to use 279–280
  Win-lose model 277–278
Complementary transactions 204–205
Conflict 264–276
  accommodation 272
  avoidance 270, 272
  collaboration 272–273
  competition 275–281
  confrontation at Intel Corp. 271
  first-line supervisors 267
  forcing 272–273
  intrapersonal conflict 265
  intergroup conflict 265
  interpersonal conflict 265
  language of 271
  management of 270–275, 283–284
  matrix organizations 435
  resolution 270–275
  third party resolution 274–275
  value 66–68
Consensus decision making 92–93
Consideration 382
Consistency 92–93
Consultative decision making 355
Contingencies of reinforcement 140–141, 147
Contingency approach 12
Contingency model of leadership 385–388
Contractual organization 490
Contrast, in perception 87
Cooperation 275–281
Cooptation 330
Coordination 427–428
Corning Glass 90
Corporate mergers, and stress 296
Correlation 16
Country-club management 384
Creativity 361–362
Crisis management 235
Cross-cultural OB
  American culture shock 493
  Arab decision making 365–366
  communication 218–219
  confrontation in Japan 282

endurance walk in Japan 254–255
individualism-collectivism 491–492
influence distribution Japan vs. U.S.A. 438
Japanese organizational structure 437–439
job enrichment 185–187
leadership 395–396
lifetime employment 75–76
motivation 128–130
negotiating with the Chinese 281–282
organizational structure 437–439
organization development 465
personality 52–53
power 333–335
power-distance 334, 465, 491–492
quality of work life 490–493
rewards: U.S. vs. Japan 158
socializing new employees in Japan 253–255
sociotechnical concepts 185–187
Soviet computer problems 466–467
stress 305–308
tardiness 157–159
time perceptions 103
theory application 128–130
uncertainty avoidance 465
values 74–76, 253
Volvo's Kalmar plant 185–187
worker comparisons 27
Crossed transactions 205–206
Culture, organizational 474–480 (see organizational culture)
Cummins Engines 177

Dana 476
Data gathering techniques 463
Decentralization 426–427
Decision making 342–367
  anarchic model 346–347
  Arab 365–366
  brainstorming 361–362
  consensus 92–93
  delegation 354–355
  delphi 363–365
  group consensus 359–360
  implicit favorite model 347
  in groups 350–365
  intuitive 348–350
  Kepner-Tregoe approach 345
  management of 366–367

nominal group method 362–363
participation in 353–358
problem solving 343–345
satisficing 345
techniques 359–365
Vroom-Yetton model 355–358
Defense mechanisms 45
Delegation 354–355
Delphi technique 363–365
Delta Airlines 7, 474, 476
Descriptive statistics 16
Deutsch's Theory of Cooperation 276
Diffusion
  of innovation 488
  conflict strategy 270, 272
Digital Equipment Corp. 7
Displacement 45
Distinctiveness 92–93
Division of labor 420, 424–425
Donnelly Mirrors 7
Dow Jones 32
Dress and impressions 99–100

Effectiveness
  goal setting 182–183, 185
  group 229–230, 250–253
  group decisions 352–353
  job enrichment 173–174
  managerial 10
  organization development 464–465
  organizational 13–14
  team 251
Ego states 202–203, 210
Eli Lilly 7
Emery Air Freight 141, 148, 163
Employee citizenship 72
Environment
  buffers 418–419
  complexity 415–416
  motivation 112
  organizational 415–419
  suprasystem 20–21
  uncertainty 415–416
Equilibrium, and change 448–449
Equity theory 126–128
ERG theory 115–116
Escalation of commitment 341
Ethics
  behavior modification 152–154
  power and politics 331–333
  values 64

Excellent companies
  lean staff 425
  management by wandering
    around 208
  principles of 476
  rewards 145
  skunkworks 431
  task forces 240
Expectancy, in perception 89
Expectancy theory 118–122
Expectations 89–90
  and change 457
Experimental research 17–18
Expert power 318
External attribution 94
Extinction 146
Extrinsic rewards 123
EXXON 7

Federal Aviation Agency 67
Feedback
  change 456
  communication 199–202
  job enrichment 168–172
  organization development 462
Females in organizations (see
  women)
Fiedler's contingency model 385–388
Field Experiments 17
Firestone Tire and Rubber Co. 310
First-line supervisors 267
Fixed interval schedule 149, 150
Fixed ratio schedule 149, 150
Flat organizations 422
Flexitime 172
Force-field analysis 454–455
Forcing 272–273
Ford Motor Company 27, 337–339,
  427
French versus American
  characteristics 52–53
Frustration-regression 116
Functional
  authority 423
  departments 425
  organizations 430
Fundamental attribution error 94
Future, organizations of 489–490

Gaines Pet Food 177
Garbage can model 346–347
General Dynamics 64
General Electric 4, 5

General Foods 177
General Motors 4, 5, 26, 427, 486
Goals
  change 455–456
  how to write 178
  job design 182–183
  organizational objectives 413–415
  superordinate 280
  transcendent 381
Goal setting 122–123, 178–183
  acceptance 179
  clarity 178
  commitment 179
  difficulty 179
  effectiveness of 182–183, 185
  Locke's theory 178
  managerial applications 188
  management by objectives
    180–183
  with loggers 180
Goldman Sachs 7
Grapevine 200
Great Britain, tardiness 158
Group
  approaches to job design 174–177,
    251–253
  characteristics 236–246
  cohesiveness 245–246
  consensus 359–360
  decision making 350–365
  development 246–249
  dynamics 228–256
  effectiveness 229–230, 250–253
  informal 233
  management of 255–256
  nature of 229–236
  norms 239–243
  roles 236–239
  self-managing 175–177
  size 231
  status 243–244
Groupthink 351
Growth need strength 169

Hackman and Oldham model 169
Hallmark Cards 7
Halo effect 95–96
Harwood Manufacturing Corp. 454
Hay Management Consultants 155
Heinz Foods 145
Heroes 479–480
Hersey-Blanchard Situational model
  388–390

Herzberg's Motivation-Hygiene
  Theory 124–125
Hewlett-Packard 7, 208, 414
Hierarchy 75
Hilton Hotel Corp. 222
Horizontal division of labor 424–425
House's Path-Goal Theory 390–393
Hybrid organization 433
Hygienes 124–125

IBM 4, 5, 7, 32, 141, 145, 207, 476
I-messages 211–212
Impoverished management 384
Implicit favorite model 347
Impression management 97–98
  dress 99–100
  ingratiation 98–99
  nonverbal 100–101
  political strategy 329
Incentive pay 154–155
Indiana Bell 172
Individual differences
  capacity to perform 111
  defined 38
  follower maturity 389
  growth need strength 169
  locus of control 51
  motives of individuals 48–49
  stress 295–297
  subordinate characteristics 392
  Type A and B behavior patterns
    295–297
Individualism-collectivism 491–492
Inequity 127
Influence
  defined 315
  U.S. versus Japan 438
Informal groups 233
Informal organization 421
Informational listening 212–213
Ingratiation 98
Initiating structure 382
Institutionalization, and change
  459–460
Integration 427–429
Intel Corp. 271
Internal attribution 93
International OB topics (see cross-
  cultural OB)
Interpersonal
  communication 202–208
  conflict 265
  listening 209–212

Interviewing 102
Intrapreneurship 489
Intrinsic rewards 123
Intuitive decision making 348–350
ITT 15

J.C. Penney 7
J.P. Morgan Co. 32
Japanese
   company principles 253
   confrontation strategies 282
   endurance walk 254–255
   lifetime employment 76
   management in the U.S. 25–27
   negotiation case 79
   open communication 218
   organizational structure 437–439
   rewards 158
   socializing new employees
      253–255
   tardiness 158
   values of 74–76
   worker compared to U.S. 27
Job characteristics 167–168, 170–171
   (also see job enrichment)
   model 167–168, 170–171
   stress 299
Job design 166–177
   (also see job enrichment)
   group approaches 174–177, 251–253
   social influences 169–170
Job enrichment 167–174
   autonomy 171
   benefits 173–174
   feedback from the job 170
   growth need strength 169
   Hackman-Oldham job
      characteristics model 168
   how to 171–174
   identifying unenriched jobs 171
   implementing concepts 171–172
   managerial applications of
      187–188
   self-help guide 174
   task identity 170
   task significance 170
Job performance 71, 111
Job satisfaction 70–71
   changes in 71
   job enrichment 173–174
   scale 70
   trends 71

Job sharing 487
Johnson & Johnson 32

Kepner-Tregoe method 345
Knowledge-based pay 156

Laboratory experiments 17
Lanoga Corp. 231–232
LEADER MATCH 389
Leaders versus managers 376
Leadership 374–397
   behavior approach 381–385
   Blake and Mouton's Managerial
      Grid 383–385
   charismatic 381
   culture 395–396
   female 393
   Fiedler's contingency model
      385–388
   Hersey-Blanchard model 388–390
   managerial applications of 397
   Ohio state studies 381–382
   path-goal theory 390–393
   power 380
   situational approaches 385–393
   social exchange 379–381
   summary of findings 394
   trait approach 377–379
   transactional 380
   versus managers 376
   Vroom-Yetton decision model
      355–358
Learning processes 13
Least preferred coworker scale
   385–386
Left-brain, right-brain 40, 348–350
Legitimate power 318
Levi Strauss, USA
Lincoln Electric Company 162
Life development stages 42–43
Lifetime employment 75–76
Line and staff 423–424
Linking 429
Listening 208–213
   active 210–211
   ego states 209–210
   informational listening 212–213
   interpersonal 209–212
   problem-ownership model 210–212
   process 209
Liz Claiborne 32
Locke's theory of goal setting 178

Lockheed Corp. 310
Locus of control 51

Management by objectives (MBO)
   180–182
Management by wandering around
   208
Managerial behavior 7–9
Managerial effectiveness 10
Managerial Grid 383–385
Managerial myopia 97
Managerial succession 450
Managing
   behavior 139–157
   change 447–460
   crisis 235
   groups 250–253
   impressions 97–98
   objectives 180–182
   stress 270–275
   reinforcement 143–151
   stress 302–305
   teams 250–253
   versus leading 376
Maslow's Need Hierarchy Theory
   113–115
Matrix organization 435–436
Maturity, of followers 389–390
Maytag 141
McKinsey & Co. 337
Merck 32
Merit pay 154
Metropolitan Life Insurance Co. 310
Minnesota Mining and
   Manufacturing Corp. 476
Moog Inc. 7
Motivation 110–128
   Alderfer's ERG theory 115–117
   capacity 111–112
   choosing a strategy 184–185
   cross-cultural applicability
      128–130
   directing behavior 118–123
   effects of social influences 117–118,
      122
   energizing behavior 112–118
   environment 112
   equity theory 126–128
   expectancy theory 119–122
   goal setting 122–123, 178–183
   Herzberg's motivation-hygiene
      theory 124–125
   impossibility of 114

job design 166–177
Maslow's need hierarchy theory
    113–115
managerial applications of
    130–131
motivators 124–125
needs 112–117
opportunity 112
organizational climate 185
performance 111–112
rewards 123–128, 144–145, 148–151,
    154–158
social influences 117–118, 122
sustaining behavior 123–128
valence 119
Motivation-Hygiene Theory 124–125
Motivators 124
Motives 48–50, 317
    achievement 48
    affiliation 48
    power 48, 317
Mountain Bell 476
Moving, and change 455–457

NASA 369–370
National Bank of North America 310
Natural observation 15–16
Needs
    achievement 48
    affiliation 48
    Alderfer's ERG theory 115–116
    frustration-regression 116
    Maslow's hierarchy 113–115
    power 48, 317
    self-actualization 113
    theories 113–116
Negative reinforcement 145–146
Negativism 45
Negotiation 279, 281–282
Neurotic organization 52
New United Motor Manufacturing
    Inc. 4, 26
Nominal group technique 362–363
Nonverbal
    communication 213–218
    cues 91
    impressions 100–101
    signals of power 324
Norms
    changing norms 242–243
    group 239–243
    job design 176

Northwestern Mutual Life
    Insurance 7
Novelty 87

Object factors in perception 86–87
Objectives, organizational 413–415
Observational research 15–16
Organization 10–11
Organization development 460–467
    action research 461–463
    confrontation meeting 464
    cross-cultural 465
    data gathering techniques 463
    differences 461
    effectiveness of 464–465
Organizational behavior 1–502
    cross-cultural (see cross-cultural
        OB)
    defined 10
    field of 11
    overview of 24
    related to systems theory 23
    research in 14–19
Organizational behavior
    modification 139–157
    avoidance 145–146
    charting 142–143
    contingencies of reinforcement
        140–141, 147
    ethics of 152–154
    examples of 131
    extinction 146
    managerial applications of
        159–160
    organizational 139–157
    positive reinforcement 144
    punishment 144–145
    rules for 151
    schedules of reinforcement
        149–151
    shaping 150
    vicarious reinforcement 150–151
Organizational change 447–460
    attitudes 73–74
    communication 456
    equilibrium 448–449
    expectations 457
    force-field analysis 454–455
    goals 455–456
    managerial applications of
        467–468
    moving 455–457

norms 242–243
power 453
participation 453–454
predicting success 452
process 449
resistance to 451–454
rewards 454, 458–459
systems perspective 447–448
transition management 456–457
unfreezing 450–454
when a new manager takes charge
    450
Organizational climate 480–481
    and motivation 185
Organizational commitment 72
Organizational culture
    assumptions 475–477
    defined 13, 475
    excellence 476
    heroes 479–480
    managerial applications of
        494–495
    rites 477–479
    Type Z 482–484
    values 477
Organizational design 410–440
    environment 415–419
    managerial applications of
        439–440
    objectives 413–415
    purpose 412–413
    structure 419–439 (also see
        organizational structure)
Organizational effectiveness criteria
    14
Organizational environment 415–419
Organizational impression
    management 101
Organizational objectives 413–415
Organizational politics 326–333
    change 453
    coalition 329
    compared with power 327
    cooptation 320
    coup d'etat 330
    defined 326
    ethics of 331–333
    managerial application of 335–336
    positive skills 327
    tactics 328–331
Organizational processes 13
Organizational purpose 412–413

Organizational socialization 247–249
  expectations 248
  group development 249–250
  realistic job previews 248–249
  reality shock 247–249
Organizational structure 12, 419–440
  (also see organizational design)
  bureaucratic 430
  centralization 426–427
  coordination 427–429
  decentralization 426–427
  functional 425, 430
  flat 422
  horizontal division of labor
    424–429
  hybrid 433
  integration 427–429
  Japanese 437–439
  line and staff 423–424, 425
  matrix 435–436
  product 425, 433
  sociotechnical 185–187, 429
  skunkworks 431
  span of management 422–423
  staff 425
  tall 422
  types of 430–436
  vertical division of labor 420–424
Organizations of the future 489–490

Participant observers 15–16
Participation
  change 453–454
  decision making 353–358
  stress 304
  Vroom-Yetton model 355–358
Paternalism 75
Path-goal theory 390–393
Pay (also see rewards)
  commissions 156–157
  contract fees 490
  gainsharing 155
  incentive pay 154–155
  knowledge-based 156
  Lincoln Electric Company case
    162
  merit, 154–155
  piece-rate 51, 155–156
  wages and salaries 154–155
People's Republic of China 281–282,
  333–335
Perception 85–92
  attribution theory 92–94

defined 86
  expectations 89–91
  halo effect 95–96
  impression management 97–101
  managerial applications 103–104
  managerial myopia 97
  object factors 86–87
  organization 91
  person factors 88–90
  process 85–86
  selective 85–86
  self-fulfilling prophecy 91
  situation factors 90–92
  stereotyping 94–95
  symbols and drama 89
  time 103
Performance
  appraisal 96, 101–102
  capacity 111
  environment 112
  opportunity 112
Person factors in perception 88–90
Personality 38–46
  AT&T management progress study
    49–50
  behavior 47–51
  characteristics of general
    managers 49
  defined 39
  development 41–43
  French versus American 52–53
  heredity 41
  left-brain, right-brain 40
  locus of control 51
  managerial applications 53–54
  motives 48–49
  neurotic organization 52
  organizations 46
  psychological defenses 45
  role playing 46
  self-concept 43–45
  self esteem 43
  situation 40
  stability 41
Philip Morris 338
Physical environment 217–218, 487
Physio-Control 7
Piece-rate pay 51, 155–156
Pitney Bowes 7
Pittsburgh Steel Co. 436
Political tactics 327–331
Politics 326–333 (see organizational
  politics)

Positive reinforcement 144
Power 314–336, 380
  assessing 319–320
  balancing 323–324
  change 453
  corporate 321
  coercive 317
  cross-cultural 333–335
  distance 334, 465, 491–492
  ethics of 331–333
  expert 318
  leadership 380, 386
  legitimate 318
  lower-level participants 324–325
  managerial applications of 335
  motivation 48, 317
  motive 48, 317
  need for 48, 317
  nonverbal signals 324
  position power 386
  process model 325
  referent 318–319
  reward 317
  social exchange 380
  sources of 315–319
  strategies 319–326
  tactics 319–322
  using 319–324
  zone of acceptance 323
Preparatory set 89
Probabilities in decision making
  347–358
Problem solving 343–345 (see also
  decision making)
Problem-ownership model 210–211
Processes 13
Proctor & Gamble 7, 177
Product departments 425
Product organization 433
Projection 45
Proximity 87
Psychological self defense 45
Psychological states 168
Punishment 144–145
Purpose, organizational 412–413

Quad/Graphics 7
Qualitative research 15–16
Quality circles 459
Quality of work life 484–488,
  490–493
  activities 486–487
  criteria for 485–486

cultural relativity 490–493
defined 485
diffusion of innovations 488–489
individualism-collectivism 491–492
managerial applications 494–495
Questionnaires 69

Rainier National Bank 20
Rationalization 45
Raychem Corp. 7
Realistic job previews 248–249
Referent power 318
Refreezing, and change 458
Reinforcement
    contingencies of 140–141
    negative 145–146
    positive 144
    schedules of 149–151
    vicarious 150–151
Reinventing the corporation 489
Repression 45
Research 14–19
    evaluation of 18–19
    experimental 17–18
    natural observation 15–16
    qualitative 15–16
    survey 16–17
Resistance to change 451–454
Reward power 317
Rewards
    change 454, 458
    extrinsic 123
    intrinsic 123
    motivation 123–128
    pay 154–157
    positive reinforcement 144–145,
        148–151
    power 317
    quality of work life 488
    targeting desired behaviors 126,
        141–143
    U.S. versus Japan 158
Right-brain decisions 348
Rites and ceremonies 477–479
Rokeach value survey 62
Roles
    ambiguity 267, 302
    analysis technique 305
    blocking 239
    clarification 305
    confliict 46, 267, 300, 302
    group 236–239
    maintenance 238–239

relationship to personality 46–47
stress 300
task 237–238
women 47
Rubbermaid 32
Rule of 100, 425

S.C. Johnson 7
S-O-B-C Model 139–140
Salience 88–89
Satisficing 345
Schedules of reinforcement 149–151
Schmoozing 245
Selection, in perception 90–91
Selective perception 85–86
Self actualization 113
Self-concept 43–45
    in perception 88
Self esteem 43–44
Self-fulfilling prophecy 91, 102–103
Self-fulfilling stereotype 95
Self-managing work groups 175–177,
    251–253
Shakey's Pizza 20
Shaping 150
Shell Oil 32
Shenandoah Life Insurance Co. 177
Shift work 303
Similarity 91
Situation factors in perception 90–92
Situational approaches to leadership
    385–393
Skills needed by managers 10
Skills of leaders 378
Skill variety 170
Skunkworks 431
Social bonds, and change 459
Social cues 169
Social exchange 379–381
Social influences
    energize motivation 117–118
    valence 122
    job design 169–170
    leadership 379–381
Social loafing 245
Social networks 235
Social orientation 128–129
Socialization 247–249, 253–255
Sociotechnical
    design 429
    systems 185–187
Span of management 422–423

Staff 423–425
State Street Investment Corporation
    338
Status, in groups 243–244
Stereotyping 94–96
Stress 290–309
    acute episodic 301
    air traffic controllers 301
    burnout 297–298
    coping methods 303–305
    cross-cultural study of 305–308
    health effects 292
    impact of events 293
    individual differences 295
    job characteristics 299
    management of 302–305, 308–309
    mergers 296
    nature of 291–297
    performance 294–295
    role 300, 302
    shift work 303
    sources of 298–303
    symptoms of 292
    Type A and B behavior 295–297
    women managers 299
Succession, managerial 450
Superordinate goals 280
Survey research 16–17
Sweden
    motivation 128
    sociotechnical concepts 185–187
Symbols and drama 90
Systems, organizational 19–24
Systems perspective, and change
    447–448

Tall organizations 422
Tandem Computers 13
Tardiness 157–159
Targeting 126, 141–143
Task forces 240
Task identity 170
Task significance 170
Teambuilding 251
Teams, management of 250–253, 384
Technology, and environment
    416–417
Tektronix Inc. 175
Thailand, motivation 129
Theory X and Y 64–67
Theory Z 483–484
Third party conflict resolution
    274–275

Time Inc. 7, 32
Time perceptions 103
Topeka Pet Food Project 177
Toyota 26, 27
Traits of leaders 377–379
Trammell Crow 7
Transactional analysis 202–208
    adult bossing style 207
    applications in organizations
        207–208
    complementary transactions
        204–205
    crossed transactions 205–206
    ulterior transactions 206–207
    ego states 202–203, 210
Transactional leadership 380
Transition management 456–457
Tupperware 145
Type A behavior pattern 295–297
Type A organizations 482
Type J organizations 482
Type Z organizations 482–484

Ulterior transactions 206–207
U.S. Civil Service 207
Uncertainty-avoidance 465
Unfreezing, and change 450–454
United Rubber Workers 310

Valence 119
Values
    air traffic controller strike 67
    changes in 61–64
    conflicts 66–68
    ethics 64
    Japanese 74–76
    management of 77
    organizational culture 475–477
    perception 88
    programming 61
    Rokeach value survey 62
    Theory X and Y 64–67
Variable 16
Variable interval schedule 149, 150
Variable ratio schedule 149, 150

Verbal impressions 100–101
Vertical division of labor 420
Vicarious reinforcement 150–151
Volvo 185–187
Vroom-Yetton model 355–358

Wages and salaries 154
Win-lose model 277–278
Win-win negotiation 279
Withdrawal 45
Women
    barriers to advancement 47
    leadership 393
    organizational structure 436
    stress 299
Work motivation 110–128 (see
    motivation)

Xerox Company 90

Zenith 141
Zone of acceptance 323

Author Index

Abegglen, J.C. 442
Aburdene, P. 502
Adams, J.S. 135
Agor, W.H. 57, 349, 371
Al-Jafary, A. 372
Albano, C. 204
Aldag, R.J. 191, 312
Alderfer, C.P. 113, 115, 135, 471
Alexander, R.A. 403
Allen, R.D. 311
Allen, R.F. 242, 501
Allen, R.W. 328, 339, 340
Alliger, G.M. 403
Alutto, J.A. 312
Andre de la Porte, P.C. 243
Angle, H.L. 340
Arbose, J. 306, 307, 312
Archer, D. 340
Argyris, C. 33, 46, 58
Ariss, S.S. 340
Armenakis, A.A. 472
Arogyaswamy, B. 158
Arpan, S. 405
Arvey, R.D. 108, 163
Asher, S.M. 262
Ashforth, B.E. 501
Astley, W.G. 339
Aterborg, J.R. 58
Athos, A.G. 82, 442, 499
Atkinson, J.W. 58
Austin, N. 15, 33, 89, 107, 225, 443, 444, 499, 501
Axley, S.R. 224
Azumi, K. 472, 502

Babb, H.W. 163
Babladelis, G. 58
Baetz, M.L. 403
Baig, E.C. 32
Baker, M. 225
Ball-Rokeach, S.J. 80
Baltes, P.B. 57
Barker, L.L. 225
Barnard, C.I. 340
Barnes, L.B. 501
Barney, J.B. 499
Baron, R.A. 57
Barrow, J.C. 403
Basadur, M. 361, 372
Bass, B.M. 403, 404, 405
Bateman, T.S. 81
Baum, C.S. 312
Bavelas, J.R. 58
Bear, J. 225
Beard, D.W. 443
Beckhard, R. 457, 471, 472
Bedeian, A.G. 183, 472
Bednar, D.A. 192
Beehr, T.A. 163, 311
Beer, M. 471, 472, 501
Bell, C.H., Jr. 135, 183, 261, 312, 461, 470, 472, 502
Bellus, D. 224
Bem, D.J. 81
Benfari, R.C. 339
Benne, K.D. 237, 260
Bennett, A. 164, 502
Benson, H. 311, 312
Berg, D.N. 472

Berg, P.O. 472
Berger, C.J. 443, 444
Berger, M. 340
Berkowitz, L. 135
Berlinger, L.R. 191
Bernardin, H.J. 107
Berne, E. 224, 225
Beutell, N.J. 286
Beyer, J.M. 163, 478, 499, 501
Billings, R.S. 261
Biondi, A.M. 372
Birnbaum, G. 370
Blackburn, R.S. 443
Blake, R.R. 286, 287, 384, 404, 405, 460
Blanchard, K.H. 389, 404, 405
Block, P. 327, 340
Blood, M.R. 261
Bluestone, I. 501
Boje, D.M. 405, 444
Boot, R. 340
Borger, D.W. 470
Bortner, R.W. 296
Bowen, D.D. 225
Bowers, D.B. 80, 312
Boyatzis, R.E. 58
Bradford, D.L. 261
Brass, D.J. 191
Braum, A. 312
Bray, D.W. 379, 380, 404
Breaugh, J.A. 261
Bridges, W. 471
Bridwell, L.G. 134
Brief, A.P. 191, 298, 312

525

Brim, O.G., Jr. 57
Brockner, J. 58, 370
Brody, M. 80, 370
Broverman, D.M. 58
Broverman, I. 58
Brown, B. 261
Brown, D.L. 286
Brown, R.V. 371
Brownwell, J. 225
Bruning, N.S. 312
Buck, R. 108
Buckley, M.R. 107
Buhrmester, D. 312
Burden, L. 382
Burke, R.J. 274
Burke, W.W. 472
Burnham, D.H. 58, 339
Burris, R.W. 32
Buss, D.D. 444
Butterfield, D.A. 501
Buxton, V.M. 501
Byham, W.C. 403

Cameron, K.S. 10
Campbell, D.T. 33
Campbell, J.P. 403, 501
Campbell, R.J. 380, 404
Campion, J.E. 108
Campion, M.A. 191
Cantor, M.G. 161
Capwell, D.F. 81
Carnegie, D. 99, 108
Carrell, M.R. 135
Carson, K.P. 403
Cartwright, D. 260, 261, 339
Cascio, W.F. 261, 404
Cash, T.F. 108
Cavanagh, G.F. 332, 337, 340
Cavender, J.W. 81
Cederblom, D. 108
Cheatham, T.R. 224
Chemers, M.M. 404
Cherns, A.B. 501
Cherrington, D.J. 80
Cherrington, J.O. 80
Cheston, R. 274
Child, J. 431, 444
Chusmir, L.H. 311
Clark, R.A. 58
Clarkson, F.E. 58
Clegg, C.W. 192
Cobb, A.T. 339
Coch, L. 471

Cohen, A.R. 191, 261
Cohen, D. 371
Cook, T.D. 33
Cooper, C.L. 298, 306, 307, 312
Cooper, M.R. 81
Cooper, W.H. 107
Copeland, L. 225
Cosier, R.A. 135, 287
Costa, P.T., Jr. 57
Costello, T.W. 45
Cotton, J.L. 17, 81
Couture, D. 371, 499
Cowan, D.A. 370
Cox, C.E. 108
Craft, R.E., Jr. 81
Crary, M. 260
Crozier, M. 339
Cummings, L.L. 32, 33, 199, 287, 340,
    404, 443, 444
Cummings, T.G. 191, 192, 472
Cunningham, D.A. 312
Curtice, H.H. 444

D'Aprix, R. 221, 224
Dabbs, J.M., Jr. 33
Daft, R.L. 199, 224, 418, 429, 431, 432,
    433, 436, 442, 443, 444
Dalky, N.C. 372
Dalton, D.R. 135, 443
Dalton, M. 161
Daniel, T.L. 135
Darley, J.M. 107
David, F. 443
Davidson, M.J. 312
Davis, G.A. 163
Davis, K. 200, 224, 261, 443
Davis, L.E. 501
Davis, S.M. 444, 502
Davis, T.R.V. 140, 163
De Vader, C.L. 403
Deal, T.E. 32, 499, 501
Dean, J.W., Jr. 191, 472, 502
Deci, E.L. 135
Delaney, W.A. 224
Delbecq, A.L. 363–364, 372
Dempsey, B.L. 340
Denny, A.T. 192
Deresky, H. 404
Dess, G.G. 443
Deutsch, M. 287
Devries, D. 163
Dewar, R.D. 443
Diamond, E.L. 311

Dienesch, R.M. 404
Dietcher, J. 370
Dinnitto, D. 58
Dipboye, R.L. 107, 108
DiStefano, T. 286
Dittrich, J.B. 135
Dobbins, G.H. 405
Donnell, S.M. 405
Donnelly, J.H., Jr. 444
Dowd, A.R. 371
Downey, H.K. 81
Doyle, R.J. 164
Drake, M.F. 108
Drasgow, F. 191
Dresner, B. 444
Drexler, J.A. 501
Driscoll, J.W. 502
Droge, C. 58
Drucker, P.F. 15, 33, 82, 192, 443
Dubin, R. 32
Dubrin, A. 339
Dukerich, J.M. 403
Dunca, K.D. 192
Duncan, R.B. 33, 443, 471
Dunnette, M.D. 33, 57, 81, 224, 260,
    286, 311, 370, 403, 471, 501
Dyer, W.G. 261, 450, 472

Easterby-Smith, M. 340
Ebbesen, E.B. 81
Eden, D. 107, 471
Edinger, J.A. 108, 225
Ehrlich, S.B. 403
Eisenberg, E.M. 225
Eisenhart, K.M. 107
Ekman, P. 225
Ellsworth, P.C. 107
Emory, C.W. 33
Epstein, C.F. 260
Ernst, F.H., Jr. 210
Esser, J.K. 135
Estes, R.W. 371
Etzion, D. 311
Evans, M.G. 405
Ewing, D.W. 80

Falkenberg, L.E. 312
Farr, J.L. 107
Fast, J. 340
Faulkner, R.R. 33
Fay, C.H. 164
Fazio, R.H. 107

Feather, N. 135
Feldman, D.C. 260, 261
Feren, D.B. 192
Ferris, G.R. 191
Festinger, L. 81, 287
Fidler, L.A. 224
Fiedler, F.E. 385, 387, 388, 404
Fielding, G.J. 443
Filley, A.C. 271, 286
Finkbeiner, C.T. 361, 372
Finkle, R.B. 403
Fischer, D. 224
Fischman, J. 311
Fisher, A.B. 108
Fisher, G. 287
Fisher, R.J. 279, 286, 287
Fitch, H.G. 163
Fitzgerald, M.P. 191
Foley, P.M. 81
Forbes, J.B. 312
Ford, C.H. 192
Ford, R.N. 191
Fordyce, J.K. 471, 472
Forsythe, S. 108
Fraser, N.M. 286
Frease, M. 502
Fredericksen, W. 163
French, J.R.P., Jr. 339, 471
French, W.L. 261, 312, 461, 470, 472,
    502
Frew, D.R. 312
Fried, Y. 191
Friedman, D.J. 371, 499
Friedman, M. 296, 311
Friesen, W.V. 225
Frohman, M.A. 472
Fromkin, H.L. 33
Fry, F.L. 163
Fu, M.Y.C. 405
Fudge, D.A. 312
Fulk, J. 405
Fuller, S.J. 501

Gabarro, J.J. 450, 471
Gadon, H. 191
Gaines, J. 311
Galbraith, J.R. 443
Ganster, D.C. 312
Gantz, J. 329
Garcia, J.E. 404
Gardner, J.W. 399
Gardner, W.L. 108
Geneen, H. 15, 33

Gershenfeld, M.K. 260
Gerstein, M.S. 443
Gilbert, J.P. 33
Gillespie, D.F. 443
Gladstein, D.L. 230
Glaser, E.M. 502
Glick, W.H. 191
Golberg, M.H. 164
Goldhaber, G.M. 225
Goldstein, S.G. 472
Goleman, D. 312
Goodman, P.S. 135, 502
Gordon, F.E. 260
Gordon, T. 81, 211, 225, 287
Gough, H. 57
Govindarajan, V. 444
Grady, J.F., Jr. 502
Graeff, C.L. 405
Graen, G. 58, 260
Grant, D.L. 380, 404
Gray, B. 340, 372, 471
Gray, J.L. 258, 285, 287, 421, 443
Greene, C.N. 81
Greenhaus, J.H. 286
Greensburg, P.D. 502
Greenwood, R. 443
Greenwood, R.G. 192
Greer, C.R. 311
Greller, M.M. 201, 224
Griffeth, R.W. 261
Griffin, R.W. 191
Griggs, L. 225
Grimes, A.J. 339
Grove, A.S. 286, 287
Grube, J.W. 80
Guare, J. 58
Guest, R.H. 501
Gumpert, R. 405
Gupta, N. 191
Gustafson, D.H. 363–364
Gyllenhammer, P.G. 185–186, 192, 501

Hackett, E.J. 502
Hackman, J.R. 70, 135, 168, 190, 191,
    192, 235, 260, 261, 443, 501
Hailey, A. 132
Hall, D.T. 108
Hall, J. 372, 405
Hambelton, R.K. 405
Hamner, E.P. 163
Hamner, W.C. 135, 163, 164
Handy, C. 502
Hare, A.P. 260

Harkins, S. 261
Harlan, A. 135
Harper, M.B. 225
Harris, P.R. 58, 82, 499, 501
Harris, R.T. 457, 471
Harrison, D. 58
Harrison, R.P. 215–216
Hartman, E.A. 311
Hasset, J. 80
Hastorf, A.H. 107
Hatfield, J.D. 135
Hatvany, N. 82, 225
Hay, T.M. 372, 471
Hayes, R.S. 163
Hebden, J.E. 261
Heenan, D.A. 472
Heider, F. 107
Heilbroner, A. 370
Heilman, M.E. 404
Hellriegel, D. 12, 81, 167, 171, 190, 191,
    192, 448
Hemming, H. 312
Hennessey, H.W. 32, 286
Henrick, H.W. 372
Herbert, T.T. 371, 404
Herold, D.M. 201, 224
Hersey, P. 389, 404, 405
Herzberg, F. 81, 124, 125, 135, 191
Hickson, D. 164
Hill, G.W. 352, 371
Hinckley, S.R., Jr. 371
Hinings, B. 443
Hipel, K.W. 286
Hitt, M.A. 311, 499
Hofstede, G. 129, 135, 334, 340, 472,
    492, 502
Hogan, E.A. 108
Hogarth, R.M. 371
Holahan, C.J. 502
Hollander, E.A. 404
Hollander, E.P. 260, 261
Hollenbeck, J.R. 192
Holliman, C.R. 372
Hollingsworth, A.T. 372
Holmes, T.H. 293
Holzbach, R.L. 107
Hom, P.W. 261
Homans, G.C. 404
Hood, J.N. 311
Hopkins, B.L. 163
Hornstein, H.A. 404
Hosking, D. 9, 404
House, R.J. 135, 403, 404, 405

Houser, R. 370
Houston, B.K. 311
Howard, J.H. 312
Howe, L.W. 80
Huber, G.P. 370
Hull, F. 472, 502
Hunsaker, J. 58
Hunsaker, P. 58
Hunt, J.G. 9, 404
Hunt, J.W. 135
Hunter, J.E. 134
Hurlock, E.B. 41
Huse, E.F. 472
Huseman, R.C. 135

Iacocca, L. 4, 15, 32, 33, 155, 337–339, 441–442
Idaszak, J.R. 191
Indvik, J. 405
Ingle, S. 472
Ireland, R.D. 499
Ivancevich, J.M. 163, 292, 311, 312, 444
Iyer, H. 57

Jablonsky, S. 163
Jackson, P.R. 192
Jackson, S.E. 312
Jacobs, T.O. 404
Jaeger, A.M. 472, 482, 501
Jago, A.G. 371, 404
Jamal, M. 311
James, L.R. 501
James, M. 224, 225
Janda, L.H. 108
Janis, I. 351, 371
Janson, R. 191
Jelinek, M. 443
Jemison, D.B. 443
Jenkins, G.D. 191
Jennings, E.E. 339
Jensen, M.A.C. 247, 261
Jermier, J.M. 311
Jewell, L.N. 261
Jobs, S. 5, 32
Johnson, C.M. 163
Johnson, D.W. 276
Johnson, J.D. 224
Johnson, R. 276
Joiner, C.W. 501
Jones, A.P. 501
Jones, E.E. 108

Jones, E.W., Jr. 107
Jones, R.A. 107
Jongeward, D. 224
Jonsson, B. 192
Joyce, W.F. 444
Jucker, J.V. 107
Jurkovich, R. 443

Kahn, R.L. 286, 312, 471
Kakabadse, A. 339
Kanter, R.M. 323, 340, 471
Kaplan, L.B. 81
Kapp, R.A. 287
Karmel, B. 163, 403
Kast, F.E. 21, 32, 33, 80, 403, 413
Katz, D. 471
Katz, M. 32
Kavanagh, M.J. 472
Kelley, H.H. 107
Kemp, N.J. 192
Kempen, R.W. 163
Kennedy, A.A. 32, 499, 501
Kepner, C.H. 370
Kerr, J. 501
Kerr, S. 126, 135, 339, 383, 404
Kets de Vries, M.F.R. 58
Keys, J.B. 82
Kilmann, R.H. 162, 472, 499, 501
Kimberly, J.R. 471, 502
King, A.S. 471
Kipnis, D. 108, 339, 340
Kirschenbaum, H. 80
Klein, H.J. 192
Klimoski, R.S. 404
Kneale, D. 32
Knowles, H.P. 80
Kolodny, H.F. 444, 501
Kondrasuk, J.N. 192
Koontz, H. 423, 443, 444
Kopp, D.G. 163
Korda, M. 340
Kotter, J.P. 32, 49, 58, 339
Kover, A.J. 410, 442
Krackhardt, D. 260
Krant, A. 396
Kreitner, R. 143, 163

LaFrance, M. 225
Landy, F.J. 107
Langseth, P. 471
Larson, J.R., Jr. 192
Larson, L.L. 404

Larwood, L. 108
Latane, B. 261
Latham, G.P. 32, 164, 179, 192, 371
Lawler, E.E., III 81, 135, 164, 235, 403, 471, 501, 502
Lawrence, P.R. 444
Leana, C.R. 371
Leavitt, H.J. 371, 405, 444
Ledford, G.E., Jr. 164
Lee, J.A. 471
Lee, S.M. 225
Leitko, T.A. 472
Lengel, R.H. 199
Lenwick, P.A. 328
Levering, R. 32
Levin, D.P. 444
Levine, M.W. 107
Levine, R.A. 57, 108
Levinson, D.J. 42, 57
Levinson, H. 57, 311, 312
Levy, A. 471
Levy, J. 57
Lewicki, P. 107
Lewicki, R.J. 286
Lewin, K. 449, 460, 471
Ley, M. 339
Liden, R.C. 192, 404
Liebowitz, S.J. 472
Likert, J.G. 286
Likert, R. 260
Lincoln, J.R. 260
Linsay, C.P. 340
Linsenmeier, J.A.W. 108
Lipman-Blumen, J. 393, 405, 444
Lippit, G.L. 471
Litterer, J.A. 286, 443
Lloyd, K. 370
Locke, E.A. 32, 82, 135, 163, 179, 185, 192, 325, 339, 340, 371
Lockwood, D.L. 9
Loher, B.T. 191
Lord, R.G. 107, 403, 404
Lorsch, J.W. 443, 444
Louis, M.B. 261
Lowell, E.L. 58
Lowenstein, R. 80
Luft, J. 260
Luthans, F. 9, 32, 140, 143, 147, 163, 286, 392

Maccrimmon, K.R. 370, 372
Macholowitz, M.M. 135
Macy, B. 192

Maddi, S.R. 57
Madison, D.L. 328, 340
Magne, M. 311
Mahr, L. 404
Maier, N.F. 371
Main, J. 225
Mainiero, L.A. 340
Malatesta, C.Z. 261
Malik, S.D. 250, 261
Manning, M.R. 311
Manuso, J. 292
Manz, C.C. 163, 261, 444
March, J.G. 370, 371
Mares, W.J. 501
Marks, M.L. 502
Marshall, E. 499
Marshall, J. 298
Marshland, S. 501
Martin, H.J. 162
Martin, J. 371
Martin, J.E. 164
Martin, P.Y. 58
Martinko, M.J. 108
Maruyama, G. 276
Maslach, C. 81
Maslow, A.H. 113, 115, 134
Massey, M.E. 63, 80
Matteson, M.T. 292, 311, 312
Matthews, K.A. 311
Maurer, J.G. 340
Mausner, B. 81, 135
Mayes, B.T. 312, 328, 340
Mayo, C. 225
McCaleb, V.M. 192
McCann, J. 443
McCaskey, M.B. 471
McCauley, C. 107
McClelland, D.C. 48, 58, 317, 339
McConkie, M.L. 192
McCormack, M.H. 354, 371
McCrae, R.R. 57
McCune, J.T. 81
McEvoy, G.M. 261
McGee, G.W. 81
McGrath, J.E. 311
McGregor, D. 64, 65, 80, 261, 460
Mead, M. 395
Megginson, L.C. 224
Mehrabian, A. 225
Meier, S.T. 311
Meindl, J.R. 403
Melcher, A.J. 158
Merton, R.K. 107

Metzcub, R. 382
Meuse, K.P. 472
Michela, J.L. 107
Miles, E.W. 135
Miles, R.E. 443, 502
Mileti, D.S. 443
Miller, D. 58
Miller, J. 260
Miller, K.I. 371
Miller, L.M. 144
Miller, T.R. 82, 134
Miner, J. 134
Miner, J.B. 403
Mintzberg, H. 370, 371, 442
Mirman, R. 163
Mirvis, P.H. 472, 502
Mitchell, R. 32
Mitchell, T.R. 33, 134, 135, 183, 192, 261, 405
Moberg, D.J. 332, 337, 340
Mobley, W.H. 81
Moeller, N.L. 191
Mohrman, S.A. 471
Molloy, J.T. 99, 100, 108
Mone, E. 404
Monge, P.R. 371
Moore, T. 58
Moorhead, G. 191
Moran, R.T. 58, 82, 499, 501
Morgan, B.S. 81
Morris, J.H. 224, 225
Morrow, P.C. 81
Moskowitz, M. 32
Moss, L. 311
Moss, P. 499
Mossop, J. 471
Motowidlo, S.J. 311
Mouton, J.S. 286, 287, 384, 404, 405
Mowday, R.T. 81, 135, 340
Muna, F. 365, 372
Munchus, G., III 472
Murphy, C.J. 383, 404
Murray, H. 379
Murray, J.V. 369, 470
Murray, V.V. 329
Musselwhite, E. 225

Nadler, D.A. 135, 235, 471, 472, 501, 502
Naisbitt, J. 489, 502
Nakane, C. 81, 82
Napier, R.W. 260
Narayanan, V.K. 191

Nath, R.A. 191, 225
Nathanson, S. 370
Nelson, D. 276
Nelson, D.L. 81, 312
Nelson, S.M. 163
Newman, J.E. 311
Nicholas, J.M. 472
Nichols, R.G. 225
Noe, R.A. 191
Noller, R.B. 372
Nonaka, I. 438, 444
Nugent, P.S. 57
Nutt, P.C. 471
Nye, R.D. 286
Nystrom, P.C. 442, 443

O'Donnell, C. 444
O'Hara, K. 163
O'Toole, J. 502
Odiorne, G.S. 192, 471
Okumura, A. 438, 444
Oldham, G.R. 70, 168, 191, 260, 261, 443
Olsen, J.P. 371
Organ, D.W. 81
Ornstein, R.E. 57, 371
Orth, C.D. 339
Osborne, A.F. 372
Oshry, B. 502
Otsubo, M. 437, 444
Otten, A.L. 80
Ouchi, W.G. 82, 443, 482, 484, 499, 501

Packard, J.S. 311
Parasuraman, S. 312
Parker, C. 339
Parkington, J.J. 501
Parks, K.R. 312
Parmerlee, M. 163
Parnes, S.J. 372
Pascale, R.T. 82, 442, 499
Passmore, W.A. 192
Patterson, M.L. 108, 225
Paulus, P.B. 312
Pava, C. 502
Payne, R. 32
Pearce, J.A., II 443
Pearce, J.L. 286
Peele, S. 57
Peponis, J. 502
Perkins, D.N.T. 501

Perlman, B. 311
Perlmutter, H.V. 472
Pervin, L.A. 58
Peters, M. 472
Peters, R.K. 312
Peters, T. 15, 33, 89, 107, 145, 163, 225, 240, 260, 372, 425, 443, 444, 474, 476, 499, 501
Peterson, M.E. 164
Peterson, R.O. 81
Petre, P. 32, 471
Pettigew, A.W. 32, 499
Petty, M.M. 81
Pfeffer, J. 13, 134, 191, 339, 340, 403
Phares, E.J. 58
Phillips, E. 274
Pickhardt, C.E. 502
Piercy, J.E. 312
Pilnick, S. 242
Pinder, C.C. 12
Pine, R.C. 163
Pinfield, L.T. 370
Pittner, M.S. 311
Platz, S.J. 405
Podsakoff, P.M. 81, 339
Ponds, S.B., III 472
Pondy, L.R. 405, 444
Popovich, P. 261
Porras, J.I. 472
Porter, L.W. 81, 107, 134, 135, 224, 328, 339, 340, 443
Pottick, K.L. 312
Powell, G.N. 501
Premack, S.L. 261
Preston, C. 311
Price, K. 108
Price, M. 58
Price, R.A. 57
Pucik, V. 82, 225
Pugh, D.S. 32
Purdy, K. 191
Pye, L.W. 108, 287

Quick, J.C. 81, 294, 311, 312
Quick, J.D. 294, 311
Quinn, R.E. 58, 471
Quinn, R.P. 286, 312

Ragan, J.W. 372, 404
Rahe, R.H. 293
Raia, A.P. 181
Ralston, D.A. 108

Randall, L.K. 225
Randolph, W.A. 443
Ranson, S. 443
Rauschenberger, J. 134
Raven, B. 339
Rechers, A.E. 250, 261
Reeder, G.D. 107
Reibstein, L. 261
Reich, R.B. 501
Reichers, A.E. 81, 501
Reichman, W. 339
Reilly, R.R. 261
Reitz, H.J. 261
Renwick, P.A. 340
Rhodes, S.R. 81
Rice, B. 57, 372, 404
Ricks, D.A. 405
Robbins, S.P. 268, 286
Roberts, K.H. 191, 224
Robey, D. 371, 442
Robinson, V. 472
Rodgers, R.C. 191
Rohlen, T.P. 253, 262
Rokeach, M. 62, 80, 81, 499
Ronen, S. 191, 396, 405, 502
Rosenbach, W.E. 191, 399
Rosenberg, H.R. 502
Rosenberg, M. 44, 57
Rosenblatt, S.B. 224
Rosenkrantz, P.S. 58
Rosenkrantz, S.A. 32, 286
Rosenman, R.H. 296, 311
Rosenthal, R.A. 107, 312
Rosenzweig, J.E. 21, 32, 33, 80, 403, 413
Rosenzweig, M. 1107
Ross, J. 370
Rotter, J.B. 50, 51, 58
Rowan, R. 224
Rowe, M.P. 225
Roy, D. 260
Ruben, J.Z. 286, 370
Rubin, D.B. 107
Rubin, D.K. 312
Rubin, Z. 57
Ruble, T.L. 287
Ruch, W.V. 225
Russell, C.J. 404

Saari, L.M. 32
Sachdeva, P.S. 339
Salancik, G.R. 108, 134, 135, 191
Sandberg, W.R. 372

Saporito, B. 471
Sari, L.M. 192
Sasaki, N. 262
Sashkin, M. 371, 472, 502
Sathe, V. 499
Saxberg, B.O. 80
Saxton, M.J. 162, 499, 501
Sayles, L.R. 248
Schein, E.H. 32, 261, 287, 339, 499, 501, 502
Schilit, W.K. 325, 339, 340
Schlenker, B.R. 108
Schlesinger, L.A. 502
Schmidt, N. 81, 134
Schmidt, S. 108
Schmidt, S.M. 339, 340
Schmidt, W. 353
Schmidt, W.H. 286, 405
Schnake, M.E. 163
Schneider, B. 501
Schneider, D.J. 107, 108
Schonberger, R.J. 33
Schoonhoven, C.B. 32
Schrank, R. 261
Schriesheim, C. 339
Schriesheim, C.A. 383, 404, 405
Schriesheim, J. 405
Schuler, R.S. 298, 310, 311, 312
Schuster, M. 164, 287, 502
Schwartz, H.S. 134
Schweiger, D.M. 371, 372
Schwendiman, G. 225
Schwenk, C. 163
Scott, D. 225
Scott, W.E. 33
Scott, W.R. 33
Sears, J. 163
Sease, D.R. 443
Segal, M. 107
Seigiovanni, T.J. 382
Sekaran, U. 58
Seligman, D. 472
Senger, J. 107, 113
Sengoku, T. 81, 164
Serpa, R. 162, 499, 501
Seyle, H. 311
Shaver, P. 312
Shaw, B. 340
Shaw, K.N. 32, 192
Shaw, M.E. 260
Sheats, P. 237, 260
Shefner, J.M. 107
Shepard, H.A. 286

Sheppard, B.H. 286
Sibey, V. 404
Sime, W.E. 312
Simmons, J. 501
Simon, H.A. 370, 371
Simon, S.B. 80
Sims, H.P., Jr. 163, 261, 444
Singer, J.E. 312
Singh, R. 404
Skinner, B.F. 152, 163
Skon, L. 276
Skrypnek, B.J. 107
Sloan, A.P., Jr. 427
Slocum, J.W., Jr. 12, 81, 167, 171, 190, 191, 192, 448, 501
Smiddy, H. 192
Smith, D.E. 108
Smith, F.J. 33
Smith, J.E. 107, 403
Smith, R. 312
Snoek, J.D. 286, 312
Snow, C.C. 502
Snyder, M. 107
Snyder, R.A. 224, 225
Snyderman, B.B. 135
Soelberg, P.O. 371
Solomon, M.R. 108
Solomon, R.H. 340
Sorenson, R.E. 471
Spector, P.E. 58
Spendolini, M.J. 443
Springer, S.P. 57
Srivasta, S. 191, 339
Stacey, M. 58
Staines, G.L. 312
Stalk, G., Jr. 442
Starbuck, W.H. 442, 443
Starke, F.A. 258, 285, 287, 421, 443
Staw, B. 108, 191, 199, 261, 287, 370, 371, 403, 404
Stead, B.A. 286
Steel, F. 472
Steele, F.I. 502
Steers, R.M. 81, 134, 135
Steil, L.K. 225
Steiner, I.D. 232
Stern, R.N. 260
Stevens, L.A. 225
Steward, P.L. 161
Stewart, R. 9
Stitt, C.L. 107, 108
Stjernberg, T. 501
Stogdill, R.M. 135, 261, 383, 403, 404

Stone, E.F. 33
Stostak, A.B. 312
Strasser, S. 81
Streufert, S. 33
Stricktland, W. 404
Strober, M.H. 260
Strube, M.J. 404
Sullivan, J.J. 80, 483, 501
Sulzer-Azaroff, B. 163
Susman, G.I. 192
Sussman, M. 135
Suttle, J.L. 501
Sutton, R.L. 107
Swartz, H. 502
Szczerbacki, D. 472

Taggart, W. 371
Tannenbaum, R. 353, 405
Tartell, R. 404
Taylor, A. 81
Taylor, R.L. 399
Taylor, R.N. 370
Taylor, T.O. 371, 372, 499
Tedechi, J.T. 108
Terborg, J.R. 57
Terkel, S. 55
Tharp, G.D. 312
Thayer, P.W. 191
Thomas, J. 191
Thomas, K. 472
Thomas, K.W. 272, 286
Thompson, J.D. 443
Thornton, G.C. 403
Thurow, L.C. 81
Tiana, K.O. 225
Tichy, N.M. 471
Tjosvold, D. 276
Todor, W.D. 443
Tosi, H.L. 163, 164
Tosi, L. 164
Toulouse, J. 58
Tregoe, B.B. 370
Trice, H.M. 163, 478, 499
Trist, E. 192
Tubbs, M.E. 135, 192
Tuckman, B.W. 247, 261
Tung, R.L. 287, 443
Tuttle, J.M. 17, 81
Twain, M. 18
Tziner, A. 261

Ulvila, J.W. 371
Umstot, D. 106

Umstot, D.D. 135, 167, 171, 183, 190, 191, 192
Urwick, L.F. 443
Ury, W. 279, 287

Vaill, P.B. 502
Van de Ven, A.H. 363–364, 372
Van de Vliert, E. 286
Van Fleet, D.D. 443
Van Maanen, J. 15, 33, 261
Van Sell, M. 298, 310, 312
Vancil, R.F. 444
Vandenberg, S.G. 57
Vandiver, K. 370
Vardi, Y. 261
Vecchio, R.P. 135, 404
Velasques, M. 332, 337, 340
Villere, M.F. 224
Vogel, S.R. 58
Von der Embse, T.J. 369, 470
Vredenburgh, D.J. 340
Vroom, V.H. 135, 355, 357, 358, 365, 371, 405

Wahba, M.A. 134
Wahlstrom, M. 499
Walker, A.H. 443
Walker, J.M. 403
Wall, T.D. 192
Wallace, M.J., Jr. 164
Walters, R.W. 191
Walton, R.E. 192, 266, 286, 420, 443, 501, 502
Wanous, J.P. 81, 249, 250, 261
Waterman, R.H. 145, 163, 225, 240, 260, 371, 425, 443, 444, 476, 499
Watson, D.J. 81
Watt, J.T. 224
Weaver, C.N. 81
Webber, R.A. 502
Weber, M. 444
Wechrich, H. 192
Weick, K.E. 403, 501
Weil, R. 471, 472
Weiss, J. 499
Welsh, A. 191
Wendler, E. 405
Wexley, K.N. 164
Wheeler, H.N. 163
Whetten, D.A. 10
White, D.D. 192
Whitney, G. 260

Whitsett, D.A. 171, 192
Whittaker, W. 108
Whyte, G. 370
Whyte, W. 164
Whyte, W.F. 260, 502
Wigdor, L. 135
Wiginton, J.S. 224
Wikinson, H.E. 339
Wilkinson, I. 339, 340
Williams, J.S. 57
Williams, K. 261
Williams, L.J. 81
Witten, M.G. 225
Wolfe, D.M. 286, 312

Wolff, E. 108
Wood, R. 472, 502
Woodman, R.W. 12, 167, 171, 190, 191, 192
Wortman, C.B. 108

Yang, C.Y. 82
Yankelovich, D. 80
Yeager, E.G. 502
Yetton, P.W. 355 357, 358, 365, 371, 405
Yorks, L. 192
Yukl, G.A. 378, 389, 403, 405

Zald, M.N. 340
Zaleznik, A. 403
Zalkind, S.S. 45
Zaltman, G. 471
Zand, D.E. 339, 471, 501
Zander, A. 260, 261
Zawacki, R.A. 472, 502
Zima, J.P. 108
Zimbardo, P.G. 81
Zuboff, S. 224